POLICE
IN AMERICA

JUSTICE IN
JACKSON, MISSISSIPPI

**Hearings
Held in Jackson, Miss.
February 16-20, 1965**

Vol. II

U.S. Commission
on Civil Rights

ARNO PRESS & THE NEW YORK TIMES
NEW YORK, 1971

Reprint Edition 1971 by Arno Press Inc.

Reprinted from a copy in
The State Historical Society of Wisconsin Library

LC# 70-154592
ISBN 0-405-03401-6

Police In America
ISBN for complete set: 0-405-03360-5
See last pages of this volume for titles.

Manufactured in the United States of America

HEARINGS

BEFORE THE

UNITED STATES
COMMISSION ON CIVIL RIGHTS

VOLUME II
ADMINISTRATION OF JUSTICE

HEARINGS HELD
IN
JACKSON, MISS.
February 16–20, 1965

II

CONTENTS

(III)

Other Proceedings

EXHIBITS

MISSISSIPPI

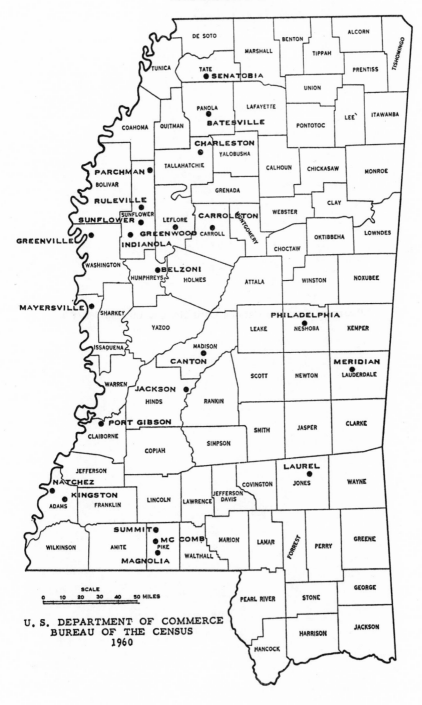

U. S. DEPARTMENT OF COMMERCE
BUREAU OF THE CENSUS
1960

Library of Congress Catalog Card No. CR 1.8:H35/965/V.2

U.S. COMMISSION ON CIVIL RIGHTS

The Commission met in the recreation hall, Veterans Administration Center, 1500 East Woodrow Wilson Drive, Jackson, Miss., at 9:30 a.m., Tuesday, February 16, 1965, the Hon. John A. Hannah, Chairman of the Commission, presiding. Testimony on the administration of justice began at 3:50 p.m., Wednesday, February 17, 1965.

Present: John A. Hannah, Chairman; Eugene Patterson, Vice Chairman; Mrs. Frankie Muse Freeman, Commissioner; Erwin N. Griswold, Commissioner; Rev. Theodore M. Hesburgh, C.S.C., Commissioner; Robert S. Rankin, Commissioner.

Also present: Howard W. Rogerson, Acting Staff Director; William L. Taylor, General Counsel; Samuel J. Simmons, Director of Field Services; Warren I. Cikins, special assistant to the Staff Director; M. Carl Holman, Information Officer; Michael O. Finkelstein, Assistant General Counsel; Charles C. Humpstone, staff attorney; Roy Littlejohn, staff attorney; Richard F. Bellman, staff attorney; Brian M. Olmstead, staff attorney; Edwin D. Wolf, staff attorney; Edward B. Beis, staff attorney; John G. Birkle, Financial Management Officer; Robert H. Amidon, Chief of Investigations; Alan Marer, staff attorney, Department of Justice.

PROCEEDINGS

Chairman HANNAH. This hearing of the U.S. Commission on Civil Rights will come to order. We now move into the second phase of the hearing which has to do with the administration of justice. Mr. Taylor, will you call the first witness?

Mr. TAYLOR. Mr. Chairman, the first county on which we will hear testimony is Pike County. I would like to ask Mr. Roy Littlejohn of the Commission staff to give some background information on that county.

Mr. LITTLEJOHN. Pike County is in southern Mississippi on the Louisiana border. The total population of the county in 1963 was estimated at 35,000, of whom more than 40 percent were Negro. As of

1962 about 64.6 percent of the voting age whites were registered to vote, while only 2.1 percent of the voting age Negroes were registered.

Pike County is in the center of an area which is developing industrially. Oil has been discovered in the area. McComb, which is the largest city in the county, has a population of 12,000 and has long been a major rail center.

In 1959, the median income for white families was $4,600; the median income for Negro families was $1,800. In 1959, the median education level for Pike County Negroes was 7 years; for whites it was 11 years. In the school year of 1960–61, the Pike County School District spent about $165 for each white child and about $115 for each Negro child.

Chairman HANNAH. Thank you very much, sir. Mr. Taylor?

Mr. TAYLOR. Yes. I would like to call Mr. Littlejohn as a staff witness.

Chairman HANNAH. Mr. Littlejohn, will you raise your right hand.

(Whereupon, Mr. Roy Littlejohn was duly sworn by the Chairman and testified as follows:)

TESTIMONY OF ROY LITTLEJOHN, STAFF ATTORNEY, U.S. COMMISSION ON CIVIL RIGHTS

Mr. TAYLOR. Mr. Littlejohn, will you give your full name and address?

Mr. LITTLEJOHN. My name is Roy Littlejohn. I live at 407 Madison Street Northeast, Washington, D.C.

Mr. TAYLOR. What is your position with the Commission?

Mr. LITTLEJOHN. I am a staff attorney.

Mr. TAYLOR. Are you admitted to the bar.

Mr. LITTLEJOHN. Yes, I am a member of the bar of South Carolina and the District of Columbia.

Mr. TAYLOR. Do you have an investigation report to present to the Commission?

Mr. LITTLEJOHN. Yes, I have.

I would like to present to the Commission a report prepared by the staff on incidents of racial violence in or near Pike County from January 25, 1964, to date. This report was compiled as a result of investigations conducted by attorneys in the General Counsel's Office during 1964 and 1965. The attorneys made a number of trips to Pike County, interviewed witnesses, law enforcement officials, and examined government records. Since the report is rather long and since witnesses will testify to some of the incidents, I will summarize only briefly the cases investigated by the staff and submit the full report for the record. The documentation for the report appears in the footnotes at the end.

During 1964, and particularly during the summer months, there was an unusual amount of vigilante violence in Pike County. Fourteen Negro homes, a Masonic meeting hall, and one church were bombed; two churches were destroyed by fire, two were damaged, and still another was the object of an arson attempt. In addition, there were incidents of assault, including four shootings.

From January through May there were three incidents: A fire bomb was thrown at the home of the president of the Pike County NAACP, Curtis Bryant, and on two different nights numerous crosses were burned throughout the county.

One night in June, three Negro homes, including Curtis Bryant's, were bombed. Within a 10-day period during the same month, two local Negroes were abducted and beaten and three northern white men were followed from McComb; two of them were assaulted while the third was held at gunpoint.

During July, after civil rights workers affiliated with the Council of Federated Organizations arrived to begin voter registration work, bombs were thrown at the home of Curtis Bryant's brother and at the COFO house; two churches were burned to the ground; fire damaged another church, and an attempt was made to burn still another; one of the organizers of the COFO project in McComb, a Northern white man, was assaulted in McComb; and shots were fired at the home of Curtis Bryant and at two Negro policemen.

In August bombs were thrown at a Negro home and at the building where NAACP meetings were held; one church was severely damaged by a flash fire; a local white man was whipped; and one night crosses were burned at two different white homes.

The violence reached a peak during the first 3 weeks of September. Seven Negro homes in Pike County were bombed; one church was destroyed by fire; and three COFO workers were assaulted on different occasions. After Negroes rioted in reaction to major incidents of violence on September 20, the State highway patrol was sent in force to Pike County to assist in law enforcement.

Prior to September arrests were made for only one of the offenses committed. Four white men were arrested following the shooting at Negro policemen in July; they pleaded guilty to charges of disturbing the peace and were fined. Three paid $22.50 and the fourth paid $47.50. At the end of September 11 men were arrested. One man was not indicted. The rest were indicted on charges of conspiracy, unlawful use of explosives, or attempted arson. The only incidents cited in the indictments were the bombing of Charles Bryant's home on

July 26, the bombing of the Baker home on September 9, the bombing of the Quin home on September 20, and the attempted arson of the Sweet Home Baptist Church on July 18.

The attempted arson indictment was passed to the file without further action. Those indicted for conspiracy pleaded nolo contendere—no contest—and were fined $500 and sentenced to 6 months in jail. The sentence was suspended during good behavior. Those indicted for unlawful use of explosives were sentenced to 5 years in jail. This sentence was suspended upon certain conditions, among which were that the defendants possess no firearms or explosives.

In imposing sentence the judge added orally—although this does not appear in his order—that he would hold all the defendants responsible for a further outbreak of violence irrespective of proof of their participation. Since there were no fines imposed, three of the defendants who were charged solely with unlawful use of explosives paid no fines.

After the sentencing of this group of defendants on October 23, there were several acts of violence against white people. One man was assaulted, two others shot at, and one family's store was vandalized. In two of these cases there was evidence that the violence was racially oriented. Six white men were arrested in November and charged with these incidents. Five of them pleaded guilty and were sentenced to one year in jail. The sentence was not suspended. The sixth man will be tried in the spring.

I would like to offer as an exhibit for the record the staff investigation report detailing these incidents.

Mr. TAYLOR. The report will be marked as Exhibit No. 11. (Exhibit No. 11 was marked for identification and received in evidence.)

Mr. LITTLEJOHN. The report contains, as an appendix, pictures of the Mount Vernon and Zion Hill Baptist Churches after their destruction by fire last year. We have some enlargements of these pictures which we would like to show to the Commission and the audience. You now see a picture of the Mount Vernon Baptist Church. This church was destroyed by fire on July 21, 1964. These pictures were taken by the Federal Bureau of Investigation. Would you display the picture of the Zion Hill Baptist Church?

Chairman HANNAH. After we have seen it, if there is no objection, you can turn it around to the cameras if you wish.

Mr. LITTLEJOHN. This church was destroyed by fire on July 17, 1964.

Mr. TAYLOR. Does that conclude your report?

Mr. LITTLEJOHN. Yes, it does.

Chairman HANNAH. Proceed.

(Witness excused.)

Mr. TAYLOR. The next witness is Mr. Willie Dillon.

Chairman HANNAH. Mr. Dillon, will you raise your right hand?

(Whereupon, Mr. Willie J. Dillon was duly sworn by the Chairman and testified as follows:)

TESTIMONY OF MR. WILLIE J. DILLON, PIKE COUNTY, MISS.

Mr. TAYLOR. Mr. Dillon, will you give us for the record your full name and address, and your occupation?

Mr. DILLON. My full name is Willie J. Dillon. McComb, Miss., Route 1, Box 17.

Mr. TAYLOR. How long have you lived in Mississippi?

Mr. DILLON. I have lived in Mississippi all my life.

Mr. TAYLOR. And in Pike County?

Mr. DILLON. I was born in Pike County.

Mr. TAYLOR. Would you state your occupation for the record?

Mr. DILLON. I am a mechanic by trade.

Mr. TAYLOR. Have you or your wife ever been involved in civil rights activities?

Mr. DILLON. Well, I haven't. My wife, she goes to the meetings at the COFO office, and my kids went to COFO school.

Mr. TAYLOR. Have you ever attempted to register to vote?

Mr. DILLON. I haven't, but my wife have.

Mr. TAYLOR. I understand that dynamite was thrown at your home on the evening of August 28, 1964. Can you tell us about that?

Mr. DILLON. It were. I always work in my yard, you know, at night, on a car or something like that. Somebody come by—and one of the COFO cars came by; his car wouldn't crank and he asked me, reckon I could make it crank? And I told him I thought I could. Well, he left the car, and during the week I worked on the automobile. And so it took me about 2 or 3 nights, you know, working it part-time when I come from my regular job. And so on the third night, well, I put another battery in the car and run it some, to see would it crank when it got hot.

Well, I worked, and guys come by and talked. But anyways, it was around 12 or 12:30 that night when I quit working on it. I went in to take a bath and shave. I got through shaving and went to step in the bathtub, and I heard the explosion go off. My wife was in the bed and she jumped up and asked me what happened, or what was it. I told her I didn't know, and we ran to the window and looked. We couldn't see anything but smoke on the outside.

So I put my clothes back on and went running out on the porch. The neighbors were beginning to come out and nobody knows what happened, and they seen a lot of smoke. So the people come and we looked to see what happened, where it was at, and so we didn't find anything. So after about 5 minutes, some other guy came and he walked over nine sticks of dynamite in my front yard.

My wife went to the telephone next door and called FBI men. They came and about that time all the officers in McComb and the sheriff and all was there around the same time. Well, they went to asking questions. Why was it put at my house. I told them I didn't know anything, why it was put there, who put it there, anything like that. Well, they questioned and questioned. Well, they asked me, you know, about anything I was involved in, about COFO. Well, I told them I didn't belong to anything; that my wife, she participated in it. Well, they questioned her, and then told us that we knowed something about who was putting the dynamite out and things like that.

Mr. TAYLOR. Who told you?

Mr. DILLON. The law officer.

Mr. TAYLOR. Do you know which law officer?

Mr. DILLON. Well, the sheriff and, well, most all of them. I didn't know, you know, all the law officers. I didn't know about them. But anyway, they all questioned me and questioned my wife and some of them questioned my kids and, well, told us we knowed about who was bombing, that the Negroes was bombing and saying the white people was doing it. And so they kept up the questioning. I said, "well, the only reason I could see that anybody would bomb at my house was because I worked on a COFO car." So then they went to the COFO car and they searched it and said it had been run. I told them "yes, it had been run because I had been working on it trying to see would it start." And so they searched and searched. I had to hang a light in a chinaball tree in the yard from my electric line coming into the house. They looked and seen that there and they said, "Well, we're going to take you to jail." And I said, "For what?" And they said, "For stealing electricity and running a garage without a license." I said "I don't have a garage. If this chinaball tree is a garage, well I guess I'm running one." And they told me "Well, we're going to take you to jail."

Well, they told me to go in and get my shoes and hat. Well, I went on and got it. They told me to go to the car, and I went in. I went and got in the car. Well, they taken me to the nearby overnight service station. Then they questioned me some more about it, said I knowed something I wasn't telling them. "You know who's doing the bombing," or something like that, and I said "I don't know anything about any bombs."

Mr. TAYLOR. Who took you to the service station?

Mr. DILLON. I was in the car with the sheriff and a deputy, I reckon. I don't know who it was.

Mr. TAYLOR. About what time of night was this?

Mr. DILLON. —It had to be about 2 or 3. It was beginning to be morning then. Well, they taken me on from the overnight station to the county jail at Magnolia and turned me over to the jailer.

Well, I stayed in jail until the next morning, and then, well someone come to question me again. I had told them what I knowed. They questioned me and told me that I was lying and things like that, and I told them, "Well, I told you what I knowed about it: nothing. I didn't see anyone put it there, so I don't know anything about who's bombing."

So I was questioned and jailed and stayed there a month. I was fined 3 months and a hundred dollars for stealing electricity and 5 months and $500 for operating a garage without a license.

Mr. TAYLOR. You said you were in jail for a month. When were you first taken before a justice of the peace?

Mr. DILLON. I was taken—that happened on a—let's see; I can't think of the date.

Mr. TAYLOR. Was it the day after you were arrested?

Mr. DILLON. I was taken that next day after the bomb was put in my yard, that next evening between 2 and 3, to the justice of the peace. And so they read off the charge, what they had me in there for. So they asked did I have a lawyer, and I replied back "no". And he said "Well, if you had a lawyer, why, it wouldn't. do any good. It would be the same if you had a lawyer or if you didn't have one."

Mr. TAYLOR. When you were taken before the justice of the peace, you were asked if you had a lawyer at that time?

Mr. DILLON. At that time.

Mr. TAYLOR. Had you been asked at any time previously if you wanted to see a lawyer?

Mr. DILLON. I hadn't.

Mr. TAYLOR. Had you been asked to see if you wanted to see any member of your family or a friend?

Mr. DILLON. I wasn't asked anything about did I want to see anyone, because I was expecting, you know, someone to come. But my wife said she came and they wouldn't let her see me, so I didn't know anything, only I was in jail.

Mr. TAYLOR. And when you came before the justice of the peace, you did not have a lawyer and you pleaded guilty?

Mr. DILLON. I pleaded guilty because I had no other choice but to plead guilty. I had no lawyer. And in the jail in McComb, whatever the law said, that's what it is. Nobody said I wasn't guilty;

nobody said anything, the way I see it. That's the way it always has been.

Chairman HANNAH. Would you speak a little louder?

Mr. DILLON. I said I didn't have a lawyer and I didn't know to ask for one, because I figured I hadn't done any crime to have a lawyer, so I figured I'd just plead guilty and pay a fine. But I was sentenced to 8 months and $800.

Mr. TAYLOR. I would just like to note for the record at this point that Mr. Dillion's sentence was appealed for a trial de novo. The case was removed to a Federal court where the appeal bond was reduced to $500, and the case then remanded to the State court. The remand order was appealed and on January 18 Mr. Dillon paid court costs of $42.60 and the case was dropped. I have no further questions at this point.

Chairman HANNAH. Mrs. Freeman?

Commissioner FREEMAN. Mr. Dillon, you are an automobile mechanic, are you not? How long have you been an automobile mechanic?

Mr. DILLON. Well, I have been a mechanic mostly all my life.

Commissioner FREEMAN. You have been working as a mechanic in the same place in McComb all the time?

Mr. DILLON. Well, for different jobs. Not at the same place all the time.

Commissioner FREEMAN. How long have you been self-employed?

Mr. DILLON. I haven't been self-employed. I always worked for other people all the time.

Commissioner FREEMAN. Have you ever repaired cars for your friends before?

Mr. DILLON. All the time. I have friends and they, you know, would ask me to repair them. Some of them I didn't have no tools, you know, to repair with, of my own. I just have a few tools. But just minor little things I do to them on my own.

Commissioner FREEMAN. Had you had occasion to know the sheriff before?

Mr. DILLON. I hadn't, no.

Commissioner FREEMAN. You knew who he was though?

Mr. DILLON. I knew who he was when I seen him. I didn't know him before.

Commissioner FREEMAN. You were never charged with operating a garage?

Mr. DILLON. I never had a garage. I would just—maybe someone come by and ask me to make their car run or something like that; that would be all. I didn't run a garage.

Commissioner FREEMAN. There is no garage on your property?

Mr. DILLON. No garage on my property at all.

Commissioner FREEMAN. When the sheriff saw the dynamite and the place where there had been an explosion, did he look to see whether there had been any damage before he started charging you?

Mr. DILLON. He looked to see if there was any damage. There was no damage done because it was maybe 10 feet from my porch.

Commissioner FREEMAN. Do you know if he did anything to try to find out who did this?

Mr. DILLON. I didn't hear anything.

Chairman HANNAH. Dean Griswold?

Commissioner GRISWOLD. Mr. Dillon, do you know whether the sheriff undertook to see if there were any fingerprints on the dynamite which was found?

Mr. DILLON. I wouldn't know that, because they took the dynamite.

Commissioner GRISWOLD. Did you see him pick up the dynamite?

Mr. DILLON. I didn't see them pick it up because I was in the house being questioned when the dynamite was picked up, I think.

Commissioner GRISWOLD. How long have you lived in this present house?

Mr. DILLON. I lived in that house about 12 years.

Commissioner GRISWOLD. And during those 12 years, have you from time to time repaired friends' automobiles as they were brought there?

Mr. DILLON. Well, there were occasions. Well, I—I guess I have all my life. I couldn't say, you know, over a period of time. But I work, anyway, on my spare time.

Commissioner GRISWOLD. Have there been several automobiles parked on your grounds from time to time during that period of 12 years?

Mr. DILLON. I have three myself.

Commissioner GRISWOLD. Have there been automobiles of other persons parked on your grounds awaiting repairs during this period of 12 years.

Mr. DILLON. Well, maybe one car, waiting for repairs. Maybe somebody will bring one by and it won't run and he will leave it sitting by the road, because I don't have much ground to park one on.

Commissioner GRISWOLD. Had the sheriff or any of his deputies or anyone else ever talked with you before about operating a garage without a permit?

Mr. DILLON. Well, they hadn't, because I didn't run any garage.

Commissioner GRISWOLD. Were you doing anything different on the evening of August 28, before the bomb explosion, with respect to other persons' automobiles than you had been doing during the preceding 12 years?

Mr. DILLON. No.

Commissioner GRISWOLD. And you had not received any arrest or complaint prior to this evening?

Mr. DILLON. No, not about running no garage; no.

Commissioner GRISWOLD. What you were doing with automobiles on your premises was not concealed in any way? I take it you worked in the front, visible from the street?

Mr. DILLON. It was in my front yard, right on the street.

Commissioner GRISWOLD. And you had no shed or other building there?

Mr. DILLON. I haven't anything there but a chinaball tree.

Commissioner GRISWOLD. Thank you.

Chairman HANNAH. Mr. Rankin.

Commissioner RANKIN. Do you work regularly in a garage?

Mr. DILLON. I work regular. I have a job working in a garage.

Commissioner RANKIN. Did anybody there tell you, warn you that you might be breaking the law?

Mr. DILLON. No.

Commissioner RANKIN. They did not think you were operating a garage?

Mr. DILLON. I am not operating a garage.

Chairman HANNAH. Mr. Patterson.

Vice Chairman PATTERSON. Mr. Dillon, let me just ask you if I got this story straight. On the night of August 28 you say there was an explosion in your yard.

Mr. DILLON. It was.

Vice Chairman PATTERSON. Your wife called the FBI——

Mr. DILLON. She called them.

Vice Chairman PATTERSON. The sheriff came to your house and put you in jail.

Mr. DILLON. That's right.

Vice Chairman PATTERSON. Thank you.

Chairman HANNAH. What about this charge of stealing electricity?

Mr. DILLON. Well, I had a light in my chinaball tree. But the reason I put the light in the tree, there had been bombing. I live in the neighborhood where Mr. Bryant's brother lived, and there had been peoples passing and stopping and parking cars, you know, by the road, unknown cars. All the people out in my area had lights on posts and hanging by trees to have lights. See, we live in the rural; there is no city lights or anything. So—well, it would be out in the tree; it was almost over the road. And I just had an old extra cord and I just hanged it over the wire and let it burn by the road.

Chairman HANNAH. But this was actually using electricity that did not go through the meter?

Mr. DILLON. It was using electricity not through the meter.

Chairman HANNAH. So to that extent it was true that you were using electricity that was not metered to you?

Mr. DILLON. Burning a light by the road, that was true.

Chairman HANNAH. Dean Griswold?

Commissioner GRISWOLD. You testified that at the time you pleaded guilty in justice of the peace court you did not have a lawyer, isn't that correct?

Mr. DILLON. I did not have a lawyer.

Commissioner GRISWOLD. Did you at some subsequent time have a lawyer?

Mr. DILLON. I never had a lawyer until afterward.

Commissioner GRISWOLD. Well, I understand that your case was then appealed to the superior court. Then it was removed to the Federal Court and appealed to the U.S. Court of Appeals. I find it unlikely that all of that was done by you without a lawyer.

Mr. DILLON. No, sir. I had a lawyer after——

Commissioner GRISWOLD. That's what I meant; after the justice sentenced you, an appeal was taken. You did have a lawyer to help you with that appeal?

Mr. DILLON. That's right.

Commissioner GRISWOLD. How did you get that lawyer?

Mr. DILLON. Well, my wife got him.

Commissioner GRISWOLD. Your wife retained a lawyer in Natchez—or in McComb, excuse me?

Mr. DILLON. In McComb. Well, I was in jail. I didn't know how she done it because I was in jail.

Commissioner GRISWOLD. Was this a lawyer in practice in McComb, or was it a lawyer from outside?

Mr. DILLON. He was from here in Jackson.

Commissioner GRISWOLD. A lawyer from Jackson came down to represent you and handled the case?

Mr. DILLON. That's right.

Commissioner GRISWOLD. Thank you.

Chairman HANNAH. Mr. Rogerson?

Mr. ROGERSON. Just one followup. Was this lawyer Negro or white?

Mr. DILLON. Well, he was a Negro.

Mr. ROGERSON. Did you say, Mr. Dillon, that the FBI did come to your house the night of the bombing?

Mr. DILLON. They did come.

Mr. ROGERSON. About the same time as the sheriff?

Mr. DILLON. Well, I don't think they got there the same time because it was I think another incident had happened before it happened. They was out somewhere else and they came shortly afterward, from what I can recall.

Mr. ROGERSON. Did the FBI agent interview you at your home?

Mr. DILLON. They did.

Mr. ROGERSON. Did the FBI ever interview you after you were taken to jail?

Mr. DILLON. No.

Mr. ROGERSON. Was the last time that you saw an FBI agent at your house?

Mr. DILLON. That was the last time I saw one.

Mr. ROGERSON. Did you say that you do not own a set of mechanic's tools?

Mr. DILLON. I do not.

Mr. ROGERSON. Did you charge your friends for work you did on their cars?

Mr. DILLON. No, I did not charge them.

Mr. ROGERSON. You do not charge any people whose cars you fix at your home?

Mr. DILLON. No, I do not charge.

Mr. ROGERSON. Thank you.

Chairman HANNAH. Mr. Patterson.

Vice Chairman PATTERSON. If you did not have a set of mechanic's tools, how did you repair the cars?

Mr. DILLON. Well, I do not have a set. I have some pieces of tools. Not a complete set. Most anyone that works on anything has something, you know, to work with. And I have automobiles of my own, and so I have some. But no equipment to run a garage. I don't have that. I cannot run one, because I don't have what it takes to run a garage.

Vice Chairman PATTERSON. You say that they found sticks of dynamite in your yard?

Mr. DILLON. That's right.

Vice Chairman PATTERSON. If this is true, what do you think made the explosion?

Mr. DILLON. Well, some of it went off that made the explosion.

Vice Chairman PATTERSON. But it did no damage to your house?

Mr. DILLON. It did no damage to my house.

Vice Chairman PATTERSON. One final question: Why were you burning that light in the chinaberry tree?

Mr. DILLON. On account of people stopping by and, you know, we didn't know who it was, and all the bombing was going on beforehand. So that's why people was burning lights. They was staying up all night watching for cars or strange cars that was passing. And so that's why I had the light there.

Vice Chairman PATTERSON. Thank you.

Chairman HANNAH. Further questions? Father Hesburgh.

Commissioner HESBURGH. Who took care of your wife and youngsters while you were in jail?

Mr. DILLON. The neighbors.

Commissioner HESBURGH. Did you phone your wife after they took you to jail that night?

Mr. DILLON. I seen her that evening after they taken me and had my trial.

Commissioner HESBURGH. I see. What time did you say they had the trial?

Mr. DILLON. They had the trial—maybe it was something to 3 o'clock.

Commissioner HESBURGH. Three o'clock in the afternoon or the morning?

Mr. DILLON. In the afternoon. The next day after the bomb was put.

Commissioner HESBURGH. And how long did you see your wife?

Mr. DILLON. What's that?

Commissioner HESBURGH. How long did you see your wife at the time of the trial?

Mr. DILLON. I didn't see her at the trial.

Commissioner HESBURGH. Did you see her after the trial?

Mr. DILLON. I saw her after they carried me back to the jail.

Commissioner HESBURGH. How long?

Mr. DILLON. It was a short while after I was back in jail.

Commissioner HESBURGH. Fifteen or twenty minutes?

Mr. DILLON. Maybe.

Commissioner HESBURGH. And then you didn't see her again until you got out of jail?

Mr. DILLON. Well, she would come, you know; I stayed there a month.

Commissioner HESBURGH. I see. Thank you.

Chairman HANNAH. Any further questions, Mr. Taylor?

Mr. TAYLOR. No, sir.

Chairman HANNAH. You are excused, Mr. Dillon. Thank you very much.

(Witness excused.)

Chairman HANNAH. Mr. Taylor, will you call the next witness.

Mr. TAYLOR. The next witness is Sheriff R. R. Warren.

Chairman HANNAH. Sheriff, will you raise your right hand?

(Whereupon, Sheriff Robert R. Warren was duly sworn by the Chairman and testified as follows:)

Chairman HANNAH. Will you introduce your attorney, sir?

Mr. WARREN. Mr. Joe N. Pigott, McComb.

TESTIMONY OF ROBERT R. WARREN, SHERIFF, PIKE COUNTY, MISS.

Mr. TAYLOR. Sheriff Warren, will you state your name and your residence and your occupation for the record?

Mr. WARREN. My name is Robert R. Warren. I live just out of McComb on the west side Highway 24. I am sheriff of Pike County.

Mr. TAYLOR. How long have you held that office?

Mr. WARREN. Since the 6th of January 1964.

Mr. TAYLOR. Prior to that time, what training had you received in law enforcement?

Mr. WARREN. I was trained in the Mississippi Highway Patrol some 20 years before that, and worked for the Mississippi Highway Patrol for 6 years. This was prior to being elected sheriff.

Mr. TAYLOR. What is the nature of your enforcement duties as sheriff of Pike County?

Mr. WARREN. Well, it covers quite a territory under the sheriff's duties, which is law enforcement, collecting taxes, selling tags—it covers quite a territory.

Mr. TAYLOR. Does it include keeping the peace and good order of the community?

Mr. WARREN. Yes, sir; it sure does.

Mr. TAYLOR. How many men do you have on your force?

Mr. WARREN. I have, I believe, 10 deputies.

Mr. TAYLOR. Do you have any auxiliaries in addition to the deputies?

Mr. WARREN. No, sir; I do not.

Mr. TAYLOR. Are any of the deputies or any of the men on your force detectives or trained as detectives?

Mr. WARREN. Most of the men have gone through some type of training school. Most of them also have been officers for as long as 10 and 15 years.

Mr. TAYLOR. Do you have any Negroes on your force?

Mr. WARREN. No, sir; I do not.

Mr. TAYLOR. Now, you have received a copy of the Staff Investigation Report on Incidents of Racial Violence in Pike County during 1964, and I believe you have had an opportunity to examine it. Did you investigate most of these incidents?

Mr. WARREN. Some of them I did. Some I didn't. Some wasn't reported to me, as sheriff of Pike County.

Mr. TAYLOR. Would it be easier to list the ones that you have not investigated or the ones that you have?

Mr. WARREN. Well, I guess it would be easier to list the ones that I did not investigate. I believe we have them marked off here.

In your report, beginning with number one—well, that was the burning of the crosses in Pike County. Of course I knew about this. Under the laws of the State of Mississippi there is no criminal charge can be made against anyone burning a cross unless the property owner makes a charge of malicious mischief or trespassing. We investigated this as best we could. Of course, when these things were set off, they were set off in good numbers. They were sometimes several miles apart, so you can understand how we were running in circles trying to find out what was going on.

Do you want me to go ahead, now, with the——

Mr. TAYLOR. I would just like you to tell me, if you would, which of the incidents did you not investigate?

Mr. WARREN. All right, sir. The Curtis Bryant, number 2, I did not investigate. It was not reported to me.

Mr. TAYLOR. That is the cross burned in front of his home?

Mr. WARREN. That's true. The number 2 there, yes, sir.

Mr. TAYLOR. And how about the other incidents concerning Mr. Bryant, the fire bomb and——

Mr. WARREN. No, sir, I didn't investigate any of the Curtis Bryant incidents because they were in the city limits and it wasn't reported to me.

Mr. TAYLOR. All right. Continue.

Mr. WARREN. The number 3 down here happened on June 8, 1964. This happened in Lincoln County, which I have no jurisdiction over whatever, the adjoining county north of Pike.

Mr. TAYLOR. That is a matter concerning three white men who were chased from your county to Lincoln County.

Mr. WARREN. That's right.

Mr. TAYLOR. And you had no communication with the sheriff of Lincoln County or anybody else on that incident?

Mr. WARREN. No, sir; I did not.

Mr. TAYLOR. Did the sheriff of Lincoln County make any request of you to investigate that case?

Mr. WARREN. No, sir.

Mr. TAYLOR. Did you feel any obligation to investigate it?

Mr. WARREN. Well, to tell you the truth, I didn't know about it. It wasn't reported to me. I read it in the newspaper.

Mr. TAYLOR. All right, continue.

Mr. WARREN. Now the Ivey Gutter, I did investigate this. I have a report. I think you have it in your records. I took a statement from Ivey Gutter in which he stated that upon arriving home from work that afternoon—he had ridden home with a Walter Lee Felder. After getting out of his car three men wearing hoods came out of the woods— would you like me to go through this or how would you like to do it?

Mr. TAYLOR. This is one of the short reports, so go right ahead.

Mr. WARREN. All right, sir. Three men came out of the woods, attacked Gutter, knocked him down three times, I believe he told me, and then put him into the car. The three men were hooded, were young men, 19 or 20, about 140 pounds. The driver was an older man.

After putting Gutter in the car, a hood was placed over his head and he was carried out into the woods. One of the men said, "You and C. C. Bryant goes to lunch every day together."

Gutter's description of the weapons used by the three men were .22 automatic pistol, .38 pistol, 20-gauge shotgun. He believed the car was a black and white Chevrolet, no tag number. He did say that he saw the tag but he didn't have the tag number.

At the time this happened, Gutter's wife had gone to the grocery store.

Mr. TAYLOR. This is the only document I have that you have submitted on this incident, Sheriff. Did you interview Walter Lee Felder?

Mr. WARREN. Yes, sir; we interviewed him. He didn't see a car, could give us no description of the car that was seen in that vicinity. We also made a trip to Walthall County which Gutter had called in later to the office. I didn't talk to him that time, but one of my employees did. He thought he knew a person over there, but the only thing, he didn't have the name, that had a Chevrolet that resembled this car. We made a trip over but we were unable to find a car that would meet this description. Not having the tag number, you can see that it would get very complicated to find a car like that.

Mr. TAYLOR. Sheriff, you were requested to bring all documents that concerned this and other investigations. Does the fact that you have no documents on this case mean that what you are telling me now was never recorded?

Mr. WARREN. It was never written down; no, sir.

Mr. TAYLOR. Continue.

Mr. WARREN. The number 5, Wilbert Lewis, this was not reported to me. I didn't investigate it.

Number 6, Freddie Bates was not reported, nor Mrs. Corine Andrews, that wasn't reported to me.

Now on your churches, I did investigate, I believe, all the burnings of the churches or attempted arson. Now the church west of Percy Quin Park, I believe, was the first church that burned. I had a call on this church about 5 o'clock on the morning of the 17th of July.

We went out to the church—some of my deputies. I called in a couple of the highway patrol investigators, also called in the fire marshal—State fire marshal. And we went through the ashes of this church, was working on it all that day and into the next day, when we were called out on the Sweet Home Church. And this church is east of McComb in the Whitestown Settlement, I believe it's called.

This church was possibly an attempted arson. They had set more or less a time bomb in this church, going in at a side door, and set the bomb in next to the pulpit.

For some unknown reason this bomb didn't go off. There was a flash fire which we think was caused when the fire hit the powder, possibly was a flash. And the church had been saturated in what we believed was diesel fuel, which is a kerosene with possibly some motor oil added to it. It charred the floors pretty bad in the church. Otherwise, there was no damage. There were several hundred dollars worth of damage.

However, in this case, after the investigation was finished up in the first of October, this case was solved and the persons were arrested, which were four of the men involved in the other bombings in Pike County.

Mr. TAYLOR. Before we get too deeply into each of these cases I would just like to understand, Sheriff, which of these cases you did not investigate, either because they were outside of your jurisdiction or for any other reason.

Mr. WARREN. All right. Now the Rose Bower Baptist Church is in Amite County, the county adjoining on the west side. I did not investigate it. You want to go through and get all we did not investigate?

Mr. TAYLOR. I just want to get all the cases you did not investigate and the reasons.

Mr. WARREN. The cross burning in front of Dr. Mayer's home, no report. The rest of them I believe I investigated. Oh, I have one more. Let's see. Now the cases involved in—that happened in the city limits of McComb, Mendy Samstein, Robert V. Stone, Rev. Russell Bennett, none of those I investigated. That was in the city limits, which they naturally would investigate.

Mr. PIGOTT. It was reported to you?

Mr. WARREN. No, it wasn't. I read of those cases in the paper. And the one on October 27, Malcolm Campbell being threatened, that case wasn't reported to me. I believe the rest of them I investigated.

Mr. TAYLOR. So the cases which you have listed as not investigated were cases which you say were not reported to you or to your office or which occurred within the city limits and therefore were within the jurisdiction of the police department rather than yours?

Mr. WARREN. That's right; sir.

Mr. TAYLOR. You have no limitation on your jurisdiction; this is an agreement?

Mr. WARREN. Naturally I have jurisdiction over the city, but we try to work together. They take care of the cases in the city limits because they have a police force, I think about 16 or 18 policemen. I have three other towns besides McComb, so I have a pretty big territory to try to cover with my 10 deputies.

Mr. TAYLOR. Did you investigate these other incidents as they were reported to you?

Mr. WARREN. Yes, sir; I did.

Mr. TAYLOR. Sheriff, did you make a statement reported in the press that one of the bombings which took place on September 21 was a "COFO plant?"

Mr. WARREN. Well, I would like to qualify that a little, if I might.

Mr. TAYLOR. I just wanted to know whether you made the statement, or if you made a statement similar to it or a different statement.

Mr. WARREN. This is September 23 you are talking about?

Mr. TAYLOR. The report is dated September 21.

Mr. WARREN. Yes, I probably made that statement, for this reason. As I said before, we could get no cooperation from the Negro people. When something would happen, an explosion or any incident, the Negro people would usually call the NAACP; it would make a round through Washington and come back through the FBI in McComb and to me.

The night of the 23d, when the bomb was thrown at Matthew Jackson's house—the stick of dynamite, rather—it landed approximately about 30 or 40 feet from his house in his yard. We located this thing. No one called us. We located this incident by shortwave radio and ear after hearing the bomb when it went off. At the time when we drove up to Matthew Jackson's house he denied that there had been an explosion there, that there had been an explosion at his place. We left, came back; we traced the call again—I mean traced the sound, came back; it had to be there. Then is when we found the hole in the ground.

So naturally, being an investigative officer, you wonder what is going on when you have an explosion and some person denies it happens in his yard. I mean, it leads you to believe something may be going on.

Mr. TAYLOR. And on the basis of that you concluded that you definitely thought the bomb was a plant? That is what you were quoted as saying?

Mr. WARREN. Yes, sir; that is probably true. And in addition to that, we were told that night at Matthew Jackson's home that a white small make of automobile followed Reverend Taylor in by his house, went down the road about three-quarters of a mile, turned around and followed Rev. Ned Taylor out. This again leads us to believe that maybe something was wrong.

Mr. TAYLOR. Sheriff, the statement that I quoted, or was recorded in the McComb Enterprise Journal, on September 21, and it is referring to the Quin bombing, not to the bombing you are referring to right now.

Mr. WARREN. Well, if I might, with the Commission's permission, I would like to go into that bombing.

Mr. TAYLOR. Well, I would just like to know whether you believed you had evidence on that date that——

Mr. WARREN. Well, as I said before, Mr. Taylor, several things pointed up to that. I mean during these investigations. There is several different things pointed up to that. I mean when we go out to a bombing or a bomb site, there was no one seen, there was no automobile seen. There was no evidence to work on.

Mr. TAYLOR. In any case, you believed on that date that the bombing was a plant?

Mr. WARREN. Yes, sir; I did.

Mr. TAYLOR. Did it turn out that you were wrong?

Mr. WARREN. Yes, sir; I was wrong.

Mr. TAYLOR. So as of September 20, your investigations hadn't led you to any of the persons who were actually responsible for this bombing or any of the other bombings?

Mr. WARREN. I don't believe I understood that question.

Mr. TAYLOR. As of the day when the bombing took place, your investigations of that bombing and prior bombings had not led you to the persons responsible for any of them?

Mr. WARREN. As of that date, no, sir, they had not.

Mr. TAYLOR. How many persons were arrested in connection with the incidents of violence which were referred to in this investigation report?

Mr. WARREN. In this report there was 11 and 6—17 persons.

Mr. TAYLOR. When were they arrested and which incidents of violence were they charged with?

Mr. WARREN. Well, we had 11 people arrested—I believe it was September 30 and October 1. Eleven people were arrested on those dates. We got a confession from them that they did the bombings and—or some of the bombings that we had been working on.

Now the other six was arrested in October. I believe it was October the 20th. There was six arrested for aiming and discharging weapons. One case was malicious mischief, I believe, or aiming and discharging—pointing a weapon at a human being. Those people were arrested on October 20

Mr. TAYLOR. So several persons were arrested for three of the bombing incidents and several others were arrested for some incidents which occurred in October or thereabout?

Mr. WARREN. That's right. Eleven persons were arrested for the bombing incidents.

Mr. TAYLOR. What were the major obstacles which prevented you from solving these cases at an earlier date, Sheriff?

Mr. WARREN. Well, there was several. As I said before, we had very little cooperation out of the Negro people. They didn't call us. If you give a crime like that 15 or 20 minutes start on you, it is hard to solve. They can move into another part of town, have a very good alibi when you get in on the case.

The FBI worked with us on these cases, right side by side with us. They made no arrests. It is just something that is hard to solve when you go out to a crime. There is no evidence, there is no description on anything, automobile, a person, anything that we could work on.

Mr. TAYLOR. I understand the highway patrol came into Pike County in force last fall. Did you request this assistance?

Mr. WARREN. Yes, sir; I did.

Mr. TAYLOR. When did you make that request?

Mr. WARREN. On the night of September 20 after the Aylene Quin bombing.

Mr. TAYLOR. Can you tell us why you made the request on that date?

Mr. WARREN. Yes, sir; I would like to. When this happened, this bombing—this explosion happened—it was possibly 11 o'clock on Sunday night. We got to the location—we wasn't called on it; we found this location as usual. We were called maybe by some people in that part of town and they said there was an explosion, they didn't know where. We found this location. An FBI agent by the name of

Frank Ford was with me. When we got to the location, he and a highway patrolman after, well, possibly 20 minutes after the bombing—when we got on the street about two blocks from the bombing site—there was a riot, you might say, in progress. There was three or four hundred Negroes. A lot of them was drinking. They were cursing, they were calling us everything except white people. They even was threatening to kill us.

When we got out of the car at the bomb site, there was only seven officers there. We tried to quiet the Negroes down so we could make an investigation. Mr. Ford talked to the Negroes, tried to quiet them down. He was cursed and his flashlight was knocked out of his hand by a rock.

We were dodging rocks, bottles, concrete—pieces of concrete. This thing was possibly, we thought—at least I thought—was out of hand. We called all my men in, the seven that was there including the FBI, Mr. Ford. We decided we would back up and get some reinforcements, which we did. We called the chief of the Highway Patrol and he talked to the Governor, and possibly 50 patrolmen were sent in down there that night.

Mr. TAYLOR. During the period between May and September 20, a number of bombings and shootings had taken place; is that correct?

Mr. WARREN. Yes.

Mr. TAYLOR. But you did not feel a need to call the Highway Patrol before the date of September 20?

Mr. WARREN. Well, maybe you misunderstood me, or I didn't say it. Now the Highway Patrol investigators were working with us at all times, possibly four or five. And about 20 or 30 FBI agents was working at all times, along with myself and my deputies and the McComb Police Department.

Mr. TAYLOR. Did you take any steps to prevent incidents of violence against Negroes from occurring once it was evident that you had a problem here?

Mr. WARREN. Well, we took steps the same as we would against anyone. I took an oath that I would enforce the laws fair and impartially, regardless as to race, color or creed. I think we took as much precaution to preserve law, you know, and for the Negro as well as we did the whites.

Mr. TAYLOR. Did your men patrol the Negro community at night?

Mr. WARREN. Yes sir; we patrolled the Negro communities; yes, sir.

Mr. TAYLOR. You told us that arrests were made in three cases. What is the status of your investigation with respect to the other cases?

Mr. WARREN. Well, I would like to say this: I am only the arresting officer. Of course, when it gets up to the courts, my authority ends. I would like for you to ask Mr. Pigott, who is the district attorney of that district down there on that question.

Mr. TAYLOR. Mr. Pigott, would you care to make a statement about the status of those cases?

Mr. PIGOTT. In that regard, those persons who were charged and indicted and pled guilty to having bombed two houses—after they had pled guilty and had been sentenced—their attorneys were requested by myself and by Mr. Reeves, the county attorney, to take a list of certain crimes of violence that had occurred involving other bombings in the county during the year. They were requested to consult with their clients, and without giving us any information to incriminate themselves—which we knew they wouldn't do—we asked them to merely check off the crimes or the acts of violence in which their clients were implicated, so that we could then concentrate our efforts more particularly toward the acts of violence that had not been solved.

This was done and the list was given back to us. All of the incidents were checked off by the attorneys for those persons. However, the investigations are continuing in all regards except for those persons who have—except for those incidents in which persons have actually been indicted. And if additional information is obtained that can be submitted to a grand jury, that will be done.

Mr. TAYLOR. Did that cover all of the incidents that have been reported here?

Mr. PIGOTT. No. You have a number of incidents that we didn't even know about until this noon when you gave that list to us. We have since gone over them and some of those that you have related we were not advised that they had occurred.

Mr. TAYLOR. I am thinking particularly of the three beatings. Now, Sheriff, you have mentioned them. I take it those are still under investigation and those cases are not closed or solved; is that correct?

Mr. PIGOTT. Now you have reference to——

Mr. TAYLOR. I am speaking particularly of the Wilbert Lewis case.

Mr. PIGOTT. So far as I know, no arrest has been made, and Wilbert Lewis has furnished no additional information as to the identity of the persons. We have no further information as to their identity.

Mr. TAYLOR. Sheriff, was any identifying information furnished to you by Federal investigators in this case?

Mr. WARREN. No, sir; there was no information furnished me.

Mr. TAYLOR. Are you sure of that?

Mr. WARREN. I am quite sure, I think.

Mr. TAYLOR. I beg your pardon?

Mr. WARREN. Yes, sir; I'm sure. It might have been discussed, but I don't think there was any report given me on it.

Mr. TAYLOR. I have no further questions of this witness.

Chairman HANNAH. Father Hesburgh?

Commissioner HESBURGH. I will defer to the lawyers.

Chairman HANNAH. Mrs. Freeman?

Commissioner FREEMAN. Sheriff Warren, I would like to have some more information about your procedure with respect to investigation. On two occasions, in referring to an incident or bombing, you have stated that no information was submitted to you by the victim. I would like to know if you require the victim to conduct the investigation to determine who has bombed or burned out a church, or if not, what steps do you take in trying to find out who did?

Mr. WARREN. Well, naturally we don't expect the victim to make the investigation. We try to find out if anyone saw the incident or heard the incident. We take testimony from, or a statement from anyone that will give it to us, that they heard the explosion or saw an automobile or anything. In other words, we work around the locations, go to the different homes close to it, ask questions as to, you know, if they heard anything, saw anything. We make a pretty thorough investigation. And as I stated before, most of these investigations Mr. Frank Ford was working side by side with me on the investigation, on most of them. But we do make a thorough investigation.

Commissioner FREEMAN. With respect to the incidents occurring to persons, have there been any arrests of persons who were alleged to have beaten people?

Mr. WARREN. Well, the only one—well, there was—the only one I investigated was the Ivey Gutter case. There hasn't been an arrest on that. The only thing we had, he gave us the number of men, the approximate age and weights, and a black—or a Chevrolet, 1954 or 1955 Chevrolet, I believe. We checked out as many of those cars as we could find in the county and in the adjoining counties through the word from Gutter that there was a car maybe in the next county that could have had something to do with it. We even went over in this county and spent quite a time trying to find this automobile. Of course, you realize in looking for a 1954, 1955, 1956 Chevrolet without a tag number, it is something like looking for a needle in a haystack. But we did attempt to find out all the information on all the incidents that occurred in Pike County.

Chairman HANNAH. Dean Griswold?

Commissioner GRISWOLD. Sheriff, as I recall your testimony, you said that reports on many of these events were not made to you, but were made to the FBI, and that you heard about it indirectly. Was that correct?

Mr. WARREN. That is true, sir.

Commissioner GRISWOLD. Do you have any idea why that was the situation?

Mr. WARREN. Well, no actual proof. I was told that COFO people probably told the Negroes to call the FBI and not to have anything to do with the local law enforcement.

Commissioner GRISWOLD. You think they had any reason for such advice if they gave it?

Mr. WARREN. I don't see why they would have because we made every investigation regardless of whether they called us or not. I mean when we finally did get the word, we made the investigation.

Commissioner GRISWOLD. Do you think what happened to Willie Dillon had anything to do with such advice?

Mr. WARREN. I don't believe I quite get you there, sir.

Commissioner GRISWOLD. Mrs. Dillon reported to the FBI that a bomb had gone off in their front yard.

Mr. WARREN. Yes, sir.

Commissioner GRISWOLD. And you came and promptly arrested Mr. Dillon on two charges and took him off to jail. He was tried without a lawyer and kept in jail for 30 days. Finally, through the aid of a lawyer and removal to the Federal courts, his problems were solved. Do you think that many people were likely to report to you thereafter about bombs going off in their yard?

Mr. WARREN. Do you mind if I explain that just a little?

Commissioner GRISWOLD. I would be glad to hear it.

Mr. WARREN. In the first place, we didn't arrest Willie Dillon promptly. We made an investigation. There was in that yard what looked like a dynamite cap had gone off and on the edge of the hole, possibly within 6 inches of this hole, lay nine sticks of dynamite.

We don't believe that that dynamite was laying there when that cap went off, because we think it would have exploded. We did quite a bit of investigating. In fact, we arrived at Willie Dillon's house somewhere around 1 o'clock and I believe Willie was arrested about 3 or 3:30 that same morning.

Now, during the investigation these violations came up which naturally I am sworn to uphold the law in the county that I am sheriff in. We had worked possibly 2 hours and a half on the investigation before Dillon was arrested.

Commissioner GRISWOLD. What evidence did you feel you had that Mr. Dillon was operating a garage on his premises?

Mr. WARREN. Well, there was three or four cars there. He admitted to us that night that he was working on this automobile, and that he had commonly worked on people's automobiles for hire. So that gave us the right to make a charge against him for operating without a license.

Commissioner GRISWOLD. Does working on a person's automobile constitute operating a garage, even when there is no equipment?

Mr. WARREN. It would under certain conditions. If he——

Mr. PIGOTT. Just a minute. Dean Griswold——

Commissioner GRISWOLD. Mr. Pigott, I didn't ask for your testimony. You can advise your client, if you care to, but, Mr. Pigott, the sheriff is the witness.

Mr. PIGOTT. I am going to object——

Commissioner GRISWOLD. You can advise your client, if you care to, but you are not the witness.

Mr. PIGOTT. I think that under the rules of the Commission, as we are advised, any witness has a right to have counsel——

Commissioner GRISWOLD. Right.

Mr. PIGOTT. And that counsel has a right to state an objection, for the record at least.

Commissioner GRISWOLD. Yes; that is correct.

Mr. PIGOTT. I would like to let the record show that there have been furnished to the Commission certified copies of the affidavits, certified copies of the transcript of the record in the justice of the peace court, wherein the defendant, Willie Dillon, pled guilty and was sentenced.

There has also been introduced in the record, or made available to the Commission, the finding of fact and opinion of the U.S. District Court wherein he found that the defendant, Willie John Dillon, did and can receive a fair trial in Pike County, Miss. Now, it is not the prerogative of the sheriff to determine the guilt or innocence of a person, but——

Commissioner GRISWOLD. Are you making an objection, Mr. Pigott?

Mr. PIGOTT. Yes, sir.

Commissioner GRISWOLD. What is the objection?

Mr. PIGOTT. The objection is that—it is not his prerogative and it is not his authority to make a determination as to whether a person is guilty or innocent. But that if he sees a violation of the law occurring, he is under oath to——

Commissioner GRISWOLD. Does he not have to make at least a determination that there is probable cause that a violation is occurring?

Mr. PIGOTT. Yes. I just wanted the record to show that the justice of the peace court and the U.S. District Court have upheld him in that decision that he made.

Commissioner GRISWOLD. In the justice of the peace court the plea of guilty was without the benefit of counsel. And all that the U.S. District Court has held is that he could receive a fair trial in the justice's court. That decision was appealed to the court of appeals, and the case was then settled. So I don't suppose that the district court decision is of any particular value on that matter.

But my question is—and it seems to me to be a relevant question—what evidence was there which would lead a fair-minded law enforcement officer to conclude that there was probable cause that Mr. Dillon was operating a garage; not repairing cars, but operating a garage on his premises? And I think that is an appropriate question.

Mr. PIGOTT. If that is the question, I will ask the witness to answer it.

Mr. WARREN. Well, in Mississippi, we think if a person is under a shade tree working on automobiles for hire, he is operating a garage. If he is working on these automobiles for hire, which he admitted that night to be doing, I could do nothing else than arrest him.

Commissioner GRISWOLD. Did you ever arrest any other person for operating a garage when he was repairing automobiles on his personal premises under a shade tree?

Mr. WARREN. No, sir; I haven't. But none of them admitted they were working on them for hire.

Commissioner GRISWOLD. You still think that what happened to Willie Dillon has nothing to do with the Negroes' reluctance to report violations to your office?

Mr. WARREN. Yes, sir. I feel like they should be reported to my office. I don't think that——

Commissioner GRISWOLD. That wasn't my question.

Mr. WARREN. I don't think it should have anything——

Commissioner GRISWOLD. My question was whether people are afraid to report incidents to your office because they encounter what seems to them to be arbitrary enforcement of the law if they make reports to your office.

Mr. WARREN. Not unless they are violating the law, and which I say that Willie Dillon was violating a law.

Commissioner GRISWOLD. I think we can leave the record as it stands.

Chairman HANNAH. Mr. Rankin?

Commissioner RANKIN. I just have one question concerning the climate around McComb. We have here 40 incidents with 8 arrests—is this a good record or not? What do you think about it, Sheriff?

Mr. WARREN. Well, Professor, I think they have got us charged up with some there that didn't happen in Pike County, so I think our percentage should run a little better than that.

Commissioner RANKIN. Well, I am just going by the record.

Mr. WARREN. Well, that's what I say. In quite a few of these records, they didn't happen in Pike County.

Commissioner RANKIN. Well, let's cut 5 of them off and say there are 35. Do you think that is still a little bad?

Mr. WARREN. Yes, sir; I will agree. However, according to our investigation and the investigation of the FBI, we feel like that these arrests—these 10 people, you might say, were causing us all of our troubles. As a people, the people of Pike County, they do not condone what was going on and we feel like this 10 or 11 people was causing all our trouble, Professor.

Commissioner RANKIN. You think it was a handful of people, then, in Pike County who were responsible for this; is that correct?

Mr. WARREN. Yes, sir; that is very correct.

Commissioner RANKIN. And you think the climate there is not bad?

Mr. WARREN. No, sir. I think the climate is very good. I think the people are more reconciled and I think the climate is better now than it was 12 months ago. But I will assure you that the people of Pike County don't go along with church burnings, bombings, or any of that type of stuff. It was just a handful of people there that decided they would take the law in their own hands and do it their way. That is my opinion on it.

Commissioner RANKIN. And you think, then, that by these arrests you have really cleared up this pretty horrible situation?

Mr. WARREN. Yes, sir; I feel like we have cleared it up. Well, we had the other little incident there in the next month. But since that time, things have been mighty quiet. The people of Pike County have gotten behind their law enforcement, their courts, and I think the thing has been cleaned up.

Commissioner RANKIN. They object to the burning of churches today, is that correct?

Mr. WARREN. Yes, sir.

Commissioner RANKIN. They object to bombings, am I correct in that?

Mr. WARREN. That is very correct, sir.

Commissioner RANKIN. And they object to cross burning?

Mr. WARREN. That is very true.

Commissioner RANKIN. And if the white people in the community are strong enough in their objection, don't you think that might have some effect in stopping these activities in the future?

Mr. WARREN. Well, I am quite sure it will, and I am quite sure it has already had quite a lot to do with quieting the temperature down down there.

Chairman HANNAH. Mr. Patterson?

Vice Chairman PATTERSON. Sheriff, when did the temperature quiet down after you made the key arrests of those men who pleaded *nolo contendere*?

Mr. WARREN. Yes, sir. It began to quiet down some at that time. Then we had the other little incident in October which was another class of people, six white people. They decided they had to do a little law enforcement, which their case didn't last as long as the other one.

I might say this: This sixth man that they stated a while ago was going to be tried next spring, his probation was revoked. He had 2 years' probation, State penitentiary, for breaking and entering. His probation was revoked in this incident and he is now in the State penitentiary to serve these 2 years. And when it is served he will be brought back to Pike County and tried on this incident. So I think that the people have quieted down and they feel very secure. I think they are at rest.

Vice Chairman PATTERSON. Do you think strong effective police work had some part in the cessation of the bombing and burning in McComb?

Mr. WARREN. Yes, sir; I really do.

Vice Chairman PATTERSON. And if some other communities were beset by similar problems, would you instruct your law enforcement officers to make prompt arrests whenever they can?

Mr. WARREN. Yes, sir; I sure would.

Vice Chairman PATTERSON. Does some of the new atmosphere that you described in McComb come from the statement of the businessmen and community leaders that was so widely publicized?

Mr. WARREN. Yes, sir; I think by reason of this statement they realized that law enforcement had gone about as far as it could go without the backing of the public, and I think that is the reason this statement was brought out.

Vice Chairman PATTERSON. Was this an important factor to you as sheriff of Pike County, that the businessmen and community leaders came out and said what they did? Did this make your job easier?

Mr. WARREN. Yes, sir; it was a very important factor. In fact, we were beginning to think we were orphan children after doing all this work until the public finally did come out and gave us this support.

I would like to make this statement, if I might: Just before these arrests were made, County Attorney Bob Reeves and myself talked to the newspaper there in McComb. We asked the public to give us $5,000 to put out a reward for any information that would lead to the arrest and conviction of any person involved in this bombing. They responded to the effect that within 3 days we had over $7,000 in this fund. This fund is still in the bank. There was no money spent out on a reward. This happened about 5 days before the arrest, and we were in process of breaking this thing at that time.

I would also like to state at this point that the churches in McComb, especially the Baptist Church in McComb, have gone out to help rebuild the burned and bombed churches. In fact, I have made personally several donations to these churches. They go around with a petition and ask you to donate, and you give them your donation. Now there is no doubt in my mind but what these churches will be built back. If the insurance doesn't cover it, they will be built back by donations from white as well as Negro people.

Vice Chairman PATTERSON. As a law enforcement officer who has been through a difficult period, and has come now to a better time, would you on behalf of all law enforcement officers in Mississippi like to see all businessmen and community leaders take this kind of stand that the leaders of McComb have taken?

Mr. WARREN. Yes, sir; I really would, for this reason: Law enforcement is just as strong as the people that is behind him. You are no stronger than the people that is behind you. If a law is unpopular, it cannot be enforced; therefore, you are just as strong as the people. So I would really like to see that happen in all the counties in Mississippi.

Vice Chairman PATTERSON. That's all I have.

Chairman HANNAH. Any further questions?

Mr. TAYLOR. Just a couple. Sheriff, on the question of why incidents have not been reported to you: During this period when, according to your testimony, you believed that Negroes might be responsible for the violence, did you interrogate Negro leaders at any length?

Mr. WARREN. Not to excess. Possibly 30, 40 minutes, 45 minutes.

Mr. TAYLOR. Wasn't the leader of the NAACP picked up by several men at his home one night and questioned for a while?

Mr. WARREN. Yes. And I'll tell you the reason. As I said, we couldn't find this location, this Matthew Jackson. This is the case involved in the one you're talking about. They first denied the bomb being thrown there. Then they denied having called anyone. The radio came back about 45 minutes later, said that Curtis Bryant in McComb had called Aaron Henry. He had in turn called the Justice Department in Washington, and they—it came back down the regular route through the FBI to McComb FBI, and to us. However, we had been in on the investigation at that time about an hour and a half. I asked the city police to pick Curtis Bryant up. I would like to talk to him and ask him why he didn't call the local officers, why we wasn't notified. This is one case had we been notified we would have caught the people.

Mr. TAYLOR. Excuse me. How many people picked him up that night?

Mr. WARREN. I do not know. City police picked him up. I wasn't there. I was out in the field.

Mr. TAYLOR. And he was interrogated for a period of time?

Mr. WARREN. Well, possibly 30, 45 minutes.

Mr. TAYLOR. I have one other question, Sheriff: During this period, particularly from May until September when the Quin house was bombed, did you ever issue any statement that was published any place calling for the maintenance of law and order in your community?

Mr. WARREN. Calling for the maintenance of law and order?

Mr. TAYLOR. That's right.

Mr. WARREN. I don't believe I know how you mean that now. You mean asking the people to cooperate, or how do you mean?

Mr. TAYLOR. Well, phrase it yourself. Either asking them to co-operate, asking for the restoration of law and order——

Mr. WARREN. Yes, I really did. I made several talks, very humbly, to different clubs and asked them to go along with the law enforcement officers and try to help us solve these problems.

Mr. TAYLOR. I have no further questions.

Chairman HANNAH. Father Hesburgh?

Commissioner HESBURGH. I just would like to refresh my memory on one that happened here. In the case of Willie Dillon, he spent, I believe, a month in jail; is that correct?

Mr. WARREN. Yes, sir. But I would like to clarify that, if I might.

Commissioner HESBURGH. Go ahead.

Mr. WARREN. This was after Willie Dillon had been sentenced by the court. Now Willie Dillon was arrested at 3:30 or 4 o'clock on that morning and at 1 o'clock that same day—not the following day—he was carried into court and advised that he could have an attorney, which he said he didn't want an attorney, didn't have an attorney. He was sentenced at this time. Now this was after he had been sentenced that he spent this time in jail.

Commissioner HESBURGH. I mean he was actually sentenced 5 months on one term and 3 on another. Now, in contrast to that, the gentlemen who were apprehended for the bombings and burnings, how long were they sentenced to spend in jail?

Mr. WARREN. Well, before the pleading of guilty, they spent some 40 days in jail. And I wouldn't like to be held accountable for this, but they were held incommunicado, some of them for 72 hours before we got the confession. They spent 40 days in jail, though, before court came up.

Commissioner HESBURGH. Then after the sentence, they didn't spend any more time in jail?

Mr. WARREN. No, sir. As I said, that is where my authority ends, at the court.

Commissioner HESBURGH. I understand.

Mr. WARREN. And I don't have anything to do with the sentence or what might happen on it.

Commissioner HESBURGH. No, I wasn't trying to relate this to your office. I was merely trying to get the fact that Mr. Dillon, whose house was bombed, spent this time in jail, and the people who admitted to many of these bombings, after their trial spent no time in jail.

Mr. WARREN. Yes.

Chairman HANNAH. Mr. Rogerson, do you have a question?

Mr. ROGERSON. I have two. Back to this Dillon case once more: Sheriff, during your term of office, have you ever arrested anyone else on the charge of operating a garage without a license?

Mr. WARREN. No, I have not. It hadn't come to my attention. If it came to my attention that they were operating a garage without a license, I would certainly arrest them.

Mr. ROGERSON. Sheriff, do you resent the fact that Negroes do not report crimes to you?

Mr. WARREN. No, I don't necessarily resent it, Mr. Rogerson. I think it would have helped in the investigations had they reported it to me. It doesn't matter; I don't resent that fact.

Mr. ROGERSON. Doesn't it bother you that a large segment of the population does not have confidence in you?

Mr. WARREN. It matters in the investigation.

Mr. ROGERSON. Well, I don't mean in a particular case, but generally, as the chief law enforcement officer in the county, doesn't it bother you that a large segment of the population doesn't have confidence in you?

Mr. WARREN. Not if they have been instructed to do so maybe by some other organization.

Mr. ROGERSON. What, if anything, have you done to establish a better relationship with the Negro community in Pike County as a result of your experiences over the last year?

Mr. WARREN. Well, we have had several meetings with the Negro leaders in Pike County and talked to them and tried to work out some programs that we could get together. They could help us, we could help them. We had several meetings like that.

Mr. ROGERSON. Do you feel your relationship with the Negro community is better now?

Mr. WARREN. Yes, I do. I feel like it is.

Mr. ROGERSON. You feel that perhaps they would have more trust and confidence in you today than they seemed to have last year?

Mr. WARREN. Yes, sir; I think so, Mr. Rogerson. I think they would call more often than they did.

Mr. ROGERSON. Thank you.

Chairman HANNAH. That is all, gentlemen. Thank you very much. (Witness excused.)

Chairman HANNAH. Mr. Taylor, I understand the chief of police is not here. Do you want to dispose of this item this afternoon?

Mr. TAYLOR. I believe his attorney is here, Mr. Wiltshire.

Chairman HANNAH. Is Mr. Wiltshire here?

Mr. WILTSHIRE. Yes.

STATEMENT OF WILLIAM A. WILTSHIRE, ESQ., ON BEHALF OF POLICE CHIEF GEORGE GUY

Mr. WILTSHIRE. Mr. Taylor and I have briefly discussed my client who was supposed to be here today. I am counsel for George Guy. I was up here expecting to be with Mr. Guy, and Mr. Guy had expected to be here also. However, while I was coming up here, I understand that one of the counsel for the Commission and Mr. Guy's doctor had been in a telephone conversation and Mr. Guy, as of today, after being examined by the doctor, has been advised that he should not appear. We have discussed this briefly, and we feel that it is past a legal matter, and I cannot advise him to appear over the objections of his doctor. And I just urge that the Commission understand that Mr. Guy wants to appear, and we have no objections to appearing.

Chairman HANNAH. He is unable because of health reasons. Would it be possible for a representative of the Commission, or a staff member, to see Mr. Guy in the hospital or wherever he is?

Mr. WILTSHIRE. I am sure, as I have discussed with Mr. Taylor, we will be willing to work this out in any manner, interrogatory statements, executive hearing, or just any way the Commission wants to work it out at a later date. We will certainly be glad to cooperate.

Chairman HANNAH. We certainly appreciate your report. The Commission will consider this in executive session and determine how they would like to proceed. Thank you very much.

We will recess until 9 o'clock tomorrow morning. Two Commissioners will remain to receive documents.

(Whereupon, at 5:27 o'clock, the public session was concluded, and a subcommittee of the Commission convened for receipt of subpenaed documents.)

The deposition of Police Chief George Guy, McComb, Miss., was taken on Friday, February 19, 1965, at 3 p.m. at the Admiral Benbow Inn.

Present: Mr. Edwin D. Wolf, staff attorney; Mr. Charles C. Humpstone, staff attorney; Mr. William A. Wiltshire, attorney for Police Chief Guy; Police Chief George Guy, McComb, Pike County; Kenneth D. Meier, court reporter.

Mr. WOLF. Chief Guy, we would like to ask you some questions. When they are transcribed, we will send you a copy, have you sign it, and have it notarized so that we can have a sworn statement.

Mr. GUY. Yes.

Mr. WOLF. Would you please state your name, residence, and occupation?

Mr. GUY. George Guy, chief of police, McComb, Miss.

Mr. WOLF. How long have you served as police chief?

Mr. GUY. Since 1955.

Mr. WOLF. Prior to becoming police chief had you had any training in law enforcement?

Mr. GUY. I was on the regular police force.

Mr. WOLF. For how long?

Mr. GUY. Sir, since 1947, the last time. I had been on previous to that time, back in 1933–34.

Mr. WOLF. Chief, do you recognize that, as police chief, you have a duty to keep the peace in the city of McComb, Miss.?

Mr. GUY. I sure do.

Mr. WOLF. You have received a copy of the staff investigation report on the incidents of racial violence in McComb and Pike County during 1964. Could you tell us which of these incidents you investigated?

Mr. GUY. Is this what you are talking about here?

Mr. WOLF. This is the chronological list.

Mr. GUY. Maybe I should take my record I brought here. That's on my writeup book.

Mr. WOLF. Chief, I believe you have the chronological index to the staff report on Pike County?

Mr. GUY. Right.

Mr. WOLF. In the chronological index there are a certain number of incidents which are marked with one asterisk. We note these as having occurred within the city of McComb. Could you tell us which of those that are marked with one asterisk you did not investigate?

Mr. GUY. The G. T. Vaccarella home is south of McComb which is outside of the city limits. That's No. 22. I believe that is all. The rest of them that are marked, I believe, did happen in McComb. Now, the Wilbert Lewis beating—No. 7—they picked him up in McComb, but the act of violence happened outside the city limits of McComb.

Mr. WOLF. Do you view that as not having been committed within the city limits?

Mr. GUY. Well, now picking him up at his work and carrying him out with the intent of fixing an automobile might be. Of course, when he got out there I understand they came out of bushes and everywhere else and tied him to a tree and whipped him. I talked to Wilbert that night. I got out of bed and went to his home. I talked to him and his father-in-law, the Reverend Dickey, and discussed the matter with them. We checked around as much as we could in McComb, and was trying to locate the possible suspects. We checked the description of the car he gave us and of the man that picked him up. As of yet we haven't the evidence on it.

Mr. WOLF. Have you investigated that case?

Mr. GUY. Oh, yes, sir; we are investigating it. Yes, sir.

Mr. WOLF. May I ask then, are there any other cases aside from those which are marked with one asterisk that you investigated?

Mr. GUY. No. All of those outside the city limits, of course, the sheriff department and the police department, the highway patrol, and the F.B.I. agent all work together on these things.

Mr. WOLF. So you as chief of police would cooperate with the sheriff?

Mr. GUY. We cooperated in a lot of them. Of course, I felt more responsibility for those that happened inside the city limits. But my services were available to anybody that needed them, inside or out.

Mr. WOLF. In those cases which you investigated, did you investigate each of them as they occurred?

Mr. GUY. I recall when we got called to go investigate, we did, yes. Lot of them we went and investigated where we didn't get called on. They would call somebody else before they called us and many of them we had to go find out where they was. Nobody called us at all.

Mr. WOLF. How did you hear about them?

Mr. GUY. The supermarket in Burglundtown, I had some men on State Street standing up talking to a couple of F.B.I. agents and they heard the bombing. They heard the bomb go off, so they went and found it and as yet we haven't got a call on it.

Mr. WOLF. Were you or your men able to solve any of these cases?

Mr. GUY. You say we. Well, in the investigation we did our part in helping solve them.

Mr. WOLF. As I understand it, there were arrests made in four of these cases. As to the others, Mr. Pigott testified that the attorneys for the men arrested checked off a number of other incidents?

Mr. GUY. Yes, sir.

Mr. WOLF. This occurred in late September. Could you tell me what the principal obstacles were which prevented you from solving these cases before the end of September?

Mr. GUY. Lack of information and lack of good hot suspects to work on. We talked to a lot of people and it lasted until September when the case broke. We just happened to talk to the right person.

Mr. WOLF. Did you have enough men to carry out this investigation properly?

Mr. GUY. Well, we more or less turned the investigation part of it over to the F.B.I. and highway patrol and sheriff's department. They came into McComb and set up offices there and they had special men that knew how to do it probably a lot better than my men did. We worked with them, like when they wanted to go pick up somebody and talk to them, we dispatched my men to pick them up and bring them back to talk to; or any information we got, we passed along.

Mr. WOLF. Are your files closed in the cases which were not the subject of actual indictments?

Mr. GUY. No, sir; no, sir.

Mr.WOLF. Did you request any assistance from the highway patrol?

Mr. GUY. I sure have.

Mr. WOLF. When did you do this?

Mr. GUY. I think the first time—I don't know if it was the first time or not. I know I did during the bombing at the Alyene Quin home.

Mr. WOLF. Did you do this before?

Mr. GUY. I'm just trying to remember. I'm not sure. I usually called the governor—in our circumstances down there—and request some assistance. Several times we had them on a standby basis, like the time we were in Biloxi down there and we had our auxiliary policeman and highway police and highway patrol working for 24 hours around the clock. We were going to be damn sure there wasn't going to be any incidents of violence down there because we had enough trouble and we don't want any more trouble. We are going to do our best to prevent anything going on.

Mr. WOLF. As the summer went on and the number of incidents increased did you feel you had a serious situation on your hands?

Mr. GUY. Yes, I did.

Mr. WOLF. Did you take any specific steps to prevent these incidents?

Mr. GUY. We doubled our forces. We had off-duty policemen working extra hours. We called in most of our auxiliary men, worked overtime, and tried to do everything we possibly could to stop these bombings and burnings.

Mr. WOLF. Did you issue any public statements calling for law and order?

Mr. GUY. I didn't, no, but there had been I think from the sheriff's department. I figured his would be just as good as mine. I talked to a lot of people and asked them to cooperate, which they have.

Mr. WOLF. Did you attempt to gain information about the plans and activities of extremist groups such as the Klan?

Mr. GUY. Oh, yes. We worked on that angle, worked on several different angles. In a case like that you can't exclude anybody. You even checked on COFO workers and everybody else. Until you put your finger on the guilty party, everybody is a suspect.

Mr. WOLF. Were you aware of the fact that on the 20th of September, following the Quin bombing, Sheriff Warren made a statement to the press that he believed the bombings at the Quin home and at the Society Hill Baptist church were plants?

Mr. GUY. I heard him make that statement all right. I think I heard him and saw it in the paper.

Mr. WOLF. Did you agree with him at the time?

Mr. GUY. Not altogether. I did at one time think that with some of the COFO workers, there was a possibility they could have done it because I understand it has been done in Tougaloo or somewhere up there. We did not exclude them from being suspects.

Mr. WOLF. Right. Well, what I am saying is this. At the time of the last incidents, the 20th and 23d of September, you had not progressed far enough in your investigation to exclude the possibility that COFO was responsible for these bombings?

Mr. GUY. No.

Mr. WOLF. Mr. Humpstone, would you like to ask some questions?

Mr. HUMPSTONE. Chief Guy, I believe you said you had trouble learning about some of these incidents. Was that because Negroes failed to bring complaints to you?

Mr. Guy. They would call their home office. They would call the FBI and lot of times the FBI would call us.

Mr. Humpstone. Now, do you have any knowledge or any belief as to why the Negroes didn't bring complaints to you first?

Mr. Guy. No, I don't. I sure don't.

Mr. Humpstone. The Commission has heard some testimony to the effect that the reason Negroes did not bring their complaints to local law enforcement officers was that they were instructed not to by the COFO workers. Do you believe that that was a reason? Or do you believe there might have been some other reasons?

Mr. Guy. I don't know what reason they had, but they didn't do it. I'll say this. That hindered us a lot of times in making a good investigation or getting started quick on an investigation of this type. Lot of times if you can get there quick enough, you may run across something that may help you. But delaying that action and not calling us, I think it hurt us from coming up with the answer, probably a month earlier and maybe better.

Mr. Humpstone. Chief Guy, do you have any detectives on your force?

Mr. Guy. No, sir.

Mr. Humpstone. Are all of your men police officers?

Mr. Guy. That is right, sir.

Mr. Humpstone. Uniformed patrolmen?

Mr. Guy. Yes, sir.

Mr. Humpstone. Are any of the patrolmen trained as investigators?

Mr. Guy. Well, they have had roughly some training. They are not trained as fully as they should be.

Mr. Humpstone. Have any of them been to the FBI school?

Mr. Guy. No, sir. Except locally—let me take this back. The local Mississippi Law Enforcement Officer's Association held a class which went into different phases of law enforcement investigation and what not—very short classes. They need more of that, I realize that.

Mr. Humpstone. When was that class?

Mr. Guy. Several years ago.

Mr. Humpstone. Do they hold them every year?

Mr. Guy. At that time they were holding them at least once a year if we requested it, but now I'm not sure how often they hold them.

Mr. Humpstone. With respect to the incidents that involved fire or burning, I understand that it is the law of Mississippi that the State insurance commissioner, who is also ex-officio State fire marshal, has a staff of trained investigators who are employed for the purpose of investigating attempted arson, but he cannot enter a case until he has been requested to do so by local law enforcement officers. Did you believe that the evidence in any of these cases indicated arson in some form or another?

Mr. GUY. Mr. Barry, who is with the fire marshal's office, was down on several occasions. He was called in, I believe, by the fire chief, Mr. Fred Smith, to investigate some of these potential arson cases where they had tried to set a thing on fire and didn't catch it on fire.

Mr. HUMPSTONE. Did you request any assistance from the fire marshal?

Mr. GUY. No; I let Mr. Fred Smith do it. You don't have to request him. If he has a suspect, he is going to call him anyway. 1 have in the past on automobiles and different things.

Mr. WOLF. Let me ask you some questions with regard to two specific cases. First of all, back to the Wilbert Lewis case. You told us that you did investigate that case. You went out to interview Wilbert Lewis and you investigated it subsequently?

Mr. GUY. Right.

Mr. WOLF. Did you report this incident to the sheriff yourself?

Mr. GUY. No. I think they called the sheriff or called the FBI and the FBI had notified the sheriff. I went up there at night. As far as I know there wasn't anybody up there except myself. I talked to Wilbert for a good length of time and talked to his father-in-law, and he explained how it happened. As far as identifying anybody, he could not, and gave us the best description he could, and that's all we had to go on.

Mr. WOLF. Did you ever discuss this case with the sheriff?

Mr. GUY. I think off and on I have discussed all of them more or less with him.

Mr. WOLF. Have you ever received any identifying information from th FBI in this case?

Mr. GUY. No.

Mr. WOLF. Chief Guy, there were arrests of 10 men at the end of September; they were sentenced on October 23. Subsequently there were several incidents. I believe, all of them in McComb, involving the Vaccarellas, a man named Wallace, and Charles Hughes. These were all directed against white men.

Mr. GUY. Yes.

Mr. WOLF. The arrests were made, as I understand it, on November 4. This was, perhaps, within 10 days of the first series of incidents. Did you investigate those cases?

Mr. GUY. We did. In fact, I put a man in Mr. Vaccarella's store for several nights down there, trying to catch the guilty party. The sheriff, myself, and Mr. Vaccarella held a meeting in my office trying to figure out the best way to handle that thing and to investigate it and try to catch the guilty party. And we put the man in the store for several different nights to watch the store. What had happened to his store was that somebody had taken either a pellet gun or nigger shooter and shot holes through the glass windows. Now, at his house—somebody shot a shotgun at his house.

Mr. Wolf. Chief, these incidents seem to be the same type as those which occurred earlier in the summer. Is there any reason why arrests were made so quickly in these incidents and not for several months in the others?

Mr. Guy. We got the information a lot quicker. We were luckier with a lot of them. It was some darn hard work on the part of all the law enforcement agencies down there.

Mr. Wolf. Could you tell us what information you have as to the reason for the attacks on the Vaccarella family?

Mr. Guy. The only thing I know is what Mr. Vaccarella told me. He got an anonymous phone call to fire, I don't know if it said a particular nigger or all of his niggers at work, and he wouldn't do it and that's when the damage began happening to his property.

Mr. Wolf. I see. Mr. Vaccarella told you that?

Mr. Guy. Right. He told me that himself.

Mr. Wolf. I believe these men were not charged with the burning of the crosses in August. Did you ascertain whether they were responsible for those?

Mr. Guy. No, I didn't. I don't know whether they were or not.

Mr. Wolf. Chief, do you have any members of the Klan or other extremist organizations on your force?

Mr. Guy. I do not.

Mr. Wolf. Is it your policy to exclude these people?

Mr. Guy. We will not have police officers on the force that belong to a Klan organization or any other organizations that are way out.

Mr. Wolf. Do you ask the FBI to check—whether these people are members?

Mr. Guy. I asked them to check it and if they found out if anybody belonged to it, to let me know, and I would strictly dismiss them. They came back and gave me a clear bill of health.

Mr. Wolf. Since you have been police chief have you ever been an officer or member of the Americans for the Preservation of the White Race?

Mr. Guy. I have.

Mr. Wolf. What office did you hold?

Mr. Guy. I held the president's office for about two meetings. I quit, didn't ever go back, so they elected somebody else.

Mr. Wolf. Are you still a member of the organization?

Mr. Guy. I don't have a card. I had been to those two meetings when they first organized.

Mr. Wolf. What led you to join this organization?

Mr. Guy. At that time I was in politics and there was a pretty good bunch of businessmen in that thing. And actually I thought I would have some votes, so I could get elected sheriff.

Mr. Wolf. As you understand them, what are the aims and purposes of this organization?

Mr. Guy. Actually I have forgotten. I read the charter and I read the bylaws and all that and could have brought it with me. I'm sure we could get a copy but I don't have it, and I don't remember what it said.

Mr. Humpstone. While we are at this point, could you obtain that and forward it to us?

Mr. Guy. Yes, I think we can.

Mr. Wolf. I would like to read you a statement of Ellis Rowan, president of the Jackson chapter of the APWR.

Say we find a Negro who is an agitator. The first thing we do is to tell his employer. Usually that takes care of it, and the Negro is fired. We don't tell our members to do anything. More than 90 percent of the people in this area feel as we do. So all we need do is just pass the word on what somebody's doing.

We don't try to get any Negro's job, unless he is an agitator. If somebody tells us about a Negro agitator he must put it in writing. Then it goes to our executive committee, and if there's any doubt about it, a five-man committee investigates. And finally it must be voted on by the whole membership at our weekly meeting. But if the situation isn't cleared up, we just pass the word. The persons who feel as we do don't have to be told to stop trading at that place where the Negro works.

Does this statement appear to you to be consistent with the aims of the organization as you understand them?

Mr. Guy. I don't know. That didn't come up as long as I was a member down there. Now, what they did after I got out, I'm not sure. I'm not responsible, because like I say, I attended two meetings and we were more or less in the process of organizing the darn thing. As far as their aims, goals and what not, I couldn't tell you right now what they are. I don't know.

Mr. Wolf. Do you know whether the APWR in McComb has ever operated in this fashion? In other words, have they boycotted a place which hired a Negro whom the organization believed to be an "agitator", whatever that means?

Mr. Guy. I don't think we have any places in McComb boycotted as far as I know.

Mr. Wolf. Why did you resign from the APWR?

Mr. Guy. By the time the election was over——I got beat—I decided to get out of it.

Mr. Wolf. Was it public knowledge in the community that you were an officer of this organization?

Mr. Guy. Yes. I didn't try to hide it.

Mr. Wolf. Did you make it public when you resigned?

Mr. Guy. I didn't make it public when I joined and when I resigned, it is just in and out. I didn't think too many people knew it. The reason they know it now is because I told you.

Mr. Wolf. Do you think that your membership in the Americans for the Preservation of the White Race was inconsistent with your duties as chief of police?

Mr. Guy. Well, after thinking about it, I think the chief should be free from all organizations that might put pressure on him. Not that they put any pressure on me, but there's a possibility any organization will put a pressure on a chief of police if he belongs to it. And for that reason I don't belong to any of them.

Mr. Wolf. Do you think that your membership in the Americans for the Preservation of the White Race had anything to do with the Negroes being reluctant to report incidents to the police force?

Mr. Guy. I don't think so.

Mr. Wolf. You don't?

Mr. Guy. I don't see how they could have known that I belonged to it. Like I say, I attended a couple meetings and that was it, and very few people were at those meetings.

Mr. Wolf. Do you think if they had known you were a member or president of the organization, they would have felt less prone to trust the police or believe they would get equal treatment from the police?

Mr. Guy. I don't know about that, what their reaction would have been if they knew about it. But I don't think you will find anyone in McComb say that they couldn't trust me or that I mistreated them.

Mr. Wolf. Do the Ku Klux Klan or related organizations exist in McComb and Pike County?

Mr. Guy. They did, and my idea is that they still do. As far as any activity, I haven't seen any lately.

Mr. Wolf. Do you have any idea how many people belong to it?

Mr. Guy. No, I don't. I just haven't.

Mr. Wolf. You don't know whether they are still active?

Mr. Guy. No, not for sure.

Mr. Wolf. Were the people who were sentenced for the bombings members of the Klan or Klan-type groups?

Mr. Guy. I'm not definite about that because I didn't talk to them. The sheriff did. My understanding is that they did that on their own.

There may be one or two of them did belong to the Klan, but I couldn't swear to it because I don't know for sure.

Mr. Wolf. When they were arrested, did you collect a substantial amount of weapons and ammunition from some of them?

Mr. Guy. The FBI did uncover quite a bit of dynamite, caps, and weapons, and what not. When I say FBI, we were all working together, you might say.

Mr. Wolf. Was it an amount that you would call an arsenal?

Mr. Guy. You could, yes; I think you could.

Mr. Wolf. Was it more than the normal amount?

Mr. Guy. More than the normal man would have just ordinarily, yes, because dynamite you got no benefit at all. It is in the construction business to blow up stuff.

Mr. Wolf. Do you believe that the people who were arrested and sentenced were the only people involved or implicated in this violence?

Mr. Guy. It's my understanding when they arrested these boys, they more or less admitted to all of the bombings. Of course, we didn't have enough evidence to prove all of them. But we feel like they was the biggest bunch and they were responsible for the biggest majority of it.

Mr. Wolf. As I understand it, they are not wealthy people. And yet they possessed a substantial amount of weapons. Does that suggest, perhaps, that there were other people in the community who were financing them?

Mr. Guy. Well, I don't know what that stuff cost, to tell you the truth. But a man working nowadays can put away a nickel or two and buy it himself, not too much. But they probably could have had financial backing, but where from I don't know.

Mr. Wolf. Do you believe there were some other people financing them?

Mr. Guy. I can't say. I don't know.

Mr. Wolf. Your investigation hasn't developed any evidence along this line?

Mr. Guy. No.

Mr. Wolf. Thank you.

(Whereupon, at about 3:45 p.m. the deposition was concluded.)

U.S. COMMISSION ON CIVIL RIGHTS

WEDNESDAY AFTERNOON SESSION, FEBRUARY 17, 1965

A subcommittee of the Commission met in the Recreation Hall, Veterans Administration Center, 1500 East Woodrow Wilson Drive, Jackson, Miss., at 5:30 p.m., Wednesday, February 17, 1965, the Hon. Erwin N. Griswold, Commissioner, presiding.

Present: Erwin N. Griswold, Presiding; Mrs. Frankie Muse Freeman, Commissioner.

Also Present: William L. Taylor, General Counsel; Michael O. Finkelstein, Assistant General Counsel.

PROCEEDINGS

Commissioner GRISWOLD. The Subcommittee will come to order. We are to receive some documents, Mr. Taylor?

Mr. TAYLOR. Mr. Davenport.

Mr. DAVENPORT. Here.

Mr. TAYLOR. Mr. Davenport is here pursuant to a subpena calling for the following documents:

All records, documents, and memoranda in your possession or control, including without limitation, all records of complaints, affidavits and warrants, records of arrests, investigative reports and statements pertaining to the beating of Bruce Payne on or near Port Gibson on or about October 31, and the assault upon Bruce Payne and George Green in Jefferson or Claiborne County on or about November 2, 1963.

Will you produce the documents, sir?

Mr. DAVENPORT. Shall I enumerate them or just hand them to you?

Mr. FINKELSTEIN. Just hand them to us. That's fine.

Mr. DAVENPORT. Those are the affidavits and warrants and bonds. I have no statements or reports that were furnished by any investigative officer. And I made those in my own office. I borrowed them from the circuit clerk and made them where I could have something to give to you all, see.

Mr. TAYLOR. These are all the documents you have concerning those two cases?

Mr. DAVENPORT. That is correct. And I prepared that affidavit. Now the second name you mentioned, we don't know anything about that Green.

Mr. TAYLOR. Let me get this clear. Do the documents you have here refer to the incident on October 31 only?

Mr. DAVENPORT. It refers to the incident of Bruce Payne only.

Mr. TAYLOR. There were two incidents concerning Bruce Payne, October 31 and November 2.

Mr. DAVENPORT. I don't know the dates, but it was the one concerning the beating, not the shooting.

Mr. TAYLOR. Those are all the documents?

Mr. DAVENPORT. Yes.

Commissioner GRISWOLD. Do you want to number the documents?

Mr. TAYLOR. No, it is not necessary.

Commissioner GRISWOLD. Then the documents will be received.

Do you have anything more you want of Mr. Davenport?

Mr. TAYLOR. No, sir.

Commissioner GRISWOLD. Is he under subpena?

Mr. TAYLOR. He is under subpena and should return here tomorrow, February 18.

Commissioner GRISWOLD. Mr. Davenport, you are excused today, but are still under subpena as indicated. Thank you.

Mr. TAYLOR. Mr. Lawrence, you are here in response to a subpena which calls for exactly the same documents called for from Mr. Davenport. Do you have such documents?

Mr. LAWRENCE. Sir, I do not, because I haven't had any information relative to any of this matter. I have written no document. I had no information of any particular until sometime in December of 1964, no documents. The affidavits would be filed—would be what is there—by the county attorney, and I wouldn't have any.

Mr. TAYLOR. So you have no documents with respect to this?

Mr. LAWRENCE. None whatever. Now if you want that, I can go and get a certified copy for you, but it will be just the same that you have there.

Mr. TAYLOR. I don't think that will be necessary, to duplicate this document.

Mr. LAWRENCE. Thank you.

Commissioner GRISWOLD. Is Mr. Lawrence under subpena?

Mr. TAYLOR. Mr. Lawrence is under subpena for the same time as Mr. Davenport.

Commissioner GRISWOLD. Mr. Lawrence, you are excused now, but remain subject to the subpena.

Mr. LAWRENCE. Thank you. Now, I beg your pardon, for the intrusion, please. Do you mean—let me say that I am going to have a term of court tomorrow——

Commissioner GRISWOLD. Would you please sit over there if you have more to say.

Mr. LAWRENCE. Now let me see if I understand Your Honor, please. I have a term of court approaching Monday morning. I am writing indictments, I am making investigations. Do you mean that I journey on until I get further notice from you, or am I to be back here in the morning?

Commissioner GRISWOLD. Mr. Taylor?

Mr. TAYLOR. Sir, you are to be back here in the morning for the sessions beginning at 9 o'clock tomorrow morning.

Mr. LAWRENCE. Thank you. Would you let me come at 9 o'clock? I am not asking any favors. I drive slowly.

Mr. TAYLOR. I cannot say for sure, but it should be in the morning session. The witness is scheduled to be called during the morning session tomorrow.

Commissioner GRISWOLD. I can say you will be heard in the morning, but I can't say you will be heard as the first witness in the morning.

Mr. LAWRENCE. That will be all right.

Commissioner GRISWOLD. Will you see that that is carried out, Mr. Taylor?

Mr. TAYLOR. Yes, sir.

Mr. LAWRENCE. That means for me to be here at nine. Thank you.

Commissioner GRISWOLD. Anything further, Mr. Taylor?

Mr. TAYLOR. No, sir.

Commissioner GRISWOLD. This session of the subcommittee is adjourned.

(Whereupon, at 5:35 p.m., the subcommittee of the Commission was adjourned.)

THURSDAY MORNING SESSION, FEBRUARY 18, 1965

The Commission met in the Recreation Hall, Veterans Administration Center, 1500 East Woodrow Wilson Drive, Jackson, Miss., at 9:00 a.m., Thursday, February 18, 1965, the Hon. John A. Hannah, Chairman of the Commission, presiding.

Present: John A. Hannah, Chairman; Eugene Patterson, Vice Chairman; Mrs. Frankie Muse Freeman, Commissioner; Erwin N. Griswold, Commissioner; Rev. Theodore M. Hesburgh, C.S.C., Commissioner; Robert S. Rankin, Commissioner.

Also Present: Howard W. Rogerson, Acting Staff Director; William L. Taylor, General Counsel; Samuel J. Simmons, Director of Field Services; Warren I. Cikins, Special Assistant to the Staff Director; M. Carl Holman, Information Officer; Michael O. Finkelstein, Assistant General Counsel; Charles C. Humpstone, staff attorney; Roy Littlejohn, staff attorney; Richard F. Bellman, staff attorney; Brian Olmstead, staff attorney; Edwin D. Wolf, staff attorney; John G. Birkle, Financial Management Officer; Robert H. Amidon, Chief of Investigations; Alan Marer, staff attorney, Department of Justice.

PROCEEDINGS

Chairman HANNAH. This hearing of the U.S. Commission on Civil Rights will come to order. Mr. Taylor, will you call the next witness.

Mr. TAYLOR. The next witness is Robert W. Brumfield.

Chairman HANNAH. Mr. Brumfield, will you raise your right hand?

(Whereupon, Mr. Robert W. Brumfield was duly sworn by the Chairman and testified as follows:)

Chairman HANNAH. Mr. Taylor, begin the questioning.

TESTIMONY OF ROBERT W. BRUMFIELD, ESQ., PIKE COUNTY, MISS.

Mr. TAYLOR. Mr. Brumfield, would you please give your full name, your residence, and your occupation for the record?

Mr. BRUMFIELD. Robert W. Brumfield. I am a resident of McComb, Miss., and I am an attorney.

Mr. TAYLOR. How long have you lived in McComb?

Mr. BRUMFIELD. All of my life, with the exception of when I was away at college and some 6 months in California.

Mr. TAYLOR. Have you held public office in Pike County or McComb?

Mr. BRUMFIELD. Yes; I have. I was police judge or city judge from 1955 to the latter part of 1962.

Mr. TAYLOR. With what community organizations are you affiliated?

Mr. BRUMFIELD. Well, during 1964 I was president of the McComb Chamber of Commerce. I am a member of the McComb Lions Club and past president of that organization, and a member or affiliated with a number of other clubs there in town.

Mr. TAYLOR. We understand that a group of white people in McComb became concerned about the incidents of racial violence which we heard testimony about yesterday. Can you tell us what they did about it?

Mr. BRUMFIELD. Well, sir; we became greatly disturbed about the incidents there in McComb and formed a group to try to determine what, if anything, we could or should do to help solve the problems. We started having meetings the latter part of October, and in November came out with a statement of principles that we felt embodied the ideas that would help solve the problems that we had in particular in McComb.

And Mr. Taylor, if you would like, I have brought for the benefit of the Commission the advertisement setting forth that statement of principles which I would like to present. This was published in the McComb Enterprise Journal in its edition of November 17, 1964.

And gentlemen, the reason for the publishing of this statement at that time was this. We started working on our group during the latter part of October. In November we had built to a group of approximately 20. We hoped to enlarge our group to some 200 before we made a public statement. In the middle or earlier part of November we had built our group to approximately 50 people. We were informed the—I believe the first Thursday before this statement appeared in the newspaper on Tuesday—that the NAACP planned to make a test of public accommodations there in McComb. Although we had not built our group up to the size which we wanted it to be at that time, we nevertheless felt that we must at that time come out with a statement of principles, setting forth our belief that although we do not favor the Civil Rights Act, it was nevertheless the law of the land and we had to learn to live under that law and abide by it, and urging our people to be peaceful while these public tests were taking place.

This statement was printed by a local printer. We started getting signatures on a Friday morning with a press deadline the following Monday night. We obtained by press time over 650 signatures to this statement of principles right there in McComb. Undoubtedly we could have gotten many more, but we had a deadline. We didn't have an ample opportunity to really present it by and large to the people of our town and our county. Since that time we have had many hundreds who have signed the statement of principles.

Mr. TAYLOR. Mr. Brumfield, the statement isn't very long. Would you care to read it or summarize its major points for the Commission?

Mr. BRUMFIELD. Yes; I will be glad to.

The great majority of our citizens believe in law and order and are against violence of any kind. In spite of this, acts of terrorism have been committed numerous times against citizens both Negro and white.

We believe the time has come for responsible people to speak out for what is right and against what is wrong. For too long we have let the extremists on both sides bring our community close to chaos.

There is only one responsible stance we can take: And that is for equal treatment under the law for all citizens regardless of race, creed, position or wealth; for making our protests within the framework of the law; and for obeying the laws of the land regardless of our personal feelings. Certain of these laws may be contrary to our traditions, customs, or beliefs, but as God-fearing men and women, and as citizens of these United States, we see no other honorable course to follow.

To these ends and for the purpose of restoring peace, tranquility, and progress to our area, we respectfully urge the following:

1. Order and respect for law must be reestablished and maintained.

(a) Law officers should make only lawful arrests. "Harassment" arrests, no matter what the provocation, are not consonant with impartiality of the law.

(b) To insure the confidence of the people in their officials, we insist that no man is entitled to serve in a public office, elective or appointive, who is a member of any organization declared to be subversive by the Senate Internal Security Subcommittee or the U.S. Army, Navy, or Air Force, or to take any obligation upon himself in conflict with his oath of office.

2. Economic threats and sanctions against people of both races must be ended. They only bring harm to both races.

3. We urge citizens of both races to reestablish avenues of communication and understanding. In addition, it is urged that the Negro leadership cooperate with local officials.

4. We urge widest possible use of our citizenship in the selection of juries. We further urge that men called for jury duty not be excused except for the most compelling reasons.

5. We urge our fellow citizens to take a greater interest in public affairs, in the selection of candidates, and in the support and/or constructive criticism of public servants.

6. We urge all of our people to approach the future with a renewed dedication and to reflect an attitude of optimism about our county.

This statement was signed, as of 7 p.m., approximately 3 days after its original circulation, by over 650 people, and the names are attached to this list.

Mr. Taylor. What would you say has been the effect of the Citizens for Progress?

Mr. Brumfield. Well, I think the effect has been very good. Now, unquestionably, the court in our county, getting a plea of guilty in these bombing cases and putting these men on probation, had a great deal of effect in calming the situation in our town and in our county. We also feel that our statement of principles has had some effect toward calming our people and toward trying to make everyone understand that we are part of the United States, these are the laws of the United States, and that we have to live with them as best we can.

Mr. Taylor. Is your group doing anything to follow up or to implement the principles that you have stated?

Mr. Brumfield. Yes, sir; we are working to implement these principles.

Mr. Taylor. You have said that the law is being accepted even though it wasn't exactly welcomed by many people. Isn't it possible while this law isn't welcomed, that improving economic and educational opportunity for Negroes, might turn out to be good business for everybody, and for the State of Mississippi?

Mr. BRUMFIELD. Well, it is possible. It very definitely is. I can't say that it is probable. Now, the Mississippi Economic Council, which is the State chamber of commerce, has a program right now underway called "75 by 75." I think presently the average income of the people in the State of Mississippi is about 52 percent of the national average. Now this program, "75 by 75," is an effort to try to raise the average income of the people of this State to 75 percent of the national average by 1975. Of course, approximately 50 percent of the population of this State is colored. We cannot raise the average income of this State to 75 percent of the national average unless we raise the average income of our colored people, along with our white people. Now, our primary problem in Mississippi is not enough employment, not enough industry. Of course, the Civil Rights Act is not going to bring us that employment and it is not going to bring us that industry.

Mr. TAYLOR. Thank you, Mr. Brumfield.

Chairman HANNAH. Father Hesburgh.

Commissioner HESBURGH. Mr. Brumfield, that is a fine statement of principles, and I am sure I speak for many people when I say that we welcome it. Is it possible to get what you have done extended throughout the State to other counties where we have had difficulty?

Mr. BRUMFIELD. Well, sir, the Mississippi Economic Council, the Mississippi Manufacturers Association, I noticed in the paper this morning, the Mississippi Association of Supervisors, the Mississippi Sheriffs Association have adopted statements very similar to the statement of principles that we formulated there in McComb. There is a little difference in the wording. There are a few items we have in our statement that are not in theirs. But as I understand, they are going to try to circulate this statement that the Mississippi Economic Council has formulated throughout the State.

Commissioner HESBURGH. Mr. Brumfield, does part of one of the points in your statement indicate that a State official should not be able to belong to the Ku Klux Klan?

Mr. BRUMFIELD. Well, sir, I won't name any organization. I will say that if the Ku Klux Klan is on the subversive list, that it certainly would be included.

Commissioner HESBURGH. I just wasn't sure. And the last question I had is that it has seemed to me, at least listening to the testimony the last few days, that at one time in McComb there seemed to be a breakdown of confidence in the law, so to speak, or in the protection of homes and life under the law. Do you think that can be rebuilt?

Mr. BRUMFIELD. Yes. We—now when I say "we" I speak primarily for white people—now we did not have any lack of confidence in our law enforcement officials there. It did appear that law and order at times was breaking down in our county. We believe that the lack of cooperation that has been brought out by previous witnesses in this hearing yesterday has been resolved by the sheriff and the other parties.

Commissioner HESBURGH. When I said that the confidence had broken down, I probably should have been more specific. The confidence of the Negro community was broken down to the extent that Negroes were reluctant to call the law when they had difficulty because it often involved further difficulty.

Mr. BRUMFIELD. Well, I don't believe that you could say that the confidence of the majority of the Negro community was broken down, because of course there were just a small portion of our colored population that was involved in these activities. I am sure that while these acts were going on and were being committed, that they were meeting other law violations that were being prosecuted in the courts where the complaining witnesses were colored people or where the defendants were colored people.

Commissioner HESBURGH. Well, I was very happy to see as part of your statement that there should be an end to arrests that simply involve harassment. I think that is a very good statement.

Mr. BRUMFIELD. Thank you, sir.

Chairman HANNAH. Mr. Taylor, can we insert this advertisement in the record.

Mr. TAYLOR. Yes, sir. This will be marked as Exhibit No. 12 and placed in the record.

Chairman HANNAH. It is received in the record.

(Exhibit No. 12 was marked for identification and received in evidence.)

Chairman HANNAH. Mrs. Freeman?

Commissioner FREEMAN. Mr. Brumfield, it is true, of course, that a declaration of principles is a necessary first step in changing a climate. However, I would like to know if you can give us some more specific information about a program of implementation, and particularly with respect to three areas.

Mr. BRUMFIELD. At this time I cannot say anything other than the fact that the program is being implemented.

Commissioner FREEMAN. Well, may I ask you further then. Does the list of persons who signed include employers?

Mr. BRUMFIELD. This list includes employers, employees, professional men, merchants, and bankers. It is a wide segment of people in the community.

Commissioner FREEMAN. Did this statement encourage more active participation in public affairs?

Mr. BRUMFIELD. That's correct.

Commissioner FREEMAN. One of the things that we have learned here is that there has·been a lack of participation. Rather, Negroes have been discouraged from participating in affairs of government. Could you say that the statement would encourage this large segment of the population, the 40 percent who are nonwhite, to participate actively in affairs of government?

Mr. BRUMFIELD. This statement urges all of our citizens to take a more active interest in public affairs.

Commissioner FREEMAN. Now, we have found there is a wide discrepancy in the educational attainment level between white and nonwhite; here to for the Negroes have achieved much less. There is also a discrepancy in the educational system. Does the statement contemplate upgrading the schools and desegregating the school system?

Mr. BRUMFIELD. What specific recommendations this group might make I do not know at the present time.

Commissioner FREEMAN. Thank you.

Chairman HANNAH. Dean Griswold?

Commissioner GRISWOLD. Mr. Brumfield, I want to make it plain that I welcome and applaud this statement and your part in attaining it. There are some facts about it that I would like to ascertain. Are there any Negro signers to this statement?

Mr. BRUMFIELD. No, sir. To my knowledge we didn't ask any to sign. We didn't ask any public officials to sign this statement.

Commissioner GRISWOLD. Why did you not ask any Negroes to sign?

Mr. BRUMFIELD. Well, we just didn't. Why, I don't know. We just didn't. Now, of course, we feel like that on this statement we have approximately between 25 percent and one-third of the people that could have been called on to sign this document in our town. Of course, we have a population of approximately 12,000 there, roughly half of whom are colored and who were not asked to sign the statement.

Another half of that remaining 6,000 you would classify as young people, college students and teenagers and infants. And a great portion of the 3,000 left would be widows in McComb. McComb is a town of elderly retired people.

And we feel like that of the people that we could have got to sign this, we got approximately 25 percent to a third. We could have gotten more, but, as I said, this was something that was new. This was not something that you just take and lay down on a fellow's desk and say "Here, sign this." This is something you had to explain to a person before you asked him to sign.

Commissioner GRISWOLD. Did you find opposition to signing?

Mr. BRUMFIELD. Not to my knowledge. Now there were some who

did not sign it; there were some that refused to sign. But most of the people who were presented with this statement did sign.

Commissioner GRISWOLD. Have you encountered any reaction as a result of your activity in obtaining these signatures?

Mr. BRUMFIELD. No, sir.

Commissioner GRISWOLD. Have you lost clients or have people refused to deal with you?

Mr. BRUMFIELD. No, sir.

Commissioner GRISWOLD. Now let me turn to another matter. You are a lawyer in McComb and a former police judge. We had as a witness here yesterday, Willie Dillon, who was arrested at 3 or 4 a.m. one day last August and by 3 p.m. of the same day was arraigned in your local court. I assume you were not the judge at that time?

Mr. BRUMFIELD. No, sir; that was the justice of the peace court, which is a county court. I was police justice. I had the same subject jurisdiction as the justice of the peace, only my territorial jurisdiction was confined to the city limits.

Commissioner GRISWOLD. According to the evidence before us, he was arraigned at 3 o'clock the afternoon of the same day, having been in jail all of the interval from his arrest to the arraignment without any counsel. He pleaded guilty to two charges. With respect to at least one of these, operating of a garage without a license, would appear to me to be at least a substantial question whether his acts constituted that offense. He received a substantial sentence; both a substantial fine and a period in jail. Is this the customary way, the ordinary way, in which offenses of this kind are handled in McComb?

Mr. BRUMFIELD. Well, now, I don't know what you mean by "Is this the ordinary way." Do you mean the speed with which it was handled, or what?

Commissioner GRISWOLD. I mean the speed and the lack of counsel and the substantial penalty.

Mr. BRUMFIELD. Well, Dean Griswold, of course I am not familiar with that case other than what I heard testified to here yesterday and other than what I read through the newspaper. Now the only thing I can tell you is the experience that I had in the 7 or 8 years that I was the judge there in McComb.

We held court every morning at 8 o'clock, and people that had committed an offense in the preceding 24 hours were brought before me and were arraigned and either tried at that time, or their case was set for a later date. Now, the justice courts operate a little bit different. They do not have regularly scheduled criminal terms of court. Generally speaking, in the justice court, the criminal hearing would be held just about any time the defendant was brought before the justice.

As to the matter of fines, I can't comment one way or the other on that. I was city judge in McComb when we had the original racial trouble in 1961, and our fines, the fines that I imposed, where there was a plea of guilty, were $100 and 30-day jail sentence suspended pending good behavior. Where the plea was not guilty and there was a conviction, I believe the sentence was $100 fine and 30 days in jail with no suspension.

Commissioner GRISWOLD. When, in this case, after the substantial sentence was imposed, counsel was obtained, he was from Jackson. Do you have any idea why they would go to Jackson to get a lawyer in such case?

Mr. BRUMFIELD. No sir; I don't. Mr. Wiltshire, who represented Chief Guy here yesterday, is president of our local bar association. The State bar and the local bar association decided that they would handle these cases. I personally could not handle them, because I am a law partner of Mr. Reeves, the county prosecuting attorney, and, of course, I would have been barred from appearing in criminal court.

Commissioner GRISWOLD. I want to make it plain, I am not seeking to be critical of you in any way.

Mr. BRUMFIELD. Yes.

Commissioner GRISWOLD. On the contrary, I greatly admire what you have done. I am just trying to find the situation, the atmosphere in McComb. Are there any Negro lawyers in McComb?

Mr. BRUMFIELD. No, sir.

Commissioner GRISWOLD. Is it the practice in McComb that substantial jail sentences are imposed in the local courts without counsel for the defendants?

Mr. BRUMFIELD. No, sir; no, sir; there again, as I say, I am barred from practicing in the criminal courts. The only thing I can tell you is the experience that I had while I was city judge. Now, take, for instance, public drunkenness. The fine was $22.50. That applied regardless of whether they were colored or whether they were white. Assault and battery, minor assault and battery would run around that. Fines in the city court would run anywhere from around $12.50 on a simple speeding charge to as much as a hundred dollars on a driving while under the influence of intoxicating liquor charge.

Commissioner GRISWOLD. These were all fines and not jail sentences?

Mr. BRUMFIELD. That's right, they were all fines.

Commissioner GRISWOLD. In this case I find myself still rather startled not merely by the arrests under the circumstances, but also by the 3-month and 5-month jail sentences on these charges.

Mr. BRUMFIELD. I myself have placed jail sentences on defendants and did place jail sentences on defendants in racial cases, in 1961, where they pled not guilty and were convicted. That involved white and colored.

Commissioner GRISWOLD. Do you think there should be a heavier sentence imposed when there is a plea of not guilty?

Mr. BRUMFIELD. Well, to my knowledge, that is more or less the procedure of courts. Where there is an admission of guilt or recognition of the fact that one has broken the law, I think the courts are generally inclined to be a little bit more lenient than they are when one just denies guilt and is later convicted.

Commissioner GRISWOLD. In this case, the defendant did plead guilty. He got an aggregate of 8 months for rather trivial offenses. Isn't that a little steep on the basis of your experience?

Mr. BRUMFIELD. Well, I think the steepest jail sentence I imposed was approximately 3 months while I was there.

Commissioner GRISWOLD. Thank you.

Chairman HANNAH. Mr. Rankin?

Commissioner RANKIN. This statement that you gave us has helped McComb a lot, hasn't it?

Mr. BRUMFIELD. Yes, it has helped. There is no question it has helped. But at the same time, the people that signed this statement did not want to take away credit from the court decision. The court decision in the bombing cases, was extremely unpopular throughout the county. Due to the manner in which evidence was procured in those cases, there was a possibility, a good possibility, that evidence would not have been admissible and that there would have been an acquittal either through preemptory instruction or through the jury finding them not guilty, and that would have ended those cases. Now when putting these people on probation, controlling their action, the judge, as was stated I believe when the statement was read on McComb early yesterday, did tell those boys that he was holding them responsible for any violence that would or might be committed in the community, regardless of the source. This had a great deal of effect.

As I say, our statement had some effect. But nevertheless, I don't want to sit up here and tell you that this statement of principles alone is what calmed the situation in McComb. I feel like it had some influence, but I also think that this probation had some influence, too.

Commissioner RANKIN. But McComb has prospered since then, hasn't it? Didn't you say a few minutes ago that it hasn't hurt them economically?

Mr. BRUMFIELD. That is true.

Commissioner RANKIN. And a few minutes ago you also made the statement that the Civil Rights Act of 1964 was of no particular economic benefit to the area; that it in itself would not bring prosperity.

Mr. BRUMFIELD. That's right.

Commissioner RANKIN. Don't you think it would help? That is my point. I have before me Frank Morgan's article in the Wall Street Journal for February 2, 1965, which he calls, "The Price of Strife." He goes into it and shows what a heavy price that you pay. Conformity to the Civil Rights Act might after all be the means whereby you might secure economic advantage.

Mr. BRUMFIELD. Well, it could possibly, Mr. Rankin, but of course, if you have a hundred jobs in the community, a possible redistribution of those jobs on different racial lines in effect would not benefit your community economically.

Commissioner RANKIN. Well, now, wait just a minute. If it were known that there was no racial strife in McComb and that there was labor in McComb, would not new industries come in? Wouldn't this be a place where they would want to locate? Couldn't that bring them?

Mr. BRUMFIELD. Well, yes, sir.

Commissioner RANKIN. Why, sure. Therefore, as it says in this article, "The Price of Strife," maybe, after all, complying with the Civil Rights Act of 1964 might be an instrument for improving economic conditions?

Mr. BRUMFIELD. That's right.

Commissioner RANKIN. Thank you.

Chairman HANNAH. Mr. Patterson.

Vice Chairman PATTERSON. Mr. Brumfield, we have had some witnesses here at this hearing who questioned whether words about change mean anything, whether deeds will follow in Mississippi. You state that following the breaking of the bombing case in McComb, plus the issuance of this statement of principles by your business leadership, some things did change. Is that an accurate assessment of what you said?

Mr. BRUMFIELD. Well, it certainly appeared to be a lot calmer. For example, I believe the residence of Aylene Quin was bombed on a Sunday night, if I am not mistaken. The next day—my office is on Main Street there in McComb, up over one of the local banks in our main business district—the next day you could look out across Main Street and three-fourths of the parking places in town were empty. People were actually afraid at that time to come on the streets. But after the solving of these cases, and the matters that took place subsequent to that, the calm was restored to the community.

Vice Chairman PATTERSON. This strikes me as a very dramatic thing. McComb and Pike County were nationally publicized as a hotbed of trouble in Mississippi for a long time. All of a sudden, after a case was cracked and after the business community issued its statement of principles, tranquillity was restored and has been maintained to this day, has it not?

Mr. BRUMFIELD. Yes, sir.

Vice Chairman PATTERSON. Would you say to any troubled community in the South that this is the proper way to restore tranquillity to a community?

Mr. BRUMFILD. I think vigorous law enforcement and unified effort by all of the citizens of the community to maintain law and order is very definitely what is needed. And we had vigorous law enforcement. I couldn't help admiring Sheriff Warren yesterday. And, of course, I am sure you gentlemen are familiar with this. Assisting Sheriff Warren in this investigation were some 25 or 30 Federal Bureau of Investigation agents working on these cases, and some 10 or 15 or more Mississippi State Highway Patrol specially trained investigators. These fellows worked round the clock and they solved these cases about as quickly as they could have been solved. And in fact, it is possible that their haste in solving them may be the reason some of the evidence would not have been admissible.

Vice Chairman PATTERSON. Mr. Brumfield, Sheriff Warren also mentioned in his testimony that his job of law enforcement became a lot easier when the business and professional power structure of McComb got behind him and issued its statement of principles. As a member of that power structure, would you have any advice for other communities in Mississippi?

Mr. BRUMFIELD. Well, I certainly think that as problems like this confront other communities, that they need to have unified leadership to try to cope with them. Through perhaps unified leadership and asking the people to abide by the laws, they would not get themselves involved in difficulty.

Now, another thing, in Sheriff Warren's testimony yesterday, he overlooked that, back prior to the actual Mississippi project coming into McComb, Sheriff Warren, Chief Guy, Mayor Burt, many others, went before community organizations in McComb, made statements in the newspapers and over the radio, asking our people to remain calm, and to maintain law and order. They asked the people to do this. We later found out it was just more or less a handful of people that were stirring up all this trouble.

Vice Chairman PATTERSON. Do you then agree with Sheriff Warren that the attitude of the business community and community leadership, does have a role in law enforcement?

Mr. BRUMFIELD. Very definitely.

Vice Chairman PATTERSON. Thank you.

Mr. BRUMFIELD. I think the business leadership or the citizens— if your citizens don't support the law, well, you have no law.

Vice Chairman PATTERSON. Thank you.

Chairman HANNAH. Thank you very much, Mr. Brumfield. You are excused.

Mr. BRUMFIELD. Thank you.

(Witness excused.)

Chairman HANNAH. Mr. Taylor, will you call the next witness?

Mr. TAYLOR. The next witness is Mr. Jessie Harris.

Chairman HANNAH. Mr. Harris, will you raise your right hand?

(Whereupon, Mr. Jessie Lee Harris was duly sworn by the Chairman and testified as follows:)

Chairman HANNAH. Mr. Taylor, will you begin the questioning.

TESTIMONY OF MR. JESSIE LEE HARRIS, PIKE COUNTY, MISS.

Mr. TAYLOR. Mr. Harris, would you please give us your full name, your address, and your occupation?

Mr. HARRIS. Jessie Lee Harris, 702 Wall Street, McComb, Miss. I am a field worker for the Student Nonviolent Coordinating Committee.

Mr. TAYLOR. How long have you lived in Mississippi?

Mr. HARRIS. All my life.

Mr. TAYLOR. How long have you been active in the civil rights movement?

Mr. HARRIS. Ever since 1961 when I was arrested here in Jackson for breach of the peace when I went into the Trailway bus station. Since then I have been active in voter registration in Mississippi.

Mr. TAYLOR. Could you tell us briefly about the program of your organization in McComb and what its purposes and goals are?

Mr. HARRIS. Well, in 1963, I was assigned to direct the third congressional district in which McComb is located in voter registration. I had been going into towns like Vicksburg, Natchez, here in Jackson, and into McComb, to set up a voter registration project—or voter education project, you might say. Since then I have been mainly working in and out of McComb.

I think that everybody knew that the summer project was about to start right after the orientation took place in Oxford. Ten of us went into McComb to set up a voter registration project.

Mr. TAYLOR. What was the object of this project?

Mr. HARRIS. Mainly voter registration.

Mr. TAYLOR. To get more people to register?

Mr. HARRIS. Voter education, you might say.

Mr. TAYLOR. Could you also tell us briefly what the problems were that you encountered in the local community in trying to carry out your project? What problems did your organization and you personally encounter?

Mr. HARRIS. Well, I think I might say practically the same thing that Wiley Branton testified about what happened in the Delta. Practically the same thing happened in McComb when people go down to the courthouse and register to vote.

I mentioned before that before the summer project, we went into McComb. There was certain things that we was expecting to happen. We didn't know too much about McComb. I mentioned before that only two or three of us had went into McComb—just to talk to people. We talked to people like Mrs. Quin, Mr. C. C. Bryant, and people that we had some type of contact with.

When 10 of us went into McComb to set up a voter registration project, we mostly expected to be arrested, you might say be beaten, or even killed. We knowed that we was going into an area where voter registration or activities had never got really off the ground before. We also knew of the atmosphere that was created down there for the last, you might say, 4 or 5 years or so, so we was afraid to go in there. And after we went in there, it was pretty much true. We went in an bought a house in the ctiy—well, you might say leased a house for a year or two. We was followed by highway patrolmen all the way from Crystal Spring into McComb. When we got into McComb we were stopped by the highway patrol and taken to the nearest town somewhere in Lincoln County for investigation. We were questioned. This was practically the same pattern which we always expected—we would be stopped, you know.

When we got into McComb, we were stopped by some deputies and we were asked our names and where we were from and what we was doing there, and we was released without charge.

And I might say we went in—it is kind of hard to really explain the whole line of fear, not only among us but among the people we worked with.

Mr. TAYLOR. Were there many arrests during the course of the summer of people in your organization?

Mr. HARRIS. Well, we had quite a few. I think after we arrived in McComb about 2 weeks—about 4 days after that, after our house was bombed—I knows in the last part of June and about a week after we arrived in McComb, we were stopped by highway patrolmens, and we was given tickets and so forth. At one time I was picked up and taken down to the jail for speeding. Most of all the staff there in McComb was arrested for food handling without securing a permit. We was arrested in October at the county courthouse for trespassing. We were stopped many times for investigation during the bombings and so forth.

Mr. TAYLOR. Were there also incidents of violence in connection with your project?

Mr. HARRIS. What do you mean when you say "incidents of violence"?

Mr. TAYLOR. Incidents of violence directed at the place where you conducted your project?

Mr. HARRIS. Well, 16 bombings took place in McComb, and we really feel that the reason for these 16 bombings, was because of our activities there in McComb. I spoke at Society Hill, tried to ask them to let us use the church for voter-registration class, and about 2 days after that the church was bombed.

Mr. TAYLOR. I mean particularly with respect to the place where you conducted your business, the Freedom House.

Mr. HARRIS. Well, the Freedom House was bombed.

Mr. TAYLOR. Do you think that the situation is improving now?

Mr. HARRIS. No; I don't think so. I have listened to the testimony of the last person who testified. He mentioned something about the 650 people who signed the statement of principles. He also mentioned that no Negroes was asked to sign the statement. I think that I can speak for the majority of the peoples who live in Pike County, or McComb, that the statement of principles to them really don't solve their problems. We think that the statement of principles in McComb—came out in McComb, you might say, was another trick to stop all the attention that was focused on McComb during the summer.

As I mentioned before, before we went into McComb, there was about two or three bombings had already occurred and there was some shooting up and down one of the main streets there and there were many cases where people that came into McComb and were practically ran out of town because they were from outside of the State. When we got to McComb I think that you might say that we was a threat. We was a threat not only to the white community, but we was a threat to the power structure there.

After all the bombing that took place there, and because of our presence, because we wanted to use churches to set up classes and because we wanted to teach Negroes how to fill out the registration card and to participate in the Government, and because we wanted to teach other subjects, like in Freedom School where we teach students courses that they never get in high school, and we want to get them involved in community organization, I think that this is a threat to the power structure there. And so I think that this is just another trick, you might say, to focus all the attention off of McComb. And you know, it really don't solve any of the problems.

Mr. TAYLOR. I would like to ask you one more question: isn't it helpful to conduct all of these activities in a calm atmosphere? And hasn't the atmosphere been calmer since the fall of last year as a result of some activities that were described here this morning?

Mr. HARRIS. I think we can work better in McComb's present atmosphere. As I mentioned before, we couldn't practically get a church in McComb in the beginning. And we couldn't practically go out and talk to people because every time a bombing would take place we were busy on getting the news out and so forth. So it is better to work now in McComb.

Mr. TAYLOR. Thank you.

Chairman HANNAH. Father Hesburgh?

Commissioner HESBURGH. Mr. Harris, your main purpose in McComb was to get people registered. How many did you get registered?

Mr. HARRIS. Well, we don't know. We can't tell, because we have tried many times to contact the registrar, you know, and he refused to give us this type of information.

Commissioner HESBURGH. Well, let me put it differently. How many persons did you train who tried to register?

Mr. HARRIS. I don't know. I think it is close to 200 people that went through the process of these classes that we set up. And we have taken down maybe 125 people.

Commissioner HESBURGH. So you trained about 125, and they in turn have gone to register?

Mr. HARRIS. Right.

Commissioner HESBURGH. Now you don't have any information on any of these 125?

Mr. HARRIS. No, we don't have any information, because when they go down to the courthouse, they take the test and the registrar will tell them to come back in 30 days to check to see did they pass or not. And in many cases these people are afraid to go back by themselves and check.

Commissioner HESBURGH. Haven't they gone back to check whether or not they are registered?

Mr. HARRIS. Most of them have went back and most of them failed.

Commissioner HESBURGH. You say most of those who went back found they failed?

Mr. HARRIS. Right.

Commissioner HESBURGH. So really the net result after this long hot summer is that not many people were registered?

Mr. HARRIS. That's right.

Commissioner HESBURGH. Mr. Harris, I appreciate the anguish that you and your fellow workers went through to try to get more people registered in a place—in a county where only 2.1 percent of the Negro population is registered. But don't you think that both sides, the white and the Negro side, would have to look forward to some kind of a break to calm down this climate and make it more constructive?

Mr. HARRIS. Well, I think we agree that the Negro community and the white community are sometime going to have to get together before they can solve any type of problem.

Commissioner HESBURGH. That's right. Now wouldn't it be better—and I'm just making this as a supposition—wouldn't it be better if your group assumed that the white group which signed this statement was serious about it and meant to do these things? Wouldn't it be better to assume these people meant to get rid of harassment, that they meant to get rid of public officials whe were trying to hurt other people, that they are trying to get responsible law, that they are trying to get fair jury trial?

These are all rather clear public statements. Wouldn't it be a good thing, now, if your group in response to that would come out with the things that you think ought to happen, maybe some of the same things and maybe some other things, and then possibly get the two groups together and discuss what are the two goals of the community called McComb? Wouldn't this be better than the first time they came out—and this is probably the first time they ever came out with such a statement—to say "I don't believe them, it is just another trick." If every time either side makes a move it is looked on as a trick, if your coming in to register people is looked on as a trick by the white people, if their statement that they want a better community is looked on as a trick by the colored people, then we never get anywhere. But somewhere along in the middle of this bad situation we have to get both sides together and we have to communicate. That was one of the points, that there has to be better communication.

Now I grant you may feel badly if they independently get out their statement, but you independently could get out your statement, and then the two groups could get together. I think if they could get together and find that they want the same kind of things and same kind of community, perhaps the immediate prize that you are looking for, that these people who are qualified get registered, could be realized sooner. I'm sure there are a lot of white people in town who can see that they do get registered.

Mr. HARRIS. Well, as I mentioned before, mainly we are working in voter education where we set up classes and talk about politics.

Commissioner HESBURGH. Yes.

Mr. HARRIS. You know, we mainly get people to express themselves, what they feel about the situation which they live in, what they think. Do they think that they are the cause of the trouble or are the people across the track the cause of the trouble? I think everyone agrees that the white community and the Negro community have to get together in order to solves some of the problems. But here, in Mississippi, where I have lived all of my life, I think that this is one of the problems, that the Negro and the white community have to get together. I think in McComb you have a power structure which is very strong there, and where it is kind of hard for the Negro community and the white community to get together.

Just to point out one case, after we got to McComb, and had worked there for probably 2 months or so, Mr. Heffner, called us on the phone and asked us our purpose there. After that telephone call was made he received telephone calls, telling him to leave town and so forth, and eventually he left. So this is one of the problems. It is kind of hard for us to work, not only the Negro community but in the white community, to get in there to really set up something.

Commissioner HESBURGH. What I am really saying, Mr. Harris, is something President Kennedy said once, looking at the bad situation in the whole world. He said, "Let us begin." Now how do you make a beginning? I would assume as an outsider that the white people are trying to make a beginning and the violence has stopped. Now suppose your group, which has a legitimate job to do, to train people to be able to register and vote and take part in the political life of your community, put down the things that you would like, and maybe you find that these things coincide with what the white group wants. You say you can't talk to the white community. I say talk to Mr. Brumfield. He started this on the white side, and you started some of this from the colored side. Why don't you talk to him and then you get something started. And then maybe you could have a get-together periodically and you say this and this and this happened which seems against your statement of principles, and he could say this and this and this happened which seems against your statement of principles. You could then talk it out. But somehow a conversation has to get started, somehow a beginning has to be made to get from what was admittedly a very bad situation all summer to what I think most reasonable citizens would like to see as a good community. Does that sound reasonable?

Mr. HARRIS. Well, it sounds beautiful, you know. But working in Mississippi, you might say, anywhere, that, you know—back to what I said before—that we think that we have certain things on our mind, most of us, as you know; that is, from our side of the State. And we don't go into a community, you might say, with this type of idea or with this purpose in mind. We go into a community just to talk to people and to listen to them; we don't get the impression that we have to go and talk to Mr. Brumfield, because we know that these people that live in Mississippi, you know, and they know Mr. Brumfield, and they know—you know, all the peoples like Mr. Brumfield. They know the response they are going to get, because they work for him every day and because they associates with him downtown, you know, and so forth. They know these people. They already talked to him, you know, and in other words, they are afraid to talk to him because they know him and so forth.

Chairman HANNAH. Mr. Harris, I would like to remind the Commissioners we have many witnesses who have been subpenaed and we are getting substantially behind schedule. I hope that the Commissioners would ask rather concise questions so that we can get back on our time schedule.

Mrs. Freeman?

Commissioner FREEMAN. Mr. Harris, will you tell me if there were any other groups working to encourage voter registration in McComb prior to July 1, 1964?

Mr. HARRIS. Well, you had the local NAACP, and then you had a citizen league, which was organized in 1961 and started the voter registration drive then.

Commissioner FREEMAN. Were Negroes permitted to use places of public accommodations in McComb following the statement that was issued?

Mr. HARRIS. Well, in some places there—you might say one. And that is the Holiday Inn, which opened up in 1964, as the result of a test made there. So I guess that is the only place there in McComb that a Negro can use. But there are no public facilities in that town where a Negro can use. So in other words, all of them are segregated.

Commissioner FREEMAN. All of the places still refuse to serve Negroes?

Mr. HARRIS. Right. Right.

Commissioner FREEMAN. I have no further questions.

Chairman HANNAH. Any questions?

Vice Chairman PATTERSON. No questions.

Chairman HANNAH. You are excused, Mr. Harris. Thank you very much.

(Witness excused.)

Chairman HANNAH. Mr. Taylor, will you call the next witness.

Mr. TAYLOR. The next witness is Mr. Curtis C. Bryant.

Chairman HANNAH. Mr. Bryant, will you raise your right hand?

(Whereupon, Mr. Curtis C. Bryant was duly sworn by the Chairman and testified as follows:)

Chairman HANNAH. Mr. Taylor, will you begin the questioning?

TESTIMONY OF MR. CURTIS CONWAY BRYANT, PIKE COUNTY, MISS.

Mr. TAYLOR. Mr. Bryant, would you give your full name, your residence, and your occupation for the record?

Mr. BRYANT. My name is Curtis Conway Bryant. My residence is McComb, Miss., Box 333—my mailing address is Box 333–B, McComb Street. My residence is Venable Extension South. I am a railroad employee, a craneman on the Illinois Central Railroad.

Mr. TAYLOR. How long have you lived in Mississippi, sir?

Mr. BRYANT. I have lived in Mississippi all my life with the exception of 6 years.

Mr. TAYLOR. And how long have you worked for the railroad?

Mr. BRYANT. Since 1942.

Mr. TAYLOR. Are you a registered voter in Pike County?

Mr. BRYANT. Yes, I am.

Mr. TAYLOR. And have you voted in Pike County?

Mr. BRYANT. Yes.

Mr. TAYLOR. What organizations do you belong to?

Mr. BRYANT. I am presently president of the Pike County branch of the NAACP, since 1954. I am local chairman for Victor Lodge 1733, legislative comitteeman for the same lodge. I am a Master Mason. I am a member of the Society Hill—deacon of the Society Hill Baptist Church, Sunday schoolteacher. And formerly a member of the Scout activities there in the same city .

Mr. TAYLOR. Could you tell us briefly what the activities and the goals of the NAACP in Pike County have been?

Mr. BRYANT. Over the years the goals of the Pike County branch of NAACP has been to eliminate all phases of segregation, whether it be in government or employment; in other words, in all aspects of human life, wherever discrimination exists. That is our goal, to banish racial discrimination.

Mr. TAYLOR. We have heard some testimony about the violence in Pike County last summer. Did it affect you personally?

Mr. BRYANT. Yes, quite a bit.

Mr. TAYLOR. Could you tell us about it briefly?

Mr. BRYANT. I think it was back in February 1964, there was a suit which came up on February 3, 1964, challenging the deannexation of the city. At that time there were signs on the premises of the Illinois Central Railroad with a person hung in effigy, "The NAACP, don't let this happen to you," with a rope around its neck. These things were found around the property and we called attention to management as regards to these things, and on January 25, I think it was, there was a cross burned on the north lawn; there were also crosses burned all over Pike and the adjacent counties. These things seemed to me were intended to intimidate, to bring fright and fear into the minds of the Negro who had been struggling for the elimination of racial discrimination. Those things affected not only me, but my entire family.

On the night of April 28 there was a bomb thrown in my barbershop. It exploded, created a large sound. It really frightened me. I had no idea that this would happen even though I had encountered many hostilities, I did not feel that this thing could happen and would happen. But to my surprise, my shop was bombed.

At the time my son was in the hospital in Jackson and my wife was there with him, and I was at home alone. We went out and some kids came to my door and told me that my barbershop had been bombed, and we went out and looked. And the bomb had knocked a hole in the barbershop and knocked a lot of the windows out. The chair was on fire. We went out and put the fire out and then immediately we called the police department. We then notified the Justice Department, I think Mr. John Doar—not Mr. Doar, Attorney Owen called him and informed him of the bombing. We also notified the police department of the cross burning. The police department did not come. We carried the cross to the courthouse and showed the cross to the police, the night clerk, or the sergeant at the police department. We, I don't think, at no time had an investigation of the cross burning. At least, no one came on the scene, no official of the law.

Mr. TAYLOR. Were there other incidents after April 28th?

Mr. BRYANT. Yes. On June 22, I think it was, 1964—I don't recall exactly when. On the night of that, my son and another boy, a young man, were guarding my home. I had reached the point where we felt that it was very hazardous. We had received numerous phone calls threatening our lives, not only my life, but that of my entire family. And the Pike County branch of the NAACP had employed this young man to guard my home. On another occasion before the June 22 bombing, two young men were seen stopping in front of my yard. One started to get out. The young man who was guarding the house got up and goes around and the men got back in the car and pulled off. They did not commit any crimes.

But on the night of June 22, the bomb was thrown—I mean the dynamite was thrown about 19 feet from the car in which my son and the other young man were sitting. It really had an impact. The first thing I thought of, that they had been killed. I immediately ran out. I had acquired a high-powered rifle in order to try and protect my home and my family. I discharged, I think, one or two shots with the rifle, and when we finally found out that my son and the other young man were safe, we felt somewhat more secure. On the same night, my son and others went in pursuit of the car to no avail. We again reported this incident to the chief of police, the night clerk, or the sergeant, I think it would be, who was on duty at night. They sent someone out to investigate as they did in the first bombing. As far as I know, no one was caught. But we did report these incidents promptly to the local law officials. I am a resident—a city resident. We felt that it was our duty to report these incidents to the city officials. That we did.

We then called the FBI, as we did in all cases. We notified the police department, the FBI, and the Justice Department. We notified all of these officials. We did not call the sheriff's office because we were residents of the city and I think the sheriff pointed out in his testimony that there was a close relationship between the city and county. Therefore, we felt that we had not been requested to notify the sheriff, but we did notify the police department of these incidents. They sent men out on both occasions to investigate. They did not come up with anything. They did take some lead pipe on the night of April 28; they pointed out that they felt that it was an explosive bomb.

Mr. TAYLOR. Apart from these incidents, were you ever interrogated or questioned by local officials concerning any of the incidents of violence?

Mr. BRYANT. Yes. On the night of September 23, I think—I don't recall exactly when. So many incidents. On the night of the 20th, the church that I am a member of, the Society Hill Church, along with the home of Aylene Quin, had been bombed. We reported these incidents to the FBI. I think the FBI pointed out that they would notify the local law enforcement. We called Attorney General John Doar—I mean the Assistant Attorney General, John Doar; informed him on the night of the 20th. We called our state president, Aaron

Henry, our director of the Washington Bureau, Mr. Clarence Mitchell, on the night of the 20th. And then on the night of the 23d, the home of Mr. Matthew Jackson and the home of one of the former police officers was bombed. We reported these incidents.

Mr. TAYLOR. What happened after they were reported?

Mr. BRYANT. I had reported the bombing of the former police officer and the home of Mr. Jackson. Mr. Jackson called my home and asked me to call the FBI. I called the FBI as he requested. He did not request that I call anyone else. The FBI stated that they would call the other officials.

Mr. TAYLOR. I understand. But what happened to you after that?

Mr. BRYANT. While I was calling these officials, Mr. John Doar, I called him, and Mr. Mitchell, and at the time I was talking to the assistant director of the FBI in Jackson, Mr. Keith, I think was his name, when the police department arrived—one auxiliary policeman, some members of the police department, and one highway patrolman. Two carloads came to my residence while I was on the phone and— with revolvers when they got out of the car—I think about four or five got out of the car with their hands on their revolvers. My wife was out on guard duty with others. She came to the gate where they were. I had a large fence around my place in order to try and get somewhat more security. She came and asked them what do you want. The assistant night chief says, "The sheriff wants to talk with your husband."

She says, "Well, now, why do you need two carloads? He is not a violent man. He has never caused any violence. Why do you need all of these cars?"

He says, "Well, they just happened to be in the area."

One carload of police, I think around four or five, got out, and as I pointed out, with their hands on their revolvers, as if I was a criminal. After she had told them that there were no violence, then the night chief came to the door shining the light in the house. I had the front door open and I could see the light, so I comes to the front door and asked what was the trouble. "What did you want." They says, the night chief, Mr. Allen, says, "The sheriff wants to talk with you at the courthouse." I says, "Am I under arrest?" He says "No. All he wants to do is talk with you." I said, "I'm on the phone talking with the assistant FBI director of the State of Mississippi." I said, "If you will permit, I would like to go in and hang the phone up and let him know that I am being detained." He consented.

I went in and notified Mr. Keith that I was going. I then went to the police department and waited for probably an hour until the sheriff came. When the sheriff came, he came in, he was very violent, very indignant. He came in cursing, says, "You damn niggers have not called me at a single bombing. All of you are damn liars."

I said, "Sheriff, I don't know what you're talking about."

He says, "This Matthew Jackson bombing. Your pastor"—the Rev. Ned Taylor was my pastor. He says, "Your pastor led the car to the bombing. Do you believe that?" I says, "No, I don't believe it, Sheriff. I know him to be a very reliable man." He said, "Even your damn preachers are damn liars."

Then he began to question me as to whether he was a member of the NAACP. I says "Sheriff, I feel that it is our policy that we do not give out the names of our members in order that we can and will protect them."

Prior to this interrogation, one of the highway patrolmen came in and asked me questions and tried to force me to tell him as to whether Mr. Jackson or the Reverend Taylor were members of the NAACP. I told him the same thing: That we were under obligation not to reveal the membership of our organization in view of the fact that we felt that it would bring personal harm and personal danger on their person, and for that reason I would like to decline.

He said, "The sheriff asked me to talk with you, and you are not cooperating." I said, "I will assure you I will cooperate with you as much as possible, but this I cannot do. It is against our policy." And I refused to tell him as to whether the two were members of the NAACP.

Going back to the sheriff, the sheriff persisted. He says, "Now, if you damn niggers don't tell me the next time there is a bombing, I am going to skin you. You call Washington, you call Henry, and you call the Justice Department. And you don't call me."

I said, "Sheriff, I have cooperated, and if this is what you want, if this will help to solve problems, then we will call you.

There had been a number of incidents; the Burglund Supermarket, for example, had been bombed. There was almost violence at that scene. And it seems to me according to the information that I gather, that there was distrust on the part of Negroes for the long harassment that had been encountered by the Negro people, not just a segment. I think at first there was not fear on the part of all Negroes. My barber shop was the first place to be bombed in Pike County. It was the first bombing, and whenever an incident would occur, the people would think that it was my home or my residence, the person that they were after. But when the bombs began to go off at a number of places, then the people began to feel that it is time that they begin to watch and guard their homes. After these incidents, the people began to guard their churches, their homes, and all of their places of business.

Mr. TAYLOR. Mr. Bryant, has the situation improved now so that you don't have to guard your home?

Mr. BRYANT. Yes, I feel that it has improved to an extent where we do not guard our home, even though we do not feel fully secure.

Mr. TAYLOR. Thank you.

Chairman HANNAH. Do any of the Commissioners have any questions?

Thank you very much. You are excused, Mr. Bryant.

(Witness excused.)

Chairman HANNAH. Mr. Taylor, will you call the next witness?

Mr. TAYLOR. Mr. Chairman, the next testimony concerns Adams County, and I would like to ask Mr. Wolf to present the brief background and statement about that county.

Mr. WOLF. Adams County is in southwestern Mississippi, along the Mississippi River. Natchez, the county seat, was once the main river port between Memphis and New Orleans. The total population of the county in 1963 was estimated at 37,000, of whom about half were Negro. As of January 1964 almost half of the voting-age whites were registered to vote; 6.8 percent of the voting-age Negroes were registered.

During the past 15 years Adams County has industrialized. The International Paper Co., which opened a large plant in Natchez in 1950, now employs more than 1,300 workers and has an annual payroll of $6 to $7 million. In addition there is a large plant of the Armstrong Tire and Rubber Co. and a small plant of the Johns-Manville Co.

As of 1959 Adams County had the fourth highest median income per family in Mississippi. The median income for white families was $6,100; for Negro families it was $2,000. Nineteen percent of the Negroes and 25 percent of the whites were involved in manufacturing.

In Natchez, as of 1959, more than one-third of the housing units occupied by Negroes were unsafe and inadequate for human shelter; 7 percent of housing units occupied by whites were in this category.

In 1959 the median level of education for Negroes was completion of 6th grade; the median for whites was completion of high school. In the school year 1960–61 the Natchez school district spent almost $220 per year for each white child and about $130 for each Negro child.

Chairman HANNAH. Thank you very much, Mr. Wolf. Mr. Taylor, will you call the next witness.

Mr. TAYLOR. The next witness is Mr. Bruce Payne.

Chairman HANNAH. Mr. Payne, will you raise your right hand?

(Whereupon, Mr. Bruce Lloyd Payne was duly sworn by the chairman and testified as follows:)

Chairman HANNAH. Mr. Taylor, will you begin the questioning?

TESTIMONY OF MR. BRUCE LLOYD PAYNE, NEW HAVEN, CONN.

Mr. TAYLOR. Mr. Payne, will you give us your full name, your residence, and your occupation?

Mr. PAYNE. My name is Bruce Lloyd Payne. I am a graduate student in political science at Yale University, and my residence is Yale University, 1566 Yale Station, New Haven, Conn.

Mr. TAYLOR. Have you engaged in any civil rights activities in Mississippi?

Mr. PAYNE. Yes, I have. In the fall of 1963 I worked on the Aaron Henry freedom ballot campaign, which was, as you know, a mock election and the preparation for voter registration work. We did some talking during that campaign about voter registration work to the people that we worked with.

Mr. TAYLOR. In what area of the State were you working?

Mr. PAYNE. I worked primarily in Natchez and a little in the surrounding area.

Mr. TAYLOR. We understand that you were assaulted on two occasions during the fall of 1963 in the Natchez area. Can you tell us briefly about it?

Mr. PAYNE. Yes. On the 31st of October, we were followed around the town. I was working with one other civil rights worker, George Green, a SNCC staff member, and we were followed during the day by a number of young white men in two different cars. At one point one of them got out of their cars and tried to attack me, or asked me to come over to him, and I didn't, and managed to escape him at that time. But later in the day, we found it necessary to drive to Port Gibson to take one of our other workers up there. She had to speak that evening. Before we left town, these two cars that I spoke about, each with two men in them, passed back and forth in front of the house where we were staying, and so did a police car driven by one of the officers of the police.

We were followed out of town, escorted out of town more or less, by the police and by these two cars. But at the edge of the town the police waved at us and didn't continue along with us. The two other cars did, however. I drove all the way to Port Gibson without stopping. These two cars followed directly behind us. I drove a little slowly so that I could keep a lot of other cars behind us so that anything that happened would be public. But as it turned out, that didn't deter them.

When we arrived in Port Gibson we stopped in a gas station to ask for directions. They got out of their cars, one of them came up to me, looked me in the eye and then began to slug me. Two others joined in while the fourth stood and watched Miss Baker and George Green. This went on for 3 or 4 minutes, interrupted occasionally by various insults and announcements that I was not to come back to Adams County any more, that I had been making trouble down there. And shortly after that, they gave up and left, with a few more of those sorts of admonitions. I drove on to Jackson then and called the police chief of Port Gibson, told him about the incident, gave him the license numbers of the cars that had been involved. And I also called J. T. Robinson, the police chief of Natchez, with whom I had had some dealings in the past, and told him about the two cars that had followed us from Natchez. That was pretty much the story for the 31st.

I went back to Natchez on the first of November, stayed at the house of a priest, Father Morrissey, who has the Negro parish there. I was staying there because I wasn't allowed to stay in a place where SNCC workers normally stayed, George Metcalf's rooming house. He had been threatened by the police chief that his license would be removed and he would get into a lot of other trouble if he didn't have me stay somewhere else. So I agreed to stay at the house of this priest. We received a couple of threatening phone calls that night—or I guess one threatening phone call. The next day we noticed we were still being watched by various people. But since this time we had a faster car, and we still needed to do some work in the little town of Fayette and some of the surrounding areas, we drove north from Natchez about 11 o'clock in the morning.

We were run off the road five times—or four times, excuse me; one time they missed—at speeds in excess of 95 miles an hour. But we only had a rented 1963 Chevrolet; they were following us in a new 1964 Impala. The last time we were run off the road it was impossible for us to turn around and go back, which is what we had done on previous times. They thought they had us stopped and started to get out of the car. One of them did get out of his car, pulled a gun on us and told us to get out, motioning apparently for us to get into his car. They had left just enough space for us to get around their car, and so George, who was driving, stepped on the gas and we sort of wheeled around their car and took off toward Fayette. The fellow with the gun at that point fired four shots at the car, the first three definitely at the tire. One of them hit the tire, which was going down as we drove toward Fayette. The last one—or I imagine the last one, I'm not sure—hit the middle of the rear end of the car. We escaped then. They chased us to Fayette, caught up with us just there, but we lost them in the town managing to create a traffic jam, and got off on the back roads and went to Jackson.

At that point we called—I spoke with the wife of the sheriff of Jefferson County, where we believe the shooting occurred, and spoke with the sheriff of Adams County, giving him the full details and leaving my address and phone number and that sort of thing.

Mr. TAYLOR. And that was the conclusion of that incident. Did you ever speak with or were you ever contacted subsequently by any Mississippi law enforcement officer about either of these incidents?

Mr. PAYNE. No, I wasn't. I believe the last time I spoke to them was on November 2, late in the evening, I spoke with the sheriff of Adams County. I believe he called me back once. I called and left a message for him, and he called me back that night at the COFO office.

Mr. TAYLOR. Did you give them any address where you could be reached?

Mr. PAYNE. Yes. The police chief of Natchez had taken my home address down—my parents' address, which is in Arlington, Va. I had left the address of the COFO office and the phone number with all of the law enforcement officers, and had said that I could be reached there. I have been reachable through the COFO office. I get mail through COFO regularly.

Mr. TAYLOR. Were you interviewed by the Federal Bureau of Investigation?

Mr. PAYNE. Yes. I have been interviewed I think four or five times. Once I was interviewed by the Justice Department late on both evenings, on the 31st and on the 2d. And on the 3d I was interviewed by the FBI in Jackson, and later on in Alexandria, Va.

Mr. TAYLOR. Did you give the FBI information identifying your assailants?

Mr. PAYNE. Yes. When I was interviewed by the FBI in New Haven I identified pictures of my assailants from both incidents. One of the fellows, the fellow who had the gun in the second incident, was one of those who was involved in the first one as well, I'm sure.

Mr. TAYLOR. I would like to note for the record, Mr. Chairman, that five men were arrested by the highway patrol in October 1964 and charged with one of these incidents. The charges against one man were dropped shortly thereafter and on January 5, 1965 the case against the remaining four men was scheduled to be presented to the grand jury. The case was dismissed because no witnesses appeared. Mr. Payne, were you ever contacted by any of the prosecuting officials, the county prosecutor or the district attorney, with reference to these incidents?

Mr. PAYNE. No, I was not.

Mr. TAYLOR. Were you ever requested to testify or to appear before any grand jury with reference to these incidents?

Mr. PAYNE. No, I was not.

Mr. TAYLOR. Just a couple more questions. You said you had had some contact with the police chief of Natchez before the first of these incidents took place. Could you describe that briefly?

Mr. PAYNE. Yes. On the night of, I guess, the 29th of October, George Green, with whom I was working, was arrested on suspicion of car theft. He was driving a car that I had brought down from New Haven to use in the project. He was later charged with running a red light, I believe. They kept him overnight, and the next morning, about 9 o'clock, I appeared at the police station and was told that I would have to see the chief of police before I could get George Green out of jail.

It took me 3 hours to get to see the chief of police. Meanwhile, I talked with a number of the other police officers there. When the police chief came and spoke to me, he said a number of things. After taking down all kinds of information about me, he warned me that I had better not bring any more civil rights workers to his town. He said that if anything happened, if anything at all happened, if any incidents were created, he said "My men have arms and they know what to do with them. If you people make trouble, I'll guarantee you there is going to be some slow walking and some sad singing." He repeated that a couple of times.

Then he spoke to me pretty directly and said, "Well, I'm not going to arrest you, but I can't save you from the local people around here. They're rough. They'll tear your head off." And sure enough, the next day I had some dealings with the local people.

Mr. TAYLOR. Did you construe that as a threat?

Mr. PAYNE. I certainly did construe it as a threat. And in fact, I told him that he was threatening me at the time.

Mr. TAYLOR. Thank you.

Chairman HANNAH. Father Hesburgh?

Commissioner HESBURGH. Just one question, Mr. Payne. If you had been called last January, would you have come down to identify these people and testify at the grand jury?

Mr. PAYNE. Yes, I would have. I thought at one time there might be some financial problem with that, but I was considering it. I didn't know when the trial was going to be originally, or where it might be, but I understand there was a Uniform Subpena Act, and that I could have been subpenaed easily. But I certainly would like to testify.

Commissioner HESBURGH. Thank you.

Chairman HANNAH. Mrs. Freeman?

Commissioner FREEMAN. Mr. Payne, are you going to continue with your voter registration activities in this State?

Mr. PAYNE. Well, there isn't much I can do in this State while I am a graduate student. But I would like to come back and do what work I can. I do spend some time raising funds for SNCC's work and speaking for the project in other parts of the country and New Haven.

Commissioner FREEMAN. Were you satisfied that you were able to make a contribution?

Mr. PAYNE. Yes. The contribution that people from the outside like myself can make is illustrated by the fact that although George Green had been shot at something like nine times before this incident, it had never made the paper and never seemingly reached the conscience of the country very clearly. But since I was a student at Yale and had been in California, apparently people were interested.

I don't know if my being white had anything to do with that. But somehow it did shock people and it did enable us to raise some money for the movement, at least, and to raise some interest in Congress and other places. I must say a number of people, Justice Department officials and Congressmen, were willing to see me and talk about the situation and expressed a good deal more concern than they had with regard to some of the other incidents in the past.

Chairman HANNAH. Dean Griswold?

Commissioner GRISWOLD. Mr. Payne, if this case should again be presented to the grand jury and you were notified or subpenaed, would you appear?

Mr. PAYNE. Yes, I would.

Commissioner GRISWOLD. Thank you.

Chairman HANNAH. Mr. Rankin?

Commissioner RANKIN. Did you ever consider a civil action?

Mr. PAYNE. Yes, I considered it, but I rejected that possibility fairly fast. There are more important things to do than lose more court cases in Mississippi.

Commissioner RANKIN. Thank you.

Chairman HANNAH. Mr. Patterson?

Vice Chairman PATTERSON. A lot of Mississippians wonder what an outsider like you from Yale University was doing down here, and they really don't understand. Could you state why you came here?

Mr. PAYNE. Yes. I worked on behalf of the civil rights movement before. And I always felt that white outsiders were probably not as effective working in the South, though I was glad to be asked by the Negro community in Mississippi to come down and help. My feeling was, quite simply, from what I had heard about Mississippi, that it was almost impossible for the Negro people of Mississippi to do anything for themselves, or to do enough for themselves to get the vote, which is what is so crucially needed. My feeling was that although I had some access to the information, that the picture of what was going on in the country, or in Mississippi, was simply not getting to the country; that unless people from the outside came in, that the tribulations of the Negroes in Mississippi, all of the troubles they had, would not get to the conscience of the country enough to get Federal enforcement of the law, which I am afraid is what we need before the people of Natchez, the law enforcement officers and the rest of the people will agree to sit down at the conference table. Until we have enforcement of the law and safety for the Negroes in Mississippi, then the other things that need to come, the dealing with economic problems and so forth, just can't be done. And so that's the kind of contribution that I wanted to make.

Chairman HANNAH. Mr. Payne, what do you hope to do after you finish your graduate program?

Mr. PAYNE. I want to teach. I have various plans of where I might teach, and a good many of them center around the South.

Chairman HANNAH. Any further questions?

Mr. Rogerson.

Mr. ROGERSON. Mr. Payne, is this activity in Mississippi all voter registration and voter participation activity?

Mr. PAYNE. Well, that was the ultimate aim of the freedom ballot campaign. That is what I was doing; we were collecting signatures and so forth to try to dramatize to the country that the Negroes in Mississippi really did want to vote, and we had the 80,000 turnout in the freedom ballot. And it was prefatory to the work done in the summer and spring in the voter registration.

Mr. ROGERSON. So all your activities were in connection with the voter registration and civil rights?

Mr. PAYNE. Right.

Mr. ROGERSON. Were you aware of arrests being made in connection with your case?

Mr. PAYNE. Yes, I was, through the papers and through communication of friends of mine in Mississippi. But I wasn't aware of the grand jury hearing until I was in Washington and I heard about it I think 3 or 4 days before, or 2 or 3 days, that it was going to take place.

Mr. ROGERSON. Thank you, Mr. Payne.

Chairman HANNAH. Thank you, Mr. Payne. You are excused.

(Witness excused.)

Chairman HANNAH. We will now take a 10-minute recess and resume at 10 minutes to eleven.

(Short recess taken.)

Chairman HANNAH. The hearing will be in order. Mr. Taylor, will you call the next witness.

Mr. TAYLOR. The next witnesses are District Attorney T. J. Lawrence, and County Prosecutor Joseph Davenport.

Chairman HANNAH. Gentlemen, will you raise your right hands? (Whereupon, T. J. Lawrence, Esq., and Joseph Davenport, Jr., Esq., were duly sworn by the chairman and testified as follows:)

Chairman HANNAH. Have chairs, gentlemen.

Mr. Taylor?

TESTIMONY OF T. J. LAWRENCE, ESQ., DISTRICT ATTORNEY, NINTH CIRCUIT COURT DISTRICT, OF MISSISSIPPI AND JOSEPH DAVENPORT, JR., ESQ., COUNTY PROSECUTOR, CLAIBORNE COUNTY, MISS.

Mr. TAYLOR. Mr. Davenport, would you state your name, your residence, and your occupation for the record?

Mr. DAVENPORT. My name is Joseph Davenport, Jr., I live in Port Gibson, Miss. I am prosecuting attorney in and for Claiborne County.

Mr. TAYLOR. And Mr. Lawrence, would you do the same, please?

Mr. LAWRENCE. T. J. Lawrence, district attorney of the Ninth Circuit Court District of Mississippi. I live in Vicksburg. And the district is composed of four counties: Claiborne, Warren, Issaquena, and Sharkey. I reside at 702 Maddingly Street in Vicksburg, Miss.

Mr. TAYLOR. Mr. Davenport, how long have you served as county prosecutor?

Mr. DAVENPORT. I finished the first year of my fourth term—13 years.

Mr. TAYLOR. Are you familiar with the Bruce Payne assault of October 1963?

Mr. DAVENPORT. I am familiar with it from reports made in October 1964, the first knowledge that I had of it.

Mr. TAYLOR. Arrests were made in that case, were they not?

Mr. DAVENPORT. They were.

Mr. TAYLOR. Is it your responsibility to prepare with Mr. Lawrence felony and misdemeanor prosecutions in your county?

Mr. DAVENPORT. Generally speaking, that is true. Frequently the offices of the JPs will prepare an affidavit, but prior to trial, if it is not in proper form, we will amend the affidavit. Generally speaking, that is true, though. We prepare them for the officers.

Mr. TAYLOR. Did you prepare the case against the persons arrested in the Payne case?

Mr. DAVENPORT. I prepared the affidavit, drafted and prepared it, personally typed it, because it was on my noon hour when I heard about it. I prepared the affidavit.

Mr. TAYLOR. In your investigation of this case, or in your preparation of this case, did you interview the victim?

Mr. DAVENPORT. No, I did not.

Mr. TAYLOR. Did you receive any information from any law enforcement official of his interview with the victim?

Mr. DAVENPORT. I received information from an FBI agent and a highway patrol investigator as to what had happened, and they wanted an affidavit to arrest them—yes, sir. Do you want me to relate what they informed me?

Mr. TAYLOR. You may, if you wish.

Mr. DAVENPORT. At noon I was at my home and Sheriff Dan McKay of Claiborne County called me and asked me to come down to the courthouse. He didn't say what it was about. When I got there he was present, an FBI agent, and a highway patrol investigator. And they related an incident of a person having been beaten up the year before, which now I know was in 1963. And they wanted an affidavit, and there was some discussion on whether it was a misdemeanor or a felony. And so it is always easier to make the felony charge; if it turns out to be a misdemeanor, you can always reduce it. So I generally in these instances recommend that a felony charge of assault and battery be made.

Now our statute provides for assault and battery with a deadly weapon with intent to kill, or if no deadly weapon is involved, it has to be in a manner and means sufficient to produce death. So I drew it on that basis, charging a felony, and it was signed by a highway patrol investigator who had, I presume, investigated the case; perhaps the FBI did. He was with the FBI agent. I do not know—I presume they both investigated the case. And I prepared that affidavit.

The FBI agent asked if I would give him a copy for his file, and I had made one, which I did. And they left the courthouse to go to the justice of the peace to get it signed. I didn't go with them; wasn't asked to. And that was signed, I know, because I seen the affidavit, and a warrant was issued for four persons. I heard something about five, but this one was for four persons. And I believe the same day, or the next day, they were arrested. There was a return of the warrant, a verifax copy of which I have furnished you, together with a verifax copy of the affidavit.

Mr. TAYLOR. Yes, sir.

Mr. DAVENPORT. And I believe it [the warrant] was executed the same day, upon hearsay information there, it is my understanding they were taken to the jail in Jackson, Miss., and presumably they were interrogated. The next day I got a call from a lawyer there, and they wanted to see about making bond, wanted a small bond as they always do, but I think I insisted—I believe the bond was finally made at $2,000. And the bond subsequently, I understand, was made. And they were released.

At the time the FBI agent and the highway patrol investigator and the sheriff called me, I informed them—or requested them, didn't tell them, it is not my job to tell them what to do—that we would want them to be there when the grand jury met on the first Monday of January, and to have the witness there, the victim, because they had all the testimony. It doesn't take as much evidence before the grand jury, but it takes some time before the grand jury can get an indictment. Without that we couldn't do anything. I advised them at what time the grand jury met. That was at the initial consultation at the time the affidavit was made. Our grand jury meets on the first Monday of January, and I think the third Monday of May is the next one. The grand jury met and the four defendants were there.

Sometimes our grand juries finish in 1 day. In this instance it went 2 days, considering the evidence. About sometime in December when Mr. Lawrence came there—he comes down usually a couple weeks before court and goes over the cases to be presented to the grand jury; he sees what they are all about, and draws up a formal indictment. Either then or after hearing the evidence. So he was notified in December when he came down that this matter was coming up.

Also, about 2 weeks before the grand jury met, I asked Sheriff Dan McKay—requested him or reminded him that this matter, among others, was coming up; not just in this case but to have the witnesses in other cases and this case—to notify them and remind them even though they had been notified. Now witnesses I am referring to are the highway patrol investigator and the FBI agent and Bruce Payne, if he knew where he was. And he advised me that he had so notified the officers involved, and he hadn't notified Payne. He did say that two FBI agents had been down there a couple weeks earlier and wanted to see the bonds; I guess to be sure there were bonds. I don't know their motive. He said at that time that he had asked the two agents where Bruce Payne was, where he could notify him, and they told him that they didn't know. So I believe that's about the extent of it. Payne wasn't at the grand jury. Apparently he wasn't notified, as he just testified to. He has been informed as to when the next grand jury meets now since he testified.

Mr. TAYLOR. You made no direct effort to get in touch with Mr. Payne yourself?

Mr. DAVENPORT. No, I didn't. In that respect I might say that the 'sheriff always notifies the witnesses. It's our custom, whether it is right or wrong. And in this instance I had no knowledge as to where Payne was. I had heard, but it was after the grand jury had completed its investigation, and the news account stated that he was a Yale University student. I did not know that prior to the time of the grand jury convening. And I would have assumed that he would have been notified; I would have assumed that the FBI, knowing their thoroughness in investigative procedures, would have had his name, address, and so forth, and perhaps erroneously I thought they would have notified him after I requested the sheriff to ask both them and the State highway patrol investigator to do so. And which he said that he did do.

Mr. TAYLOR. I have no further questions at this time.

Chairman HANNAH. Dean Griswold?

Commissioner GRISWOLD. Mr. Davenport, is it your responsibility to present the cases to the grand jury in Claiborne County?

Mr. DAVENPORT. My responsibility is to assist the district attorney in the presentation of cases. I do not sign the indictments. The district attorney does.

Commissioner GRISWOLD. Well, who is responsible for presenting cases to the grand jury in Claiborne County?

Mr. DAVENPORT. I would say the district attorney with my assistance.

Commissioner GRISWOLD. Are you responsible for the preparation of cases which are to be presented to the grand jury?

Mr. DAVENPORT. While they are in the justice of the peace court.

Commissioner GRISWOLD. Well, my question had nothing to do with the justice of the peace court. It had to do with the preparation of cases for presentation to the grand jury.

Mr. DAVENPORT. I beg your pardon. In working with the district attorney, it is to that extent. He is in charge of the cases.

Commissioner GRISWOLD. Do you regard it as part of your responsibility to take the steps which are necessary to have the needed witnesses present at the time of the presentation to the grand jury?

Mr. DAVENPORT. In conjuction with the district attorney as to what witness we would desire there, yes, sir.

Commissioner GRISWOLD. Did you think that there was any basis for an indictment in this case without the presence of Mr. Payne or Mr. Green?

Mr. DAVENPORT. There was a possibility. He should have been there. Bruce Payne should have been there to testify to the extent of the beating that he received. Very definitely I think that he should have been there.

Commissioner GRISWOLD. Why would you present the case to the grand jury without the presence of either one of those witnesses?

Mr. DAVENPORT. We present all cases that have been bound over to the grand jury. We tell them what they have to consider and it is presented, and if they don't act on it, it does not bar it from a presentation to the next grand jury. It does no harm at all.

Commissioner GRISWOLD. It does no harm except to delay things until the next grand jury and to create a very definite impression that the county prosecuting officers had no interest in obtaining an indictment in this case.

Mr. DAVENPORT. I beg your pardon. I thought your question was why did I present it if Bruce Payne was not there at that time.

Commissioner GRISWOLD. That was exactly my point. And did you expect to obtain an indictment without the presence of either Mr. Payne or Mr. Green?

Mr. DAVENPORT. Well, I didn't know. Many indictments have been made without the victim being there.

Commissioner GRISWOLD. Are you giving consideration to presenting this again to the grand jury, sir?

Mr. DAVENPORT. Oh, definitely, yes, sir. Dean, he has been notified and requested to appear at the next grand jury since his testimony.

Chairman HANNAH. Mrs. Freeman? Father Hesburgh?

Commissioner HESBURGH. No questions.

Chairman HANNAH. You are excused, gentlemen.

Mr. DAVENPORT. Thank you very much.

Mr. LAWRENCE. Gentlemen, may I make this statement?

Chairman HANNAH. Go ahead.

Mr. LAWRENCE. Please bear with me just a few minutes.

Chairman HANNAN. Sit down, Mr. Lawrence, so the microphone will pick up your voice.

Mr. LAWRENCE. Thank you. Thank you. I am proud to say that I have been district attorney of this district for 30 years. I have never dodged an issue in 30 years nor failed to present any evidence that came to my attention within that period of time. It matters not who they are, nor the extent of the nature, character, and kind of the matter before the court.

Long about December the 20th of the past year, I drove into Port Gibson. I made a partial investigation personally, myself. I came down for that purpose.

The grand jury is convening in January, the first Monday in January. I was closing a term of court in Vicksburg, in the dying days of December 1964—just a few days. We got into—I got into Port Gibson, and I was informed about this matter for the first time. Between the 15th of December 1964 and the 1st of January, Mr. Davenport—I will have to rescind that statement. Mr. Davenport had mentioned it to me maybe 30 days prior thereto. Now, the grand jury was in session, I was informed that these parties would be in the grand jury to offer testimony. Now, in my judgment as district attorney, it is pretty close on the two indictments. One would be for a misdemeanor; secondly, a felony if any instruments were used, or instrumentalities were used of sufficient force and means to produce death. Now, I have been happy to inform Mr. Bruce Payne—I think that is Mr. Bruce Payne I just recently conferred with.

Chairman HANNAH. Here this morning?

Mr. LAWRENCE. Yes.

Chairman HANNAH. Since he testified.

Mr. LAWRENCE. Let him stand up and see if I can identify him. Yes, sir, that's the man. That's the man. And I have informed him, personally, and officially, that on the third Monday of May 1965 there will be a grand jury in Claiborne County, Miss. I do not go into the Natchez district; just a few miles below Port Gibson is the end of our district. I am not only inviting him to come; now his partner there, George Green—I wouldn't know him if he would walk up here. I am now publicly inviting George Green to come to Port Gibson and also Bruce Payne, on Monday, the third Monday of May 1965 to offer testimony. And may I say this, please, and I am through. And I'm sorry for taking your time. I do wish that they would give me a report. If they don't want to give me a report, if they will give me a sufficient amount of facts to prepare an indictment that will hold water—you know what I'm talking about?—on the two questions involved—and I'm asking them here and now to please let me have that. Meet us in Port Gibson. And it has been a pleasure to see all of you.

Chairman HANNAH. Just a minute, Mr. Lawrence.

Mr. LAWRENCE. Oh. Excuse me.

Chairman HANNAH. Dean Griswold?

Commissioner GRISWOLD. I find myself wondering, Mr. Lawrence, why we have all this zeal with respect to the grand jury which will meet in May, and as far as I can see, no traces of any zeal or interest with respect to the grand jury which met in January?

Mr. LAWRENCE. I knew nothing about this case, these matters involved, save and except from December 20, along about that time, until the convening of the grand jury. And the sheriff informed me that the department, either—I don't want to say the FBI department, but he said "they" had been notified to be here, and I have the information that they were before the grand jury. Yes, sir, that's it.

Commissioner GRISWOLD. You testified that the sheriff advised you that he was informed that Mr. Payne and Mr. Green would be before the grand jury in January?

Mr. LAWRENCE. Let me strike the words—names. "They" would be here that is involved in this matter. "They."

Commissioner GRISWOLD. Who is responsible for presenting cases to the grand jury in Claiborne County?

Mr. LAWRENCE. Who's responsible? Now, you know what I—I think that——

Commissioner GRISWOLD. It seems to me that that question is susceptible to an answer and not a speech.

Mr. LAWRENCE. Yes, sir.

Commissioner GRISWOLD. Who is responsible for the presentation of cases to the grand jury in Claiborne County?

Mr. LAWRENCE. I would say the sheriff.

Commissioner GRISWOLD. Well, that's an interesting observation. You are the district attorney of Claiborne County, and Mr. Davenport is the county attorney of Claiborne County?

Mr. LAWRENCE. Yes, sir.

Commissioner GRISWOLD. Is the sheriff a member of the bar?

Mr. LAWRENCE. Yes, sir.

Commissioner GRISWOLD. Is the sheriff a member of the bar?

Mr. LAWRENCE. No, sir.

Commissioner GRISWOLD. You are testifying here that under the law and policy of the State of Mississippi, it is the responsibility of the sheriff to present cases to the grand jury?

Mr. LAWRENCE. My answer will be, please, to have the witnesses at the door of the grand jury and Mr. Davenport and myself present it to the grand jury.

Commissioner GRISWOLD. I don't want to be misunderstood. I am not really meaning to be critical of you. It seems to me that what we have really got here is a serious inadequacy in the system of the administration of justice in the State of Mississippi. You have a sharply divided responsibility in which each person expects somebody else to see that the witnesses are available. And in particular, the persons, whom it seems to me are clearly charged by law with the responsibility, do not regard themselves as responsible for seeing that the cases are properly presented to the grand jury, that is, that the witnesses are there and are ready to present the cases. As far as I can see, had we not come to Mississippi, you would have regarded yourself as having no further responsibility with respect to this crime which is alleged to have been committed in Claiborne County. Is that right?

Mr. LAWRENCE. No, sir; that isn't correct in its entirety.

Commissioner GRISWOLD. What would you have done if we had not come to Mississippi?

Mr. LAWRENCE. If you had never come to Mississippi, and I had had the information, and Mr. Payne, or either of these assaulted parties, or any person had furnished me with the information, there had been a violation of law done in my district, I would have then and there taken action, as Mr. Davenport did in filing that affidavit upon sufficient evidence.

Now let me say this, please, sir. And I am very happy to see you and very happy you are talking about this serious matter. Now, you are getting into the matter of the grand jury in Mississippi. Mr. Davenport and I will go out 2 weeks before court convenes, and we will interview parties regarding said assaults, killing, murders, or a murder case. We will go out and see those parties, and every time we see them, we say now we want you before the grand jury on a certain date to offer testimony in this case. They say "All right; I'll sure come."

Now, Mr. Davenport and I will leave the scene. The sheriff has— the sheriff can request attendance of witnesses, but I would say it wouldn't be legal. Mr. Davenport and I can't compel the attendance of a witness. We make that statement. We would then convene the grand jury. The grand jury is in session, and the foreman of that grand jury would issue a subpena subpenaing in the witnesses to offer testimony. The sheriff, Mr. Davenport, and myself would name what we determine would be the proper witness to be in court.

Commissioner GRISWOLD. Well, now we've got a further division of the responsibility. It seems that it is the foreman of the grand jury who is responsible to bring in the witnesses. The foreman of the grand jury, the sheriff, the district attorney, the county attorney. And in the process, nobody brings in the witness.

Mr. LAWRENCE. Well, I beg your pardon now. I'm sorry. Excuse me. Do you want me to answer?

Commissioner GRISWOLD. Yes.

Mr. LAWRENCE. Yes. Well, that's the procedure. Now, under the law of this State, the district attorney, the statute says, is to appear before the grand juries, and the circuit courts, and prosecute for the State—appear before the grand juries and in the circuit court. But I have been throwing in a little extra good measure. I have been going out myself digging into it and trying to get the facts to present to the Fatal Twelve.

Commissioner GRISWOLD. What digging did you do on this case?

Mr. LAWRENCE. I knew nothing about it on December 20.

Commissioner GRISWOLD. Then you didn't put the extra measure in on this one?

Mr. LAWRENCE. No, sir; I didn't. No, sir; I didn't. I didn't have time.

Commissioner GRISWOLD. What did you do after December 20, when you did know something about it?

Mr. LAWRENCE. I didn't do anything because I had information that they would be in the open courtroom on that occasion, and I felt that I could interview them then and there at that time. And I didn't have the time. I was closing a term of court in Warren County.

Commissioner GRISWOLD. And when you found that they were not present in January, did you do anything about it?

Mr. LAWRENCE. Yes. I held up the grand jury from about 12 o'clock that day until 4 o'clock in the afternoon, begged them to stay. No, I didn't beg them; I said "Will you please stay, and let's see if they come." I went out into the courtroom; no, they were not there. I said, "Mr. Sheriff, our people here?" "No, not yet." I went back into the grand jury, and they said "Well, we're going home. You don't have any authority to hold me." And I said, "Well, wait now, we've got to write up a report." And just a little after 4 o'clock, on the second day, the grand jury adjourned. The term was over.

Commissioner GRISWOLD. And when you found that these witnesses had not appeared, did you take any steps to find out why?

Mr. LAWRENCE. No, sir. I asked the sheriff could he tell me why, and he said he didn't know why.

Commissioner GRISWOLD. Did you take any steps to see that they would appear at the next session of the grand jury?

Mr. LAWRENCE. I didn't know who to contact. I saw the names when I got this important document to come here to Jackson. I saw the names, and that's the first time as far as I recall definitely, who the parties were. Now, I got here and this morning I heard the fine young man testify. And he came back down, and I said "Maybe I better get permission from your department to talk to you." He was kind enough.

I said "Son"—I called him son; you know, I'm getting a little old. I said "Son, would you—do you mind talking to me about it?" He said "No." I asked him the instruments used, the weapons, and so forth. And he gave me some names. And he told me that "I'll be there the third Monday in May of 1965." That pretty well concluded our conference.

Commissioner GRISWOLD. But you had made no effort yourself to get in touch with him, to find where he was, even to find out what his name was, until today?

Mr. LAWRENCE. No, sir; I had not. Please let me say why. I had to stay in the courtroom in Warren County until all the prisoners were sentenced. That is in December. January, the first Monday morning, journey to Port Gibson, and then right behind that, journey to a term of court in Issaquena County, and from there to go into term of court on next Monday in Sharkey County. So all of my time has been consumed. And I have made no effort to try to find out. I knew—I found out in Port Gibson this would be the names of the parties. And of course, I was going to make some effort to find out between now and May, as soon as I got a little breathing spell.

Commissioner GRISWOLD. Do you think it might be a good idea if the legislature of Mississippi would reorganize the prosecuting function in this State so as not to divide responsibility quite so widely?

Mr. LAWRENCE. Your Honor please, let me refrain from interfering with the Mississippi legislature.

[Laughter.]

Commissioner GRISWOLD. Well, on the contrary, sir. I understand you are a district attorney. And you are confronted with a situation where through someone's fault a case has been very inadequately presented. And I am trying to assist you to develop a system here under which the law can be effectively enforced and where we won't have situations like this where the chief witnesses were not notified, where the district attorney took no steps to see that they were notified, and where, even after they had not appeared and he knew that they had not been notified, he took no steps to see that they were made available at the next session of the grand jury. My purpose is to assist you. Don't you think there ought to be a better system of enforcing the law in Mississippi than there is now?

Mr. LAWRENCE. Please. I can't say over the State, but I can tell you over in the Ninth Circuit Court District, we are making every effort possible to enforce the criminal laws that appear upon the statute books of this State.

Commissioner GRISWOLD. That is an interesting statement, but the facts of this case are not consistent with it.

Mr. LAWRENCE. Yes, sir.

Commissioner GRISWOLD. In this case you made no positive effort to have the witness appear before the grand jury, in a case for which you were responsible.

Mr. LAWRENCE. I don't believe that I could concur that it was my responsibility to bring the witnesses here.

Commissioner GRISWOLD. Whose responsibility was it?

Mr. LAWRENCE. The responsibility—oh, yes, one time I was responsible. When they didn't appear there, then I could have written and asked the foreman of the grand jury to issue a subpena for the witnesses, and he could have then called his secretary around and wrote the subpena. And he said, "Well, where would you find them?" The sheriff walks in and says "Where would you find them?" "I don't know. I don't know where you'd find them."

Commissioner GRISWOLD. Can you find anyone if you make no effort to find them?

Mr. LAWRENCE. No sir, I don't believe you could. I don't believe you could find them if you didn't make an effort.

Commissioner GRISWOLD. We had no difficulty in finding him and bringing him here today, no difficulty whatsoever.

Mr. LAWRENCE. Yes, but you had that strong arm of the majestic law to reach out and bring him in.

Commissioner GRISWOLD. You don't have any arm of the majestic law to assist you in Mississippi?

Mr. LAWRENCE. Yes, sir. Yes, sir. But I have got to locate them first before I can reach them.

Commissioner GRISWOLD. You have got to try to locate them?

Mr. LAWRENCE. Yes, sir.

Chairman HANNAH. Any further questions?

Thank you, gentlemen. You are excused.

Mr. LAWRENCE. Thank you, gentlemen.

(Witnesses excused.)

Chairman HANNAH. Mr. Taylor, will you call the next witness.

Mr. TAYLOR. The next witness is Mr. Leonard Russell.

Chairman HANNAH. Mr. Russell, will you raise your right hand?

(Whereupon, Mr. Leonard Russell was duly sworn by the chairman and testified as follows:)

Chairman HANNAH. Mr. Taylor, will you begin the questioning.

TESTIMONY OF MR. LEONARD RUSSELL, ADAMS COUNTY, MISS.

Mr. TAYLOR. Mr. Russell, would you give your full name, residence, and occupation for the record?

Mr. RUSSELL. Leonard Russell, 18 Irving Street, Natchez, Miss., employed at the International Paper Co.

Mr. TAYLOR. How long have you been working at the International Paper Co.?

Mr. RUSSELL. Ever since August 8, in 1952.

Mr. TAYLOR. Are you a member of the union at that plant?

Mr. RUSSELL. I am.

Mr. TAYLOR. Is that a segregated local union?

Mr. RUSSELL. Yes, sir.

Mr. TAYLOR. And do you hold any position in that local?

Mr. RUSSELL. A steward.

Mr. TAYLOR. We understand that your house was attacked in November of 1963. Is that correct?

Mr. RUSSELL. That's correct.

Mr. TAYLOR. Could you tell us about it?

Mr. RUSSELL. Well, on the 21st of November 1963, I was fixing a closet on the inside, reconditioning a closet in the house. And at 11:15 someone came to my front and called. And I went to the side door and answered, and he asked me to come help him push his car. So I asked him who he was and he said, "I'm a Jones." And I said, "Jones?" I said, "I don't know no Jones." He said, "Oh, you know Jones from Meadville."

So I said "Well, let me get my car." He said, "You don't need no car," he said. "It is very easy to start. We'll just shove it by hand."

Well, that made me feel funny, if he didn't want me to use the car, just push it off by hand. So I told my wife. She said, "Why don't you go and help him. There might be some day when you'll need help." So I said, "Well, you come on and drive," I said. And I gotten over on the other side. And he said "You are going in your car?" And I said, "Yes."

Well, the car was just about I imagine a hundred feet from my house, up on the dark side, the north side of it. So she started to pull in behind. He went there and stooped down behind the bumper with a flashlight to hide the tag. But I just caught the last three letters of the tag, "AMS." It was an Adams County tag.

Mr. TAYLOR. You did not live in Adams County?

Mr. RUSSELL. No, sir, I live in Franklin County, 7 miles from Meadville.

Mr. TAYLOR. That is an adjacent county?

Mr. RUSSELL. Yes, sir.

Mr. TAYLOR. But the tag was an Adams County tag?

Mr. RUSSELL. Yes, it was an Adams County tag.

Mr. TAYLOR. Go ahead, please.

Mr. RUSSELL. So he said, "Go around to the front and push it." I said, "Okay, just as soon as we turn around." So I had her to drive on up and turn around, and I said, "Now don't you stop when you get back. Pull up just like you're going in front of the car."

Well, when we passed the car there was a tall fellow with a hood over his head, at the car that was stopped there. He had the hood up and he just stuck his head under the hood; so we drove on up and turned around and come back and kept straight on to the house. Well, I got up, when I pulled up in the driveway, and went in the house and got my gun. Well, they pulled off. So it just upset my wife after she had seen the fellow with the hood over his head. And she went to questioning me and asked me if I had any trouble with anyone in the Klan or something. And I told her no, I don't know what it is. So she stayed awoke. Well, I laid down on the davenport.

And around the 22d—that was that morning about 12:15, well the car came back and stopped down below the house and one up above the house. So she called me; she said, "Those cars are back." So I got up and got in the chair set in between the living room and the bedroom, with my shotgun across my lap, and I sat there about 10 minutes and a gun shot said "dai," like a rifle, and there was a grenade come in from the window, one of those smoke grenades or bomb, or whatever they call it. Well, it came in the north window and busted the north window. I just put a new screen all the way up on the south side, and it broke that window and went through and hit it and fell back in the window. Well, I shot out that window and one shot at the door just about shoulder high at the side of the door, so my wife screamed, and I told her to bring me two buckets of water; the curtain was burning. So I throwed the water on there and finally got the fire out.

And I just taken me a towel and put it over my face and told her to take one and put over hers; and by knocking that window out, the north and south window, why, the air was pulling the smoke out. And I put the fire out. So we came out the house after they pulled off and went up side the road to some of our neighbors and I stayed not too far from the house, to watch the house while she called for the sheriff. So she called for the sheriff, and the sheriff wasn't there and he sent one of his deputies; at least one of his deputies is the one that came.

So the fellow where we went to call from, well he brought my wife back down to the house, and he asked her where I was and she told him, "Well, I was up the road a piece." So he blowed for me. Well, I didn't come out right then. So he come back down there and then went back up the road and on his way back down one of his near neighbors come out and asked what's the matter. So he say, "Some so-and-so done throwed something in the kid's house down there, tried to set it on fire, run him out." And this fellow said, "Well, I told them boys not to do that." That's what this fellow told me what brought my wife back down to my house.

Mr. TAYLOR. This was a neighbor of yours?

Mr. RUSSELL. This was a neighbor of mine where we called from. Another one told him that, you see.

Mr. TAYLOR. Did you ever find out what he meant by that statement?

Mr. RUSSELL. I sure didn't.

Mr. TAYLOR. Did the sheriff interview you?

Mr. RUSSELL. Yes, sir.

Mr. TAYLOR. Without mentioning any names, do you have any idea of why this incident might have happened?

Mr. RUSSELL. I sure don't.

Mr. TAYLOR. Did anything happen at the plant where you work which might have provoked this?

Mr. RUSSELL. Well, I don't know anything that could have. Unless a few months—about a month or so before this, we had a grievance turned in and I don't know whether that could have caused it or not. I wouldn't say that was what it was.

Mr. TAYLOR. You had filed a grievance on behalf of Negro workers?

Mr. RUSSELL. Yes, I had.

Mr. TAYLOR. Has anything happened to you since that time?

Mr. RUSSELL. Nothing.

Mr. TAYLOR. Did you move out of your house after this happened?

Mr. RUSSELL. Yes. I had the deputy sheriff stay with me until the next morning. And then we went out to a place they called Bude, Miss., where my wife's sister lived, and then I got in the truck and then the sheriff and the deputy came back out there with me to move my things. So I moved out there. It being bad weather during Christmas, I didn't get to move to Natchez until 26th day of December. On the 26th day of December I moved to Natchez.

Mr. TAYLOR. So you have left that house and now you live in Natchez?

Mr. RUSSELL. Yes, I left it the next morning.

Mr. TAYLOR. No further questions, Mr. Chairman.

Chairman HANNAH. Mrs. Freeman?

Commissioner FREEMAN. Mr. Russell, do you know of any prosecution of the persons who threw the bomb, the incendiary bomb, into your home?

Mr. RUSSELL. No, I don't.

Commissioner FREEMAN. Are facilities segregated or integrated at the plant where you work?

Mr. RUSSELL. Segregated.

Commissioner FREEMAN. Has there been any effort to desegrate them?

Mr. RUSSELL. Only water fountains.

Commissioner FREEMAN. The water fountains are desegregated?

Mr. RUSSELL. That's the only thing desegregated.

Commissioner FREEMAN. What about the lavatory facilities?

Mr. RUSSELL. They're segregated.

Chairman HANNAH. Mr. Rogerson?

Mr. ROGERSON. Mr. Russell, was the neighbor white or Negro who allegedly said, "Now I told those fellows not to do that"?

Mr. RUSSELL. He was white.

Mr. ROGERSON. I see.

Chairman HANNAH. Any further questions?

Mr. TAYLOR. No, sir.

Chairman HANNAH. Thank you very much, Mr. Russell. You are excused.

(Witness excused.)

Chairman HANNAH. Will you call the next witness.

Mr. TAYLOR. The next witness is Mr. Archie C. Curtis.

Chairman HANNAH. Mr. Curtis, will you raise your right hand?

(Whereupon, Mr. Archie C. Curtis was duly sworn by the Chairman and testified as follows:)

Chairman HANNAH. Mr. Taylor?

TESTIMONY OF MR. ARCHIE C. CURTIS, ADAMS COUNTY, MISS.

Mr. TAYLOR. Mr. Curtis, would you give us your full name, your residence, and your occupation for the record?

Mr. CURTIS. My name is Archie C. Curtis. I live at 66 Brenham Avenue, Adams County, Natchez, Miss. I am owner of the Curtis Funeral System, Inc.

Mr. TAYLOR. How long have you been in Mississippi?

Mr. CURTIS. Approximately 30 years.

Mr. TAYLOR. And how much of that time have you been in Adams County?

Mr. CURTIS. All that time.

Mr. TAYLOR. Where did you go to school, sir?

Mr. CURTIS. Natchez College.

Mr. TAYLOR. Are you a registered voter in Adams County?

Mr. CURTIS. I am.

Mr. TAYLOR. Mr. Curtis, are you active in voter registration work?

Mr. CURTIS. I am.

Mr. TAYLOR. To what civic or civil rights organizations do you belong?

Mr. CURTIS. I am a member of the Natchez Business Civic League and I am chairman of the Political Action Committee. That committee is to try to get our people registered and consequently to become voters. I have been active in trying to get people registered. I have made talks at churches, at clubs and societies, and contacted people personally.

Mr. TAYLOR. We understand that on February 15, 1964 you were attacked. Could you tell us about that incident?

Mr. CURTIS. Well, on the night of February the 15th, 1964, approximately at 12:45, I received a call in Curtis Funeral Home. I replied, "This is the Curtis Funeral Home." The caller said, "I want to speak to Archie Curtis." I said, "This is he talking." He said, "My name is Mr. Bogard. I am Joe Gooden's foreman. His wife has had a heart attack, and he wants your ambulance to come and carry her to the hospital." I replied, "I don't know Joe Gooden, or where he lives." He answered and give description and said, "Come on to Palestine Road, and when you get to the end of the Palestine Road on the blacktop, there will be a man with a lantern to direct you the way to Joe Gooden's home."

I woke my wife and told her where I was going. I immediately called Mr. Willie Jackson, a part-time worker, told him to get ready immediately; we had an emergency ambulance call to make. I began to get ready, not fully dressed. I put my suit over my pajamas and my overcoat on, and raced on around to Willie Jackson's home, and we went on to the funeral home and got my ambulance, and then proceeded to make the call.

I goes on the Palestine Road, and when I gets to the end of the blacktop, blowed my horn. I didn't see nobody with a lantern. I told Willie, "I believe this is a false call." Just then he looked in the mirror on the side and seen a car approaching the rear of our ambulance at a distance, and he said "A car is coming behind us." I looked in my mirror, and I seen it. I said, "Well, I'm going on to the end of this road until I get to the road that comes in from Washington. I'll stop there and ask do they know where Joe Gooden lives."

I gone on down to the end of that road, and when I got there, they was at the back of my ambulance. Instead of them coming on around—I taken my hand out of the window and motioned for them to come on around—their lights was on. Two men with white hoods over their head and down to their waist, pistols in their hand, got out and came to my ambulance, and two on Willie's side. They said, "Get out of this ambulance." I said, "Oh, go away, men. I came out here for Joe Gooden's wife who had a heart attack."

Just then the third man came, which was a shorter fellow than these two other gentlemen, and he had a shotgun, a Winchester. He said "Didn't you"—he used a curse word. He said, "Didn't you hear those men say get out of that ambulance? They mean for you to get out or we'll blow you to pieces."

Well. I didn't rush to get out. I taken my time in turning around.

I got on out the ambulance, and when I got out, they hit me on the hand with one of the pistols, jerked my glasses off, throwed them away, and blindfolded me. Then led me to the car and put me in the car they had. They did Willie the same. They taken him out of the ambulance on the other side and brought him around my ambulance; and when they got him around the ambulance, he told me they blindfolded him with his handkerchief. They put him in the car, and the driver got in on his side and four more men got in the rear and told the driver to drive on. He drove on, down to Duck Pond, and out to some oil wells. He stopped his car at a distance and taken us out, led us over from the car, a distance from the car, I don't know just how far it was, but it was a good distance, and said "Get out, get out them clothes."

Well, they taken Willie from me. They led him over a distance from where I was. I pulled off my overcoat. He said "Take off the other coat." I taken it off. He struck me two licks on my back, and say "Give me that NAACP card that you have in your pocket."

I said, "I don't have no NAACP card in my pocket." He said, "Oh, yeah, you and that damn West got NAACP cards in your pocket and you know who else got them." I said, "I don't have no NAACP card in my pocket, and I haven't never heard West say he had no NAACP card in his pocket."

Mr. TAYLOR. Who's West?

Mr. CURTIS. George West, a competitor of mine who is in the same business as I am. And then said "Drop them pants." So I dropped the pants, and they started whipping me with a whip. And whipping me with the whip, I said, "Man, don't be whipping me like this. What have I done?" They never said anything. I say, "I've had a stroke and I'm just getting up from a stroke, and don't be whipping me like this."

Then one said, "We ought to kill them out here." Another one said, "No, let's leave them." I heard them telling Willie when they was whipping him, "What you doing with him? What you doing out here with him," or "What you doing with him?" So they was ready to leave and I heard them say, "You better not say anything about it. You better not tell nobody about it."

As soon as they began to walk off, I pulled the blindfold from over my eyes to see if I could recognize them, or recognize the car. But it was a late hour in the night and I couldn't recognize the car, but I did see it was a white tag similar to Adams County tag, but I couldn't make out the number. I couldn't recognize their voices; they said but a very few words. And by them being hooded I only recognized their eyes being white and their mouth. But I couldn't recognize any of them, any of their voices.

Mr. TAYLOR. How did you get back home?

Mr. CURTIS. Well, when they left, I told Willie, "Well, we got to get out of here now, Willie." And we dressed and got ready to leave and walked down one road and came into an oil well on that road. I said, "Well, this is the wrong road. Let's turn around." We went back to the same spot we were. I said, "The only way we can get out from here, Willie, is to go down the road they went out."

Willie said, "No, don't we go out that road. They may be laying out there to kill us." And I said, "Well, we've got to get out, so let's go." So finally I convinced him, and we went on down the road they went out. We finally came back to the road where our ambulance was. I left my red lights on, but I had pulled my headlights off. And when I got to my ambulance, the battery was down. I tried to start it; put it on the side of the road, further on the side of the road, and we couldn't start it. So we finally put to the side of the road while waiting for the battery, and I said, "Well, now, Willie, we have got to go now and try to get home." I said, "I know a friend on this road who will probably get us home, Norman Bell." So we started walking up to Norman Bell's home.

Well, we got to Norman Bell's home about 4 or 5 o'clock in the morning, I imagine. I woke them up; they came to the door, excited. I told them the story. Then I rang my wife, told her what happened. I asked Norman Bell to carry me into town, I wanted to go to the sheriff's office. He got dressed and brought us on to town, and we went to the sheriff's office. I asked the desk sergeant could he get in touch with the sheriff for me, Sheriff Anders. He said, "I don't know; I'll try."

So he called, but he couldn't get him. And finally Deputy Blough and Deputy Smith came. When they came I told them the story. They said, "What in the world happened?" So I told them again. They said, "Well, Curtis, we have but little to go on. You don't recognize the men's voices; you don't know them. But we'll do what we can to apprehend them."

Before I left I told Deputy Blough that my car was out where they stopped me. He said, "Well, what's the trouble with it?" I said, "Couldn't get it started." So he and Deputy Smith taken a jump cable, and carried us out where the car was, got it started. Before it got started, Willie went with them over to where they carried us to whip us, showed them the place, came on back and got the ambulance started. Mr. Jackson and I came on back home.

Mr. TAYLOR. Were you treated by a doctor, Mr. Curtis?

Mr. CURTIS. After I went home and taken a bath, I went to my physician. I feared my blood had ran up, and my wife was quite excited. She insisted I go, so I did. I went to my family physician and he examined me and my blood pressure wasn't higher. He seen the bruises on my back, and advised me to go home and take some rest.

Mr. TAYLOR. Your physician is Dr. McAmis?

Mr. CURTIS. Dr. McAmis.

Mr. TAYLOR. We have an affidavit here from Dr. McAmis. In part it reads, "On physical examination, he had multiple bruised, discolored areas of the skin, shoulders, back, arms, hands, buttocks, thighs and legs. These bruised areas varied in width from very narrow to areas approximately 2 inches in width or slightly more than. The injury sustained by the patient was in the nature of multiple bruises and abrasions of the skin apparently produced by being struck with great force by objects of at least three different widths."

Mr. Curtis, do you have any idea why this happened to you?

Mr. CURTIS. The only thing that I feel is because of my interest in trying to get people registered and voting.

Mr. TAYLOR. Thank you.

Chairman HANNAH. Any of the Commissioners have any questions? Father Hesburgh?

Commissioner HESBURGH. Mr. Curtis, is this sort of thing unusual in Adams County?

Mr. CURTIS. Well, up until that time we haven't had any. There had been some previous beating by some other fellows but I had none to threaten or beat me.

Commissioner HESBURGH. I don't mean unusual for you, but unusual for people generally. Does this sort of thing happen very often?

Mr. CURTIS. It has happened very often since that time; yes.

Commissioner HESBURGH. Thank you.

Chairman HANNAH. Mrs. Freeman?

Commissioner FREEMAN. Mr. Curtis, are you aware of any efforts of the sheriff to try to apprehend the persons responsible for the beating or keep these incidents from occurring?

Mr. CURTIS. My wife called the sheriff that Sunday. And we couldn't get him; so we called again, and we finally got hold of him, and he said he would be out. He didn't come Sunday, and he didn't come Monday. He eventually came out Tuesday. And I told him the story. He said that he would do all he could apprehend the men. But I haven't heard from him.

Commissioner FREEMAN. You haven't heard anything since?

Mr. CURTIS. No.

Chairman HANNAH. Mr. Rankin?

Commissioner RANKIN. I noticed you were interviewed by the highway patrol, is that correct?

Mr. CURTIS. Yes, sir.

Commissioner RANKIN. Did anything result from that?

Mr. CURTIS. No, sir. I haven't heard anything. They've been to see me several times, the FBI and the highway patrol. But they said they had no leads on that.

Chairman HANNAH. Is that all, Mr. Taylor?

Mr. TAYLOR. Just one further question. Do you know, Mr. Curtis, when the deputies went back with Mr. Jackson to the place where you were beaten, were they able to pick up anything? Any article of clothing?

Mr. CURTIS. No, not that I know of. They never told me they picked up anything; had no trace of anything. They shot at my ambulance too around about August. It was parked on the side of the funeral home. They shot in it and also shot in the funeral home.

Mr. TAYLOR. That was this past August?

Mr. CURTIS. Past August.

Mr. TAYLOR. Was this reported?

Mr. CURTIS. I called the police department and told them about it. In fact, when I heard of the shooting in the ambulance, the police department was out at the funeral home then. A neighbor called me and told me there was some shooting going on out at the funeral home. One of the officers called me and asked me if my ambulance been out that night, and I told him, "Yes, it had." And he said it had been shot at. I rushed out to the funeral home and found it had been shot through the windshield, and on the side of the ambulance.

Mr. TAYLOR. Did any law enforcement officer examine the ambulance?

Mr. CURTIS. Yes, they did.

Mr. TAYLOR. Thank you.

Vice Chairman PATTERSON. Mr. Curtis, you say you assumed you were beaten because of your voter registration activity?

Mr. CURTIS. Because of my activity in trying to get people registered and voting.

Vice Chairman PATTERSON. Do you think the purpose of beating you was to frighten you so you would stop these activities?

Mr. CURTIS. I think it was.

Vice Chairman PATTERSON. Was this your reaction, or what was your reaction to the beating?

Mr. CURTIS. I still tried to get them to register. I never did stop.

Vice Chairman PATTERSON. Thank you.

Chairman HANNAH. Thank you very much, Mr. Curtis. You are excused.

(Witness excused.)

Chairman HANNAH. Would you call the next witness, Mr. Taylor.

Mr. TAYLOR. The next witness is Mr. Alfred Whitley.

Chairman HANNAH. Mr. Whitley, will you raise your right hand?

(Whereupon, Mr. Alfred Whitley was duly sworn by the Chairman and testified as follows:)

Chairman HANNAH. Mr. Taylor, will you begin the questioning.

TESTIMONY OF MR. ALFRED WHITLEY, ADAMS COUNTY, MISS.

Mr. TAYLOR. Mr. Whitley, would you give us your full name and address?

Mr. WHITLEY. Alfred Whitley, Route 4, Box 244, Natchez.

Mr. TAYLOR. What do you do for a living, sir?

Mr. WHITLEY. I am employed at the Armstrong Tire and Rubber Co.

Mr. TAYLOR. In what capacity?

Mr. WHITLEY. Janitor work.

Mr. TAYLOR. How long have you lived in Mississippi?

Mr. WHITLEY. Ever since 1922.

Mr. TAYLOR. And has that time been in Adams County?

Mr. WHITLEY. Yes.

Mr. TAYLOR. Have you registered to vote?

Mr. WHITLEY. No, sir.

Mr. TAYLOR. Have you ever been involved in civil rights activity of any kind.

Mr. WHITLEY. No, sir.

Mr. TAYLOR. We understand that you were attacked about a year ago. Could you tell us about the night that you were attacked?

Mr. WHITLEY. Yes, sir. On February 6, when I got off at the plant, we all left. I was rushing to come home in our car, just a plain car. When we hit the main highway, coming 61 north, we were all lined up coming home. Everybody was driving in a pretty good rush, around 60 miles an hour. When we got down there to the first red light, why I could see the light was going to come on and I pulled over to the right, and all the cars was lined up to the left, and I passed them cars. When the light clicked on they had to start off, but I had about a 30-mile speed and I passed them.

And when I got to the second set of red lights, I slowed down for that light and another car passed me. When it passed me, it cut in over in front of me. I wasn't driving no more than about 40 miles an hour. And then after I got about half a mile out, I started going on home, I picked up my speed, and I cut over to pass him, and he shot out and got up to 70 miles an hour and then I cut back in behind him and then I could discover that a car was trailing me then. And so I drove on until I came to my fork. When I came to my fork, this car wouldn't let me by, he kept going. So I turned in and the car was right behind me turning in. And so when I got to the airport fork—well, when I got to my little road to go into my house, I turned in there and it turned in right behind me. And got out the road about a hundred yards down there two cars were parked there, and I couldn't get by.

Mr. TAYLOR. This is a dirt road?

Mr. WHITLEY. Yes, gravel road. So I stood there and blowed about a minute. Nobody moved or nothing. So I guess it must have been the man behind covered me, and then all of them come out then with their guns, out of their cars in front of me.

Mr. TAYLOR. About how many men were there?

Mr. WHITLEY. Eight. So when they come out of the car, straightened up out of the car, my lights were shining down through there, and they had their hoods back, and no sooner than they straightened up they could see their faces was in the light, they done like that (indicating). They covered themselves with one hand, and they had their guns pointed on me and in my car. And so I just got out and when they got there I got out and they said, "If you don't say nothing, you won't get hurt."

So then they took everything, my glasses and everything I had on me. And then they told me, they said, "Put your hands behind you." I put my hands behind me. They said, "Close your eyes." I done that. And they tied my hands behind me. They taken me on to their car then. And one said something I couldn't understand. But anyway, he was talking about the car and the hood. He said, "Let's put him in this Olds," and they put me in an Oldsmobile and I reckon they drove about 40 minutes before they stopped. And they stopped way out in the swamp somewhere; I didn't know where I was.

Mr. TAYLOR. Could you see where you were going?

Mr. WHITLEY. No, sir, I couldn't see. So when they stopped, the one that was in the car in front asked the one who was in the car ahead with me, he said, "What have he said?" They said "Nothing."

So then they got me out then, and they pulled my clothes off, tore them off, cut them loose, took them off. And they reeled out two bull-whips then and say, "You hear this?" They pops it around over my head a little and then they shoved me down on my stomach. Well, they had all of my clothes off, and when they shoved me down on my stomach, then they started beating. And they beat there until they got tired of beating, and went to blaspheming and said, "You the toughest we ever beat on," said that, "He won't talk and we know he ain't dead."

By that time I asked him a question, I said, "You all brought me out here, and I didn't know what you brought me for, and you all didn't asked me nothing. I didn't know nothing to tell you."

And he said "Well, don't you know we know you're the leading nigger in Natchez, the NAACP and the Masonic Lodge? And you have a white leader, and you're going to tell us who he is." And I said, "I'm sorry, I can't tell you."

So they beat me thataway the third time and asked me them questions. So then they got me up to my knees and put a double-barreled shotgun right at the end of my nose and said, "Well, now, you're going to tell a white man the truth." And I said, "I done tell the white man all the truth that's in me."

Then one had what you call a riding strap; he beat me in the face until he knocked me over. And then they jumped me back up on my knees and then they said, "Now, you'll tell the white man the truth." I said, "Well, I done tell him all the truth that there is that I know. I told you about the church, and that's all I belong to, nothing else." I said, "I can't tell you nothing else." And I said, "Now, Lord—," and he said, "That's right, call your God."

And I said, "Well, you got a Lord." And I said "I don't know who you is with the gun, but whoever you is, you pull the trigger."

And that time he took the gun out of my face, and they handed me a bottle of castor oil and told me to drink every bit of it, and I drank it. And about that time one shoved a single-barrel gun across my nose, laid right across like that (indicating), and said, "Nigger, smell what you're going to die of." And that time, the other one had the double-barrel shotgun, said "Get up on your feet."

I stood up and looked at him—looked at the hood; I couldn't look him in the eye. Just looked at the hood. And he said "Nigger, run." And I took off and run just about as far as from here to the wall there, and they had a flashlight lantern shining on me, and I just fell on my stomach. And when I fell, they carried that light just like that and they didn't see me, and they clamped the light out and they shot right where they seen me last. They just emptied guns over my head, and I was laying there.

Mr. TAYLOR. Did they leave then?

Mr. WHITLEY. Then they got in their cars and left.

Mr. TAYLOR. And did you manage to get back home?

Mr. WHITLEY. Yes, I managed to work my way back out to the road and caught a truck to come out to the cycle plant, called my wife and she come got me.

Mr. TAYLOR. Were you treated by a doctor after this?

Mr. WHITLEY. Yes, sir. I called a doctor and the doctor told me to go to Jeff Davis Hospital. And he asked me did I call the law, and I told him no. And he said "Call the law and tell the law to meet you at the hospital." And I done that.

Mr. TAYLOR. Were you admitted to the hospital?

Mr. WHITLEY. Yes, in Jeff Davis Hospital.

Mr. TAYLOR. And how long were you out of work as a result of this?

Mr. WHITLEY. 10 days.

Mr. TAYLOR. I would like to read at this point the medical report provided by Dr. Springer, who treated Mr. Whitley.

It says, in part, "Numerous abrasions and contusions, swelling about both eyes and across both cheeks. He appears alert and well oriented. He is weak, however, apparently from having been forced to drink approximately 2 or 3 ounces of castor oil."

Mr. TAYLOR. Did you say the sheriff did come to the hospital to interview you?

Mr. WHITLEY. Yes.

Mr. TAYLOR. Were you able to give him any information about the event which would have identified people involved?

Mr. WHITLEY. Well, I didn't know none of them and I just told him they was all hooded. I just saw their faces and they looked like they were white. And they said they were white when they was beating me, you see. So that's all the identification I could give him.

Mr. TAYLOR. When you were able to make your way home and get a ride, were you able to recover your clothes? Or were your clothes left where you were?

Mr. WHITLEY. Well, I got some of my clothes. But I recovered the rest of them later, about 4 days later after I was out of the hospital. The game warden, the doctor told me, picked them up and brought them to his office.

Mr. TAYLOR. Do you know where the beating took place?

Mr. WHITLEY. Well, they tell me it was in the government forest. That's all I know; the place, I don't know where it is.

Mr. TAYLOR. Were you ever reinterviewed by the sheriff?

Mr. WHITLEY. No, sir.

Mr. TAYLOR. Did he ever come back to see you again?

Mr. WHITLEY. No, sir.

Mr. TAYLOR. Now, going back to the beginning of this night, you said that the car pulled out ahead of you, and wouldn't let you pass. I don't want you to give me the name, but did you recognize any person in this car?

Mr. WHITLEY. Well, I knowed the car. I knowed the man that drove that car. I knowed the car.

Mr. TAYLOR. Was he somebody who worked with you?

Mr. WHITLEY. Yes, he worked at the plant. And they called him——

Mr. TAYLOR. I don't want to know his name.

Mr. WHITLEY. Don't you? Okay.

Mr. TAYLOR. Do you have any idea why this happened to you, Mr. Whitley?

Mr. WHITLEY. Well, I don't have no—just I never thought that it would happen, because hadn't nobody said nothing to me about anything like that, and I didn't have no idea anything like that would happen because I didn't belong to no kind of organization or nothing. But I had a few discussions in the plant, but it wasn't concerning no NAACP or nothing.

Mr. TAYLOR. A discussion about civil rights, or did somebody ask you something about civil rights?

Mr. WHITLEY. No, sir. They did ask me about the school situation, and asked me what I thought about it. I told them, I said, "Well, now, at the present time," I said, "I think the school situation is pretty good." I said, "We have several schools here in Natchez, and the school buses, and the children are beginning to get a learning." And so then I asked him, I said, "Would you allow me to ask you a question?" And he said, "Oh, yes." And I said, "Well, now, what I would like to know is if the State of Mississippi would go to work in schooling about four or five thousand children," I said, "Now how much you think it would cost to school them children, per head?" He said, "Oh, around about five, six thousand dollars per head."

And I said, "Well, if he schooled all of those children, and after they get their learning nothing in Mississippi for them to do, they got to go to another State to get work to do." I said, "What profit is that to Mississippi?" I said. I said, "We who live here in Mississippi ought to be trying to fix a way for them to go to work after they get their learning, or something for them to do. Or Mississippi will just be growed up in bushes, won't be nothing here but us old folks if we don't do nothing about it." He just shook hisself and walks off then.

Mr. TAYLOR. Were you ever taken back to the spot where you were beaten by the sheriff or anybody else?

Mr. WHITLEY. No, sir; never was.

Mr. TAYLOR. Thank you.

Chairman HANNAH. Father Hesburgh?

Commissioner HESBURGH. Mr. Whitley, did you tell the sheriff everything you have told us?

Mr. WHITLEY. Yes, sir.

Commissioner HESBURGH. And after that you never saw him again?

Mr. WHITLEY. No, sir.

Chairman HANNAH. Mrs. Freeman?

Commissioner FREEMAN. Mr. Whitley, you said that in telling the sheriff everything that you have told us, you gave the sheriff the name of the person whom you recognized?

Mr. WHITLEY. Yes, ma'am.

Commissioner FREEMAN. And there have been no arrests made?

Mr. WHITLEY. Nothing. Nothing has been done about it.

Chairman HANNAH. Mr. Rankin?

Commissioner RANKIN. Did these men refer to each other by name, like Jack or Joe, or anything like that?

Mr. WHITLEY. Who's that? That taken me out?

Commissioner RANKIN. Yes.

Mr. WHITLEY. No, they didn't give no name. They didn't call no name.

Commissioner RANKIN. Did they say they were a member of any organization at all?

Mr. WHITELY. No, sir.

Commissioner RANKIN. In fact, they just didn't say anything much to you.

Mr. WHITLEY. No more than the questions that they asked me and they knowed I was answering.

Chairman HANNAH. Mr. Patterson?

Vice Chairman PATTERSON. Do you think they really had you mixed up with somebody else, Mr. Whitley, or do you think they thought they knew who you were?

Mr. WHITLEY. Well, evidently they had to know who I was, because from the way they stated when they beat me up. They said, "We've been after you 5 days." They said, "you're the hardest one we ever tried to catch."

Vice Chairman PATTERSON. Do you think it might have resulted from what you said at the plant that day?

Mr. WHITLEY. That's the only thing I can see.

Vice Chairman PATTERSON. Thank you.

Commissioner RANKIN. Has anything happened since then?

Mr. WHITLEY. No, sir.

Chairman HANNAH. Mr. Rogerson?

Mr. ROGERSON. Mr. Whitley, was this the sheriff of Adams County with whom you talked?

Mr. WHITLEY. Well, it was a deputy sheriff.

Mr. ROGERSON. And you only saw this deputy?

Mr. WHITLEY. That's all.

Mr. ROGERSON. That's the only one who came?

Mr. WHITLEY. Yes.

Mr. ROGERSON. And you never saw anyone from the state police, the highway patrol?

Mr. WHITLEY. Well, one time after that out there at the church—I live right at a church—there was some white folks came out there and done a lot of shooting right there in front of the church. I called the sheriff and Mr. Smith, I think, he does police work or something, but he ain't the deputy sheriff. But anyway, he came out and checked on that. He said "Oh, they're just hunting places to target shoot. They're just target shooting out there." He said he thought they wasn't harming nothing, so they came out there once after that and done the shooting like that, and I walked out there and looked to see who they was, but I didn't let them see me—a bunch of white folks down there shooting pistols, shooting in the bank over there.

Mr. ROGERSON. And you live outside of Natchez in Adams County?

Mr. WHITLEY. Yes, I live about 10 miles out.

Mr. ROGERSON. And the man who came at the time of the shooting at the church, you think, was from the sheriff's office?

Mr. WHITLEY. No, sir, I don't think they was from the sheriff's office that done the shooting. I don't think he was a police. I don't know just what he is, but he wasn't an officer. But the first time he come and said that they were just target shooting. Well, the next time they come I didn't call him because I just figured they was trying to learn how to shoot, I reckoned, and they wasn't going to bother me. I wasn't going to bother them.

Mr. ROGERSON. Thank you.

Chairman HANNAH. Do you continue to live in the same house?

Mr. WHITLEY. Yes, sir.

Chairman HANNAH. Do you have children?

Mr. WHITLEY. One grandchild lives with me.

Chairman HANNAH. Your children are all educated and they have left home? You have no children at home?

Mr. WHITLEY. Yes.

Chairman HANNAH. You told us about the beating. After the beating was over, they told you to run. You ran for a distance and then fell flat on your stomach. And then the guns were shot where you had been. Do you think that they were actually trying to shoot you, or just trying to frighten you?

Mr. WHITLEY. Well, I really believe they was trying to shoot me because with the looks of the blazes coming from the gun, this part of the body couldn't have missed catching it; the blazes was coming right straight over my head.

Chairman HANNAH. Thank you very much, Mr. Whitley.

Mr. Taylor, one more question?

Mr. TAYLOR. Mr. Finkelstein?

Mr. FINKELSTEIN. Mr. Whitley, was it raining the day that you were beaten?

Mr. WHITLEY. No, sir.

Mr. FINKELSTEIN. It was dry?

Mr. WHITLEY. Yes, sir.

Chairman HANNAH. Thank you very much, sir. You are excused. (Witness excused.)

Chairman HANNAH. Mr. Taylor, may we have one more witness before we break?

Mr. TAYLOR. The next witness is a staff witness, Mr. Edwin D. Wolf. He will present the staff report.

Chairman HANNAH. Will you raise your right hand?

(Whereupon, Mr. Edwin D. Wolf was duly sworn by the Chairman and testified as follows:)

TESTIMONY OF EDWIN D. WOLF, STAFF ATTORNEY, U.S. COMMISSION ON CIVIL RIGHTS

Mr. TAYLOR. Mr. Wolf, will you give your full name and your address?

Mr. WOLF. My name is Edwin D. Wolf. I live at 1869 Mintwood Place N.W., Washington, D.C.

Mr. TAYLOR. What is your position with the Commission?

Mr. WOLF. I am a staff attorney.

Mr. TAYLOR. Are you admitted to the bar?

Mr. WOLF. I am admitted to the bar of the Supreme Court of Pennsylvania and the Court of Common Pleas of the city of Philadelphia.

Mr. Taylor. Would you present your report, please?

Mr. Wolf. I would like to present to the Commission a report prepared by the staff on incidents of racial violence in and near Adams County from September 1963 to date. This report was compiled as the result of investigations conducted by attorneys in the general counsel's office during 1964 and 1965.

We made a number of trips to Adams County, interviewed witnesses, and examined government records. Since the report itself is rather long and since witnesses have already testified to certain incidents occurring in 1963 and the winter of 1964, I would like to summarize rather briefly the remaining cases investigated by the staff and submit the full report for the record.

There has been little civil rights activity in Adams County. When a group of freedom riders came to Natchez in 1961, they were not permitted to leave the bus. In October and November 1963 a small group of civil rights workers came to Adams County to assist in the Aaron Henry freedom vote campaign, an effort to stimulate Negro interest in registration and voting. About this time a series of incidents began in and around the county. I will report briefly on them in chronological order.

On the night of September 21, 1963, the Mount Plains Baptist Church burned to the ground. The sheriff was notified. The State fire marshal's office investigated and found evidence of arson. No arrests have been made.

James Carter Winston is a 40-year-old Negro who was employed by the Pickett's Cafeteria at the International Paper Co. plant in Natchez. On February 15, 1964, at 9 p.m., Winston left work and began walking down the road by the plant to go home. As was his usual practice, he attempted to hitchhike a ride home. A car stopped and a hooded white man carrying a rifle got out and ordered him into the car. Winston was ordered to lie down on the floor and a hood was placed over his head and tied around his neck. There were two other white men in the car, one of whom put a rifle against his head. During the ride Winston was asked if he were a member of the NAACP and the names of the local members of the NAACP. When the car stopped, about 12 or 13 miles from Natchez, he was forced to crawl through the mud to a spot where other hooded men were waiting. His clothes were stripped off and he was whipped. He was given a bottle of castor oil to drink and beaten a second time. Then he was forced to run naked down the road. Winston wandered about until he found a house where the people took him in. They gave him clothes and drove him to Natchez a few hours later. Later that day a deputy sheriff who had been notified of the incident came to his home and was informed of what had occurred. Winston did not go to a doctor and he went to work the next day. No arrests have been made.

Clifton Walker was a Negro laborer who worked in the woodyard of the International Paper Co. in Natchez. He had worked for the company since 1950 and was considered a good employee who was regular in his attendance. He lived in Woodville in Wilkinson County. He was married and had children. He drove to work in a car pool with another Negro and three whites. On February 28, 1964, he worked his regular shift, from 3 p.m. to 11 p.m. He never returned home. About noon the next day he was found dead in his car near the Poor House Road in Wilkinson County. He had been shot in the back with buckshot and rifle slugs. Sheriff Charles T. Netterville of Wilkinson County investigated. No arrests have been made.

Richard Joe Butler is a Negro farm laborer who lived in the Kingston Community. He had not been active in civil rights, and his whereabouts at the present time are unknown. Sometime in March 1964, Butler's car was stopped by two cars driven by white men. He managed to escape. A few days later the Identification Division of the Mississippi Highway Safety Patrol in Natchez was notified of a threat against Butler. Nightly surveillance of Butler's home was set up by the patrol and the Adams County sheriff's office. The surveillance generally ended about 2 a.m.

On April 5, 1964, about 8 a.m., Butler was shot four times with a shotgun on the property of his employer, near Kingston. He was seriously injured and taken to Jefferson Davis Hospital in Natchez. That same day he named five men as those who shot him. On April 7, 1964, the highway patrol arrested two men and charged them with assault with intent to kill. Charges against one were dropped when a lie detector test indicated his probable innocence; charges against the other man were dismissed on December 18. On October 27, 1964, two other men were arrested and charged with the shooting. Charges against both were dismissed without prejudice on November 17, 1964. County prosecutor Edwin Benoist gave lack of evidence as the reason for the dismissal in all the cases.

On April 24, 1964, six crosses were burned in Adams County, as part of a statewide demonstration by the Ku Klux Klan. No arrests were made.

On the morning of June 7, 1964, the assistant pastor of St. Mark's Baptist Church went to the church and found it vandalized. Sheriff Anders investigated. No arrests have been made.

The Riverview Motel is a modern, brick motel operated by a Negro businessman in Natchez. It was opened for business for Negro guests on about March 1, 1964. Before the motel opened, vandals cut down a billboard advertising the motel and shot out the motel sign. On June 20, 1964, between midnight and 1 a.m. a cross was burned on the property next to the motel. The proprietor did not call the police. In addition, since the opening of the motel, the sign has been shot at on three occasions. Each time the police were notified. No arrests have been made.

On July 12, 1964, the Jerusalem Baptist Church burned to the ground. Rev. Baldwin, the pastor of the church, learned of the fire early that morning. He reported the fire to the sheriff's office. The State fire marshal concluded that the fire was the result of arson. No arrests have been made. A photograph of this church is part of Appendix A to the staff report. An enlargement is available for the benefit of the audience.

On July 12, 1964, the same night on which Jerusalem Baptist Church burned, the Bethel A.M.E. Church burned to the ground. The sheriff and the State fire marshal investigated; the marshal found evidence of arson. No arrests have been made.

Willie Washington is a Negro contractor who has been a successful bidder on municipal jobs in Natchez. He is a registered voter and is a member of the Business and Civic League. He is not active in the civil rights movement. On the night of July 12, 1964, the same night the churches were burned, while sitting in his living room, he heard the sound of breaking glass on the front steps of his porch. He went to the door and saw a car pulling away from the curb. He called the police who discovered that a glass bottle stuffed with a rag wick and filled with kerosene had been thrown at the house. The bottle was broken, and the fluid did not ignite. The fragments were sent by the police to a police laboratory. No arrests have been made.

Extremist literature circulated in the community after the incident suggested that all three incidents of July 12 were plants. A copy of the literature is in Appendix B to the staff report.

On August 5, 1964, the Mt. Pilgrim Baptist Church burned to the ground. The sheriff investigated. The State fire marshal found evidence of arson. No arrests have been made. A photograph of this church is part of Appendix A to the staff report, and an enlargement is available for the Commission and the audience.

Jake Frishman is a 58 year old white man who operated a tavern for Negroes called The Wall Street Grocery. The tavern was in a frame building next door to a house rented and used by civil rights workers last summer. On the night of August 14, 1964, about 60 persons were inside the tavern when it caught on fire. The building was evacuated, and within a minute there was an explosion and flames shot through an open window. The fire spread rapidly and gutted the interior of the building. Investigating law enforcement officers discovered evidence of arson at the rear of the building. The sheriff believes the fire was set by whites. No arrests have been made.

On the night of September 15, 1964, stink bombs were thrown into two Jitney Jungle food stores owned by Mayor John J. Nosser, and bricks and a stink bomb were thrown into a Cadillac car agency owned by Orrick Metcalfe and his son. The bombs were thrown 10 days after pro-civil rights statements attributed to both men appeared in an interview published by the Chicago Daily News. No arrests have been made. An earlier interview by Nosser had been the subject of extremist literature, which is in Appendix B to the staff report.

Mayor Nosser testified before the Commission last week, and his testimony is hereby entered into the public record with his consent.

On September 26, 1964, at about 9:20 p.m. dynamite was thrown at the home of Mayor John J. Nosser. The mayor and his wife were sitting in the living room at the time of the explosion. The blast cracked every wall in the house and knocked the front columns askew. The police investigated. No arrests have been made.

On September 26, 1964, the home of Willie Washington was attacked again. About 9:30 p.m., while Mrs. Washington was alone, a bomb exploded in front of the house. The blast damaged the roof, gutters, and woodwork, cracked plaster, and broke two windows. Prior to the bombing, Mr. Washington had received a number of threatening phone calls. No arrests have been made.

George Metcalf is a 53-year-old Negro who works for the Armstrong Tire Co. He lives at 9 St. Catherine Street, Natchez, Miss. He is president of the Adams County chapter of the NAACP. On the night of January 25, 1965, a shot was fired at his house, striking a window frame and shattering the window. Metcalf was in the house at the time. He called the FBI and the police, who arrived that night and investigated. The police returned the next morning and continued the investigation. No arrests have been made.

Other incidents during the period covered by this report have affected white citizens of Natchez. None of the persons affected were willing to testify at this hearing because of fear of reprisal. In addition to these incidents, there were others reported which we were unable to confirm because of the victims' unwillingness to be interviewed. Several white citizens of Natchez related to us that they had received threats following actions on their part indicating sympathy for the Negro community. Several persons received anonymous telephone calls, usually in the middle of the night. Another person was warned of an impending bombing of his house. Another person reported that he was under surveillance and that his car had been followed by a car occupied by a group of white men. One family's home was watched on New Year's eve by an occupant of a car and then guests were followed by several cars when they left at 4 a.m. There were also threats of economic boycott and actual boycotts against persons who hired Negroes or were otherwise identified as favorable to Negroes. Finally, the Catholic clergymen in the area were attacked by extremist literature as a result of visiting a Negro in jail and permitting civil rights workers to stay at the rectory. This literature is in appendix B to the staff report.

Mr. TAYLOR. Does that conclude your report?

Mr. WOLF. That concludes the report. I would like to submit it for the record.

Mr. TAYLOR. The staff report and the appendices will be received in the record. (Exhibit No. 13 was marked for identification and received in evidence.)

Chairman HANNAH. Any questions you would like to ask Mr. Wolf?

Mr. TAYLOR. No, sir.

(Witness excused.)

Chairman HANNAH. And Mayor Nosser's testimony is included in the record?

Mr. TAYLOR. It will be included in the record.

(Following is the testimony of Mayor John J. Nosser, given before the Commission on February 11, 1965:)

(Whereupon, Mayor John J. Nosser was duly sworn by the Chairman and testified as follows:)

TESTIMONY OF JOHN J. NOSSER, MAYOR, NATCHEZ, MISS.

Mr. TAYLOR. I would just like to inquire of Mayor Nosser, since it was originally contemplated that he would appear at public session but cannot for medical reasons, whether the testimony we take today may be printed in the public record.

Mayor NOSSER. Yes, sir.

Mr. TAYLOR. Thank you. Mayor, would you please give us your full name and your residence?

Mayor NOSSER. My name is John J. Nosser. I live on 207 Linton Avenue, Natchez, Miss.

Mr. TAYLOR. And your full-time occupation is mayor?

Mayor NOSSER. At this time, yes. I am the mayor of the city of Natchez.

Mr. TAYLOR. Mayor, can you tell us where you were born?

Mayor NOSSER. I was born in a small village by the name of Al Monsif, in Lebanon.

Mr. TAYLOR. And how long have you lived in Mississippi?

Mayor NOSSER. I lived in Mississippi ever since 1919.

Mr. TAYLOR. All that time in Natchez?

Mayor NOSSER. No, sir. I lived in Vicksburg most of the time, and I moved to Louisiana. We didn't live there too long; we came back to Vicksburg again, and I lived in Clarksdale, Miss., for a while. I have been in Natchez now for 25 years.

Mr. TAYLOR. How long have you been mayor of Natchez?

Mayor NOSSER. This is my third year. Let's see, the first term I was elected to was a 2-year term only, but this last term that I was elected to was 4 years, so by July 1968, I will have served 6 years.

Mr. TAYLOR. Your first successful campaign for mayor was in 1962?

Mayor NOSSER. Yes, sir.

Mr. TAYLOR. Were you, during that campaign, the subject of any attacks which were based upon race or upon racial grounds?

Mayor NOSSER. Well, there was more or less of a whispering campaign, that I was a foreigner and—well, let's stop at that. Of course, the whispering campaign, of course you know I've got a lot of friends in Natchez. And just like anybody else, you have friends and foes wherever you go. And I say that whatever rumors were circulated about me was based on strictly prejudice.

Mr. TAYLOR. Did this happen again in 1964?

Mayor NOSSER. In 1964, yes. It was much more—let's say much more emphatic and open.

Mr. TAYLOR. Can you tell us what kind of an attack this was? Was there literature distributed?

Mayor NOSSER. Yes, they had literature distributed accusing me mostly of not being a man understanding the tradition of the South, trying to change the tradition of the South.

Mr. TAYLOR. During the past year or so has there been violence in the Natchez area which has been of a racial character?

Mayor NOSSER. Oh, yes. It was last year.

Mr. TAYLOR. Several incidents that you know of?

Mayor NOSSER. Well, I won't say several. I will say a few.

Mr. TAYLOR. Have you, yourself, been a victim of violence?

Mayor NOSSER. Yes. Two stink bombs had been thrown into stores of my family. And one explosive bomb was thrown in the front yard of my house.

Mr. TAYLOR. About when did this occur?

Mayor Nosser. Sometime last summer, I can't recollect the exact date.

Mr. Taylor. Do you know of any reason why this should have occurred to you?

Mayor Nosser. Well, I think some people were misguided. You know, you have a few people in every organization and every race who are hot-headed and don't use much logic in their actions. I think it was purely misunderstanding, and people were misguided.

Mr. Taylor. What about the other violence that has occurred in the area to other people?

Mayor Nosser. Well, of course, I can't tell you. I don't know who committed the violence and I don't know why. And any answer that I give you certainly wouldn't be authentic, because I don't know.

Mr. Taylor. Well, let me ask this: Do you believe there are extremist groups in the area, such as the Klan, which are responsible for any of this violence?

Mayor Nosser. There is no question there is an extreme element in there.

Mr. Taylor. Does the group go by any name?

Mayor Nosser. Well, the way I understand it, in every organization, regardless of whether it is an organization being religious, secular or political, there is an element in that organization that does not live up to the principles of the organization. I dare say that there are some people in churches that are church members and certainly don't live up to their obligation as church members.

Mr. Taylor. So you are saying that perhaps this is not the organization as such, but particular members?

Mayor Nosser. No. This is my experience with organizations, and I don't know. Because I am not a member of these organizations.

Mr. Taylor. In your opinion has local law enforcement been effective in dealing with these incidents of violence which have occurred?

Mayor Nosser. No. Well, we judge effectiveness of law enforcement by the accomplishment, and they haven't found out anything about these people. They haven't discovered anything about them. Even when the FBI came down there—I am talking about the Natchez locality now—and we had State troopers down there, and we had a State detective down there. And it seems to me they haven't been able to find anything.

Mr. Taylor. They haven't been able to find anything with respect to the two incidents that occurred?

Mayor Nosser. The people who committed these crimes.

Mr. Taylor. Is that true of the incidents directed against you, the stink bombs at your store?

Mayor NOSSER. That's right.

Mr. TAYLOR. Did the bomb explode on the lawn of your house?

Mayor NOSSER. Right on the porch.

Mr. TAYLOR. Did it do any damage?

Mayor NOSSER. $10,000 worth of damage.

Chairman HANNAH. $10,000, that's a lot of damage.

Mayor NOSSER. It's a large house. It's a two-story building. The foundation was shook up. It's got about 15 rooms or more in that house, and the sides of every room were split, and the ceilings were split.

Mr. TAYLOR. In addition to the violence which has occurred, has there been any economic pressure directed against white people in the community that you know of?

Mayor NOSSER. Well, I know that our stores—we have four stores in Natchez, which I don't have anything to do with the stores since I was elected mayor of Natchez. My three sons and son-in-law run these stores. They had a campaign, or boycott was conducted, and it affected our business a great deal.

Mr. TAYLOR. Who are "they"?

Mayor NOSSER. The element that you and I are talking about. In fact, our stores were boycotted by whites for a period and then again by colored for a short period. But my situation was this: I ran for the mayor's office for one purpose only. I am not a politician; I have been a businessman all my life. I just felt like I owe it to the community to serve the community and give them as many years of my life as possible. I went into the office to do the right thing by everybody, to bring progress and prosperity to the community.

I wasn't taking sides in this racial trouble at all. I am trying to do what I think is right, either way and anyway, at any time. When some of them white people thought that I was pro-Negro, why they boycotted my stores. When some of the colored people thought I was not, I was a pro-white, they boycotted our stores. But the truth of the matter is this: I am trying to do what is right under any circumstances, whether it benefits colored or white. I kept communication wide open between the mayor's office and the colored citizens, which no mayor had done that before; it was the first time in history. I am trying to do what is right by both races. I caught the worst of it from both of them.

Mr. TAYLOR. Would you tell us a little bit more about the steps you have been trying to take to improve the situation?

Mayor NOSSER. Well, when I went into the mayor's office, I made some proposals to the board of aldermen, such as we ought to give the colored funerals police escort. We ought to have some colored policemen on the police force. And immediately there was a certain complaint and criticism and that is when the boycott started with white people. And later on, my house was bombed one Friday night.

The attitude of the government down there in Natchez, including the mayor, was, until that time, an unusual attitude. The administration sitting on the side watching two camps, one on each side, fight. And they were sitting up there enjoying the fight. I felt like it is my duty to establish peace in the community, knowing that I had—the colored people and I would get along fine. I attended to their grievances. I did all I could for them within the law. I felt like it is my duty to open the lines of communication between the Klan—between that element and the mayor's office.

And Thursday, before the Friday that my house was bombed, I called the head of the Klan. I inquired who he was. I knew who he was. I called him. I never seen him before. I didn't know him until I called him and then met later. I called him one Thursday night. He agreed to meet with me in my office Saturday morning. Friday night my house was bombed. But I was in my office Saturday morning to talk with him. That was the beginning of the opening of the lines of communication between me and that element. And it has done a lot of good.

I met with that man quite often in order to tell him what I am trying to do to keep peace in this community under the law. And—when the colored people found out that I was negotiating with that man—I wouldn't say negotiating; I am trying to open lines of communication between the mayor's office and that element. I feel the mayor is the mayor of all people. Well, they thought that probably I am joining the Klan now, and they start boycotting me. But the boycott by colored people wasn't as severe as the one I had by the white people. Of course, I have always met with the colored leaders in the community, and I told them my position, just like I am telling you now. I didn't have anything to hide.

And before the freedom riders went into Natchez to integrate Natchez, some local colored people up there went into Kress' Store. They have a lunch counter up there, and they invaded that counter and everything was peaceful. When the freedom riders came down there and integrated most of our motels and hotels and restaurants, well, everything was peaceful. And I believe that was due to me opening the line of communication between that element and the mayor's office. You see, the point is this. These white people and the colored people, ain't none of them scared. They're not scared. Whatever they do, the reason is not fear. They are trying to accomplish something according to their own ideas, whether they are right or wrong.

But I am trying to prove to you that opening the line of communication between the mayor's office and that element, let's say the radical element in there, has opened the way to a peaceful situation in the community which had never existed before.

Mr. TAYLOR. Would you say that this group that you have discussed things with, or negotiated things with, is in a position of strength in the community? Would you be negotiating with them if they were not in a position of strength?

Mayor NOSSER. Well, state your question again. Let me understand what you say.

Mr. TAYLOR. You say that the night before your house was bombed, you called this group and asked to have a discussion with them. Then your house was bombed. Do you think that was an indication that they wanted to show you they were in a position of strength in the community?

Mayor NOSSER. Well, of course, I don't know about that. But—I could talk for myself. I think the duty of the government and being the head of the government is to do all I can within my power. It makes no difference how high I could go or how low I could go in order to establish peace in the community. I don't mind meeting with anybody if my meeting is going to be to accomplish more peace in the community.

Mr. TAYLOR. I have no further questions.

Chairman HANNAH. Mr. Patterson?

Vice Chairman PATTERSON. Mayor, what do you say to the head of the Klan when you have conversations with him?

Mayor NOSSER. I told him that I am at the head of the government; I am responsible for our people, for the fate of our people, and all I am doing, I am trying to enforce the laws. I am trying to help our colored citizens if they need a lot of help, trying to provide jobs for them in the industries, trying to provide jobs for them in the government. And I don't think there is anything wrong with that. I asked them, "Do you see anything wrong?" They said, "No, we don't see anything wrong with that." And I said, "All right." I said, "I took the oath of office that I would enforce the laws of the city of Natchez and the State of Mississippi." I said, "I am doing the best I can under the oath, and as far as I am concerned, all the citizens are entitled to the same privilege, and anything that I give anybody that is deprived of their privilege, I am going to give them under the law."

Vice Chairman PATTERSON. Did he make demands on you?

Mayor NOSSER. No, sir.

Vice Chairman PATTERSON. Did he tell you his intentions?

Mayor NOSSER. No, sir. He said he is glad that I called him. In fact, he told me, later on after we had some integrated motels and hotels and restaurants, that if it were not for the fact that I had called him and had a talk with him and he knew about my intentions, that probably there would have been bloodshed in the streets of Natchez.

Vice Chairman PATTERSON. Did you tell him that you would enforce the law?

Mayor NOSSER. He didn't keep me from enforcing the law.

Vice Chairman PATTERSON. No questions.

Chairman HANNAH. Mr. Mayor, what is the population of Natchez?

Mayor NOSSER. Oh, I would say about 25,000.

Chairman HANNAH. And what percentage of them are Negroes?

Mayor NOSSER. Say about 40, 42 percent.

Chairman HANNAH. Mrs. Freeman?

Commissioner FREEMAN. Mr. Mayor, will you tell me something about the Negro population. What is the industry, what are the skills, what are the kinds of jobs they do?

Mayor NOSSER. Well, as you well know, the Negroes in Mississippi— in Natchez, just like the rest of them down South; they haven't had the opportunities for having a good education, and under the circumstances, they do the best they can, and they work. We have got a lot of them working in these big industries right next to the white people. We have the colored and white, and they get along fine all these years.

Commissioner FREEMAN. As mayor do you have the responsibility for appointing the various officers of the city government? Are a certain number of your employees department heads?

Mayor NOSSER. Yes, we have. We have employees. Of course, each department has a head who is responsible for that department. He hires the employees, and he makes the recommendation that a man be promoted, and if they think that he is doing the right thing, we approve his recommendation.

Commissioner FREEMAN. Do you appoint these department heads? What are some of the departments that you have?

Mayor NOSSER. Some of the department heads are elected and some are appointed. The head of the Public Work Department is appointed. The chief of police is elected. The head of the—the city treasurer is elected, tax assessor is elected, judge is elected.

Chairman HANNAH. The chief of police is elected?

Mayor NOSSER. Yes. We have an old antiquated charter up there that certainly there is a lot of changes in it should be made, but people could never see to change any of it. We have tried two or three times to change the charter, but was defeated.

May I say a word or two before I leave. I want to say this. The way I feel about things now, I didn't come up here to discuss the past, because discussing the past is not going to do me or anybody any good unless we can learn our lessons from the past to implement our experience in the present and in the future. I believe at this time— and I am being very frank; I came up here with one purpose. I know you told me to come up here, but my purpose in coming up here before you is not trying to take sides in this controversy. And as long as you are going to find people taking sides you are going to have trouble. What we need today is more people who are neutral, who see the good points on this side, and the good points on this side, and try to get the two sides, the people together.

And with this in my mind, I want to say this. That now since the civil rights law is the law of the land, I don't think that mass demonstrations anywhere is doing the cause of peace any good. I believe that any citizen, white or colored, or group of citizens who may think that their civil rights are being violated, I think they ought to resort to the laws and the courts of the land. Now when you do that, they will be justified and they will get what is coming to them without any violence, without any hatred, without any prejudice. Now this is my opinion.

The next point, I want to say this. Since the civil rights law is the law of the land, I think what contributes to opening the wounds that may exist in some people's hearts is the presence—and I am being very frank now—the presence of some white people with colored when they have demonstrations. I think that is the worst thing. It hurts the cause of peace. And it hurts the cause of restoring justice. Now, you may not believe me, you may not agree with me, but I know—I think I know what I'm talking about. The law of the land should be obeyed. It should be enforced. And the regular due process of law should be followed in every case. And mass demonstrations are not contributing to the get-together of the two races or to the peace of the two races in any community in the South. And the presence of white people with colored people in demonstrations is doing the cause of justice and the cause of peace more harm than ever. This is my experience. That is what I hear. And gentlemen, and lady, I am telling you what I know. I didn't come up here to hurt anything. I came up here to try to do some good, to try to give you my honest opinion about the situation.

Chairman HANNAH. Well, as you know, sir, this Commission is trying to find out what the facts are.

Mayor NOSSER. Yes, sir.

Chairman HANNAH. And we would like to do what we can to assure progress in the elimination of the unquestioned grievances which have existed in the past. And we appreciate your coming. I am sure Father Hesburgh has some questions.

Commissioner HESBURGH. Mayor, do you think the mayor can use much leverage in creating a good community?

Mayor NOSSER. Yes, definitely. I have tried it. You know, I have tried it. And I know. Of course, sometimes you experience a lot of obstacles in your way, and sometimes you get to the point where you want to throw up your hands. But I believe with patience that any mayor of any town can help the situation a lot.

Commissioner HESBURGH. How much can you do about controlling violence? I know this is a police function, but I mean how much can you do about the police?

Mayor NOSSER. Well, you see, in Natchez it is different, just like I told you before, the police are elected by the people. There is very little that the mayor and Board of Aldermen can do with him.

Commissioner HESBURGH. Can't you even say something, that it is not working very well for example. We have long lists of violence. I think we have as long a list out of Natchez as out of any city in the United States, which doesn't make anybody very proud. But when you go down this long list, almost every single account finishes with these words, "No arrests were made." Now, in your time as mayor, can you think of anybody, any white man, who has created violence or bombing or burning or beating of Negroes ever being brought to trial and convicted and sent to jail for doing that, the way he would be in any other part of the country?

Mayor NOSSER. Well, I have to agree with you that there is some prejudice. There is no question about that. I am not denying that. But I just believe there is more than one way of restoring peace, as long as the peace has been restored.

Commissioner HESBURGH. Mayor, I was listening to what you said. You said we ought to do this by equality before the law. But where is the equality of the law when a man can beat a Negro and bomb or burn, and nothing happens? Then the Negro has only one alternative; maybe the only alternative he has is to protest.

If you have bombings, burnings, beatings year in and year out, and there is no arrest made, or if the arrest is made, the man puts up a few dollars and walks out free; if nobody goes to jail for this and nobody is going to do anything about it, the Negro feels, "My life is as cheap as anybody who wants to take it. I have no protection. It is no better than the will of any guy that would want to kill me." So the law is meaningless in this case.

Mayor NOSSER. I see your point. We have brought the FBI down there, brought the State troopers up there, and the State police, and they were honest, and they are trying all they can to catch those people, to find evidence to catch anybody, and they haven't been able to do it. So I mean, it is a hard case. I mean these cases could happen in Chicago, Ill. or anywhere. But let's assume that the local people, the local police didn't want to do anything. Let's assume that. Then what about the FBI or what about the State troopers, and what about the State secret service?

Commissioner HESBURGH. Well, let me ask you something else. Suppose they do catch somebody in an act of violence and they bring them in to trial—will they ever be convicted?

Mayor NOSSER. Well, that I don't know. That is just up to the courts.

Commissioner HESBURGH. Did you ever see a white man convicted for an act of violence against a Negro in Natchez? Did you ever hear of one, ever?

Mayor NOSSER. Well, there have been instances, yes.

Commissioner HESBURGH. Could you tell me about one? I would like to hear about one.

Mayor NOSSER. Of course, I don't know. I can't relate these instances, but there have been instances.

Commissioner HESBURGH. There have actually been instances where a white man was sent to jail for committing violence against a Negro, for example, killing one?

Mayor NOSSER. You would have to go to the records of the court. I don't know.

Commissioner HESBURGH. But do you recall any such case?

Mayor NOSSER. Well, I tell you, prior to getting in the government, I never had any time to record any case like that. I was a business man; I attended my business. So I don't know. But I am almost sure if you investigate you will find out some of them were penalized or punished for doing wrong.

Commissioner HESBURGH. But with all the violence in Natchez in the last 3 years, you don't recall a single white person—and I am assuming the white persons committed the violence against Negroes— you don't recall a single case during these years of your government where a white person has been brought to trial and convicted?

Mayor NOSSER. No, sir. No.

Commissioner HESBURGH. Well, let's assume now you and I are Negroes, not whites. And we are living in Natchez, and this is the situation we find ourselves in. Anybody can do anything to us and he will never be brought to trial because he either never gets caught or if he is caught, there is not enough evidence, or somebody won't talk. So what are we going to do now to try to get equality for ourselves, or even human dignity in this situation? Maybe if enough of us stand up in the street and say "All right, try to kill us all right out in the open."

Mayor Nosser. What do you propose?

Commissioner Hesburgh. All I am saying is the Negroes' only alternative, when this kind of thing is going on, is to get up and protest. This dates back to the Boston Tea Party which was a protest. They marched. And I would say the only thing—if the only thing a Negro can do is march and protest, then God bless the white people who are willing to stand up and be counted with him because somebody has to make a protest in this type of situation. Now when you say this is wrong, I respect your opinion, but I have to disagree with you, because I think the protest is the only thing left in the situation.

Mayor Nosser. Well, you are trying to approach the problem from a different angle. I am trying to approach the problem through the people who are the cause of this thing. That's the only difference.

Commissioner Hesburgh. I think it needs all kinds of approaches, but I think——

Mayor Nosser. I'm trying to educate the white and the colored to try to understand each other; that's the only way you can get along, by understanding. But your approach is not doing any good, because you had the FBI down here and you had the State troopers down here. It don't do anything.

Commissioner Hesburgh. It did this much good. Do you think there would be equal opportunities for Negroes to go into restaurants today if it weren't for the protests that were made when they went and sat there?

Mayor Nosser. That's not a protest; it's a law.

Commissioner Hesburgh. No, but how was the law passed? Discrimination had been going on for a hundred years. How was the law passed?

Mayor Nosser. The Negroes protested the separate school facilities. Was it demonstrations that caused the Supreme Court to decide to integrate the schools?

Commissioner Hesburgh. I don't think——

Mayor Nosser. They did that without any demonstrations.

Commissioner Hesburgh. But that was easier to do because that was just changing the law, whereas this case was different.

Mayor Nosser. Then why didn't they pass laws to cure our ills?

Commissioner Hesburgh. This gets into a good philosophical discussion, and I am probably talking too much.

Mayor Nosser. It is plain as daylight. The local authorities could not do nothing about the violence, and I agree with you. All right, by the same token, the FBI couldn't do anything about it.

Commissioner Hesburgh. I think they could if they wanted to.

Mayor Nosser. Then there is something wrong with the FBI all over the country. And the State troopers couldn't do anything about it. So I say this: Let's resort to getting the people to understand one another. Understanding—I mean that's what we need down there.

Commissioner Hesburgh. I'm not against understanding but sometimes a human situation gets to a point where all you can do is get up and protest, and sometimes if enough people get up and protest—

Mayor Nosser. I think anybody's policy is wrong when they are going to sit in one camp and say "This is the camp, and we don't want anything to do with you." This is not the solution to our problems. I think understanding, understanding and recognizing one another's rights, and belief in God, that we are all children of God; that's the only thing that is going to cure our problem.

Commissioner Hesburgh. I agree with you, but I merely say that there are times when things get so bad that people have to protest. And I understand it when they do; that's all.

Mayor Nosser. When you have a law, why should you protest? You've got the laws; all you have to do is resort to the courts. What do you have laws for?

Commissioner Hesburgh. Mayor, let me just tell you one thing. We sat here a few minutes ago talking to a chief of police. There is a law. The law says you can go in and get a coke at a lunch counter. So a kid goes in to get a coke at a lunch counter and is hit over the head with a baseball bat. The chief of police is in the room; he arrests the man. What happens? Nothing. The chief sets bond at $25; the man raised the money and is released. Now if you were the kid in the case, what is your respect for the law or for the equality?

Mayor Nosser. I don't believe in that kind of—what are you going to do? Declare war?

Commissioner Hesburgh. No. You do a lot of things. You do what you're doing, and I think it is right.

Mayor Nosser. I think it is the only solution.

Commissioner Hesburgh. But you also understand that people get so fed up they protest. That's all I'm saying. You do everything you can.

Mayor Nosser. My reasoning is this, before you have the law, I wouldn't be against protest at all. But since you have the law now, protest isn't doing any good. You ought to follow the course of the law. If you are not satisfied with the State courts, you can go to the Federal courts, according to law.

Commissioner HESBURGH. Yes. But do you know what it costs? Well, I think we've gone far enough on this issue.

Chairman HANNAH. Mr. Taylor, do you have another question?

Mr. TAYLOR. Just a question or two. Could a Negro citizen of Natchez walk down to a restaurant that was covered by the law and ask for a cup of coffee or a meal and be served today?

Mayor NOSSER. Yes.

Mr. TAYLOR. He can?

Mayor NOSSER. Yes. In fact, before the freedom riders went to Natchez, we had a few local people, colored people that integrated Kress' lunch counter, and everything was peaceful.

Mr. TAYLOR. Do Negro citizens actually use the restaurants?

Mayor NOSSER. If they want.

Mr. TAYLOR. You don't know of any who do, or do you?

Mayor NOSSER. Well, I don't know them. But I know four or five of them came to Kress' several times day after day up there and nobody bothered them. They were served.

Mr. TAYLOR. Do you know whether there are businessmen or merchants in the white community who have been boycotted or subjected to pressure aside from yourself?

Mayor NOSSER. I have heard rumors, but I don't know for sure whether they have or not.

Mr. TAYLOR. You have heard some rumors that this has happened?

Mayor NOSSER. I think there was just one more merchant in town.

Mr. TAYLOR. As I understand it, the State highway patrol came to Natchez sometime last spring. Didn't violence subside after they came for a while?

Mayor NOSSER. That's right. We haven't had any violence since.

Mr. TAYLOR. Are they still there?

Mayor NOSSER. No, sir. They pulled out a couple of months ago. But we haven't had any violence during their presence, and after they left we haven't had any violence.

Mr. TAYLOR. Mr. Finkelstein has one question.

Mr. FINKELSTEIN. Mayor, we have a copy of a newspaper advertisement with the headline "We Believe," which appeared in the Natchez Miss., Democrat on October 18 and then again on December 10. The statement has three paragraphs condemning violence and urging government officials and law enforcement officers to further their efforts to protect citizens, all the citizens of your community. Do you know about this statement? Can you tell us something about it?

Mayor NOSSER. Yes.

Mr. FINKELSTEIN. Why don't we mark this as exhibit No. 14. (Exhibit No. 14 was marked for identification and received in evidence.)

The document referred to is quoted in part as follows:

1. That this community is on the threshhold of a great economic, cultural and industrial development period, and to assure such growth we must have a reputation as a law-abiding community of people fully aware not only of the privileges, but more urgently of the responsibilities of living here.

2. That violent and unlawful acts of a few, determined to impose their will upon us, not only endanger our personal security but threaten the hopes and whole future of this area, and such acts must be met with overwhelming determination by all of us to end them.

3. That "fear of being involved" by responsible people is the very blood on which these hoodlums thrive, and we must not only put aside such fear, we must seek ways to participate actively in bringing to our governing officials and law enforcement officers, local, State, and national, any fact, matter or suspicion which might help them in their efforts to protect us.

Mayor NOSSER. That was made by several civic and religious organizations; is that right?

Mr. FINKELSTEIN. That's right.

Mayor NOSSER. I've seen it.

Mr. FINKELSTEIN. Were you involved in the preparation of that statement?

Mayor NOSSER. No, sir.

Mr. FINKELSTEIN. Do they consult you?

Mayor NOSSER. They have. In fact, I was involved once before, and I wanted a statement like this a long time before this appeared, when the first violence took place. And we weren't very successful in doing that.

Mr. FINKELSTEIN. Did you as mayor issue any statement similar to that or any statement calling for law and order when the violence first occurred?

Mayor NOSSER. I did.

Mr. FINKELSTEIN. When was that? Do you recall?

Mayor NOSSER. I don't know, sir. It is sometime during the last summer.

Mr. TAYLOR. That's all.

Chairman HANNAH. Mayor, did they ever apprehend those responsible for the bombing of your own home?

Mayor NOSSER. No, sir.

Chairman HANNAH. You never knew who was responsible?

Mayor NOSSER. No, sir.

Chairman HANNAH. You indicated that you were born in Lebanon. How old were when you came to this country?

Mayor NOSSER. I was 19.

Chairman HANNAH. You have done very well. We appreciate the expressions you have made here today. How much education did you get in this country after you came, or did you start in business?

Mayor NOSSER. Well, in those days, I graduated from high school. I was practically raised by a Presbyterian missionary and I remember I went to Sunday school when I was 5 years old. I graduated from the University of Beirut, American University of Beirut in 1919, and right after graduation I came to the United States. I came here to live because we had a good many American teachers and professors in high school and college, and I admired them. So I just made up my mind to come over here to live. And I proudly say that the people that I got acquainted with, the Americans I got acquainted with in the American institutions, were really ideal Americans in every respect. However, then I came to this country, and I began to get disappointed gradually, because the picture I had in my mind of all the American people was one thing, and what I found out was another. But nevertheless, you've got a good country here and knowing that we have our own failings and our shortcomings, sooner or later we get over most anything.

Chairman HANNAH. Did you come directly to Mississippi?

Mayor NOSSER. Yes, sir.

Chairman HANNAH. You have lived in Mississippi all the time?

Mayor NOSSER. Yes, sir.

Chairman HANNAH. You said that you had four stores. What sort of stores?

Mayor NOSSER. Well, it is three supermarkets and one discount store.

Chairman HANNAH. The food business primarily?

Mayor NOSSER. Yes.

Chairman HANNAH. Thank you, sir.

Commissioner RANKIN. Mayor, have the churches helped you much in your position or not? Have the churches taken any stand or any position—or the ministers of the churches?

Mayor NOSSER. Well, some of the ministers were for me. I tell you, I got my support from the average citizen, not from the rich, not from the real poor. But substantial citizens.

Commissioner RANKIN. Not from the ministry?

Mayor NOSSER. Well, I got some help from them. But I can't tell you who voted for me or who didn't vote for me.

Commissioner RANKIN. You are in the position here of trying to communicate.

Mayor NOSSER. Oh, yes, indeed. As a matter of fact, I had a meeting, asked them to come and talk to me.

Commissioner RANKIN. Have they suffered for their stand?

Mayor NOSSER. Well, I think Monsignor Fullham there did; he suffered a little bit. They put out some pamphlets about him which were not exactly nice.

Commissioner GRISWOLD. Who's this?

Mayor NOSSER. Monsignor Fullham. And I talked to the Ministerial Association and I told them in brief that it is just as much their duty as it is mine to keep the people straight and to work for peace. They are actually more responsible than the government as far as people being Christian or being unchristian. And it is up to them to call the people to their duty as Christian people and to create peace in the community. I worked with them.

In fact, the people that were behind this actually the main factor there was the past presidents of the chamber of commerce. Of course I happened to be one of them. I asked the city and county officials one time after the first instance that we go and put something in the paper like that, and we didn't get anywhere. Most of them, they weren't against them, but most of them said "Well, we swore to uphold the laws of the city and State and this is just a reinformation, and what's the use of doing it?"

But we have had a lot of people, the great majority of our people— let me say this again. The great majority of our people in Natchez, and probably just like anywheres in the South, they are righteous people. They see the right, and they see the wrong. They want to do what is right. But our trouble comes from small elements here, and I believe that if the people are given enough time, we can solve our problems down there. I know right now in Natchez you would be surprised; Natchez today is so much different from Natchez last year. And it is due to people like me and—I'm not bragging about myself, but who will go out and explain things to people and study with people and talk things over with people, both colored and white. I meet with all of them. And my mission is peace, understanding. I think the only way you can overcome violence is understanding. And I think when the majority of our people down there, both colored and white, understand the present law we will have peace, and we will have peace with honor.

You see, it is so hard, right or wrong. The tradition in the South is a way of life. It has been there for so many generations, and I haven't been raised in the South and I know, and you ought to know as much as I do, at least; and it is a way of life. I may think it is wrong, you may think it is wrong, but that is the way of life. Now you want to change the way of life for a generation. You can't change it overnight unless you have violence; there is no question about that. You make a sudden change, you are going to have violence.

Commissioner FREEMAN. How many Negroes are registered to vote in Natchez?

Mayor NOSSER. We have about 600, I believe.

Commissioner FREEMAN. Six hundred?

Mayor NOSSER. Yes, ma'am.

Commissioner FREEMAN. What is the total population?

Mayor NOSSER. The population is about 25,000.

Commissioner FREEMAN. And 42 percent Negro?

Mayor NOSSER. Forty-two percent Negro.

Commissioner FREEMAN. And you have 600 registered to vote?

Mayor NOSSER. That's right. And I tell you now, and I can tell you honestly, when Negroes go to register in Natchez, they have not been discriminated, as far as the test is concerned. As I stated before, most of them haven't had the education. Now you have young people coming out now all having opportunity to go to school.

Commissioner FREEMAN. Are the schools desegregated in Natchez?

Mayor NOSSER. No.

Commissioner FREEMAN. You said that of course you are in favor of all persons asserting their rights under the law.

Mayor NOSSER. Yes, certainly.

Commissioner FREEMAN. And that desegregation is now the law of the land.

Mayor NOSSER. Well, let's not go into details about that.

Commissioner HESBURGH. Who is going to have the understanding?

Mayor NOSSER. See, what I want to do, see—the press did not help the situation in the South. It didn't help it at all. They didn't help it at all. And by having people like me to be misunderstood by our people in the South serves only to hurt the cause of peace. So I am not going to say anything that would hurt the cause of peace. I have to work with both sides. You know what my goal is. And approaching that goal is going to be gradual approach, and it is going to take a lot of diplomacy to approach that goal. I just don't believe in a sudden change, when a sudden change is going to bring violence. Violence is not getting anybody anywhere.

Commissioner GRISWOLD. How slow does the change have to be so as to keep it from being sudden?

Mayor NOSSER. The change now is on its way. It's making progress.

Commissioner GRISWOLD. The law as to schools has been clear now for nearly 11 years, and nothing has happened in Natchez. Is this a sudden change?

Mayor NOSSER. Well, all they have to do, the colored people have to go ahead and say "We want to integrate," and that's all it is. I know the white people are not going to come and say "We want to integrate." It is up to the colored people, and if they are satisfied, it is their business. If they are dissatisfied they ought to let the people know about it.

Commissioner GRISWOLD. It is not the business of the public officials of Natchez?

Mayor NOSSER. Is it the function of a public official to go to your house and tell you "Now, listen, I don't like the looks of your house and you ought to get a better house, and your rooms are not well decorated?" Is that the function of the public officials?

Commissioner GRISWOLD. I don't think that is at all relevant. The fact is that you are administering, the officials of Natchez are administering the school system of Natchez and you have taken no steps, as I understand it——

Mayor NOSSER. The city government has nothing to do with the school system whatever. The school system is run by a school board.

Commissioner GRISWOLD. Which is a part of the overall city administration.

Mayor NOSSER. No, sir. It has nothing to do with the city. The money raised to run the school and education system is raised by the county government.

Commissioner GRISWOLD. Have you undertaken to suggest to the county government that they ought to comply with the law with respect to schools?

Mayor NOSSER. I don't think it is my function to tell anybody——

Commissioner GRISWOLD. Your idea is that there will be peace if everybody just accepts things as they are and does not try to do anything?

Mayor NOSSER. No, sir. My idea is I understand the people down there, and you don't. And I know what is the best way to work with these people to accomplish what you have in mind. What you have in your mind would not be accomplished unless you have bloodshed, and I just don't believe in bloodshed.

Commissioner GRISWOLD. Well, you may not be entirely clear as to just what is in my mind.

Mayor NOSSER. I know what's in your mind. You want a sudden change. Now I just made the statement a sudden change doesn't do anything. If you pardon me, this is the goal (indicating), and these are the people (indicating). The shortest line between two points is a straight line, right?

Commissioner GRISWOLD. Not always.

Mayor Nosser. In this case it is not always, that's right. That's right. You're right about that. Now you want to follow this straight line. I'm going all over the world around here to get back to the goal, and while on my route I don't have any trouble, and you may have trouble before you get to that point. That's the only difference.

Commissioner Griswold. But you misinterpret my approach entirely. I don't seek sudden change, just some change, and in this area you have made no change whatever.

Mayor Nosser. I have mentioned Kress has been integrated for the first time in history.

Commissioner Griswold. But in the area of schools you have made no change.

Mayor Nosser. Schools, I'll tell you now—and I want to be fair. We have just as good colored schools as we have white, and if you don't believe it, I'll drive you down to Natchez and you look at it.

Commissioner Hesburgh. Well, the Natchez school district spends almost $220 a year for each white child and $130 for each Negro—that's not equal.

Mayor Nosser. Well, I tell you; when did you get this report?

Commissioner Hesburgh. Yesterday.

Mayor Nosser. Probably they didn't take into consideration the new school up there; they just put one up.

Commissioner Hesburgh. I don't want to get into this argument, but I want to make one point. The city put up a new school for colored, despite the fact that 10 years ago the law said they should be integrated.

Mayor Nosser. I'm not arguing with you. You don't have any argument with me about the situation that exists. We all know that. And I am not here to discuss these conditions, because I agree with you on these conditions. But I think we are here not to discuss the past. Now I just made the statement discussing the past is not going to help anybody. But we are going to discuss the present and the future, and we are going to get somewhere.

Commissioner Hesburgh. Mr. Mayor, I'll end with this. You get yourself in a very vicious circle, I think, at the moment. Mrs. Freeman says how many are voting? You say about 600 out of 42 percent of 25,000. Why not more? Well, they're not educated. How many in city offices in responsible positions? With 42 percent of the population Negro, how many Negroes have something to do with their own government?

You say they're not well educated. Dean Griswold makes a point that the law was changed because the reason they are not well educated is that they have been segregated and poorly educated in a segregated situation. So we are going to correct the fundamental system we are talking about. And the answer is this year you build a new school for segregated education. This is no change; this is going backwards.

Mayor NOSSER. The reason some of the colored people are not educated is not because of lack of schools; it is because of the economy.

Commissioner HESBURGH. Why is that? They're poor because they don't have schools. I mean it is just a circle.

Mayor NOSSER. Well, let me ask you this. Up North Negroes enjoy any rights that white people enjoy, right?

Commissioner GRISWOLD. Not always.

Mayor NOSSER. However, the schools are integrated, right?

Commissioner HESBURGH. No, no, no. Most of the schools in the North are just as segregated, but for other reasons, because of the housing patterns.

Mayor NOSSER. Then why don't you integrate them?

Commissioner GRISWOLD. We're trying.

Mayor NOSSER. Let me say this. Any Negro can go into any school he wants to—

Commissioner HESBURGH. But they can't live where they want to. And because they can't live where they want to, they can't go to school where they want to. We have just as many problems in the North; this is the point.

Mayor NOSSER. I have half a dozen colored families living right by me.

Commissioner HESBURGH. We have problems up North, but we happen to be here now.

Mayor NOSSER. Well, the economy—that's what I'm saying. There you have a lot of trouble up North. And I mean it is not racial; it is an economical problem.

Commissioner HESBURGH. It is racial.

Mayor NOSSER. People have full stomachs and live in nice homes, you don't have any trouble with them. It is poor people we have problems with.

Chairman HANNAH. Do you have Negroes living in fine homes in Natchez?

Mayor NOSSER. Yes. Not too many of them; we have a few, yes.

Commissioner RANKIN. You talk about the future. What are you going to do about this ruling that HEW has made about funds going to schools?

Mayor NOSSER. I think they are going to comply with it.

Commissioner RANKIN. What does that mean, then, if they are going to comply? Does that mean integration of the school?

Mayor NOSSER. It could mean integration of schools. I mean if we all are patient, we'll get things passed. I am not just fighting the past.

Commissioner RANKIN. I'm going up to the future there.

Mayor NOSSER. Yes. Now let me tell you something. Here you agree with me that discrimination is all over the country, right? It is just as bad up North as it is down here. Yes——

Commissioner HESBURGH. It is a different type.

Mayor NOSSER. Here you are, they send turkeys down here to feed the poor, and I dare say not every family in Mississippi eats turkey on Thanksgiving, and I don't. I don't like turkey.

Commissioner HESBURGH. I don't either.

Mayor NOSSER. And I'll tell you something else. Every Negro family living in Natchez or anywhere in the State of Mississippi, any white people around, if they don't have any turkey or chicken, they'll get some turkey or chicken. And I'll tell you something else. These turkeys are probably more needed in Harlem than in Mississippi. And here I want to get to this point, Mr. Chairman, before I leave. You are trying to give Mississippi a bad image, much worse than it is. And you have in this movement for equalization of privileges, which I believe in, you have in this movement some mercenary people. All they care about, the colored and white, is as far as the dollar that comes into their pocket. And those people are hurting this movement.

Chairman HANNAH. Well, Mr. Mayor, I'm sure you realize that this Commission is not sponsoring these groups that come into Mississippi. We are trying to find out what the facts are.

Mayor NOSSER. I know that; you're trying to find facts.

Chairman HANNAH. So that we can make recommendations to the Congress, to the President, and anyone else who will listen. It will bring about the kind of progress that you are talking about. And I'm sure you understand this.

Mayor NOSSER. Yes, I understand. Just like I told you, Mr. Chairman, I came up here not to antagonize anybody. I don't want anybody to antagonize me. I came up here for one purpose, and that purpose is to give you my opinion, my experience of what I think would be in the best interests of both races and the best interests for peace and progress and equal rights and everything else.

Chairman HANNAH. We appreciate your coming. I would like to ask just one more question. You have made comments about the undesirable results of northern groups entering your State.

Mayor NOSSER. Yes.

Chairman HANNAH. And I know in the State from which I come, Michigan, that if there is a political issue and there is a group from New York which comes in to advise the people of Michigan as to what they should do about it, you can be quite sure that they will not prevail because the people resent outsiders telling them what to do. And I assume this is true here. But would you like to say anything more about demonstrations in Natchez—whether the driving force came from the North? You have said this was bad.

Mayor NOSSER. Well, see, we have got what they call COFO, and they're mixed, white and colored. I know they're mixed in Natchez; they're probably mixed everywhere in the South where they are, COFO people. That is what it appears to the white people there, and it is not doing any good.

Chairman HANNAH. But do you think that these people who come down from Chicago or Ohio would be less resented if they were Negroes instead of whites?

Mayor NOSSER. I'm sure of that. I'm sure of that.

Chairman HANNAH. But even they would be resented?

Mayor NOSSER. Probably they will. But they won't be resented as if you have white people. You see, to give you an instance, when they integrated Kress' there was no whites with them; they came in, colored, four or five young people. They had no trouble at all. We had one policeman up there; they called a policeman in order to keep peace. Not to put them out, but to keep peace. And he stood right in front on the sidewalk to see that while they were there nobody would go and bother them.

Chairman HANNAH. Do any other Commissioners have any questions? Well, we are very grateful for your coming.

Mayor NOSSER. I thank you for letting me come, and I assure you again I am working for peace and harmony. I want to tell the lady up here who represents the colored citizens, I am not biased. I love these colored people. They are as good as white people. In fact, I will do more for them. They call me about something wrong with the street or the paper or the trash or something, I'm just right there to help them. I'll do all I can for them. And I'll tell all of you, it is just going to take patience, a little patience. Things are progressing much faster now than in the past. And I appreciate the opportunity to come before you, and I am very glad to have met with you and talked with you. I know your mission is a mission of peace. I wish you the best luck and God bless you.

Chairman HANNAH. Thank you very much.

(Witness excused.)

Chairman HANNAH. We will now recess until 1:45, 1 hour and 20 minutes from now.

(Whereupon, at 12:25 p.m., the Commission recessed, to reconvene at 1:45 p.m., the same day.)

THURSDAY AFTERNOON SESSION, FEBRUARY 18, 1965

Chairman HANNAH. The hearing will please come to order. Mr. Taylor, will you call the next witness.

Mr. TAYLOR. George West and Rev. Willy Scott.

Chairman HANNAH. Gentlemen, will you raise your right hand.

(Whereupon, Mr. George West and Rev. Willy Scott were duly sworn by the Chairman and testified as follows:)

Chairman HANNAH. Mr. Taylor, will you begin the questioning.

TESTIMONY OF GEORGE F. WEST AND REV. WILLY S. SCOTT, ADAMS COUNTY, MISS.

Mr. TAYLOR. Mr. West, will you give your name, residence, and occupation for the record.

Mr. WEST. George F. West, Sr., licensed mortician and funeral director, residence, 729 North Pine Street, Natchez, Miss.

Mr. TAYLOR. How long have you lived in Mississippi?

Mr. WEST. All my life.

Mr. TAYLOR. And in Adams County?

Mr. WEST. All my life.

Mr. TAYLOR. Are you a registered voter in Adams County?

Mr. WEST. I am, sir.

Mr. TAYLOR. Do you belong to any organizations or hold any position?

Mr. WEST. I belong to the Natchez Business and Civic League. I am a member of the State Funeral Directors and Morticians Association, and a member of the National Funeral Directors and Morticians Association.

Mr. TAYLOR. Could you describe briefly for us the activities of the Business and Civic League?

Mr. WEST. The Natchez Civic Business League is a chartered organization that has as its objective to work for the improvements in general of all mankind in Natchez, Adams County, and specifically to improve the life of the Negro by encouraging them to engage in businesses, to learn about the government and how it operates, to register and vote and take an active part in electing the officials of the town in which we live.

Mr. TAYLOR. Reverend Scott, will you please give your full name and residence for the record?

Rev. SCOTT. I am Willy S. Scott. I live Route 2, Box 531, Natchez.

Mr. TAYLOR. How long have you lived in Mississippi, sir?

Rev. SCOTT. I lived in Mississippi for 21 years.

Mr. TAYLOR. Are you a registered voter in Adams County?

Rev. SCOTT. I am.

Mr. TAYLOR. How long have you been in the ministry?

Rev. SCOTT. Twenty-six years.

Mr. TAYLOR. Do you have a congregation in Adams County?

Rev. SCOTT. I have.

Mr. TAYLOR. Gentlemen, you are aware of the incidents of racial violence in Adams County, are you not?

Mr. WEST. Yes, I am. We are.

Rev. SCOTT. Yes.

Mr. TAYLOR. What effect would you say these have had upon the Negro community there?

Mr. WEST. Well, number one, it has a grave effect, a detrimental effect upon the Negro community in Natchez and Adams County.

Mr. TAYLOR. Has any of this violence caused members of the Negro community to take steps to ensure their own safety?

Mr. WEST. Yes, it has, sir.

Mr. TAYLOR. Have you yourself taken such steps?

Mr. WEST. Well, yes I have, sir. The community, after these violent acts that have been mentioned here, armed itself so to speak. I think more guns and ammunitions were sold in Natchez and Adams County than at any time in the history of Adams County. You said have we taken steps? Yes, we have. We have naturally armed ourselves, too, and along those lines. I would like to point out, sir, that after the incident affecting Mr. A. C. Curtis, Mr. Anders' deputy, Mr. Blough, suggested to us that any time we get a call to call his department, and they would check it out to see if it was legitimate call or whether it was somebody trying to pull one of these acts, and which we did. Many times we were escorted to the scene of an accident and to pick up bodies and so forth.

Mr. TAYLOR. But you did not feel, I take it, that you could simply rely upon protection of the police in the community. You felt you had to supplement that by having arms of your own?

Mr. WEST. Well, the community felt that self-preservation is one of the first laws of nature I think, and we felt that maybe by being protected in this way it might help. Because we never knew and we don't know today what happens in these situations and therefore we just didn't know where the perpetrators of these incidents were coming from, who they were, and so therefore naturally we were on the lookout for any situation at any time.

Mr. TAYLOR. Are either you Reverend Scott or Mr. West a regular reader of the Natchez newspaper?

Mr. WEST. Yes, I am.

Rev. SCOTT. I am.

Mr. TAYLOR. Were these incidents of violence reported in the newspaper?

Mr. WEST. Very rarely, if any; it might have been one time maybe but not much. They didn't get newspaper coverage on this to my knowledge, in the local paper. We got it out of the other papers, maybe Jackson or Times-Picayune, but not the local paper.

Mr. TAYLOR. Is that your experience also?

Rev. SCOTT. That is my experience.

Mr. TAYLOR. Mr. West, has there been any improvement in the situation in recent months?

Mr. WEST. I think so, sir.

Mr. TAYLOR. To what do you attribute that improvement?

Mr. WEST. Number one, we haven't had violence in recent weeks and months. Number two, quite a number of organizations took a full-page ad in one of the papers condemning violence and incidents of that nature. And number three, the sheriff department, the sheriff himself has indicated he would like to have a meeting with our group to discuss law enforcement as it applies to all citizens. This we feel is an improvement.

We have been trying to get Negro policemen on the force in Natchez for quite a few years and I understand that the chief of police, Mr. James T. Robinson, has indicated to me and to the group of colored in Natchez and Adams County that if Negro policemen pass the civil service examination that they would be hired and work for him and with me. That was unheard of 2 or 3 years ago.

Mr. TAYLOR. When all this violence took place in the winter and spring of 1964, was the highway patrol present? To your knowledge did it come into the Adams County area during that period?

Mr. WEST. Yes, they did.

Mr. TAYLOR. Did they stay for a considerable period of time?

Mr. WEST. Yes, sir; they did.

Mr. TAYLOR. Did they have a calming effect on the situation?

Mr. WEST. Very much so, sir.

Mr. TAYLOR. Thank you.

Chairman HANNAH. Father Hesburgh?

Commissioner HESBURGH. Reverend Scott, is there much communication between the Negro and white community in Adams County?

Rev. SCOTT. Well, very little that I can recall just now.

Commissioner HESBURGH. Do you think it is necessary to have more
communication to clarify this whole situation?

Rev. SCOTT. I think so.

Commissioner HESBURGH. Do you think it is possible to create some
mechanism for having more conversation about the aims and desires
of the Negro community?

Rev. SCOTT. We should have.

Commissioner HESBURGH. Is anyone really working to bring this
about?

Rev. SCOTT. No, sir. We are not working to bring that about. We
have talked about it as a group of ministers in our area, organizing a
group. We have talked about it, but we have not effected the plans
as yet.

Commissioner HESBURGH. Do you have hopes for it?

Rev. SCOTT. We have hopes for it.

Commissioner HESBURGH. What would you think is the most important single thing that should be done to have a better situation in
Adams County?

Rev. SCOTT. Well, the greatest thing that we hope for, the greatest
relationship was that we could meet with members of the power
structure in our community and know each other and understand what
this situation may be.

Commissioner HESBURGH. Thank you, Reverend Scott.

Commissioner FREEMAN. Reverend Scott, would you give us an
estimate of the number of churches in Natchez?

Rev. SCOTT. Well, within the city limits in Natchez we have about
27 churches, I believe.

Commissioner FREEMAN. How many of them are Negro and how
many are white?

Rev. SCOTT. We have, maybe, we might say 40 with all of the
churches there, with the white and colored.

Commissioner FREEMAN. Have any of the pastors or church laymen
made any overtures towards——

Rev. SCOTT. They have not. Heretofore, in the late years we used
to fellowship together with Southern Baptist's activities and in the late
years we was called Communists and, of course, that made a coolness
between the fellowship.

Commissioner FREEMAN. Have the members or the pastors or

leadership of the white churches made any statement of concern in opposition to the savagery that has gone on?

Rev. Scott. Not to my knowledge. They have not.

Chairman Hannah. Dean Griswold?

Commissioner Griswold. Reverend Scott, do the white ministers and the Negroes ministers of Natchez ever meet together?

Rev. Scott. No, sir, we do not.

Commissioner Griswold. Have you ever met together at any time in the past?

Rev. Scott. Well, in my beginning years in Natchez we had. We had hoped to organize a race relationship organization at the time a good friend of ours was there, Brother Elkins. We made several attempts, but we never were successful with the efforts.

Commissioner Griswold. Would there be any place in Natchez where you could meet together?

Rev. Scott. Oh, yes, sir.

Commissioner Griswold. What sort of places?

Rev. Scott. Well, we could meet together in any church there, to come together. Or we have the city auditorium.

Commissioner Griswold. Would there be any place where you could eat together?

Rev. Scott. No, sir, nobody eating together. None of them eat together.

Commissioner Griswold. Break bread together?

Rev. Scott. We don't break bread together.

Commissioner Griswold. Do you think that an avenue of communication or at least a start towards general communication would be opened if the white ministers and the Negro ministers of Natchez could meet together and did meet together?

Rev. Scott. I think so. I think we could. But usually the trouble has been the white minister who would like to work with Negro ministers. He has also been threatened and, of course, that is the thing that is really keeping us apart. We are afraid to meet with each other.

Commissioner Griswold. I can understand that if it were one minister alone. But suppose that all of the white ministers of Natchez met with all the Negro ministers of Natchez, let's say in an open public meeting, so that anybody could come and make sure you weren't patching up some dreadful conspiracy. Would that be constructive?

Rev. Scott. That would be constructive.

Commissioner Griswold. Would that provide some protection to the white ministers?

Rev. Scott. It would, yes.

Commissioner GRISWOLD. What do you think would be the general reaction in Natchez if the white ministers as a group invited the Negro ministers to meet with them?

Rev. SCOTT. Well, I think that would be a great step forward.

Commissioner GRISWOLD. Do you think it would be so regarded by the white community in Natchez?

Rev. SCOTT. I don't know about the white community. I don't think it would be so pleasant.

Commissioner GRISWOLD. Would there be members of the white community who would welcome it?

Rev. SCOTT. There would be some.

Mr. WEST. Some.

Chairman HANNAH. Mr. Rankin?

Commissioner RANKIN. I noticed that you have been active with the NAACP. Am I correct in that?

Rev. SCOTT. Yes, sir.

Commissioner RANKIN. Did you hear the testimony of the witnesses this morning? Were you present this morning?

Rev. SCOTT. Yes. Mr. Curtis happens to be a member of our congregation.

Commissioner RANKIN. And you noticed that some of them thought their trouble possibly came from the fact that they were affiliated with the NAACP. They were asked that question.

Rev. SCOTT. Yes, sir.

Commissioner RANKIN. Do you have any idea why you escaped all this trouble and they had the trouble?

Rev. SCOTT. No, sir, I don't have any idea.

Commissioner RANKIN. Were you just a little bit bigger? Do you think that had anything to do with it?

Rev. SCOTT. Well, one of the things is that I denied being a member.

Commissioner RANKIN. Is there anything else? You said that is one of the things. Anything else?

Rev. SCOTT. Well, you know, we had a little trouble once at a meeting at my church when they attempted to put pressure on me as being a member of the NAACP. Of course, I denied that fact at that time.

Commissioner RANKIN. Peter denied one time also. [Laughter.]

Chairman HANNAH. Mr. Patterson?

Vice Chairman PATTERSON. Mr. West, you heard the testimony this morning from the Negro man who appeared to me to be rather gentle. He said they were taken out in the nighttime by hooded men, forced to take off their clothes and beaten until they were bruised?

Mr. WEST. Yes, right.

Vice Chairman PATTERSON. You know the white people of Natchez from your years there. Do you consider these acts to be representative of the white people of Natchez, Miss.?

Mr. WEST. Not the entire community; there are some who are better. But the great majority of the people in Natchez and Adams County don't feel this way.

Vice Chairman PATTERSON. If the great majority of the people wouldn't do that, why is it still being done in Natchez?

Mr. WEST. Because the great majority have stayed silent on this issue. They haven't spoken out and I think that is the reason that these things happen. Those that did speak out, their places were bombed or things of that nature. But the great majority of the white people in Natchez and Adams County that I come in contact with don't feel that way.

Vice Chairman PATTERSON. You say things calmed down after the highway patrol arrived in Natchez?

Mr. WEST. Right.

Vice Chairman PATTERSON. Why do you think this is so?

Mr. WEST. Well, let me first go back a little if I may. The community has been very much disturbed because of the inability of the local law enforcement officers to apprehend any of the perpetrators of these particular incidents. Well, naturally when the highway patrol came in and made arrests and confiscated ammunition from cars and things of that sort, things quieted because they searched all cars and got guns and ammunition out of quite a few on both sides.

Vice Chairman PATTERSON. Thank you.

Chairman HANNAH. Mr. Scott, what is the denomination of your church?

Rev. SCOTT. Baptist.

Chairman HANNAH. Any further questions?

Mr. TAYLOR. No, sir.

Chairman HANNAH. Thank you very much, gentlemen. You are excused.

(Witnesses excused.)

Mr. Taylor, will you call the next witness.

Mr. TAYLOR. Sheriff Odell Anders.

Chairman HANNAH. Sheriff Anders, will you raise your right hand?

(Whereupon, Sheriff Odell Anders was duly sworn by the Chairman and testified as follows:)

Chairman HANNAH. Gentlemen, will you introduce your attorney?

Mr. ANDERS. Mr. Joseph Zuccaro from Natchez.

TESTIMONY OF JAMES ODELL ANDERS, SHERIFF, ADAMS COUNTY, MISS.

Mr. TAYLOR. Sheriff, would you please state your full name and residence for the record.

Mr. ANDERS. I am James Odell Anders, sheriff and tax collector in Natchez, Miss., and I reside at 309 Holly Drive, in Natchez.

Mr. TAYLOR. How long have you served as sheriff?

Mr. ANDERS. Around 13 months.

Mr. TAYLOR. Do your law enforcement duties include keeping the peace in the community of Adams County?

Mr. ANDERS. It surely does, yes, sir.

Mr. TAYLOR. We have heard a great deal of testimony this morning on incidents of racial violence in Adams County in 1964. Has your office made any arrests in any of these cases.

Mr. ANDERS. We have made, I believe of the things that are listed here, I think we made one arrest in the Richard Joe Butler shooting.

Mr. TAYLOR. That arrest was made by the highway patrol with your assistance?

Mr. ANDERS. No, sir. This arrest was made by me, about a week after the shooting, or something like that. Of course the highway patrol was there and meeting with the district attorney and county attorney and highway patrol and with the evidence we had collected we did arrest this one man. I arrested him.

Mr. TAYLOR. Have there been any convictions in any of these cases?

Mr. ANDERS. No, sir.

Mr. TAYLOR. Why have you been unable to solve these cases, sheriff?

Mr. ANDERS. Well, to start with you don't have anything to go on. Well, we had, I believe it was four beatings. The first started about February 6, and then the next three were the same day, on February 15. I didn't call anybody on February 6, and then on February 15 when these other whippings took place, I called the FBI and the Mississippi Highway Patrol. No, I called the FBI on the 15, which was Sunday, and I came to Jackson to see the Governor on Monday and asked him for assistance, and he sent them down on Monday. And, you don't have anything to go on. You take the witnesses and it isn't their fault, I know. They tell you maybe it is a short man or a tall man. They don't know where they are whipped and no finger prints or anything like that. You have nothing to go on, nothing whatsoever to go on. You just can't make an arrest when you don't have anything to go on. We did not, on the Whitley case. At that particular time we thought possibly it was maybe that he was trying to get a better job through the union or something like that.

The name that he gave us of the man that followed him out, we questioned him and then we questioned I should say 25, 30 or 40 men in the plants in the unions down there. Maybe something would come out of that, and we found nothing on that.

Mr. TAYLOR. Sheriff, may I interrupt you.

Mr. ANDERS. All right.

Mr. TAYLOR. You mentioned the Whitley case, and we heard testimony on that from Mr. Whitley this morning.

Mr. ANDERS. Yes.

Mr. TAYLOR. And you submitted to us some records on the case; is that right?

Mr. ANDERS. Yes, Monday.

Mr. TAYLOR. In the Whitley case, the only record I find is a single sheet of undated paper which contains the name of the man who Mr. Whitley mentioned?

Mr. ANDERS. Yes.

Mr. TAYLOR. But, it does not indicate anything about any suspects being interviewed. Isn't it a customary practice to make a record of such interviews?

Mr. ANDERS. Let me tell you this. Any time that you hold an investigation, you run across things that in no way pertain to a case like this, but in a lot of ways it will tend to hurt the reputation of people. If we don't find that they know anything about this particular crime that we are talking about, then we destroy the records so that it won't incriminate these people.

Mr. TAYLOR. Are you saying that there *were* records in this case?

Mr. ANDERS. Well, with all our notes we keep records like that. I don't have any now on that.

Mr. TAYLOR. As the number of incidents increased, did you feel you had a serious situation on your hands?

Mr. ANDERS. I did. If you will notice this happened on the 6th of February, the Whitley case. And then the 15th was Archie Curtis and Willie Jackson that was with Archie Curtis, and the Winston. Those all happened the same date. And too, I want to tell you this. Archie said that one of the deputies talked to him, that I never did see him until Tuesday. I was working on the other cases is why I didn't see him. I was on the Winston case, which was from the 6th to the 15th—was 9 days. I felt that we had something big. I knew that we had to stop it some way and that's when I called the FBI, that afternoon. The next day I came to Jackson to see the Governor.

Mr. TAYLOR. Is Mr. Curtis well known to you?

Mr. ANDERS. Yes, he's well known.

Mr. TAYLOR. As these incidents went along, did you take any different steps, such as placing additional patrols in the Negro community to try to add preventive power to the situation?

Mr. ANDERS. I'll say at times that we would have 25, maybe 30, men working.

Mr. TAYLOR. In the Negro community, sir?

Mr. ANDERS. Well, in Adams County. In Natchez you don't have white and Negro like that. You have, I mean you have a white person living here and a Negro right next door to him. There's a few places where you can tell this is a colored community and this is a white community, but not much. Especially did we have a lot of men employed when these churches started being burned down there. That's when we employed a lot of men.

Mr. TAYLOR. After these church burnings began, did you make any effort to bring in additional patrols and try to protect the churches?

Mr. ANDERS. The preacher—I heard you all ask him a little bit ago how many churches was in Adams County. I think it is 68 Baptist churches in Adams County, colored Baptist churches. It's impossible for the highway patrol, the sheriff's department, the police department, the constables and everything together, to completely guard all the churches in the county. We couldn't do that. So, I called all the preachers together. Now, see, we had two churches burned one day and then we had one burned maybe 2 weeks later, something like that. I called all the preachers of all these churches together, explained to them that we didn't have personnel enough to watch their churches and suggested to them, asked them for their help to watch their own churches. I guess we had 50 preachers that afternoon when we had this meeting.

Mr. TAYLOR. Did you tell them to shoot to kill?

Mr. ANDERS. I surely did.

Mr. TAYLOR. Sheriff, did you consider the situation to have been seriously deteriorated when you had to advise people to protect their own property with guns?

Mr. ANDERS. Well, it is a deterioration, I know that. But like I say now, no matter how many law enforcement officers we have, you couldn't watch these churches day and night. It's impossible. And now let me say this. That along with the FBI and the highway patrol and all, we have stayed up night after night after night watching these places and watching people that had been threatened and things like that.

Mr. TAYLOR. To your knowledge are there extremist groups such as the Klan operating in Adams County?

Mr. ANDERS. I think there were. Now whether they are, I think they are very inactive now.

Mr. TAYLOR. Do you have any knowledge as to their strength and activities when they were active?

Mr. ANDERS. I surely don't. The strength nor activities. I have no idea.

Mr. TAYLOR. Do you have any opinion as to the size of the group that was responsible for this violence?

Mr. ANDERS. It's the opinion of all law enforcement officers that there are maybe not over 10 or 12 or 15 people doing every bit of the violence in Adams County; yes.

Mr. TAYLOR. In selecting your own recruits do you check their backgrounds with the Federal Bureau of Investigation to determine whether they have been convicted of any offense?

Mr. ANDERS. You mean the people working for me?

Mr. TAYLOR. The people working for you.

Mr. ANDERS. I don't have to check with the Federal Bureau; I know them.

Mr. TAYLOR. Do you know that they have not been convicted of any offense?

Mr. ANDERS. I do; yes.

Mr. TAYLOR. Do you also know what their affiliations are or whether they might belong to any of these organizations?

Mr. ANDERS. Let me tell you. Anybody working for me belonging to any of these organizations would be immediately dismissed.

Mr. TAYLOR. Reverend Scott and Mr. West indicated that there were a great many arms and weapons in Natchez. Do you know whether there have been any automatic weapons or high-powered weapons in the community, or anything resembling an arsenal?

Mr. ANDERS. No. Not in one spot, not too many guns. Now, of course that's a hunter's paradise down there and you find a lot of people with shotguns and high-powered rifles shooting deer and things like that, quite a few people—but as far as any arsenal is concerned, no.

Mr. TAYLOR. There was a report that on October 26, the Federal Bureau of Investigation and the Mississippi Highway Patrol seized a large number of weapons, ammunition, and knives following one of the arrests.

Mr. ANDERS. That's right. Yes.

Mr. TAYLOR. Have any automatic weapons or high-powered rifles been registered with you under the provision of Mississippi law?

Mr. ANDERS. No, sir.

Mr. TAYLOR. Do you know that they are required to be registered?

Mr. ANDERS. Yes; but they haven't been registered.

Mr. TAYLOR. No further questions.

Chairman HANNAH. Father Hesburgh?

Commissioner HESBURGH. Sheriff Anders, do you think that this whole situation could be stopped if you could somehow find out who these people are—this small group that you think is——

Mr. ANDERS. Reverend, I think it can and I think eventually we will find out.

Commissioner HESBURGH. In other words——

Mr. ANDERS. We have evidence in cases. It will take time, but eventually I think that with what we have that we possibly will work things out.

Commissioner HESBURGH. It would seem to me that within a comparatively small community where people know each other, there are probably a large number of people who know who is doing these things since there is a certain pattern involved.

Mr. ANDERS. I doubt it. One disadvantage we have is as you know, we live right on the Mississippi River. Let me say this, too, about the whippings and why I say that it isn't a pattern. First, Whitley was whipped. He had nothing to do with any voter drive or any voter registration, I mean anything like that. He was whipped. Next, Archie Curtis and his driver were whipped. They had had some affiliations with the Natchez Business League. And then Winston, the one that was whipped down there, he had no affiliations whatsoever. The masks used by the men that whipped him were these little Halloween masks over the eyes, so we feel that possibly the first was maybe because of seeking a better job. The second possibly was because of voter registration, and the third was maybe thrill seekers or something like that.

Commissioner HESBURGH. You don't think the fact that a couple of them used castor oil and things of that sort——

Mr. ANDERS. It could be. I don't know.

Commissioner HESBURGH. I'm out of my field. I would just like to say it is one of the most savage situations I have heard of in my life, as bad as anything I have heard of in many countries of the world which we condemn. And I do hope you can get to the bottom of it.

Mr. ANDERS. Sir, we hope so too.

Chairman HANNAH. Mrs. Freeman?

Commissioner FREEMAN. Sheriff Anders, how long have you lived in Natchez?

Mr. ANDERS. All my life.

Commissioner FREEMAN. Do you know most of the people?

Mr. ANDERS. I'd say 90 percent of them, yes.

Commissioner FREEMAN. Well then, do you know those who have good reputations and those who have bad reputations?

Mr. ANDERS. I have learned more about that in the last year than I previously knew, but I know now pretty well, yes.

Commissioner FREEMAN. During the time that you have been sheriff, when complaints have been made to you, have you in cases other than those we are discussing arrested persons on the basis of a description, made inquiry, questioned them about the particular complaint involved?

Mr. ANDERS. What do you mean?

Commissioner FREEMAN. Some persons from time to time have said that they were arrested, then questioned, and then released. But in these cases you only arrested one person; was that correct?

Mr. ANDERS. One person, and the highway patrol and FBI then arrested two more on the strength of my records there. I don't follow what you are trying to get.

Commissioner FREEMAN. Let me ask it another way. What training did you have in law enforcement?

Mr. ANDERS. I had about 5 years previous to this.

Commissioner FREEMAN. Prior to the time you assumed your present office?

Mr. ANDERS. Yes.

Commissioner FREEMAN. In your training in law enforcement wasn't it considered to be a good policy for the law enforcement officer to know his community so that when an incident occurs he can at least bring in for questioning some individuals who might be considered guilty?

Mr. ANDERS. That's right, and I mean it still remains like that.

Commissioner FREEMAN. But you did not do that in these cases?

Mr. ANDERS. We did it in every case. We questioned people in every case. We didn't always arrest people and bring them in and question them, but we have questioned people in every case that's happened.

Commissioner FREEMAN. In all of these cases were you satisfied that the persons questioned had not participated in these incidents?

Mr. ANDERS. That's right.

Commissioner FREEMAN. Thank you.

Chairman HANNAH. Dean Griswold?

Commissioner GRISWOLD. Sheriff Anders, you said you have had several years experience in law enforcement. Could you tell us what that was?

Mr. ANDERS. I was a deputy under Robert Burns down there, and then I was affiliated with the motor vehicle comptroller, which is part law enforcement, investigative work.

Commissioner GRISWOLD. How many deputies do you have in Adams County?

Mr. ANDERS. We have five.

Commissioner GRISWOLD. Who determines how many deputies you should have?

Mr. ANDERS. I guess I do.

Commissioner GRISWOLD. How are they paid?

Mr. ANDERS. By me.

Commissioner GRISWOLD. How are you paid?

Mr. ANDERS. On a fee basis.

Commissioner GRISWOLD. Fees from what?

Mr. ANDERS. Fees from tax collecting and, well, tax collecting, serving of papers and things like that.

Commissioner GRISWOLD. In this situation did you need more than five deputies?

Mr. ANDERS. Yes, sir, and I hired more than five.

Commissioner GRISWOLD. At your own expense?

Mr. ANDERS. Yes, sir.

Commissioner GRISWOLD. Was there any way available to you under the laws of Mississippi through which you could have increased the size of your force except at your own expense?

Mr. ANDERS. Not that I know; no, sir.

Commissioner GRISWOLD. Did you increase the number of deputies to the point where you were losing money on the activity?

Mr. ANDERS. At that time, yes, sir.

Commissioner GRISWOLD. Do you think that there ought to be some means by which you could have hired at public expense the number of deputies which you need to maintain law and order in Adams County?

Mr. ANDERS. I did think that until this past summer when the Governor beefed up the highway patrol. Now then, I mean he has a State highway patrol force that you can call on and that he will send to you any time you need them, or he has with us at any time.

Commissioner GRISWOLD. That wasn't available until the summer of 1964?

Mr. ANDERS. That's right; yes.

Commissioner GRISWOLD. Do you have any sort of scientific laboratory in your sheriff's office in Natchez?

Mr. ANDERS. No, we don't.

Commissioner GRISWOLD. Are you qualified to take fingerprints?

Mr. ANDERS. Yes, sir.

Commissioner GRISWOLD. Where have you received training with respect to taking fingerprints?

Mr. ANDERS. At the University of Mississippi law school.

Commissioner GRISWOLD. Is this part of a police course that is made available there?

Mr. ANDERS. Yes.

Commissioner GRISWOLD. How do you have other sorts of scientific analyses made?

Mr. ANDERS. Well, of course, the State has a lab here. There's one in Baton Rouge, the Louisiana State Police lab, that we use some because it is closer. And then, of course, the FBI is right there with us to offer us any and all kind of help that we need.

Commissioner GRISWOLD. In one of these cases where arrests were made, did you use a so-called lie detector test?

Mr. ANDERS. On one. We made one arrest. Another boy was brought to Jackson, and he did take a lie detector test which showed that he had nothing to do with it. And we had checked his alibi as to where he was and everything else, but since the victim did name him, well, we did pick him up anyway.

Commissioner GRISWOLD. Who administered the so-called lie detector test?

Mr. ANDERS. I believe Patrolman Ivey, Sam Ivey of the Mississippi Highway Patrol.

Commissioner GRISWOLD. It was not done by you or one of your deputies?

Mr. ANDERS. No, sir.

Commissioner GRISWOLD. Do you think that lie detector tests have any reliability?

Mr. ANDERS. Dean, I don't know about that. I'd say yes.

Commissioner GRISWOLD. On what basis do you think they have reliability?

Mr. ANDERS. I don't know enough about it to discuss it, Dean, really.

Commissioner GRISWOLD. But you just testified that the lie detector tests showed that he had nothing to do with it, and therefore he was discharged?

Mr. ANDERS. I also said, Dean, that I checked every place that he said he was at the particular times that these things happened, and they also checked out.

Commissioner Griswold. I should think that might have been a good reason for discharging him, but I am suggesting that either holding or discharging people on the basis of a so-called lie detector test has no scientific weight.

Mr. Anders. I don't know about that, but after we did bring him here and after checking the story down there and after the lie detector test on top, we did let him go.

Commissioner Griswold. Have things been better in Adams County in the last 2 months than they were last year?

Mr. Anders. Yes, sir.

Commissioner Griswold. Have you any opinion as to why that is the case?

Mr. Anders. No. Well, actually what we had—you have 2 weeks of beatings and then nothing happened until the shooting of Richard Joe Butler. Nothing happened there until the three churches were burned. In other words, we had about 3 weeks of violence all through the year. And I just hope it doesn't start back. But I mean we had about 3 weeks of it. In between those times it was good. I think the highway patrol, the FBI, the citizens of the community—during these troubled times I received letters and telephone calls from every civic club, people from all walks of life extending their help that they could give to us. I would like to say at this point that there isn't 1 percent of the people in Adams County that think of beating people and burning churches and things like that.

Commissioner Griswold. Well, I would like to think that that is true but I find myself a little puzzled at that being the case. Isn't it possible to get some clues to the identity of the persons who are doing these things? I should think that some skilled and conscientious, hard-working detective would lead you to some information about these groups.

Mr. Anders. Dean, in October of this past year, we had approximately 75 highway patrol. We had around 30 FBI investigators in there, with my force, with the police force in Natchez. I don't know how we can come up with it. We have tried. I think eventually we will.

Commissioner Griswold. I think that what you said shows that you have tried, and I hope that you will continue to try and be successful. I wonder a little. You said nothing about any detective force or any undercover work. I can understand how you might not want to talk about that, but that would be the way, I would suppose, that a group such as this would be uncovered.

Mr. ANDERS. Police investigation or anything is only as good as their informers. We do have them. We are working.

Chairman HANNAH. Dr. Rankin.

Commissioner RANKIN. At one time I was a very incompetent municipal officer, as these questions will probably show. But I was never allowed to destroy records. Your comments on that subject interested me. Who has access to your records?

Mr. ANDERS. We don't necessarily destroy them but just not keep them. If they don't pertain to the case, then all it can do is be detrimental to someone.

Commissioner RANKIN. Well, a lot of information in my files was detrimental, but I didn't show it to everybody. You don't show your files to everybody who wants to see them, do you?

Mr. ANDERS. During the months of October and when all the highway and FBI were there my files were open completely to them.

Commissioner RANKIN. To the FBI?

Mr. ANDERS. To all of them. I lost a lot of them during that time.

Commissioner RANKIN. Well, they were police officers?

Mr. ANDERS. Yes, sir.

Commissioner RANKIN. You mean you just can't trust the other police officers?

Mr. ANDERS. I didn't say that, no, sir, I trust all police officers.

Commissioner RANKIN. But you certainly don't give access to the general public. Don't you think it would be well to keep records?

Mr. ANDERS. Well——

Commissioner RANKIN. What would other law enforcement officers have done if nobody kept records?

Mr. ANDERS. Let me tell you, anything pertaining to the case that comes up we keep the record. But when something doesn't pertain to the case, and you know that you find a lot of things, hidden skeletons, you don't want to bring those up, I would rather throw them away. I don't want anybody hurt through an investigation like that.

Commissioner RANKIN. Well, in my town everybody knows about all the hidden skeletons. There's another point I want to bring up. I don't know much about police work but you said less than 1 percent caused this trouble in Natchez, isn't that right?

Mr. ANDERS. Yes.

Commissioner RANKIN. Now, you would call Natchez a law-abiding community, wouldn't you?

Mr. ANDERS. I certainly would, yes.

Commissioner RANKIN. And, yet you say that 1 percent of the population——

Mr. ANDERS. Less than 1.

Commissioner RANKIN. Less than 1 might have done this?

Mr. ANDERS. Yes.

Commissioner RANKIN. How many potential church burners do you think you have in Natchez?

Mr. ANDERS. I would like to think that we have none.

Commissioner RANKIN. But, you know you have some, don't you?

Mr. ANDERS. No, sir, I don't know that.

Commissioner RANKIN. You don't know that?

Mr. ANDERS. I don't know that. I don't know that the people that burned the churches are from Natchez.

Commissioner RANKIN. Obviously you don't, because you never arrested anybody.

Mr. ANDERS. And, I hardly think that they are from Natchez.

Commissioner RANKIN. Well, then, one thing to do is to watch the people as they come in from the outside, isn't that right? It seems to me that instead of sitting around in 68 church yards waiting for somebody to come, you might make a list of potential church burners. And if there are 68 of them, watch a bit. Now you see I am a very incompetent police officer, but it is something.

Mr. ANDERS. Yes, sir.

Commissioner RANKIN. But did you ever think about shadowing some of these people?

Mr. ANDERS. We shadow them all the time.

Commissioner RANKIN. You didn't come up with any?

Mr. ANDERS. We didn't come up with anything, nor did the FBI, nor the highway patrol, nor the Fire Commissioner nor any individual that doesn't condone this. They didn't come up with anything.

Commissioner RANKIN. If these people get into some large jewelry stores, they could really become millionaires, couldn't they?

Mr. ANDERS. Well, the first thing you have to do you know, you have to have a motive, robbing a jewelry store, you would have a motive. Burning a church, you don't have a motive. You have hate or something like that.

Commissioner RANKIN. Isn't that a motive?

Mr. ANDERS. But, you can't sell hate. You can't do anything with that. You don't have anything concrete to work on.

Commissioner RANKIN. I admit it is difficult. But people who hate quite frequently make known their hates, don't they? And I would watch them a little bit.

Mr. ANDERS. I can assure you that if anybody ever made known their hate, they were questioned. Whether it be in Adams County, Wilkinson, Jefferson, or any other county.

Chairman HANNAH. Mr. Patterson?

Vice Chairman PATTERSON. Sheriff, do you have the Ku Klux Klan headquarters of Natchez or Adams County infiltrated?

[Laughter.]

Mr. ANDERS. Would you repeat that, please?

Vice Chairman PATTERSON. Do you have the local Ku Klux Klan infiltrated?

Mr. ZUCCARO. We are going to object to that question, Mr. Chairman, as being immaterial and irrelevant.

Vice Chairman PATTERSON. Do you have access to the information that the FBI might gather from its infiltration of the Klan?

Mr. ANDERS. I do.

Vice Chairman PATTERSON. Do you have reason to believe that some of these acts have been committed by the Ku Klux Klan?

Mr. ANDERS. The hooded—I mean when your victim says they are hooded, yes.

Vice Chairman PATTERSON. Isn't that membership fairly limited, to your knowledge?

Mr. ANDERS. Fairly limited, yes, sir.

Vice Chairman PATTERSON. Do you feel that you have taken all possible precautions to investigate those men?

Mr. ANDERS. Yes.

Vice Chairman PATTERSON. In connection with these crimes?

Mr. ANDERS. Yes, sir; yes, sir.

Vice Chairman PATTERSON. Sheriff, you say that in your estimation fewer than 1 percent of the people of Natchez engage in things like stripping a man at night at gunpoint and beating him?

Mr. ANDERS. Yes.

Vice Chairman PATTERSON. You said earlier it might be 10, 12, 15 men?

Mr. ANDERS. That's what all enforcement officers—agencies that have worked in that community—that's what we think, yes.

Vice Chairman PATTERSON. We had a witness, the sheriff of another county, yesterday, who also said it was only a handful of men that gave his county a bad name—as in Adams County. And we asked him how he stopped it, as he apparently has, and he said two things. One is that he made a big arrest. He got into that handful of men, and he made an arrest. Second, he got the support of his business community, which he felt was a help to law enforcement. Are you getting adequate backing in Natchez and Adams County from your business community?

Mr. ANDERS. I doubt that there would be one businessman in Adams County, I know that there isn't one businessman in Adams County that would condone anything like this or who would not go out of their way to help us in most any way.

Vice Chairman PATTERSON. But have they made this manifest so that it has an effect on the climate prevailing in Natchez?

Mr. ANDERS. Yes, sir. I don't know that it has been published— I mean, your Chamber of Commerce, all your civic clubs and things like that, yes, sir.

Commissioner RANKIN. Were there any monetary rewards offered by this group?

Mr. ANDERS. Yes.

Commissioner RANKIN. Were they sizable?

Mr. ANDERS. I think $5,000 was one reward, yes.

Commissioner RANKIN. Who put up the money for this?

Mr. ANDERS. I believe the city of Natchez did.

Commissioner RANKIN. And that one did no good?

Mr. ANDERS. Did no good at all.

Vice Chairman PATTERSON. Sheriff, what was it the highway patrol could do in Adams County that you couldn't do?

Mr. ANDERS. I don't know that they could do any more, only bigger force and talk to more people. I don't think that they could do any more like I say, except more people and talking to more people.

Vice Chairman PATTERSON. But you say you still haven't made a big arrest because, as I believe you said earlier, you hope this violence doesn't start again?

Mr. ANDERS. I don't think it will start back, and I think that we will eventually make these arrests on this.

Vice Chairman PATTERSON. But you don't feel you can make them yet?

Mr. ANDERS. I know we haven't.

Vice Chairman PATTERSON. You think these men are still at large?

Mr. ANDERS. Yes, sir.

Vice Chairman PATTERSON. Do you think you know who they are?

Mr. ANDERS. Yes, sir.

Vice Chairman PATTERSON. What are you waiting for?

Mr. ANDERS. To bring a man before a court without any evidence is useless.

Vice Chairman PATTERSON. You are building a case?

Mr. ANDERS. That's right; yes, sir.

Vice Chairman PATTERSON. Are you hopeful that that case is going to stand up?

Mr. ANDERS. I'm most hopeful.

Vice Chairman PATTERSON. One other question, Sheriff, and that's all. It has nothing to do with law enforcement, but I would like to know what you think about it. What kind of man could do the kind of thing that has happened?

Mr. ANDERS. I don't know. I can't picture a man doing it. Can you?

Vice Chairman PATTERSON. No sir, we don't think that way. But then you know people in the criminal element. You're the sheriff. I just though you might have an idea of what motivates them. What kind of fellows are they?

Mr. ANDERS. I don't know. You take an instance right across the river from Natchez, maybe 2 months or 3 months ago, some men threw gasoline on a man and burned him to death over there. I don't know what kind of man it takes to do that. I couldn't tell you that.

Vice Chairman PATTERSON. Pretty sorry fellow, isn't it?

Mr. ANDERS. To me, I think so.

Chairman HANNAH. Mr. Rogerson, do you have a question?

Mr. ROGERSON. Sheriff, what kind of training do your deputies get? You mentioned you have your own. Where do you get them?

Mr. ANDERS. Well, each man I have working for me—I expect that the deputies I have, the total law enforcement years put together would be close to a hundred.

Mr. ROGERSON. These men have probably had experience as deputies for a number of years?

Mr. ANDERS. Yes.

Mr. ROGERSON. Sheriff, about what percentage of your time, outside of these crisis situations, is spent as sheriff and what percent of your time as tax collector?

Mr. ANDERS. Oh, I never did think of it much. Of course we have— you take different times of the year. Now, you take in January, and January is when all land taxes and things like that are paid. Then in October, then you have your automobile sales and things like that. Now, these, of course, we have a complete different crew for your tax collecting and for your law enforcement. Were you talking about my time?

Mr. ROGERSON. I'm talking about your time, but I am interested in that point too.

Mr. ANDERS. I would say about 14 hours a day on law enforcement and maybe 2 or 3 on the tax part of it.

Mr. ROGERSON. Have you worked closely with the chief of police in Natchez?

Mr. ANDERS. Yes, sir; yes, sir. We are right next door to each other.

Mr. ROGERSON. Close day-to-day working relationship?

Mr. ANDERS. Yes.

Mr. ROGERSON. Where are your headquarters as sheriff—in Natchez?

Mr. ANDERS. In Natchez. That's the only town we have in Adams County, Natchez.

Mr. ROGERSON. Thank you.

Chairman HANNAH. Sheriff, we have subpenaed the mayor of Natchez. Because he was going to be hospitalized this week, he volunteered to come in last week and appear before us. We have heard some reference today to the bombing of his home. When you described the burnings and beatings, I don't think you made any reference to the bombing of the mayor's home. Did this occur in one of these same 3 weeks you referred to?

Mr. ANDERS. Well, you had the bombing of—let's look over this list—you have the Jitney Jungle stores—you have the two Jitney Jungle stores and the Cadillac car agency down here. That's three of them. That's on the 15th, three bombings were on the 15th, and then the mayor's home was on the 26th and Willie Washington's home was on the 26th, all in September, all within a 2-week period right in there.

Chairman HANNAH. I recognize the mayor's home is in the city and within the jurisdiction of the chief of police rather than the responsibility of your office. But its the same small group involved in these store bombings in Natchez which is involved in the churches and the beatings out in the county.

Mr. ANDERS. Yes, sir.

Chairman HANNAH. Are there further questions?

Vice Chairman PATTERSON. You think you know who they are?

Mr. ANDERS. I think so, yes.

Vice Chairman PATTERSON. That ought to make them pretty nervous.

Mr. ANDERS. I hope so.

Chairman HANNAH. Any other questions? You are excused, gentlemen. Thank you.

(Witness excused.)

Mr. Taylor, will you call the next witness?

Mr. TAYLOR. The next witness is Chief of Police J. T. Robinson.

Chairman HANNAH. Mr. Robinson, will you raise your right hand?

(Whereupon, Police Chief James Theodore Robinson, was duly sworn by the Chairman and testified as follows:)

Chairman HANNAH. Will you introduce your attorney.

Mr. ROBINSON. Clifford Pintard, Jr., from Natchez.

Chairman HANNAH. Mr. Taylor, will you begin the questioning.

TESTIMONY OF JAMES THEODORE ROBINSON, CHIEF OF POLICE, NATCHEZ, ADAMS COUNTY, MISS.

Mr. TAYLOR. Chief Robinson, will you give your full name and residence for the record?

Mr. ROBINSON. My full name is James Theodore Robinson. I live at 2752 Miller Avenue in Natchez.

Mr. TAYLOR. How long have you served as chief of police?

Mr. ROBINSON. I have started my second term. It will be a 4-year period.

Mr. TAYLOR. You are elected to office?

Mr. ROBINSON. Yes, sir.

Mr. TAYLOR. Do your responsibilities as chief of police of Natchez include keeping the peace within the city limits of Natchez?

Mr. ROBINSON. Yes, sir.

Mr. TAYLOR. We have heard some testimony here today about a large number of incidents, some of which occurred in Natchez. Have you made any arrests in any of these cases?

Mr. ROBINSON. No, sir. I assisted in arrests that the State made in the beating of Bruce Payne in Jefferson or Claiborne County.

Mr. TAYLOR. That arrest was made in 1964, about a year after the case occurred?

Mr. ROBINSON. Yes, sir.

Mr. TAYLOR. Why has there been such difficulty in solving these cases

Mr. ROBINSON. Mr. Taylor, the first thing you don't have very much to go on. I have called for assistance from the FBI. Every case of violence that we have had in the city, I have asked the assistance and I have gotten it on each case that I have called them on, and I have called them on every one of them. You don't have much to go on, as I was saying. The witnesses don't give you any clues at all, and there are very few witnesses that you can come up with.

Mr. TAYLOR. You don't mean that they withhold clues; they just don't have any clues to give you, is that right?

Mr. ROBINSON. That's right.

Mr. TAYLOR. Sheriff Anders indicated there were extremist groups operating in the county. Do you know anything about such groups?

Mr. ROBINSON. Yes, sir. I have been well aware that there are some extremist groups operating in the county.

Mr. TAYLOR. Would that include the group calling itself the Klan?

Mr. ROBINSON. I wouldn't know what they go by. I don't know any of them personally. I have some thoughts of who might be members, but I don't know what they belong to.

Mr. TAYLOR. Does the Klan operate openly, or does any extremist group operate openly, hold meetings, and so on?

Mr. ROBINSON. The Klan, the Grand Wizard, lives in Adams County.

Mr. TAYLOR. Do they hold meetings in the county?

Mr. ROBINSON. I don't know. I couldn't tell you.

Mr. TAYLOR. How large do you think the group is which is responsible for the bombings?

Mr. ROBINSON. Like the sheriff and myself and the general thought of all enforcement agencies that operated in these acts of violence, that have helped down there and investigated them, we believe it is very few. I mean, it is a very few people doing it and we have our ideas who they are. We think we know who they are and Mr. Taylor, I have lost a many hour sleep at night trying to catch them.

Mr. TAYLOR. I would like to ask you a personal question. I was in Natchez several months ago interviewing a person who had some difficulties. I won't identify him because he is concerned about reprisals. While I was interviewing him, across the street somebody was snapping a bullwhip and looking up at the house. Does that happen very frequently to your knowledge in the city?

Mr. ROBINSON. No, sir, it does not. That's the first I have known about it.

Mr. TAYLOR. You haven't heard of bullwhips being displayed or openly used by anybody?

Mr. ROBINSON. I have heard of them being used.

Mr. TAYLOR. But they are not flourished openly ordinarily? This was an odd occurrence that happened while I was there?

Mr. ROBINSON. Could you tell me where it was?

Mr. TAYLOR. I will, but not right now.

Mr. ROBINSON. No, sir, it is not an everyday occurrence.

Mr. TAYLOR. In selecting your own recruits, do you check their background with the Federal Bureau of Investigation?

Mr. ROBINSON. Mr. Taylor, I do not select any police officers.

Mr. TAYLOR. How are they selected?

Mr. ROBINSON. Civil service. They are screened through the civil service and the only way I know they are fixing to be hired, civil service will give me a call and say they have three or four that have passed an examination and will I step over for a personal interview. And I sit in on the interview and that's all I do. I don't grade them or anything else.

Mr. TAYLOR. Is there a security check connected with this?

Mr. ROBINSON. Yes, sir.

Mr. TAYLOR. But, you don't have to satisfy yourself that persons are not members of any subversive organizations. Somebody else makes this determination?

Mr. ROBINSON. Right.

Mr. TAYLOR. Do you know whether it is the policy to exclude from membership on the force persons who are members of subversive organizations or persons who have been convicted of offenses?

Mr. ROBINSON. Mr. Taylor, if a police officer applicant has a police record, he's automatically excluded from the examination. That don't mean minor traffic. I mean, it does mean fighting, drunk or anything like that, he's excluded automatically. He never gets to take the test.

Mr. TAYLOR. What if he is a member of an organization which would be described as an extremist organization?

Mr. ROBINSON. Mr. Taylor, I personally talked to the Civil Service Commission Chairman then—it's a new Chairman now—and I told him I would hold an investigation of any department and to see if I could find if there are any members of any subversive organizations on the department. And he assured me that if we could come up with any names that could be proven, that they would be terminated from the police department.

Mr. TAYLOR. Did you hold such an investigation?

Mr. ROBINSON. Yes, sir.

Mr. TAYLOR. And you have satisfied yourself that there is no person on your force who is connected with any of these organizations?

Mr. ROBINSON. Could you specify these organizations for me, please, sir?

Mr. TAYLOR. Well, I am not sure I know the names of the organizations as well as you might; the Klan or the Americans for the Preservation of the White Race. Is that an organization operating in your area?

Mr. ROBINSON. Yes, sir.

Mr. TAYLOR. Would membership in that organization exclude them?

Mr. ROBINSON. No, sir, it would not.

Mr. TAYLOR. It would not exclude somebody as a member of your force?

Mr. ROBINSON. No, sir.

Mr. TAYLOR. How about membership in the Klan?

Mr. ROBINSON. I believe it would exclude them. I know it would. I don't have to believe.

Mr. TAYLOR. How much can you tell us about the Americans for the Preservation of the White Race?

Mr. ROBINSON. Mr. Taylor, I attended one meeting of the Preservation of the White Race and I was invited as a guest speaker. I attended and my topic of my speech that night was: "What the general public could do to assist law enforcement". I don't know if they kept notes or anything of that, but I talked from 8 until 11 o'clock to them. That's a pretty long speech.

Mr. TAYLOR. Sounds like a pretty long speech.

Mr. ROBINSON. And I asked everyone of them out there in case we had any demonstrations or anything uptown would they stay out of the area and let the local law enforcement officers handle it. And I was assured by them that they would, and that they wouldn't come up.

Mr. TAYLOR. Do you know what the objectives of the organizations are?

Mr. ROBINSON. No, sir, I don't.

Mr. TAYLOR. Has there been any evidence of economic boycotts or threats against white merchants or anybody else within the city of Natchez?

Mr. ROBINSON. Mr. Taylor, I heard—this is hearsay—that they were, not the Preservation of the White Race, but that they were planning something, but I don't know. I mean, if it ever took place, it never happened.

Mr. TAYLOR. You heard somebody was planning something, but you don't know whether it was this group or another group?

Mr. ROBINSON. No, sir, I don't know what it was.

Mr. TAYLOR. Now, Bruce Payne testified that he was followed from Natchez in the latter part of October 1963 and beaten in Port Gibson and that he called you and he gave you the precise license plate number of the cars involved. Do you recall that situation?

Mr. ROBINSON. Mr. Taylor, I would hate to call Bruce something, but he did not call me and give me any license.

Mr. TAYLOR. Did he call your office?

Mr. ROBINSON. He could have called my office. I understand he called the ex-sheriff, but he did not call me.

Mr. TAYLOR. I think he said he called the ex-sheriff on another occasion. There were two beatings involved.

Mr. ROBINSON. I'm not going to say that he could not have called my office. He could have called my office.

Mr. TAYLOR. What would you do with such information given the fact it occurred in another county?

Mr. ROBINSON. Usually if the desk sergeant answered the phone and if a man who would say I was beaten say in Port Gibson or Fayette, they would immediately tell him to call the sheriff in Fayette or the city marshal and in Port Gibson the same thing. They would tell him to call them and would assist him in trying to find out who the chief was or the sheriff was in the county.

Mr. Taylor. Would you also call the sheriff in Port Gibson or Fayette?

Mr. Robinson. Yes, sir, I would.

Mr. Taylor. And would you conduct an investigation in Adams County?

Mr. Robinson. Mr. Taylor, I'm getting ahead of your question—I would if the sheriff of another county or chief of another city would ask me to conduct an investigation, I would make a thorough investigation.

Mr. Taylor. But, if you got the information and you called him, wouldn't it ordinarily be the case that he would ask you to conduct the investigation?

Mr. Robinson. He might, but in this case I wasn't. I wasn't requested to make any investigation.

Mr. Taylor. Well, you didn't know. You received no such call personally, but you can't say whether or not anybody from your force did?

Mr. Robinson. No, sir. But, if it was, Mr. Taylor, he would keep records and we keep them pretty good, and I would have seen a report on it.

Mr. Taylor. Do you remember Mr. Payne? Did you have an encounter with him?

Mr. Robinson. Yes, sir.

Mr. Taylor. A day or two before?

Mr. Robinson. Yes, sir, I did.

Mr. Taylor. He described a discussion with you. Is that about right?

Mr. Robinson. No, sir, it wasn't.

Mr. Taylor. Would you care to tell us?

Mr. Robinson. Yes, sir, I'll tell you some of it. I got a call at the station. I was at the front office when the call came in, and it was an anonymous call, and I'm going to tell you just what the call said. It said, "There's some bomb on the highway out here," and said, "you can get hurt."

And I said. "Where is it at?"

He said, "Wood Avenue."

Well, I dispatched a car out there immediately. I don't know what we had. I didn't know what the call was, if it was a fictitious call or what. One of my officers picked up a British subject by the name of Bosenquet and they brought him to the jail. I charged him with vagrancy. He was filthy, I'll tell you the truth. He was absolutely filthy.

Mr. TAYLOR. Did he have any money in his possession?

Mr. ROBINSON. I don't remember. It wasn't much if he did.

Mr. TAYLOR. All right, continue.

Mr. ROBINSON. So we brought him in and we charged him and I talked to him myself. He told me that he was from England. They got an accent and I couldn't hardly understand his accent. And I asked him, I said, "Son," that's just a general speaking term a police officer uses. "Son," I said, "what in the world are you doing over here?" And, he said that he was over here working for a civil rights movement and he was working for COFO. And I asked him why didn't he stay in England. I said, "There's discrimination over there." And I asked him, I said, "Son, do you have any reason, I mean do you care what happens to you or what happens to the world or anything?" And he told me it didn't make any difference to him who ruled the world. He was wishing it would be the United Nations, would police the South. Mr. Taylor, I couldn't understand him too well and I let it drop at that.

Mr. TAYLOR. I see. How did this relate to Mr. Payne?

Mr. ROBINSON. Well, I had George Green arrested. He was arrested for running a red light. Then I charged him with investigation for auto theft, merely to check on him and to see who he was and to give us a legal charge to charge him. And Bruce Payne told me that the car belonged to a friend of his in Connecticut and under the law I could ask him—make him produce ownership papers. And I didn't want to put him to that much trouble. I asked him would he get a wire from the owner to me and he did. He got the wire to me and released the car to him. I talked to Bruce Payne; I talked to him just like he was my brother. I sit down and enjoyed talking to him and see what he had in mind. We don't know these people when they come into town, we don't know what they were for. And the sentiment of the people were kind of high at this time. Mostly we wanted to know where he was or what he was doing, where we could protect him. He needed some protection. I mean, he really needed it, and he thinks constant surveillance or police arrest was not for his protection. Of course, you can't make him believe that, Mr. Taylor, but that's the truth.

Mr. TAYLOR. Did the presence of Mr. Payne and others complicate life for you as a law enforcement officer?

Mr. ROBINSON. Yes, sir, they did.

Mr. TAYLOR. Did you resent it in any way?

Mr. ROBINSON. Mr. Taylor, I resented it, but I am a professional law enforcement officer. I have been in police business 18 years, and I have come up the hard way from the beat patrolman to the chief of police and I am proud that I got a chance to get ahead. And I did get ahead and I done it through hard work, and it don't make any difference to me if it is protecting the COFO workers, the citizens on the street. I'll do my utmost just to uphold the law to the best of my ability.

Mr. TAYLOR. Thank you.

Chairman HANNAH. Mr. Robinson, you excite my curiosity. It really hasn't much to do with what we are dealing with today. You say the Wizard of the Klan lives in Natchez. Is that the State or national figure?

Mr. ROBINSON. That's the State.

Chairman HANNAH. Is that the highest official in the Klan?

Mr. ROBINSON. Mr. Hannah, I don't know. I really don't know. I saw my first Klan open meeting at the Liberty Ball Park and I was born and raised in Natchez and I saw my first Klan meeting, and it impressed me. It was about 800 to 900 people there at the meeting, and Mr. Shelton talked. I think he is as high as you can get in it. But he gave the talk and it was very impressive to me.

Chairman HANNAH. He's from outside of Mississippi?

Mr. ROBINSON. Yes, sir. He's from Alabama.

Chairman HANNAH. When was this meeting that you talked about?

Mr. ROBINSON. It was in 1964, Mr. Hannah. I don't know just the exact date.

Chairman HANNAH. Father Hesburgh, do you have any questions?

Commissioner HESBURGH. Chief Robinson——

Mr. ROBINSON. May I explain why I was out at the meeting. It sounded kind of funny. I had police officers in plain clothes in the place and the FBI was there. And also I went to see and listen and observe as much as I could, and I couldn't see anything that night that would make you think they were anything but upstanding people.

[Laughter]

Chairman HANNAH. Father Hesburgh?

Commissioner HESBURGH. Chief, is it the Klan that burns these crosses?

Mr. ROBINSON. I don't know, Father.

Commissioner HESBURGH. Is it generally assumed that they are the ones that burn crosses? Is this part of the tradition?

Mr. ROBINSON. Father, one night we had a call on a cross being burned. We made very few reports. We usually call the fire department and douse the flame and pull the debris out of the street. If it is not burned real bad we take it in the police car and take it to the station and throw it in the trash can. But there were two small children, they described them as 12, 14 years old, burned one, and we checked the neighborhood and we couldn't come up with anybody that could identify the children.

Commissioner HESBURGH. Do you know the significance of this cross burning? Does it have any significance?

Mr. ROBINSON. Not that I know of. I know what I have heard.

Commissioner HESBURGH. What is that?

Mr. ROBINSON. It stands for unity. That's what I have been told.

Commissioner HESBURGH. Also, it stands for trouble, doesn't it.

Mr. ROBINSON. Yes, sir.

Commissioner HESBURGH. One last question, Chief. Most of these problems of violence have involved the Negro community, correct?

Mr. ROBINSON. Father, it has happened to the Negro mostly. As Sheriff Anders was saying, it's not a Negro district in Natchez as it is in other towns or anything. I have lived next door to colored myself, and there are some colored school teachers.

Commissioner HESBURGH. But the victim has usually been a colored person?

Mr. ROBINSON. Yes, sir.

Commissioner HESBURGH. Do you think it would help their morale or give them some sense of communication with the police force if there were some Negroes on the police force?

Mr. ROBINSON. It is now in process of hiring two colored policemen to work exclusively in the colored district. However, I won't have anything to do with hiring them. They will be hired and screened through the Civil Service Commission.

Commissioner HESBURGH. I think it's a fair statement. Dr. Hannah knows more about this than I do. In many places in the North we have found that having Negro policemen on the force gives the Negro community some sense of participation; at least they feel the idea merits consideration.

Chairman HANNAH. Mrs. Freeman?

Commissioner FREEMAN. Chief Robinson, how many members do you have on the police force?

Mr. ROBINSON. Forty. Now that includes the school guards, the meter maids, the impounder, and myself.

Commissioner FREEMAN. You are considering employing two Negroes?

Mr. ROBINSON. That is right. That is the wishes of the mayor and the board.

Commissioner FREEMAN. When you arrested George Green, you were aware that he had been engaged in civil rights activities. You said that you wanted to check on him to see who he was. It seems to me that there's a contradiction here. Earlier the question had been posed as to why you had not made any arrests relating to the attempts of violence. It was said that the violators constitute only about one percent of the populace. But here is one person who comes in and who is arrested for running a red light, then charged on a trumped-up charge to find out who he is. But you didn't proceed in this manner and at least arrest other people in order to stop the whippings and bombings and the fires. Do you see any distinction in your methods?

Mr. ROBINSON. I have no distinction between a COFO worker, a Klan member, an average citizen that violates the law. George Green and Bruce Payne happened to come in town and I was called immediately when they went to a certain place and told me—the man there told me some troublemakers are in Natchez and said, "I don't want them out here." He gave me the license number of the car they were driving and how many was in the car. And naturally we sent a car out that way looking for them to see who they were. We didn't make an illegal arrest.

Commissioner FREEMAN. In the course of your investigation have you had occasion to question any members of the Klan?

Mr. ROBINSON. I don't know if they were Klan members or not. We interrogated a lot of people. I think my records will show that we have talked to a good many on a lot of acts of violence that have happened there.

Commissioner FREEMAN. Thank you.

Chairman HANNAH. Dean Griswold?

Commissioner GRISWOLD. Chief, are places of public accommodation in Natchez segregated or desegregated?

Mr. ROBINSON. They are desegregated now.

Commissioner GRISWOLD. How long has that been the case?

Mr. ROBINSON. It has been since the Civil Rights Act. Dean, Charles Evers, and some local citizens from Natchez desegregated the Holiday Inn, the Eola Hotel, the Albert Pick Motel, Dumas Motel, the Clark Theater, the Ritz Theater and the Baker Grand Theater.

Commissioner GRISWOLD. Was there any scene or episode of violence or threat of violence in connection with this?

Mr. ROBINSON. No, sir; none whatsoever.

Commissioner GRISWOLD. Was you or your force called by anyone in connection with these activities?

Mr. ROBINSON. Dean, I had every man on the force working. I have 13 members on the auxiliary force, and I had them to stand by. We did not make a big showing at these places. We had men there and men at close distance around all these places. We did have plain-clothes men following each place that they went to. We did not have any, and I was amazed. And frankly, the citizens of Natchez, the responsible citizens of Natchez, should be commended for it.

Commissioner GRISWOLD. If I recall the testimony this morning, it was that, as of today, only the Holiday Inn is desegregated in Natchez; is that your understanding?

Mr. ROBINSON. I didn't get your question good there.

Commissioner GRISWOLD. I believe it was stated this morning that only the Holiday Inn is desegregated in Natchez?

Mr. ROBINSON. That's false. All of them are desegregated.

Commissioner GRISWOLD. Do you know whether Negroes are from time to time using these other places today?

Mr. ROBINSON. I don't know. I have very seldom gone out to lunch. I go home usually for lunch. Either I might go to the Holi-day Inn or Eola or Tops Grill for a sandwich or something. I got very irregular hours. I was at the Eola Hotel one day when the Freedom Democrats were taking depositions around at the courthouse, and it was desegregated that day, and that was just here just——

Commissioner GRISWOLD. What I was trying to get at is simply this. I think one day various places are desegregated. A Negro enters and is served. But that's the last that is heard of it. It doesn't last. It doesn't continue that way. It is your understanding that these places have continued to serve Negroes in places of public accommodations?

Mr. ROBINSON. They are at Kress every day. Kress is uptown and you can see that, it's right on Commerce and Franklin, and its desegregated.

Commissioner GRISWOLD. Well, I think it's very much to the credit of Natchez and to your credit for the steps you took to see that there wouldn't be violence and it has worked out so well.

Mr. ROBINSON. Mr. Griswold, I have worked long hours.

Commissioner GRISWOLD. I have no doubt of that. May I ask you just one other question, which is not in any sense a reflection upon you. How are you chosen for your office? Are you appointed or elected?

Mr. ROBINSON. No, sir; I'm elected.

Commissioner GRISWOLD. For what term?

Mr. ROBINSON. Four-year term.

Commissioner GRISWOLD. Are you paid a salary or fee?

Mr. ROBINSON. A salary.

Commissioner GRISWOLD. Are the members of your force—paid a salary or by you?

Mr. ROBINSON. They are paid by salary, the city pays them.

Commissioner GRISWOLD. Are you eligible for reelection in your term?

Mr. ROBINSON. Yes, sir.

Commissioner GRISWOLD. Is it the regular practice in Mississippi that chiefs of police of cities are elected?

Mr. ROBINSON. Mr. Griswold, in some cities they are appointed. It's got its good points and it's got its bad points. It's good points is you can retire after 20 years and the bad points of being elected, I cannot retire after 20 years. I have got 18 years in now and I wish I could retire after 20.

Commissioner GRISWOLD. Perhaps this is an unfair question and I won't press you on it, but do you think that the chief of police should be elected or appointed?

Mr. ROBINSON. I think he should be elected.

Chairman HANNAH. Dr. Rankin?

Commissioner RANKIN. Chief, I have only one question. Do you think things are better in Natchez?

Mr. ROBINSON. Yes, sir, I know it is.

Commissioner RANKIN. And you think that the public accommodations section of the 1964 Civil Rights Act is being obeyed?

Mr. ROBINSON. Yes, sir, I do.

Commissioner RANKIN. Has this made your work a little bit easier?

Mr. ROBINSON. I'll tell you to start off with, the first day that the Clark was integrated, it kind of kept us on pins and needles. This is from my own opinion because I believe that the people that integrated it that day wanted only trouble. They didn't want to integrate the Clark because they didn't try, but they did cause quite a bit of confusion on the streets. But we didn't have any incidents. We did move on some whites, and we moved on some colored until we broke it up. I just went around and told them to break it up and go in and they broke it up and we didn't have any more trouble. The next time they come they bought tickets and went to the show.

Commissioner RANKIN. But now things are going pretty well, is that right?

Mr. ROBINSON. Yes, sir.

Commissioner RANKIN. And, it's not a bad thing to have on the statutes? It cleared the atmosphere. I've heard how bad this law was since I have been here. I heard two or three people say it is terrible; but, really, a lot of the evidence has shown that it helped a little bit to clear up the situation.

Mr. ROBINSON. That's a matter of choice, though. If I want to go to the show, I will go, and if I don't, I'll stay home.

Chairman HANNAH. Mr. Patterson?

Vice Chairman PATTERSON. Chief, I also have just one question. We have seen here in testimony today quite a list of violations in your city. We have heard the sheriff say that he hopes that there won't be any new outbreak, but he admits that some of the people whom he thinks are guilty are still at large. I assume you agree with him?

Mr. ROBINSON. Yes, sir.

Vice Chairman PATTERSON. He also adds that he thinks he knows who they are, even though he doesn't know if he can make a case against them. Do you think you know who they are?

Mr. ROBINSON. Yes, but I don't think we can make a case stick.

Vice Chairman PATTERSON. Do you think that they think you are going ahead with that case as soon as you can?

Mr. ROBINSON. Yes, I do.

Vice Chairman PATTERSON. Do you think that is an important matter in law enforcement?

Mr. ROBINSON. My house has been threatened to be bombed.

Vice Chairman PATTERSON. This is really the question. The police and sheriff have tried to break these cases according to you and Sheriff Anders. But no arrests have been made in both cases. The mayor, as I understand it, has made some efforts at racial understanding in Natchez. His house has been bombed. Now, who takes the next step in a city like Natchez? Do you think the business community could help you with a more forward attitude and a more specific statement of what it wishes in the community?

Mr. ROBINSON. Mr. Patterson, the people made their statement. A lot of the civic organizations are giving me their wholehearted support, and there was a statement made in the Natchez Democrat signed by some of the civic clubs in Natchez that they do not condone any act of violence. And I believe that the acts right now have stopped. I think the parties responsible, they might not be from Natchez and again they could be. I think they know that we are determined and if we can make a case stick, we are going to take them into court. And I believe the responsible people in Natchez that will serve on a jury will convict them.

Chairman HANNAH. Mr. Rogerson?

Mr. ROGERSON. Chief Robinson, I have been a little confused this afternoon as to whether members of the Klan are known or are not known in Natchez and Adams County. Now, I assume that you would pretty easily know who the grand wizard is or with whom he is associated. Now, on the one hand, you seem to say that the Klan is a clandestine operation. And then you talked about the big session in 1964 at the Liberty Ball Park.

Mr. ROBINSON. Yes, sir.

Mr. ROGERSON. Is that in Natchez?

Mr. ROBINSON. Yes, sir; it's in Natchez.

Mr. ROGERSON. I assume that was widely advertised. Some 800 people were there. These people were all observed, I assume, by you, the FBI and others. Now, I don't know how many of the 800 were people like you, Chief, but 800 is a sizable number of people to be interested in this activity. Were the people there in these robes and so on?

Mr. ROBINSON. No, sir; they were in plain dress clothes.

Mr. ROGERSON. But some of them were officers and focused some attention on themselves at some point in the rally?

Mr. ROBINSON. Mr. Rogerson, I was impressed myself with the type people I saw there. I saw some local businessmen. They could have been observers. I saw school boys and girls. I saw some older people, and outside the gates there was two or three little colored boys riding bicycles. It impressed me.

Mr. ROGERSON. When in 1964 was this Liberty Ball Park session held?

Mr. ROBINSON. I don't remember the date.

Mr. ROGERSON. Was it before most of the bombings and burnings in 1964?

Mr. ROBINSON. No, sir, it was after, I do believe. I'm not positive. I do believe it was after.

Mr. ROGERSON. Now, in other places Klan meetings in the community and in the county are either obviously advertised or they seem to be passed along by word of mouth? Do you know when local Klan meetings are being held in Adams County?

Mr. ROBINSON. No, sir, I don't.

Mr. ROGERSON. Just one other thing. Apparently membership in the Americans for the Preservation of the White Race, if that's the correct title, is not a bar to employment on the police department in Natchez. And now you are making moves to hire Negroes, and I assume that membership in the NAACP would not be a bar.

Mr. ROBINSON. I rightly don't know. I imagine it would, though.

Mr. ROGERSON. You imagine it would? Why is that?

Mr. ROBINSON. Yes, sir.

Mr. ROGERSON. Is the NAACP equated to the Klan in your eyes?

Mr. ROBINSON. No, sir.

Mr. ROGERSON. Why would it be a bar?

Mr. ROBINSON. I didn't hear your question.

Mr. ROGERSON. Why would it be a bar? Why would membership in the NAACP be a bar to membership on the Natchez police force?

Mr. ROBINSON. I assumed it may. I said, I imagine it would. I really don't know. I shouldn't answer that question because I really don't know.

Mr. ROGERSON. Your position reflects an attitude, and that's interesting.

Mr. ROBINSON. I really don't know if it would or not, and I really doubt if it would.

Mr. ROGERSON. Thank you.

Chairman HANNAH. Mr. Taylor?

Mr. TAYLOR. You said there was a test of public accommodations in several places that serve Negroes?

Mr. ROBINSON. Right.

Mr. TAYLOR. You also said you eat in the Eola Hotel when you get a chance?

Mr. ROBINSON. Yes.

Mr. TAYLOR. And Tops Grill and a couple of other places?

Mr. ROBINSON. Yes, sir.

Mr. TAYLOR. Have you ever seen Negroes in any of those places while you have been there?

Mr. ROBINSON. Yes.

Mr. TAYLOR. On how many occasions?

Mr. ROBINSON. Two or three occasions.

Mr. TAYLOR. Eating at the lunch counter?

Mr. ROBINSON. No, sir, not eating at the counter, they were eating at the table.

Mr. TAYLOR. This must be a recent development. Do the Negroes in Natchez know they can use these facilities?

Mr. ROBINSON. I don't think that they want to. I'm going to tell you the truth.

Mr. TAYLOR. You don't think they want to?

Mr. ROBINSON. No, I think they could if they did.

Mr. TAYLOR. One other question. You say there are two other Negroes coming on the force. When they come on will they have full power of other patrolmen on the force?

Mr. ROBINSON. Yes.

Mr. TAYLOR. Will their duty be limited only to the Negro community?

Mr. ROBINSON. No, sir. Of course, that is where they will work in the—that's what the plans are, if they are hired, to work in the colored community.

Mr. TAYLOR. Will they have authority to arrest a white person for a crime committed in Natchez?

Mr. ROBINSON. Oh, yes, sir, yes, sir.

Mr. TAYLOR. I'm glad to hear that.

Mr. ROBINSON. Delegate authority to one and not another.

Chairman HANNAH. That's all, gentlemen. Thank you very much. You are excused, and we will take a 10- minute break. We will resume at 3:30.

(Witness excused.)

(A short recess was taken.)

Chairman HANNAH. The hearing will come to order. Mr. Taylor, will you call the next witness.

Mr. TAYLOR. The next witness is Dr. Benjamin Murph.

Chairman HANNAH. Is there a staff witness first?

Mr. TAYLOR. I'm sorry. The next testimony comes from Jones County, and Mr. Wolf will give us background information on Jones County.

Chairman HANNAH. Mr. Wolf?

Mr. WOLF. Jones County is in the southeastern portion of Mississippi. The total population of the county in 1963 was 59,000 of whom about one-fourth were Negro. In 1958, 50 percent of voting age whites were registered but only 10 percent of the voting age Negroes were registered.

The largest city in Jones County is Laurel, with a population of 28,000, of whom about one-third are Negro. Laurel, a county seat, is a manufacturing center, primarily of wood products. Thirty-two percent of the whites and 23 percent of the Negroes are involved in manufacturing.

Jones is a relatively prosperous county. In 1959 the median income for Negro families was about $2,200; the median income for white families was about $4,700.

In 1959, the median level of education for whites was 11 years; for the Negroes, 7 years. In the school year 1960–61, the Laurel County School District spent about $185 for each white child and about $120 for each Negro child.

Chairman HANNAH. Thank you, Mr. Wolf.

Dr. Murph, will you raise your right hand?

(Whereupon, Dr. Benjamin E. Murph was duly sworn by the Chairman and testified as follows:)

Chairman HANNAH. Mr. Taylor, will you begin the questioning.

TESTIMONY OF DR. BENJAMIN ELORY MURPH, JONES COUNTY, MISS.

Mr. TAYLOR. Dr. Murph, will you give your full name, your residence, and your occupation for the record?

Dr. MURPH. My name is Benjamin Elory Murph, 118 Harrison Boulevard, Laurel, Miss.

Mr. TAYLOR. And your occupation, sir?

Dr. MURPH. I am a doctor of dental surgery.

Mr. TAYLOR. Where did you obtain your D.D.S.?

Dr. MURPH. From the dental department of Meharry Dental College in Nashville, Tenn.

Mr. TAYLOR. How long have you lived in Mississippi, Dr. Murph?

Dr. MURPH. I will have lived in Mississippi 30 years, June 14, 1965.

Mr. TAYLOR. Has most of that time been in Laurel or Jones County?

Dr. MURPH. Yes, sir.

Mr. TAYLOR. Are you affiliated with any civic or civil rights organizations in Laurel?

Dr. MURPH. Yes, sir. I am a member of the National Association for the Advancement of Colored People, member of the Masons, Knights of Pythias, and other organizations.

Mr. TAYLOR. Since the passage of the Civil Rights Act, July of last year, have Negroes in your community attempted to use places of public accommodation?

Dr. MURPH. Yes, they have.

Mr. TAYLOR. Has this happened on several occasions?

Dr. MURPH. Yes, it happened in July of last year, very shortly after the civil rights bill was passed and also recently.

Mr. TAYLOR. What happened when Negroes attempted to use these facilities?

Dr. MURPH. First occasion was at a sandwich shop and they met some resistance from many people who were gathered there to see that they would not be able to use these facilities.

Mr. TAYLOR. When you say they met some resistance, what kind of resistance are you talking about?

Dr. MURPH. They had some fights. They had some fights with those who carried clubs and sticks against those who attempted to gain first-class citizenship at the counters.

Mr. TAYLOR. Did this happen on more than one occasion?

Dr. MURPH. Yes, it did.

Mr. TAYLOR. About how many times?

Dr. MURPH. It happened at Kress and Woolworth, to my knowledge.

Mr. TAYLOR. Did you ever attempt to get service at a place?

Dr. MURPH. Yes, I attempted to get service at the same sandwich shop, John's Cafe, and the Travel Inn. At John's Cafe the policeman were called and our driver's licenses were examined and we were asked to continue. At the Travel Inn we were refused service.

Mr. TAYLOR. You say at the John's Cafe you were asked to continue?

Dr. MURPH. Asked to continue on down the street after we were examined.

Mr. TAYLOR. Did you do so?

Dr. MURPH. Yes.

Mr. TAYLOR. Are there desegregated establishments, places of public accommodation in Laurel today, sir?

Dr. MURPH. Yes. The railroad station, the bus terminal and several other eating establishments have been desegregated.

Mr. TAYLOR. As to the eating establishments, can a Negro citizen use these facilities in the same way that a white citizen can?

Dr. MURPH. I have my doubts about that because of incidents of the past. Negroes are still fearful of using these facilities. They have been intimidated. They have been shoved off the counters. They have been knocked around at these facilities and some of them still fear going into them.

Mr. TAYLOR. Has there been any improvement in the situation? Do you think these fears are still justified?

Dr. MURPH. Well, some and then some not. We have opened up lines of communication between white and Negroes, and I think that we are facing a new day. I believe that a brighter day is in front of us. But we hope that the day will come when every man can vote and register regardless of the color of his skin and to get an education, not just a Negro education.

Mr. TAYLOR. Thank you.

Chairman HANNAH. Father Hesburgh?

Commissioner HESBURGH. Dr. Murph, wasn't there a burning in Laurel within the last day or so?

Dr. MURPH. I believe there was.

Commissioner HESBURGH. Was it a church?

Dr. MURPH. It was an office, I think the COFO office.

Commissioner HESBURGH. That would at least indicate that the new and brighter day is not yet here?

Dr. MURPH. Yes.

Commissioner HESBURGH. Thank you.

Chairman HANNAH. Mrs. Freeman?

Commissioner FREEMAN. Dr. Murph, on the occasions when you said people have been intimidated and pushed around, were the police officials notified of this?

Dr. MURPH. Yes, they have been notified.

Commissioner FREEMAN. What happened after that?

Dr. MURPH. We have had one arrest and otherwise nothing happened.

Commissioner FREEMAN. What is the attitude of the Negro community about the police department? Do they have confidence in it?

Dr. MURPH. Well, I doubt seriously whether they have confidence in the policemen because we have had to suffer many incidents and suffered brutality in the past. All of these build up to make us suspicious and doubtful as to the confidence that we can have in the policemen.

Commissioner FREEMAN. When you say brutality, are you referring to police brutality?

Dr. MURPH. We have had it in the past. We haven't had it recent.

Commissioner FREEMAN. Are there Negroes on the police force?

Dr. MURPH. Yes, we have eight.

Commissioner FREEMAN. It is your impression that the situation has improved because of the presence of the Negro members on the police force?

Dr. MURPH. I believe so.

Commissioner FREEMAN. Thank you.

Chairman HANNAH. Mr. Taylor, did you have any other questions?

Mr. TAYLOR. No, sir.

Chairman HANNAH. You are excused, sir. Thank you.

(Witness excused.)

Chairman HANNAH. Call the next witness, Mr. Taylor.

Mr. TAYLOR. The next witness is Jack Lohner.

Chairman HANNAH. Mr. Lohner?

Mr. Lohner, will you raise you right hand?

Whereupon, Mr. Jack Lohner was duly sworn by the Chairman and testified as follows:

TESTIMONY OF MR. JACK ELLIS LOHNER, WINSTON-SALEM, N.C.

Mr. TAYLOR. Mr. Lohner, will you give us your full name, residence, and occupation?

Mr. LOHNER. My name is Jack Lohner, Jack Ellis Lohner. I reside in Winston-Salem, N.C., and I'm a variety store manager.

Mr. TAYLOR. You presently manage a variety store in Winston-Salem?

Mr. LOHNER. Winston-Salem.

Mr. TAYLOR. During the year 1964, and up until recently were you manager of a Kress Store in Laurel, Miss.?

Mr. LOHNER. Yes, I was.

Mr. TAYLOR. Following the passage of the Civil Rights Act last July did your store adopt the policy or did your company adopt a policy of serving Negroes at the lunch counter?

Mr. Lohner. Yes.

Mr. Taylor. And did Negroes attempt to use the lunch counters during that month of July when the Civil Rights Act was passed?

Mr. Lohner. Yes.

Mr. Taylor. What happened to Negroes who attempted to use these facilities?

Mr. Lohner. At first few Negroes tried to use the facilities and nothing happened.

Mr. Taylor. And did something happen subsequent to that?

Mr. Lohner. We had some instances, yes.

Mr. Taylor. Of what?

Mr. Lohner. Of violence.

Mr. Taylor. Negroes were attacked?

Mr. Lohner. Yes.

Mr. Taylor. By whom were they attacked?

Mr. Lohner. White people.

Mr. Taylor. On how many occasions did that occur?

Mr. Lohner. I think it was on four, three occasions at the lunch counter, four occasions altogether in my particular store.

Mr. Taylor. Did you have some conversations with any police officials about that?

Mr. Lohner. Yes. I talked to Chief Nix, yes.

Mr. Taylor. And did he offer to help you in preventing these incidents in any way?

Mr. Lohner. Yes, he came to me and offered help.

Mr. Taylor. What did he say he would do?

Mr. Lohner. He said that he would—well, to quote him, "stop all this foolishness and not let any of this violence occur." He was going to try to keep control of it.

Mr. Taylor. Did he station a man—a patrolman—in your store at any time?

Mr. Lohner. Yes.

Mr. Taylor. What month was this?

Mr. Lohner. I don't know exactly. I think it was in August.

Mr. Taylor. This was after July, after several incidents?

Mr. Lohner. After one incident. I don't know of any other.

Mr. Taylor. Do you know of anyone that has been arrested for acts of violence at your store?

Mr. Lohner. I personally know that Chief Nix made one arrest when I was right there with him.

Mr. Taylor. That was one of the early incidents?

Mr. Lohner. That was one one the first incidents.

Mr. Taylor. To your knowledge were these persons convicted?

Mr. LOHNER. I know of one instance where he made the arrest. I know that that person was arrested and taken to jail.

Mr. TAYLOR. You don't know whether he was convicted or not?

Mr. LOHNER. No.

Mr. TAYLOR. Were you or anybody at your store called upon to testify in those proceedings?

Mr. LOHNER. Not to testify, no.

Mr. TAYLOR. Did you say there were a couple more incidents in July and August? Was there one more recently than that?

Mr. LOHNER. Yes.

Mr. TAYLOR. When was that?

Mr. LOHNER. November sometime, the last of November.

Mr. TAYLOR. What happened on that occasion?

Mr. LOHNER. A Negro boy and a white boy sat down at the lunch counter and the Negro boy, I beg your pardon, the white boy was hit in the face.

Mr. TAYLOR. With a fist?

Mr. LOHNER. Yes.

Mr. TAYLOR. Do you know whether arrests were made on that occasion?

Mr. LOHNER. No, I don't know.

Mr. TAYLOR. Did you file a complaint or did anyone in your store do so?

Mr. LOHNER. Yes.

Mr. TAYLOR. You did call the police?

Mr. LOHNER. Yes.

Mr. TAYLOR. Did these incidents injure your business in any way?

Mr. LOHNER. Yes.

Mr. TAYLOR. Sales declined?

Mr. LOHNER. Particularly right after the incident you could notice a drop in the sales.

Mr. TAYLOR. Thank you.

Chairman HANNAH. Father Hesburgh?

Commissioner HESBURGH. Mr. Lohner, do you notice any change in climate between operating a store in Laurel and operating a store in North Carolina?

Mr. LOHNER. I wish I could truthfully say, but I'm just ordering the merchandise for the store and haven't even hired the people. It will be opened as soon as I can do all that.

Commissioner HESBURGH. Good. Thank you sir.

Chairman HANNAH. Mr. Rogerson?

Mr. ROGERSON. Mr. Lohner. When you saw Chief Nix arrest somebody, did you see what happened?

Mr. Lohner. No, sir.

Mr. Rogerson. You didn't see the violence occur?

Mr. Lohner. I didn't see the actual incident.

Mr. Rogerson. Thank you.

Chairman Hannah. Any further questions? Mr. Taylor?

Mr. Taylor. Just one or two. When these incidents started, did you make it a practice of stationing somebody by the telephone every time a Negro came in your store?

Mr. Lohner. We were ready in case anything happened that we could notify the police for some help.

Mr. Taylor. You were expecting trouble?

Mr. Lohner. No, not——

Mr. Taylor. After the first one or two incidents?

Mr. Lohner. Yes.

Mr. Taylor. And were there groups of white people who frequently congregated outside your store?

Mr. Lohner. When was this?

Mr. Taylor. During the month of July or August.

Mr. Lohner. Before an incident, usually.

Mr. Taylor. Thank you.

Chairman Hannah. You are excused, sir. Thank you very much. (Witness excused.)

Chairman Hannah. Call the next witness, Mr. Taylor.

Mr. Taylor. I would like to call on Mr. Wolf again, to present a short investigation report.

Chairman Hannah. Mr. Wolf.

TESTIMONY OF EDWIN D. WOLF, STAFF ATTORNEY, U.S. COMMISSION ON CIVIL RIGHTS

Mr. Wolf. The following is the first part of a report of the staff's investigation of incidents of violence against Negroes and others attempting to use public accommodations under Title II of the Civil Rights Act of 1964 and violence against members of Local 5–443 of the International Woodworkers Association in Jones County, Miss. The report is based on affidavits of victims and witnesses, interviews with law enforcement officials and information in Government files.

On July 11, 1964, Larry McGill, age 11, and several other Negro youths decided to eat at a previously segregated lunch counter at the S. H. Kress store in downtown Laurel. Larry and his group were driven downtown by his mother, Mrs. Bertie Mae McGill. When they arrived in the downtown area, the children got out of the car, went into the Kress store and sat at the lunch counter. Mrs. McGill parked her car and followed. The police chief of Laurel, L. C. Nix, was present.

Before the Negroes could be served two white men armed with bats, who had been in the store, attacked the Negroes as they sat at the counter. Jessie Harrington was struck on the head and blood ran out of his mouth. Larry McGill was hit across the back and knocked down as he was leaving his seat. The police chief stopped the attack and arrested one of the assailants. The Negroes were taken to the hospital, treated and released. The police did not interview Mrs. McGill or any of the victims of this attack. The person arrested forfeited an appearance bond of $25.

On the afternoon of August 15, 1964, Larry McGill and other Negro boys again went to the S. H. Kress store. A group of white men was standing in the store with baseball bats as they entered. As they sat at the lunch counter, Larry was approached by a white woman who pointed a pistol at him and ordered him to leave his seat. His mother, who was in the store and observed the scene, was also threatened. Another of the youths was struck on the back of the neck with a baseball bat by one of the men. The Negroes left the store and reported the incident to a policeman. They also swore out warrants for the arrest of their assailants. Both were subsequently tried on charges of assault and found not guilty.

On the morning of August 11, 1964, Eugene Keys, an 18-year-old Negro resident of Laurel, went to the S. H. Kress store to buy a notebook. A white man whom Keys did not know approached him from the front of the store. The man accused him of eating at the lunch counter, threatened him, and then took brass knuckles out of his pocket and tried to hit Keys two or three times. Keys grabbed the man's arm and was not hit. Keys fled when the white man took out a knife. The incident was reported to the police. A few days later Keys pointed out his assailant to Federal officials. No arrests have been made.

On August 14, 1964, Sharon Diane Jefferson, a 13-year-old Negro girl, was accosted by three white men as she sat at the lunch counter at the Woolworth store in downtown Laurel. One of the men pulled her from the stool and another kicked her as she was being pushed out of the store. No arrests have been made for this assault.

On the afternoon of November 28, 1964, two civil rights workers, John T. Foster, Jr., white, and John Handy, Negro, went to the S. H. Kress store in downtown Laurel. They sat at the lunch counter and were served. About halfway through the meal a white man came up behind Foster, spun him around and hit him on the nose and the back of the head with his fist. The man then walked away. After the assault Foster and Handy went to the police station and swore out a John Doe warrant for the arrest of the man based on a description given to the desk sergeant. No arrests have been made.

On December 16, 1964, six persons, four Negroes and two whites, went to the Pinehurst Cafe in the Travel Inn and attempted to obtain service. They entered the cafe and sat in two groups. They were not served. There was no crowd or disturbance. When they refused to leave upon request of the management they were arrested by the police chief on warrants sworn out by the attorney for the management. Some of the group went limp and were carried out of the cafe and dragged up the steps of the city hall. The others walked to jail. All were charged with breach of the peace. The four demonstrators who went limp were also charged with resisting arrest.

Mr. TAYLOR. The next witness is Police Chief L. C. Nix.

Chairman HANNAH. Mr. Nix? Mr. Nix, will you raise your right hand?

(Whereupon, Police Chief L. C. Nix was duly sworn by the Chairman and testified as follows:)

Chairman HANNAH. Will you introduce your attorney, sir.

Mr. NIX. Mr. William Deavours.

TESTIMONY OF L. C. NIX, CHIEF OF POLICE, LAUREL, JONES COUNTY, MISS.

Mr. TAYLOR. Chief Nix, will you please give your full name and residence for the record?

Mr. NIX. My name is L. C. Nix. I live at 26 Oakcrest Drive, Laurel, Miss.

Mr. TAYLOR. How long have you served as chief of police in Laurel?

Mr. NIX. Little better than 6 years.

Mr. TAYLOR. Do your responsibilities include keeping the peace and preventing violence in the city of Laurel?

Mr. NIX. Yes, sir.

Mr. TAYLOR. We gather from testimony that there was some violence attending the desegregation of the stores in Laurel last summer; is that correct?

Mr. NIX. Yes, sir.

Mr. TAYLOR. Did you make an arrest in one of these early incidents of violence?

Mr. NIX. I did.

Mr. TAYLOR. What was the offense involved?

Mr. NIX. On this occasion I happened to be down at Kress and my attention was called to a disturbance near the lunch counter. There was a white man had one of these small child's baseball bat hitting a nigger boy over the head with it. I ran over to him, placed him under arrest and got the ball bat and everybody else cleared out from that, and I didn't even know who the Negro boy was.

Mr. TAYLOR. What was the date of that; do you recall?

Mr. NIX. I would have to look at the records.

Mr. TAYLOR. Perhaps this was the incident involving Larry Mc-Gill, a boy of about 11 on July 11?

Mr. NIX. I later learned that it was Larry McGill and a Jessie Harrington.

Mr. TAYLOR. Can you tell us what the subsequent disposition of that case was?

Mr. NIX. This fellow was arrested and carried into court, and he forfeited $25 cash bond on it.

Mr. TAYLOR. What was the charge against him?

Mr. NIX. Assault with a stick.

Mr. TAYLOR. And he was able to simply fail to appear and forfeit the cash bond, and that was the end of the matter?

Mr. NIX. No one appeared against him.

Mr. TAYLOR. Now, did you witness the incident yourself?

Mr. NIX. Yes, sir.

Mr. TAYLOR. You did not appear against him either?

Mr. NIX. I was present.

Mr. TAYLOR. Now, one of the last of these incidents, if not the last, was on November 28, 1964, in Kress' store. Are you familiar with that incident?

Mr. NIX. We have a record of an incident happening down there.

Mr. TAYLOR. You just brought in some of your reports on these cases, and the complaint I have in front of me simply says Mr. Lohner, that refers to Jack Lohner, reported that some colored and white persons were at the lunch counter and a "WM", white male, hit one of them.

Mr. NIX. Yes.

Mr. TAYLOR. Is that the complete report on this case?

Mr. NIX. That is the complaint that was made.

Mr. TAYLOR. Well, in other cases there are other documents attached to the complaint. Was there any followup on this case?

Mr. NIX. This was a complaint that we received by telephone from the Kress store.

Mr. TAYLOR. Would your records reveal any subsequent investigation of this complaint?

Mr. NIX. I believe there was a John Doe warrant made in this case, but no arrests have been made. It hasn't been located.

Mr. TAYLOR. John Doe warrant made by the parties who were the victims in this case?

Mr. NIX. That's right.

Mr. TAYLOR. I believe, chief, that it has been testified that since the passage of the Civil Rights Act you have arrested, on charges of disturbing the peace or other charges, Negroes who have attempted to use places of public accommodation. Can you tell us what the circumstances of those arrests were?

Mr. NIX. These were arrested on warrants preferred by the owner or manager of the place of business.

Mr. TAYLOR. What places of business were these?

Mr. NIX. The Pinehurst Coffee Shop, Travel Inn Hotel.

Mr. TAYLOR. Were you aware as a law enforcement officer that the persons who were arrested had a right under Federal law to use these public accommodations?

Mr. NIX. The charge against them was not for using the accommodations. The charges were made and I'm obliged to serve any charges that are made.

Mr. TAYLOR. My question was not about the arrest. My question was about whether you were aware that they had a right to be served at these facilities?

Mr. NIX. Yes, sir.

Mr. TAYLOR. And you say they had a right, but you had to arrest them on a warrant?

Mr. NIX. The warrant was charged with breach of the peace.

Mr. TAYLOR. Knowing of this right, did you inform the proprietor that these persons had a right to be there before you served the warrant of arrest?

Mr. NIX. In this case it was an attorney himself and he made out the warrants.

Mr. TAYLOR. You thought he would know of this without your informing him, so you didn't feel you had any obligation to tell him these persons had these rights?

Mr. NIX. He is past district attorney of the district up there.

Mr. TAYLOR. Who is that?

Mr. NIX. Paul G. Schwartsfager.

Mr. TAYLOR. And he is the justice of the peace?

Mr. NIX. No, sir.

Mr. TAYLOR. He is the owner of the establishment?

Mr. NIX. One of the owners, yes.

Mr. TAYLOR. How about the owner of the other establishment, is he also someone who would know of the law in this regard?

Mr. NIX. Which other establishment?

Mr. TAYLOR. You said Pinehurst Cafe and Travel Inn, I believe.

Mr. NIX. That's all one business. It's a hotel and coffee shop.

Mr. TAYLOR. I see. Before making this arrest did you attempt to determine whether any breach of the peace had in fact occurred?

Mr. NIX. I believe that would be up to the courts to decide a thing like that because we have had a call to this establishment and when we arrived there was no breach of peace, but we know not what happened before we arrived.

Mr. TAYLOR. Breach of the peace is a conclusion, is it not? Were the facts upon which this conclusion was based stated to you?

Mr. NIX. Charges were not made before me. The charges were made and served by me and my men.

Mr. TAYLOR. The affidavit reads: "Willfully and unlawfully, with intent to provoke a breach of the peace, refused to leave the Pinehurst Coffee Shop when ordered to do so by affiant." Those were the charges in this case.

Mr. NIX. Yes, sir.

Mr. TAYLOR. Will you provide protection for places of accommodation, chief, when they serve Negroes in compliance with the Civil Rights Act?

Mr. NIX. We have told all the people there that we will try to keep the peace.

Mr. TAYLOR. Do you feel that today Negro citizens in Laurel can go downtown to any place of public accommodation and have nothing to fear if they sought service?

Mr. NIX. Much more so now than in the past. As a matter of fact, the last few days several of them have.

Mr. TAYLOR. Thank you.

Chairman HANNAH. Dean Griswold?

Commissioner GRISWOLD. Chief Nix, as I understand the situation with respect to the episode at the Kress store on July 11, you were personally present.

Mr. NIX. Yes.

Commissioner GRISWOLD. And, you saw the white man with the small baseball bat hit the Negro boy?

Mr. NIX. Yes, sir.

Commissioner GRISWOLD. And, you then arrested the white man?

Mr. NIX. Yes, sir.

Commissioner GRISWOLD. As I recall your testimony, when the case came up for trial, no one appeared to prosecute; is that correct?

Mr. NIX. No one did appear. I made the charges myself.

Mr. GRISWOLD. Why shouldn't you have prosecuted the case as the chief police officer of the city who had personally witnessed the crime committed in your presence?

Mr. Nix. When a person is arrested and posts a cash bond which is set up by the courts as a minimum that would be fined, he has a right to appear or not to appear.

Commissioner Griswold. He has a right to appear or not to appear?

Mr. Nix. If he does not appear there will be a forfeiture on his bond.

Commissioner Griswold. Is there no alternative? Couldn't he be taken on a *capias* and brought into court on the charges?

Mr. Nix. Not on that.

Commissioner Griswold. Did you move that he be arrested and brought before the clerks?

Mr. Nix. We don't have such in city court.

Commissioner Griswold. Are you sure that that is the law in Mississippi?

Mr. Nix. That's—other than that, would have been to go before the grand jury.

Commissioner Griswold. Concerning the charges which were made, why wasn't it your duty to go out and arrest him and bring him in to meet the charges made before the court which you had personally witnessed?

Mr. Nix. He has a right to appear when he posts his cash bond or not to appear.

Commissioner Griswold. I asked you if you were sure that's the law of Mississippi, and I suggest to you that on motion by the prosecuting officers, he can be arrested and brought before the court. The forfeiture bail is simply an alternative.

Mr. Nix. I don't believe that is part of my job. I believe it would be the court's or the attorney's to handle that.

Commissioner Griswold. The amount of bail that was forfeited in this case was $25 as I understand it?

Mr. Nix. Yes, sir.

Commissioner Griswold. On July 11, which is the same day, was Arthur Harmon arrested in the city of Laurel?

Mr. Nix. Arthur Harmon? If I recall correctly.

Commissioner Griswold. Do you have other copies of the record that you can hand to Chief Nix. See if that will refresh his recollection.

Mr. Nix. Yes, sir. Arthur Harmon was arrested on July 11, 1964.

Commissioner Griswold. What was the charge against Mr. Harmon?

Mr. Nix. Disturbed the peace, violent and profane language. This affidavit was signed by C. P. Cantrell who is assistant manager of Kress store at that time.

Commissioner GRISWOLD. And one of the other papers indicates that the charge is public profanity. Can you tell us what was the disposition of that case?

Chief NIX. He posted $25 cash bond and according to the records here he was find $25 in court.

Commissioner GRISWOLD. In other words, there was a $25 fine for public profanity in Laurel and a $25 cash bond for hitting a boy on the head with a baseball bat so that blood came from his mouth; is that right?

Mr. NIX. I didn't see any blood come from the boy's mouth.

Commissioner GRISWOLD. Well, let's leave the blood out then. You saw him hit him on the head with a baseball bat?

Mr. NIX. Yes, sir.

Commissioner GRISWOLD. So then I understand that piety is such in Laurel that public profanity and hitting people on the head with a bat are regarded as small offenses?

Mr. NIX. Any other charge would have had to go before the grand jury and into the State courts.

Commissioner GRISWOLD. I don't see what you mean by that. One of the things we are interested in during these hearings is the even-handed administration of justice in Mississippi or, to put it another way, how much equal protection of the law there is in Mississippi. To what degree people are treated alike in the administration of law, not merely in the courts, but by the police, regardless of their color or any other irrelevant circumstance. Here we find a case of a Negro boy being hit on the head with a baseball bat in the presence of the chief of police who personally made the arrest. The case is disposed of by a $25 bail forfeiture. And we find another man—and I don't know whether he was white or Negro, and I don't care—who was charged with public profanity, and he is fined $25. I find myself puzzled as to whether there is an equal administration of the law in Laurel, Miss.

Mr. NIX. I did not set the cash bonds on either of those.

Commissioner GRISWOLD. Do you think that forfeiture of a $25 cash bond was an appropriate disposition of the offense which was committed in your presence?

Mr. NIX. As far as I know at that time because the boy ran off. He was able to travel. He did not make any complaint. Neither did his mother.

Commissioner GRISWOLD. This offense occurred in your presence.

Mr. NIX. Yes, sir.

Commissioner GRISWOLD. Did you seek to interview the boy or his mother?

Mr. Nix. No, sir, I didn't know his mother was there. I didn't know who the boy was.

Commissioner Griswold. You think there was any way you could have found out?

Mr. Nix. Possibly was.

Commissioner Griswold. Did you make any effort to find out?

Mr. Nix. No, sir.

Commissioner Griswold. Did you regard it as any of your responsibility to find out?

Mr. Nix. I regard it as a routine.

Commissioner Griswold. Hitting people on the head with a baseball bat is routine in Laurel? Is that what I'm to understand from your answer?

Mr. Nix. This was just an assault.

Commissioner Griswold. Yes, but quite a serious assault, was it not?

Mr. Nix. If it had been any other charge on it, it would have gone into the State courts. It would have been assault with intent.

Commissioner Griswold. Now let's turn to the event of the 16th of December when you or one of your officers arrested John P. Foster. Do you recall the event at the Pinehurst Cafe?

Mr. Nix. I know of the event, yes, sir.

Commissioner Griswold. The complaint of which I have a copy here says: "Willfully and unlawfully, with intent to provoke a breach of the peace, refused to leave the Pinehurst Coffee Shop after being asked by affiant, being a duly authorized representative of said place." Now, do you understand that complaint and charge and offense of the law?

Mr. Nix. Any charges that are made, I am obligated to serve them, not to prove them.

Commissioner Griswold. Not unless they state a legal offense?

Mr. Nix. I believe that——

Commissioner Griswold. If somebody filed an affidavit with you and said, "I hereby complain against John Smith because he didn't talk to me when he passed me on the sidewalk this morning," you wouldn't serve it, would you?

Mr. Nix. If the same charge was made against you in Laurel, Miss., I would be obliged to serve it.

Commissioner Griswold. The charge that I wouldn't talk to somebody when I passed him on the sidewalk?

Mr. Nix. No, sir; the same charge stated in there.

Commissioner Griswold. The charge I am referring to is the one here, and I'm simply asking you whether you understand this charge in this complaint to state a violation of the law? "Willfully and unlawfully with intent to provoke a breach of the peace, refused to leave the Pinehurst Coffee Shop after being asked by the affiant." Now, do you understand that to be a violation of the law?

Mr. Nix. I believe that's up to the courts, the judge, to decide on that, sir. I can't set myself up as a judge.

Commissioner Griswold. Do you have any obligation to enforce the Federal law in Mississippi?

Mr. Nix. My obligations are to enforce State laws, local ordinances, and to preserve the peace.

Commissioner Griswold. And to ignore Federal law?

Mr. Nix. No, sir.

Commissioner Griswold. Have you heard of the Civil Rights Act?

Mr. Nix. I have no civil authorities—criminal—until it becomes criminal.

Commissioner Griswold. I'm only talking about criminal charges. Have you heard of the Civil Rights Act?

Mr. Nix. Yes, sir.

Commissioner Griswold. Have you heard of the public accommodations provisions of the Civil Rights Act?

Mr. Nix. Yes, sir.

Commissioner Griswold. Do you regard them as law in Mississippi?

Mr. Nix. Yes, sir.

Commissioner Griswold. Do you regard it as your responsibility to enforce them in Mississippi?

Mr. Nix. I don't believe I can enforce the segregation or the desegregation of a place.

Commissioner Griswold. Have you not taken an oath to support and defend the Constitution of the United States?

Mr. Nix. Yes.

Commissioner Griswold. Do you not regard that oath as binding?

Mr. Nix. Yes, sir.

Commissioner Griswold. Well, I would suggest to you that you consult your counsel on the question whether a warrant or complaint such as this does state an offense under the laws of Mississippi, including the Constitution of the United States. It is quite plain, I believe, that under the Civil Rights Act, the statute of Mississippi which you were undertaking to enforce in this case is invalid and was invalid on the day in December when you served this warrant.

Mr. Nix. I was only serving the warrant. I believe it's the court's obligation to decide whether or not the charges are in order.

Commissioner Griswold. Well, I suggest to you that you have some responsibility to decide whether a complaint states an offense, which I tried to illustrate by my foolish complaint that someone wouldn't talk to me as I walked down the street. Now, this is not a technical matter. This is a matter which has been much publicized over the past 6 months and has in fact been decided by the Supreme Court of the United States. Do you regard yourself as bound by decisions of the Supreme Court of the United States?

Mr. NIX. To the extent of carrying out State laws and local ordinances.

Commissioner GRISWOLD. Well, I suggest you seek advice as to the effect of the decisions of the Supreme Court of the United States on the statute which you sought to enforce in that case.

Mr. NIX. Well, I would like to say this. That in this instance we had a call to this establishment. We don't know what happened prior to our arriving at the establishment, so I believe that it would be up to the affiant to prove whether or not there was any disturbance there.

Commissioner GRISWOLD. There's no disturbances indicated in the complaint. The complaint is "willfully, and unlawfully, with intent to provoke a breach of the peace," no suggestion that a breach of the peace occurred. "With intent to provoke the breach of the peace refused to leave the Pinehurst Coffee Shop after being asked by the affiant." I suggest that you seek advice from your proper legal counsel as to whether that constitutes an offense and as to whether you should hereafter serve such a complaint.

Chairman HANNAH. Mr. Patterson?

Vice Chairman PATTERSON. Chief, you said that things were better now in Laurel. You felt that Negroes could be served in public accommondations with less trouble than before.

Mr. NIX. Yes, sir. Latter part of last week several places did serve them.

Vice Chairman PATTERSON. Why do you think this improvement has taken place?

Mr. NIX. Things have just more or less leveled off. We don't have the influx of people downtown who are standing around that we one time had.

Vice Chairman PATTERSON. Have you had any expression of conviction or opinion by your community leadership and business leadership that you think might have had some effect on the public attitude?

Mr. NIX. We have had the Chamber of Commerce and all working toward more unity between the two races and I believe that it has had quite a big effect on it.

Vice Chairman PATTERSON. Chief, does a thing like that help you in the enforcement of the law in a community?

Mr. Nix. What is that?

Vice Chairman Patterson. This expression on the part of the community's leaders?

Mr. Nix. Yes, sir.

Vice Chairman Patterson. Does that help you as a law enforcement officer in your job?

Mr. Nix. Yes, sir.

Vice Chairman Patterson. Thank you.

Chairman Hannah. Mr. Rogerson?

Mr. Rogerson. Chief, I'm a little confused about your concern about bringing a charge in this McGill case that would put you in the State court. You seemed to indicate that this would be a big problem. Now, we have heard some testimony in assault cases since we have been here and have heard about this assault which would constitute a felony where there is intent. Perhaps you can state it for us, what intent is necessary for an assault to constitute a felony?

Mr. Nix. Assault with intent to kill, is that what you have in mind?

Mr. Rogerson. Well, is that the Mississippi law?

Mr. Nix. Yes, a felony, assault which constitutes a felony.

Mr. Rogerson. Well, we have also heard from others that where there might be doubt the tendency would be to bring the greater charge. Is that a common practice, where there is reasonable doubt as to whether it should be a misdemeanor charge or felony charge?

Mr. Nix. I didn't see any reasonable doubt at that time.

Mr. Rogerson. You didn't. What was the charge that you made?

Mr. Nix. Assault.

Mr. Rogerson. Would you read the charge?

Mr. Nix. It's an assault. One thing I would like to say. Maybe it would clear that thing up just a little for you. On this charge we are limited to misdemeanors in our courts, and in the State courts a case would have to be initiated by the parties involved of which I would be a witness in.

Mr. Rogerson. I have trouble with that, chief. Let's say you saw a murder committed in your presence. The person is dead. There was a victim. Perhaps you didn't catch the individual or perhaps you did, but let's say you did catch the individual. You would have no recourse to your State courts on the felony charge of murder?

Mr. Nix. That would be carried as felony report into the grand jury with action on it.

Mr. Rogerson. The machine is there and you are the one who touches off the machinery, whether it goes into your police courts or higher courts.

Mr. Nix. At that time I did not think that it constituted a felony.

Mr. Rogerson. All right. As I remember it, the charge was that this man hit this child with a stick, isn't that the way it is written, with a stick?

Mr. Nix. Yes.

Mr. Rogerson. Now the fact that a man hit a child with a baseball bat—now it wasn't a full-sized bat, it was a child's bat. But it was a club, it seems to me.

Mr. Nix. This was not a small child.

Mr. Rogerson. Eleven years old. I don't know how large they grow in Mississippi, but it was a child.

Mr. Nix. He was a pretty good-sized boy. I would like to say I wouldn't know who he was if he walked up here now.

Mr. Rogerson. Well, isn't it also true that to determine what the intent was in an assault case, the seriousness of the injury is relevant?

Mr. Nix. I believe that if the boy had been confined to the hospital, in a serious condition, there would have been a full investigation of it and turned over to the State courts.

Mr. Rogerson. You didn't try to find the child or determine the extent of injuries? I think you testified to that?

Mr. Nix. Yes.

Chairman Hannah. Mr. Finkelstein?

Mr. Finkelstein. Chief, do you know what the bond was in the Pinehurst Coffee Shop case?

Mr. Nix. Yes. I believe they set those for a hundred dollars.

Mr. Finkelstein. $100?

Mr. Nix. $100, I believe.

Mr. Finkelstein. Was that for $100 for each person?

Mr. Nix. Yes.

Mr. Finkelstein. And, what was the bond again in the baseball bat case?

Mr. Nix. $25.

Mr. Finkelstein. Do you think it is appropriate, chief, that the bond in the so-called breach of peace cases should have been four times as high as the bond in the assault case?

Mr. Nix. I didn't set the bonds. As a matter of fact, when the bond was set for the boy that was arrested at Kress, I was still around Kress's.

Mr. Finkelstein. Did you make any recommendation with respect to the bond?

Mr. Nix. No, sir. We have a list up there to go by on those bonds.

Mr. Finkelstein. And, does the list indicate breach of peace at $100?

Mr. Nix. That's the top, I believe.

Mr. Finkelstein. And, does it list assault with a weapon as $25?

Mr. Nix. From $10 to a hundred dollars.

Mr. Finkelstein. No further questions.

Chairman Hannah. Further questions?

Thank you very much, Mr. Nix. You are excused.

(Witness excused.)

Mr. Taylor. The next testimony concerns events occuring at the Masonite Company. Mr. Wolf will give us a statement on that.

Chairman Hannah. Mr. Wolf, will you make your statement?

Mr. Wolf. This is the conclusion of the staff report which I began a few moments ago.

The Masonite plant in Laurel employs about 2,800 men. Prior to 1964 the plant was entirely segregated. In March 1964, the signs over the drinking fountains and the restrooms were taken down and the seniority lists at the plant were integrated.

Four Negro employees at Masonite were the victims of Klan violence during March and April. Two of them had crosses burned at their homes after they used formerly white drinking fountains. The other two Negro employees had been promoted to new nontraditional jobs. One man had a cross burned on his lawn and received a telephone threat, "You got your warning and you had better straighten up at Masonite."

Another Negro had a cross burned on his lawn. Two weeks later, three rifle shots were fired at his home. The following day he reported the incident to the sheriff, and shortly after he returned home two shotgun blasts were fired at his home. At this time I would like to introduce into the record the staff report of investigations of racial violence in Jones County, Mississippi.

Chairman Hannah. The report is of record.

(Exhibit No. 15 was marked for identification and received in evidence.)

Call the next witness, Mr. Taylor.

Mr. Taylor. The next witness is Mr. Ottis Matthews.

Chairman Hannah. Mr. Matthews, will you raise your right hand.

(Whereupon, Mr. Ottis Matthews was duly sworn by the Chairman and testified as follows:)

Chairman Hannah. Mr. Taylor?

TESTIMONY OF MR. OTTIS MATTHEWS, JONES COUNTY, MISS.

Mr. TAYLOR. Mr. Matthews, will you give your full name and residence?

Mr. MATTHEWS. I am Ottis Matthews and I live at Route 4, Laurel.

Mr. TAYLOR. What is your occupation, sir?

Mr. MATTHEWS. I am employed at Masonite, but currently I'm on leave of absence, and I'm serving as assistant business agent at Local 5443, IWA, International Woodworkers of America. I hold the elective office of financial secretary and I'm a member of the Negotiating Committee.

Mr. TAYLOR. Would you describe briefly what your duties are as business agent for the IWA local?

Mr. MATTHEWS. It principally involves administering the contract, but I perform any other duties related to my work.

Mr. TAYLOR. During the summer of 1964 did the Masonite management in your union discuss any steps for dealing with racial integration of the job departments or job lines at the plant?

Mr. MATTHEWS. Mr. Dean Thatcher, who is the vice president, general manager of the Mississippi operations called me to his office. Present were Mr. Labyrds, Ed Labyrds, who is manager of industrial relations, and one of his assistants, Mr. Louis Cater, and a lawyer by the name of Culman, and they told me they had received an order from the President's Commission on Equal Opportunity that required them to integrate the plant.

Mr. TAYLOR. What was decided as a result of these discussions?

Mr. MATTHEWS. They asked me did I intend to carry the integration out, and I wouldn't advise them until they stated their intent. And they stated they did, so I told them the Union would co-operate. We decided at that time to approach the Governor, the Lieutenant Governor, the mayor, the police officials, and a list of the news medium and tell them what we were going to do and see if they had any alternative so that we wouldn't get in a public squabble. I also requested that he call in his managerial force and tell them the occasion and tell them that there was no alternative and that we agreed that we wouldn't attempt to take advantage of the situation by accusing each side as being at fault. The rest of the plant integration occurred at later dates principally with Mr. Louis Cater.

Mr. TAYLOR. So it was decided to take some particular steps to prove equal opportunity at the plant?

Mr. MATTHEWS. That's correct.

Mr. TAYLOR. Now, did you have any trouble or opposition to these steps?

Mr. MATTHEWS. Not to my knowledge, that was overt, that came out in the open, but I learned there was a great deal going on, you might say, behind the scene. There were a number of things that did occur. I wouldn't know whether you are asking for them now or not.

Mr. TAYLOR. Well, was there a unit of the Ku Klux Klan active at the plant?

Mr. MATTHEWS. I believe their organizational drive really began after the date set for integration of the plant. The plant has also been partially integrated, but it was partially segregated as well. The segregation was a result between colored leaders and the white leadership at the union because we do have integrated plants in that local union, and the local union is not segregated and has never been. But, at that time when they did actually get full rights, they began to appear in their organizational leaflets that identified themselves as the white knights, the Ku Klux Klan, and a great deal of indirect activity began right at that time.

Mr. TAYLOR. Was the Klan unit actively recruiting members in the plant?

Mr. MATTHEWS. I couldn't say of my own knowledge, but the evidence all pointed that they got a great many members of the plant.

Mr. TAYLOR. Were they distributing literature intending to have that effect?

Mr. MATTHEWS. Yes, and they carried it in and distributed it in several points in the mail.

Mr. TAYLOR. Did Klan elements challenge the leadership of your union?

Mr. MATTHEWS. Yes, on three or four occasions. One occurred at the time we were running for reelection and, of course, there were always other things involved other than segregation in a union election or integration, and we won that by a small majority. There was a challenge to the election and we won that by substantial majority, by four to one. And then we had one occasion immediately after I was beaten up, and we made the issue personal and direct and we won that by a four to one margin.

Mr. TAYLOR. The election events occurred during the summer of 1964, is that right?

Mr. MATTHEWS. Best of my knowledge about the last week in August and first week in September.

Mr. TAYLOR. During the course of this election campaign had you been openly critical of the Klan?

Mr. MATTHEWS. Very openly critical. I referred to them as drunks and the drags of the society. I also stated that they were led by business people that didn't have the laboring people's interest at heart.

I accused them of meeting in secrecy and laying plans and enticing people into things they didn't know about, and over a period of weeks I must have said a great deal more, too. I'm not very quiet.

Mr. TAYLOR. We understand that on November 16 you were attacked. Could you tell us briefly about what occurred on that evening?

Mr. MATTHEWS. I held the union meeting due to the absence of Mr. Jolly, the president, and as far as I can remember it was a routine union meeting. But afterwards they first wanted to see me about a problem, and I went to my office with him. When I finished I came out and a small group of people were discussing civil rights in the waiting room there in the union hall. I sat down and joined them. Conversation mostly revolved around what effect it would have on Mississippi, and the best I remember I took the view that Mississippians were big enough that this thing wouldn't drown Mississippi, that we had the intelligence and the strength to live in such society and whether we did or not we had it to do.

We talked about the way things used to be and the way they are now because it seemed to us that integration was a little better way long ago than it has been in the last few years. But when we were all done with the conversation, I went to my car and frankly had nothing on my mind. But as I went over a railroad track on a long stretch of road heading towards a creek, I noticed a car's lights blink behind me. It attracted me because it was unusual, and it did it three or four times. I said, "Now if there are signaling somebody, they will be blocking this bridge," and just before I got to the bridge the lights came on, and a car was parked. Somebody blocked the bridge. I drove up and there's a man bent over looking under the hood. And this car behind came up immediately behind me, a man ran up front, yanked open the door and shoved a gun in my face.

Some got in the front and back. They tied my hands and drove, put a blindfold over me, over my eyes. They drove me a short distance into a dump ground. They pulled me out of the car and asked me did I know who they were. I said,"No, I don't."

"Well," they said, "you have been talking about some organizations, hadn't you?"

I said, "Well, I don't know."

He said, "Well, such as the Ku Klux Klan and you have been calling them some names and some of them are not even members of the Ku Klux Klan." He said, "Do you know who we are now?"

I told them that I did, so they layed me down on the ground—tore my pants off and laid me down on the ground and began to administer a beating along with a lecture on keeping my mouth shut. I was told to quit my activities, that I had been engaged in, and at one point I told them that if they didn't quit beating me they were going to kill me, but they continued a short time. When he finished, he told me, "Now from here out you keep your mouth shut." They cut the wires on my——one of the wires off from my spark plugs, tore the others loose and advised me to lay there 5 minutes. The others left while one stood over me and eventually he left.

I got up and drove part of the way home. And while I was trying to decide what I was going to do, about half way there I decided that I would rather be dead than to have people know they beat me up and I ran from it. So I went back, searched the area and went home and called the sheriff. The deputy came and carried me to the clinic where I was treated. The beating was severe enough, they tore my underclothes off. And I was trailed to the clinic very obviously and I was treated at the clinic.

Mr. TAYLOR. After the beating what did the union do?

Mr. MATTHEWS. I'm afraid we took quite an exception to it. We put an ad reciting what had happened and stated in the ad that if these people wished to join a law-abiding community and help us build the community, we invited them to join us. If they didn't, then we were going to put them in the cemetery and we meant it. I sent you a copy of that. I meant to bring it, but I don't have it with me.

Mr. TAYLOR. What's the situation today?

Mr. MATTHEWS. Up until a very short time ago it was continual harassment of my family, my friends, and my neighbors. After I cornered some of them and advised them that I was looking for them to try again, why they stayed away from me personally. But for a short period of time there seems to have been a truce of some sort.

Mr. TAYLOR. Just in the past few weeks or so?

Mr. MATTHEWS. Yes, you can name it in weeks.

Mr. TAYLOR. During the period of time when you were harassed, did you take any steps for your own protection?

Mr. MATTHEWS. Yes. I go armed, and it is loaded at all times. And everyone in my family is a fairly good shot, too. My wife is not very scared, although they generally stay where it would be illegal to shoot.

Mr. TAYLOR. Thank you.

Chairman HANNAH. Father Hesburgh?

Commissioner HESBURGH. Mr. Matthews, will you describe what kind of people these are? I'm not talking about their names or anything of that sort, but what kind of people do things like this?

Mr. MATTHEWS. They are mentally defective. It generally shows up in alcoholism or pomposity, bully-type people. And some of them are businessmen and should be better type of people than that. They seem to be getting something personal out of it, whether it is money, prestige or what, I don't know, if you can say prestige.

Commissioner HESBURGH. You think this type of person generally can be spotted in the community?

Mr. MATTHEWS. I think they are well known.

Commissioner HESBURGH. Why doesn't the community do something about it?

Mr. MATTHEWS. I wouldn't be able to answer that question. The union did do something and that's as far as our authority goes. As citizens we are in too small a minority to have any effect.

Commissioner HESBURGH. But these people are like a government within a government and try to rule people by fear and force.

Mr. MATTHEWS. No question about that. And they also try to take over key positions, which is what they intend to do, to take over key positions.

Commissioner HESBURGH. What is their main motivation—hatred or what?

Mr. MATTHEWS. I don't think so. I observe them being more friendly with the Negro than I am. I think that they want power, money, same motivation that drives most people.

Commissioner HESBURGH. Thank you.

Chairman HANNAH. Mrs. Freeman?

Commissioner FREEMAN. Mr. Matthews, there are about 2,800 employees of the Masonite company, are there not?

Mr. MATTHEWS. That's approximately correct.

Commissioner FREEMAN. And the union represents all of them?

Mr. MATTHEWS. Yes.

Commissioner FREEMAN. And the position that has been taken by the union is to receive the endorsement of the majority of the membership?

Mr. MATTHEWS. The vast majority of the membership, and it's 100 percent, accepted whether it is liked or not.

Commissioner FREEMAN. And these plants continue to be integrated?

Mr. MATTHEWS. It is totally integrated. There are some areas that takes time to straighten out because you can't go by some areas, but we do not have any segregation.

Chairman HANNAH. Dean Griswold?

Commisioner GRISWOLD. What proportion of the employees are white and what proportion are Negro?

Mr. MATTHEWS. At the time we kept such records we had agreements that compelled one-third of them to be colored, but we ordered those types of records abolished and I don't keep them any more. I don't know.

Commissioner GRISWOLD. You think it is still approximately one-third?

Mr. MATTHEWS. It still should be. There's a normal turnover and I don't know whether that turnover has reflected a change in balance or not.

Commissioner GRISWOLD. Are both Negroes and white people members of your union?

Mr. MATTHEWS. Yes.

Commissioner GRISWOLD. You represent all the employees in the plant?

Mr. MATTHEWS. As the boys say, if they pay $4, I represent them. [Laughter.]

Commissioner GRISWOLD. You reported this beating to the sheriff as I understand it?

Mr. MATTHEWS. That's correct.

Commissioner GRISWOLD. Do you feel that you have had good cooperation from the sheriff's office?

Mr. MATTHEWS. I got good cooperation from all law enforcement agencies. They have been very active.

Commissioner GRISWOLD. And yet, as far as I have heard, no arrests have been made?

Mr. MATTHEWS. No, there hasn't. It would be a difficult case, but the investigation I know is very active still at this time.

Chairman HANNAH. Dr. Rankin?

Commissioner RANKIN. The corporation was asked to integrate its union, am I correct?

Mr. MATTHEWS. No, it wasn't asked to integrate its unions. The union was integrated before it began. But, we had an agreement with the company that certain jobs belonged to the colored and certain jobs would be white. Now, they wasn't all colored on the bottom and white on the top. It was a fairly cross section of the mill. And to that extent we were segregated and to the extent that we had a colored sublocal.

Commissioner RANKIN. I see. The corporation might lose Government contracts unless it completed the integration, is that correct?

Mr. MATTHEWS. Well, that's true, but that wasn't our concern. We knew this had to be done and it was just merely pick the right time because we see the law changing.

Commissioner RANKIN. And if the corporation lost business it would mean a loss of jobs or working hours?

Mr. MATTHEWS. You couldn't sell masonite in these United States unless you integrated that plant.

Commissioner RANKIN. Now, you must have become an expert on the Klan. Can you tell me the difference between the United Klan and the United White Knights of the Ku Klux Klan?

Mr. MATTHEWS. The difference I found is they both tell the same lies to each other.

[Laughter.]

Commissioner RANKIN. One is not worse than the other or more reprehensible than the other? Is one open and the other secret or are both secret?

Mr. MATTHEWS. They don't even let each other know what they are doing.

Commissioner RANKIN. They generally operate in groups of six in attacks upon a single individual; is that correct?

Mr. MATTHEWS. I doubt if six of them would tackle anybody over 11 years old. It is generally in 10 or 15, and they normally make sure he is unarmed, that there's no witnesses, and that he's caught completely by surprise.

Commissioner RANKIN. One last question. Did the corporation management take any interest in these events?

Mr. MATTHEWS. I secured their cooperation in checking defenses because these people, in my opinion, were supposed to be on the job while they were out committing these offenses. They closed up several unofficial gates all around the plants.

Commissioner RANKIN. Well, you really received support from management. Did you or did you not, or did the Ku Klux receive support from the management?

Mr. MATTHEWS. The top management in that plant I consider to be honest men, and I don't believe they were in it. But when you get below that level, yes, sir, I believe there were supervisors that belong to the Klan.

Chairman HANNAH. Mr. Patterson?

Vice Chairman PATTERSON. Mr. Matthews, you indicated in your testimony that you think there are some reasonable, respectable people who are using these fellows, like the ones who beat you up, because they don't have the working people's interest at heart?

Mr. MATTHEWS. I didn't say respectable people. I said business people.

[Laughter.]

Vice Chairman PATTERSON. My question is this: Do you think there are still communities in Mississippi where the business people are doing that?

Mr. MATTHEWS. Would you mind repeating that? I missed the last.

Vice Chairman PATTERSON. Do you think there are any particular communities in Mississippi—I'm not asking you to name them—where this is still going on, where men like those who beat you up are being encouraged by men who are using them?

Mr. MATTHEWS. Yes, sir.

Vice Chairman PATTERSON. Do you think the men like those who beat you up know it, or do you think they don't know what they are doing?

Mr. MATTHEWS. I don't think they are too intelligent or they wouldn't belong to the Klan in the first place.

Vice Chairman PATTERSON. Thank you.

Chairman HANNAH. Father Hesburgh, do you have one more question?

Commissioner HESBURGH. I was just curious, Mr. Matthews, about the response of the law enforcement officials when you told them the union was going to defend itself.

Mr. MATTHEWS. They did not object to us defending ourselves. They cautioned against the carrying of guns which is their duty, but they, as far as I know, they are completely free of Klan influence. I know they have rejected the help from people they suspected of being Klansmen and, frankly, I have a great deal of respect for them if the people would support them.

Commissioner HESBURGH. Are the law enforcement officials generally supported by the better elements in the community?

Mr. MATTHEWS. They would have to answer that question because I circulate so little that I don't know.

Commissioner HESBURGH. And one last question. Is it likely that these people are going to be brought to justice, these people who beat you?

Mr. MATTHEWS. We are going to exert every influence to see that they are brought to justice and tried because I was talking of self-defense to prevent any further beatings, but the only way you will ever have a good community is trial.

Commissioner HESBURGH. And you don't think this type of person should be walking around loose?

Mr. MATTHEWS. Certainly not.

Commissioner HESBURGH. Thank you.

Chairman HANNAH. That's all, Mr. Matthews. Thank you very much.

(Witness excused.)

Chairman HANNAH. It has been a long day, but we are going to call one more witness. We request the audience to be a little more quiet than they were yesterday as we came toward the end of the day. They began to move around, and it became a confused setting. We are going to call one more witness and then recess until tomorrow morning. The documents that have been subpenaed to be presented at the close of today will be put over until tomorrow, and will be so received at 9 o'clock. Mr. Taylor, will you call the last witness of the day?

Mr. TAYLOR. Mr. Claude Ramsay.

Chairman HANNAH. Mr. Ramsay, will you raise your right hand?

(Whereupon, Mr. Claude Ramsay was duly sworn by the Chairman and testified as follows:)

Chairman HANNAH. Mr. Taylor?

TESTIMONY OF MR. CLAUDE RAMSAY, JACKSON COUNTY, MISS.

Mr. TAYLOR. Mr. Ramsay, will you give your name, address, and occupation for the record?

Mr. RAMSAY. My name is Claude Ramsay. My address is Route 1, Pascagoula, Miss. I am president of the Mississippi AFL-CIO.

Mr. TAYLOR. How long have you lived in Mississippi, Mr. Ramsay?

Mr. RAMSAY. All of my life. My family is one of the older families in this State. As a matter of fact, they moved here before the State was chartered in 1808.

Mr. TAYLOR. You heard Mr. Matthews tell us about the difficulties that the local of the Woodworkers had in Laurel. To your knowledge do other union locals in Mississippi experience difficulties with extremist groups?

Mr. RAMSAY. Yes. We have a real problem in this State with the extremist groups trying to infiltrate the trade union movement, the churches, PTA's and other organizations. They don't necessarily all belong to the Klan.

Mr. TAYLOR. Can you tell us about it with respect to unions in particular?

Mr. RAMSAY. Unions in particular. Well, we have the John Birch Society rather active in Mississippi, and this group is operating very much as the Communists did in the early 1930's. They infiltrate your organization, create turmoil in your meetings, try to run your good members off, and eventually take over control of the organization. Of course I think, as Mr. Matthews pointed out, some of the problems they have had with the Klan groups, but these other groups are doing the same thing as well.

Mr. TAYLOR. You have mentioned the John Birch Society and the Klan. Are there any others involved?

Mr. RAMSAY. Well, as far as I know the group was touched on here this morning or was it this afternoon by the people from Natchez. That group in that particular area of the State as I understand it has infiltrated some of our unions in that particular area.

Mr. TAYLOR. What kind of success have groups of this kind had with their efforts to infiltrate and take over unions?

Mr. RAMSAY. Well, it's a little bit difficult to tell really. We have a number of local unions where we have reason to believe that these groups have got control of the organization, but at the present time I don't think they actually have control of too many of them. But they are active in a number of them. They are trying to get control at the present time.

Mr. TAYLOR. Do the activities of these groups interfere with your efforts at union organization in the State?

Mr. RAMSEY. Absolutely. We have a tremendous problem created by the atmosphere that has developed by these groups. They start out with a base of racial prejudice, but it don't take them long to move elsewhere. Now, I would like to say this. That we have been discussing this question of civil rights and applying only to the Negroes. In the State of Mississippi we have civil rights of white people being invaded and trampled upon. We have an organization today, International Brotherhood of Electrical Workers, that have a suit in the Federal courts at the present time because the civil rights of one of their organizers has been invaded. In an organizing campaign just south of here in Simpson County, and if you have the time I would like to read part of that suit, the points raised.

Mr. TAYLOR. Time is a little bit short and I would be glad to receive it for the record.

Mr. RAMSAY. We can put it in the record. Okay, let's do that.

Chairman HANNAH. Would you summarize it in a sentence or two, and we will receive the whole document.

Mr. RAMSAY. There's only a couple points I wanted to really read. It won't take but just a minute. I think that you need to hear this. These are the questions posed in the suit.

On March 11, 1964, two police officers identifying themselves as representatives of the sheriff's office of Simpson County, Miss., willfully and without justification prevented plaintiffs from peacefully distributing printed handbills on a public thoroughfare at the exit from the Universal plant in Simpson County, Miss.

On April 29, 1964, Mississippi State highway patrolmen, acting in concert with Universal's agents, willfully and without justification humiliated, harassed, and intimidated plaintiffs while they were distributing handbills on a public thoroughfare near the Universal plant, successfully preventing such distribution.

On May 24, 1964, defendants Mann, Grum, Lewis, Welch, and others whose identities are not now known to plaintiffs, identifying themselves as citizens of Simpson County, Miss., invaded plaintiff's lodgings in Simpson County and informed plaintiffs Fiering and Wicklife that they would be killed or injured if they did not cease organizing Universal's place, and if they did not leave Simpson County within 12 hours.

On May 2, 1964, despite repeated requests for protection, defendant Harold Varner willfully and without justification refused to furnish protection to the plaintiffs by threats made against them by defendants, Mann, Grum, Lewis, Welch, and others, thereby requiring plaintiffs to comply with the ultimatum of the mob. I would like to give you a copy of this and have the thing tendered into the record.

Chairman HANNAH. Received. (Exhibit No. 16 was marked for identification and received in evidence.)

Mr. TAYLOR. Without going into any details of this, Mr. Ramsay, I would like to know whether you think there is any relationship between incidents of violence or harassment directed at union organizing efforts and such incidents directed against Negroes?

Mr. RAMSAY. Yes, there's no question about that, I don't think. You see, lot of the plants have got some of them—racial movement and employment will run close to 50 percent. We organize them all, the black and the white. And in order to keep organization out, these groups move in and create dissension. This is one of their motives.

Mr. TAYLOR. What is the Labor Council of the AFL–CIO doing to help locals resist these continuing efforts by these extremist groups?

Mr. RAMSAY. We don't view this thing as being just a labor problem. We view them as being a State problem, a problem affecting all of the people in this State. And I might say that I'm very much encouraged at the present time concerning the recent action of the business community, the leadership of this State, the political leadership of this State. If these people had come forward and stated about 3 years ago, we wouldn't have the problems we have today. They are the ones that can solve them. I would like to cite you an incident we had happen in the city of Pascagoula, my hometown, about 3 years ago. All of you are familiar with the Oxford situation which happened on the campus of the university. We happen to have in that town one of the better newspapers. A paper that was friendly to the trade union movement. The editor of that paper wrote a series of editorials condemning the action on the campus of the university. After the sheriff had come back to Jackson County from the Oxford fiasco, a group of thugs, part of an organization similar to the Klan, and proceeded to terrorize that community. The windows of that building were shot out, the life of the editor was threatened.

They were holding meetings in the courthouse. I was in and out of there most of the time on weekends when I got in there. I checked with the—the political leadership as to why didn't it move in and do something about this. They were all intimidated to the point that they wouldn't open their mouths. I made arrangements to meet with the Metal Trades Council, the group bargaining group and shipyards, and went before that group and told them what a few of the facts of life were.

The Ingall Shipbuilding Corp. is a major industry in that town. They have had, of course they have gone in compliance since that time with Executive Order, but the fact remains that most of the work in that yard was subsidized with Federal funds to one degree or another. And I certainly knew that if we had a serious racial disturbance in this county that this shipyard would possibly shut down, and this is what I told the people in this meeting. As a result I called the editor of the paper and gave him the text of my remarks, which I won't read because of the time, but I would like for it to be shown in the record the part concerning the movement designed to destroy, found on page 7.

I would like to read you part of what he had to say in his foreword to this booklet, this is the series of editorials he wrote. He won the Pulitzer Prize as a result of the editorials. I want to read you this. This was 3 years ago.

The only person to speak publicly in favor of the Chronicle was Claude Ramsay, a Jackson County resident who is president of the Mississippi Labor Council, AFL–CIO. Ramsay's address to the Pascagoula Metal Trades Council is subject of the editorial on page 7. The U.S. Justice Department announced in Washington that it had ordered the FBI to conduct an investigation to determine if the civil rights of the Chronicle's editor to speak were being violated.

Mr. TAYLOR. That was Mr. Harkey?

Mr. RAMSAY. Mr. Harkey. His were the editorials I referred to.

Mr. TAYLOR. Just one last question: Do you feel you now have some company in this fight?

Mr. RAMSAY. Well, I feel better now than I have felt for some time. I'd be honest with you about it. It's pretty lonesome out there by yourself when you are trying to do it. I have got some things I want to get into since I have got up here. You asked me what we have been doing. It is unfortunate that I have got to get here at the tail end of the thing. I brought a stock of things along as you can see.

Chairman HANNAH. Can't we receive these things in the record?

Mr. RAMSAY. Right. To start with I have the proceedings of the Mississippi AFL–CIO. I have got several things marked in here that I would very much have liked for you to get into the record.

Chairman HANNAH. If you mark them and deliver them we will put them in the record.

Mr. RAMSAY. All right. The main thing here that I really want to get in here is a resolution adopted by us at our last convention branding these groups for what they are. That's the main thing. I have got some speeches. Our last convention made a sincere effort to put this situation in its proper prospective.

Chairman HANNAH. We commend you, Mr. Ramsay, and Mr. Matthews for your attitude.

Are there any questions the Commissioners would like to ask?

Commissioner HESBURGH. Just one quickly. Mr. Ramsay, you have been involved in this a long time in this State. Everything you said gets back to violence, trying to overturn a normal progression in government and in other organizations.

Mr. RAMSAY. Yes.

Commissioner HESBURGH. What's the answer to this? What is your recipe for getting rid of this problem the moment it appears?

Mr. RAMSAY. I think, as I told you, I'm more encouraged now than ever before now that the business leadership has taken the position that we have to have law and order in the State. It has taken a certain amount of courage in this State to be in favor of law and order. The way these people operate campaigns of hate and intimidation, you can't blame some of them. It has been pretty rough on me. I have been threatened on numerous occasions. So far they haven't caught me and run me off like they have Matthews. But, steps have been taken recently, the position of the M.E.C., the Manufacturers Association and now the position taken by the Governor. Now, my only thinking about this is that I hope the Governor and applications of the laws of this State will make sure that the rights of trade union members are also protected.

Commissioner HESBURGH. You haven't answered my question, really. My question is, what would you do the moment violence arises in a community in this State?

Mr. RAMSAY. What would I do?

Commissioner HESBURGH. Well, what do you think has to be done to quell it immediately?

Mr. RAMSAY. There's not any question this is on the shoulder of the local law enforcement agencies and if they don't put it down they are themselves negligent of their duties.

Commissioner HESBURGH. What about the business community, the people that wink at it, the people that let it go and are afraid to speak out. What about them?

Mr. RAMSAY. Of course, they hold the key to the whole thing. There is no question that the business people hold the key to the solving this State's only problems.

Commissioner HESBURGH. And if they say there is a violation and prosecute it immediately, do you think that would be good?

Mr. RAMSAY. I think so.

Commissioner HESBURGH. Has anyone ever been arrested here for handing out Klan literature?

Mr. RAMSAY. Not to my knowledge. They have been arrested around here for handing out union literature.

Commissioner HESBURGH. What about COFO and other organizations?

Mr. RAMSAY. I want to give you a couple of city ordinances.
[Laughter.]

Chairman HANNAH. You give them to the clerk. We will put them in the record.

Mr. RAMSAY. All right. I might say that I notice there have been some comment lately about Congress investigating the Klan. You had Congressman Weltner from Atlanta making that suggestion, and I would like to suggest that we have some other groups added to that list that needs to be investigated in the State of Mississippi. I'm referring to the Birch Society in particular. These are the people that create the climate for the violence that we are having in this State, even though they themselves might not be doing any violence. I have one ordinance here from the city of Canton where it cost a labor union organizer a thousand dollars to organize in Canton, Miss. I have an ordinance here from the city of Jackson where we had some union representatives arrested as a result of passing out union literature at some of the plants in this area. The same union that is carrying this case to court has this one in the courts also to establish the fact also that this is unconstitutional.

Chairman HANNAH. They will be put in the record.

Chairman HANNAH. Mr. Taylor, do you have any further questions?

Mr. TAYLOR. No further questions.

Mr. RAMSAY. As part of our campaign to try to get down the influence of the right wing extremists in this State, we have filed a suit, objections with Federal Communications systems that the license of a certain TV station in this State not be renewed. The facilities of this station have been used for years in the past as a propaganda outlet for extremists of the far right. I want to give you a copy of that petition and ask that exhibit 2, ground 3 be placed into the record.

Chairman HANNAH. Mr. Ramsay, we receive it and are grateful to you for your testimony.

Thank you very much and you are excused.

(Witness excused.)

Chairman HANNAH. Today's hearings is adjourned.

(Whereupon, at 5:10 p.m. the hearing was adjourned until the following day at 9:30 a.m.)

FRIDAY MORNING SESSION, FEBRUARY 19, 1965

The Commission met in the recreation hall, Veterans Administration Center, 1500 East Woodrow Wilson Drive, Jackson, Miss., at 9:30 a.m., Friday, February 19, 1965, the Hon. John A. Hannah, Chairman of the Commission, presiding.

Present: John A. Hannah, Chairman; Eugene Patterson, Vice Chairman; Mrs. Frankie Muse Freeman, Commissioner; Erwin N. Griswold, Commissioner; Rev. Theodore M. Hesburgh, C.S.C., Commissioner; Robert S. Rankin, Commissioner.

Also Present: Howard W. Rogerson, Acting Staff Director; William L. Taylor, General Counsel; Samuel J. Simmons, Director of Field Services; Warren I. Cikins, special assistant to the Staff Director; M. Carl Holman, Information Officer; Michael O. Finkelstein, assistant general counsel; Charles C. Humpstone, staff attorney; Roy Littlejohn, staff attorney; Richard F. Bellman, staff attorney; Brian Olmstead, staff attorney; Edwin D. Wolf, staff attorney; John G. Birkle, financial management officer; Robert H. Amidon, chief of investigations; Alan Marer, staff attorney, Department of Justice.

PROCEEDINGS

Chairman HANNAH. This hearing of the U.S. Commission on Civil Rights will come to order.

Mr. Taylor, what is the first item this morning?

Mr. TAYLOR. Madison County is the first county on which testimony will be heard this morning. I would like to ask Mr. Littlejohn to present some brief background information.

Chairman HANNAH. Mr. Littlejohn?

Mr. LITTLEJOHN. Madison County is located in central Mississippi, just north of Jackson. The population of the county in 1963 was estimated at 33,000 persons of whom almost 70 percent were Negroes. As of 1964, about 100 percent of all voting age whites were registered while only 2 percent of voting age Negroes were registered.

Madison is a rural county. In 1959, Canton, the county seat, had a population of about 9,000 almost two-thirds of whom were Negro. One-half of the Negroes in the county were employed in agriculture; 14 percent of the whites were so employed. In 1959, the median income for white families was $4,800; for Negroes it was $1,100. In 1959, 2 percent of the white homes in Canton and more than one-third of the Negro homes were unsafe and inadequate for human shelter.

The median level of education for whites was 12 years, for Negroes it was 6 years. In the school year 1960–61, the Madison County school district spent about $220 for each white child and $115 for each Negro child.

Chairman HANNAH. Thank you, sir. Mr. Taylor?

Mr. TAYLOR. The next item, Mr. Chairman, is a staff investigation report and I would like Mr. Littlejohn to be sworn.

(Whereupon, Mr. Roy Littlejohn was duly sworn by the Chairman and testified as follows:)

TESTIMONY OF ROY LITTLEJOHN, STAFF ATTORNEY, U.S. COMMISSION ON CIVIL RIGHTS

Mr. TAYLOR. Mr. Littlejohn, do you have a staff investigation report to present?

Mr. LITTLEJOHN. I have.

Mr. TAYLOR. Please proceed.

Mr. LITTLEJOHN. I would like to present to the Commission a report prepared by the staff on incidents of racial violence in Madison County beginning June 25, 1963, to date. This report was compiled as a result of investigations conducted by attorneys in the General Counsel's office during 1964 and 1965. We interviewed witnesses and law enforcement officials and examined Government records.

On June 25, 1963, five young Negroes were hit with birdshot from a shotgun fired at them by a middle-aged white man as they were walking home on West Peace Street in Canton. A white man was arrested several days later on a warrant signed by civil authorities. After four continuances of his trial he pleaded nolo contendere and was fined $500. Half of the fine was suspended upon good behavior.

In January 1964, the Madison County Movement, a local Negro civil rights organization, announced an economic boycott against white merchants in Canton. The aims of the boycott were to obtain jobs for Negroes and better treatment for Negro customers. At its peak the boycott was about 90 percent effective. Within weeks three white businesses closed and business in a large white-owned super-market dropped by 40 percent. At the same time, business in Negro-owned stores increased by 100 percent.

In early February the Madison County Herald reported the re-organization of the once-dormant White Citizens Council under a steering committee of 40 prominent white men. These included the sheriff, chief of police, mayor, city attorney, a State senator from Madison County, a former sheriff and deputy, as well as bankers, lawyers, physicians, industrialists, and businessmen. The policy of the Madison County White Citizens Council, as determined from staff interviews with members and from public announcements of the Council, was to avoid violence and to present a unanimous white resistance to the Negro majority in the county.

On February 28, 1964, the first Freedom Day in Madison County was held. Police preparation for that day included 75 special high-way patrolmen on standby alert at Jackson about 23 miles away.

On the evening of May 7, 1964, a man wearing a white hood fired shots at the Freedom House from a passing car. The license number and a description of the car were given to the Canton city police. No arrests have been made.

On the night of May 20, 1964 a white man fired several shots at the Freedom House while Negro civil rights workers were inside. A description of the man and his car was given to the police. No arrests have been made.

A second Freedom Day was held in Madison County on May 29, 1964. Armed deputies and city policemen prevented any marching. Negroes remained massed at two Negro churches. Fifty-three persons were arrested during the day. A Negro youth was knocked unconscious and arrested by a policeman.

Shortly after midnight, on June 12, 1964, a bomb was thrown at the home of Mrs. Alberta Robinson of Second Firebaugh Avenue, Canton. The bomb landed on the corner of her lawn and did little damage. A few minutes later a second bomb exploded on the lawn of the Pleasant Green Church of Christ on Walnut Street, causing minor damage. The church was used for civil rights meetings. The incidents were reported to the police. No arrests have been made.

On July 11, 1964, about 7 p.m., a fire bomb or molotov cocktail was thrown at the Freedom House from a light green Volkswagen. The license number of the automobile was given to the city police and to a special city prosecutor who investigated the incident. Three white youths were arrested. All three pleaded nolo contendere to a charge of breach of the peace and were fined $50 each. This fact was concealed from the Negro community by the prosecutor who stated to Federal investigators that he did not want members of the civil rights movement at the Freedom House to know of the arrests.

On Sunday, July 19, 1964 Michel Piore and William Carney, two white civil rights volunteers, were assaulted by a local white man as they walked by his gas station on West Peace Street. They swore out a warrant for the arrest of their assailant. Two continuances were granted in this case. In late August both Piore and Carney returned home. The city attorney then dropped the prosecution because the complaining witnesses had left Canton.

On the night of July 19, 1964, the Christian Union Baptist Church in Ridgeland burned to the ground. The incident was reported to the sheriff. No arrests have been made.

On August 2, 1964, shots were fired at the Freedom House from a car containing white teenagers. George Washington, Jr. fired back. The white youths fired again and drove away. Information describing the car was given to the police by Washington. A few days later he was arrested for unlawful possession of a firearm. No other arrests have been made.

On August 11, 1964, around 11 p.m., the meeting hall of the Willing Workers Society of the Mount Pleasant Church of Gluckstadt burned to the ground. Sheriff Cauthen investigated the incident. On August 28, 1964 he arrested Joe Lee Watts, a Negro civil rights worker, on suspicion of arson. Watts posted $500 bond. When the case was presented to the grand jury he was not indicted. No other arrests have been made.

On the night of September 5, 1964, dynamite exploded inside Joe & Barb's Curb Market on West Peace Street in Canton. The business is owned by Joe Ferguson who is white. It had been on the boycott list of the Madison County Movement until April 1964. He was the only white store owner taken off the boycott list. The incident was reported to the police. No arrests have been made.

Shortly after the explosion at Joe & Barb's, George Washington, Sr. inspected his store. He found a 5-foot fuse leading from the foundation of the store. The police investigated and found eight sticks of dynamite.

On the night of September 17, 1964, two Negro churches that had been used for civil rights meetings burned to the ground. The incidents were reported to the sheriff . No arrests have been made.

Mr. TAYLOR. Does that conclude your report?

Mr. LITTLEJOHN. Yes, on this portion of the investigation. I would like to offer this portion of our investigation report on Madison County for the record.

Chairman HANNAH. Received.

(Exhibit No. 17 was marked for identification and received in evidence.)

Mr. Taylor?

Mr. TAYLOR. The next witness is the Rev. James F. McCree.

Chairman HANNAH. Reverend McCree, will you raise your right hand?

(Whereupon, Rev. James F. McCree was duly sworn by the Chairman and testified as follows:)

Chairman HANNAH. Mr. Finkelstein will conduct the questioning.

TESTIMONY OF REV. JAMES F. McCREE, MADISON COUNTY, MISS.

Mr. FINKELSTEIN. Will you please give us your name, residence and occupation?

Reverend McCREE. My name is James F. McCree. I am a resident of Canton, Miss. I am a Methodist minister, pastor of the Asbury Methodist Church.

Mr. FINKELSTEIN. How long have you lived in Mississippi?

Reverend McCREE. I have lived in Mississippi 45 years.

Mr. FINKELSTEIN. Where were you educated, Reverend McCree?

Reverend McCREE. I was educated in the public schools of Mississippi. I graduated from the high school in Alabama and I attended college in Tennessee and also in Atlanta, Ga.

Mr. FINKELSTEIN. When did you enter the ministry?

Reverend McCREE. I entered the pastor of ministry in 1957.

Mr. FINKELSTEIN. How long have you been a minister of the Asbury Church in Canton?

Reverend McCREE. I have been minister of the Asbury Church of Canton for 19 months.

Mr. FINKELSTEIN. Are you active in civil rights?

Reverend McCREE. I am.

Mr. FINKELSTEIN. What do you do?

Reverend McCREE. I'm the executive director of the Madison County Movement.

Mr. FINKELSTEIN. What type of activity does the Madison County Movement engage in?

Reverend McCREE. The Madison County Movement is an organization of local Negroes of Madison County. We have opened it to whites if they desire to join, but none have desired except one and she is afraid to come out and say she has joined: We are trying to promote racial harmony in Madison County. We have tried and we have consistently sent letters to the elected officials of Madison County asking them to come and sit down and let us discuss this problem and then we can solve it.

Mr. FINKELSTEIN. Has there been much violence or other types of interference with your work?

Reverend McCREE. There has.

Mr. FINKELSTEIN. Can you tell us something about that, briefly?

Reverend McCREE. Well, there was a man, a white man, who followed me everywhere I would go, he would follow me. He didn't have on a uniform but I did see him on two occasions get in a police car, and eventually, I decided, he must have been a policeman. Then there were three cars parked in front of my house one night around 12 o'clock and there were cars parked back of my house and they were all whites in the cars. I have received telephone calls threatening my life and on numerous occasions I have received calls. I received one call and they said I would be killed the next day, and I told these people, I said, "Thank you for notifying me. The next time you find out anything that is going to happen to me, call again and I'll appreciate it very much."

Mr. FINKELSTEIN. We have heard, from the staff witness, evidence of a large number of incidents of racial violence in Madison County. Do you think that the police have been effective in controlling this violence?

Reverend McCREE. Not as effective as they could be if they wanted to. A lot of this violence, I believe, and we believe, is done with the knowledge of the law enforcement officers of Madison County. I have consistently exhorted and tried to keep Negroes from resorting to violence, and every time they say something about violence I will get after them about it. But consistently there have been violence and I believe that the law enforcement officers know about it.

Mr. FINKELSTEIN. You said a moment ago that you had attempted to communicate with city officials about your problems. Can you tell us something more about that?

Reverend McCREE. Yes. Here are two of the letters that we wrote to them. Even before anything happened we sent letters to all of the elected officials and they have ignored every letter that we sent to them. They have refused. May I read one?

Mr. FINKELSTEIN. Before you read it, let me ask you one question. Have you received any response to any of your letters?

Reverend McCREE. None whatsoever.

Mr. FINKELSTEIN. Go ahead, Reverend McCree.

Reverend McCREE. This is one of the letters that was sent:

"Gentlemen:

"These are the objectives that Negroes of Madison County are working for. We believe that these are the rights that we are entitled to as citizens of Canton and Madison County, Miss. We have been accused of being agitators and we have been accused of trying to take over the city of Canton and the county of Madison. Economic pressure has been placed on us. Law officers have beaten some of us.

"The following are the objectives that we are struggling for and we will continue until they are obtained.

"(1) Stop all discriminatory practices in regard to Negro voting rights. The adult white population all with the exception of approximately 200 individuals, 5,700 are registered voters. Of the 12,000 Negroes of voting age only about 400 are registered. Why? Discriminatory practices have been shown by the county registrar.

"(2) We demand that Negroes be placed in supervisory jobs in the city hall and in the county courthouse.

"(3) Because Negroes are in a majority in Canton and in Madison County and contribute largely to the economic well-being, we demand that Negroes be employed as sales clerks and cashiers in downtown places of business. This new situation would replace the old one of employment of Negroes exclusively as janitors and maids.

"(4) We demand that Negroes be placed on the city school board.

"(5) We demand that Negroes be allowed to take the examination for the police force and be hired with full authority like that of any other officer."

Mr. FINKELSTEIN. Thank you, Reverend McCree. Did you receive any answer to that letter?

Reverend McCREE. None whatsoever.

Mr. FINKELSTEIN. You said a moment ago that you didn't believe that the law enforcement officials effectively attempted to prevent violence. Do other Negroes in the community share that opinion?

Reverend McCREE. Yes. I served a number of years in the Armed Forces. I was in the invasion of France. I have never seen the fear in people, even during the invasion of France, as I saw in the Negroes of Madison County when I went there. Some of them even left my church, left my congregation because of my activities in the civil rights movement. They were even afraid to come to church. And now they will not come to church at night because they are afraid and they say, "I may get beaten and the church may be bombed. Anything may happen." These people are fearful.

Mr. FINKELSTEIN. The staff witness testified a moment ago that the sheriff and the chief of police were members of the steering committee of the White Citizens Council. Did you know that to be a fact?

Reverend McCREE. Well, everybody should know all about it. It had the mayor's name on the steering committee of the Citizens Council and it was published in the paper. They don't keep it a secret.

Mr. FINKELSTEIN. Do you think that affected the attitude of the Negro community towards law enforcement?

Reverend McCREE. Yes. It affected it because Negroes associate the White Citizens Council with the Ku Klux Klan.

Mr. FINKELSTEIN. What is the situation now in Canton, Reverend McCree?

Reverend McCREE. There is still a lot of fear. There was a report to us yesterday, and there the lady was afraid to report it to the law, that somebody shot at her and she was afraid to report it to the law.

Mr. FINKELSTEIN. No further questions.

Chairman HANNAH. Father Hesburgh?

Commissioner HESBURGH. Reverend McCree, how many belong to your organization?

Reverend McCREE. Approximately 500.

Commissioner HESBURGH. You are registered to vote, I imagine?

Reverend McCREE. Yes, I am.

Commissioner HESBURGH. Thank you, sir.

Chairman HANNAH. Mrs. Freeman?

Commissioner FREEMAN. Reverend McCree, you mentioned there are only 400 Negroes registered to vote. I would like to know whether Negroes are threatened when they attempt to vote, or is it just the examination?

Reverend McCREE. If you would see the people that have been fired from their jobs and kicked off their farms because they have simply gone to the courthouse to attempt to register to vote.

Commissioner FREEMAN. Would you give us an estimate of the number of people who have been fired because they tried, just tried to register?

Reverend McCREE. I could give you a rough estimate.

Commissioner FREEMAN. That's what I mean.

Reverend McCREE. Well, approximately a hundred or more.

Commissioner FREEMAN. Have been fired?

Reverend McCREE. Fired.

Commissioner FREEMAN. You also mentioned the police force and the examinations. Are you familiar with the requirements for being admitted to the police force? Do you know what they are?

Reverend McCREE. I don't know what they are in Canton, Miss., because I have never seen it advertised in the paper that there would be examinations. But there are Negroes just as able to serve on the police force as some of those they have on the force now.

Commissioner FREEMAN. Have any Negroes applied to take the examination?

Reverend McCREE. You have got to be a qualified elector.

Commissioner FREEMAN. Before you can take the examination for the police force?

Reverend McCREE. That's right, and if you are not a qualified elector and if you are not registered, you cannot take the examination.

Commissioner FREEMAN. With respect to the school board, are members of the school board elected or appointed?

Reverend McCREE. In the county they are elected and I think they are appointed in the city by the city council.

Commissioner FREEMAN. Do they also have to be registered voters, electors?

Reverend McCREE. Yes.

Commissioner FREEMAN. Thank you.

Chairman HANNAH. Dean Griswold?

Commissioner GRISWOLD. Mr. McCree, approximately how many Negro clergymen are there in Madison County?

Reverend McCREE. Approximately 50. But all of them are afraid, even the whites.

Commissioner GRISWOLD. No, I asked you how many Negro clergymen there were?

Reverend McCREE. That's what I'm speaking about, Negro.

Commissioner GRISWOLD. Do the Negro clergymen ever meet together?

Reverend McCREE. They will meet sometime but they are afraid. To give you an example, we had a meeting of the Negro clergy that were meeting regularly and they got afraid. They said, "I'm afraid to meet with you," meaning me, because of my activities in the civil rights field.

Commissioner GRISWOLD. How many white clergymen are there in Madison County?

Reverend McCREE. I don't know how many white.

Commissioner GRISWOLD. Could you make an approximate estimate?

Reverend McCREE. Well, I would say approximately 25 or 30.

Commissioner GRISWOLD. Do the Negro and the white clergymen ever meet together?

Reverend McCREE. No. There was one during the summer while some white ministers were there. I asked them if they would talk with the white clergy and I told them maybe if we clergymen could get together maybe we could start some dialogue between the white and the Negro. And there was one white clergyman who said he would call me and meet with me, but as of now he have never called.

Commissioner GRISWOLD. Do you think it would be helpful if the white and the Negro clergymen of Madison County did meet together?

Reverend McCREE. I do believe so.

Commissioner GRISWOLD. Do you think there's any prospect that this can be brought about?

Reverend McCREE. Not unless there is a change of heart in those people up there in the power structure, it will never happen unless that happens.

Commissioner GRISWOLD. Do you think that there is fear among the white clergymen?

Reverend McCREE. There's just as much fear among the white as there is among the Negro. I have had white people anonymously to call me and say, "Reverend McCree, we are with you, but can't do anything because we are afraid."

Commissioner GRISWOLD. Thank you.

Chairman HANNAH. Mr. Rankin?

Commissioner RANKIN. Your testimony up to now is that fear is rampant all over the county, not just among Negroes but among whites as well. Is that correct?

Reverend McCREE. That's correct; that's correct.

Commissioner RANKIN. Would you not also agree that the crux of the situation is the right to vote?

Reverend McCREE. Yes.

Commissioner RANKIN. In the demands that you made, the most important one was the right of registration and voting, is that right?

Reverend McCREE. Sure.

Commissioner RANKIN. Would it be better then, as a matter of policy, to concentrate on that one right rather than so many and keep on pursuing that particular goal rather than a number of them? I'm just asking you as a matter of policy.

Reverend McCREE. Sometimes when you try one thing and it won't work, you are better off trying something else. Maybe if you try something else you will get that thing to work. That is most important.

Commissioner RANKIN. But there is no use trying to get Negroes to be policemen if you have to be a voter and you can't vote?

Reverend McCREE. Maybe if we contend that we want Negro policemen, maybe they will let some of us register to vote.

Commissioner RANKIN. Then you are going at it in any door you can, that's what you are saying?

Reverend McCREE. If you lived in Mississippi, you would find out that you have to try any door that you can.

Chairman HANNAH. Mr. Patterson?

Vice Chairman PATTERSON. Has the situation improved in recent months in Madison County?

Reverend McCREE. Very little.

Chairman HANNAH. Any further questions?

Mr. ROGERSON. I just have one. Reverend McCree, have you ever approached the city authorities with the proposition of sitting down and talking? I mean, not a letter listing a series of demands, but let's sit down and talk about the situation?

Reverend McCREE. The first letter that we wrote, we asked them even before we had our Freedom Day, we asked them to let us sit down and talk. It was signed by 28 Negro ministers. We said if we sit down and talk we can solve this problem. Our efforts were blocked. They never gave us the courtesy of replying to our letter.

M. ROGERSON. Thank you.

Chairman HANNAH. You are excused, Reverend McCree. Thank you very much.

(Witness excused.)

Chairman HANNAH. Mr. Taylor, will you call the next witness?

Mr. TAYLOR. The next witness is Father Luke Mikschl.

Chairman HANNAH. Father Mikschl, will you raise your right hand?

(Whereupon, Father Luke Mikschl was duly sworn by the Chairman and testified as follows.)

TESTIMONY OF FATHER LUKE MIKSCHL, MADISON COUNTY, MISS.

Mr. FINKELSTEIN. Father, will you please give us your full name, your residence, and your occupation?

Father MIKSCHL. I am Father Luke Mikschl, a member of the Missionary Society called the Missionary Servants of Most Holy Trinity. We are working in sections of the South where there is a great need for priests. My residence is Holy Child Jesus Mission,

Box 366, Canton, Miss. I am pastor of one of the Catholic churches in Canton. All of our members are Negro. We have a school of about 270 from primary to high school. We have nine sisters teaching from LaCrosse, Wis. They are members of the Franciscan Sisters of Perpetual Adoration.

Mr. FINKELSTEIN. How long have you been working in Canton?

Father MIKSCHL. I have been in Canton 4½ years.

Mr. FINKELSTEIN. Would you describe very briefly the activities of your Mission?

Father MIKSCHL. We came to Canton in 1946. We had, I believe, two Catholics when we came. Our sisters came in 1948. We consider our mission a true missionary endeavor—working here in Mississippi. Our purpose has been twofold and they are very simple purposes, religious and educational. We are trying very hard to give our children a good solid Christian academic education.

Mr. FINKELSTEIN. What can you tell us of the attitude of local Negroes towards law enforcement?

Father MIKSCHL. The attitude of the Negro towards local law enforcement? To begin with I would say our relationship, the Mission's relationship to law enforcement in the county has been normal and good. Seldom if ever have I had to call on any law enforcement whatsoever, very seldon. And when I have it has been a serious problem and they have responded quickly, but that has been very seldom.

The people's attitude is different. As pastor and superintendent of our school, I have felt in the past year, particularly, that if I have ever had to call upon any law enforcement, that I would be obliged in conscience to remember the distrust that our Negro people, citizens, seem to have and apparently do have. We have been hearing this all week. They seem to have this distrust and I would have to respect that. But I certainly would definitely call on our law enforcement if the need would arise, but I would have to respect that they definitely have this distrust and this seems to have been built up over many, many, many years.

Mr. FINKELSTEIN. No further questions.

Chairman HANNAH. Father Hesburgh?

Commissioner HESBURGH. Father, what's the reason for the distrust?

Father MIKSCHL. The reason? I live as pastor, as a a white pastor and a white priest working in the community. As far as Negro citizens are concerned, I live in a world of, I would say, hearsay, and I hear many things from many, many people, Negro people. The reason I would say would be these long, long frustrations over the years of some type of unequal protection. I just can't pin it down myself. I just know it exists.

Commissioner HESBURGH. You have heard the testimony all week of acts of violence, in which the victims reported cars and license plates and gave descriptions of people who were involved?

Father MIKSCHL. Yes.

Commissioner HESBURGH. Even at times the actual pointing out of the person. You have heard the fact that in the majority of cases there were no arrests made. It seems almost like a litany, no arrest made, no arrest made, and when the arrest is made the trial is put off, put off or carried over. Finally you found that after page after page after page of these incidents there's no action—or if there is action—someone gets off with a $50 fine. Or if it is a larger fine, part of it is suspended. You must see this and hear this in your work, don't you?

Father MIKSCHL. Yes. Those are the things that we are hearing. That's true. I would say that would be part of the distrust.

Commissioner HESBURGH. Let me ask you something. Father, would you like to be a Negro living in Madison County?

Father MIKSCHL. No, I would not.

Commissioner HESBURGH. Why?

Father MIKSCHL. I believe, as the Reverend McCree has very well pointed out, there's this element of fear and this is not confined just to the Negro. This includes the white. We in this county definitely are living in an atmosphere of fear. I have felt this since I came here 4½ years ago. Now, this is on both sides. Not just Negro. Whites also, more so with the whites now than had been in the past. There are many good white people in our city and in our county who I am sure are afraid to come out and make themselves known.

Commissioner HESBURGH. Father, do you have meetings with the Negro clergymen in Canton?

Father MIKSCHL. I know them all. Meet with them? I have not met in any type of meeting, as such. In the past I have not; no.

Commissioner HESBURGH. Thank you.

Chairman HANNAH. Mrs. Freeman?

Commissioner FREEMAN. Father, you say that you yourself have not personally experienced any of the threats.

Father MIKSCHL. No, none whatsoever.

Commissioner FREEMAN. So you are in sort of a favored position?

Father MIKSCHL. I would say because of our past record, and we have been respected by I'm sure white and Negro for what we are trying to do for our people and for our children, giving them a very good education. In that sense I feel that we have been respected and appreciated in the past, both by the white and by the Negro, yes.

Commissioner FREEMAN. Does the curriculum at your school include instruction concerning not only the right but the responsibility of exercising the right to vote?

Father MIKSCHL. Yes.

Commissioner FREEMAN. So you do encourage the members of your parish to vote?

Father MIKSCHL. Yes.

Commissioner FREEMAN. Have you been successful in getting them to make the attempt?

Father MIKSCHL. Well, very, very little. We haven't made a definite program of voting. We have tried over and over to teach our people what is right and what is wrong and what they do personally would be strictly up to them. Now, beyond that, very, very few of our people are voting; I know that. Perhaps a few more than have been in the past.

For what reasons, it is built on fear. If I may give one practical solution to eliminating some of this fear that has built up over the years, I would suggest very practically that one of the biggest things that has kept them from trying to vote is that we have the practice of listing all the applicants in our local paper. That I would say in my mind has been the number one point of fear in their mind, and this was chiefly because of some loss of job or economic consideration. I honestly have to say that that is the fear in their minds that I know of.

Commissioner FREEMAN. Thank you.

Chairman HANNAH. Mr. Rogerson, go ahead.

Mr. ROGERSON. Father, what is the dropout situation in your school?

Father MIKSCHL. Very little.

Mr. ROGERSON. So that you have quite a number that complete the 12th grade?

Father MIKSCHL. Yes, definitely, yes. Over the years it's getting better and better.

Mr. ROGERSON. I see. And this is in contradiction to the average schooling in the country?

Father MIKSCHL. Well, ours would be better, I'm sure.

Mr. ROGERSON. Yes, the average is sixth grade.

Father MIKSCHL. Oh, yes. Most of our children are graduating from high school and well over half of them are going to college.

Mr. ROGERSON. One other question, then, Father. Where do these children go? What do they do after they finish the 12th grade? What kind of counsel can you give them for employment and so on?

Father MIKSCHL. We estimate that one out of five is remaining in Canton.

Mr. ROGERSON. One out of five?

Father MIKSCHL. About one out of five. I would say of all the objects and goals of our Negro people, the foremost is job opportunity. I think the greatest thing that we must do, the first thing before anything else is ever, ever solved in our community and in Mississippi, in general, we will just have to have some communication between the races. Nothing else is going to be solved first before this. And these conditions that we have, have not just cropped up overnight since some of our outsiders, so called, have come in. These conditions have existed. We have to have some talking about our problem and I'm positively convinced that if we don't have some talking soon, as the Reverend McCree has been trying to encourage over the years here, if we don't have some, I believe that our condition is going to really degenerate into a worse relationship. Our white citizens have the choice here now, the clear choice of solving this on a local basis with some of our intelligent, perhaps professional, dignified Negro citizens. If that doesn't come about, I'm afraid that we are going to have more people coming in from the outside and it will lead to violence because many of them do not understand our prejudices and our histories and our traditions in Mississippi. The ideal is to have this solved by our local people, but to my knowledge there has not been any communication between the races, any kind of a formal communication. This must come. I think we are at that point where we have to make this choice. We have been described as a closed society. I think that is a very apt title.

And what does our Negro citizen want? They want what everyone else wants, nothing spectacular or revolutionary, nothing extra. The first thing is job opportunity, and that is our number one problem. The basis of our problem in the school are children having no home life because the parents, if the children are with the parents, are working, both of them. And it is very difficult to raise a child when you are so involved in economic survival.

Mr. ROGERSON. Thank you.

Chairman HANNAH. Father, you indicated that when you first arrived in Canton and established your school there were few Catholics. And I think you said you now have 248 students or something like that?

Father MIKSCHL. 270, and one out of seven of them is Catholic.

Mr. HANNAH. Many of them are not Catholic?

Father MIKSCHL. Six-sevenths are not.

Chairman HANNAH. You testified that you have no real attendance problems, that most of them will attend very faithfully?

Father MIKSCHL. No. We insist they be on time, wear uniforms and come to school every day, and try to work their best.

Chairman HANNAH. Do you have any observations about the optional attendance laws in Mississippi? We haven't been going into education this week, but it bothers me a good deal to learn that there is no requirement for school attendance. Many people go to school, many do not. Do you have any observations on this?

Father MIKSCHL. I believe this is true. We have no truant officer. I believe that's true, and that's about all I know about the situation. I know there is a great deal of absenteeism within the Negro school system, public school system. I know that for sure.

Chairman HANNAH. You know there are many Negroes of school age who should be in the first, second, third, or fourth grade but who are not in school at all?

Father MIKSCHL. They are registered but how much they are in school during the school year is very pitiful at times. We see them walking the streets constantly.

Chairman HANNAH. Are the sisters teaching in your school white or colored?

Father MIKSCHL. Eight of them are white and one is Negro.

Chairman HANNAH. I have no further questions. Are there further questions? Dean Griswold?

Commissioner GRISWOLD. Father, is tuition required for the students in your school?

Father MIKSCHL. Yes, but we have kept the tuition very, very low. We have to get a great deal of help from the outside, particularly through our community, the Missionary Servants of the Most Holy Trinity based in Silver Spring, Md. Our tuition for the high school is $3. This is a month. The grade school tuition is $2. The tuition for the second, third, and fourth child is a dollar, and no family pays over $5 a month. We definitely do not meet expenses from our children.

Chairman HANNAH. But you have, I take it, some 210 non-Catholic children whose parents find it desirable to send their children to your school with a tuition charge, which small as it is, must be a considerable sum for many of them to spend rather than to have their children go to the public school?

Father MIKSCHL. Yes.

Chairman HANNAH. Have you any explanation for that?

Father MIKSCHL. Well, simply because, as our people say, we take pains with their children. We have an excellent group of sisters who love the work very much and have been there many years. One of them, in fact, has been with us for 16 years. The Negro children are sent to our school, we feel, because education is first in the parents' minds and they want their children to have the best education that they did not have or were deprived of because of the times in which they lived.

Chairman HANNAH. You said, if I recall correctly, that half of your high school graduates go on to college.

Father MIKSCHL. I would say that, about half.

Chairman HANNAH. Where do they go to college?

Father MIKSCHL. It's about evenly divided between our Negro State colleges and the other ones going to various parts of the country. We had a boy leave last year, graduated. He went to Marquette University. He's attending law school. We have two boys hoping to get into Creighton University on scholarship. They don't have the means at all.

Chairman HANNAH. Mr. Patterson?

Vice Chairman PATTERSON. Father, do you have white children in your school?

Father MIKSCHL. No. Our school is completely Negro. Our Bishop now has integrated the schools and we feel we will have more integration in the future. But at the present time we are completely Negro. We have over the years told everybody that anybody is invited to come to our school, but we have no white children whatsoever.

Vice Chairman PATTERSON. Would you accept the white children?

Father MIKSCHL. Definitely.

Chairman HANNAH. Any further questions? Thank you very much, Father. You are excused.

(Witness excused.)

Chairman HANNAH. Mr. Taylor, will you call the next witness.

Mr. TAYLOR. The next witness is Mr. George Washington, Sr.

Chairman HANNAH. Mr. Washington. Will you raise your right hand?

(Whereupon, Mr. George Washington, Sr., was duly sworn by the Chairman and testified as follows:)

Chairman HANNAH. Mr. Finkelstein?

TESTIMONY OF MR. GEORGE WASHINGTON, SR., CANTON, MADISON COUNTY, MISS.

Mr. FINKELSTEIN. Will you please give us your name, your residence and your occupation?

Mr. WASHINGTON. George Washington, Sr., 819 Lutz Street, Canton, Miss., and I operate as store operator and real estate.

Mr. FINKELSTEIN. What kind of store do you operate?

Mr. WASHINGTON. A grocery store.

Mr. FINKELSTEIN. You say you have real estate. Do you lease property to the Council of Federated Organizations?

Mr. WASHINGTON. Sure do.

Mr. FINKELSTEIN. Is that the Freedom House?

Mr. WASHINGTON. Freedom House, that's the Freedom House.

Mr. FINKELSTEIN. Then you are COFO's landlord, is that right?

Mr. WASHINGTON. Yes, sir.

[Laughter.]

Mr. FINKELSTEIN. Do you recall hearing an explosion on the night of June 8, 1964?

Mr. WASHINGTON. I sure do.

Mr. FINKELSTEIN. Can you tell us what happened?

Mr. WASHINGTON. When I heard the explosion, my son was sleeping up in the front room. I went up there and said, "What is that that happened out there?" He said, "Somebody threw a bomb or something up to the house." He said, "I saw the car when it passed by the window," and he said, "I know who was driving the car."

So, I got up, I went back and dressed, put my clothes on and dressed and went up there to see what had happened, did it do any damage. And, I didn't see no damage, no more than just little small hole in the ground that was there and I looked at the house, and I didn't see no damage to it, and I didn't wake the people up in the house. I went on back and decided I would go to bed. I went back and went to bed. The next morning I got up, and went to open the store. About 7 o'clock my wife came out to the store and she say, "Well, I believe I'll go up there and see if I see any more damage that was done to the Freedom House."

And I say, "Okay, go up there and see." So she goes up there. She went up there to see what damage there was to it, and she came back and said she discovered a couple windows were broken in the house. So, I said, "Well, we better call the policeman and let them know about it so they can come out and make an investigation."

While we were waiting there one of the men that lived in the Freedom house, James Collier came over. I asked him. I said, "James, did you all call the law last night?" He said no. I said, "Why?" He said, "There wasn't any use calling because they wasn't going to do anything about it."

So, I told my wife, "Call the law, and let them come out and make an investigation." She got on the phone and called the law and told them there was a bombing out there last night.

A car drove up with two policemen. They got out and my wife went to the door to see to tell them about what had happened. She was looking over to the house. Looked like they wanted to go over to my house. My wife said, "The bombing was up at the Freedom House. It was up there, up the road across the street." They replied, "Where is George?" She said, "He is in the store." They said, "Tell him to come out here."

I came by to see what they want. They said, "What about this bombing last night?"

I said, "Well, something threw a bomb up there in the Freedom House last night." "Why didn't you call us?" I said, "I didn't think it was my responsibility to call you all because there are people living in the house and they have a telephone in the house and I thought it was their responsibility to call you all."

"It was your responsibility to call us. That's your property. We don't care if you own property and it's 10 miles from you, you are supposed to notify us; that's your responsibility to notify us. We are going to send your so-and-so to the penitentiary."

I won't say what they said. I said, "For what? Somebody bombed my house and you are talking about sending me to the penitentiary?"

They said, "Yes, we are going to send you to the penitentiary and try to get you 10 years."

"Get in the car," and some profane language.

I said, "Get in the car? Do you have a warrant for me?"

"No, we don't need a warrant. Get your so-and-so in the car."

They shoved me in the car and I got in there. We headed for the police station. I didn't say anything. They didn't say too much. As I was going down through the colored neighborhood there, I saw some of my friends standing on the sidewalk and I put up my hand and waved at some of them. I always wore a smile and wanted to be friends with everyone. The policeman said, "Get your hand down there. If you don't I will take my pistol and break it off. You want them to see you in the car?"

Mr. FINKELSTEIN. What happened when you got to the station?

Mr. WASHINGTON. When I got to the station they said, "Get your so and so out." One of the policemen, Mr. Cook, unlocked the door. I got out and he said to me, "Get your so-and-so in the jailhouse." I said, "You are going to allow me to make a phone call and get a lawyer." He said, "No, I ain't going to let you talk to nobody. Get in the jailhouse." Just as I went in to the jailhouse, I wasn't expecting anything, I was struck right up over the right eye.

Mr. FINKELSTEIN. What were you doing at the time you were struck?

Mr. WASHINGTON. I wasn't doing anything, just going in jail.

Mr. FINKELSTEIN. Go ahead, Mr. Washington.

Mr. WASHINGTON. It only kind of staggered me. I couldn't see too well. I had to throw my hand up over my eye and hold it because it was hurting. There were two more fellows in jail, Lyman Jones and I don't know the other fellow's name. I know him but I can't recall his name. He asked me, "Didn't that policeman hit you?" I said, "He sure did," and I went on back over there and sat down on the bunk with him.

About 15 minutes later the policeman came back and said, "We are ready for you, George, in the interview room." Well, I was a little bit slow about going out. I said, "They might be going to attack me again when I go out," and I was a little bit slow. He called me second time and I looked out there and I didn't see but one and I said, "Well, maybe he won't bother me." So I went on with him and went in the interview room.

He told me, "Have a seat there and sit down at the front of the table." I sat down.

Mr. FINKELSTEIN. Who was in the interview room at that time?

Mr. WASHINGTON. Mr. Cook and Mr. Chance and one more policeman. I don't know his name. But, he began to question me when I sat down, asking me questions about the march and so forth, and about me letting those people stay in my house. They said the men already had to move from one place in our town. He heard that I was giving them free rent, wasn't charging them anything. He said I was backing the movement 100 percent, and I ought to leave town and go on to Washington, D.C., somewhere where there was COFO headquarters, go there and stay.

Mr. FINKELSTEIN. Mr. Washington, excuse me, were you struck again at any time?

Mr. WASHINGTON. I was struck again. I was sitting up there smiling. He said, "Wipe that smile off your face. You act like you ain't concerned." He went to strike me again and I threw my hands over there and caught part of it. He said, "It just makes me sick to look at you."

Mr. FINKELSTEIN. During the entire interrogation did they ask you any questions about the bombing of the COFO house?

Mr. WASHINGTON. Yes, sir; he asked me about it. I told him I didn't know who did it. But he told me I did know who did it. He said it wasn't nobody but some of those COFO workers. I told him I didn't think they would do anything like that.

Mr. FINKELSTEIN. How long did your interrogation last?

Mr. WASHINGTON. I didn't have any watch on but something like 3 or 4 hours, something like that.

Mr. FINKELSTEIN. Do you recall when you were released?

Mr. WASHINGTON. It was about 11 o'clock. Yes, sir; about 11 o'clock.

Mr. FINKELSTEIN. Did you subsequently report this to anyone?

Mr. WASHINGTON. I did.

Mr. FINKELSTEIN. Whom did you report it to?

Mr. WASHINGTON. Well, I told my wife when I got back to the store and there was some more people there waiting to see what happened to me, and I called the chief the next day and reported to him.

First I went to the doctor to see about my eye. On that day I had come to Jackson to a specialist. I was afraid to go to the doctor in Canton because I knew they knew what was going on, some of them. I came to Jackson and I didn't have an appointment to see the doctor that day and I didn't get a chance to see him and I had to go back and the next day I had to come back.

I called Mr. Dan, the chief, but he wasn't in. I didn't tell him what I wanted with him and that was before I went to Jackson I was going to tell him what happened. When he came in the office he called for me. But I was gone and the reason I didn't tell him what I wanted because I figured, you know, if I had told him that I was going to Jackson, somebody would have had the highway patrol waiting for me. Because they had my tag number and my name was about the fourth name on the list of the agitators, chief agitators, and because I was letting the people stay in my house there.

I slipped a jacket on and I went on in. I didn't see him, so the next day I went back and saw the specialist. So, this specialist said, "Your eye, I can't do it any good. I'm going to call this other man down to the Medical Arts Building." He said, "I can't do your eye any good."

Chairman HANNAH. Do you still have trouble with your eye?

Mr. WASHINGTON. Yes, I still have trouble with it, I sure do.

Mr. FINKELSTEIN. One more question. Did you report this to anyone else, any other official?

Mr. WASHINGTON. Well, some of the other officials in town, they told me they were sorry it happened and Mr. Dan, he told me he was sorry it happened then. He told me if I had any trouble any way to always call him. Mr. Dan, I give it to him, he was always very nice. He always was. He was very nice.

Mr. FINKELSTEIN. Is Mr. Dan the police chief?

Mr. WASHINGTON. He's the police chief; yes, sir. He is nice.

Mr. FINKELSTEIN. Thank you.

Chairman HANNAH. Mrs. Freeman.

Commissioner FREEMAN. Mr. Washington, when you reported to Mr.

Dan, did he indicate that there is any provision in the laws of Mississippi against a policeman beating you up?

Mr. WASHINGTON. He sure didn't. He was sorry that it happened and he told me he guaranteed that it wouldn't happen any more. So from that day somebody did something about it because those particular police haven't been to my place of business since then, so it's likely they had a meeting after that.

I told the policeman that morning in the police station that I had lots of friends, white and colored. I said "I got lots of friends here," and he said, "We don't think so. You have no friends among the whites. None of them think anything of you." I said, "I don't know that." He said, "How do you know that?" I said, "They call me and I go to their house at night and to the office in the daytime." He said, "I wouldn't call a man a friend if he wouldn't come out to your house in the daytime and talk to you."

And I said, "Well, they are under pressure like we are. They want to do things like we but they can't because they are under pressure. So I imagine he found out that when they had that meeting that I did have some friends."

Chairman HANNAH. Mr. Rankin?

Commissioner RANKIN. Are there any other houses closer to the Freedom House than your home?

Mr. WASHINGTON. Yes, sir.

Commissioner RANKIN. Did they report this bomb explosion? Did anybody else report it?

Mr. WASHINGTON. Well, the folks that live in the Freedom House, they reported it.

Commissioner RANKIN. They reported to the police that night?

Mr. WASHINGTON. No, sir, they didn't report it that night. They called headquarters. They reported it I think to Washington, D.C. Yes, sir.

Commissioner RANKIN. And none of the neighbors reported it to the police?

Mr. WASHINGTON. No, sir. They had the opinion, I imagine like James Collier said, it wasn't any use reporting it to them because they wasn't going to do anything about it. And then I was informed by some of the people who would be out late hours at night that a policeman was involved in that bombing.

They knew who was doing it if they wasn't doing it. They back the story up the morning in the police station. One of them said to me, he said, "I saw George, Jr. I passed the other night and he was out there squatting behind that car watching out there." And he said, "If I catch him out there I am going to bring him in and put him in jail."

I said, "For what, him watching my property and you are going to lock him up?" And he said, "yes."

I thought that if someone was out there watching and told the policeman, he would have aided them in catching them. It looked to me like they wasn't particular about seeing them.

Chairman HANNAH. Mr. Rogerson?

Mr. ROGERSON. Mr. Washington, when you reported being hit did Chief Thompson ask you whether or not you wanted to file a charge against his officer?

Mr. WASHINGTON. No, sir. He sure didn't.

Chairman HANNAH. Any further questions?

Mr. FINKELSTEIN. No further questions.

Chairman HANNAH. You are excused, Mr. Washington. Thank you very much.

Mr. Taylor, will you call the next witness.

(Witness excused.)

Mr. TAYLOR. The next witness is Mr. Mirza Hamid Hasan Kizilbash.

Chairman HANNAH. Mr. Kizilbash?

Whereupon Mr. Mirza Hamid Hasan Kizilbash was duly affirmed and testified as follows:

TESTIMONY OF MR. MIRZA HAMID HASAN KIZILBASH, MADISON COUNTY, MISS.

Mr. FINKELSTEIN. Mr. Kazilbash, will you please give your name, your residence and your occupation?

Mr. KIZILBASH. My name is Mirza Hamid Kizilbash. I am assistant professor of political science at Tougaloo College and I live on the campus of Tougaloo College.

Mr. FINKELSTEIN. Mr. Kibilbash, where is Tougaloo College?

Mr. KIZILBASH. Tougaloo College is located a few miles north of Jackson on the old Highway 51, I think, between Jackson and Canton.

Mr. FINKELSTEIN. What is your nationality?

Mr. KIZILBASH. I am a citizen of Pakistan.

Mr. FINKELSTEIN. How long have you taught at Tougaloo?

Mr. KIZILBASH. I came to teach at Tougaloo in September 1963.

Mr. FINKELSTEIN. Is Tougaloo in Madison County?

Mr. KIZILBASH. As I understand it, part of it is in Madison County and part of it is in Hinds County.

Mr. FINKELSTEIN. Did you have occasion to go to Canton on May 29, 1964?

Mr. KIZILBASH. Yes, I did. I was on the campus and one of the students came to me and asked me if I would drive some people over to a meeting in Canton. At that time I happened to be playing tennis and I wasn't at all prepared for going out, but I said, "If you need to go there, I'll be happy to drive you." And then at about 7:15 that evening two of the faculty members at Tougaloo, Mr. King and Mrs. King and two of our students, Joan Trumpauer and Eli Hochstedler— all of these people are white, incidentally—got in my car and we drove to Canton. But we didn't know where the meeting was to which we were going. Do you want me to proceed with it?

Mr. FINKELSTEIN. Yes, please go ahead.

Mr. KIZILBASH. And we had to stop in what appeared to be the Negro section of the town. This is just my guess, I think it was at a grocery store and ask for directions to this particular church where the meeting was to be held. One of the youngsters there agreed to accompany us to the church. I would not have gotten off of this un-paved road without the help of the directions the youngster was giving, but I noticed another car was driving at a very close distance to mine behind me with its bright lights on.

Now ordinarily I wouldn't pay any attention, but since it had its bright lights on, I tried to wave to him to lower the bright beams be-cause they were bothering me. He didn't and he continued to follow closely as I turned back and forth on the streets of Canton trying to get to this particular location.

Finally we reached the spot where the meeting was to be held. This other car—I pulled into the parking lot of the church—this other car pulled in along the road and turned around and stopped there. I noticed this because when I got out of the car I looked out to the road and this car was parked there. I could see these two bodies, which looked white, sitting in the car, as I walked up to the church and went inside. The meeting didn't last very long. I think about 30 or 35 minutes my own guess is.

Mr. FINKELSTEIN. What kind of meeting was it?

Mr. KIZILBASH. I think it was a meeting to either review or to discuss the events of that day, which I found out, were the attempt of Negroes to register in Canton to vote. I had not been aware of this, but as the conversation went on I realized it was an attempt to discuss what had happened, how many people were in jail and so on, an attempt to sort of get some of the strength back from the events of the day is what it appeared to me.

Mr. FINKELSTEIN. What happened after you left the meeting?

Mr. KIZILBASH. After we left the meeting—I remember during the meeting someone mentioned there was to be a curfew in Canton or something of this sort and people were not to be seen on the street after a certain time; that's one of the reasons the meeting ended so quickly. So we were in a hurry to get away without defying the curfew. As soon as I started the car and started back, immediately I noticed that another car—I don't know which car—it could have been the same car or another one, with its bright lights on, was again behind me.

I drove along back and forth, trying to get out of town. It sort of weaves around; it is a complex town to get out of. And then I got to the highway which leads to an access to the new highway. There's a little island and you have to go around it and go up to the main highway.

Well, there was a truck parked which had stopped at a stop sign on the other side. I was approaching from this side and I wasn't sure if the truck was going to come through, so I slowed down and decided to go around the island. The car that was behind me pulled around and blocked me at the island, straight across the island. I consider that act the most illegal parking on a main highway that I have ever seen. It parked straight across. I noticed a large truck parked right behind my car and another car. I couldn't say if that was just a car passing or not, but the truck had me blocked from the back and the car from the front. And about, this would be a guess, but I would say at least 10 people emerged from the different cars, from the car and truck. One white man who appeared to be the spokesman came to my car, approached the car. I would say now that in my ignorance I rolled down the window and tried to ask him "What can I do for you, why have you suddenly parked in front of my car?"

Mr. FINKELSTEIN. Was he masked?

Mr. KIZILBASH. No, he was not—nothing on his face. He had a hat on and he was built heavy. He had a short sleeve shirt on. I remember him rather distinctly but not as distinctly as I did for a few weeks after the incident.

Mr. FINKELSTEIN. Go on.

Mr. KIZILBASH. He asked me, "What is your business here." While he was asking me, he reached in and someone from behind, the other people in the car, had locked the car. Well, the window was down so he just pulled open the thing which opened the car and pulled the door open and before I had a chance to answer what my business was— I was getting out the sentence, teaching at Tougaloo, teacher—the other man by him just grabbed me by the tie and the shirt, and tried to pull me out.

In my 5 years in this country I never had such a thing happen, so I didn't know how to handle myself. All I tried to do was lean away from being pulled out of the car.

When this happened, the shirt tore and the tie went rather tightly around my neck. When he couldn't succeed in pulling me out, he let go and this other fellow began to question me, what is your business here? Don't you know better than to come into our town? I didn't— know what he was saying. I must say after that particular physical assault I wasn't able to hear everything he was saying as clearly as I would have liked to have done.

In the meantime the man who had tried to grab me or someone who had replaced him at the side of the man who was questioning me had some sort of a club, either a baseball bat or a billy club. He reached in and just bashed me on the back of my head twice. I felt that it was a rather hard blow.

So, at this time, of course, my head went down to try to keep him from hitting me right on the top. And then after he had finished he withdrew and I heard mutterings and sounds and someone said, "Let's finish them," and "Let's kill them." The most dominant one was, "Let's have a party." I don't know what that meant, but I never forget the sentence, "Let's have a party." At that time someone in the car tried to tell the group that I was not an American, that I was a foreigner. Somebody was saying—I think Mr. King was saying—I am Indian or something of this sort just to get the idea across that I am a foreigner. He didn't think Pakistan would be as easily understood as India.

[Laughter.]

At that point someone else looked through the window. The door now is opened. I should say looked through the door and said to Mr. King in the back, "You hardhead, we will get you," or something of this sort. And the threats were being continuously made and a number of obscenities which I'm sorry I cannot repeat.

Mr. FINKELSTEIN. Go on.

Mr. KIZILBASH. I wouldn't know how they were being constantly thrown because there were two ladies, Mrs. King and a student in the car—a number of things were said. After a while this particular man that hit me with the club apparently was so violent and so angry that his only interest was in trying to get at some object and bash it so he came back and bashed me again, this time claiming that I was trying to look at him. When they were talking I would look and see who was talking and as soon as I was looking at the person, the man got mad. I don't know why. Apparently he thought I would identify him or something.

Mr. FINKELSTEIN. Did they let you go?

Mr. KIZILBASH. Yes, at that time after a few minutes of this continued exercise I was told that I could proceed, and someone apparently went and moved the car from the front.

Mr. FINKELSTEIN. Did you drive to Jackson?

Mr. KIZILBASH. Yes. We started out but immediately I noticed that another car, now I don't know which car this was, was following. It even became more obvious because I was in a hurry to get away from Canton. I took the initiative in moving into the outside lane and passed a lot of cars and traveled the maximum speed I could within the limit, I think, and this car kept pursuing us very closely.

When I got very near Canton, some of us saw that one of the cars with some faculty members of Tougaloo College was going along. But we couldn't say anything because we were in a hurry and this car was behind us. Finally, on the campus of Millsaps College we turned in. I wouldn't go into Tougaloo as we normally would, because it is a dark road, so we went into Millsaps College. This car came behind me and I think when the car noticed it was being followed in turn, it pulled away and we pulled up in Millsaps and stopped.

Mr. FINKELSTEIN. Were you or one of the persons from Tougaloo able to get the license number of the car which followed you?

Mr. KIZILBASH. Yes, all the people in the car, behind the car that was following me, individually, got the number. All of them knew it and at least three of them told me the number immediately.

Mr. FINKELSTEIN. Did you contact the sheriff of Madison County on this case?

Mr. KIZILBASH. Not immediately.

Mr. FINKELSTEIN. When did you do so?

Mr. KIZILBASH. I did it 2 days later, 3 days later.

Mr. FINKELSTEIN. Did you write him a letter?

Mr. KIZILBASH. Yes.

Mr. FINKELSTEIN. Would you read us the letter, please?

Mr. KIZILBASH. This was a letter to the sheriff of Madison County, Canton, Miss.

I wrote him:

Dear Sir: On Friday, May 29, 1964, some friends of mine and I were returning in my car from a meeting in Canton when we were stopped by three cars full of white people. These people cursed and threatened us and I was beaten with a billy club on the head. As it is, out of the beating I had to get medical attention and had to stay in bed for a day. One of the cars involved in the beating followed me all the way to Jackson and we were able to get its Mississippi license plate number.

I am a citizen of Pakistan and have informed my Government as well as the Governor of Mississippi of the incident. I have reported the incident to the highway patrol in Jackson. If you would like further details, please get in touch with me.

Sincerely yours.

Mr. FINKELSTEIN. Thank you.

We would like to enter this as an exhibit.

Chairman HANNAH. It is received.

(Exhibit No. 18 was marked for identification and received in evidence.)

Mr. FINKELSTEIN. Let me note for the record that letter is dated June 2. Did you ever hear from the sheriff following this letter?

Mr. KIZILBASH. No, I never heard from the sheriff of Madison County.

Mr. FINKELSTEIN. Did you write a similar letter to the Governor of Mississippi?

Mr. KIZILBASH. Yes, I did.

Mr. FINKELSTEIN. Did you ever hear from him?

Mr. KIZILBASH. No, I didn't, and in that particular letter to the Governor I pointed out the exact number of the car, and in the one to the sheriff I didn't.

I won't go into why. I felt that it would be better for him to come and then I could tell him more because there might be some problem. For if it is as I hear—and this I wouldn't say except that I have heard that—there is supposed to be some connection between the officers of law and the people that usually create trouble, I felt that this might lead him to remove the plate or something.

Mr. FINKELSTEIN. Is the sheriff's office in Canton?

Mr. KIZILBASH. Yes.

Mr. FINKELSTEIN. How far is Canton from Tougaloo?

Mr. KIZILBASH. I don't know the exact distance, but I have driven it in less than half hour.

Mr. FINKELSTEIN. No further questions.

Chairman HANNAH. Father Hesburgh?

Commissioner HESBURGH. Mr. Kizilbash, are you from east or west Pakistan?

Mr. KIZILBASH. West.

Commissioner HESBURGH. Karachi?

Mr. KIZILBASH. No, I'm from Lahore.

Commissioner HESBURGH. I would gather this didn't make a very good impression on you of our country?

Mr. KIZILBASH. No, sir; it didn't. It was the first time I think in my whole stay here—and I have spent a lot of time in the South and in other States—I have never felt as helpless and as really afraid and scared as I did at that time.

Commissioner HESBURGH. Have you heard of other such incidents?

Mr. KIZILBASH. Well, a number of things that had happened to me prior to that which made this more fearsome. In one particular incident I was on the main street in Jackson when I was accosted by an individual who was not dressed in any official clothes or anything that would identify him and told to get off the street.

I was standing there that time it happened. I knew there was supposed to be some kind of demonstration and I happened to be walking down the street. I stopped because they were picking up some of the people who were involved and putting them in paddy wagons. I was far away from the incident just looking on like 15 other people and this man said as someone very lightly said, "I will put your so and so into the paddy wagon if you don't move on." Well, I must say, the first time I reacted with anger because he had no right to say that, and I told him to let my hand go and if he continued any further I was ready to become violent myself.

Commissioner HESBURGH. Thank you.

Chairman HANNAH. Mr. Rankin?

Commissioner RANKIN. Yes, I have a few questions to ask. I remember talking to you soon after this occasion and it was your belief that except for the fact that you were a citizen of Pakistan, all of you might have been killed. Am I correct in that?

Mr. KIZILBASH. That's right, Dr. Rankin. I think that it sort of struck me at that time that if it had not been for me perhaps there might have been more trouble. It apparently got across to the people eventually for obvious reasons that I was a foreigner, and it was not necessarily the wise thing to do, to get rid of me at this time.

Commissioner RANKIN. Have you received similar treatment elsewhere in the United States or do you think this is peculiar to this area?

Mr. KIZILBASH. On the basis of my having seen a good many States of the United States I would say this is peculiar to this State, shockingly peculiar.

Commissioner RANKIN. What courses do you teach?

Mr. KIZILBASH. I teach political science, a course in American Government, a course in European comparative government and a course in international relations.

Commissioner RANKIN. Well, how do you handle this subject when you get down to the government of Mississippi and law enforcement? Do you believe in democracy itself? You have a military dictatorship in Pakistan, is that correct?

Mr. KIZILBASH. No, Dr. Rankin, I will have to say no, that's not true. We have a constitution and we have a very, very fair, as I understand it, type of election. There might be some question on that, but we do have a democracy. And I do believe in it except I have my own views on what it means to different people. And certainly I think democracy can easily lead to the most violent type of activity within it as a dictatorship can. There seems to be much room for dictatorship within democracy, I think, today.

Commissioner RANKIN. That's quite interesting. Have you observed dictatorship within democracy in the United States?

Mr. KIZILBASH. This would be an opinion now because I was here when the last election took place in Mississippi.

[Laughter.]

And I would be quite honestly willing to defend this and to go into some detail, if it were necessary, to show why I think so, but it seems to me politics always works on the level where the people want it to. And my conclusion is that in Mississippi only those issues are discussed and brought to the public which seem usual to arouse the greatest response from the people. Unfortunately the issues happen to be ones that I wouldn't consider to be important to Mississippi today. That's to say, terribly important, in the sense that there are other things they should be discussing and which aren't mentioned and this one thing is mentioned. I think you can call it civil rights or racial discrimination.

Commissioner RANKIN. Do you have any remedy for this situation?

Mr. KIZILBASH. Yes. I would say that if I could count on the law enforcement authorities—this is not peculiar. There is violence everywhere. As long as I would have the faith that I can go to a sheriff's office and not be threatened or not be—I didn't mention this but the highway patrol that examined me at great length here in Jackson after the incident, they took all the testimony I had to offer but were very rude and very disconcerned with respect to my feelings and how I felt and seemed much more concerned with proving that I had no business being here or being in Canton. I would say the evidence is that we have to find law authorities that I could count on. If I could depend on them I would say democracy anywhere in the United States or in the world could work.

Vice Chairman PATTERSON. Does it strike you as an irony that the defense that the American citizens in this automobile offered for you was, "Wait a minute, he's not an American?"

Mr. KIZILBASH. Yes. I would say that's the greatest irony of my existence here. I can't explain how much. To see people that are fairer than me get worse treatment. By "fairer," I mean people who are supposedly Negro who I think are a lot fairer and probably more deserving than I am. My stay is very limited. My rights should be limited to an extent, but certainly they should have much more rights. I think the irony is very much. I think Shakespeare would have enjoyed working in Mississippi.

[Laughter.]

Chairman HANNAH. Mr. Kizilbash, how long do you expect to stay in the United States?

Mr. KIZILBASH. In Mississippi until May. In the United States, I might be here for a while longer. I think until about January. I have to complete a dissertation at Duke University where I am getting my Ph. D.

Chairman HANNAH. You have been in this country for 5 years?

Mr. KIZILBASH. That's right, sir.

Chairman HANNAH. And, with the exception of the period of teaching at Tougaloo, you have been a student?

Mr. KIZILBASH. Yes, sir.

Chairman HANNAH. Always at Duke University?

Mr. KIZILBASH. That's right, sir.

Chairman HANNAH. You indicated you traveled around the country a good deal.

Mr. KIZILBASH. Yes, I did.

Chairman HANNAH. And I gather from what you said that the situation you found in Mississippi is not typical of the United States.

Mr. KIZILBASH. No. I don't think so. I don't think it's typical at all.

Chairman HANNAH. I hope you're right.

Commissioner GRISWOLD. Mr. Kizilbash, where did you study before you came to the United States?

Mr. KIZILBASH. In Pakistan.

Commissioner GRISWOLD. Where in Pakistan?

Mr. KIZILBASH. Forman Christian College, University of Punjab in Lahore.

Commissioner GRISWOLD. And, you learned English in Pakistan before you came to the United States?

Mr. KIZILBASH. That's right, sir.

Commissioner GRISWOLD. Your instruction at the University of the Punjab was in English?

Mr. KIZILBASH. Yes, all work on the college level, unless you ask for it, is given in English. That is to say, there are certain colleges which provide education in Urdu, which is the language of west Pakistan, but most colleges teach in English.

Commissioner GRISWOLD. On the basis of your experience did you have confidence in the law enforcement officers in Lahore?

Mr. KIZILBASH. Yes.

Chairman HANNAH. Any further questions? Thank you very much Mr. Kizilbash. You are excused.

(Witness excused.)

Chairman HANNAH. Since it is 10:30, we will recess for 10 minutes and will begin again at about 18 minutes to 11.

(Whereupon a short recess was taken, after which the hearing resumed.)

Chairman HANNAH. The hearing will come to order. Mr. Taylor, will you call the next witness?

Mr. TAYLOR. The testimony to follow, Mr. Chairman, concerns an election held by the Agricultural Stabilization and Conservation Service in Madison County, and I call as the first witness Mr. F. W. Blease of the Agricultural Stabilization and Conservation Service.

Chairman HANNAH. Mr. Blease. Will you raise your right hand, please?

(Whereupon, Mr. Wayne Wright Blease was duly sworn by the Chairman and testified as follows:)

Chairman HANNAH. Mr. Taylor or Mr. Finkelstein?

TESTIMONY OF MR. WAYNE WRIGHT BLEASE, DIRECTOR, SOUTH CENTRAL AREA, AGRICULTURAL STABILIZATION AND CONSERVATION SERVICE

Mr. FINKELSTEIN. Mr. Blease, will you please give your name, your residence, and your occupation for the record?

Mr. BLEASE. My name is Wayne Wright Blease. I live in Falls Church, Va. I am Director of the South Central Area Agricultural Stabilization and Conservation Service, U.S. Department of Agriculture, Washington, D.C.

Mr. FINKELSTEIN. Mr. Blease, we are going to hear some testimony about an Agricultural Stabilization and Conservation Service election which was conducted in December 1964. Would you please give us some background so that the Commission and the audience can understand the purpose of these elections?

Mr. BLEASE. The Agricultural Stabilization and Conservation Service is an agency of the U.S. Department of Agriculture. The ASCS administers farm programs, which includes allotment and quarter programs for cotton, rice, peanuts, and tobacco and various price support programs, which include the price support program for cotton. We administer the wheat and certificate program, feed grain programs, agricultural conservation program, the cropland conversion program, and programs dealing with defense and disaster. Most of these programs are administered through State and county committees. The ASCS is also administering export, domestic sales and donation programs of the agricultural commodities that we acquire through the price support route. There is an ASCS State office in each State in the Nation. There is a county office in each agricultural county. Programs administered by this agency mean much to the economy of Mississippi. Last year direct payments and cost sharing to Mississippi farmers amounted to approximately $23 million. These payments do not include indirect payments which Mississippi farmers received through certain price support programs. The price support program on cotton alone increased the income of farmers in the State of Mississippi by a minimum of $72 million in 1964 when compared with the world price of cotton. Cotton is the most important cash crop in Mississippi. Most Negro farmers grow cotton.

Action farm programs are directly affecting farmers and are administered through the committee system. These county committees are not interposed by the Department of Agriculture. The Secretary of Agriculture is directed by law to use farmer committeemen to administer these programs. Regulations of the Secretary of Agriculture for election of ASCS community and community committeemen emphasize the requirements of advance public notice of election. In addition to using regular publication media such as newspaper, radio, et cetera, ASCS procedure requires an individual notice of the community committee election to be mailed to each eligible voter of record. This notice, among other things, explains the right to nominate eligible farmers by petition. As a further means of obtaining information concerning members of minority groups ASCS employees visiting farms to measure crop acreages are now required to secure the names and addresses of all persons who have an interest in the farm as owner, tenant, or sharecropper. These persons are then included in the office records. Our field employees must depend on a large extent on the farm operator or his agent to list the names of other persons who share in the crop. Admittedly the names of every tenant or sharecropper in 1964 was not obtained, but we believe, we obtained the names of the vast majority of these people. Any person who is a tenant or sharecropper and is missed is encouraged through public media to come to the ASCS county office and have his name added to the list of eligible voters.

The committee elections in 1964 in Mississippi differed from past years in that for the first time a concentrated effort was made by an organized group to place Negroes on the ballot. Negro farmers have voted in ASCS committee elections in large numbers since the inception of the committee system. But until 1964, Negro farmers were generally on the ballot only in all-Negro communities.

Participation by all farmers in community elections has been high in the Southern States, including Mississippi. In recent years we have encouraged balloting by mail as a means of increasing participation in elections. In nine Southern States, 96 percent of the counties used this method in 1964. In Mississippi, 68 counties used the mail-ballot method while 14 counties used the polling-place method. Each method has strong points over the other. The polling-place method does ensure that the person who casts the ballot is an eligible voter whereas the mail-ballot method has a weakness in that farm operators, or some organization, can put pressure on tenants or sharecroppers to mark the ballot in their presence and mail the ballot for the voter. It is very difficult in some communities to find a suitable place to hold a polling-place election. In years gone by the rural schoolhouse was used for this purpose, but today, generally speaking, these buildings no longer exist. We strongly believe when all angles are considered that balloting by mail is preferable.

We have recently modified our election procedures—effective elections were held in 1965—to prohibit an incumbent community member who is a nominee from performing any functions pertaining to the conduct of the election. The functions he would have performed will be carried out by another farmer eligible to participate in that community's election and such farmer will be appointed by the county committee for this purpose.

We began preparation nearly 6 months prior to the 1964 elections in Mississippi to ensure that free and open elections would be held. Special precautions taken for Mississippi elections were:

1. Special efforts were made to ensure that every voter was on the roll and that these individuals were given notice of the community committee elections.

2. We agreed that the Council of Federated Organizations or any other organization could have observers present at polling places in counties using the polling-place method of election. We agreed that such observer or any other person of the voter's choice could assist those voters who were unable to read or write to mark his ballot if the voter so requested, provided that the marking of a ballot by a person other than the voter was done in the presence of an ASCS committeeman or ASCS employee assisting with the polls. This information was passed on to the ASCS State office in Jackson and the State office issued instructions to this effect to the counties.

3. Sample ballots with the name of candidates, including those put on by petition, were mailed to all known eligible voters in the 14 counties using the polling-place method of election. These sample ballots were mailed at least 10 days in advance of the election.

4. A procedure was developed to ensure the security of challenged ballots.

5. Special training sessions in election procedures and regulations were held for county and community committeemen.

6. Procedures were worked out for notifying local officers, the FBI in Jackson, and the Department of Agriculture in Washington in the event of violence or misconduct at any polling place.

7. A representative of the ASCS State office was assigned to each county on election day where the polling-place method of election was in effect.

8. My staff assistant was assigned on election day to the ASCS State office in Jackson to assist with any problem.

9. The Agricultural Stabilization and Conservation Service requested the Office of Inspector General of the Department of Agriculture to contact the Department of Justice for the purpose of determining what action that department might be able to take to ensure that the forthcoming ASCS elections in Mississippi would be carried out without harmful incident.

The ASCS State executive director for Mississippi also contacted the Federal Bureau of Investigation agent in Jackson in regard to this problem. We were informed that the Federal Bureau of Investigation was not the appropriate agency to take the action requested and that that function pertains rather to the State and local law enforcement authorities in Mississippi. The FBI did offer full cooperation in all matters where it had jurisdiction.

We believe the plans worked out for the election by the Mississippi ASCS State office and the various ASCS county offices and county comittees were prudent and precautionary. Fifty-two Negroes were placed on the ballot by petition in 10 counties. In six of these counties the election was held by mail. Nine Negroes were elected as either community committeemen or alternates in five different counties. Two of these counties used the mail-ballot method and the other three the polling-place method. In addition five Negroes placed on the ballot by the community committee in Bolivar County were elected as has been the case in this county since the inception of the committee system. There is a total of 2,720 community committeemen and alternates in the state of Mississippi, 14 of which are Negroes. Nationwide, 88 Negroes were elected as community commiteemen in 1964, 80 of which were in Southern States. Also, there are 62 Negro farmers who are on review committees, all of which are in Southern States. Review Committeemen are appointed by the Administrator of ASCS under the authority delegated by the Secretary of Agriculture.

Charges of violence, threats, and intimidation against Negro voters and persons observing the polling-place elections have been made.

These charges have received national and congressional attention and inquiry. All allegations dealing with the breakdown in existing procedures are now under order of investigation of the Secretary of Agriculture. If these charges are supported, action to remedy the situation will be taken. On Wednesday of this week I was briefed by persons in charge of investigation work in Madison County. According to the investigators, ASCS officials in Madison County complied with the regulations in the conduct of the committee elections last fall. That completes my statement.

Chairman HANNAH. Mr. Finkelstein?

Mr. FINKELSTEIN. I have one question. Do I understand you correctly, Mr. Blease, that it was the policy of the Department of Agriculture in conducting this election in December 1964, to permit the Council of Federated Organizations or any other organization to have observers at the polling place?

Mr. BLEASE. We had that agreement made in Washington back in September or October, I would guess.

Mr. FINKELSTEIN. Did that policy apply to Madison County?

Mr. BLEASE. That policy applied to all counties in the State of Mississippi where the polling-place elections were in effect. And Madison County did use the polling-place method.

Mr. FINKELSTEIN. Thank you.

Chairman HANNAH. Any of the Comissioners have any questions? Mr. Rogerson?

Mr. ROGERSON. Sir, do you know the percentage of Negro farmers who are in the South?

Mr. BLEASE. No, I do not. We show no race on our records. We have no way, agencywise, to break it down as to Negro or white farmers.

Mr. ROGERSON. Thank you.

Chairman HANNAH. Any other questions? If not, Mr. Blease, you are excused.

(Witness excused.)

Mr. Taylor, will you call the next witness.

Mr. TAYLOR. The next witness is Claude Moore.

Chairman HANNAH. Mr. Claude Moore? Mr. Moore, will you raise your right hand?

(Whereupon, Mr. Claude Moore was duly sworn by the Chairman, and testified as follows:)

TESTIMONY OF MR. CLAUDE MOORE, MADISON COUNTY, MISS.

Mr. FINKELSTEIN. Mr. Moore, I just have a few questions. Will you please give your name, your residence, and your occupation?

Mr. MOORE. My name is Claude Moore. My address, Post Office Box 43, Sharon, Mississippi.

Mr. FINKELSTEIN. What is your occupation?

Mr. MOORE. Farmer.

Mr. FINKELSTEIN. Do you own your own farm?

Mr. MOORE. I do.

Mr. FINKELSTEIN. Are you a registered voter?

Mr. MOORE. I am.

Mr. FINKELSTEIN. We understand that you are president of the organization known as the Madison County Farmer's League?

Mr. MOORE. I am.

Mr. FINKELSTEIN. Can you tell us very briefly what the League does?

Mr. MOORE. Well, the purpose of the Madison County Farmer's League is to educate our people to things that concern us such as agriculture, education, housing program, farm lending agencies, and so on.

Mr. FINKELSTEIN. Did the League, as part of its activities, conduct a campaign to nominate and elect Negro farmers to the ASCS committee in Madison County?

Mr. MOORE. We did.

Mr. FINKELSTEIN. That was last December?

Mr. MOORE. That's right.

Mr. FINKELSTEIN. Did you succeed in electing any?

Mr. MOORE. Well, we had one to be elected.

Mr. FINKELSTEIN. Why weren't more Negroes elected to the committee?

Mr. MOORE. Well, we have a feeling that because of the intimidation around the polling places had something to do with it.

Mr. FINKELSTEIN. Were Negroes afraid to vote?

Mr. MOORE. They were.

Mr. FINKELSTEIN. Why do you feel it is important to elect Negroes to these committees?

Mr. MOORE. We think it is a means by which food can be placed on their tables and money in their pockets.

Mr. FINKELSTEIN. No further questions.

Chairman HANNAH. Mr. Moore, how large is your farm?

Mr. MOORE. 225.8 acres.

Chairman HANNAH. What's the principal crop?

Mr. MOORE. Cotton and corn.

Chairman HANNAH. Now how many Negro farmers are there in Madison County?

Mr. MOORE. I'm not able to quote the exact amount.

Chairman HANNAH. Are there more Negro farmers than white farmers?

Mr. MOORE. There are. As we have closely observed the record to the best of our ability, approximately—probably 65 or 70 percent is Negro farmers.

Chairman HANNAH. How many ASCS directors were elected altogether last December?

Mr. MOORE. One.

Chairman HANNAH. You elected one Negro, but how many whites were elected?

Mr. MOORE. Well, all the rest were white.

Chairman HANNAH. Was that 5 or 8 or 10?

Mr. MOORE. Five. Four were white.

Chairman HANNAH. Four were white?

Mr. MOORE. That's right.

Chairman HANNAH. And you think the reason there was only one elected is because the Negroes were afraid to vote?

Mr. MOORE. Well, particularly before now all the time when we had the polling, the poller, the person operating the polling booth, would come and ask you to cast your ballot or maybe you would pass by where it was. There wasn't any law enforcement officer or any other people standing around to intimidate or whatsoever. But this time, when some of us were placed on the ballot and were attempting to cast ballots, there were various white people that stood around the polling places—quite a few law enforcement officers—and for that reason we feel a vast amount of our people were afraid to vote because actually they would lose their homes. They would have to move if they were found standing around there and in these polling places at these private stores. We would be—didn't have no limit to the amount of white people standing around but when four or five colored people stand around they were asked to move up, get away. You know in a high tone of voice and that itself would make people shaky, you see.

Chairman HANNAH. Were these polling places usually in white stores or gas stations or something of that nature?

Mr. MOORE. At white stores.

Chairman HANNAH. Do you think there were fewer Negro farmers participating in the elections this year than there were last year, or in other years?

Mr. Moore. Well, I think more Negro farmers attempted to participate than usually because this organization of ours has discussed the meaning—what it meant to them, why it boost their interest more. And they have taken more interest in going to the polls this time than they generally have.

Chairman Hannah. Father Hesburgh, any questions?

Commissioner Hesburgh. Mr. Moore, was this the first time there was a Negro candidate?

Mr. Moore. To my knowledge.

Commissioner Hesburgh. And there was no worry about voting as long as you were voting for white candidates?

Mr. Moore. No worry whatsoever. We were asked heretofore.

Commissioner Hesburgh. As soon as you vote for Negro candidate—

Mr. Moore. That's right. In other words, after we advised our people to go and charge one person out of each community, we first attempted to get their name placed on the regular ballot so people would be really familiarized with who was running. But after being denied getting our names placed on the ballot, then we started out to campaign, you know, for the post. And that's why we became defeated. And, of course, we have various numbers of names here where they were turned down. Never was the question asked a man before this time whether his wife had any part of the farm and all that. You know they didn't know if she had the deeds. They had to go get the deeds and see if the name was on the farm contracts and by that time the polling was over, you know.

Chairman Hannah. Mrs. Freeman?

Commissioner Freeman. Mr. Moore, how many members do you have in the Madison County Farmer's League?

Mr. Moore. Well as a rough guess, approximately 500 or better.

Commissioner Freeman. How many of those are registered voters?

Mr. Moore. Not too many.

Commissioner Freeman. During the time of the polling—of the voting for the committee—were there representatives of the Department of Agriculture present at the polling places?

Mr. Moore. Well, once in a while you would see representatives from ASCS office or something around the polling places.

Commissioner Freeman. So, those representatives saw these law enforcement officers and other large groups around the polling places?

Mr. Moore. I'm sure they did.

Commissioner Freeman. Thank you.

Chairman Hannah. Dean Griswold?

Commissioner GRISWOLD. Mr. Moore, when the ballots were cast in these polling places was it a secret ballot? That is, was there a booth or a place where the voter could go and mark the ballot without others seeing how he marked it?

Mr. MOORE. Well, it was a secret place. But lot of time where we think the real defeat come in, these people who was on—these white people who were on the ballot—they were the ones that managed the polling places, you see. And when he go to show someone how to cast his ballot, he would show them the five men placed on there. There wasn't any of us on there and when he go to help him out, he know what to do, to fill out those other names there.

Commissioner GRISWOLD. Did your candidates have to have their names written in on the ballots?

Mr. MOORE. That's right.

Commissioner GRISWOLD. Because they were not printed on the ballot?

Mr. MOORE. That's right, sir.

Commissioner GRISWOLD. After the ballot was marked what did the voter do next? Was the ballot folded so that it couldn't be changed?

Mr. MOORE. That's right, sir.

Commissioner GRISWOLD. And then was it placed in a single ballot box?

Mr. MOORE. In a single ballot box.

Commissioner GRISWOLD. There weren't two boxes, one for white and one for colored?

Mr. MOORE. No, sir.

Commissioner GRISWOLD. Single ballot box?

Mr. MOORE. Single ballot box.

Chairman HANNAH. Mr. Patterson?

Vice Chairman PATTERSON. One question. Why did you want to run Negroes for these offices? Was it as a result of past injustices in your opinion?

Mr. MOORE. That's right, sir.

Vice Chairman PATTERSON. By the ASCS committee?

Mr. MOORE. That's right.

Vice Chairman PATTERSON. In what ways were you not getting what you felt was a square deal?

Mr. MOORE. We felt like we wasn't getting a square deal in cotton allotments and other things pertaining to agriculture.

Vice Chairman PATTERSON. Cotton acreage allotments?

Mr. MOORE. Cotton acreage allotments and other things pertaining to agriculture that this office had anything to do with.

Vice Chairman PATTERSON. And this is the first year that you have ever elected a Negro?

Mr. MOORE. That's right, sir.

Vice Chairman PATTERSON. One out of five?

Mr. MOORE. That is right.

Vice Chairman PATTERSON. Thank you.

Chairman HANNAH. Any further questions?

Mr. TAYLOR. No, sir.

Chairman HANNAH. Thank you very much, Mr. Moore. You are excused.

(Witness excused.)

Call the next witness, Mr. Taylor.

Mr. TAYLOR. Mr. Chairman, I would like to call on Mr. Littlejohn to complete his staff report on the committee election.

Chairman HANNAH. Mr. Littlejohn?

Mr. LITTLEJOHN. The following is a report of a staff investigation of incidents of violence occurring in connection with the Agricultural Stabilization and Conservation Service elections held in Madison County on December 3, 1964. Hawkins General Store was the designated polling place in the town of Flora in the southwestern part of Madison County. Civil rights poll watcher, Miss Euvester Simpson, a Negro from Tougaloo College, was forcibly ejected twice from the polling place by the owner of the store. When she entered a third time the owner asked a town policeman to arrest her. She was held overnight in the Flora jail on a charge of disturbing the peace in a public place.

The Madison Health Center in the town of Madison was used as a polling place. Constable Carl W. Holley was the officer on duty. During the afternoon a group of white teenagers began harassing three civil rights poll watchers. One of them, Marvin Rich, white, from New York City, remained outside the building. The whites began throwing stones at him. He tried to enter the building, but two teenagers blocked the doorway. One punched him in the face and another struck him in the face with the buckle end of a belt. Constable Holley came outside and asked Rich if he wanted to make a complaint, adding that he thought the boy would not have hit Rich unless he had been provoked. Rich said he did not wish to make a complaint. No arrests were made.

Eric Orr, a white civil rights worker, was punched in the face by a white man as he walked into the polling place in Ballard's Gin. Orr swore out a warrant and the man was arrested. Orr failed to appear at the trial and the man was released.

Community E is the Gluckstadt area of the county. The polling place was the office of the R&N grocery. The civil rights worker who observed was Miss Elayne DeLott. Space in the office was crowded, but ASCS manager Robert Hodges arranged things so that Miss DeLott could observe the balloting and assist any Negro farmer who requested her help. Sometime after 9:30 a.m. Sheriff Cauthen arrived and asked Miss DeLott to leave the store. She was told that she could see all she needed to see from the outside. She complied with his order. After the sheriff left, an ASCS committeeman asked her to come back inside the store. An hour or so later Sheriff Cauthen returned. He discussed the situation with the ASCS committeemen, and, over their objection, ordered Miss DeLott to leave the store. He told her that he was in charge of keeping the peace and that if she remained in the store four or five white men might decide to rough her up. He advised that she would be safer outside. Later she went back and was arrested when Sheriff Cauthen returned to the store. After Miss DeLott had been arrested, Eartis Crawford, a Negro civil rights worker, attempted to enter the R&N grocery. A group of white men stopped him at the entrance to the store. One of them got a gun from behind the counter, but was restrained by other men in the store. Someone struck Crawford on the back of the head and he was shoved out of the store.

Mr. TAYLOR. Does that conclude your report?

Mr. LITTLEJOHN. Yes, it does.

Chairman HANNAH. Mr. Taylor, will you call the next witness?

Mr. TAYLOR. The next witness is Robert Hodges.

Chairman HANNAH. Mr. Robert Hodges?

Mr. Hodges, will you raise your right hand?

(Whereupon, Mr. Robert Hodges was duly sworn by the Chairman and testified as follows:)

Chairman HANNAH. Mr. Finkelstein?

TESTIMONY OF MR. ROBERT R. HODGES, MADISON COUNTY, MISS.

Mr. FINKELSTEIN. Will you please give us your name, your residence, and your occupation?

Mr. HODGES. My name is Robert R. Hodges. My address is 521 Lion Street and I am office manager of the Madison County ASCS office, Canton.

Mr. FINKELSTEIN. How long have you held this position?

Mr. HODGES. I have held this position for 15 years and 4 months.

Mr. FINKELSTEIN. There was an ASCS election in December 1964, in Madison County, is that right?

Mr. HODGES. That is correct.

Mr. FINKELSTEIN. What preparation did you make for that election?

Mr. HODGES. The preparations that were made for the election were those specified in the instructions and the regulations. All of those instructions and the regulations were adhered to by our office.

Mr. FINKELSTEIN. Mr. Blease has testified that it was the Department of Agriculture's policy to allow civil rights workers or other persons to be present at the polling places as watchers. Is that your understanding?

Mr. HODGES. We were informed that the civil rights workers or poll watchers would be at the poll. It was our understanding that the committeemen, as far as they were concerned, were to allow them to observe. We had no control over the people who owned the buildings as far as any action they may take or any action a sheriff or officer may take.

Mr. FINKELSTEIN. But, it was the Department of Agriculture's policy to allow these persons to be present at the polls, is that correct?

Mr. HODGES. As far as I understand, it was, yes, sir.

Mr. FINKELSTEIN. And did you convey the substance of that policy to the law enforcement officers in Madison County?

Mr. HODGES. They were advised that the poll watchers would be at the polls.

Mr. FINKELSTEIN. Did you convey that policy to Sheriff Cauthen?

Mr. HODGES. Yes, sir, I did.

Mr. FINKELSTEIN. What was his response?

Mr. HODGES. His response was that the law enforcement officers would be in the vicinity, probably, and would probably come by the polls in case they were needed for any disturbance that might take place.

Mr. FINKELSTEIN. Did you convey this policy to the local businessmen in Madison County, the ASCS committeemen?

Mr. HODGES. The policy was conveyed to them. This was discussed with them at several times.

Mr. FINKELSTEIN. Did you explain this policy to the store owners?

Mr. HODGES. This policy was explained to the store owners. As far as we were concerned, there would be poll watchers. We had been advised there would be poll watchers present.

Mr. FINKELSTEIN. Did any of the store owners object to the presence of poll watchers?

Mr. HODGES. To my knowledge, they did not object.

Mr. FINKELSTEIN. Did any ASCS committeeman, to your knowledge, cause any civil rights observer to be arrested or forcibly ejected from a polling place?

Mr. Hodges. To my knowledge they did not.

Mr. Finkelstein. Do you know that Elayne DeLott, a civil rights worker acting as a poll watcher, was arrested by Sheriff Cauthen at one of the polls?

Mr. Hodges. I was advised that she was.

Mr. Finkelstein. Prior to her arrest, did you have any discussions with Sheriff Cauthen about this matter?

Mr. Hodges. Not about her being arrested.

Mr. Finkelstein. Prior to her arrest, did you have any discussions with Sheriff Cauthen about her presence at the polling place?

Mr. Hodges. Not her individual presence, no.

Mr. Finkelstein. Was she there when you had this discussion with Sheriff Cauthen?

Mr. Hodges. What community was she in?

Mr. Finkelstein. I believe it was the Gluckstadt area of the county, community E.

Mr. Hodges. I had no conversation with Sheriff Cauthen regarding this lady.

Mr. Finkelstein. Did you have conversation with Sheriff Cauthen at the Gluckstadt area polling place?

Mr. Hodges. Community E is the northeast Canton community and it is not the Gluckstadt community.

Mr. Finkelstein. Community E—did you have any discussions at community E with Sheriff Cauthen?

Mr. Hodges. No, sir.

Mr. Finkelstein. No further questions.

Chairman Hannah. Any of the Commissioners have any questions? Mrs. Freeman?

Commissioner Freeman. Mr. Hodges, you indicated that your office had no control over the buildings. I would like to know what arrangements were made between the Service and an owner for the use of his building?

Mr. Hodges. Throughout the years the store owners have voluntarily permitted our organization to use these various places as polling places. Most of the places—I would say all of these are places that both races felt free to come to and we had discussed with them—we had asked them if we could hold the election there this year and they had also agreed.

Chairman Hannah. Mr. Rogerson?

Mr. Rogerson. All the polling places are in white stores or in white facilities in your area?

Mr. Hodges. All of the polling places are in white stores with the exception of one, which is a public place in the B community and that is a health center at which colored—Negro and white come for services.

Mr. ROGERSON. Thank you.

Chairman HANNAH. Thank you. Any further questions, Mr. Finkelstein?

Mr. FINKELSTEIN. No further questions.

Chairman HANNAH. You are excused, Mr. Hodges. Thank you. (Witness excused.)

Mr. Taylor, will you call the next witness.

Mr. TAYLOR. The next witness is Sheriff Jack Cauthen.

Chairman HANNAH. Sheriff Cauthen, will you raise your right hand? (Whereupon, Sheriff Jack Cauthen was duly sworn by the Chairman and testified as follows:)

Chairman HANNAH. Will you introduce your attorney?

Sheriff CAUTHEN. This is my attorney, Mr. William Sterling King.

Chairman HANNAH. Mr. Finkelstein?

TESTIMONY OF JACK S. CAUTHEN, SHERIFF, MADISON COUNTY, MISS.

Mr. FINKELSTEIN. Will you state your name, your residence, and your occupation?

Mr. CAUTHEN. My name is Jack S. Cauthen. My residence is Madison, Miss., and I'm the sheriff of Madison County.

Mr. FINKELSTEIN. How long have you served as sheriff of Madison County?

Mr. CAUTHEN. Since January 6, 1964.

Mr. FINKELSTEIN. Prior to your election, what was your occupation?

Mr. CAUTHEN. Vocational agriculture teacher.

Mr. FINKELSTEIN. Where were you a teacher?

Mr. CAUTHEN. At Madison Regional School in Madison County.

Mr. FINKELSTEIN. Is that a high school?

Mr. CAUTHEN. Yes, sir.

Mr. FINKELSTEIN. Did you have any experience or training in law enforcement prior to becoming sheriff?

Mr. CAUTHEN. I did not.

Mr. FINKELSTEIN. Do you have a duty to keep the peace in your county as sheriff?

Mr. CAUTHEN. Will you repeat that, please.

Mr. FINKELSTEIN. As sheriff do you have a duty to keep the peace in your county?

Mr. CAUTHEN. Yes, sir.

Mr. FINKELSTEIN. Sheriff, Hamid Kizilbash has testified that he was beaten by a gang of white men after attending a voter registration meeting in Canton and that he sent you a letter offering to identify one of the cars which had been involved. Did you investigate this case?

Mr. CAUTHEN. As I told you the other day, I told the committee the other day that I received no formal complaint on this alleged incident.

Mr. FINKELSTEIN. Would you speak up a little, sheriff?

Mr. CAUTHEN. I received no formal complaint on this question, this incident. The letter that was read here this morning addressed to me from Mr. Kizilbash, I did not receive.

Mr. FINKELSTEIN. Did you investigate this incident?

Mr. CAUTHEN. I understand about a week, after this incident happened, Dr. Beittel, who at that time was president of the college of Tougaloo, called me on the phone and asked me if any arrests have been made—what I had found out regarding this matter. I told him that there had been no formal complaint made to me and I knew nothing of the matter. There had been no arrests made. By the way, I have that in this report that I was to hand in to this committee today.

Mr. FINKELSTEIN. When Dr. Beittel called you about a week later, isn't it true, sheriff, that he gave you the license plate numbers of one of the cars which had been involved and the name of the owner of the car?

Mr. CAUTHEN. He gave me the license plate of the car. The owner was not mentioned. He asked me if I could run it down. That was done.

Mr. FINKELSTEIN. And did you run it down?

Mr. CAUTHEN. Beg pardon?

Mr. FINKELSTEIN. And, you did run it down?

Mr. CAUTHEN. I did.

Mr. FINKELSTEIN. And you investigated the case; is that right?

Mr. CAUTHEN. That is right, sir, to that extent.

Mr. FINKELSTEIN. And did you find out who had been responsible?

Mr. CAUTHEN. I found out that the owner of that car, who is a very responsible person in Canton, said he had no control over that car that night. The car was taken. It was beyond his knowledge, without his knowledge. He didn't know anything about it whatsoever.

Mr. FINKELSTEIN. Did you ever make any attempt to contact Mr. Kizilbash?

Mr. CAUTHEN. No, sir.

Mr. FINKELSTEIN. Why?

Mr. CAUTHEN. That was about a week later that Mr.—Dr. Beittel called me in regard to that question. I had never seen Mr. Kizilbash. I can't pronounce his name. I figured if he wanted to file a complaint, if he had a complaint to make, I felt that my office was the place to make that complaint.

Mr. FINKELSTEIN. Sheriff, were you aware in December 1964 of the Department of Agriculture's policy in connection with the ASCS election which said that civil rights workers and other members of the public would be allowed as poll watchers at the poll? Were you aware of that policy?

Mr. CAUTHEN. That poll watchers would be allowed at the polls?

Mr. FINKELSTEIN. Yes.

Mr. CAUTHEN. Yes, sir.

Mr. FINKELSTEIN. You were aware of that policy; is that right?

Mr. CAUTHEN. Yes, sir.

Mr. FINKELSTEIN. And did you arrest Elayne DeLott, a civil rights worker, at the poll place of the ASCS election on December 3?

Mr. CAUTHEN. I wouldn't be sure about the date because I haven't got my notes open. I didn't come prepared to answer questions on that, but I arrested a white girl at the R&N grocery polling place. I arrested her myself.

Mr. FINKELSTEIN. What was she doing at the time that led you to arrest her?

Mr. CAUTHEN. She was blocking the polling booth. They had two booths, cloth booths I call them, in this store. She was standing directly in front of one of those booths. I asked her if she would move. People who go into the booths would have to walk absolutely around her to get to the booths. I asked her if she would move to just outside the door. I asked the poll workers whether they would if necessary turn the booths around so she could observe or see into the booths. She agreed to move outside the door. That's the first time I was out there.

We left, were called back sometime later, some disturbance. I went to no polling place unless I was called. We went back the second time. This girl was back inside the store in front of the booth, same place she was before, the first time. I asked her again if she would move and she informed me that she had called, I believe Washington, and they informed her that she had a perfect right to observe at the polls. I said, "You have a perfect right to observe at these polls, that right I will give you, but not standing where you are now. Will you please move back outside where you were before?"—where I placed her the first time. I asked her to go the first time. She moved back outside. That's the second time.

All right. The third time when I walked in she was back in the same place. I placed her under arrest and carried her to jail.

Mr. FINKELSTEIN. Was there a complaint from an ASCS committeeman, who was at the polls against her?

Mr. CAUTHEN. None other than her being inside. Right in front of the polls, the booths.

Mr. FINKELSTEIN. Did an ASCS committeeman make a complaint to you about her presence in the polls?

Mr. CAUTHEN. They made a remark. I said "There she is standing there, I can see it."

Mr. FINKELSTEIN. Did they ask you to remove her?

Mr. CAUTHEN. No, sir.

Mr. FINKELSTEIN. They did not?

Mr. CAUTHEN. No, sir.

Mr. FINKELSTEIN. Did the owner of the store ask you to remove her?

Mr. CAUTHEN. No, sir.

Mr. FINKELSTEIN. You took it upon yourself to remove her. Isn't that right, then, Sheriff?

Mr. CAUTHEN. That's correct.

Mr. FINKELSTEIN. Sheriff, do you recall the charges which you brought against Miss DeLott? Maybe it will refresh your recollection if I show you a copy of your records marked as Exhibit 19 which you produced in response to our subpena. We have underlined her name there in the records.

Mr. CAUTHEN. Would you show me that please, sir?—Investigation.

Mr. FINKELSTEIN. The charge was investigation, is that right?

Mr. CAUTHEN. That's right.

Mr. FINKELSTEIN. What were you investigating, Sheriff?

Mr. CAUTHEN. My main purpose was to get her out of that store, to get her to keep from blocking the poll booths as I told you at first.

Mr. FINKELSTEIN. Had she committed a crime?

Mr. CAUTHEN. If you don't mind, I would like to answer that my own way.

Mr. FINKELSTEIN. I beg your pardon?

Mr. CAUTHEN. May I answer that in my own way?

Mr. FINKELSTEIN. Yes.

Mr. CAUTHEN. She had deliberately twice disobeyed my request. I informed her that there could possibly be friction or she could cause trouble. And it is my job to preserve the peace and dignity in Madison County. That is why I asked her in the first place to move from in front of the polling booth to the door. To me she was a threat to the peace and dignity of that polling place, of the city of Canton, and Madison County. That is why I charged her with investigation and later released her.

Mr. FINKELSTEIN. Did you release her on bond, Sheriff?

Mr. CAUTHEN. I think she was released without bond, as well as I remember.

Mr. FINKELSTEIN. I'll show you your records and perhaps this will refresh your recollection?

Mr. CAUTHEN. $250 bond.

Mr. FINKELSTEIN. Would you say that louder, Sheriff, please.

Mr. CAUTHEN. $250 bond she was released on.

Mr. FINKELSTEIN. Is it your practice when you arrest persons for investigation to release them on bond?

Mr. CAUTHEN. Not without a charge being made.

Mr. FINKELSTEIN. Did you make any charge?

Mr. CAUTHEN. I don't remember.

Mr. FINKELSTEIN. Is there any charge indicated in your records?

Mr. CAUTHEN. You had those records the other day. I didn't come prepared to answer questions on that.

Mr. FINKELSTEIN. I'll show you your records again, then.

Mr. CAUTHEN. May I keep this over here?

Mr. FINKELSTEIN. Yes, you may.

Mr. CAUTHEN. By this record there is no charge.

Mr. FINKELSTEIN. No further questions.

Chairman HANNAH. Dean Griswold?

Commissioner GRISWOLD. Sheriff, when you say that you requested or ordered Miss DeLott to stand outside, outside of what did you mean?

Mr. CAUTHEN. Just right outside the door to the store.

Commissioner GRISWOLD. Outside the store?

Mr. CAUTHEN. Just, yes, sir.

Commissioner GRISWOLD. Away—not within the polling place at all?

Mr. CAUTHEN. As you walk immediately in the front door, immediately to your left as you walked in was your polling booth, two, I believe. She was standing at the second booth over there.

Commissioner GRISWOLD. How can anyone be a watcher at the polls and not be allowed in the polling place?

Mr. CAUTHEN. She was in plain sight of the polling both at all times.

Commissioner GRISWOLD. But outside the store?

Mr. CAUTHEN. Yes, sir.

Commissioner GRISWOLD. Were there other people in the store?

Mr. CAUTHEN. Yes, sir.

Commissioner GRISWOLD. Did you order them to stand outside?

Mr. CAUTHEN. No, sir.

Commissioner GRISWOLD. Why did you not order them to stand outside?

Mr. CAUTHEN. They wasn't blocking anything, disturbing anything.

Commissioner GRISWOLD. Couldn't she have stood inside without blocking anything?

Mr. CAUTHEN. Beg pardon?

Commissioner GRISWOLD. Couldn't she have stood inside without blocking anything?

Mr. CAUTHEN. Well, in that particular corner, sir, there the way that thing was arranged, the way the store and the polling place was arranged and the place she was standing, it was very crowded.

Commissioner GRISWOLD. Why didn't you suggest that someone else stand outside to make a place for her to stand inside?

Mr. CAUTHEN. That would have suited me fine. That's the first thing that came to my mind to ask them to stand outside this door.

Commissioner GRISWOLD. Ask who to stand outside the door?

Mr. CAUTHEN. This girl.

Commissioner GRISWOLD. Why didn't you ask one of the other persons to stand outside?

Mr. CAUTHEN. It didn't occur to me.

Commissioner GRISWOLD. If it was too crowded, why didn't you suggest some alternative?

Mr. CAUTHEN. It didn't occur to me.

Commissioner GRISWOLD. Was there some disturbance there at any time in your presence?

Mr. CAUTHEN. No, sir.

Commissioner GRISWOLD. Did anyone make a complaint to you at any time?

Mr. CAUTHEN. Complaints regarding what?

Commissioner GRISWOLD. Her presence in the store?

Mr. CAUTHEN. Yes, sir.

Commissioner GRISWOLD. What kind of complaint?

Mr. CAUTHEN. That she was blocking the polling booth and would probably sooner or later cause trouble.

Commissioner GRISWOLD. Any complaint that she had caused trouble?

Mr. CAUTHEN. That she would probably cause trouble.

Commissioner GRISWOLD. My question was, was there any complaint that she had caused trouble?

Mr. CAUTHEN. No. sir.

Commissioner GRISWOLD. I understand that you arrested her for investigation?

Mr. CAUTHEN. Yes, sir; by this record here.

Commissioner GRISWOLD. Is investigation a crime in Mississippi?

Mr. CAUTHEN. No, sir.

Commissioner GRISWOLD. On what basis did you arrest her or any person for investigation?

Mr. CAUTHEN. Would you repeat that, please.

Commissioner GRISWOLD. On what basis did you arrest her or any person for investigation?

Mr. CAUTHEN. I'm not quite sure.

Commissioner GRISWOLD. Let me put the question another way. Do you understand that you have authority under the laws of Mississippi to arrest any person for investigation?

Mr. CAUTHEN. Yes, sir.

Commissioner GRISWOLD. Could you or through your counsel tell me what the authority is for that answer.

Mr. CAUTHEN. Well, my answer would be this, if you care for me to answer.

Commissioner GRISWOLD. Without a warrant and without a complaint, you have authority to arrest a citizen of Mississippi or indeed of a foreign country for investigation; is that your understanding of your power?

Mr. CAUTHEN. On information and belief for disturbing the peace; yes, sir.

Commissioner GRISWOLD. Was there any evidence that she was disturbing the peace?

Mr. CAUTHEN. To me; yes, sir.

Commissioner GRISWOLD. What had she done that gave you evidence that she was disturbing the peace?

Mr. CAUTHEN. She blocked the polling booth where it was extremely crowded, which I had no control over—the facilities at the polling place. And she was standing in front of the polling booths as I said, and people going into the booths would have to walk around her to get into the booth. And, sir, going back quite some time back there had been quite a friction, quite a bit of friction, a lot of friction in Canton and Madison County regarding these people up there. When I say people—I mean the COFO workers, and I didn't know until this morning we were quite so bad or as bad as we were, but there was an intensive amount of friction that morning. To me there was enough to cause serious trouble in the way of a small riot or someone getting physically hurt. To me that was sufficient reason to remove that person from the polling place.

Commissioner GRISWOLD. I'm still trying to get any suggestion, any indication of information which you had that she was in fact committing a breach of the peace. So far you have given me no such information. You have said that you feared that maybe a breach of the peace might happen. Was she making a loud noise?

Mr. CAUTHEN. No, sir. I told you all I know to tell.

Commissioner GRISWOLD. Was she throwing herself around and pushing people?

Mr. CAUTHEN. No. She had a very decidedly strong odor that was very unpleasant.

[Laughter.]

Commissioner GRISWOLD. Do you understand that an odor constitutes a breach of the peace?

Mr. CAUTHEN. In some instances; yes.

Commissioner GRISWOLD. That having an odor is a breach of the peace?

Mr. CAUTHEN. No, sir; I didn't say that.

Commissioner GRISWOLD. I think that's what you said.

Mr. CAUTHEN. Well, I'll retract that statement. I misunderstood you, sir.

Commissioner GRISWOLD. What evidence did you have, Sheriff—and I ask this in all sincerity and I think we are entitled to have an answer—what evidence, if any, did you have that she was committing a breach of the peace?

Mr. CAUTHEN. After defying my suggestions, sir, for the second time.

Commissioner GRISWOLD. Your suggestions are law in Madison County, I gather?

Mr. CAUTHEN. No, sir; only in certain cases.

Commissioner GRISWOLD. A person who does not comply with your suggestions commits a crime in Madison County?

Mr. CAUTHEN. Absolutely not.

Commissioner GRISWOLD. Well, then, what had this person, Miss DeLott, done which constituted a crime in Madison County?

Mr. CAUTHEN. I tried to answer that for you twice, sir. I'm afraid I am incapable of giving you the correct answer.

Commissioner GRISWOLD. You have said you had fears that something might happen in the future. But you have not given me one scintilla of evidence available to you, either by way of complaint or by actions in your presence, that she had in fact committed a breach of the peace. Now, if I'm wrong in that statement, will you please tell me what the evidence was that enabled you to conclude that she should be arrested for committing a breach of the peace.

Mr. KING. If it please the Commission, I think that it is the duty of any peace officer to preclude or to avoid any known instances, known and shown to him by his own visible eyesight, as well as to make arrests where there have been violations. Now, you ask what the law was.

Commissioner GRISWOLD. Under what section of the Mississippi code is it his duty to take such action?

Mr. KING. It is his duty—I cannot quote the section, sir—but it is his duty as chief law enforcement officer in Madison County, Miss., to preserve the peace.

Commissioner GRISWOLD. May I question the witness? It is your duty to preserve the peace against threats of a breach of the peace?

Mr. KING. The answer is yes.

Mr. CAUTHEN. Yes.

Commissioner GRISWOLD. What threat to the breach of the peace was there, in your presence or by complaint, made to you?

Mr. KING. I'd like the record here to show——

Commissioner GRISWOLD. I have asked the question to the witness. If you want to make an objection I think you are entitled to, but I would like to have the witness answer the question.

Mr. KING. I would like to have the record show that I object to the question as being asked repetitiously. It has been asked, asked, asked, and answered, answered, answered.

Commissioner GRISWOLD. No, Mr. Attorney. I have not asked about any threat to the peace. That was introduced by you in response to the question I put to the sheriff. I'm now asking the sheriff as to what information he had that there was a threat of the breach of the peace.

Mr. CAUTHEN. Sir, I have tried to explain to you twice. It seems that I can't get the understanding across to you.

Commissioner GRISWOLD. No, I'm afraid I have no information yet as to a threat of a breach of the peace. Do you regard yourself as having an obligation to protect COFO workers in Madison County?

Mr. CAUTHEN. Yes, sir.

Commissioner GRISWOLD. Do you have an obligation—did you have an obligation to protect Miss DeLott in Madison County?

Mr. CAUTHEN. Yes, sir.

Commissioner GRISWOLD. Why, instead of arresting Miss DeLott, did you not protect her in the performance of her legal function to act as a watcher at the poll? Or let me put it another way. If there was a threat of the breach of the peace was not the threat on the part of other people? Was there any evidence that Miss DeLott was going to hit people or make loud noises or do anything else which would constitute a breach of the peace?

Mr. CAUTHEN. None.

Commissioner GRISWOLD. Thank you. That's interesting. If there was a threat to the peace, in your opinion, was not the threat from people other than Miss DeLott?

Mr. CAUTHEN. To me, sir, that threat came from Miss DeLott.

Commissioner GRISWOLD. What came from Miss DeLott?

Mr. CAUTHEN. The threat you keep talking about.

Commissioner GRISWOLD. That she would make loud noises?

Mr. CAUTHEN. Make a breach of the peace or cause a breach of the peace.

Commissioner GRISWOLD. Was not the threat to the breach of the peace from the other persons rather than from Miss DeLott?

Mr. CAUTHEN. To me, sir; Miss DeLott was the cause of it.

Commissioner GRISWOLD. You have just testified under oath that you had no fear that she would either make loud noises or hit people. What do you understand to be a breach of the peace?

Mr. CAUTHEN. A fight, a riot.

Commissioner GRISWOLD. You had no information that she would start a fight or start a riot. Therefore, if there was going to be a fight or a riot it was going to be started by somebody else. Why didn't you arrest the other people there?

Mr. CAUTHEN. You said that, sir. I didn't.

Commissioner GRISWOLD. Well, who did you think was going to start the fight?

Mr. CAUTHEN. Miss DeLott.

Commissioner GRISWOLD. In what way would she start the fight or the riot?

Mr. CAUTHEN. Sir, I won't answer any more. I refuse to answer any more questions along that line of questions.

Commissioner GRISWOLD. On what grounds?

Mr. CAUTHEN. That I have tried my best to answer them for you, sir. I can't seem to get an understanding between us.

Commissioner GRISWOLD. I simply would like to have any trace of evidence that you had that Miss DeLott was herself, through any actions which she might take, a threat to the peace in Madison County. Now, I'll ask you that question and it seems to me that it should be answered.

Mr. CAUTHEN. I have tried to answer it three times for you, sir.

Commissioner GRISWOLD. Well, can you answer it once more and then I will stop.

Mr. CAUTHEN. No, sir.

Commissioner GRISWOLD. I hope that you can get me a better answer this time than you have so far.

Mr. CAUTHEN. Well, no, sir. I don't care to answer the question again.

Commissioner GRISWOLD. You are under subpena, Sheriff.

Mr. CAUTHEN. Yes, sir.

Commissioner GRISWOLD. You are under oath.

Mr. CAUTHEN. Yes, sir.

Commissioner GRISWOLD. Let's turn to the case of Mr. Kizilbash. What investigation did you make as a result of the information which was brought to your attention in that case?

Mr. CAUTHEN. I checked this tag out. In other words, I ran an identification on the tag and found who the tag belonged to. I went to that person and questioned him. He told me and said he had witnesses to prove that his car was taken without his knowledge, that he knew absolutely nothing in regard to where that car was that night.

Commissioner GRISWOLD. Did you interview Mr. Kizilbash?

Mr. CAUTHEN. No, sir.

Commissioner GRISWOLD. Did you make any effort to interview Mr. Kizilbash?

Mr. CAUTHEN. No, sir.

Commissioner GRISWOLD. Why not?

Mr. CAUTHEN. Because I didn't hear about it. I didn't get the complaint on the incident until approximately a week later through a telephone call from Dr. Beittel, as I told this gentleman before.

Commissioner GRISWOLD. What relevance is there to the fact that you didn't get the information until a week later?

Mr. CAUTHEN. Well, sir; if you are going to investigate a happening of a week's time, that can mean quite a bit of——

Commissioner GRISWOLD. This was not a theft, sheriff.

Mr. CAUTHEN. Beg pardon.

Commissioner GRISWOLD. This was not a theft. This was an assault.

Mr. CAUTHEN. Yes, sir. I said that a lapse of time—a lapse of time of a week means quite a bit of difference in the information you get—if you wait a week to start your investigation.

Commissioner GRISWOLD. I have no doubt that that's true, but if you make no efforts to get information at all, then you get no information. How do you know what information you could have got from Mr. Kizilbash if you made no effort to get it?

Mr. CAUTHEN. I felt that if Mr. Kizilbash wanted to make a complaint, he could have called himself. He could have come to my office, sir.

Commissioner GRISWOLD. You regard it as your duty to maintain the peace in Madison County?

Mr. CAUTHEN. Yes, sir.

Commissioner GRISWOLD. You regard Miss DeLott as a greater threat to the peace of Madison County than the person who had assaulted Mr. Kizilbash?

Mr. CAUTHEN. That's what you say, sir.

Commissioner GRISWOLD. No, I ask you a question. Did you?

Mr. CAUTHEN. I'm afraid I will have to ask you to rephrase that question again or restate it.

Commissioner GRISWOLD. Did you regard Miss DeLott as a greater threat to the peace of Madison County than the person who assaulted Mr. Kizilbash in Madison County?

Mr. CAUTHEN. You want me to answer that?

Commissioner GRISWOLD. Yes.

Mr. CAUTHEN. I didn't consider Miss DeLott—I can't contrast the two. I don't quite get what you mean throwing the both together.

Commissioner GRISWOLD. You arrested Miss DeLott for doing nothing, according to your own testimony. She did not make a loud noise. She did not threaten anyone. What she did was to fail to comply with your orders which you say are not law in Madison County. But you arrested her. Now, you have a vicious assault on the highway in Madison County and you made no effort to get in touch with the person who was the victim of that assault. My question is this: Did you regard Mis DeLott as a greater threat to the peace and order of Madison County than the person who assaulted Mr. Kizilbash?

Mr. KING. No.

Mr. CAUTHEN. I didn't know anything about the assault of Mr. Kizilbash until a week later. On Miss DeLott, yes, sir, I considered her a threat to the peace.

Commissioner GRISWOLD. Let me turn to one other matter. Four churches have been burned in Madison County within the past 12 months, is that correct?

Mr. CAUTHEN. Yes, sir.

Commissioner GRISWOLD. At least four?

Mr. CAUTHEN. Yes, sir.

Commissioner GRISWOLD. That's considerably higher than the average of that activity in Mississippi, is it not?

Mr. CAUTHEN. I don't know about the average, sir, but that's mighty high for Madison County.

Commissioner GRISWOLD. What investigation have you made of those four church burnings?

Mr. CAUTHEN. I have the report here. I have these reports here.

Mr. KING. For the record we would like the record to show we agreed when we were here the other day we didn't have reports but we would prepare and furnish reports, and at this time we would like to submit those.

Chairman GRISWOLD. The reports are received.

(Exhibit No. 20 was marked for identification and received in evidence.)

Commissioner GRISWOLD. Have any arrests ever been made as a result of these investigations?

Mr. CAUTHEN. Of the church burnings?

Commissioner GRISWOLD. Yes.

Mr. CAUTHEN. No, sir.

Commissioner GRISWOLD. Thank you. That's all.

Chairman HANNAH. Mrs. Freeman?

Commissioner FREEMAN. Sheriff Cauthen, this Commission has received testimony this morning concerning the allegations that certain of the law enforcement officers are members of groups that have been organized for the purpose of resisting the attempts of Negroes to exercise their constitutional rights. I would like to know if you are a member of the White Citizens Council?

Mr. CAUTHEN. I don't know officially whether I am or not, whether my name is on the roll, I don't know. I mean, I do not know whether my name is on the roll of the steering committee of the Citizens Council, but I do attend the meetings.

Commissioner FREEMAN. Do you believe that your membership in such a group, organized, as I said, for the purpose of resisting the attempts of Negroes to exercise their constitutional rights, is consistent with your responsibilities as sheriff?

Mr. CAUTHEN. May I answer that in my own way?

Commissioner FREEMAN. Yes.

Mr. CAUTHEN. As a member of the Citizens Council back when voter demonstrations first started in Canton and Madison County, we had no way of knowing. It was advertised, televised, broadcast that there would be some 2,000 people in Canton at that time. Now, going back to the Citizens Council—the way the Citizens Council has been invaluable to me as chief law enforcement officer—they assisted me in holding meetings throughout the county, explaining to the general public that we expected unknown trouble on these voter administration demonstrations. And we would request through these meetings that these people please let the law enforcement officers handle whatever trouble might come. Now, the Citizens Council, as far as my being a member of it or the steering committee—that was one of its major advantages to me as a group. So I'm proud to be a member of the Citizens Council.

Commissioner FREEMAN. Sheriff, have there been numbers of Negroes who have attempted to register as voters in Madison County during the past year?

Mr. CAUTHEN. Yes. Yes.

Commissioner FREEMAN. How many have been added to the voting roll?

Mr. CAUTHEN. I don't know.

Commissioner FREEMAN. Thank you.

Chairman HANNAH. Father Hesburgh?

Commissioner HESBURGH. Sheriff, in getting back to the R&N grocery store, we received a report in testimony this morning that after Miss DeLott had been arrested, Eartis Crawford, a Negro civil rights worker, attempted to enter the R&N grocery. A number of white men stopped him at the entrance to the store. One of them got out a gun behind the counter, but was restrained by other men in the store. Someone struck Crawford in the back of the head and shoved him out of the store. Would you consider this a breach of the peace?

Mr. CAUTHEN. Yes, sir.

Commissioner HESBURGH. Was anything done on that?

Mr. CAUTHEN. Nothing.

Commissioner HESBURGH. On that same day, or the occasion of the same election, we read that Marvin Rich, white, was at the scene of one of these elections. He tried to enter the building because the teenagers surrounding him were throwing stones at him. When he tried to enter the building, teenagers blocked the doorway. One punched him in the face and the other struck him with the buckle end of the belt. One of your constables, I believe, was on the scene. Maybe he isn't your constable. I'm not sure how the law is organized.

Mr. KING. He is an independent officer.

Commissioner HESBURGH. Independent officer. But, in any case, no arrest was made there. Would you consider this a breach of the peace, this throwing of stones at a person standing before a store and blocking his entrance to the store and then hitting him in the face with the fist and belt buckle?

Mr. CAUTHEN. If that happened, yes, sir; definitely.

Commissioner HESBURGH. I believe this is the result of testimony received by the staff of the Commission. Sheriff, we also read this morning a long list of bombings, burnings, beating. The list almost always notes that no arrests were made. On the other hand, we have heard of a few arrests that have been made and in many—almost every case they are arrests of people who have tried to help other people obtain their civil rights. In almost every case the fine is completely out of balance with what other fines are for similar arrests. We find, for example, that a white man literally shot and hit five young Negroes with birdshot and was fined $500 of which $250 was suspended for good behavior. Do you really think, Sheriff, there is an even-handed administration of justice in the county?

Mr. CAUTHEN. An even-handed?

Commissioner HESBURGH. Administration of justice in the county, in Madison County? Let me put it more bluntly. Do you think whites and Negroes get the same kind of justice in Madison County?

Mr. CAUTHEN. Sir, I have a lot of Negro friends in Madison County.

Commissioner HESBURGH. That isn't the question, though.

Mr. CAUTHEN. Yes, sir. I do.

Commissioner HESBURGH. Do you think Negroes and whites get the same kind of justice in the county?

Mr. CAUTHEN. Yes, sir.

Commissioner HESBURGH. Thank you.

Chairman HANNAH. Mr. Rankin?

Commissioner RANKIN. I recognize being a peace officer is a very difficult job, but there are a lot of crimes that are not discovered until a week or two after they have been committed; isn't that correct?

Mr. CAUTHEN. Yes, sir.

Commissioner RANKIN. Sheriff, even though you didn't find out about the Kizilbash episode until after a week, it seems to me that it would be serious enough to question the man as to what went on in this assault case. Don't you really think so?

Mr. CAUTHEN. That would seem so, but it seems to me like Doctor or Mr. or Professor Kizilbash could have easily come to me in person or called me on the phone.

Commissioner RANKIN. You heard the letter read that he wrote to you, didn't you hear the letter this morning?

Mr. CAUTHEN. For the first time this morning, yes, sir.

Commissioner RANKIN. Well, isn't it possible that he thought that was a notice—that he was giving you notice of the affair?

Mr. CAUTHEN. Yes, sir. Had I received that letter I would have considered it a formal complaint, too, sir.

Commissioner RANKIN. I still think you could have looked into the matter when you heard about it even though you didn't have a complaint. That's my point. Don't you see?

Mr. CAUTHEN. I believe you said that you are a former lawyer in—law enforcement officer?

Commissioner RANKIN. No, sir. I have been a local officer in the sense that I was on a local governing board.

Mr. CAUTHEN. Yes, sir. Well, you know we receive many, many calls.

Commissioner RANKIN. That is correct.

Mr. CAUTHEN. That amount to nothing. You go with that.

Commissioner RANKIN. Sure.

Mr. CAUTHEN. Now, at the same time we keep talking about Mr. Kizilbash. I understand that this was reported to just about every agency—investigative agency, the FBI, the Justice Department, possibly the Mississippi Highway Patrol before it came to me. As chief law enforcement officer, in Madison County, we get many calls, sir, that materialize into nothing, just harassing calls.

Commissioner RANKIN. Wasn't there something in the paper about this, or didn't you hear any rumor of this episode?

Mr. CAUTHEN. Yes, sir. I heard a rumor of it.

Commissioner RANKIN. But you still preferred not to investigate it.

Mr. CAUTHEN. It was several days, by the date after it happened. Yes, sir, I heard some rumors.

Commissioner RANKIN. Well, I can understand a lot of your reasons. But I can't understand that you decided not to investigate it because it was a week late.

Mr. CAUTHEN. Well, the FBI and the Justice Department have been called in on every incident that had occurred up there, especially regarding the Freedom House, the bombings, the burnings of churches. The FBI, Justice Department, COFO conducts their own investigation.

Commissioner RANKIN. I go back to the week. You were notified by the president of Tougaloo, were you not?

Mr. CAUTHEN. Yes, sir, by phone.

Commissioner RANKIN. And then even after that, you did nothing about it?

Mr. CAUTHEN. You understood about the tag a while ago?

Commissioner RANKIN. Understood about what? Excuse me.

Chairman HANNAH. License tag.

Commissioner RANKIN. Yes, sir. I understand that but you didn't talk with the man, that's my point.

Mr. CAUTHEN. No, sir.

Chairman HANNAH. Mr. Patterson?

Vice Chairman PATTERSON. On the tag, sheriff, you said that the owner of the car said that the car was not in his possession at that time—at the time it was connected with the Kizilbash case, is that right?

Mr. CAUTHEN. That's correct.

Vice Chairman PATTERSON. Did the owner say that the car had been stolen from him for that period?

Mr. CAUTHEN. He said he had no knowledge whatsoever of his car being used that night.

Vice Chairman PATTERSON. The car was back in his possession the next day?

Mr. CAUTHEN. Yes, sir. The car belonged to the man's wife. The tag was registered in this man's wife's name.

Vice Chairman PATTERSON. Did the man or his wife have any idea who had used their car overnight?

Mr. CAUTHEN. No, sir.

Vice Chairman PATTERSON. Sheriff, we have begun to see a pattern in Mississippi. Some counties are doing pretty well after a long time of trouble. Some aren't doing so good in keeping harmony and peace and getting out of their period of racial trouble. Now, would you agree with me that your county of Madison is still pretty troubled in this area?

Mr. CAUTHEN. After coming here this morning it seems quite troubled.

Vice Chairman PATTERSON. Well, in this pattern that I'm describing it seemed that some of the law enforcement officers—sheriffs to whom we have talked—pretty much agree that a great amount of the responsibility to get that county out of trouble by enforcing the law rests on them. Would you agree with that?

Mr. CAUTHEN. Yes, sir.

Vice Chairman PATTERSON. Would you agree then that improvements and racial harmony in Madison County considerably rests on you?

Mr. CAUTHEN. Yes, sir.

Vice Chairman PATTERSON. Do you say that the Negro citizens and white citizens of your county get equal justice from you?

Mr. CAUTHEN. I have been in office just about a year—13½ months, I believe. What went on before in the sheriff's office I have no idea. As I told before, I was a vocational agricultural teacher for approximately 20 years. There have been considerable changes made in the policies in our office and the Canton sheriff's office. There will be more changes. Now, would you ask your question again, please, sir?

Vice Chairman PATTERSON. You have just testified that you think Negro citizens and white citizens get equal justice from you?

Mr. CAUTHEN. Yes, sir.

Vice Chairman PATTERSON. As sheriff?

Mr. CAUTHEN. Yes, sir.

Vice Chairman PATTERSON. Do you think the Negro citizens of Madison County feel that way?

Mr. CAUTHEN. I couldn't answer that, not after coming down here this morning. Until I came here this morning, I thought so, yes, sir.

Vice Chairman PATTERSON. Well, we have had witnesses from Madison County who said they did not feel Negroes always get equal justice there. Do you think that your membership on the White Citizens Council reassures the Negroes of Madison County about the equality of justice there?

Mr. CAUTHEN. The Citizens Council has not met in approximately 6 months, the White Citizens Council.

Vice Chairman PATTERSON. Is it now inactive, sheriff?

Mr. CAUTHEN. Inactive?

Vice Chairman PATTERSON. It is inactive?

Mr. CAUTHEN. At the present time, yes, sir.

Vice Chairman PATTERSON. But you are still a member, aren't you?

Mr. CAUTHEN. Yes, sir, right.

Chairman HANNAH, Mr. Rogerson?

Mr. ROGERSON. Sheriff, do you work pretty closely with the State highway patrol on matters arising in your county?

Mr. CAUTHEN. They are very cooperative.

Mr. ROGERSON. And if something is reported to the State highway patrol which has happened in your county, do they usually get in touch with you about it?

Mr. CAUTHEN. If something happens in my county do they get in touch with me about it?

Mr. ROGERSON. Yes?

Mr. CAUTHEN. Normally, yes, sir.

Mr. ROGERSON. Did you ever hear anything from the State highway patrol about the Kizilbash case?

Mr. CAUTHEN. Oh, sometime later. Three or four days, a week later.

Mr. ROGERSON. Was it after the call from Dr. Beittel or before?

Mr. CAUTHEN. Before.

Mr. ROGERSON. So it was less than a week after the incident, correct?

Mr. CAUTHEN. As to how much time, just what period of time, I don't know, sir. I don't remember.

Mr. ROGERSON. Well, you said Dr. Beittel called you a week after the incident?

Mr. CAUTHEN. Yes, sir.

Mr. ROGERSON. So that if the highway patrol called you before that, it was less than a week after the incident?

Mr. CAUTHEN. Yes, sir.

Mr. ROGERSON. On the basis of the call from the highway patrol, did you take any steps to investigate the matter?

Mr. CAUTHEN. Yes, sir, a lot of times I request their assistance.

Mr. ROGERSON. So, even before Dr. Beittel called you, you had started to investigate the Kizilbash case?

Mr. KING. Mr. Cauthen is a little hard of hearing and I don't believe he can hear you, sir.

[Laughter.]

Mr. ROGERSON. What I'm asking, Sheriff, is that first of all you have testified that the State highway patrol was in touch with you about the Kizilbash case before you received the call from Dr. Beittel.

And I think you have just said that you began investigating or doing something about that case after you heard from the State highway patrol. Is that or is that not correct?

Mr. CAUTHEN. I got the tag number from Dr. Beittel and the—in a telephone conversation that I already brought out before.

Mr. ROGERSON. After you heard——

Mr. CAUTHEN. That's the only time I heard of or seen the tag number.

Mr. ROGERSON. I wasn't asking anything about the tag number, sheriff. I was asking whether or not you began investigating the Kizilbash case after the state highway patrol reported it to you, which was prior, by your own testimony, to the call from Dr. Beittel.

Mr. CAUTHEN. I started investigating the case—the investigation I did was after the call from Dr. Beittel.

Mr. ROGERSON. Well then you have just changed your response—your prior response to me. You did not investigate the Kizilbash case until after Dr. Beittel's call, is that correct?

Mr. CAUTHEN. Yes, sir.

Mr. ROGERSON. But you had heard about this case from the state highway patrol prior to Dr. Beittel's call, is that correct?

Mr. CAUTHEN. Yes, sir.

Mr. ROGERSON. But you did nothing about it based on the information received from the state highway patrol?

Mr. CAUTHEN. That was a casual conversation. There was no formal notification or anything like that.

Mr. ROGERSON. Thank you.

Chairman HANNAH. Sir, I would like to ask a question on a little different subject. You indicated that you have been serving as sheriff for 13 months. And before that you were a Smith Hughes agricultural teacher for 20 years. I know a good deal about agricultural education. It's a responsible job in the community. I'm impressed in this State with the fact that the sheriff has many responsibilities other than enforcing the law. As I understand it one of your roles is as tax collector?

Mr. CAUTHEN. That's correct.

Chairman HANNAH. What fraction of the time and energy of your office is involved in law enforcement and what fraction is involved in the collection of taxes, other duties, sale of licenses, and so on?

Mr. CAUTHEN. The proportionate amount of time to each?

Chairman HANNAH. Approximately?

Mr. CAUTHEN. Well, I would hardly know how to answer that because we got a crew that stays in the office—the secretaries stay in the office all the time. We have our rush season in October which is tag month. January through March is a very, very busy time for tax, as far as tax collection is concerned. But, as the old saying goes, we make our money on tax collection and lose it on law enforcement.

Chairman HANNAH. How much money do you collect in your county from taxes or the sale of licenses? Approximately how much money do you collect in your county each year?

Mr. CAUTHEN. Total amount?

Chairman HANNAH. Yes, all kinds of taxes and licenses?

Mr. CAUTHEN. Sir, I'm sorry but I don't have that.

Chairman HANNAH. Well, I said approximately? Is it several hundred thousand dollars?

Mr. CAUTHEN. Approximately three, four hundred dollars.

Chairman HANNAH. Three or four hundred thousand dollars?

Mr. CAUTHEN. Yes.

Chairman HANNAH. It's a sizable operation. I recognize you didn't write the Mississippi law. This is the job that you were elected to fulfill. This is what I'm leading up to. If you were going to set up an organization concerned with law enforcement, the maintenance of peace, do you think it would be a pretty good idea to have the sheriff or the law enforcement officer so financed that they weren't concerned with tax collections or something else? Would you get better law enforcement? Would it be a more attractive job?

Mr. CAUTHEN. That's possible. I have no way of knowing the answer to that, sir. But, I think possibly it would.

Chairman HANNAH. I recognize that it is a difficult question to answer because the job is what it is. This is the one you were running for and you are elected and you intend to fulfill it. But it occurs to me, as an outsider, that if the State of Mississippi wants to improve the enforcement of laws at the county level they might well take a look at the policies and procedures used in most other States and divide the responsibility for law enforcement from that of tax collection and license collection and so on. Are there further questions?

Commissioner GRISWOLD. Sheriff, earlier this morning you handed in a letter dated February 18, which has been marked as exhibit No. 20, in response to the request for documents and information which was served on you. This includes what appears to be a copy of your report of the burning of the St. John Baptist Negro church in your county on September 17, 1964. In this report you record that you visited the church and found that it was completely destroyed by fire and state that a thorough search of the scene failed to disclose any evidence as to how the fire started. You then state that one of the deacons of the church came to you and gave the names of other deacons, several of whom were contacted. Your report then says the ones contacted admitted the Freedom School but seemed unwilling to cooperate. I find myself wondering why you use that word, "admitted," with respect to Freedom School?

Mr. CAUTHEN. Figure of speech, matter of speech.

Commissioner GRISWOLD. In what way was that an admission? Is it a crime or an offense to conduct a Freedom School in Madison County?

Mr. CAUTHEN. No, sir.

Commissioner GRISWOLD. Then why did you record it as "admitted the Freedom School?"

Mr. CAUTHEN. I call it a figure of speech, if you care to, sir.

Commissioner GRISWOLD. Now, further reading the report, it appears that you interviewed a number of COFO workers and the results of your interview are reported in your report. Did you interview anybody other than the deacons of the church and the COFO workers?

Mr. CAUTHEN. I believe that's all, sir.

Commissioner GRISWOLD. Why did you think it appropriate to interview COFO workers in connection with this burning?

Mr. CAUTHEN. That's where the first information came from as to to burning of the churches. There were quite a few of them in the vicinity of the church. That's a very logical place to start.

Commissioner GRISWOLD. By "in the vicinity," what do you mean?

Mr. CAUTHEN. That's exactly what I mean.

Commissioner GRISWOLD. How close?

Mr. CAUTHEN. Within a mile, mile and a half, two, three miles.

Commissioner GRISWOLD. They were at the Valley View COFO house, as it is called?

Mr. CAUTHEN. That's right.

Commissioner GRISWOLD. Which is down the road a mile and a half or more from the site of the church? Is that right?

Mr. CAUTHEN. Approximately, yes, sir.

Commissioner GRISWOLD. They were not standing by the church.

Mr. CAUTHEN. No, sir.

Commissioner GRISWOLD. Thank you.

Chairman HANNAH. Any other questions?

Commissioner RANKIN. I have one. Sheriff, I know you agree with us. You don't like these things any better than we do, am I correct—this church burning for example?

Mr. CAUTHEN. You are absolutely correct, sir.

Commissioner RANKIN. Now, how can we improve things? What can be done to stop this? Do you have any suggestion that you would like to make to this Commission on how we could improve the climate?

Mr. CAUTHEN. I'd say through education, mostly, sir. I'm not very inclined to enter discussions this morning. In fact, I feel kind of antagonistic to this group this morning. But, to answer your question, sir, I believe through education mostly. I would like to state that when this first church where we had the burning—the one at Ridgeland—we don't think any of our people, white or colored, burned that church. We don't know, but that's my personal feeling. And the same with most of those other churches. We don't think our people did it. We don't think our people did it.

Commissioner RANKIN. And the eventual solution of this problem is education?

Mr. CAUTHEN. That's my answer to you.

Commissioner RANKIN. As a teacher to another teacher you say it is education?

Mr. CAUTHEN. That is right, sir.

Chairman HANNAH. Thank you very much, Sheriff.

You are excused.

(Witness excused.)

In spite of the fact that it's late, I think we should have one more witness and close up Madison County, and recess until 2 o'clock. Mr. Taylor, will you call the last witness before we recess.

Mr. TAYLOR. Dan C. Thompson, chief of police.

Chairman HANNAH. Mr. Thompson, will you raise your right hand?

(Whereupon, Police Chief Dan Thompson was duly sworn by the Chairman and testified as follows:)

Chairman HANNAH. Will you introduce your counsel?

Mr. THOMPSON. Mr. Robert C. Goza.

Chairman HANNAH. Mr. Finkelstein?

TESTIMONY OF DAN C. THOMPSON, CHIEF OF POLICE, CANTON, MADISON COUNTY, MISS.

Mr. FINKELSTEIN. Will you please state your name, your residence, and your occupation?

Mr. THOMPSON. Dan C. Thompson, 164 East Center Street, Canton, Miss., chief of police of Canton, Miss.

Mr. FINKELSTEIN. How long have you served as chief of police?

Mr. THOMPSON. 21 years and 6 months.

Mr. FINKELSTEIN. Do your law enforcement duties include keeping the peace?

Mr. THOMPSON. Yes, sir.

Mr. FINKELSTEIN. Chief Thompson, we have heard testimony that during the past year there have been a number of instances of racial violence in Canton. Has your office made arrests in any of these cases?

Mr. THOMPSON. In one case that I can recall.

Mr. FINKELSTEIN. In one case?

Mr. THOMPSON. Yes—two, two cases.

Mr. FINKELSTEIN. Two cases. And in no other cases, is that correct?

Mr. THOMPSON. That's correct.

Mr. FINKELSTEIN. During the summer there were five attacks on the Freedom House at 838 Lutz Street in Canton. Did you make arrests in any of those cases?

Mr. THOMPSON. I did not.

Mr. FINKELSTEIN. Did you receive any identifying information in any of those cases?

Mr. THOMPSON. I want to correct that. In one case we did make three arrests at the Freedom House—explosion that happened at the Freedom House.

Mr. FINKELSTEIN. There was one case in which you made an arrest?

Mr. THOMPSON. July 11 incident arrests were made.

Mr. FINKELSTEIN. And in no other cases arrests were made, is that right?

Mr. THOMPSON. That's right.

Mr. FINKELSTEIN. Was there identifying information given to you in any other case, such as a license place number or description?

Mr. THOMPSON. A license plate number and the car was given to us on this case we made the arrest on. On another case the description of a car was given, but we never did locate the car. It didn't have a tag number and we got lost in the investigation.

Mr. FINKELSTEIN. Why have you been unable to solve these cases, Chief?

Mr. THOMPSON. Well, to begin with we have a small police department, but I think we have a good department. On every one of these incidents the FBI were called in to assist us, also the highway patrol and evidently the three agencies haven't been big enough to solve them yet.

Mr. FINKELSTEIN. That is not quite responsive. What are the reasons that you have not been able to solve them?

Mr. THOMPSON. We just haven't had enough information.

Mr. FINKELSTEIN. Lack of information?

Mr. THOMPSON. Lack of information.

Mr. FINKELSTEIN. Have you received information from the Negro community?

Mr. THOMPSON. Very little. We have had little cooperation from the Negro or any one else to amount to anything. It has been mostly get out and try to dig it up yourself.

Mr. FINKELSTEIN. Do you think that the lack of cooperation from the Negro community is a reason why you have been unable to solve these cases?

Mr. THOMPSON. I wouldn't say that was the reason, but I think if we had more cooperation we would have had a better chance to solve them.

Mr. FINKELSTEIN. Reverend McCree has testified that Negroes believe, rightly or wrongly, that members of your force have been involved in acts of racial violence or have otherwise maltreated Negroes. Do you know of such allegations?

Mr. THOMPSON. I do not.

Mr. FINKELSTEIN. You are not aware of any of them?

Mr. THOMPSON. No, sir.

Mr. FINKELSTEIN. Do you recall George Washington, Sr., making a complaint to you as he testified here today, that one of your officers had struck him when he was brought in for questioning?

Mr. THOMPSON. I do.

Mr. FINKELSTEIN. So you do know of at least one allegation, is that right?

Mr. THOMPSON. I was still following at the Freedom House, excuse me.

Mr. FINKELSTEIN. I see.

Mr. THOMPSON. I do know of that.

Mr. FINKELSTEIN. What did you do after you received that complaint?

Mr. THOMPSON. I went over to the store and talked to George Washington and his wife. When I walked in, George said, "Now I don't want any court case, and I don't want any law suits. I just want to tell you what has happened."

So I talked to George and I said, "George, you know I don't approve of that. I'm glad you reported it and I will look into it." So I went back and questioned the officers involved and they denied it and, of course, I talked to them very strong about mistreating anyone—which I don't believe in, which we haven't done, and we haven't had an incident like that happening any more.

Mr. FINKELSTEIN. One more question, Chief. Without mentioning any names, have you received any other complaints against this particular officer?

Mr. THOMPSON. I don't recall one right now.

Mr. FINKELSTEIN. That's all.

Chairman HANNAH. Father Hesburgh?

Commissioner HESBURGH. Chief, I know this isn't your responsibility so I'm just asking for an opinion rather than implicating you in it. But I noticed this in one of the cases that was solved. They found the people who then pleaded nolo contendere. They had driven by this house, which isn't very well liked, and threw a molotov cocktail, which is a very dangerous thing in a place where human beings are living. You can blow up a tank with one, so they are pretty terrible kind of weapons for people to be using in public. But, anyway, three youths were apparently involved in this incident. They were apprehended, brought to trial and pleaded *nolo contendere*. They were given $50 fines. It seems to me, in view of the excessive fines we have found given several civil rights workers, that this kind of thing just defies any effort you might make to bring people before the law because they are not prosecuted when they are brought before the law. Do you think it would help in your upholding of the peace in the city of Canton if people who threw a molotov cocktail at an inhabited house were brought before the law and something happened besides this $50 fine?

Mr. THOMPSON. Father, I wouldn't like to criticize the courts, so I would rather not answer that.

Commissioner HESBURGH. I would like to say that, in my own opinion, your work becomes rather difficult if you do apprehend someone and the courts let him off as if it were a big joke to throw a molotov cocktail. I don't think it is a big joke. I'm not afraid to criticize the courts and I do hereby criticize them in this. Thank you, Chief.

Chairman HANNAH. Any other questions? Mr. Taylor?

Mr. TAYLOR. Chief, in response to the subpena you submitted a report on the bombing of the Freedom House on June 8, 1964, an incident which has been referred to. It is very brief. I would like to read it.

It says: "Rembrant Washington reported to the police department by telephone at 7:15 on June 8, 1964, that someone threw a bomb at Freedom House, 838 Lutz Street, between the hour of 1 a.m. and 1:30 a.m., reported about 6 hours after explosion. I asked Rembrant why she didn't report when it happened. She said she thought that James Collier had reported it. I went to the Freedom House and talked to James Collier and asked him why he didn't report it to the police. He stated he had only three dimes and he used them first to call Clair I. Bone, who was an FBI agent in Jackson. Second, COFO office in Jackson and advised them as to what had happened. Third, the Justice Department in Washington. He stated that he could not call the police because he did not have another dime. Upon investigation I found out that George Washington owned the building known as the Freedom House and that he knew about the bombing and was on the scene very soon after it happened.

"We brought George to the station and questioned him as to why he didn't report it to the police. He would not give any reason at all. He was released after questioning. Special Investigator Gwynn Cole of the Mississippi Highway Patrol was called in to help with the investigation. An investigation was made at the scene and all evidence appeared that the window which was broke out, had been broke from the inside, also, at the spot where the explosion was supposed to have been there was no evidence of any kind of powder burns or smoke stains. The area was searched very closely and no kind of evidence was found to determine what made the marks on the sidewalk."

Chief, there is no date on that report. Was that prepared shortly after the incident?

Mr. THOMPSON. This was prepared by Assistant Chief Russell Cook, and he had written it up in longhand and he typed this up after I got the subpena. He did fail to sign it.

Mr. TAYLOR. So this was done just recently?

Mr. THOMPSON. Yes.

Mr. TAYLOR. No report was made at the time?

Mr. THOMPSON. Yes, sir; at the time a report was made in longhand.

Mr. TAYLOR. In longhand?

Mr. THOMPSON. Yes, sir, at the time; well, he copied it and failed to put the date or sign it.

Mr. TAYLOR. His signature was on the original report?

Mr. THOMPSON. Yes, sir; it was.

Mr. TAYLOR. Is this the complete report of the investigation of that case?

Mr. THOMPSON. As far as I know it is all we have in writing, but it is still being worked on. We are trying to pick up leads and pick up anything we can to help solve the case.

Mr. TAYLOR. Well, Chief, the only observation I would make about it is that the report is one page long and approximately two-thirds to three-quarters of it is devoted to questions about why COFO did not—why the people of the house did not call the police and called somebody else. Was this a greater concern than the damage to the house itself and the perpetrators of that?

Mr. THOMPSON. I think it's a great concern when something that serious happens and we are not notified. I think the quicker we get on a problem like that, the better chance we have to make headway. But——

Mr. TAYLOR. But isn't that something that could be deferred until after the investigation has begun?

Mr. Thompson. As I mentioned before, the FBI worked—we have called them in every case. They have took samples and sent them into the Federal laboratories and they, you might say, have taken over the investigation. I'm sure they can give you a much more detailed report.

Mr. Taylor. Thank you. No more questions.

Chairman Hannah. Father Hesburgh?

Commissioner Hesburgh. Chief, I am sure you found this whole experience a little unpleasant, and I'm sure we have and some of the other law officers involved have, but what we really would like to do, and I think everybody should try to understand this, is to bring about a better situation. Just speaking for one member of the Commission, I would like to say that I think one great move towards a bettering of the situation would be much better communications. I think you are probably discouraged that some of the colored people believe that your force is not protecting them as well as white people. And I think the only way to solve this kind of thing would be to get the white and Negro community together in your town so people could say freely what they think the problem is and what might be done about it. What they need is a place to get their opinions out in the open because this is not a very effective way of cleaning up a situation—it looks very bad on paper.

Mr. Thompson. Father, I'm glad you mentioned that because until I came down here I thought Canton and Madison County had improved tremendously since last summer because I know that most of the Negro people and the white people feel free to talk to me or come in my office any time they want to about any problem. We can see a big change and feel like it's going to continue.

Commissioner Hesburgh. I would hope there is some way of getting the leaders of the community together and really getting a little free conversation, some of which we had here. This is particularly desirable in the local community where the local people can do something about it, and where the local business people could get behind it too. We would hope that this thing won't just be an exercise in frustrations as it is somewhat right now. Thank you.

Chairman Hannah. Chief, the chief of police has only one duty and that's to enforce the law and maintain peace. You are not involved in tax collection or any of that sort?

Mr. Thompson. No, sir. Law enforcement.

Chairman Hannah. And you have served 21 years?

Mr. Thompson. Twenty-one years.

Chairman Hannah. And your assistants are hired also for their skill in police work. They have no other duties?

Mr. Thompson. No other duties.

Chairman HANNAH. And the city of Canton can give you as much help as seems to be necessary to maintain the peace?

Mr. THOMPSON. Right.

Chairman HANNAH. You don't have the problem of having to pay the deputies out of your own pocket or anything of that sort?

Mr. THOMPSON. No, sir; the city pays them.

Chairman HANNAH. Any other questions? If not, we are recessed until 2 o'clock.

(Witness excused.)

(Whereupon, at about 12:40 p.m. the hearing was recessed until 2 p.m. of the same day.)

FRIDAY AFTERNOON SESSION, FEBRUARY 19, 1965

Chairman HANNAH. The hearing will come to order. Before we begin this afternoon's session, I should like to comment on the last part of the program this afternoon. We are going to hear witnesses from two counties and then we are going into something of a little different nature. We have invited seven distinguished attorneys from Mississippi to appear in a panel on this date. Tomorrow there will be two panels: the first, consisting of representatives of the business community; and the second, representatives of the clergy. It is the hope of the Commission that as a result of these hearings, and as a result of these panels, moderate whites may be encouraged to step forward and take a real public interest in the solution of the civil rights problems of Mississippi. We start this afternoon with the intention of proceeding with the witnesses from these two counties and then moving to the panel discussion. And of course we hope that the members of the audience who are interested will stay on for the panel session.

Mr. Taylor, will you call the first witness?

Mr. TAYLOR. Mr. Chairman, the testimony to be heard next concerns Leflore County and I will ask Mr. Wolf to give a brief background of that county.

Mr. WOLF. Leflore County is in the Delta, a broad alluvial plain extending along the east bank of the Mississippi River from Memphis to Vicksburg and principally used for growing cotton. The total population of the county in 1963 was estimated at 48,000, of whom about two-thirds were Negroes. As of 1963, 1.6 percent of the voting age Negroes were registered, while 71.6 percent of the voting age whites were registered.

Leflore is a rural county. The county seat and largest community is Greenwood, with a population of about 20,000, of whom more than half are Negro. In 1959, the median income for white families was $5,200, and the median income for Negro families was $1,400. One-half of the Negroes are employed in agriculture. The median level of education for whites in Leflore County is 12 years. For Negroes, it is 5 years. In the school year 1960–61, the Leflore County School District spent about $220 for each white student and about $120 for each Negro student.

Mr. TAYLOR. I would now like to call upon Mr. Wolf to present a staff investigation report concerning fines and sentences imposed by courts in Greenwood, Mississippi.

Mr. WOLF. The following is a report on an analysis of city court records in Greenwood, Miss., conducted by the staff of the Commission. The purpose of this analysis is to determine whether civil rights workers appearing before the court received more onerous fines and sentences for the same offenses than other persons not involved in civil rights. I will read a summary of this report and submit the entire report for the record.

The city court docket of Greenwood during 1963 shows that five civil rights workers were charged with blocking the sidewalk, running a stop sign, operating a car with improper equipment and reckless driving. All were found guilty. Except for the worker charged with reckless driving, all received fines which grossly exceeded fines given to other persons during the year. Court records also show that during 1963 approximately 35 persons were arrested during demonstrations in connection with attempts to register to vote. They were charged with breach of the peace, disorderly conduct and disturbance in a public place. The majority received fines of $200 and jail sentences. The fines were 15 to 20 times greater than the average fine imposed for similar violations of city ordinances during the preceding year.

In 1964 the Department of Justice filed an action under the Civil Rights Act of 1960 against Greenwood city officials and others alleging, among other things, that persons engaged in voter registration activity were given substantially heavier sentences than other persons for comparable offenses. The Commission staff analyzed the city court docket pertaining to the period in 1964 after the institution of the Attorney General's action. The analysis shows that during the last 6 months of 1964 civil rights "offenders" still received discriminatory sentences and fines, although to a lesser degree.

During the last half of 1964 four civil rights workers were charged with profanity and driving with an improper license. All were found guilty. They were required to post a cash bond or were fined amounts which were greatly in excess of fines given to other persons during this period. Court records also show that approximately 130 persons were arrested during demonstrations at the courthouse in connection with attempts to register. They were charged with a variety of violations of city ordinances. All were found guilty. The majority were fined $100 and sentenced to 30 days on the county farm. These sentences were substantially more severe than sentences imposed on all other persons for violations of city ordinances during the same period.

Mr. TAYLOR. Mr. Chairman, I would like at this point to note for the record that O. L. Kimbrough, police justice of the city of Greenwood, Mississippi, was given notice and an opportunity to appear in Executive Session with respect to these matters, but that he did not do so. And I would like to enter the staff report into the record.

Chairman HANNAH. It is received.

(Exhibit No. 21 was marked for identification and received in evidence.)

Chairman HANNAH. Call the next witness.

Mr. TAYLOR. The next witness is District Attorney George C. Everett.

Chairman HANNAH. Mr. Everett, will you raise your right hand?

(Whereupon George A. Everett, Esq. was duly sworn by the Chairman and testified as follows:)

Chairman HANNAH. Mr. Taylor?

TESTIMONY OF GEORGE A. EVERETT, DISTRICT ATTORNEY, FOURTH JUDICIAL DISTRICT OF MISSISSIPPI

Mr. TAYLOR. Mr. Everett, I believe at the time you appeared in Executive Session you submitted all of the documents that you had that were relevant to this case; is that correct?

Mr. EVERETT. Yes, sir.

Mr. TAYLOR. Would you please state your name, your age, and your occupation?

Mr. EVERETT. My name is George A. Everett—you have it "C", which is incorrect.

Mr. TAYLOR. Sorry.

Mr. EVERETT. I am 52 years of age. I am the District Attorney for the Fourth Judicial District of Mississippi.

Mr. TAYLOR. When were you elected district attorney, Mr. Everett?

Mr. EVERETT. I was first appointed to take office September 1, 1963. I had previously been elected to take office the first of the year—January 6 I believe—of '64. However, due to a vacancy, I was appointed to fill out the unexpired term.

Mr. TAYLOR. Mr. Everett, you have received—and I would like to read into the record the following summary: James Travis, a Negro voter registration worker, was shot and seriously wounded while riding in a car with two companions on February 28, 1963, in Leflore County. Wesley Kersey and William Hester Greenlee were indicted for assault with a deadly weapon in connection with this incident on May 8, 1963. The sheriff was the sole witness. Defendants' first motion for continuance was filed May 20, 1963, and the case was continued to the November 1963 term of the court. There were no opposing papers in the file. Defendants' second motion for a continuance was filed November 25, 1963, and the case was continued to the May 1964 term of the court. On May 18, 1964, the prosecution moved that the case be continued to the November 1964 term on the ground of the illness of Sheriff Cothran, a material witness. The motion was granted. When the case came up in November the prosecution moved that it be remanded to the file or passed. This is the equivalent of a permanent adjournment.

I would like to ask, Mr. Everett, what happened when the case first came up for trial in May, 1963?

Mr. EVERETT. I, of course, was not district attorney at that time, and had no official connection with the case at that time.

Mr. TAYLOR. To your knowledge, did the State oppose the postponement?

Mr. EVERETT. I do not know, but I would venture the guess that it did not.

Mr. TAYLOR. Can you tell us what happened when the case next came up in November, 1963?

Mr. EVERETT. In November, 1963, I was then, of course, the district attorney. The case was prepared for trial and the State was ready to go to trial with the matter.

Approximately 3 days before the trial date, the witnesses had been subpenaed and all had been served with the subpenas. Approximately 3 days before the trial date, President Kennedy was assassinated. In view of that, the defense made a motion—filed a motion in view of the publicity and the feelings with regard to the assassination of the President—and I'm not sure whether or not Oswald had been shot at that time or not. I don't recall. The motion was made for a continuance. That continuance was neither agreed to nor opposed by me, the State. I announced ready for trial and stated to the judge that I neither agreed to nor opposed the motion and left it in his hands. He granted the continuance.

Mr. TAYLOR. The case was then postponed for a period from that time until May, 1964, is that correct—from November, 1963 until May, 1964 because of the matters you have stated?

Mr. EVERETT. That's right.

Mr. TAYLOR. What happened at that time?

Mr. EVERETT. At that time, in preparing the case for trial—getting it ready for trial—we ascertained that the sheriff was in a serious condition physically. He had just been released from the hospital and he presented—I say just been released. I don't recall the dates. I don't mean it was that day. He had presented to the judge a medical excuse stating that he was physically unable to appear in court. Therefore, the State had no alternative but to move for a continuance because of the materiality of his testimony.

Mr. TAYLOR. And it was then postponed from May, 1964 until November, 1964, is that correct?

Mr. EVERETT. That's correct, the next term of court.

Mr. TAYLOR. What happened when the case came up in November, 1964?

Mr. EVERETT. Shortly prior to the November term of court, I learned that there was some question about the validity of the alleged confession involved in the matter. I learned it then for the first time. On interrogating the officer who had taken the confession, I learned facts which caused me to believe that the confession would not be admissible in court over the objection of the defense.

For that reason I felt that we had no case, no evidence. That was the basic evidence in the case concerning Greenlee himself. We had no evidence against Kersey that we could introduce. I felt then that we had no possible way of obtaining a conviction or even getting to the jury with the case. Therefore, I moved to pass the case to the files.

Mr. TAYLOR. And what is the meaning of passing the case to the files?

Mr. EVERETT. Passing the case to the files means that it is removed from the docket. The indictment is not dismissed, the case is not closed, but it is held in what you might say is a period of suspended animation until something else is done at a later time.

Mr. TAYLOR. Mr. Everett, do I understand that you are saying that between November 1963 and November 1964, you had no knowledge of the nature of the way the confession was obtained, and that this first came to your attention in November 1964?

Mr. EVERETT. About then. I don't know whether it was October or November—what month it was in. But I had no reason prior to that time to believe that the confession had not been obtained in a proper manner.

Mr. TAYLOR. Do you have any memorandum of this conversation that you had with the official involved?

Mr. EVERETT. I do not.

Mr. TAYLOR. Did you have any other evidence in this case except the confession against the persons indicted?

Mr. EVERETT. Yes, sir. Of course we had the evidence of the automobile from which the shots were no doubt fired. The inside of that automobile was also shot. Bullets had hit in it and done considerable damage. We had evidence from the FBI laboratory relating to two bullets, the projectiles from two cartridges, one of which was removed from the neck of Travis. The other had been removed or found in the automobile used in the shooting. And that evidence or that testimony was that the two bullets were fired from the same weapon.

Mr. TAYLOR. Could you identify that weapon? You didn't, did you?

Mr. EVERETT. The weapon, no, sir.

Mr. TAYLOR. What kind of weapon was it?

Mr. EVERETT. The FBI laboratory report stated that it was an automatic weapon, possibly a Thompson submachinegun. They did not positively identify the type of weapon but concluded that that was the best possibility.

Mr. TAYLOR. Just one more question, Mr. Everett. Were you connected with this case in any capacity other than as district attorney—county attorney?

Mr. EVERETT. District attorney.

Mr. TAYLOR. District attorney, I'm sorry.

Mr. EVERETT. Yes, sir. I had participated in the original FBI investigation of the case when it first occurred.

Mr. TAYLOR. In what capacity?

Mr. EVERETT. As a special agent of the FBI.

Mr. TAYLOR. No further questions.

Chairman HANNAH. Do you have any questions, Dean Griswold?

Commissioner GRISWOLD. Did you interview James Travis, the victim of this incident?

Mr. EVERETT. No, sir; I did not.

Commissioner GRISWOLD. Why would you not have interviewed him as a part of the preparation of this case?

Mr. EVERETT. I would have interviewed him prior to the trial, sir. He was not interviewed prior to that because he was, of course, not in Greenwood. When I first went to the hospital when this shooting incident occurred to try to interview all three of the persons who were in the car, of course, Travis was under medical care and could not be interviewed. Travis was subsequently interviewed by the FBI agent in Jackson, Mississippi, and I had access at that time as an FBI agent to the report of his interview. Therefore, I was familiar with the facts to which Travis could testify.

Commissioner GRISWOLD. And was he in a position to give any sort of identification of the persons in the car from which the shots came?

Mr. EVERETT. No, sir; other than to state that there were three white men.

Commissioner GRISWOLD. With respect to this confession which you concluded that you couldn't use, was that reduced to writing?

Mr. EVERETT. No, sir. It was an oral statement.

Commissioner GRISWOLD. Is it the practice in Leflore County not to make written records of confessions?

Mr. EVERETT. Some are and some are not. Depending on the willingness of the person interviewed.

Commissioner GRISWOLD. I can understand how there may be a problem as to whether the person interviewed will himself make and sign a written confession. But don't you think the police officer should at least have made a prompt memorandum of a confession if such had been—when he took such a confession?

Mr. EVERETT. I certainly do.

Commissioner GRISWOLD. When did you first learn that there was a confession?

Mr. EVERETT. When I first entered the case, when I first became district attorney.

Commissioner GRISWOLD. Did you——

Mr. EVERETT. Of course—I beg your pardon there—I knew prior to that, that there had been a statement made to the sheriff.

Commissioner GRISWOLD. When you became district attorney, did you suggest that a memorandum should be made of the events?

Mr. EVERETT. No, sir; I did not.

Comissioner GRISWOLD. Would you think that would be a good practice, to make a memoradum of such an important matter?

Mr. EVERETT. Yes, sir.

Commissioner GRISWOLD. Did you question the police officer—I forgot whether it was sheriff or police chief. Was it the sheriff who took the confession?

Mr. EVERETT. I will have to refer you there to my Executive Session testimony. I don't wish to call names or identify people publicly in matters which may embarrass them, if I may not do so.

Commissioner GRISWOLD. Well, I understand that the confession was given to the——

Mr. EVERETT. An officer.

Commissioner GRISWOLD. To an officer. Did you question him shortly after you became district attorney as to the circumstances of the confession?

Mr. EVERETT. I questioned him concerning the confession. I did not go into any detail with regard to the circumstances of it because I did not have any reason to believe that he might have made the confession bad by his actions in taking the statement.

Commissioner GRISWOLD. Did he then tell you anything about threats made to the accused at the time the statement was taken?

Mr. EVERETT. No. sir.

Commissioner GRISWOLD. When did you first learn about these threats?

Mr. EVERETT. Shortly before the November 1964 term of court when I learned it from one of the defense counsel.

Commissioner GRISWOLD. Did you then talk with the police officer—the officer involved?

Mr. EVERETT. Yes, sir.

Commissioner GRISWOLD. What did he say?

Mr. EVERETT. He related to me then the circumstances of his having obtained the statement.

Commissioner GRISWOLD. And you felt that this was enough to make the confession inadmissible? Did you conclude that you did not have enough evidence to go to trial?

Mr. EVERETT. Yes, sir; we had no other way to identify the defendants as being in the automobile in which the—from which the shots were fired.

Commissioner GRISWOLD. You could prove that—at least you had evidence tending to prove that the shots which hit Mr. Travis were fired from this other car?

Mr. EVERETT. Yes, sir.

Commissioner GRISWOLD. Did you know anything about the ownership of the other car?

Mr. EVERETT. Yes.

Commissioner GRISWOLD. Did you have any evidence or results of investigation with respect to the use of that car at this time?

Mr. EVERETT. Yes, sir; we knew that one of the persons indicted had possession of that automobile approximately 3 hours before the shooting when he was last seen.

Commissioner GRISWOLD. But not closer than 3 hours?

Mr. EVERETT. No, sir.

Commissioner GRISWOLD. Thank you.

Chairman HANNAH. Mrs. Freeman?

Commissioner FREEMAN. Mr. Everett, this indictment of Wesley Kersey and William Hester Greenlee was on May 8. Who would have presented the information or evidence to the grand jury? Would it have been the district attorney?

Mr. EVERETT. Well, the district attorney would have presided over the presentation, would have—yes. He would not have presented the evidence. The witnesses, of course, would have presented it. But the district attorney would normally call the witnesses and question them before the grand jury.

Commissioner FREEMAN. In this case, witnesses were called and gave evidence to the grand jury. Based upon the evidence that was given to the grand jury there was an indictment. Is it customary for the district attorney, after there has been an indictment by the grand jury, to determine thereafter to pass the case to the files?

Mr. EVERETT. Oh, certainly. Depending on what develops during the course of events. I have passed cases to the file in the same term that the grand jury has returned an indictment, if I didn't think it were properly prosecutable.

Commissioner FREEMAN. Mr. Everett, will you tell me if Mr. Kersey and Mr. Greenlee were out on bond pending the trial of this case?

Mr. EVERETT. They were.

Commissioner FREEMAN. What was the amount of their bond?

Mr. EVERETT. I could not tell you.

Commissioner FREEMAN. You do not know?

Mr. EVERETT. I do not know.

Chairman HANNAH. Father Hesburgh?

Commissioner HESBURGH. Mr. Everett, what would have happened to this case if the law officer involved who obtained the confession happened to have dropped dead?

Mr. EVERETT. The same thing as happened to it without his having dropped dead. We could not have proceeded.

Commissioner HESBURGH: Isn't it a little difficult where justice depends on a single confession not to reduce it to writing?

Mr. EVERETT. It wouldn't have mattered, sir, if it had been writing or not. He could not have testified. If he had been the one who took the confession, it would be he who would have to introduce it in evidence.

Commissioner HESBURGH. But if he had left a written record of that, wouldn't that——

Mr. EVERETT. I don't think so.

Commisisoner HESBURGH. All right.

Chairman HANNAH. Mr. Rankin?

Commissioner RANKIN. Has anything turned up since it's been passed—any new information to your office—new information on this case?

Mr. EVERETT. No, sir.

Commissioner RANKIN. Not a thing?

Mr. EVERETT. No, sir.

Chairman HANNAH. Mr. Patterson?

Vice Chairman PATTERSON. Mr. Everett, as I understand it, before you became district attorney—November 1963—or were you district attorney?

Mr. EVERETT. I was then, yes.

Vice Chairman PATTERSON. You subpenaed witnesses and were ready to go to trial before you continued the case?

Mr. EVERETT. Yes.

Vice Chairman PATTERSON. In May you postponed the case again because of the materiality of the sheriff's evidence.

Mr. EVERETT. Yes, sir.

Vice Chairman PATTERSON. Or I mean the law officer who had taken the confession. But then it was November of '64 before you determined the conditions under which he had taken that confession; is that correct?

Mr. EVERETT. Basically so. As I stated, I do not know exactly which month I learned it in, but it was prior to the November 1964 term of court, between the May and November terms.

Vice Chairman PATTERSON. Thank you.

Chairman HANNAH. Mr. Rogerson?

Mr. ROGERSON. I take it, sir, that the weapon has not been found?

Mr. EVERETT. No, sir.

Mr. ROGERSON. If the weapon were found and connected to the defendants, this would be something you feel you could proceed on?

Mr. EVERETT. If it were connected to the defendants, yes. But, we would still have to have the evidence of who was there to shoot it, not just ownership, of course.

Mr. ROGERSON. Do you know anything about this weapon? Does the search continue for it? I mean, is the case active in the sense that investigation is still going forward?

Mr. EVERETT. I rather doubt it. There is a completely new sheriff's administration in office and I doubt that they are doing anything about it.

Mr. ROGERSON. There is no carryover between administrations in the sheriff's office?

Mr. EVERETT. Only insofar as the incoming sheriff would want to do so. I could, of course, request further investigation and have done so. However, I doubt seriously if any investigation of an active nature is being made.

Mr. ROGERSON. Thank you.

Chairman HANNAH. Mr. Taylor?

Mr. TAYLOR. Mr. Everett, what were the facts which led you to conclude that the confession was coerced in this case?

Mr. EVERETT. Well, I will refer you there, Mr. Taylor, to my testimony in Executive Session, if you don't mind, because I don't want to get into too much in my personal opinion in the public session.

Mr. TAYLOR. I don't think this is a matter of personal opinion, is it, sir? You must have had facts upon which you made a determination that the confession was coerced.

Mr. EVERETT. That is quite true. And you have access to what I stated in Executive Session there, sir, and I refer you to that and ask you to consider that my answer.

Mr. TAYLOR. Let me ask you this: Was there any physical coercion involved in this confession?

Mr. EVERETT. No, sir.

Chairman HANNAH. Any further questions?

Commissioner GRISWOLD. Mr. Everett, would you consider it good police practice to obtain such a confession as this in writing and with witnesses?

Mr. EVERETT. Yes, sir.

Commissioner GRISWOLD. Do you regard it as any part of your function to advise police officers in your district as to the circumstances under which confessions should be obtained and the way in which they should be recorded?

Mr. EVERETT. Yes, sir, and I have done so.

Commissioner GRISWOLD. Thank you.

Chairman HANNAH. That is all, Mr. Everett. Thank you. You are excused.

(Witness excused.)

Chairman HANNAH. Call the next witness.

Mr. TAYLOR. The testimony following concerns Washington County. And the first witnesses are James Edwards and Dr. Noble Frisby. Let me state for the record at this point, Mr. Chairman, that an opportunity was given to John N. Cothran, Humprey Highway, Greenwood, Mississippi, to testify concerning the events we have just been over. We have a report from his doctor saying he is unable to appear for medical reasons.

Chairman HANNAH. Now, the next witness is?

Mr. TAYLOR. Dr. Noble Frisby and Mr. James Edwards.

Chairman HANNAH. Mr. Frisby and Mr. Edwards, will you raise your right hands?

(Whereupon, Dr. Noble Frisby and Mr. James Edwards were duly sworn by the Chairman and testified as follows:)

Chairman HANNAH. Mr. Taylor?

Mr. TAYLOR. Mr. Finkelstein?

TESTIMONY OF DR. NOBLE L. FRISBY AND MR. JAMES EDWARDS, WASHINGTON COUNTY, MISS.

Mr. FINKELSTEIN. Mr. Edwards, will you please give your name, your residence and your occupation?

Mr. EDWARDS. James Edwards, residence Greenville, Mississippi. Occupation, a mortician.

Mr. FINKELSTEIN. And Dr. Frisby, will you do the same, please?

Dr. FRISBY. Dr. Noble L. Frisby, 576 East Alexander, Greenville, Mississippi, physician.

Mr. FINKELSTEIN. Mr. Edwards, are you a registered voter?

Mr. EDWARDS. I am.

Mr. FINKELSTEIN. Dr. Frisby, are you a registered voter?

Dr. FRISBY. I am.

Mr. FINKELSTEIN. Mr. Edwards, how long have you lived in Mississippi?

Mr. EDWARDS. About 33 years.

Mr. FINKELSTEIN. How long have you lived in Greenville?

Mr. EDWARDS. Twenty-one years.

Mr. FINKELSTEIN. Are you an officer in any civil rights organizations in Greenville?

Mr. EDWARDS. I am.

Mr. FINKELSTEIN. Which ones?

Mr. EDWARDS. I am chairman of the board of the Washington County Branch of the NAACP. I am president of the Washington County Business League.

Mr. FINKELSTEIN. What are the principal activities of those organizations?

Mr. EDWARDS. The Washington County Business League is an organization composed of the business and professional men of the town and the purpose of it is to work in closer harmony among all the businesses of the city—certain Negro businesses.

Mr. FINKELSTEIN. Are these activities of your organization interfered with in any way by incidents of violence or problems of law enforcement?

Mr. EDWARDS. No, they are not. No, sir.

Mr. FINKELSTEIN. Have you had incidents of racial violence in Greenville during the past year?

Mr. EDWARDS. No, sir.

Mr. FINKELSTEIN. Has there been extensive civil rights activity in Greenville?

Mr. EDWARDS. There has been.

Mr. FINKELSTEIN. What is the attitude of the Negro community toward the law enforcement authorities in Greenville.

Mr. EDWARDS. The attitude of the Negro community toward the law enforcement in Greenville is good. We think perhaps we have one of the best police forces in the State, one of the best police forces that you will find around. We are sorry we can't say the same for the sheriff's force, which are also law officers. The only violence that we had within the last year occurred among—I mean with the sheriff's force. Now we had an officer who was stationed at the hospital—an incident at the hospital which was built partially with Hill-Burton funds—and we had an officer there who did strike an orderly—a hospital orderly—across the head with a club or a pistol. However, the police department did arrest him. And after they arrested this officer from the hospital, we found out then that this officer was a deputy sheriff. So they in turn had to release him. But he was arrested and tried. And our police department also arrested—at the time when we had a cross burning in Greenville—the police department arrested those men that burned the crosses, tried them, and fined them, and one of them fell dead.

Mr. FINKELSTEIN. I understand that he fell dead from a heart attack, is that right?

Mr. EDWARDS. From a heart attack, yes.

Mr. FINKELSTEIN. In your opinion, what are the reasons for effective law enforcement in Greenville?

Mr. EDWARDS. I believe one of the reasons is we have a liberal newspaper. And the next thing, we have a fine chief of police. I think that he has trained officers. And we have a young mayor, which we haven't always had. But ever since we have had the present chief of police and the last, just before him, we had a good police force. In addition to that, we have seven Negroes on the police force and about five Negro women on the force. And I think along with that, and with the cooperation that they have been able to get from the power structure in the city fathers, I believe it has enabled Greenville to have a good police force. Our chief of police and the majority of the policemen are well trained and they are trained men in their profession.

Mr. FINKELSTEIN. Dr. Frisby, would you like to add anything to what Mr. Edwards has said about these problems?

Dr. FRISBY. Well, I would like to say that it is due to the power structure. The police force can't do it alone. It has to have some help. And I think that certain individuals have helped the police force—and then he said the newspapers. It has often been said the pen is mightier than the sword. If you have a good newspaper, I think you will have a good community. I think that is the reason why some of these communities don't have the racial differences—have more racial differences than Greenville does, because the newspapers are afraid to speak out. And that is not true in Greenville. The newspapers in Greenville will speak out, whether he thinks it is wrong or right. He will pass his opinion. And I think that is what most of these communities need. And then he says a good police force and the other members of the community. No community can have a good city unless they are supported by the citizens, police force, and a good newspaper. I would like to read an article here. It says, "Were it left to me to decide whether we should have a government without newspapers or newspapers without government, I should not hesitate a moment to prefer the latter." And that was said by Thomas Jefferson. So you can see how important a newspaper is.

Mr. FINKELSTEIN. Thank you, Dr. Frisby.

Dr. FRISBY. And as I say, the power structure behind the newspaper and the other citizens is why Greenville doesn't have the trouble that many cities have.

Mr. FINKELSTEIN. Thank you.

Chairman HANNAH. Mr. Patterson, after such favorable testimony for newspapers I should give you the first opportunity to ask questions.

Vice Chairman PATTERSON. Doctor, I should just like to extend my profound thanks to the witnesses.

Chairman HANNAH. Father Hesburgh?

Commissioner HESBURGH. I think it is a pleasant thing at the end of this day, somewhere near the end, anyway, to hear such good news about Greenville. And it seems to me the witnesses have put their fingers right on important things; that a community is as good as it wants to be. As you both say, if law enforcement is backed up by the city fathers and the business people and the power structure, as you call it, if a good newspaper is there to criticize things when they do go wrong, as they will in any community once in a while, well, then people get what they deserve. But you say that the Negro community in Greenville has confidence in its police force?

Dr. FRISBY. I beg your pardon?

Commissioner HESBURGH. Do you believe that the Negro community in Greenville has confidence in its police force and in the law and order that is kept there?

Dr. FRISBY. I do. But I might add that we have other grievances, so far as jobs are concerned.

Commissioner HESBURGH. The police can't create those. I mean this is another problem and I agree it is an important problem.

Dr. FRISBY. I see.

Commissioner HESBURGH. But it would seem to me, after what we have been hearing the last 2 or 3 days, that you have to begin with peace in a community and you can't get peace unless you get law and order.

Dr. FRISBY. That's right.

Commissioner HESBURGH. And if you don't have law and order, then everything is bad in the community.

Chairman HANNAH. Any further questions?

Commissioner HESBURGH. No.

Chairman HANNAH. Mrs. Freeman?

Commissioner FREEMAN. Dr. Frisby or Mr. Edwards, how many Negroes in Greenville are registered voters?

Dr. FRISBY. Approximately 2,000.

Commissioner FREEMAN. Approximately 2,000, out of a total voting age population of how many?

Dr. FRISBY. Total population? You mean over-all, white——

Commissioner FREEMAN. Negro.

Dr. FRISBY. I guess approximately 5,000.

Commissioner FREEMAN. Then you have about the highest percentage of any community in the State?

Dr. FRISBY. Yes.

Commissioner FREEMAN. I am interested in knowing the extent of compliance with Title II of the Civil Rights Act of 1964, the public accommodations section. Do Negroes freely use the places of public accommodations in the city of Greenville-

Mr. EDWARDS. We use quite a few of them, and some are not being used. We have tested them in some of the leading places, and they have gone along with us nicely. But some of the smaller places that we don't know of, that we haven't tested ourselves, and some of them that the kids are testing—they are not responding so nicely. But the better places are responding and going along with the program. But we have that other group that is not going along with us as yet.

Dr. FRISBY. I might say that one place served the Negroes, but they say they are not welcome. The Negroes said, "We didn't come for your welcome; we came to get something to eat," so they eventually served them.

Commissioner FREEMAN. Thank you.

Chairman HANNAH. Dean Griswold?

Commissioner GRISWOLD. Mr. Edwards, has there been COFO activity in Greenville?

Mr. EDWARDS. Yes, sir.

Commissioner GRISWOLD. Has this been extensive?

Mr. EDWARDS. Yes, sir.

Commissioner GRISWOLD. What is the object of the COFO activity in Greenville?

Mr. EDWARDS. It has been to get out the people to register and vote and to help to integrate places and to help to see that the law—the 1964 Civil Rights Act was carried out. I would like to say, too, that I think regardless of what we do in Greenville or other places, unless the literacy test in Mississippi is eliminated as a prerequisite to voting, we are not ever going to get enough voters to do much good. Unless we can get Federal registrars in the State of Mississippi, we won't get enough Negro voters to do much good.

Commissioner GRISWOLD. With respect to the COFO activity in Greenville, what has been the attitude of the police department?

Mr. EDWARDS. Very cooperative.

Commissioner GRISWOLD. Have there been any incidents arising out of the COFO activity?

Mr. EDWARDS. No, sir.

Commissioner GRISWOLD. Have the police sought to prevent it in any way?

Mr. EDWARDS. We haven't had any clashes at all.

Chairman HANNAH. Mr. Rankin?

Commissioner RANKIN. You have spoken well of the newspapermen, represented on my right, in relation to the good condition in Greenville. What about the clergy on my left? Has the clergy played any part?

Mr. EDWARDS. The clergy in Greenville has done about what they can do. They too are under pressure like they are in other places. And we don't condemn them for not being able to come out like some of these businessmen can do. Yet in all of the churches there is a certain segment of the membership that—after all, it's the power they've got to serve too.

Commissioner RANKIN. Why can't they come out? Can you answer that question?

Mr. EDWARDS. I beg your pardon?

Commissioner RANKIN. Why can't they come out and take a stand?

Mr. EDWARDS. Well, they depend upon their membership for a livelihood—number one. And I think that they have found out that those who don't necessarily go along with the civil rights program don't necessarily go along with the powers to participate in it, and for that reason I think it makes it a little bit hard for him to be able to get his support from them too. The churches are going to have to depend upon the support of all of their congregation.

Commissioner RANKIN. So support is the important thing?

Mr. EDWARDS. I think so, that is the important thing.

Chairman HANNAH. Mr. Patterson?

Vice Chairman PATTERSON. Dr. Frisby, how did you get this good law enforcement in Greenville?

Dr. FRISBY. I beg your pardon?

Vice Chairman PATTERSON. How did you get this good law enforcement in Greenville?

Dr. FRISBY. I think it is coming down the line probably from the forefathers, that we always had since I have been there.

Vice Chairman PATTERSON. What factors exist that make it possible in Greenville when it doesn't seem to be possible in some other cities?

Dr. FRISBY. Well, as I mentioned before, I think it is the police force——

Vice Chairman PATTERSON. But I am speaking of the police force. How did you get a good police force in Greenville?

Dr. FRISBY. We elected a good man.

Vice Chairman PATTERSON. You think it goes back to the vote, do you?

Dr. FRISBY. I think it goes back to the vote in selecting a good police officer.

Chairman HANNAH. Thank you very much, gentlemen. We appreciate your being with us.

(Witnesses excused.)

Chairman HANNAH. Call the next witness.

Mr. TAYLOR. The next witnesses are Mr. Leroy Percy and Mr. Albert Lake.

Chairman HANNAH. Mr. Percy, Mr. Lake?

(Whereupon, Mr. Leroy Percy and Mr. Albert Lake were duly sworn by the Chairman and testified, as follows:)

Chairman HANNAH. Mr. Finkelstein?

TESTIMONY OF MR. LEROY P. PERCY AND MR. J. ALBERT LAKE, WASHINGTON COUNTY, MISS.

Mr. FINKELSTEIN. Mr. Lake, will you please give us your name, your residence and your occupation?

Mr. LAKE. My name is J. A. Lake, Greenville, Mississippi, an attorney.

Mr. FINKELSTEIN. How long have you lived in Mississippi, Mr. Lake?

Mr. LAKE. I have lived in Mississippi all of my life except while I was in school and a year or two working elsewhere, and the time I have been in the Army.

Mr. FINKELSTEIN. How long have you lived in Greenville?

Mr. LAKE. All of my life, 59 years.

Mr. FINKELSTEIN. Have you been active in civic and political life in Greenville?

Mr. LAKE. Yes. I served for a number of years in the state legislature, served as city attorney for some 10 or 12 years; Chamber of Commerce activities, served as president of that group. And the normal activities in which a practicing lawyer participates.

Mr. FINKELSTEIN. Are you a member of a firm of attorneys?

Mr. LAKE. Yes.

Mr. FINKELSTEIN. What is the name of the firm?

Mr. LAKE. Firm name is Wynn, Hafter, Lake and Tindell.

Mr. FINKELSTEIN. Mr. Percy, would you give your name, residence and occupation?

Mr. PERCY. Leroy P. Percy. I live just outside of Greenville. I am a cotton farmer.

Mr. FINKELSTEIN. How long have you lived in Mississippi?

Mr. PERCY. Oh, about 35 years.

Mr. FINKELSTEIN. And in Greenville?

Mr. PERCY. That length of time.

Mr. FINKELSTEIN. Have you been active in civic and political life of Greenville?

Mr. PERCY. I suppose quite active. Maybe not quite as much as Mr. Lake, but more or less along the same line except not the legal end of it.

Mr. FINKELSTEIN. What business positions do you hold?

Mr. PERCY. Well, I am chairman of the board of one of the banks, the First National Bank. And I am president of the Greenville Compress Company in town. I also serve on other business boards.

Mr. FINKELSTEIN. Let me go back to you, Mr. Lake, for a moment. Did the business and professional community in Greenville contribute in any way or assist the law enforcement officials in carrying out their duties?

Mr. LAKE. Well, first let me say I would like to agree with Dr. Frisby's answer to one of your last questions, that the situation in Greenville is nothing that has developed in the last few years. I give full credit to the efforts of our newspaper and to our good friends there, but I think it could well be said that Greenville had as much to do with making the newspapers as the newspapers had to do with making Greenville.

Recently, it became apparent to anyone who was interested, that problems might arise in connection with the school segregation problem and the civil rights laws. There have been groups, voluntary groups from—a voluntary group or more, consisting of people, you might say, on the right, on the left, in the middle, who have discussed and who have, I think, come to conclusions as to what the community feeling on matters was. And they have determined how far things could move at what time. And they have basically operated to give support to the governing body of the city and to the police force and to see that law and order was maintained. Not that we felt that it was necessary to support them in that activity, but to give them the support that we thought they were entitled to.

Mr. FINKELSTEIN. Mr. Percy, I believe that your family name is a famous name in the Delta, isn't that right, sir?

Mr. LAKE. That is correct. Let me answer that, yes.

Mr. FINKELSTEIN. Can you give us some idea of why Greenville, from a historic point of view, seems to be different from the other communities?

Mr. PERCY. Well, first, Mr. Finkelstein, let me say this. I don't think Mr. Lake, or I, or the other people from Greenville want to set up Greenville as a Utopia or as anything better than any other community in the State. I think that we do feel that we are making every effort that we can make in these difficult times to—for local responsible leadership to take responsibility for trying to solve these problems as they come up from day to day. Greenville has been a community of—I don't know, it has had an atmosphere of tolerance, a feeling of live and let live. There is no particular pressure to be a conformist. You don't have to—you can believe whatever you want to believe. You can do most anything you want to do as long as you keep out of the chief of police's way over there and as long as you don't bother other people.

I think the basic reason for Greenville being the community that it is, is this: There has been a long history of responsible citizens willing to participate in local government, not only to involve themselves in voting and getting the vote out, but to serve as city councilmen, as members of the school board and so forth. I think that is basic.

And I have got to say, like Dr. Frisby said, that any community—I'm sure Mr. Patterson will agree—that has a live-wire, progressive, aggressive newspaper, it kind of keeps everybody on their toes. And boy, we got one in Greenville, I tell you. And it don't respect persons or organizations, and they are willing to take sides on controversial issues. I think it is very important.

Mr. FINKELSTEIN. Thank you. No questions.

Chairman HANNAH. Father Hesburgh?

Commissioner HESBURGH. Mr. Percy or Mr. Lake, or both of you, I gather you haven't had any church bombings up in Greenville?

Mr. PERCY. No, sir.

Mr. LAKE. No, sir.

Commissioner HESBURGH. You haven't had the usual reign of terror we have been seeing in other parts of the State.

Mr. PERCY. No, sir.

Mr. LAKE. We have none, no, sir.

Commissioner HESBURGH. Well, I think if I might override your modesty for a moment, this is a kind of model that I think every State needs because there are very bad parts of the State I come from, Indiana. And I am sure the other gentlemen can say the same. And there are very good parts. And it seems to me what we have been reaching for here the last few days is what is the formula for law and order in a good, healthy, peaceful, progressive community. I don't think we are looking for anything other than that. I think you gentlemen have given us some ideas as to how that might be accomplished. I think you put your finger right on the heart of it when you talk about responsible leadership on the part of the outstanding citizens of the community. I don't want to ask any questions. I just want to congratulate you for what you are doing.

Mr. LAKE. Well, Father Hesburgh, I think the credit there should probably go to our granddaddies rather than us.

Commissioner HESBURGH. Well, then I will congratulate your granddaddy.

Chairman HANNAH. Mrs. Freeman.

Commissioner FREEMAN. Mr. Lake or Mr. Percy, I wonder if either of you would identify for the record that live-wire newspaper that has had such a positive effect?

Mr. PERCY. I would be happy to—the Delta Democrat Times.

Commissioner FREEMAN. Thank you.

Chairman HANNAH. Dean Griswold?

Commissioner GRISWOLD. Mr. Perry, has the atmosphere in Greenville been good for business.

Mr. PERCY. I think it has very definitely been a factor, Dean Griswold. Yes, sir.

Commissioner GRISWOLD. Have any industries located in Greenville because it has a reputation of having good race and community relations?

Mr. PERCY. I think that is correct.

Commissioner GRISWOLD. Does this contribute to the general prosperity of Greenville?

Mr. PERCY. It certainly does, to quite a degree.

Commissioner GRISWOLD. Would you agree with that, Mr. Lake?

Mr. LAKE. Yes. I think without a doubt that we have realized that—that we all realize that disturbances that take men's minds off of their business and sort of make you, you might say, look down a dark hole of despair, will kill off any economic progress.

Chairman HANNAH. Mr. Griswold, in your modesty, I think Mr. Lake is a graduate of your law school.

Commissioner GRISWOLD. I didn't want to pin that on him, but it is true. He is not only a graduate of my law school, but a classmate of mine.

Mr. LAKE. May I say this. I have enjoyed the friendship for a long time, but Erwin Griswold was so far above me in the ratings in that class that you might say he was almost in another class.

Chairman HANNAH. Mr. Rankin?

Commissioner RANKIN. Mr. Percy, wouldn't you say you are giving us one of the answers, too much centralization in Washington? When you have communities like yours which can meet their responsibilities, isn't that the best way, if we don't believe in centralization or too much power, to keep our power at home?

Mr. PERCY. I think that is correct, sir. I think we all must know that the problems that arise out of our racial situation happen at the local level.

Commissioner RANKIN. That's right.

Mr. PERCY. And they have to be dealt with at the local level. And I think that if responsible citizens will involve themselves in trying to solve these problems, it just doesn't get past the local level.

Commissioner RANKIN. The problems of government sometimes increase to the square of the distance. Isn't that right?

Mr. PERCY. That's correct, sir. That is correct.

Chairman HANNAH. Mr. Patterson?

Vice Chairman PATTERSON. Mr. Percy, I have noticed that in the last 10 days the County Supervisors Association has come out with a law and order statement, the Sheriff's Association of Mississippi, the circuit clerks or voting registrars—the Governor and the Attorney

General have both mentioned that law and order must prevail in Mississippi. There is a lot of talk in the press corps about a change in this State, a distinct change—of this year being a watershed, a time of turning. You and your family are active leaders of Mississippi history, past and future. Could you comment on the validity of the supposition that a major change is underway at present?

Mr. Percy. I think that is correct, Mr. Patterson. I think that we in Mississippi have realized or are in the process of realizing that this doctrine of massive resistance, this posture of inflexibility that has been in effect in certain parts of the State for the last 10 years, is just no longer possible or practical. It just doesn't work. I think the people in Mississippi want to be in the main stream of American life. They do not want to be in the backwater. I think that they are tired of being led by the dead hand of the past. They want something—they want hope in the future; they want partialism, and I think we are going to get it.

Vice Chairman Patterson. Thank you.

Chairman Hannah. Mr. Rogerson?

Mr. Rogerson. Gentlemen, we have heard a lot in the last few days about Klan activity and various other kinds of terrorism and extremist activity. Have you had any recent history of Klan activity or organization in your community or county?

Mr. Lake. The only thing that I personally have heard that would indicate any attempted Klan activity was the burning of three crosses and, as the previous witnesses testified, those people were arrested— I think Bill Burnley told me within 30 minutes. And as has been said, one dropped dead.

Mr. Percy. From a heart attack.

Mr. Lake. From a heart attack. That is all that I know of—all that I heard of anything.

Mr. Rogerson. Thank you.

Chairman Hannah. Mr. Taylor?

Mr. Taylor. Mr. Percy, earlier you said that your community did have some problems, but I take it that you look forward with some confidence to the ability of the community to solve the problems in a way which will improve opportunity for all persons. Is that right?

Mr. Percy. That's correct.

Mr. Taylor. How important is open communication between members of the races in working toward that kind of solution?

Mr. Percy. I think it is very important, Mr. Taylor, and I think that we have very good communications in Greenville. I think the responsible citizens in the Negro race and the white race do work together on a very good basis.

Mr. TAYLOR. Thank you.

Chairman HANNAH. Father Hesburgh?

Commissioner HESBURGH. I would think the best evidence of good communication is that this is practically the first time since we have been here that a white delegation and Negro delegation from the same county have said the same thing.

Mr. PERCY. It looks like it's rigged testimony, doesn't it, Father?

Commissioner HESBURGH. It is beginning to sound like a love feast.

Mr. PERCY. I would like to make this statement. We haven't solved all our problems by a long shot. We have got a lot more to solve. But I think we have the will to make reasonable solutions.

Chairman HANNAH. Well, as we excuse you, I should like to say to you gentlemen and to your predecessors, Dr. Frisby and Mr. Edwards, that it has been a breath of fresh air to find a community where the leadership on both sides is willing to recognize their problems and that they think the problems are going to be solved only when responsible leadership recognizes they exist and recognizes that the best solutions are those that are worked out by the local people who are going to have to live with them.

Thank you very much. You are excused.

(Witnesses excused.)

[Applause.]

Chairman HANNAH. Call the next witness.

Mr. TAYLOR. The next witness is Mayor Patrick Dunne.

(Whereupon, Mayor Patrick Dunne was duly sworn by the Chairman and testified, as follows:)

Chairman HANNAH. Mr. Finkelstein?

TESTIMONY OF PATRICK A. DUNNE, MAYOR, GREENVILLE, WASHINGTON COUNTY, MISS.

Mr. FINKELSTEIN. Will you please state your name, your residence and your occupation?

Mayor DUNNE. Patrick A. Dunne, 517 East Moore Street, Greenville, Mississippi.

Mr. FINKELSTEIN. How long have you been mayor of Greenville, Mr. Dunne?

Mayor DUNNE. Thirteen months.

Mr. FINKELSTEIN. How large is Greenville?

Mayor DUNNE. 47,000.

Mr. FINKELSTEIN. What is its racial composition?

Mayor DUNNE. About 48 percent Negro and 52 percent white.

Mr. FINKELSTEIN. When you learned last spring, Mayor Dunne,

that civil rights workers would be coming to Greenville, did you take any steps to insure that there would be law and order?

Mayor DUNNE. Yes, sir.

Mr. FINKELSTEIN. What did you do?

Mayor DUNNE. We got together several of the people that Mr. Lake and Mr. Percy mentioned. We discussed this thing as to how the city was going to be harassed by people coming in and what was the best solution to this problem so that there would not be any violence. And we took a cue from Governor Johnson's inaugural address, that we were in the mainstream of America. And we issued a statement that law and order must prevail in our community and that we were not going to tolerate extremists. And this we meant and the people knew that we meant it.

Mr. FINKELSTEIN. Do you have a copy of that statement?

Mayor DUNNE. Yes, sir. I would like to enter it into the record, if I may, sir.

Chairman HANNAH. It is received.

(Exhibit No. 22 was marked for identification and received in evidence.)

Mayor DUNNE. This is one.

Mr. FINKELSTEIN. There was more than one such statement, Mayor?

Mayor DUNNE. Yes, sir.

Mr. FINKELSTEIN. Who made the statements?

Mayor DUNNE. The City Council—myself and the City Council.

Mr. FINKELSTEIN. Did you have any discussions with any members of the business community?

Mayor DUNNE. Yes, sir; and here is the third statement.

Mr. FINKELSTEIN. There were three such statements?

Mayor DUNNE. One of them was pertaining to laws, that we are a society of laws and not of men. That was brought out in another thing of city government there so that the people would know how the City Council felt about laws and how they should be obeyed and must be obeyed.

Mr. FINKELSTEIN. What are the major industrial plants in your city?

Mayor DUNNE. Chicago Mill, U.S. Gypsum Company, Mohasco, Atkins Saw, Moeller Manufacturing, Midstates Metal, Cleaver-Brookes, Moso Screw Company.

Mr. FINKELSTEIN. Are you fairly industrialized compared with other cities in the Delta?

Mayor DUNNE. Yes, sir.

Mr. FINKELSTEIN. Have you been successful in attracting new industries to Greenville?

Mayor DUNNE. Yes, sir.

Mr. FINKELSTEIN. Do you think that effective law enforcement has been a factor which has helped you to attract such industry?

Mayor DUNNE. Yes, sir.

Mr. FINKELSTEIN. No further questions.

Chairman HANNAH. Father Hesburgh?

Commissioner HESBURGH. Mayor Dunne, when the COFO workers, who seemed to be at the center of much of the agitation or difficulty, or whatever you want to call it—we have heard this from other counties and other cities—when the COFO workers did come to Greenville, was there an attitude of letting them do whatever they felt they wanted to do, as long as they did it in an orderly and legal way?

Mayor DUNNE. Yes, sir. We were prepared. We—I have here a statement that—an article that appeared in the Democrat Times that "COFO says Greenville to be Pushed to the Limit." And these are the type things that we were—all through the summer.

And in the same story, in a little box, you will also notice that "The City Police Thoroughly Prepared." "We want to try to prevent violence or demonstrations if we can help it." This is a statement by Chief Burnley which I would like to enter into the record, if I may, which showed these people came in to do their best to prevent strife and turmoil, which they readily announced that they would. And we were doing our best to see that there was no violence and that law and order was maintained.

Commissioner HESBURGH. Did COFO do anything good?

Mayor DUNNE. No, sir.

Commissioner HESBURGH. You don't think so. Well, did they get anybody registered to vote?

Mayor DUNNE. I do not know, sir, because in Washington County, any person that—as in the past, all he has to do is go to the courthouse and register—and also to City Hall.

Commissioner HESBURGH. Good. Thank you very much.

Chairman HANNAH. Mr. Rankin?

Commissioner RANKIN. In addition to having a good law enforcement group, is it good to have a good city council also?

Mayor DUNNE. Yes, sir, and good citizens.

Commissioner RANKIN. All three are necessary, is that true?

Mayor DUNNE. Yes, sir. Yes, sir; and we do have good citizens, all 47,000 of them.

Chairman HANNAH. Mr. Patterson?

Vice Chairman PATTERSON. Mr. Chairman, I am going to withhold any further questions to the mayor because it is my experience that when a man is coming out this far ahead in a hearing, he may go home and find the city hall burned down. I don't want to stretch his luck.

Chairman HANNAH. Mr. Rogerson?

Mr. ROGERSON. I would just like to ask one thing. We introduced some staff background on Washington County when we were talking about voting the other day. And I just noticed that we haven't separated Greenville out from Washington County. But we have been concerned about this educational gap in the State and the fact the State does not have a compulsory school law. Do communities have any power to enact compulsory school attendance laws in this State?

Mayor DUNNE. I do not know. This is a school board matter and these are complete separate entities. I cannot answer your question, sir, because I do not know the answer.

Mr. ROGERSON. Thank you.

Chairman HANNAH. Thank you very much, Mayor. You are excused. Call the next witness.

(Witnessed excused.)

Mr. TAYLOR. The next witness is William Burnley, chief of police.

Chairman HANNAH. Mr. Burnley, will you raise your right hand?

(Whereupon, Mr. William C. Burnley, Jr., was duly sworn by the Chairman and testified, as follows:)

Chairman HANNAH. Mr. Finkelstein?

TESTIMONY OF WILLIAM C. BURNLEY, JR., CHIEF OF POLICE, GREENVILLE, WASHINGTON COUNTY, MISS.

Mr. FINKELSTEIN. Will you please state your name, your residence and your occupation?

Mr. BURNLEY. William C. Burnley, Jr. My occupation is the chief of police, Greenville, Miss. I live at 410 South Rebecca Drive in Greenville.

Mr. FINKELSTEIN. How long have you served as chief of police?

Mr. BURNLEY. Six years, sir.

Mr. FINKELSTEIN. Prior to being chief, how much experience or training did you have in law enforcement?

Mr. BURNLEY. I have been with the department 19 years and I am a graduate of the FBI National Academy in Washington.

Mr. FINKELSTEIN. How many men do you have on your force?

Mr. BURNLEY. Fifty-three.

Mr. FINKELSTEIN. Do you have any men trained as detectives?

Mr. BURNLEY. Yes, sir, I do.

Mr. FINKELSTEIN. In selecting your recruits, do you check their background to determine whether they have been convicted of any offense?

Mr. BURNLEY. Yes, sir; they are fingerprinted. These fingerprints sent to the FBI in Washington and a return is made before we employ them.

Mr. FINKELSTEIN. Do you attempt to determine whether they are members of any extremist organizations?

Mr. BURNLEY. I do, sir.

Mr. FINKELSTEIN. How do you do that?

Mr. BURNLEY. First we ask them. And if they do belong, it will come out, sir. You will know it.

Mr. FINKELSTEIN. Do you give them any tests to determine that?

Mr. BURNLEY. We give them the IQ test, also, the lie detector test.

Mr. FINKELSTEIN. What is your policy if you find they do belong to such an organization?

Mr. BURNLEY. Membership in any organization of extremist groups is not tolerated.

Mr. FINKELSTEIN. In the spring of 1964 when you learned that civil rights workers would be coming to Greenville, were you concerned about possible racial violence?

Mr. BURNLEY. Yes, sir.

Mr. FINKELSTEIN. What did you do to prevent such violence?

Mr. BURNLEY. I thought it was necessary that our personnel be informed as to the issues, as to the law and our policy regarding enforcement during this period.

Mr. FINKELSTEIN. When you say your policy regarding enforcement, what was that policy?

Mr. BURNLEY. The policy was this. Arrest no person regardless of who they are or what group they belong to unless they have violated the law.

Mr. FINKELSTEIN. Did you conduct any special instruction or training classes for your policemen?

Mr. BURNLEY. Yes, sir; we had instruction periods on this type of thing that I have just explained.

Mr. FINKELSTEIN. Did you give policemen who felt they couldn't carry out your policy a chance to be transferred?

Mr. BURNLEY. There was no place to transfer, sir. I gave them this—I merely said to our entire group, "This is the policy; this is the way that we must operate. If there are those among you who feel that you cannot operate along this policy line, I would appreciate it if you would come and talk with me about it and I will not hold it against you. You may resign or leave the department."

Mr. FINKELSTEIN. Did you attempt to advise yourself of the activities of Klan-type groups in Washington County or in Greenville?

Mr. BURNLEY. Yes, sir.

Mr. FINKELSTEIN. Do you feel that you knew pretty well what they were doing?

Mr. BURNLEY. I feel that I did, yes, sir; I hope that I did.

Mr. FINKELSTEIN. Were there any incidents of racial violence in Greenville during the summer or fall of 1964?

Mr. BURNLEY. There were minor incidents. I have some newspaper releases, if you would like to go into them. Assaults between the races, Negro on white, white on Negro. The usual assault and battery cases that you would have. Nothing unusual.

Mr. FINKELSTEIN. About how many were there?

Mr. BURNLEY. Perhaps three or four.

Mr. FINKELSTEIN. And were arrests made in these cases?

Mr. BURNLEY. Arrests were made in each and every case and they were brought before the court.

Mr. FINKELSTEIN. And were they convicted?

Mr. BURNLEY. Yes, sir.

Mr. FINKELSTEIN. Did you arrest any civil rights workers who were in Greenville?

Mr. BURNLEY. No, sir.

Mr. FINKELSTEIN. None at all?

Mr. BURNLEY. No, sir.

Mr. FINKELSTEIN. No further questions.

Chairman HANNAH. Father Hesburgh?

Commissioner HESBURGH. I would gather, chief from our prior conference with the other gentlemen from Greenville that you had a good deal of support from the local community?

Mr. BURNLEY. Yes, sir.

Commissioner HESBURGH. The fact is you did?

Mr. BURNLEY. I had tremendous support from the community.

Commissioner HESBURGH. Do you think you could have done what you did without strong support from the local community?

Mr. BURNLEY. No, sir. However, I do say this. I would not have yielded my stand on law enforcement.

Commissioner HESBURGH. You say, then, that you need a philosophy of law enforcement which I gather in your case——

Mr. BURNLEY. A philosophy of professionalism.

Commissioner HESBURGH. That's right.

Mr. BURNLEY. Yes.

Commissioner HESBURGH. You need good training of yourself and your officers and you need the backing of the community.

Mr. BURNLEY. That's true. Backing of the community is very, very important, one of the utmost factors.

Commissioner HESBURGH. Would you say, without undue modesty, that you and your officers probably have more training in law enforcement technique than many of the other officers in this State?

Mr. BURNLEY. I would not know, Father, how to compare with the rest of the State. I do know that the rest of the State is now making progress in this area. For instance, Governor Johnson talked with Mr. Hoover, when Mr. Hoover was in Mississippi, and as a direct result of this conversation numerous men with the Highway Patrol are now being sent to the Academy in Washington. Where these men are now distributed throughout Mississippi, you do not have the breakdown in law enforcement. You have a professional-type job.

Commissioner HESBURGH. Did you find that you learned a good deal at the FBI Academy?

Mr. BURNLEY. Yes, sir; I sure did.

Commissioner HESBURGH. And you are able to pass that on to your men?

Mr. BURNLEY. Yes, sir. And also, my entire staff has been to the FBI Academy.

Commissioner HESBURGH. They have all been there too?

Mr. BURNLEY. Yes, sir, seven men.

Commissioner HESBURGH. Thank you, chief.

Chairman HANNAH. Dean Griswold?

Commissioner GRISWOLD. Chief Burnley, how many officers are there on your force?

Mr. BURNLEY. Fifty-three, sir.

Commissioner GRISWOLD. Are there any Negroes on the force?

Mr. BURNLEY. Yes, sir.

Commissioner GRISWOLD. How many?

Mr. BURNLEY. We have seven officers, five—maybe six or seven police crossing guards.

Commissioner GRISWOLD. How long have there been Negroes on the police force in Greenville?

Mr. BURNLEY. Since 1950.

Commissioner GRISWOLD. That would be 15 years ago.

Mr. BURNLEY. Yes.

Commissioner GRISWOLD. Do you find the presence of Negro police officers on your force useful and desirable?

Mr. BURNLEY. Yes, sir; I sure do.

Commissioner GRISWOLD. You said a moment ago that you had good support from the community in Greenville. Does that include the Negro community as well as the white community?

Mr. BURNLEY. Yes, sir.

Commissioner GRISWOLD. How is that evidenced to you?

Mr. BURNLEY. It is evidenced in the very fact that these people came here to testify in behalf of good law enforcement in Greenville. It is evidenced in daily activity by their respect for our department.

Commissioner GRISWOLD. This wasn't news to you when you heard them testify today, I assume?

Mr. BURNLEY. No, sir; it wasn't news to me.

Chairman HANNAH. Mr. Rankin?

Commissioner RANKIN. In your work, have you had to call frequently upon the Highway Patrol?

Mr. BURNLEY. No, sir.

Commissioner RANKIN. FBI?

Mr. BURNLEY. No, sir.

Commissioner RANKIN. In other words, you have handled things pretty well at home, is that correct?

Mr. BURNLEY. Yes, sir.

Commissioner RANKIN. And the courts have done pretty well too?

Mr. BURNLEY. The courts have done extremely well.

Commissioner RANKIN. It is pretty hard for a law enforcement officer to do his job unless the courts do well also, is that true?

Mr. BURNLEY. Very much so.

Commissioner RANKIN. Thank you.

Chairman HANNAH. Mr. Patterson?

Vice Chairman PATTERSON. Do you have any problems, chief?

Mr. BURNLEY. Problems every day, sir.

Vice Chairman PATTERSON. Thank you.

Chairman HANNAH. Mr. Taylor.

Mr. TAYLOR. Chief, what kind of records do you keep? Can you just outline generally for us what——

Mr. BURNLEY. Many records, sir. And you would have to specify— give me some specific type of records.

Mr. TAYLOR. Well, when a complaint is made to you, is that generally recorded?

Mr. BURNLEY. Generally when a complaint is made, someone calls in or appears in person, they call or come to the desk, it is—the complaint is then given to the man on duty at the time. He makes a typewritten record of it. If it is of a serious nature, it is also backed up with a process that shows the results of investigations on it.

Mr. TAYLOR. Are memoranda generally made of telephone conversations when they relate to a case?

Mr. BURNLEY. Only the complaining conversation.

Mr. TAYLOR. Do you keep records of investigative interviews?

Mr. BURNLEY. Yes, sir.

Mr. TAYLOR. Are these records destroyed for any reason?

Mr. BURNLEY. No, sir.

Mr. TAYLOR. Just one further question. During the course of this summer or before it, were public statements made either by you or by others—or specifically by you—making it clear that violence would not be tolerated in the community?

Mr. BURNLEY. Yes, sir. I would like to introduce this into the record, which is a newspaper account of Klan activity at its first, and the action taken by the police; an editorial by the Democrat Times; also an article where I was invited to the International Association of Chiefs of Police Civil Rights Conference at the University of Oklahoma and did attend; where assaults had occurred and our action and statements released; an editorial plugging professionalism in our department; our city court, the court of His Honor George Earl Solomon and his wisdom therein; and editorial——

Mr. FINKELSTEIN. Excuse me. This editorial is entitled "Cheers for Police."

Mr. BURNLEY. I also have a letter here I would like to read for the benefit of this body. It is from a lady whom I do not know, Mrs. Edward C. P. Thomas, from 241 Barklindale Circle, Rosemont, Pennsylvania.

To the Chief of Police, Greenville, Mississippi.

Dear Sir: As the mother of Morton Thomas, a student worker in the Student Non-violent Coordinating Committee, I would like to express my admiration and grateful thanks for the splendid work you and your police force have been doing in maintaining law and order under extremely difficult conditions. My son has told us last night on the telephone that your police force has protected them in their job. We all recognize the tremendous problem which has confronted you this summer and are grateful for your attitude and your efficiency.

Commissioner RANKIN. Can I ask you a question?

Mr. BURNLEY. Yes, sir.

Commissioner RANKIN. If you would hear of an assault somewhere in the city, would you investigate that without a complaint?

Mr. BURNLEY. It is according to what I heard, sir. Hearsay is not a basis for too much action. If I thought it was a serious offense and I should investigate it, I am sure I would, sir.

Commissioner RANKIN. Thank you.

Chairman HANNAH. Mr. Burnley, before you are excused, we said some nice things about the witnesses, colored and white, who appeared. The Mayor indicated the degree of support that the Mayor of the City Council—officials of the city, have given to progress in the area of civil rights over a long period. This Commission in its recommendations to the President and to the Congress has recommended several times that the Federal Government concern itself with the possibility of doing what it can do to improve the training of police officials. This is a problem that is not only important in Mississippi; it is important all over the country. And one of the areas in which the whole Nation could well concern itself to its own advantage would be in the professionalization of its police forces. And this Commission has recommended this over and over again. And, of course, in some States real progress is being made. Your testimony here today emphasizes what is perfectly evident. This is an important part of assuring progress in this area.

So as we excuse you, we again commend all the people of Greenville who have been here and I am sure what you say is right and that we have heard the bright side of it. There are probably many problems to be solved, but with the kind of people you have in the county and the city, if you keep the same attitude, you can expect these will be solved. And after the rather depressing testimony we have had from some communities and some counties, this is a good note upon which to conclude most of the questioning. We are going to have a witness or two in the morning, but you are the last witness representing a community.

Before you leave and before we take a recess, I want to again comment with reference to the first of these panels.

This is a lawyers panel. While we are in recess they will rearrange the tables and chairs here on the stage. Those who will be participating this afternoon are the President of the Mississippi Bar Association, Mr. Thomas; the former Dean of the University of Mississippi Law School, Mr. Farley; Mr. Brocato of Clarksdale; Mr. Campbell of Greenville; and Mr. Grantham, Mr. Pyles and Mr. Wise, all attorneys in Jackson.

(Witnesses excused.)

Chairman HANNAH. Mr. Taylor has an announcement.

Mr. TAYLOR. I wanted to enter into the record at this point, Mr. Chairman, some information on Commissioner Walter Dell Davis's concern that under Mississippi law records we sought from him could not be produced. The objection has now been removed by the consent of the district attorneys involved and the records have been produced for the Commission.

Chairman HANNAH. We will reconvene at 3:40.

(Whereupon, the Commission took a short recess, after which they proceeded with the lawyers panel.)

LAWYERS PANEL, FEBRUARY 19, 1965

The Commission met with the lawyers panel in the Recreation Hall, Veterans Administration Center, 1500 East Woodrow Wilson Drive, Jackson, Miss., at 3:40 p.m., Friday, February 19, 1965, the Honorable Erwin N. Griswold, presiding.

Present: Erwin N. Griswold, Commissioner (Presiding); John A. Hannah, Chairman; Eugene Patterson, Vice Chairman; Mrs. Frankie Muse Freeman, Commissioner; Rev. Theodore M. Hesburgh, C.S.C., Commissioner; Robert S. Rankin, Commissioner.

Panel Members: Earl T. Thomas, Esq., President, Miss. Bar Association, Jackson, Miss.; Robert J. Farley, Dean Emeritus, University of Miss. Law School, Oxford, Miss.; Vincent J. Brocato, Esq., Clarksdale, Miss.; Roy D. Campbell, Esq., Greenville, Miss.; R. Gordon Grantham, Esq., Jackson, Miss.; Dixon L. Pyles, Esq., Jackson, Miss.; Sherwood W. Wise, Esq., Jackson, Miss.

PROCEEDINGS

Commissioner GRISWOLD. The recess will conclude and this session will be in order. We have, as the remaining part of the hearing this afternoon, the privilege of hearing from a group of distinguished Mississippi lawyers. I will first introduce them to you.

On my left, your right, is Mr. Dixon L. Pyles, of Jackson, Miss. Next to him is Mr. Vincent J. Brocato, of Clarksdale, Miss. And next to him is Robert J. Farley, whom I will introduce as of Oxford, Miss., because everyone knows of Dean Farley and his long distinguished connection with the law school at Oxford. He is currently serving on the faculty, I believe, of the Stetson University Law School, is that correct?

Mr. FARLEY. Florida.

Commissioner GRISWOLD. Of the University of Florida Law School, having retired last summer from the University of Mississippi Law School. On my immediate right, your left, is Mr. Earl T. Thomas of Jackson, who is President of the Mississippi Bar Association. Next to him is Mr. Sherwood W. Wise, of Jackson, Miss. And the next to him is Mr. Roy D. Campbell of Greenville, Miss. On my extreme right, your left, is Mr. R. Gordon Grantham of Jackson, Miss. And to my immediate left, of course, is the other lawyer member of the Commission, Mrs. Frankie Freeman of St. Louis, Mo.

Gentlemen, we have asked you to meet with us to give us the benefit of your experience and advice, both about problems in Mississippi and about what can or should be done about them. This might relate particularly to what lawyers can or should do about the problems. But I do not think that it need be limited to that. Lawyers are, or ought to be, leaders in any community and any information or advice which you can give to the members of the Commission as to steps which you think can be taken or ought to be taken to bring about a better climate of race relations in Mississippi will be very welcome and very helpful. I think we might first call on Mr. Thomas and see if he has any observations he would care to make.

Mr. Thomas. Thank you, Dean Griswold. We appreciate—the Mississippi State Bar and its members—your offering us this opportunity to appear before the Commission. And we would like to play our part in attempting to solve the many pressing problems which are before us. I might say, Dean, that shortly after I took office in June of last year as President of the Bar, we had our first meeting of the Board of Bar Commissioners, a board consisting of 19 members from as many circuit court districts of Mississippi, and it was there that the problems came down, not singly or doubly, but in multiples. And the pressing problem which eventuated, Dean—I imagine you would have some reference to—would be a resolution, would it not, Dean? May I comment on it?

Commissioner Griswold. Yes, I would appreciate it if you would tell us about the resolution. And if you have a copy of it, give it to me so the full text can be included in the record.

Mr. Thomas. Thank you, Dean Griswold, I shall. And I would like to take the opportunity of identifying this particular resolution to which you refer which consists of four pages. I would like, if you please, sir, with the Commissioner's permission, to have it entered as a part of the record. I believe Mrs. Freeman has a complete copy, Dean. I believe this is short a page.

Commissioner Griswold. Will you please give it to Mr. Taylor and mark it is an exhibit.

(Exhibit No. 23 was marked for identification and received in evidence.)

Mr. Thomas. Dean, since you kindly invited me to comment on the passage of this resolution—after concluding a rather heavy agenda, we came to what we considered the greatest problem facing our board. And that was with reference to the very problems that we are here discussing because at that time there was pressing down on us—had filtered down as it does, because we feel its impact here—the force of

Gideon v. *Wainwright*, decided by the U.S. Supreme Court on March 18, 1963. It reached down after being held off because of the ABA meetings and all the interpretations and the like going on. This came down, but it was—it came down as a cataclysm on us because we——

Commissioner Griswold. Might I say, Mr. Thomas, just to identify the case for the audience——

Mr. Thomas. Yes, Dean.

Commissioner Griswold. And you correct me, if I misstate it. Gideon and Wainwright is the decision of the U.S. Supreme Court holding that the States are required to provide counsel for any person charged with serious crime in the State.

Mr. Thomas. Thank you, Dean. They are not—not any correction to the Dean. The Dean is the dean of Harvard University Law School. I appreciate the Dean coming to my aid at this time. *Gideon* v.*Wainwright* was pressing down upon us because our court had interpreted our Constitutional requirement of the assistance of counsel to apply only to capital cases or wherein death might be taken. That, too, had been more or less until 1938, the province of the U.S. Supreme Court until *Johnson* v. *Zerbest* came along. And then when *Gideon* v. *Wainwright* came on March 18, 1963, with its companion cases, then all the bars of this country, particularly our bar and others comparably situated with us, were faced with a gigantic problem, the defense of indigent defendants or poor people.

And that was only because our State does not have—because of funds or otherwise—does not have in any place a public defender. There are some of our counties that do not even have a county prosecuting attorney, although all, of course, have a district attorney who carries on the same duties, supervisory or otherwise. We have only one place in Mississippi where we have a legal aid bureau, and that is here in Jackson. And because of understaffing or because of its infancy, it, too, could not handle any problems in the defense of indigents or paupers or poor people. But that does not complete the picture. Because where counsel could be provided in felony cases—up to now I believe that is as far as it has gone, although the overtones—Dean, you teach it—the overtones seem to indicate to me that wherever imprisonment can be enforced, even if it is in the misdemeanor field—and I would say that if it analogized itself and runs parallel with the criminal justice act of '64—it said that other than petty offenses—it looks to me that the eventual holding is going to be that counsel must be furnished indigent people unable to employ counsel in that case.

But that would then end our story or our problem, although that was particularly grave in itself, a matter of—a moment of mountainous proportions for us, because alongside of it, but not necessarily in mutual exclusion of it, or even a part of it, was the proposition of the defense of unpopular defendants. They might or might not be the indigents. And imbedded in that, to compound the matters worse, is the representation of unpopular defendants, the raising of an unpopular defense or systematic exclusion of the Negro from the jury or— of the constitutional requirements and the like. There were many things, and these were all placed on us. And our bar is not—we don't even have the trial bar, more or less divorced from the practicing or from the office practice of the counsel.

Second, we don't have the cleavage of the sanction of England between the barrister on the one hand, the trial segment, and the solicitor, on the other. Yet, we—or course—we have no Erskine tradition reflected in that man's statement that, whenever he could stand or not stand between the crown and the subject, then his love for England would end.

But that tradition is taught us in law school and it comes down. We could take both the solicitor and the barrister, but we are so far divorced from representation in criminal cases that this was just a shot out of the blue to us when it came to us. And, of course, we knew that there was descending on us, both from the lawyer fold and also from those colleges and elsewhere, those who come into Mississippi. The trail actions when they were first brought up, we got a fee to pay like everybody else and a number said well, wait a minute, now; it is a case of the beam and a moat. Who are they to tell us what from. But we knew after a while, though. When the shaking down—when the lawyers were referred to their oath and to their duties and going back to the Erskine tradition and what we learned in law school, we knew we had a problem at hand that couldn't be solved by recriminations. It couldn't be solved by holier than thou. We knew that we had to do something.

So—and in our talk there, it was amazing. This—a lot—we have been criticized in some other States for this being a mere scrap of paper. I can assure you, Dean Griswold, and the other distinguished members of the Commission, it is more than that. It took three and a half hours for agreement, and it was reached unanimously to come to pass on that. And there was a lot more heat than light came out, I assure you, during the first 2 hours on that, even in our own group.

Commissioner GRISWOLD. Can you summarize what the statement says?

Mr. THOMAS. Yes, I can, Dean. Dean, I will say that the resolution, which is a verbal act or an overt act as we see it—more than a scrap of paper—simply says that the Mississippi Bar recognizes that

Mississippi through the years has had inbedded in its own constitution, in Sections 24, 25, and 26, the requirement that people shall be furnished with counsel in civil and criminal cases. Court shall always be open. Justice will not be denied or delayed. We were up against it. We didn't need *Gideon* vs. *Wainwright*, but it is here. And we recognize our obligation and we now here affirm and tell ourselves and tell the bar that we stand ready to discharge the duties to any person regardless of higher or lower state, whether rich or poor, resident or nonresident, or any race, color, creed or national origin, that we are—actually we are going to say that we are going to carry out our duties as lawyers. Essentially I was directed as President of the bar here to appoint a special liaison committee for all the districts of Mississippi. That is essentially it.

Commissioner GRISWOLD. Thank you very much, Mr. Thomas. Perhaps I might call on Mr. Farley to see if he has any comments on any aspects of the problem. Then perhaps I will open the floor for general discussion on not merely the resolution, but on any other matter. Dean Farley?

Mr. FARLEY. Well, I have nothing to say, other than that I think that we in Mississippi—and I don't think it is restricted to Mississippi, or even to the South—have in late years, I think, either overlooked, forgotten or ignored the first in the canon of ethics. And that has to do with the defense of courts from unjust criticism—not criticism, but unjust criticism and clamor. The members of the bar over the country, in part, and particularly in the South, have spent a good deal of time, not only in unjustly criticizing the Supreme Court of the United States which has sifted down into other courts, as well as joining in the clamor. I think that was one of the finest things that Mr. Thomas has done in addition to getting this resolution through, was to make a speech—when was that, Earl?

Mr. THOMAS. Annual Judges Conference.

Mr. FARLEY. Yes, Annual Judges Conference, at which he brought that out so clearly and so forcibly and to their delight—because it is realized now—we are realizing so many things, that all of life is coordinated and our ethics—I mean legal ethics are really not very different from any other ethics. And we can't go on—we can't teach disrespect for one area and respect for another and hope to obtain any sort of a government. I just want to add that as an additional thing that Mr. Thomas has done as president of the bar.

Commissioner GRISWOLD. Thank you, Dean Farley. I wonder if there are any of the other lawyers who would care to comment on this or any other matter.

Mr. WISE. Dean, may I have a word?

Commissioner GRISWOLD. Yes, Mr. Wise.

Mr. WISE. It seems to me at this point, since Mr. Thomas has pointed out the resolution and has referred to the lawyer's obligation— I think it is very important that the public understand the obligation which a lawyer undertakes when he becomes a member of the bar. These are governed not only by the canons of the profession but by a number of cases to which Mr. Thomas has alluded. At the risk of boring you with a little reading, I would like to bring these things out. Canon 5 of the American Bar Association, to which we are subject, says "It is the right of the lawyer to undertake the defense of a person accused of crime regardless of his personal opinion as to the guilt of the accused." Canon 15 says "No fear of judicial disfavor or public unpopularity should restrain the lawyer from his full discharge of his duties." Canon 31 says that "Every lawyer upon his own responsibility must decide what employment he will accept as counsel."

Now, the American Bar Association has elaborated on that by resolutions which have been adopted. In 1953, it adopted a resolution which says this: "The American Bar Association reaffirms the principles that the right of defendants to the benefit of assistance, of counsel and the duty of the bar to provide such aid, even to the most unpopular defendants, involves public acceptance of the correlative right of a lawyer to represent and defend in accordance with the standards of the legal profession, any client without being penalized by having imputed to him his client's reputation, views or character. The Association requests state and local associations to cooperate fully in implementing these declarations of principle."

And another statement from the American Bar Association, adopted in 1962, says that "While any lawyer should retain the right to decline employment under Canon 31, there is a group, if not an individual responsibility of the bar, to see to it that defendants in unpopular cases obtain competent counsel to defend them and that such counsel are not prejudiced or damaged by undertaking such representation when requested."

Now I might also point out that the Mississippi Supreme Court has likewise followed *Gideon* vs. *Wainwright*. And I think for the benefit of the record that it might be well if I were to cite a few cases which I think should rightly be in the record.

Commissioner GRISWOLD. Let's not make it too many.

Mr. WISE. All right.

Commissioner GRISWOLD. This is not a judicial hearing.

Mr. WISE. Yes, sir. In 1964, the Mississippi Legislature, by Section 2505 of the Mississippi Code of 1942, amended this section so as to require that a person charged with a felony less than capital who is indigent may have counsel appointed for him at the discretion of the court. Now that was an added portion to the section which already provided counsel for capital cases. Now, the Mississippi Supreme Court in *Conn* vs. *State*, 170 Southern 20, has decided that under *Gideon* vs. *Wainwright* there is no option in the court, but that the court must appoint counsel in cases less than capital unless there be an intelligent and competent waiver of counsel and so forth.

So as not to override the Dean's admonition, I will cite him the other cases later. But what I am saying is that *Gideon* vs. *Wainwright* is recognized by the Supreme Court of the State of Mississippi, and counsel must be provided in felony cases less than capital. So that the lawyers in Mississippi are bound not only by the case law, but they are bound by the canons to which they are bound and to which they must subscribe. Now this, of course, gets into an area of public acceptance and public education, and I think that my one suggestion right here, if I may make it, is that the law profession needs itself and needs the assistance wherever it can get it to educate the public to the fact that this obligation rests on the legal profession and that it must carry it out. Now I have some suggestions—I won't talk too long—as to how to implement this, but I am sure some of these other gentlemen would like to comment.

Commissioner GRISWOLD. We would be glad to have them, Mr. Wise, perhaps a little later.

Mr. WISE. Yes, sir.

Commissioner GRISWOLD. Mr. Pyles?

Mr. PYLES. Yes, sir; I think that one of our big problems here is that the Mississippi State Bar has not properly educated Mississippians as to the role of the lawyer in society, and they don't understand when we take these cases as to why we are doing it. If we could get some sort of an educational program to keep—get the public informed as to our duties and obligations, I think that a good deal of the problem would disappear.

Commissioner GRISWOLD. What do you think could be done about that, Mr. Pyles?

Mr. PYLES. I think a sustained educational program on the part of the bar, using all mediums of communication, so that everybody is aware and informed of the role of the lawyer in society and his duties and his obligations. And I think it is the duty of the bar to undertake that.

Commissioner GRISWOLD. Let me just suggest a question, Mr. Pyles. It is intended with every friendly motive.

Do you regard the obligation to represent indigent defendants charged with serious crime as solely a responsibility of the bar or is it a responsibility of the people of Mississippi?

Mr. PYLES. Well, it is a responsibility of the people of Mississippi and of the bench. And once the bench calls on a lawyer to defend a man, I think it is his duty to undertake that defense. There may be exceptions to that, but by and large I think you could generally say when a court calls upon a lawyer to defend an indigent defendant, it is that lawyer's duty to do so.

Commissioner GRISWOLD. Without compensation?

Mr. PYLES. If necessary, without compensation.

Commissioner GRISWOLD. And suppose the lawyer gets called on 50 times in a year? Should he still do it without compensation?

Mr. PYLES. No, he could not. I think you would have to depend upon the fairness of the courts in assigning these things. And I think our courts would be fair.

Commissioner GRISWOLD. What I am trying to suggest is that there should be some system established by law to assist the judges in appointing counsel under which—perhaps in cases of difficulty requiring a substantial amount of time—appropriate but modest payments could be made to counsel.

Mr. PYLES. That is true. We do have a law that makes very modest payments, and I think the Federal Government is most remiss in that field. They don't have any——

Mr. CAMPBELL. I beg your pardon. I believe there is a recent statute which takes effect in just a month or two. The compensation is not handsome, but the prospect of it exists.

Mr. PYLES. I am glad to hear that. Good.

Commissioner GRISWOLD. What about the costs of investigation in these criminal cases to which a lawyer is assigned—bringing on of witnesses, obtaining expert testimony? Should the lawyer be expected to cover those costs out of his own pocket or should something else be done?

Mr. CAMPBELL. Well, of course I think the answer to that question is almost obvious. The lawyer can't always do it. I think it is a real problem which exists not only in State courts, but it also exists, to my amazement, in the Federal courts. And it is a problem. The lawyer can't just dig in his pocket and do it because one lawyer might have a bigger pocket than another, or he might dig deeper. So that is a precarious reed on which to lean this knee.

Commissioner GRISWOLD. Mrs. Freeman?

Commissioner FREEMAN. I would like to go beyond the representation by counsel to the whole concept and idea of local administration of justice. Some of you may have heard the testimony that related to what we considered to be improper, inadequate preparation of cases by members of the bar who are county attorneys or district attorneys. What is the role of the Mississippi Bar with respect to recommendations for this sort of thing?

Mr. CAMPBELL. I think Mr. Thomas probably can answer better. But I can say this to you. The Mississippi State Bar has time and again made recommendations to the legislature in various phases of the administration of justice. I do not know of a specific recent recommedation in the particular connection. But, for example, the Mississippi State Bar has in times past repeatedly suggested in urgent terms that the legislature take a long look at our justice of the peace system, for example, with the idea of perhaps revising it, perhaps eliminating it and replacing it with something else. So I think the answer in general terms is that the Mississippi State Bar has a definite obligation in this area.

Commissioner GRISWOLD. Mr. Thomas, does the Mississippi State Bar have committees which are considering problems like these, including committees who expect to make recommendations for changes in legislation?

Mr. THOMAS. Yes, sir; they have two. One—two primary committees, Dean Griswold. One is the Criminal Law Committee headed by Mr. O'Donald down on the Gulf Coast. And the Study Committee, which is a very large committee, would in themselves address themselves to criminal aspects in one of its big subcommittees, Dean. They have two very fine working committees of their own.

Commissioner GRISWOLD. Do they make reports from time to time?

Mr. THOMAS. Yes, sir; they send out reports to the Board of Bar Commissioners prior to the annual meeting of the bar. And then half a day's session is taken up with discussion of their reports, on the adoption, deletion or the like.

Mr. WISE. Then there is the legislative committee of the Mississippi State Bar which follows through and actually presents these matters to the legislature for consideration.

Commissioner GRISWOLD. Mr. Grantham, I wonder if you have any——

Mr. GRANTHAM. Well, just on this recent Federal act which I think requires, as I recall it, that each Federal court district present or prepare a plan for the appointment of lawyers to represent indigent clients. One thing we have done in the Hinds County Bar is—that I have done as president—is to appoint a committee that is composed of—the chairman is the district attorney—the Federal district attorney—United States district attorney. And then we have the district attorney—and the State district attorney, the county attorney and the city attorney—all on that committee. And they are preparing now a plan on the local level to supplement the Federal plan, and they are working with the State bar committee on that.

Commissioner GRISWOLD. Would this be a plan with a view to legislation or to action by the bar?

Mr. GRANTHAM. No. This particular committee is to set up a feasible plan whereby lawyers will be available to be appointed by the court. And it will be rotated to keep any one lawyer from having an undue burden.

Commissioner GRISWOLD. I think we have heard from everyone except Mr. Brocato. I wonder if you have any comment?

Mr. BROCATO. I want to correct one impression about the attorney being paid in a capital case. He only receives $75—if two attorneys—which is intended to cover the expenses of investigation. I am impressed with Dean Griswold's statement about it being the responsibility of others than the lawyer. I mean not to raise any racial overtones, but since the registration program began in Coahoma County, in which I live, in 1961, there have been 14 Negroes who killed 14 Negroes. Thirteen of those Negroes were defended by white lawyers without any outside assistance from any outside agency. One of the Negroes had employed a white lawyer. Now no assistance was rendered to those defense counsel. I personally know that one of them expended a sum in excess of $250 on the defense of that indigent Negro. It is not entirely the responsibility of the bar. It is our responsibility when we take the oath that we cannot shirk. But certainly the general public, following Mr. Pyles' suggestion, needs to understand that the lawyer in the representation of the indigent defendant is discharging a solemn duty that he is taking on his oath as an attorney.

Commissioner FREEMAN. Mr. Brocato, how many Negroes reside in Coahoma County?

Mr. BROCATO. The 1960 Census had a population of 34,000.

Commissioner FREEMAN. Thirty-four thousand Negroes?

Mr. BROCATO. Yes.

Commissioner FREEMAN. How many of them are registered voters?

Mr. BROCATO. I can't tell you, although I am chairman of the Coahoma County Election Commission. In the city of Clarksdale there are 997 that are registered. My best guess would be that there would be close to 1,500 to 1,750 Negroes who are qualified to vote if they obtain their exemption certificates or pay their poll tax.

Commissioner FREEMAN. Less than 5 percent?

Mr. BROCATO. Well, your computation I'm sure is correct. Now let me make this suggestion, since that observation has been made. I think that when you speak of registration and voting you are going at the problem from the wrong angle. I think this I think that the registration will not make a good citizen. I think a good citizen will register if he can. I know that in 1927 three naturalized Italians took it on themselves to naturalize every Italian in Coahoma County. It didn't take 6 months; it took them 15 years. Now there are three of those naturalized Italians who still cannot vote. They were naturalized, but they cannot take—they cannot pass, they can take—they cannot pass the voter registration test. When we say registration will cure that ill, we are saying that registration will qualify you to vote and that will make you a good American citizen. I think that the answer is in reverse; that when you become a good American citizen, like the Italians that went to school for 3 years—if that didn't do it, for 4 years every night, and the school was paid for by these Italians—I think there is the answer. I think that it is your responsibility and my responsibility.

Insofar as the registration is concerned, there has been a great deal of testimony about people who refused to register applicants. I am chairman of the Coahoma County Election Commission. We pass on every application that the registrar takes in Coahoma County. We had failed—the only woman Phi Beta Kappa in Coahoma County, white, failed the examination. Well, you say, it was a mistake. It was a mistake on our part. We had 2 public accountants in the 44 names who were submitted to the Department of Justice, and it was—I learned this from the Department, and not from my own observation—it developed that 22 of the reversals of the registrar by the Election Commission were white and 22 were Negro. I don't think that the registration—I mean the registration is the answer to our problem.

Commissioner GRISWOLD. I wasn't sure that any of us had introduced the subject of registration at this point. The subject of this panel is what can lawyers do about the situation in Mississippi. Mr. Thomas has introduced the question of the representation of indigent defendants. And I would like to say, not only as a member of the Commission but as a lawyer and a law teacher, that I welcome the resolution which has been adopted by the State Bar of Mississippi and I commend the leadership of Mr. Thomas and others in obtaining that resolution.

Mr. Thomas, perhaps it would be appropriate for me to ask you. What has been done to implement the resolution?

Mr. THOMAS. Yes, sir; because that is what we get into, Dean, and properly so both from inside and outside. Otherwise, as William Percy, who is a relative of Leroy Percy who was on the stand, said on April 1, "What do you say, you spoke so loudly I cannot hear what you say." So we downed the implementation. I might say, Dean Griswold, that we have some men here on this panel that have represented either the COFO workers or those in whom COFO was interested. Here is Mr. Roy Campbell of Greenville; Mr. Vincent Brocato, chairman of the board of bar examiners and practicing lawyer at

Clarksdale, and Mr. Dixon Pyles, who Judge Cox has sent for several times and who has appeared on a number of cases.

Mr. PYLES. Forty-two.

Mr. THOMAS. So Dean, they are the actual——

Commissioner GRISWOLD. Excuse me. How many, Mr. Pyles?

Mr. PYLES. Forty-two.

Commissioner GRISWOLD. Forty-two. All right.

Mr. THOMAS. And that is the implement—those of us who can speak directly on the implementation.

Commissioner GRISWOLD. And that is since the adoption of the resolution?

Mr. THOMAS. Yes, sir.

Commissioner GRISWOLD. Have you set up any committees or panels in sections or counties of the State——

Mr. THOMAS. (Interposing). Yes, sir.

Commissioner GRISWOLD. (continuing). To whom a judge or an indigent defendant may turn for help?

Mr. THOMAS. Dean Griswold, I should have brought the list with us. I have this—this resolution directed me as president to appoint the special liaison committee for the entire State of Mississippi, dividing it properly up for the divisions of each of the Northern and Southern Federal Court Districts of Mississippi. That I did. There are 283 practicing lawyers on that committee in the composite. The chairman of each division of the committee in either the northern or southern district is either a member of the board of bar commissioners, or chairman of the board of bar examiners, or former president of the bar, or the like. A number—not all of them, Dean, we are deficient in that respect. Most of them have met. The one at Hattiesburg had an early meeting and they decided on a plan—had the sheriffs and had the justice of the peace and the city judges and others—and the lawyers present, and told them what the problem was. And they decided that in the Federal court that a list—one list would be given of all the practicing lawyers, whether they practiced or whether they did not. And they go in pairs—not one by one, but in pairs. And the Federal court will begin at the top.

For instance, when Judge Cox or Judge Mize in the southern district out of the Federal court would call for representation for an indigent, he would say all right, who's—the list would be before him. And they would check off and take the first two coming on that list. Now if one of those did not practice criminal law or was disabled, he could get someone else, but he had to pay the fee or he had to make arrangements because each one had to take their turn at the mill, as it was, two by two. The State courts, the justice of the peace, the municipal courts, the county courts and the circuit courts would take the reverse list—the other list—which began at the bottom so that they would try to avoid as much duplication of effort, trying to concentrate on one man. Now, in Mr. Campbell's division I believe that they didn't use the pair system, because the judge had been—he has been—the circuit judge has been using this list some time.

Mr. CAMPBELL. That's quite right. He started it some time ago.

Mr. THOMAS. And here president of the Hinds County bar, Mr. Gordon Grantham—they are working there on different ways. But the Meridian bar was working on the double way. And I believe—you do yours on the single way, beginning one court—the Federal court begins at the top and the State courts at the bottom?

Mr. BROCATO. Yes.

Mr. THOMAS. Dean, this is essentially it—I mean for the whole State. Now I will admit it has not been done unanimously. And I have not tried to keep behind them, but we've simply got—its an education process demanding some patience, but we are trying to follow up as best we can.

Commissioner GRISWOLD. Do I understand, Mr. Thomas, that any indigent person charged with any crime, including one with civil rights aspects, can obtain a lawyer to represent him in the State of Mississippi?

Mr. THOMAS. Under this plan, they can, Dean, if they are—if imprisonment is involved.

Commissioner GRISWOLD. That is why I said serious crime.

Mr. THOMAS. Yes, sir, yes, sir.

Commissioner GRISWOLD. I know the problem. It isn't necessarily a misdemeanor or a felony, but either serious crimes or whatever the Geidon case applied to.

Mr. THOMAS. Yes.

Commissioner GRISWOLD. Now let me ask you another question. Suppose a man isn't indigent. Suppose he is a COFO worker and COFO is perfectly ready, willing and able to pay a fee—or some other organization such as CORE or SNCC—can that man obtain a lawyer to represent him in the courts of Mississippi?

Mr. THOMAS. In Mr. Brocato's division, the Delta division, and Mr. Campbell's division, that is so, and in some of the other divisions that has been done.

Commissioner GRISWOLD. What about divisions other than Mr. Brocato's and Mr. Campbell's?

Mr. THOMAS. Well, now, in the Hattiesburg division—I can't say it is in all of them, Dean—we have an educational process. But the resolution and the committee lists and the calls for representation regardless of indigence. In fact, one of the instances it provoked—

17 out of the 19 who were present, the commissioners—two of them were out of the State and couldn't get there—was an instance that occurred in a certain part of this State or where they couldn't get any local members of the bar to represent them, this particular COFO defendant. And then they called in an outside lawyer. And then he is blocked under one of our statutes by two lawyers coming in. And word was had by our group, both from the Federal judge and the State judges, that that is a paper conviction. They were not going to allow it to stand and no decent person, or no decent judge would let it stand. And that is one of the instances that came—made the bar see instantly that going back to our oath, Dean—so that's the problem.

Commissioner GRISWOLD. Well, I want to make it plain that I recognize the problem and the way it is handled in some communities. I am wondering if you could make it a collective responsibility of the bar. That is, the president of the bar association—I don't know to what extent you have local bar associations in Mississippi—but the executive committee of the bar association designates a lawyer and says, "You represent him." And that makes it perfectly plain that he is not carrying on the representation because he likes the client or is associated with his ideas but is carrying out his responsibility as a member of the bar. I wonder if you have taken any steps of that sort? Because as I see the problem in Mississippi, it is perhaps more serious with respect to the defendant who is able to pay a lawyer than it is with respect to the defendant who can't pay a lawyer.

Mr. THOMAS. Yes, sir; I'll judge that's so, Dean Griswold. The former president of the bar, Mr. Wise, and Dean Farley, and we have other former presidents here—our governing board is the board of bar commissioners. We have no executive committee out of it. It is simply the board of bar commissioners. And they are scattered all over the State and the meetings are not too regular, Dean. But, we do have—that's why each bar commissioner or commissioners residing in a particular division or district was charged with representation of all defendants who were able to pay counsel and because of the unsavory or so-called present stigmatized representation of indigent or the like, they are charged with it. And I have faith in the Mississippi bar, Dean. While in some respects it may be a little slow or it may be imperfect at times, at heart I do believe they will be reckoned to the oath. It is a case of both education and patience, and it just happens that—we say, Mr. Campbell and Mr. Brocato—it looks like we have had a lot of local firepower put on those places among others, Dean. Now some places we have had none; I mean we have had no incidents, had nothing to call on them. But I do know that we do have, I think, very able members of the board of commissioners and I believe absolutely they'll do their duty.

Mr. CAMPBELL. May I make a comment there, if you please?

Commissioner GRISWOLD. Yes, Mr. Campbell.

Mr. CAMPBELL. Yes. First of all, in order to avoid any more hypocrisy and the inevitable, I want to say this: If tomorrow a COFO worker should come to me in Greenville and say, "I have the money, I have been arrested, will you represent me," my answer to him would be I would prefer not to if you can get another lawyer. Why? I do not practice criminal law. And as in the case of most lawyers, when I started again right after World War II, I did anything I could to make a living. When I got to the point where I did not have to deal with criminal cases, I tried to quit. Now that is a pragmatic factor which is necessarily present here all the way. Now, you do not want to find yourself in a forum which is playing by rules with which you are not really familiar. You haven't kept your tools sharp. Practicing criminal law is a different kettle of fish from going into court and trying civil cases. Now this is a burden which the bar of this State must face and must accept now. In my particular district, it is doing so.

But I think ultimately this involves a philosophical concept as well as many pragmatic considerations which are going to compel, in my judgment, that the State—and I mean the State and not the United States—that the State shall make some provision. I think that if it is left indefinitely as a burden which the profession should carry, then you are going to get results which are good in some cases and not so good in others, and it is going to look like Robert Bench and his stock market chart.

Commissioner GRISWOLD. Mr. Campbell, I sympathize with your position in that. I don't think anyone who asked me to represent him in a criminal case would get very good service. About how many lawyers are there in Mississippi

Mr. CAMPBELL. In Mississippi, the whole State?

Commissioner GRISWOLD. Yes.

Mr. WISE. Twenty-two hundred.

Mr. PYLES. Practicing lawyers?

Commissioner GRISWOLD. Yes, practicing lawyers.

Mr. WISE. That's right.

Commissioner GRISWOLD. Would any of you have an estimate of how many practice criminal law to any appreciable extent?

Mr. CAMPBELL. Half of them.

Mr. WISE. Half of them. But I would emphasize, generally speaking, in smaller counties where there are very few lawyers, say four or five members of the bar, ordinarily those lawyers handle both civil and criminal work. As you get to the larger towns, you find of course, more specialization and more lawyers who do not handle criminal work. Now this point that he brought out, of course, is extremely important. There are other considerations in addition to the unpopularity of the case which I think we all understand, and which bears down on the lawyers to some extent. There are other things, such as situations where there are mass arrests and the need for a great amount of representation all at once. That presents a problem. Then you have to get, as I see it the only solution to any of these things is to get back to the organized bar, to the education of the people, to the making of a list and a rotation system so that all of the lawyers in the particular county get into the act, so to speak. Then this takes whatever stigma there may be in it, this takes it off. This relieves the burden of an undue amount of criminal practice. And those of us who don't know anything about it possibly can get some help if necessary. But it gets down to a proposition, I think, of a list of lawyers preferably composed of all the lawyers in the county work on a rotation basis at the election of the court and by the appointment of the court. And this would get at it.

Now you asked Mr. Thomas about—you say it is done in Clarksdale. It is done in Greenville. It is done in Hinds County. It is done elsewhere. How about those other counties? This is again a matter of getting to them. This is a matter again of education. This is a matter of organization. And while it will be slower in some places than in others, it will occur, in my opinion, everywhere in the State. I know the lawyers of Mississippi well enough. There is no distinction between lawyers in Greenville, lawyers in Jackson, and lawyers in any other town in Mississippi. They are a dedicated group of people. They are professional people. And in my judgment, they will do their duty when it is properly brought to their attention.

Commissioner GRISWOLD. Thank you, Mr. Wise. Let me ask you another question which is suggested by what you have just said. You have said the only way to handle it is through these lists which the courts can use. It occurs to me that another way to handle it is to have these cases handled by lawyers from outside the State who are paid by the people who can pay them. There have been some occasions and some efforts to have lawyers from outside the State handle them. I wonder if you have any attitude about that?

Mr. WISE. Yes, sir, I definitely do. I think it depends a great deal on who these lawyers are. Last summer and the summer before, we were—we had the National Lawyers Guild with us. I assume that this Commission probably knows more about the National Lawyers Guild than I do. But I don't think it has a particularly good reputation in the bar of the United States.

This group circularized the entire Mississippi State Bar with questionnaires, and most of those questionnaires went into the wastebasket. Now on the other hand, there have been some suggestions from the Siegel-Tweed Committee that possibly lawyers will come in who are not only qualified but whose standing and whose ability and whose integrity is recognized.

Commissioner GRISWOLD. If such lawyers were designated by that Committee and came to Mississippi, would they be received by the members of the bar of Mississippi?

Mr. WISE. I could only say that I hope they would, personally. I believe Mr. Thomas is prepared to say that—as Mr. Thomas told me—I was going to speak for him, but I understand that the commissioners of the State bar have looked with some favor on that.

Commissioner GRISWOLD. Almost inevitably they would not be members of the bar in Mississippi?

Mr. WISE. Yes, sir.

Commissioner GRISWOLD. Would they be allowed to practice in this type of case in Mississippi?

Mr. WISE. In my opinion, this type lawyer, with this motivation, would.

Mr. PYLES. Dean Griswold, we have a rule in our Federal district court here that was adopted in 1940 that when an out-of-State lawyer comes into this district, he must associate with a local counsel. And that—they may have to change the rule or they may have to make some special dispensation of that rule. And I understand there is a State statute where two members of the bar can protest and they would have to—he would not be allowed to practice.

Commissioner GRISWOLD. Well, what I am really trying to say is what do you think the attitude of Mississippi lawyers will be? Frankly, what I am suggesting to you is a way of relieving you of a professional burden. And I am wondering whether the bar of Mississippi will cooperate with efforts to that end or whether they will obstruct it.

Mr. PYLES. Well, the bar is made up of individuals. I couldn't speak for all the lawyers. As far as I am concerned, I would accept it.

Commissioner GRISWOLD. Mr. Thomas, do you have any idea what the organized bar would do?

Mr. THOMAS. Not as the organized bar, Dean. All I could say—because no official action has been taken either by the bar in its annual session or by the board of bar commissioners—I will say, however, that in some of my talks unofficially with the members of the board of bar commissioners about this problem, or related problems and also with Mr. Brocato, the chairman of the board of bar examiners and the other members, of which I happen to be one, of his group—that we view it with favor, coming from—whether you come from a reputable firm or are a sole practitioner or come from a firm or not, certified as they are. We feel this way because there is tremendous pressure which is being placed on the Mississippi bar, even under *Gideon* v. *Wainwright*—outside of the racial overtones, the unpopular cause, or where there is raised an unpopular defense. So reputable lawyers—we—my personal opinion and those other commissioners that I have talked unofficially to on the board of bar examiners was that it would be welcomed additionally because it would help the strain and because it—under the bar of Mr. Wise there—that *NAACP* v. *Button*, and the *Virginia Railway Trainmen* case—that they probably would get even this law that—even this statute—to which Mr. Pyles referred to. And I think Judge Cox and Judge Mize of the southern district who have this rule requiring a local attorney—that is how Mr. Pyles was being sent for—when Judge Cox said we want you to sign with these lawyers from New Orleans, he did. I would too. But anyway, what Judge Clayton of the northern district says, Dean Griswold, is, if anyone is qualified—has no black marks as far as he knows—he is going to practice in his court.

So I would think that the overall thinking among those with whom I talked was that they would not resent, but on the contrary, would come to appreciate and accept. Because, as I understood from your Commission, after Mississippi had picked up all the slack—we have got to reeducate ourselves in criminal law because *Gideon* vs. *Wainwright* is going to make us go back to the criminal law—after we have done that, as I understood, the polecats can go out. And furthermore, we think that those coming down would have a more absolute appreciation of the problems involved in the overnight transition period with which we are faced after a hundred years of problems. We think it would be—the two sides of the coin would be helpful to the Mississippi Bar in the transition period, particularly being a little more patient and understanding with our problems in the transition period.

Commissioner FREEMAN. Mr. Thomas, with respect to the provision of the Mississippi law, if I understood correctly—or maybe it was Mr. Brocato who said an outside lawyer could practice unless two local lawyers objected?

Mr. THOMAS. Yes.

Commissioner FREEMAN. How does that operate? Does it mean any two of the 2,200 lawyers?

Mr. THOMAS. I believe it is the local bar, isn't it?

Mr. BROCATO. Mr. Pyles was the one that referred to it, that the statute provides that if any two of the lawyers of that local bar object to his participation in any case, then the question of his practicing in that case must be submitted to the board of bar commissioners.

Commissioner FREEMAN. May I take that further. We cannot avoid the racial overtones here. We assume there may be in any community two lawyers that might object to a Negro lawyer who would be qualified. Has the bar considered this and the need for repeal of this legislation?

Mr. THOMAS. Now that is being considered by the study committee, Mrs. Freeman. Now, how they come out of the reformation I do not know. Because that was one of the instances that provoked this resolution.

Commissioner GRISWOLD. Mr. Thomas, just one last question about this. If outside lawyers of good reputation came in under the auspices of what is called the Tweed-Siegel Committee—which is in fact one appointed at the request of President Kennedy, would they have reasonable access to law library facilities in Mississippi?

Mr. THOMAS. I would say so, Dean. So far as I am any judge of it.

Commissioner GRISWOLD. Are there county law libraries in Mississippi?

Mr. CAMPBELL. Some.

Commissioner GRISWOLD. What are they?

Mr. CAMPBELL. Some are poorly kept up, but generally most counties have a fair working library.

Commissioner GRISWOLD. Is there one in Jackson?

Mr. WISE. Yes, there is a very excellent State library here in Jackson. There is a very excellent library at the University of Mississippi.

Commissioner GRISWOLD. Would such lawyers have access to either of those libraries without difficulty?

Mr. WISE. Yes, no question about it.

Commissioner GRISWOLD. Now, one or two references have been made to Negro lawyers. How many Negro lawyers are there in Mississippi? Do you know, Mr. Thomas?

Mr. THOMAS. I believe there are three or four.

Mr. PYLES. There are four.

Mr. BROCATO. There are four.

Mr. THOMAS. There are four.

Commissioner GRISWOLD. In active practice?

Mr. THOMAS. Yes.

Commissioner GRISWOLD. Half the population of Mississippi is Negro, and out of 2,200 lawyers, 4 are Negro. Do you think that is a good situation—a sound situation or a justifiable situation?

Mr. THOMAS. Well, that is——

Commissioner GRISWOLD. I am asking any of you.

Mr. THOMAS. I couldn't account for that because there are so many variables in that equation. All I know is when I was coming up—of course Bob is a little older than I am, Dean Farley is, but I was actually there when he tried to teach me some law—and at that time—and Vincent and I—we were in one class together—there were seven Negro lawyers and some of them were very capable lawyers in Mississippi at that time. I don't know how you would account for only four now, except as the Dean says, the educational qualifications for all lawyers have gone up considerably by statute since then. Instead of the high school academic requirement prevalent then, you now have to have at least 2 years of college.

Commissioner FREEMAN. How many law schools are there in this State?

Mr. THOMAS. Let's see. Dean, help us out, Dean Farley.

Mr. FARLEY. Only one. One accredited law school and a night school in Jackson, an approved law school.

Commissioner GRISWOLD. How many Negro students are there in these two law schools?

Mr. FARLEY. I don't think they've ever had any in the Jackson law school.

Commissioner GRISWOLD. I think you have one now?

Mr. CAMPBELL. No, I don't think so.

Mr. FARLEY. I don't think we have one in law school now, no.

Commissioner GRISWOLD. Didn't you have one in the summer term?

Mr. FARLEY. I think we had one last year that got expelled.

Commissioner GRISWOLD. Yes. I wonder if any of you have any comments to make on whether it wouldn't be in the interests of all the people in Mississippi, including the white lawyers in Mississippi, to have more Negro lawyers in this State.

Mr. FARLEY. I will make a comment on that——

Mr. GRANTHAM. I can't figure out how we are going to get them here if they don't come. We can't make them.

Mr. FARLEY. I don't think that there has been any—there may have been for 2 or 3 years—some disposition to overcome those stumbling blocks. And we have Negro lawyers, but I know up until the Brown case, as far as I know, there was no disposition to—I talked to a number of Negro students, several from Howard, who spoke of locating in Mississippi and came to talk with me. And after considering it, I decided he was faced with this situation—that all the judges and all the jurors at that time, except an occasional one in Federal court, were white, and that a Negro lawyer just didn't get much business. He got none from white people and he got very little from Negro clients. It is just this late trouble that has given the Negro lawyers a tremendous business—I mean a diversion of business, particularly criminal matters. I will give you an example, there.

Daryl Howard, for example, who you possibly know—he practiced law in Jackson for a number of years and just gave up behind his father-in-law—Boone, I believe, was his name—and they both quit. They didn't get enough business. He moved on to Washington and spent the rest of his life there. He was a very good lawyer and certainly was entitled to get the business, but the Negro people in Jackson just didn't hire them.

Commissioner FREEMAN. Are the bar associations in this State open to Negro lawyers?

Mr. THOMAS. We have the integrated bar, automatically.

Commissioner FREEMAN. Do you have any other bar association in this State?

Mr. THOMAS. We have no voluntary—well, we have locals——

Commissioner FREEMAN. That's what I mean.

Mr. THOMAS. Like Hinds County does, that's right. Let's see, Mr. Grantham, would know that. Mr. Grantham, you are president of the Hinds County bar.

Mr. GRANTHAM. The two Negro lawyers practicing here are not active members of our local bar association. But I do know from my personal knowledge that when we had the last law institute, that they were invited to attend. They did not.

Commissioner FREEMAN. Have they ever been invited to membership?

Mr. GRANTHAM. They have not been invited to membership, no. Not to my knowledge. Now I am speaking solely for myself.

Mr. BROCATO. Mrs. Freeman, to clarify your question about—and I may answer as to whether or not more lawyers in Mississippi would help our situation. I think unquestionably it would. And I think that if there were 7 Negro lawyers in Mississippi 35 years ago, that there should be 14 by now, relatively. Everything else is doubled. But Pine Bluff, Arkansas, has three Negro lawyers, and they all make an excellent living. Insofar as the board of bar admissions is concerned, we have had only one application. And I know nothing that the bar admissions as a body can do to encourage Negroes who are graduates of other law schools to come in and take our bar examination. It seems like—I don't want to get into racial overtones—but it seems like that is a thing for the Negroes to persuade some young active law graduate to come to Mississippi.

When I started practicing law, there was a Negro lawyer in Clarksdale who made a good living. He was a graduate of Harvard, Dean. There was a Negro lawyer in Mount Bayou who was also a graduate of Harvard. And they represented defendants in every court. As a matter of fact, when I was in Pine Bluff trying to litigate a matter in court there, Mr. Wiley was representing a white client in the court. I mean I had never seen that. But the lawyer that was with me expressed no surprise over it.

Commissioner GRISWOLD. I would like your comments on this. Can the fact that there are so few Negro lawyers here, and that means that not many are willing to make the try, be explained by the extremely frustrating situation which they encounter. Reference has been made to no Negro jurors or very few, and I gather that they are almost unknown in this State, half the population of which is Negro. Does a Negro lawyer who tries to practice here encounter so many frustrations—and I will go on and say so many injustices—that he just can't take it and goes someplace else?

Mr. PYLES. I don't think so, Dean. Of course, we—all lawyers encounter frustrations, but I think Dean Farley hit the nail on the head. It is primarily from an economic standpoint. With white judges, white jurors, largely, a Negro client feels that he would rather be represented in most instances by a white lawyer.

Mr. CAMPBELL. Can we broaden this inquiry just one step. We are emphasizing Negro lawyers. Now I don't know how many Negro doctors there are in Mississippi, but there are many. I doubt, without knowing, that there are very many Negro electrical engineers, structural engineers, mechanical engineers, and so forth. Now whatever that is, I suspect the reason for it is the same reason for the dearth of lawyers and I dare say it has its roots in economic facts of life. I don't actually know.

Commissioner GRISWOLD. I am wondering if they are just economic facts of life or whether they do not in some large measure go back to your legal and social systems which make it extraordinarily difficult for a Negro, even of considerable ability, to make his way in Mississippi. And I find myself wondering if, in the interests of the lawyers and the white people of Mississippi, that's a healthy situation.

Mr. CAMPBELL. Well, I think we would all agree that the sooner the economic wealth of this whole State increases, and the sooner the earning power of every man and of every woman who works is greater, the better for this State. I think we would agree that the sooner more people have better education and more skills and are able to command the income which will come from that, the better off the whole community will be.

Mr. PYLES. Dean, in 1957, I was the Chairman of the Professional Economics Committee and we made an economic survey of this State. We found that for any lawyer, without regard to color, who came out of school and hung up his shingle and started out, it was 5 years before he was able to make a living. Those are economic facts of life. And unless you have a family or friends, or you can get into some firm, I think it is too hard a pull up the hill for an individual just to start out economically, from the results of our survey. And I think our survey revealed a situation not too far different from the other States— in what was found in the other States. Now I can't quote you the figures because I don't have them, but I have the book that we published on them.

Commissioner GRISWOLD. Mr. Farley, do you think that is still true of the typical graduate of the University of Mississippi Law School? Can't he break even until 5 years after he has left law school?

Mr. PYLES. I think it is even more true today in Mississippi than it was——

Commissioner GRISWOLD. I was asking Mr. Farley on the basis of his——

Mr. PYLES. Oh. I thought you said me.

Mr. FARLEY. I wouldn't put it at 5 years. I would say it is a little earlier than that, if you can last. I agree with you that you have got to have some sort of way of getting along for at least 2 years. That's true, I found from my own experience, even if you are doing good business, because the litigation and various and sundry other returns from your work—it doesn't begin to come in regularly for 2 years, no matter how much practice you are getting. I mean you still have to borrow money to live on, ordinarily. But most of our graduates now that they have a little bit of backing I think can get on their feet inside of 3 years. It all depends on the breaks that they get. I think that a Negro lawyer in Jackson during this late unpleasantness—that he would have been very much in demand, but with a limited type of practice.

Commissioner GRISWOLD. Mr. Taylor?

Mr. TAYLOR. I wonder if I might make an observation of a somewhat utopian nature. A number of people on the panel have agreed that it would be greatly desirable to have more Negro lawyers in the State for various reasons. I think many people have agreed that one of the big problems is starting out. Of course, one way a lawyer starts out when he has economic problems is to associate with a good law firm. I say this as a utopian observation because there aren't very many law firms in the country where Negroes and whites practice together. But I say it hopefully in this State because 42 percent of the population is Negro, and we are looking toward a day when economic and educational opportunities for Negroes get better. Someday it may be very good business for lawyers, I would think, to have an integrated law firm. I say that as a utopian observation and leave it at that.

Commissioner GRISWOLD. Mr. Thomas, let me raise another question to which we haven't made reference but which arises out of my experience. You have a system of bail in this State, as I understand it, which I never heard of in any other State in the country. Bail cannot be made by posting cash, is that right?

Mr. THOMAS. Well, except in traffic violations, that is essentially correct.

Commissioner GRISWOLD. Do you think that is a sound system?

Mr. THOMAS. No, sir; I was district attorney 10 years and I did not think it was a sound system then and I don't think so now. We have tried, the district attorneys associations, to do something about that. But it has not been done. But that has been in the statute—in the code for years and years.

Commissioner GRISWOLD. What do you think is the purpose or objective of having that in the statute—the code?

Mr. THOMAS. Dean, I would just not know how to answer that—to project the reason behind it—a lot of courts have read into it by decisional law, but so many of our statutes refer to two individual sureties. There are a lot of them—the compilation is not brought up to date as regards to them, but I just can't give you the answer to that, Dean, why.

Commissioner GRISWOLD. I wonder if any of the lawyers have any opinion on this. Mr. Wise?

Mr. WISE. I don't know why it is. But I might just say that it is not confined just to criminal situations; it is true in civil, too. There is no way to post a bond—an appeal bond—for instance, a supersedeas bond in a civil case, except by sureties or by a surety company. I have clients who would like to put up some negotiable instruments and bonds and take the case up so as to save the interest while the case was on appeal, and they can't do it. I don't know why it is, but it is there. And if you try—if you are thinking of something in connection with the criminal situation, I would just like to clarify it and say it applied to the——

Commissioner GRISWOLD. I don't see that saying it is twice as wrong as I said it was really helps us.

Mr. WISE. Well, no, but possibly I misinterpreted your questioning. I thought possibly you felt that it had something to do with criminal justice and I don't think it does.

Mr. PYLE. Dean Griswold, if you have got the money, it doesn't present as big a problem as you may imagine. If you've got the money to put up for your bail or for your supersedeas bond, you can always find a surety company who will accept that cash and write the bond.

If you haven't got the money, you're in trouble anyway. Anybody who is poor is in trouble.

Commissioner GRISWOLD. You have to pay the premium to the surety company, of course.

Mr. PYLES. Of course.

Commissioner GRISWOLD. Although you have the full amount of money available. Is there any reason why a person should be responsible for the premiums for the benefit of the surety company?

Mr. PYLES. Well, except that the surety companies in order to exist have got to have premiums. And I don't hold any——

Commissioner GRISWOLD. Well, what risk does the surety company take when it has the full amount of cash deposited with it? Why should it get a premium for that?

Mr. PYLES. Well, it doesn't, except that they charge it.

Commissioner GRISWOLD. You said, Mr. Pyles, that anybody who had the cash could get a surety bond.

Mr. PYLES. That's right.

Commissioner GRISWOLD. But I had personal knowledge of a situation in this State about 2 years ago where no company authorized to do business in Mississippi would write a surety bond. And we were advised that they were afraid that their right to do business in Mississippi would be terminated if they wrote bonds in cases of this type. Do you have any comments on that?

Mr. PYLES. Yes. I represent a good many labor unions, and we go into communities somewhere where there is an agent in that community who does not want to write the bond because it would jeopardize his other business. But we have also been able to come to Jackson here and get the bond written at Jackson. And I think that your advice was not quite correct. I believe you can get them written here in the city of Jackson.

Commissioner GRISWOLD. Well, this was in connection with the so-called Freedom Riders. I don't remember whether it was 3 years ago or 2 years ago. There were several hundred of them. And determined efforts to get a surety company to write bonds were unsuccessful. There was then an effort to get a company outside the State—not authorized to do business in the State, so it couldn't lose any business in the State—to write the bond and get the State authorities to accept it for this purpose. And for a while it looked as though that would work—then that fell through. Now here is a situation where you won't take cash and where you cannot get a surety company. Is that a sound way to administer justice?

Mr. PYLES. No. We do have at the present time here in Jackson—and I can't speak for other places—certain bail bond brokers who represent various and sundry insurance companies, who, if you deposit the cash with them, regardless of what the charge is, will write the bond.

Commissioner GRISWOLD. Well, this was not the situation in these cases of 2 or 3 years ago.

Mr. WISE. Dean, I don't gather from what these gentlemen said that they are defending this system either from a criminal standpoint or a civil standpoint. But you asked why, and I don't know why. I know—I represent—I handle civil business entirely. And I would like to see the civil part of it changed because, as I say, I have got clients who don't like to have to pay those premiums. Some of them can put up some securities of their own, save the premium. And from a civil point of view I would like to see it changed, and I would say it could carry over just as well to the other.

Commissioned GRISWOLD. Is anybody doing anything about it?

Mr. WISE. Not to my knowledge.

Commissioner GRISWOLD. Do any of you think that this is something that might be worth looking into?

Mr. WISE. I think definitely it would be.

Mr. THOMAS. That's right.

Commissioner GRISWOLD. Now let me turn to another matter which has developed in our hearings. In connection with the handling of criminal cases in Mississippi, there seems to be a great division of responsibility which leads, on the one hand, to a passing of the buck, and, on the other hand, to a "Well, I assume he's going to do it." The result is that nobody does it. I mention, for example, the fact that you have both a county attorney and a district attorney who seem to share responsibility for the prosecution of felonies in the circuit court. In addition there are sheriffs and foremen of the grand jury and others. Do you regard the present system for the handling of prosecutions in Mississippi as soundly organized? I wonder if any of you would make any comments on that?

Mr. PYLES. You mean the present—the district attorney and the county attorney?

Commissioner GRISWOLD. Yes.

Mr. PYLES. Well, I think the system is soundly organized. We may have some instances where the individuals involved are not too good or don't have a high standard.

Commissioner GRISWOLD. Why should there be a county attorney and a district attorney, each sharing responsibility with respect to a matter? Is it not the experience in the law and elsewhere that when responsibility is divided it is not accepted by either party in many cases?

Mr. Pyles. In the few criminal cases that I have had, both the county attorney and the district attorney have been awfully vigorous about it. They haven't shirked their duties in any way that I know of. And perhaps in our rural system here when this thing was set up, the district attorney was in one place and the county attorney was in another. When these things would come up, the county attorney usually handles the prosecutions in the county court and in the justice courts, in these counties where they do have a county court. And I think there is a real need. Now there may be some need to delineate the duties of them, but I don't think there is any real problem of that in Mississippi.

Mr. Thomas. Dean, I was county attorney 5 years—Mississippi Delta, from which Roy and Vince come—and then I was district attorney for 10 years. I see no particular improvement in that field for this reason. The county attorney is captain of the ship, so far as the justice of the peace and the county court is concerned. He is the responsibility for law enforcement, the prosecution, is directly on him. And by statute, he is made, as it were, the assistant district attorney in the circuit court presided over by the circuit judge, who may have seven counties. And the district attorney's district is coterminous with that of the circuit judge. When they come in, he assists the district attorney. So as regards circuit court prosecutions, the local responsibility and sole responsibility of the district attorney is shared as an assistant by the county attorney. But the county attorney takes over as captain of the ship or is solely responsible for the county court and the justice of the peace. I think you have reference to a little colloquy that occurred here yesterday.

Commissioner Griswold. Yes, but that was only illustrative of a broader problem.

Mr. Thomas. Yes, sir.

Commissioner Griswold. The problem seemed to arise out of a system in which nobody quite knows who is supposed to do what and the result is, often enough, that it just doesn't get done.

Mr. Thomas. When I was county attorney, the formal prosecutions were bound over—came through the justice of the peace to the county courts, and I kept a record of that and kept the grand jury docket posted so when the district attorney came and we both went to the grand jury—and under the statute we're authorized to appear before the grand jury—they were there and the sheriff executed the process to get the witnesses in on a grand jury subpena to be present. But the dockets were made up from the justice of the peace hearings as regards felony prosecution—that is county prosecutions. And the other dockets, on appeal for misdemeanor convictions, went another way. But it seemed to work at that time. Unless something has arisen since then, Dean, I thought it was a satisfactory way.

Commissioner GRISWOLD. Mrs. Freeman?

Commissioner FREEMAN. Somewhat along these same lines, I would like to refer to the duties of the sheriff. He seems to have law enforcement duties and also tax collection duties. His fees come from the taxes that are collected and the time which is spent on law enforcement is left entirely up to the particular sheriff. Is this correct? I would like to know your opinion on the fact that one person is charged with all of these responsibilities. Can such a person adequately perform all of the duties and functions of his office?

Mr. THOMAS. Well, that has been the subject of very heated—not only debate, but constructive legislation in the making with the Mississippi Economic Council for the last 2 years, to my knowledge. And they have a bill to that effect—on the divorcement of those duties for that reason—to make law enforcement a duty of the sheriff as such, but to throw tax collection to the tax assessor or combine it with another office. Let the offices be entirely separated. And it has been given terrific research study by some of the men out of the University of Mississippi—Bob—who were assigned to work on that project. I do know that has been a problem, but——

Mr. FARLEY. But there has to be a constitutional amendment——

Mr. THOMAS. Yes, it does, that's right.

Mr. FARLEY. It has been advocated, but it hasn't ever come out in legislation.

Mr. THOMAS. It has a very definite relevance—bearing on law enforcement. You're right, those two—the combination of the two offices.

Commissioner GRISWOLD. Any others care to comment on the sheriff's offices?

Mr. PYLES. Well, the sheriff cannot succeed himself under Mississippi law, and in these suggestions—

Commissioner GRISWOLD. Which means that there can never be a professional sheriff.

Mr. PYLES. Well, it also means they cannot build a political empire in the county, too, which may be good or bad, and I—personally, I like the system. And the proposal has been made that if they separate these services, that the sheriff will have law enforcement duties and will be able to succeed himself. My personal opinion is that that is going to be worse than it is at the present time.

Commissioner GRISWOLD. If the duties were separated, I assume the sheriff would be paid a salary and not by fees.

Mr. PYLES. I would assume so.

Commissioner GRISWOLD. Do you think it is sound to pay any public officer by fees—any county-wide public officer?

Mr. PYLES. Well, I couldn't give a blanket—say it is unsound or sound, but I would prefer a salary system myself.

Commissioner GRISWOLD. One of the things that we have been concerned with at these hearings, on which we have received a great deal of evidence and with respect to which we have a statutory responsibility—because under the statute setting up this Commission, we are charged with investigating denials of the equal protection of the laws any place in the United States—one of the things that has given us concern is what might be called the even-handed administration of justice in Mississippi. What I am about to say does not concern the superior courts of the judicial system in which you gentlemen practice. The place where the impact of the law is felt by most citizens of the State—of any State—is at the level of the police officers, the sheriff, the sheriff's deputies, and perhaps in the very lowest local courts, which, in this State, I take it, are justice of the peace courts. We get the impression—in fact, we have not merely received the impression but have received a great deal of evidence to support it—that the law is not evenly applied in Mississippi by police officers, sheriffs and justice of the peace courts; that Negroes frequently, especially when they are involved in civil rights activities, are held subject to higher bail and receive more severe sentences than are white persons who are charged, perhaps, with more serious offenses; that police officers and sheriffs undertake to exercise authority with respect to Negroes and civil rights workers which they don't undertake to exercise with respect to white persons.

I wonder if any of the lawyers has any comment or observation to make on that; whether it's true, and, if so, what can and ought to be done about it. What can lawyers do to seek to have an even-handed administration of justice in Mississippi so that everyone is treated alike by the police and by the courts? Mr. Grantham?

Mr. GRANTHAM. We would like to have that, frankly. We have got to recognize that what you have found is true. You have ample evidence of it. Speaking as a former FBI agent with experience in a number of our northeastern cities, I can also say that I found that it was also true there; that it is not peculiar to Mississippi. It was at that time. It's something that we have—now I think I disagree with Mr. Pyles down there—I think making our sheriffs professional law enforcement men would go a long way toward solving that problem and I advocate the change in our system so that he can succeed himself. Having been a law enforcement officer, I feel that. So better education, better personnel, better paid personnel would go a long way toward solving those problems.

Commissioner GRISWOLD. Mr. Wise?

Mr. WISE. I think I would have to disagree with Mr. Pyles, too. I know you don't expect a panel of lawyers to agree.

Commissioner GRISWOLD. If we get a flve-to-four decision, we'll be doing very well.

Mr. WISE. I think the system needs to be changed. I think the Mississippi Economic Council's effort in this direction is good. I think the sheriff should succeed himself, and he should be a professional law enforcement officer. And I also agree that paying any public official by fees is an antiquated approach to a problem, and that all of them should be on salary. Now as to what the lawyers can do about the equal enforcement of justice. I think perhaps that this gets down to a question more of citizenship than of professional life. Now when we become lawyers, we don't cease to be citizens. And as citizens, we should, of course, have an interest in this thing. And I think this is true of all citizens. What we can do about it, I don't know. But what we do about it I think has to be in common with the citizenship of the State generally.

Commissioner GRISWOLD. Well, I agree with you fully, except for the notion I have lurking in the back of my head that lawyers are leaders in the community—not only ought to be, but that they are. And I am just wondering how far the lawyers of the community should undertake active leadership on the development of these problems.

Mr. WISE. Well, I hope you're right. And I do believe that you are, that lawyers are among the leaders of the State. They are not the only ones.

Commissioner GRISWOLD. No.

Mr. WISE. But I think whatever situation in life we happen to be in, as good citizens we need to work on this problem whether we are lawyers, doctors, ministers or what have you. And I think it is not an obligation peculiarly befitting to the lawyer. I think it is an obligation to everybody. If he happens to be in a better place to work on the problem, well and good.

Commissioner GRISWOLD. Mr. Pyles?

Mr. PYLES. This is also the responsibility of the courts. And while I have the floor here, I would like to say it is not unusual for Gordon and Sherwood to disagree with me. But I would like to point out that simply separating the office of sheriff and tax collector doesn't mean that you are necessarily going to get a professional as a sheriff. More than likely you are going to get a courthouse politician who is going to perpetuate himself in office, and I don't think that is good. But this—the even administration of justice is, I think, the dual re-

and the southern jurisdiction, which is the white, until such time as this can be rectified. These will develop a program to help us in our missionary activity in the Delta system that has created such a great problem for all denominational groups in Mississippi.

In addition to that, within the last several hours, we have at our State, denominational schools, signed Federal compliance on education, which I think is a tremendous step in doing something here to meet the issues that confront us.

Now we do have pressures from within. We have people who are differing with those who are attempting to follow the patterns of the church as a whole. These have created a great deal of problems both for the bishop and his cabinet who work out the affairs of our Methodism in Mississippi. But I think in many, many instances we made progress. We tried as best we could, and I hope the others would say the same thing, to be as faithful and even more so if we can, to cooperate with the denominational groups in this State as they have with us. These gentlemen who are here with us on the platform today have given me the privilege of chairing the Committee on Concern. And I have had delightful experiences in that and have had an opportunity to share any sort of ability that I have and any sort of influence that I have to ask people to share in that. I think, Mr. Chairman, if I were to analyze things in Mississippi from August of 1964, until this moment, I think that great progress has been made, notwithstanding the fact that much information has been to the contrary.

Commissioner HESBURGH. Thank you very much, Bishop Pendergrass. I want to say a special word of thanks to the next gentleman who is going to speak since he was very helpful in getting this panel together this morning. Also, although he was officially scheduled for a much longer statement I would like to ask him to make this statement as a matter of record. I am very happy to present to you the Reverend William P. Davis of the Mississippi Baptist Seminary.

Reverend DAVIS. Mr. Chairman, I would like for the printed copy to become a part of the official record. The press has a copy and will handle it as it thinks best.

Commissioner HESBURGH. It will be copied into the record as if read.

STATEMENT OF REV. WILLIAM P. DAVIS, MISSISSIPPI BAPTIST SEMINARY

I have been invited to discuss the Committee of Concern—its background, when and how it was formed, what it has accomplished, and its purposes for the future.

are going to carry this out to the police. Everybody has been touched by it. Those that haven't been have been intimidated by it. We are beginning to get out from under that thing. The lawyers are taking the lead, I think, in getting out from under that. And I think it should be a part of their program, and I feel that it will be, to get some of these tenacious State laws—this legislation—repealed.

Commissioner GRISWOLD. Thank you, Mr. Farley. I think I would like to say that, believe it or not, I am a great believer in State's rights.

Mr. FARLEY. I have never seen anybody who wasn't.

[Laughter.]

Commissioner GRISWOLD. The difference between me and other people who talk about State's rights is that I am also a great believer in State responsibilities. And I am sure that when Mississippi comes to understand and accept its responsibilities, it will have far less trouble with interference from the Federal Government.

On behalf of the Commission, I would like to extend sincere thanks to all the members of the bar who have come to the meeting this afternoon and have given us the benefit of their experience, which, of course, is far more intimate with the situation and affairs in Mississippi than we can have in a brief visit here. With those thanks I declare this afternoon session—this panel meeting—adjourned.

(Whereupon, at 5:20 p.m., the Commission adjourned to reconvene at 9:00 a.m., Saturday, February 20, 1965.)

SATURDAY MORNING SESSION, FEBRUARY 20, 1965

The Commission met in the Recreation Hall, Veterans Administration Center, 1500 East Woodrow Wilson Drive, Jackson, Miss., at 9:00 a.m., Saturday, February 20, 1965, the Hon. John A. Hannah, Chairman of the Commission, presiding.

Present: John A. Hannah, Chairman; Eugene Patterson, Vice Chairman; Mrs. Frankie Muse Freeman, Commissioner; Rev. Theodore M. Hesburgh C.S.C., Commissioner; Robert S. Rankin, Commissioner.

Also present: Howard W. Rogerson, Acting Staff Director: William L. Taylor, General Counsel; Warren I. Cikins, special assistant to the Staff Director; Mr. M. Carl Holman, Information Officer; Michael O. Finkelstein, Assistant General Counsel; Charles C. Humpstone, staff attorney; Roy Littlejohn, staff attorney; Richard F. Bellman, staff attorney; Brian Olmstead, staff attorney; Edwin D. Wolf, staff attorney; John G. Birkle, Financial Management Officer; Robert H. Amidon, Chief of Investigations; Alan Marer, staff attorney, Department of Justice.

Chairman HANNAH. This hearing of the U.S. Commission on Civil Rights will be in order. The first item of business this morning will be a presentation by two Negro attorneys from the State of Mississippi. Mr. Taylor, will you introduce our first guests this morning.

Mr. TAYLOR. Yes. Our guests are Mr. Jack Young and Mr. Jess Brown.

Chairman HANNAH. You are guests this morning.

TESTIMONY OF JACK YOUNG, ESQ., AND R. JESS BROWN, ESQ., JACKSON, MISS.

Mr. YOUNG. Thank you.

Chairman HANNAH. Mr. Taylor will have some questions and some of the other Commissioners may have some. Mr. Taylor, will you introduce the program?

Mr. TAYLOR. Yes. Mr. Jack Young and Mr. Jess Brown, you are both practicing attorneys in the State of Mississippi, is that right?

Mr. YOUNG. Yes, that's right.

Mr. BROWN. That's right.

Mr. TAYLOR. How long have you been practicing here?

Mr. YOUNG. Since 1951.

Mr. BROWN. Practicing in the State of Mississippi since 1954. I have only been in Jackson, that is, had an office here, since about '62, or something like that.

Mr. TAYLOR. We have been hearing a good deal of testimony which concerns, in one way or another, the problem of legal representation for Negroes in this State. Would you say that a large share of your practice is concerned with civil rights cases?

Mr. BROWN. Yes, that's correct.

Mr. TAYLOR. Mr. Young, it may be a hard estimate to make, but how many cases which would be classified as civil rights cases did you handle in the year 1964?

Mr. YOUNG. Perhaps I could break it down in this way if it would make it a little more understandable. There are three Negro lawyers who are associated in the handling of local civil rights cases in this area. Those lawyers are Mr. Brown, Mr. Carsie Hall, and myself. In 1961 we had the cases which were known as the Freedom Rider cases in Jackson, and, of course, the three of us handled those cases. Of the Freedom Rider cases, there are now 29 cases on appeal for a writ of certiorari in the U.S. Supreme Court. Ninety-one of those cases are still in the Mississippi State Supreme Court. And

Students from Oberlin and other colleges, in cooperation with the local congregation, rebuilt the Antioch Baptist Church and raised the money for the construction and furnishing of the building. Students from Queens College, New York, spent 2 weeks, from January 29 through February 12, working on three churches. A number of college students, both inside and outside of Mississippi, have indicated a desire to help. At the YWA House Party, Gulf Shore Assembly, over 400 high school and career girls gave $184.30 and expressed a deep concern in helping rebuild the churches. If the remaining 20 burned churches are to be rebuilt, the Committee of Concern must have an additional $100,000.

The immediate and future purpose of the Committee of Concern was clearly stated by a spokesman for the Quakers in explaining their role in the church reconstruction program:

"As we see it, the most important thing about this entire effort is not so much the buildings being replaced as the manner and fact of their reconstruction. Thus, we have endeavored to explore the opportunities which a cooperative building program might provide for bringing the white and Negro communities into a more meaningful relationship. We have chosen to work with the Mississippi Committee of Concern because we have felt this constructive new response to violence and hatred might serve as an appropriate vehicle for the establishment of new bridges of interracial understanding."

In addition, let it clearly be added that anarchy, bigotry, demagoguery and violence shall not be allowed to prevail in Mississippi—that we, the people of Mississippi, will not stand for it. A new sunrise of interfaith and biracial good will stands at the gate of the morning in Mississippi "to bind up the brokenhearted and give unto them beauty for ashes, and to build the old waste places, the desolations of many generations. Let no man's heart fail." Indignities and injustices shall not prevail. Tyranny must go! A power structure designed to deprive citizens of their voting rights and to discriminate in the administration of justice because of race or creed is tyranny. It is not treason to challenge tyranny. It is the highest act of patriotism and obedience to the eternal command of Almighty God: "Let My People Go."

Any citizen worthy of the name is entitled to his civil rights. Intimidation or discrimination used to deny a citizen his civil rights should not be tolerated in Mississippi or anywhere in the United States of America. There should be no place for such practices in the wide, wide world. Human beings matter more than empty tradition.

Reverend DAVIS. I would like to say that I am not a Johnny-come-lately. I have spent most of my life in Mississippi with the exception of about 14 years during which time I was abroad visiting our mission fields and other places of interest—studying humanity. I returned to Mississippi in 1948 and have been officially connected with interracial mission work in Mississippi almost since that time. I have seen this work grow from infancy to a position which today covers a State like—as one of the newspapers described its spread—the dew. We have 1,900 students enrolled in our seminary system, 22 schools, 44 extension centers of those schools. So it was easy for the department, which I am trying to lead, to become identified with the leadership of the Committee of Concern which was organized September 9, 1964, in the Baptist Building of the Mississippi Baptist Convention.

It has been, since its beginning, interracial and interfaith. There isn't anything fraternalistic about the Committee of Concern. Presently we are engaged in rebuilding 18 of the 38 burned churches. Six of the churches have been completed and if we have the money we intend to rebuild or help rebuild the remaining 20.

I think that because of the efforts of the Committee of Concern, we have created a different situation in Mississippi. The lawyers supported the Mississippi Baptist Convention, the covention board, the executive committee. And these gentlemen here on the panel with me and thousands of Mississippians not here this morning, but who probably are listening to this panel discussion, have been most helpful in making this work a reality.

Now, I would like to say as a final word, let it clearly be added that anarchy, bigotry, demagoguery, violence shall not be allowed to prevail in Mississippi—that we, the people of Mississippi, will not stand for it. A new sunrise of interfaith and biracial good will stands at the gate of the morning in Mississippi to bind up the brokenhearted and to give unto them beautiful ashes and to build the old waste places the desolation of many generations. Let no man's heart fail in dignity and injustices shall not prevail. Tyranny must go. A power structure designed to deprive citizens of their voting rights and to discriminate in the administration of justice because of race or creed is tyranny. It is not treason to challenge tyranny. It is the highest act of patriotism and obedience to the eternal command of Almighty God. "Let My People Go."

Any citizen worthy of the name is entitled to his civil rights. Intimidation or discrimination used to deny a citizen his civil rights should not be tolerated in Mississippi or anywhere in the United States of America There is no place for such practices in the wide, wide world. Human beings are more important than empty tradition. I think we are establishing lines of communication and good will by racial lines of communication. And for that we are dedicated and in that direction I believe we are moving.

will go on bail, he doesn't have too much problem. But here again, the bail has to be approved by the sheriff. Well, after you have had a lot of people arrested in the community, this source is exhausted and you no longer have people who are able to go on bonds. And then people are reluctant to go on the bonds for people they don't know, which means then you have to resort to either surety bonds or to cash bonds. And unfortunately, surety companies in Mississippi won't go on bail bonds for civil rights workers, which means then that the only other resort is to cash bonds.

Now I have heard some of the gentlemen on the panel mention the fact yesterday that under our law cash bonds are not permitted. I think this is in error. The 1960 Mississippi legislature amended the bail bond act so that you can now post cash bonds at the discretion of the court, and that is what we have been forced to do in most of these cases. But here again, the bonds as a rule are so high that your big problem is finding the money. For instance, in the cases we have now on appeal to the county court, the bond is $1,500. From the county courts, it is $1,500. When you have a hundred defendants, that is $150,000 worth of bonds. And it is difficult to come about this sort of money. Sometimes the defendants stay in jail because we haven't been able to raise the cash to post the bond.

Mr. TAYLOR. Do you consider this an abuse of the purpose of bail, which is to secure the attendance of persons at the trial?

Mr. YOUNG. Well, as I understand it, the purpose of bail, as you have just said, is to assure the attendance of the defendant at the trial. And when we notice that in some cases the bond is much less for similar offenses committed by people who are not civil rights workers, then we don't have any other recourse except to think that perhaps this is an abuse.

Mr. TAYLOR. Do you have any recommendation or——

Mr. YOUNG. As to what should be done or what could be done? If by some means the courts could be persuaded to reduce the bond in these cases, or at least to make the bond comparable to that which would be charged in other offenses, it would help a great deal.

Mr. TAYLOR. Let me ask about criminal defense in cases other than civil rights cases, particularly the defense of Negroes who are charged with crimes. Are there problems in this area too?

Mr. BROWN. There are a number of problems connected with this area. You see, most of your legal defense organizations which furnish legal assistance and money, particularly to defendants involved with civil rights cases, are all pretty well burdened all over the country. And that being true, where defendants become involved in noncivil rights cases, it makes the load tremendous. As you very well know, in criminal law, generally, and particularly in this area—just practicing criminal law where the client has to pay you—there is not very much money in it. And most lawyers say they don't fool with criminal law. So it does pose a problem. And sometimes what we do is carry the load ourselves in many instances. In some cases I have lost money representing defendants because they didn't have the money.

Mr. TAYLOR. I have been noticing a number of decisions, including a recent decision of the Supreme Court of Mississippi, which indicate a full recognition that exclusion of Negroes from juries is a defense and will invalidate the prosecution. I think that was a very recent decision of the Mississippi Supreme Court.

Mr. BROWN. I represented the defendant in that case. The recent case I think you are talking about was one where the Mississippi Supreme Court reversed or remanded a case coming out of, I think, Scott County, Forest, Mississippi. And we raised the question of systematic exclusion of Negroes from the jury. Now, when I started with that case, a boy got in jail and his father came to my office. And he had, I think as I recall, maybe $150, $200; that's all he had to start with. And he came to my office maybe a day or two before he was to be arraigned and tried. As I recall, I think he came in on Saturday. It took me a couple of days to prepare the necessary preliminary motions for arraignment. And on the morning I went there I had about $200 in my pocket. That's all I had been paid. I couldn't see my way in that case. I went ahead, filed the motions, spent about 3 days down there representing this client with these motions. And luckily, Mr. Wulf, who is the joint counsel for the American Civil Liberties Union out of New York City, was here on another occasion and I discussed my problem with him. I said, "I'm bogged down. I don't know what I'm going to be able to do here." And that was before we went into the merits of the case.

And he says, "Is your man able to pay?" And, of course, I indicated to him he was not. And I got help from the American Civil Liberties Union. That's the way that case was able to go on through to the Mississippi Supreme Court. But sometimes when I start, I don't know where I'm going to end.

Mr. TAYLOR. It is a hit-or-miss proposition because of the limited resources available.

Mr. BROWN. Yes, that's right.

Mr. TAYLOR. I understand, and I think it was discussed here yesterday, that in the criminal defense of Negroes, white lawyers are sometimes or frequently involved in various parts of the State. But isn't it a real problem, the raising of the constitutional defense? Is it frequently raised? And if it is not, why not?

do unto you," and most of our race relations problems will be solved.
[Applause.]

Commissioner HESBURGH. Thank you very much, Mr. Rankin. I think everyone has had a chance to say something. I would like to put a hypothetical question to this group since it represents a wide sweep of the religious element in Mississippi. We have heard a number of times during the course of this week and, of course, on other occasions—and we heard it from the good Bishop Allin this morning when he spoke about getting the groceries cut off—what would happen to the clergymen of this State if they really came out for the things that have been spoken about this week—the things Mississippians yearn for in this new day.

If they came out with the statement that every registrar in the State of Mississippi should act on what has been said by the business community and by the legal community and by many of your fine leaders who have spoken here, including your Governor; if they said that they believe every capable citizen of this State should have the right to vote, not 20 years from now, not 50 years from now, but right now, even if we have to keep the registration places open all night long to register people who are qualified; if every single religious representative in this State came out and said he believes that equal opportunity in education is important because no State moves forward without education and he thinks we all ought to put our shoulder to the wheel and come out for adequate education right now so that every single citizen of this State would have a much greater opportunity to be educated to the full extent of his talents; if they said they think that every citizen of this State should have an equal opportunity to a decent place in which to live, so far as that is possible, and should be accepted as a human being on his own personal capability and his own personal dedication, his performance as a human being, not his color; if they went beyond that and said they are going to try to invigorate aspiration among all people, white and colored, that they are going to make of this State a kind of new South which people haven't seen before. And are going to do it quickly, ignoring those people in their congregations who think this is a bad idea. Because part of religion is prophecy, and part of prophecy is having the courage to stand up and say what is right, what is right today, not next year or when it is easy to be right, not what is right because it is popular or what is right because it is profitable, but right because this is the will of God for His people, and we are His people. What would happen if every religious person in this state would sign such a statement?

They can't drive all the ministers and all the priests from the State. There wouldn't be any religion here, and I think there is a great deal of religion here. As a matter of fact, I think there is a lot more religion here in Mississippi than in many other States of the Union. We have heard some wonderful people during this past week who said, "I'm afraid to go into that booth alone, but I am not really alone because I have prayed, and God is with me. But I have been afraid. And yet I realize all I can do is die. And if something is right, you should be willing to be a martyr for it as evidenced by others who have gone through great indignity and great injustices." Vice chairman Patterson asked one little old lady about 80 years old, "Do you like the white people."

And she said, "of course I likes them. I loves them. I wouldn't be Christian if I didn't."

I think I would like to ask the panel this question, and I would like a little open discussion on it. What would happen if every religious leader in this State came out in one swoop and said, "This is our manifesto, and this is what we believe. We are going to begin preaching this doctrine day in and day out. We are going to live it in our church associations and our church activities. And if you don't like it you are going to have to drive out every one of us." I just don't think that's going to happen.

Reverend WHITNEY. Mr. Chairman, I think this is hypothetical.

Commissioner HESBURGH. That is all right.

Reverend WHITNEY. But I think really that you have a situation here which is much deeper than most people recognize because there are a lot of persons who preach the Gospel who don't believe it, who really believe that God made several groups and put some groups here and other groups there and there should be no communication between these groups. I don't think you could get the ministers of this State to really come out with a statement stating that this is the will of God, and we should follow it. I think Mr. Golden, in his book, "Mr. Kennedy and the Negroes," talks about it very beautifully when he says the society is sort of moving on the middle class and most of the ministers are no longer leading the people but the people leading the ministers.

I think this is the problem we have, for example, in our congregation. I have said to the people when a white man or woman cannot come into our congregation and worship with us, then I am not going to accept this church as my pastorate. I am not going to work with you. This is my conviction, that any person who wants to come to X church can. A person comes to worship God and I don't think we should deny him the right. I believe this, but I'm not sure whether someday almost every person will find himself legally involved in some way.

Now he may be on a jury today, but he could be a defendant tomorrow. And the day that he is a defendant, he is going to then realize, you understand, that he himself also wants a fair and impartial trial when sitting as a defendant before a court. You understand—that the defendant who is sitting there was previously in the jury box. And another thing, too, they seem to, in many instances, identify the lawyer with the client he represents. If he is an accused rapist, then the lawyer looks like a rapist. If he is a bank robber, then when you walk in, you look like a bank robber. And another thing, too, as a lawyer, our position as a lawyer is to represent the client. A man comes in my office and says he wants to get a divorce from his wife. And he says that his wife has been untrue to him or he raises some other ground. That is his ground; he says that. I wasn't there. I don't know whether she was untrue or not. He says so, and it is my duty to represent him and for the court to determine. I don't care whether he stays with her or not. All I know is I am defending that client.

Mr. TAYLOR. Thank you.

Chairman HANNAH. Mrs. Freeman?

Commissioner FREEMAN. Mr. Young and Mr. Brown, it is apparent that you and the other lawyer—the two of you and the other Negro lawyer in the State have had to carry a disproportionate share of the burden of the legal profession in representing clients. We learned yesterday that there are 2,200 lawyers in this State, of whom only 3 are Negro. I would like to hear your comments as to what could be done to get more lawyers of the Mississippi Bar interested in representing those persons and what needs to be done to get more Negro lawyers in this State.

Mr. YOUNG. I think, Mrs. Freeman, the reason perhaps that we don't have more Negro lawyers than we have is quite simple. Until James Meredith went to the University of Mississippi, Negroes were not admitted to the University of Mississippi. Mississippi is the only accredited law school in the State. And if a Negro wished to study law, he had to go outside of the State to do it. I dare say that 80 percent of the lawyers who practice in Mississippi are graduates of the University of Mississippi. And upon graduation they are automatically admitted to the bar without the necessity of taking the examination. If he is a graduate of Yale, Harvard, Oxford, or any other place than Mississippi, he has to come back to Mississippi and take the Mississippi bar examination—which doesn't necessarily encourage lawyers who are going out of the State to come back to Mississippi.

In addition to that, I think that our problem has been in the past that after having been forced to go out of the State to school and after having had a taste of integrated life or life in an integrated society where people are treated as men and as women rather than as boys and as girls, the young Negro is reluctant to come back to Mississippi and bring his family to live in Mississippi in a condition similar to that which he left. So he doesn't have any incentive to come back to Mississippi. Now we have had some few—and very few Negroes who have been admitted—or rather who have been to law school, make application to take the Mississippi State Bar. And I think that the only Negro who is interested in taking the bar in Mississippi would be one who actually feels that he has a job to do, that he has a contribution to make, and that he can best make it in Mississippi. If he is interested in practicing law to make a living for his family, then he just doesn't come back to Mississippi.

Now, what can be done to interest lawyers of other groups to take this sort of practice, I don't know. There is no reluctance on the part of white lawyers to take non civil rights cases. They take civil cases, they take criminal cases where Negroes are involved with Negroes or even where Negroes are involved with whites, as long as the cases have no civil rights connotation because they have nothing to fear from the community at large. But when a white lawyer is asked to take a civil rights case, he immediately has problems. I mean economic problems. He can be subjected to serious economic pressure, and most people think about their families before they jump out into these sorts of things. Now, the program that was suggested by the members of the State Bar Association yesterday—wherein they proposed to set up a system where you automatically are assigned to the case, is perhaps the best solution I know at this point. But that is certainly not a perfect solution.

Commissioner FREEMAN. One of the other questions that was raised yesterday was about the participation of Negro lawyers in the programs and committees of the State Bar Association. I would like to know from you and Mr. Brown the extent to which you have participated in the committee assignments.

Mr. YOUNG. Well, we have not participated in the committee assignments. I think you heard the president of the State bar in answer to a question of one of the members of the Commission that we have an integrated bar. We do have an integrated bar. By law we are required—all members of the bar are required to belong to the State Bar Association. However, heretofore, all State Bar Association meetings have been held in segregated hotels. And since we are Negroes, the inference was we weren't expected to attend. I don't

Bible," there has been encouragement for people. And there are thousands of similar people in this State who have been looking for some kind of leadership.

Mr. Chairman, this morning—and this is the first time I have been here because I have been out of town—this morning I heard certain industrialists say some things about what's going to happen and the hopefulness now. Mr. Owen Cooper, who is the past president of a Mississippi Baptist convention board, tried not to talk religion but was talking religion all the way through here. He was trying to talk as an industrialist. And Mr. Cooper, I think, reflects the dilemma that has been in existence here for many, many years, and not just since 1954—the exact roll of religion in the going problems of living, and this is every facet of living.

I think the time has come for the teachers of religion to say this is what we believe in. This is what we think is God's word. Now, Bishop Brunini said that. I think the time has come for us to say that in a united voice—if only for the sake of somebody like myself because that old song about hanging together or hanging separately is very true—if only for the sake of the Negro preacher on this issue. And to me, it's the greatest challenge that has confronted our State and our Nation and it's a challenge that we all know is going to be with us for the rest of our lives. In this issue we as religious leaders must do some teacher work and, if you please, then some leading without deprecating all the fine sacrificial efforts that people on this panel here—that people in this room have been engaged in for all these years.

If there is one thing that I resent—and I'm going to say this in public—I don't think Bishop Allin was strong enough and here I agree with you, John. I resent the image that has been created by our colleagues in other parts of the country that we are the weaklings, that we have accepted the status quo. I resent it. I resent the type of clergymen who have come into Mississippi and on an overnight investigation has become an expert on the problems of Mississippi and all of these areas in which this Commission is concerned. I have the highest respect in the world and I have met hundreds of those who have come into the State to make witness, and to make witness is something else besides coming in and becoming an expert on a 24-hour basis. I had a young rabbi come this past summer. He called me up on Monday morning with one foot on the plane and said to me he came in on Sunday. And he had came down to take a look-see. And he had seen and he called me up and said, "Rabbi, I admire you. I know what you are going through." My answer to him was—Well, I can't give it in public.

[Laughter.]

You haven't the faintest idea what is happening in Mississippi. There have been too many such clerical experts who have come down into our State. Come down and share with us—not as the voice of the North telling us simple-minded folk of the South what to do.

Commissioner HESBURGH. I think one thing is coming through. They aren't dead yet.

[Laughter.]

I would like to wind this up in about 10 minutes. I don't want to arbitrarily say who should speak or not speak, but I think we have something rolling here and I think it's terribly important. Would you like to say something again, sir?

Reverend DAVIS. Well, I would like to say, sir, that the roll of the minister is in behalf of the welfare of all the people of the State and of the Nation. That is his primary concern. The concern of God is not for things but for people. And, our concern likewise becomes a concern for the total welfare of humanity in this State. I think that more ministers and more leaders have been aware of that and working in that direction than we have recognized. We are fellow laborers in a common cause; I see no defeat—I see victory. I think that we will resolve our tensions. We will settle our disputes and difficulties. We will come through to victory. I don't think we are going to do it tomorrow, but I think we will do it. I think we shall do it.

Commissioner HESBURGH. Thank you very much, sir. Now, would you like to say something again, Bishop Pendergrass?

Bishop PENDERGRASS. May I say this. Since 1940—these are facts that people do not altogether understand—the church that I represent has been totally integrated at the upper level. We have representatives on the major boards of our church. We have bishops in the Methodist church. And when I spoke a moment or two—and this is in rebuttal—that I'm a Johnny-come-lately, I meant by that, that while I have come to Mississippi as a Johnny-come-lately, I have not been totally unaware of the problem that exists. And with my deep and sincere appreciation for Rabbi Nussbaum's presence here, if he will permit me, I would like to say just this one word. Almighty God has never done anything overnight. In the beginning he made a world and spoke unto chaos and said, "Let there be light, and there was light." He put a perfect man and a perfect woman in a garden and they could not deal with the problem—there were problems of disobedience and an unwillingness to abide by the principles of God. Then He gave us the patriarchal fathers, but they were not enough. He then gave us the law giver, but he was not enough. He then gave us the prophets, but they were not enough. And then He reached in the coffers of love, as we Christians say—and for this I apologize to my friend here.

I have never seen a Negro teacher up there bringing Negro students into that legislative hall and into those places so that at that time they become indoctrinated—just like where a 2-year-old Catholic is a Catholic at 90—he has to be indoctrinated then. He will have the desire to become the governor of Mississippi, become the mayor of Jackson. And there is another thing I have always believed, and that is this,—: I don't believe in inferiority. You can call me inferior. Simply because you call me that, that doesn't mean that I think so. Because I am free in that respect, completely free.

And we are going to have to indoctrinate our students. We have a twofold job. Not only our problems, not only the matter from the other side—the problem is also from our side—trying to free our minds. And the only way we can free our minds is to be able to bring people into these schools and let them speak and be able to—you don't have to always agree with them. I wouldn't agree with everybody on this panel if I heard every one of you speak on the same subject. But I will take a little bit from each one of you and form my conclusion. And that is the type of teaching that is going to have to be done. That is why you don't have Negro lawyers. You don't have them because it is not started in the 1st, 2d, 3d, 4th, on up to 12th grade. That is why you have to build it.

Now the next thing, as Mr. Young has already pointed out, we also have a Jackson School of Law. Whites work in the post office, serve as clerks and other things during the day, and go to school in the evening and finally come to be a lawyer. Now, that is not only the problem with lawyers; that is the same thing true with doctors. Somebody said we had plenty of doctors. Yeah, about 65 doctors and a little less than a million Negroes. Is that plenty of doctors?

And another thing, they said this. I heard some say that Negroes won't use Negro lawyers. That is a mistake. It has been, but the Negroes now are beginning to get confidence in Negro lawyers. They are beginning to get confidence in them because they read the paper—they know what's happening. They know men like Thurgood Marshall, Bob Carter, others that I could go on naming, so they begin now to become interested and believe in Negro lawyers. They have confidence in them. There was a time they didn't believe in Negro doctors, Negro lawyers, Negro anything, because they had been brainwashed. And they themselves believed that they were inferior. I never worry about a white man calling me inferior, but I become worried when I begin to think it. That is the only time I begin to worry. And those are the things that will make Negro lawyers, that will make Negro ministers, that will make Negro doctors, that will make Negro dentists. That is why we don't have them. Once we get that we will be able to move, and not move against the other side—move with the other side.

Chairman HANNAH. Thank you very much, Mr. Brown. Mr. Rankin?

Commissioner RANKIN. Mr. Young, I would like to ask you one question: Are misdemeanors in this State usually punished by fine or imprisonment?

Mr. YOUNG. Yes.

Commissioner RANKIN. Do you think fine or imprisonment is fair punishment? In other words, if a man has 15 cents in his pocket and he gets 30 days or $300, he is forced to take the 30 days, is that correct?

Mr. YOUNG. I misunderstood your question. He isn't given an election.

Commissioner RANKIN. He has no choice at all?

Mr. YOUNG. It is not "either/or." It is "and."

Commissioner RANKIN. It is both.

Mr. YOUNG. That's right.

Commissioner RANKIN. Does this lead to suspended sentences?

Mr. YOUNG. Often you do have suspended sentences.

Commissioner RANKIN. Have you ever made a study of suspended sentences to see how the court hands them out.

Mr. YOUNG. As far as Negroes are concerned?

Commissioner RANKIN. Yes, as far as Negroes are concerned.

Mr. YOUNG. Well, as far as I know, Negroes get about as many suspended sentences as do whites.

Commissioner RANKIN. And so the courts have been fair in that respect, is that correct?

Mr. YOUNG. Well, I can only speak with regard to suspended sentences in courts in Hinds County where I practice. I have no complaint on the question of suspended sentences in ordinary misdemeanor cases in Hinds County.

Commissioner RANKIN. And you don't know if this is true of the rest of the State?

Mr. YOUNG. Well, I can't say that as a fact with regards to the rest of the State.

Commissioner RANKIN. Thank you.

Chairman HANNAH. Thank you very much, gentlemen. We are grateful to you for being here this morning. We appreciate it.

Mr. BROWN. Thank you.

Chairman HANNAH. Mr. Taylor, I think you have two more presentations before we proceed with the panel?

Commissioner HESBURGH. Ladies and gentlemen, we have used up our time but I promised Rabbi Nussbaum I would let him close with an aphorism famous among the rabbis.

Rabbi NUSSBAUM. Well, everybody has gotten in a lick for their religion and I want to say something in behalf of mine. When the children of Israel came to the Red Sea and they heard about the Egyptian hords pursuing them, as we are all aware, they got scared and started crying to the Lord. And according to a rabbinic comment, the Lord said, "Moses, you tell those people to get up from their knees and stop praying and let them do something." This is what we have to do. We have a rabbinic aphorism that says, as I remember most of it, "The day is short, the work is much, the matter is urgent. It's not up to you to complete the work. But, neither are you free to desist from it." And I say thanks to the Commission for being here to give us the kind of encouragement that we need to continue with this work that has gone on for many years in this State of Mississippi which we all love.

[Applause.]

Commissioner HESBURGH. Ladies and gentlemen, on behalf of all of you and, I presume, on behalf of all those who are seeing us on television, I want to thank each and every one of these gentlemen for the wonderful hour they have given us. I think it has taken courage on their part to say what they have said. I think we have tried to blend courage with realism, but also with idealism which, after all, will get us where we are going. It is customary at both the beginning and the close of Commission meetings to have an official statement from our Chairman who, as you know, is Dr. John Hannah, president of Michigan State University.

Chairman HANNAH. Thank you, Father Hesburgh.

As we bring this Mississippi hearing to a close the Commission on Civil Rights extends its appreciation to the U.S. District Court in Jackson. And then I want to say a few words about the hearing. First we want to express our appreciation to the Federal district judges who made possible the use of the Federal courtroom for last week's executive session. We are very grateful to the director of the Veterans' Administration Center and his staff members whose cooperation greatly facilitated the conducting of this week's public sessions. We are also grateful to Chief U.S. Marshal Jack T. Stuart and his deputies who have ably assisted us during all sessions of the hearings.

A special measure of appreciation must go to the members, past and present, of the Mississippi State Advisory Committee to this Commission who have worked so patiently and courageously to help awaken the consciences of their fellow Mississippians. Their work has been performed under conditions which have sometimes been extremely trying. It is reassuring that so able and dedicated a group of Mississippians will remain in constant communication with us and will be continuing their important work long after the Commission has left Mississippi. We thank the many members of our own staff who have worked so hard in making this hearing possible. In the view of all the Commisisoners, they have done very well indeed.

Most of all, we should like to express our appreciation to all those who have appeared before the Commission during these hearings. It was encouraging to us that the Hon. Paul B. Johnson, Governor of Mississippi, not only came before the Commission to discuss the problems and progress of his State but urged other responsible Mississippians to seize upon this hearing as an opportunity to put the facts about Mississippi in perspective. We are grateful to State Attorney General Joe T. Patterson and Mayor Allen C. Thompson of Jackson and to the scores of other private citizens and public officials from whom we have sought information during the past 2 weeks.

For some of these, it was not an easy experience to testify before the Commission, but we would assure them that our sole concern has been to elicit facts, not to cause any person discomfort or embarrassment. We are aware, too, that some of those who testified here had already paid a substantial price in physical suffering or economic loss for speaking their convictions or attempting to exercise their rights. It is a tribute to Mississippi that such citizens have been willing to appear at this hearing and the Commission hopes, with them, that the climate of opinion in Mississippi is now such that people can speak the truth as they see it without risking reprisals or abuse.

When the Commission opened these hearings 2 weeks ago, we announced that we intended to call a broad range of witnesses so that we might examine allegations of racial discrimination in voting and law enforcement objectively and in context. We have conscientiously sought to do this, both in the executive session and in the public session. Since the beginning of the hearings, the Commission has heard the testimony of some 100 Mississippians of both races, representing a wide spectrum of experience and opinion. The hearing itself was the outgrowth of months of preparation and research, including many field trips by staff members and the sifting of voluminous records and complaints in an earnest attempt to examine as fully as possible the conditions which have produced civil rights problems, in certain parts of this State, of a kind and intensity rarely encountered elsewhere. It was determined long before the Commission arrived here that our major interests would be the present status and future prospects of civil rights in Mississippi rather than an exháustive and largely profitless review of past injustices.

is of significance. By median age, of course, I mean that age whereby you have half of the population above and half below that age. In 1900 we had a median age of about 18 years. By 1960 it had moved to 24 years of age. So consequently we would say that the population is growing older, at least in respect to average or median age. There is almost no change for nonwhites, but there was a considerable change for the median age of the whites. There is about a 10-year spread between the median age of the whites and nonwhites in 1960. This changing age pattern, I think, is due largely to the out-migration of the nonwhite element of the population. This is specifically so, I find, in the age group of 20 to 44 years of age.

During the thirties, this age group increased some, but it dropped considerably from 1940 to 1960. We had about a 200,000 drop in population at that age level, and about 150,000 of this 200,000 were nonwhite. So you can see that the young adults in their very productive years who were leaving the State essentially were nonwhite. Now, not all of it is due to out-migration. Some is due to birth rates and death rates, and somewhat also, I suppose, to the declining birth rate of the depression years. So much for the characteristics of the population from the standpoint of size, location, concentration, and so forth.

Moving on to the income of the population, let me talk briefly about family income in accordance with the way the U.S. census defines it and evaluates it. I find that nonwhite Mississippians as a group live on a substantially lower income than do whites, as a rule. In 1959 the median family income was $1,450 for nonwhites and a little better than $4,200 for whites. In other words, half the families had incomes above that point; the other half, below. A point of significance, I think, is that 80 percent of the nonwhites had a median income of less than $3,000. Now this $3,000 level, of course, is the so-called dividing line in the war on poverty that the Federal Government is talking about so much and beginning to take action on. We also have a substantial number of white families, incidentally, that had a median income below $3,000—about 34 percent. Still, a great disparity exists between whites and nonwhites. But, nevertheless, it indicates, of course, that Mississippi is not a wealthy State. In contrast, we had about 26,000 white families with $10,000 income or more; less than a thousand nonwhites were that affluent. In other words, less than a thousand nonwhite families had that annual income of $10,000 or more.

Let me look briefly now at the median earnings of the experienced civilian labor force by occupation group. Nonwhite males in professional categories had a median income about 52 percent of the whites' median income—about $2,700 as contrasted to approximately $5,200. In no occupation group is the nonwhite median income above the $3,000 level for males. I think by way of contrast and comparison, also, we ought to know that there were 5 occupation groups out of the 12 where the male white median income was below $3,000, again pointing up the fact that Mississippi is not wealthy.

Education is often viewed as a panacea for all the problems of society. But, yet, I think most of us will admit it is not the complete panacea. Still, we recognize that there are decided advantages for well-trained and educated citizenry. We know that in today's complex society, for example, that economy absorbs the well-trained better than it does the not so well educated. We find a striking and rather pronounced upward trend in incomes for both the white and nonwhite portions of population as the years of education increase. It is extremely low, as I think might be expected, for both white and nonwhite persons below the high school level. You find a greater disparity of income between the whites and nonwhites as you move upward in the educational scale. For example, the nonwhite male median income was about 89 percent of its white counterpart when they had no education, but only about 52 percent of that white median when you had a college education involved.

The disparity, I found, of income between white and nonwhite women is not as pronounced as in the case of the males. You had a median income of nonwhite women, though, who were high school graduates that was about the same as white women with only elementary education. But contrast that, though, to the median income of nonwhite women completing college with that of white women with college degrees and you find that the nonwhite median was about 90 percent of the whites' median for females—not a great disparity there.

There is a manner in which we sometimes make these comparisons; that is, by type of family, one being the husband and wife type family. We find that the nonwhite income was a little more than a third of the whites during the productive years to age 65. Beyond that, the disparity is not so great. The median income of the nonwhites, for husband and wife families beyond 65, is about 61 percent of the white median. The families that are headed by females only, as contrasted to husband and wife categories, don't fare very well in either case. But the nonwhite fare considerably worse than the whites, I think, with a median income of less than a thousand dollars, about 38 percent of the white median. Then, of course, it has been said that we have a substantial number of nonwhite families headed only by a female person, so to the extent that this is substantial, of course, the problem becomes worse. And I have no statistics on that type of a situation.

Looking briefly at employment characteristics—and I will try then to conclude my remarks—looking at this very briefly from the stand-

U.S. COMMISSION ON CIVIL RIGHTS

MONDAY AFTERNOON SESSION, FEBRUARY 15, 1965

The Commission met in the Recreation Hall, Veterans Administration Center, 1500 East Woodrow Wilson Drive, Jackson, Miss., at 2:00 p.m., Monday, February 15, 1965, the Hon. John A. Hannah, Chairman of the Commission, presiding.

Present: John A. Hannah, Chairman; Eugene Patterson, Vice Chairman; Mrs. Frankie Muse Freeman, Commissioner; Erwin N. Griswold, Commissioner; Robert S. Rankin, Commissioner.

Also Present: Howard W. Rogerson, Acting Staff Director; William L. Taylor, General Counsel; Michael O. Finkelstein, Assistant General Counsel.

PROCEEDINGS

Chairman HANNAH. Ladies and gentlemen, the Civil Rights Commission is in session this afternoon for the purpose of receiving certain documents that have been subpenaed.

Let the record show that I am John A. Hannah, the Chairman of the Commission.

On my right is Mr. Eugene Patterson, the Vice Chairman; on his right is Dr. Robert Rankin; and on my left is Mrs. Frankie Freeman, all members of the Commission.

We will ask the audience to remain quiet and to terminate any of their activities with reference to arrangements that they are making for wires until this session has been concluded. Mr. Taylor, will you call the first witness.

Mr. TAYLOR. The first witness is Sheriff Jack Purvis, Sheriff of Humphreys County.

Chairman HANNAH. Mr. Purvis, will you raise your right hand?

(Whereupon, Mr. John D. Purvis was duly sworn by the Chairman and testified as follows:)

Chairman HANNAH. Have a chair, sir. Mr. Purvis, who is the gentleman accompanying you?

Mr. PURVIS. Mr. James T. Bridges.

Mr. BRIDGES. I am an attorney at law and his counsel.

Chairman HANNAH. All right, Mr. Taylor, will you handle the proceedings?

(417)

Another reflector of economic well-being, I think, can be called the welfare statistics. Since the welfare program is administered by professionally trained workers, it provides a fairly reliable index to poverty. We have in this State a public assistance program which includes some 161,000 persons. That adds up to 7.4 percent of the population. Racially, that breaks down to 38.34 percent white, 61.66 percent nonwhite.

In certain programs, of course, the disparity is greater. In this category is the aid to dependent children program. The amount of monthly payments in our assistance program varies, of course, slightly between the different categories of aid. But they are remarkably uniform in that they run around $40. The average monthly old age assistance in Mississippi for September 1964 was $37.20. The point that might be made there, however, is that our reports indicate that cases of dependent children mean households, so the payments per dependent child is only $12.37. We have made some study in our report of the trend in the assistance statistics over the last 5 years, made by comparison with the statistics of 5 years ago. We find relatively little change; a slight increase in the number of nonwhite recipients, a slight decrease in the number of white recipients. The biggest change is in the number of white dependent children, which has decreased 24.2 percent, while the number of nonwhite children has increased 27.4 percent.

By way of adding the final factor, we have considered educational level as a reflector of economic status. Statistics there indicate that of the total population, 3.8 percent have no schooling at all and the median years of schooling completed is 8.9 percent in the entire population. Of the whites, 1.2 percent have no schooling; of the non-whites, 8.4 percent have none. The median year of schooling for whites is 11; the median year for nonwhites is 6. The number of whites who have completed 4 years of college is 7.7 percent; the number of nonwhites is 1.8 percent.

By way of summarizing what I have said, I simply have made a point or two, I think, about housing which adds up to the fact that it is woefully inadequate for the total population. It is particularly inadequate for the nonwhite portion of the population, which means something over 900,000 people. A large part of this element of the population, 26.3 percent, live in overcrowded housing. More than two-thirds of them have nonflush toilets or none. More than three-fourths live in houses which have no bath facilities. Nearly a third of them live in dilapidated houses.

As to the welfare status reflecting the picture, one might conclude, of course, that the welfare payments are woefully inadequate. They are well below that of any other State in all categories. They are less than half the national average in all categories. That is not to say, of course, that there isn't a reason for it. The reason, I think, is simply the inability of the State to pay more. Finally, the educational level, which I touched on, showing that we have 8.4 percent of the nonwhite males with no schooling should be remembered. Concluding then, I think one might say that in regard to these things, such as housing, welfare, and education, Mississippi has many problems.

Chairman HANNAH. Thank you very much, Professor Fortenberry. Gentlemen, these are fine reports. And they will be included in the record in their entirety. Copies have been furnished to the press. We are very grateful to you. Thank you very much. Well done.

REPORT ON THE ECONOMIC STATUS OF NEGROES IN MISSISSIPPI

Much has been said about the plight or condition of the Negro in the United States and in Southern States such as Mississippi. Much more needs to be done in the way of ferreting out facts pertaining to the economic status of the Negro element of the population. This paper sets forth, through generous use of tables and a more limited textual discussion based on those tables, some of the economic characteristics of the nonwhite (essentially Negro) portion of the Mississippi population. No effort is made to compare the relative position of the Mississippi Negro to that of Negroes in other parts of the country. This is not to say that Negroes in Mississippi are in any better or any worse position, relatively speaking, than in any other State or the United States as a whole. Rather, it is simply an attempt to set forth some essentially economic characteristics. Except for a few exceptions, the data is drawn from Bureau of the Census publications and reflects 1959 or 1960 situations. There are no available data since the 1960 census to indicate any substantial changes from relative positions stated in this paper.

SIZE AND LOCATION OF THE POPULATION

At the time of the 1960 census, the total population of Mississippi numbered 2,178,141 persons, almost identical with the 1940 population of 2,184,000. Of this 1960 population, more than 920,000 or about 43 percent were nonwhite, virtually all of whom were Negroes; as contrasted to slightly more than 50 percent nonwhite in 1930 and almost exactly 50 percent in 1940. Thus, there has been a substantial decline in the percentage of the total population which is nonwhite. Table 1 shows the 1960 population of the State by color and broken down according to urban and rural.

A majority of Mississippian's—both white and nonwhite—lived in rural areas in 1960. The rural proportion of nonwhite population was somewhat higher than that of the white population—68 percent of the nonwhite portion of the population lived in rural areas while 58 percent of the white portion of the population lived in rural areas.

Mr. TAYLOR. These documents will be marked and a receipt given to Sheriff Purvis. Mr. Chairman, I recommend that the witness be kept under subpena until Tuesday, February 16, at 1:30 in the afternoon, during which session the documents will be returned to him.

Chairman HANNAH. Is this all that you need from Sheriff Purvis?

Mr. TAYLOR. Yes, sir.

Chairman HANNAH. Thank you, gentlemen. You are excused.

We will see you again tomorrow afternoon. If you are here by 1:45 tomorrow, it will be time enough because I think that we will go through until about 12:30 and therefore may not be back until about 1:45.

Mr. BRIDGES. All right, sir.

(Witness excused.)

Chairman HANNAH. Call the next witness.

Mr. TAYLOR. The next witness is G. H. Hood, Circuit Clerk for Humphreys County.

Chairman HANNAH. Mr. Hood, will you raise your right hand?

(Whereupon, Mr. G. H. Hood was duly sworn by the Chairman and testified as follows:)

Chairman HANNAH. Mr. Hood, would you introduce your counsel?

Mr. BRIDGES. James T. Bridges of Belzoni, Miss., counsel for Mr. Hood.

Chairman HANNAH. Mr. Taylor, will you handle the proceedings?

TESTIMONY OF G. H. HOOD, CIRCUIT CLERK, HUMPHREY'S COUNTY, MISS.

Mr. TAYLOR. Mr. Hood, you are currently the Circuit Clerk or Registrar for Humphreys County, is that correct?

Mr. HOOD. I am.

Mr. TAYLOR. You are here pursuant to a subpena which calls for the following records:

"All written applications for voter registration submitted to the Registrar, Humphreys County, during the period from August 1, 1964, to date."

I ask you to produce the documents called for.

(Documents handed to Mr. Taylor.)

Mr. HOOD. They are numbered on the top, sir, right under that clip.

Mr. BRIDGES. Mr. Chairman, these records are a part of the permanent records of Mr. Hood's office, and we can't leave the originals here except for a short time. We have to have them back.

Chairman HANNAH. Can we keep them until tomorrow and return them then?

Mr. BRIDGES. Yes, sir.

Chairman HANNAH. That will be satisfactory.

Mr. TAYLOR. Mr. Hood, are these all of the documents called for in the subpena?

Mr. HOOD. That's right.

Mr. TAYLOR. They are. In that case, the clerk will give a receipt to Mr. Hood for the documents. I recommend that the witness remain under subpena and be excused until tomorrow, February 16, at 1:45.

Chairman HANNAH. Thank you very much, gentlemen. You are excused until tomorrow.

(Witness excused.)

Chairman HANNAH. Mr. Recorder, will you indicate on the record that Dean Griswold, another member of the Commission, is now in attendance.

Mr. TAYLOR. Mr. Chairman, the next witness is Dan C. Thompson, Chief of Police, Canton, Miss.

Chairman HANNAH. Mr. Thompson, will you raise your right hand?

(Whereupon, Mr. Dan C. Thompson was duly sworn by the Chairman and testified, as follows:)

Chairman HANNAH. Will you introduce your counsel?

Mr. GOZA. Mr. Robert Goza, city attorney, Canton.

Chairman HANNAH. Mr. Taylor, will you proceed.

TESTIMONY OF DAN C. THOMPSON, CHIEF OF POLICE, CANTON, MISS.

Mr. TAYLOR. Chief Thompson, you are currently the Chief of Police of Canton, Miss., is that correct?

Mr. THOMPSON. Yes, sir.

Mr. TAYLOR. You are here under subpena to produce the following documents:

All records, documents and memoranda in your possession or control including, without limitation, all records of complaints, affidavits and warrants, records of arrests, investigative reports medical reports, and statements pertaining to the beating of Mirza Hamid Kizilbash, in Canton on or about May 29, 1964.

Secondly—

All records, documents, and memoranda in your possession or control including, without limitation, all records of complaints, affidavits and warrants, records of arrests, investigative reports, and statements pertaining to the following matters:

(a) All incidents of violence at the building known as the Freedom House, 838 Lutz Street, Canton, Miss., from January 1, 1964, to date, including, without limitation, the bombing on or about June 8, 1964, the attempted bombing on or about July 11, 1964, and the shootings on or about May 7, 1964, May 20, 1964, and August 2, 1964.

larger than that for nonwhites, partly because of the different death rates and partly because of migration differences.

"The potential for future increases in the number of older persons is found in the age group from 45 to 64 years of age * * * Persons of this age increased by about 45 percent from 1930 to 1960 with the white rate of increase greater than that of nonwhites.

"Young adults, from 20 to 44 years of age, increased during the 1930's, but dropped by about 200,000 between 1940 and 1960. Most of this decline, 150,000, is represented by the decreasing number of nonwhites at these ages. Part of the decline is the result of lower birth rates during the depression years, but the bulk of the loss is the result of migration from the state.

"The youngest segment of the population, under 20 years of age, is composed essentially of preschool and school age young people. The size of this group remained fairly stable from 1930 to 1950, but rose during the 1950's * * * Young whites represented a smaller proportion of the white population in 1960 than in 1930, whereas nonwhites showed a higher proportion."

INCOME OF THE POPULATION

Viewed in any one of several ways for measuring economic well-being, nonwhite Mississippians, as a group, live on substantially lower incomes than do whites. Table 4 sets forth one measure, family income [4] for 1959, for the total population as well as the white and nonwhite portions. In 1959, the median yearly income for nonwhite families in the State was only $1,444; the median for whites was almost three times as high at $4,209.[5] During that year more than 80 percent of nonwhite families in the State existed on less than $3,000 family income—the basic income level which the Federal Government deems to be the dividing line for the war on poverty—while a substantially smaller but still very significant percentage of white families, 34 percent, had incomes below than level. At the other end of the income scale, about 26,000 white families enjoyed incomes of $10,000 or more, but only 775 nonwhite families were that affluent. In between the two extremes are almost 58 percent of the white families with incomes from $3,000 to $10,000, but only 17 percent of the nonwhite families with such incomes.

The income differences between the white and nonwhite population of Mississippi are sharply portrayed when comparison is made on such criteria as occupation, years of schooling completed, and family type and age. Nonwhite males in professional and technical occupations, for example, had a median income only slightly more than one-half that of the white males in the same occupation in 1959. In no occupation groups does the nonwhite male population have a median income above the $3,000 level, of which we hear so much of late. It should be noted also that for 5 of the 12 occupational groupings in Table 5, the white male median income figure is below the $3,000 level, pointing up the fact that Mississippi is not a wealthy state.

---

[4] The 1960 census definition of "family" is "two or more persons living in the same household who are related to each other by blood, marriage, or adoption; all persons living in one household who are related to each other are regarded as one family." Family income does not include nonmonetary income such as imputed rent.

[5] Median income in 1959 for families and unrelated individuals as reported in the 1960 census was $1,168 for nonwhites and $3,565 for whites, again a ratio of about 1 to 3. Unrelated individuals are defined as "(1) a member of a household who is living entirely alone or with persons all of whom are not related to him, or (2) a person living in group quarters who is not an inmate of an institution."

TABLE 4.—*Family income in Mississippi by color—1959*

	All families		White		Nonwhite	
	Number	Percent	Number	Percent	Number	Percent
Under $1,000	98,462	19.7	32,751	10.1	65,711	37.1
$1,000–$1,999	90,262	18.0	38,622	11.9	51,640	29.1
$2,000–$2,999	69,825	13.9	40,216	12.4	29,609	16.7
$3,000–$3,999	56,128	11.2	41,954	13.0	14,174	8.0
$4,000–$4,999	46,822	9.3	39,443	12.2	7,379	4.2
$5,000–$5,999	39,598	7.9	36,009	11.1	3,589	2.0
$6,000–$6,999	29,028	5.8	26,967	8.3	2,061	1.2
$7,000–$7,999	21,176	4.2	19,795	6.1	1,381	0.8
$8,000–$8,999	14,393	2.9	13,799	4.3	594	0.3
$9,000–$9,999	9,303	1.9	8,896	2.7	407	0.2
$10,000–$14,999	18,032	3.6	17,382	5.4	650	0.4
$15,000–$24,999	5,769	1.2	5,675	1.8	94	0.1
$25,000 or more	2,123	0.4	2,092	0.6	31	
Total	500,921	100.0	323,601	99.9	177,320	100.1
Median Income	$2,884		$4,209		$1,444	
Percentage nonwhite to white median			34.3			

Source: United States Census of Population, General Social and Economic Characteristics, Mississippi 1960.

Education is often viewed as the panacea for all the ills of society. While it probably is not the cure-all, politicians, economists, and, in fact, most educators stress the advantages of a well-trained and well-educated citizenry. There is no question that today's complex society and economy more readily absorb the well-educated while tending to reject the not-so-well educated. Certainly there is little question that income tends to increase with increased education.

Table 6 shows 1960 median incomes of persons age 25 and over by color, sex, and years of school completed. There is a striking and pronounced upward trend in incomes for both the white and nonwhite portions of the population as the years of education increase. As might be expected in today's economy, the median income for both white and nonwhite males is extremely low for those with less than a high school education. The disparity of income between white and nonwhite males, while substantial in some cases below the high school level of education, is of greater magnitude beyond that point.

For example, the nonwhite male median income is 89 percent of the white income where no education has been obtained, but only 52 percent when a college education has been obtained. Median income for the nonwhite male college graduate is $3,258 as compared with $6,288 for the white college graduate. The disparity of income between the white and nonwhite women is not as pronounced as in the case of males. Yet it is interesting to note that the median income of nonwhite women who were high school graduates was approximately the equivalent of that of white women completing elementary school. However, the median income of nonwhite women completing college was 90 percent of that for white women with college degrees.

July 11, 1964, and arrests that were made in connection with that bombing. And that is the only further information we have.

If I may make a request of the Commission, that is a permanent jail docket and we would certainly like to have it back as quickly as possible.

Chairman HANNAH. Would tomorrow be soon enough?

Mr. GOZA. Yes, sir, Mr. Chairman, it would. One of those documents has nothing whatsoever of interest to this Commission in it, and if we may take it back with us, we would appreciate it.

Mr. TAYLOR. Mr. Chairman, I would recommend that we copy the relevant portions of these documents and return them before the witness leaves today, and the other items can be returned on the return date of the subpena, which is later in the week. Would that be satisfactory?

Mr. GOZA. That will be satisfactory. Could we have a determination by the Commission or its representative that one of the dockets has nothing of interest in it; the little black book is merely a log which could be probably photostated. Could we have such a determination at this time?

Mr. FINKELSTEIN. Well, we will have to examine the books.

Mr. GOZA. Fine. But will we have that determination before we leave?

Mr. TAYLOR. We will return the books to you.

Mr. GOZA. Fine.

Chairman HANNAH. Anything further, Mr. Taylor? When are these gentlemen to return?

Mr. TAYLOR. Well, the clerk will give a receipt for the aforementioned documents, and I recommend that the witness be kept under subpena and excused until Friday, February 19, at 9 a.m.

Chairman HANNAH. You are excused.

(Witness excused.)

Mr. TAYLOR. The next witness is Sheriff Jack Cauthen, Sheriff of Madison County.

Chairman HANNAH. Sheriff, will you raise your right hand?

(Whereupon, Mr. Jack Cauthen was duly sworn by the Chairman and testified as follows:)

Chairman HANNAH. Will you introduce your counsel, sir?

Mr. CAUTHEN. This is Mr. W. S. Cain.

Chairman HANNAH. Mr. Taylor, proceed.

TESTIMONY OF JACK CAUTHEN, SHERIFF, MADISON COUNTY, MISS.

Mr. TAYLOR. Mr. Cauthen, are you the Sheriff of Madison County?

Mr. CAUTHEN. Yes, sir.

Mr. TAYLOR. You are here pursuant to a subpena calling for precisely the same documents as I read with respect to Police Chief Thompson.

Mr. CAUTHEN. Yes.

Mr. TAYLOR. Unless you would like me to, I will not repeat——

Mr. CAUTHEN. I heard it all, so that's all right.

Mr. TAYLOR. I ask you to produce the documents called for in the subpena.

Mr. CAUTHEN. Can I start with No. 1, please?

Mr. TAYLOR. Yes, sir.

Mr. CAUTHEN. There was no complaint made. I have no records or documents pertaining to No. 1.

Mr. TAYLOR. That is the——

Mr. CAUTHEN. This is Mr. Kizilbash.

Mr. TAYLOR. Yes, sir; proceed.

Mr. CAUTHEN. No. 2(a), I have no records. All this is pertaining to the city, what happened within the city of Canton. Everything there was more or less handled by the police and—just a second. Any records that I have would be contained in this jail docket of arrests, convictions and so forth pertaining to that.

Mr. CAIN. We would submit this jail docket, if it please the Commission, but we would like to have it back as soon as we can get it, under the same conditions that the marshal of the city submitted his.

Mr. TAYLOR. With the Commission's permission, we can copy any relevant information from the docket and make it available tomorrow morning if someone wishes to claim it at that time.

Mr. CAIN. Thank you, sir.

Mr. CAUTHEN. That will be available tomorrow morning?

Mr. TAYLOR. Yes, sir, at our office in this building.

Mr. CAUTHEN. Would that be this same office?

Mr. TAYLOR. That is Room C–125.

Mr. CAUTHEN. Is that the address on the subpena?

Mr. TAYLOR. Yes.

Mr. CAUTHEN. All right. That's fine.

Mr. TAYLOR. You may proceed.

Mr. CAUTHEN. Pertaining to (b), that will be the same answer.

Mr. TAYLOR. The only record you would have of (b) is any record contained in the jail docket that you have already submitted?

Mr. CAUTHEN. That's right. And there will be no record in there because there was no arrest made by my office. As for (c), there was an investigation by the Canton police, one representative of my office, the Mississippi Highway Patrol, and the FBI. I have no records on (c).

TABLE 7.—*Median 1959 incomes of families and unrelated individuals in Mississippi, classified by family type, age, race and sex*

Age of Family Head or of Individual	Medians		Percentage nonwhite to white medians
	White	Nonwhite	
Husband-wife families:			
Under 35	$4,591	$1,737	37.8
35–44	5,422	1,886	34.8
45–64	4,301	1,579	36.7
65 and over	1,958	1,189	60.7
All	4,406	1,583	35.9
Other families—male heads	2,889	1,412	48.9
Other families—female heads	2,479	950	38.3
All families	4,209	1,444	34.3
Unrelated individuals—male:			
Under 35	1,042	823	79.0
35–44	3,318	1,060	31.9
45–64	1,557	843	54.1
65 and over	869	599	68.9
All	1,119	765	68.4
Female:			
Under 35	719	607	84.4
35–44	2,897	653	22.5
45–64	1,491	586	39.3
65 and over	755	532	70.5
All	882	575	65.2
All unrelated individuals	957	644	67.3

Source: United States Census of Population, Detailed Characteristics, Mississippi 1960.

TABLE 8.—*Employment in major industry-groups in Mississippi employing 20,000 or more persons—1960, and percentage change in totals from 1940–60*

	Number	Percent of all employed	Number	Percent of all white employed	Number	Percent of all non-white employed	Percent change in total number employed 1940–60
Agriculture	142,860	20.9	54,865	12.8	87,995	34.9	66.0
Construction	44,849	6.6	33,218	7.7	11,631	4.6	84.2
Manufacturing	130,804	19.2	100,377	23.3	30,427	12.1	95.6
Furniture and lumber and wood products	34,197	5.0	17,842	4.1	16,355	6.5	8.9
Apparel and other fabricated textile products	27,060	4.0	26,625	6.2	435	0.2	274.5
Retail trade:							
Other than food and dairy product stores or eating and drinking places	60,411	8.9	50,159	11.7	10,252	4.1	95.6
Private households	52,090	7.6	4,123	1.0	47,967	19.0	5.2
Other personal services	21,480	3.1	11,983	2.8	9,497	3.8	41.2
Public (Government) educational services	30,167	4.4	18,928	4.4	11,239	4.5	85.5
Public administration	24,573	3.6	22,723	5.3	1,850	0.7	112.7

Source: United States Census of Population, General Social and Economic Characteristics, Mississippi 1960.

TABLE 9.—*Median 1959 family income in Mississippi by industry of head, experienced labor force—1960*

Agriculture, forestry, and fisheries _____ $1, 437
Construction _____ 3, 601
Manufacturing _____ 4, 091
Retail trade _____ 3, 964
Personal services _____ 1, 668
Public administration _____ 5, 655

Source: United States Census of Population, Detailed Characteristics, Mississippi 1960.

The furniture, lumber and wood products industry, which accounted for the largest number of manufacturing employees in 1960, expanded only slightly between 1940–60. It accounted for a higher percentage of total nonwhites employed than whites but at the same time employed about as many whites as nonwhites. On the other hand, Mississippi's rapidly expanding apparel industry, the industry employing the second largest number of manufacturing employees, with 27,000 workers in 1960, employed fewer than 500 nonwhites that year.

Retail trade (other than food and dairy product stores or eating and drinking places), where jobs increased about 96 percent in the 20-year period from 1940 to 1960, accounted for only 4 percent of all nonwhite employed persons in 1960 compared to approximately 12 percent of whites. The median 1959 income for families whose head was employed in the retail trade was $3,964, yielding only to manufacturing and public administration for higher median incomes in industries employing more than 20,000 persons.

In private household work, where total employment has remained almost unchanged since 1940, nonwhites constituted over 90 percent of all employees in 1960. About 19 percent of all nonwhites employed in Mississippi were in this category as contrasted to 7.6 percent of total whites employed. Public education contained about the same percentage of nonwhite total employment (4.5 percent) as that for whites (4.4 percent). In public administration, where 1959 median income was $5,655 for families whose head was so employed, there was less than one percent of the total nonwhites employed compared to over five percent of total whites employed in the State.

OCCUPATIONAL DISTRIBUTION

Turning to the kinds of jobs that persons occupy—the occupational distribution of employed persons in 1960—there is generally a concentration of nonwhites in occupations in which there has been a declining or static demand for workers between 1940 and 1960. This holds true for the male farmers and farm managers, for farm laborers and foremen, and for laborers exclusive of farm and mine work, as well as for the female private household workers, farm laborers, and foremen. Noteworthy exceptions are male operatives and kindred, and females employed as service workers outside private households. Generally, the median incomes were lowest in the occupations showing a heavy concentration of the nonwhite population. This is not so pronounced in the two exceptions mentioned above, however, where the median income of the family head is $3,410 and $2,719, respectively.

Mr. TAYLOR. Yes, sir. Next item is (g), I believe.

Mr. CAUTHEN. The burning of the Willing Workers' Meeting Hall at Gluckstadt was investigated by a member of my office, a member from the Fire Marshal's office, at our request, and two investigators from the Mississippi Highway Patrol. Practically the same answer there.

Mr. TAYLOR. All right.

Mr. CAUTHEN. And for the last one, same thing.

Mr. TAYLOR. Will you submit that report also?

Mr. CAIN. We will have to prepare them. You understand we don't have them. We are going to prepare them.

Mr. TAYLOR. The report of your own investigation.

Mr. CAIN. That's correct.

Mr. TAYLOR. And you have no other documents in your possession?

Mr. CAIN. No.

Mr. TAYLOR. All right. Proceed.

Mr. CAUTHEN. Exactly the same answer for the others, (h) and (i).

Mr. TAYLOR. Investigations were made by persons under your supervision along with other investigative agencies.

Mr. CAUTHEN. Yes, sir.

Mr. TAYLOR. Do I understand your answer is that you have no documents relating to this, but you can submit a report to be prepared by an investigator? Is that correct?

Mr. CAUTHEN. That is correct.

Mr. TAYLOR. You have no documents of your own or of any other authorities such as the Highway Patrol?

Mr. CAUTHEN. We do not.

Mr. TAYLOR. In that case, the clerk will give you a receipt for the document submitted. I recommend that the witness be kept under subpena and excused until Friday, February 19, at 9 a.m.

Chairman HANNAH. Mr. Cauthen, you indicated that you had recently come into office when some of these incidents occurred. When did you assume the office of sheriff?

Mr. CAUTHEN. January 6, 1964.

Mr. TAYLOR. My last statement was that you were excused for the time being but are still under subpena and are to return February 19—that's a Friday—at 9 a.m.

Mr. CAUTHEN. At the same place?

Mr. TAYLOR. At the same place, yes, sir.

Mr. CAIN. We will bring in the report from the Highway Patrol tomorrow morning. We will bring in these others Friday morning, if that meets with your approval. We will have to prepare them.

Chairman HANNAH. But he will bring in copies of what you now

TABLE 11.—*Median 1959 family income by occupation of head, Mississippi—1960*

Professional, technical and kindred	$6,315
Farmers and farm managers	1,557
Managers, officials and proprietors, except farm	6,296
Clerical and kindred	5,287
Sales workers	5,467
Craftsmen, foremen and kindred	4,555
Operatives and kindred	3,410
Private household workers	1,064
Service workers, except private household	2,719
Farm laborers, unpaid family workers	806
Farm laborers, excluding unpaid and foremen	1,159
Laborers, excluding farm and mine	2,343

Source: United States Census of Population, Detailed Characteristics, Mississippi, 1960.

REFLECTORS OF ECONOMIC STATUS

The preceding information relates largely to income and employment as an index of the economic well-being of the people of Mississippi. Other indices of the welfare of the population may be found in statistics on the conditions or circumstances of human existence such as housing, welfare status, and education. While these facts may be considered as a product or result of income, they may also be considered as reflecting the income status of the individual. At any rate, they are necessary to complete the picture of the economic and social environment of the population.

HOUSING

Of fundamental importance to the material welfare of people is housing. In addition to supplying a basic physical necessity, housing—or the quality of housing—has significance in other respects such as physical and mental health, work performance, and self-respect. Economists agree that there tends to be a relationship between home ownership and income. Table 12 reveals that 57.7 percent of the 580,070 dwelling units in Mississippi are owner-occupied while 42.3 percent are occupied by renters. This ratio is practically the same when broken down into urban and rural residents, with rural residents showing 1.1 percent more home owners than urban dwellers. When divided along racial lines, however, there are more noticeable contrasts. While 69 percent of white housing units are owner-occupied, only 38.1 percent of nonwhite units are in this category. The differences are slightly less among urban residents where 64.5 percent of the white units are occupied by owners compared to 42.3 percent of the nonwhite units. The spread is greater, however, in rural units where the percentage of owners is 72.5 percent for whites and 35.6 percent for nonwhites.

Of greater importance than ownership, perhaps, is the adequacy of the dwelling unit. One standard of adequacy is size, measured by the number of persons per room. Table 13 contains information on occupants per room for the entire State, and broken down into rural and urban and white and nonwhite categories. It will be noted that 35.3 percent of the occupied units have .50 or less persons per room and that this ranges downward to 12.1 percent with 1.50 or more persons per room. The percentage of units with 1.50 or more residents is less for urban residents (8.4) and slightly higher (14.8) for rural residents. Considerable variation is noted between white and nonwhite residents. Of the most spacious residences (.50 or less persons per room), 40.4 percent are white and 26.4 percent are nonwhite. Large variation also exists for the less spacious units and is particularly evident in the least spacious category (1.50 or more persons per room) where the figure is 4 percent for whites and 26.3 percent for nonwhites. These disparities between whites and nonwhites do not vary greatly when divided into urban and rural categories.

Another standard of adequacy or comfort in housing is the facilities with which the dwelling units are equipped. Among the facilities usually considered most important are water supply, toilet facilities, and bathing facilities. Of the total of 628,945 housing units in Mississippi (see Table 14), 54.7 percent have hot and cold water piped inside while 27.8 percent have no piped water. In white housing 71.9 percent of the units have hot and cold water inside. If the figures are confined to nonwhite residences, however, only 19.7 percent are so equipped while nearly half (48.2 percent) have no piped water.

TABLE 12.—*Tenure of occupied housing units, by color, urban and rural, Mississippi—1960*

	All units		White		Nonwhite	
	Number	Percent of Total	Number	Percent of white	Number	Percent of nonwhite
THE STATE Total occupied units	568,070	100.0	360,459	100.0	207,611	100.0
Owner-occupied	327,894	57.7	248,835	69.0	79,059	38.1
Renter-occupied	240,176	42.3	111,624	31.0	128,552	61.9
URBAN Total occupied units	233,260	100.0	155,436	100.0	77,824	100.0
Owner-occupied	133,170	57.1	100,257	64.5	32,913	42.3
Renter-occupied	100,090	42.9	55,179	35.5	44,911	57.7
RURAL Total occupied units	334,810	100.0	205,023	100.0	129,787	100.0
Owner-occupied	194,724	58.2	148,578	72.5	46,146	35.6
Renter-occupied	140,086	41.8	56,445	27.5	83,641	64.4

Source: United States Census of Housing, State and Small Areas, Mississippi 1960.

The disparity between facilities is further noted in the table which shows that while 73.9 percent of all white units have flush toilets, only 33.6 percent of the nonwhite residences have such equipment. This means that 66.4 percent of nonwhite units have nonflush toilets or no toilets facilities at all. In bath facilities it will be noted that 73.1 percent of white residences have bathtubs or showers compared with 22.7 percent of nonwhite units which have such facilities. Thus 77.3 percent of nonwhite residences have no bathtub or shower. As may be expected, a breakdown of these statistics into urban and rural categories reveals that of all urban residence units, 78.7 percent have hot and cold water piped inside, 91 percent have flush toilets, and 81.6 percent have bathtubs or showers. Among all rural housing units the percentages are 38.9, 40.6 and 40 respectively. The nonwhite residences vary greatly from the white units on these items. Of the white urban units 95.1 percent have hot and cold water piped inside, 97.7 percent have flush toilets, and 96.5 percent have bathtubs or showers. Of the nonwhite urban units 42.6 percent have hot and cold water inside, 76.4 percent have flush toilets, and only 49 percent have bathtubs or showers. The figures on rural residences vary even more widely. While 56 percent of rural white units have hot and cold water piped inside, only 5.9 percent of nonwhite houses are so equipped; 57.5 percent of white houses and 7.9 percent of nonwhite houses have flush toilets; 57.1 percent of white units and 7 percent of nonwhite units have bathtubs or showers. The highest percentages on lack of facilities thus reveal that 92.1 percent of nonwhite rural units have nonflush toilets or none, and that 93 percent have no facilities for bathing.

A third standard for measuring housing adequacy is the physical condition of occupied units. For such statistics we use three classes of residence units designated as sound, deteriorating, and dilapidated as shown in Table 15. It will be noted that of all units in the State 61.1 percent are classified as sound and only 13.4 percent as dilapidated. As the figures show the urban units are in better condition than those in rural areas. Considered in white and nonwhite categories it will be observed that 76.8 percent of white units are classified as

TABLE 13.—*Persons per room in occupied housing units, by color, urban and rural, Mississippi—1960*

	All units		White		Nonwhite	
	Number	Percent of all units	Number	Percent of white units	Number	Percent of non-white units
THE STATE						
Persons per room:						
0.50 or less	200,307	35.3	145,448	40.4	54,859	26.4
0.51 to 0.75	114,914	20.2	82,290	22.8	32,624	15.7
0.76 to 1.00	119,421	21.0	84,267	23.4	35,154	16.9
1.01 to 1.50	64,453	11.3	33,982	9.4	30,471	14.7
1.51 or more	68,975	12.1	14,472	4.0	54,503	26.3
Total occupied units	568,070	100.0	360,459	100.0	207,611	100.0
URBAN						
Persons per room:						
0.50 or less	87,587	37.5	63,959	41.1	23,628	30.4
0.51 to 0.75	51,277	22.0	37,779	24.3	13,498	17.3
0.76 to 1.00	52,477	22.5	38,151	24.5	14,326	18.4
1.01 to 1.50	22,419	9.6	11,847	7.6	10,572	13.6
1.51 or more	19,500	8.4	3,700	2.4	15,800	20.3
Total occupied units	233,260	100.0	155,436	100.0	77,824	100.0
RURAL						
Persons per room:						
0.50 or less	112,720	33.7	81,489	39.7	31,231	24.1
0.51 to 0.75	63,637	19.0	44,511	21.7	19,126	14.7
0.76 to 1.00	66,944	20.0	46,116	22.5	20,828	16.0
1.01 to 1.50	42,034	12.6	22,135	10.8	19,899	15.3
1.51 or more	49,475	14.8	10,772	5.3	38,703	29.8
Total occupied units	334,810	100.0	205,023	100.0	129,787	100.0

Source: United States Census of Housing, State and Small Areas, Mississippi 1960.

sound and only 5.2 percent as dilapidated. Figures on nonwhite units, in considerable contrast, show only 33.6 percent sound and 27.8 percent dilapidated. The breakdown into urban and rural housing shows no great difference from the contrast between white and nonwhite in the whole State.

TABLE 14.—*Selected facilities in housing units, by total, white, and nonwhite heads of household, urban and rural, Mississippi—1960*

	All units		White		Nonwhite	
	Number	Percent of all units	Number	Percent of white	Number	Percent of nonwhite
THE STATE						
Total housing units	628,945	100.0	421,334	100.0	207,611	100.0
Water supply:						
Hot and cold piped inside	343,802	54.7	302,932	71.9	40,870	19.7
Only cold piped water inside	74,477	11.8	35,376	8.4	39,101	18.8
Piped water outside	35,610	5.7	8,108	1.9	27,502	13.2
No piped water	175,056	27.8	74,918	17.8	100,138	48.2
Toilet facilities:						
Flush toilet	380,974	60.6	311,604	73.9	69,730	33.6
Other toilet facilities or none	247,971	39.4	110,090	26.1	137,881	66.4
Bathing facilities:						
Bathtub or shower	355,282	56.5	308,084	73.1	47,198	22.7
No bathtub or shower	273,663	43.5	113,250	26.9	160,413	77.3
URBAN						
Total housing units	249,156	100.0	171,332	100.0	77,824	100.0
Water supply:						
Hot and cold piped inside	196,199	78.7	163,018	95.1	33,181	42.6
Only cold piped water inside	36,220	14.5	5,844	3.4	30,376	39.0
Piped water outside	11,600	4.6	1,371	.8	10,229	13.1
No piped water	5,137	2.1	1,099	.7	4,038	5.2
Toilet facilities:						
Flush toilet	226,804	91.0	167,358	97.7	59,446	76.4
Other toilet facilities or none	22,352	9.0	3,947	2.3	18,378	23.6
Bathing facilities:						
Bathtub or shower	203,401	81.6	165,261	96.5	38,140	49.0
No bathtub or shower	45,755	18.4	6,071	3.5	39,684	51.0
RURAL						
Total housing units	379,789	100.0	250,002	100.0	129,787	100.0
Water supply:						
Hot and cold piped water inside	147,603	38.9	139,914	56.0	7,689	5.9
Only cold piped water inside	38,257	10.1	29,532	11.8	8,725	6.7
Piped water outside	24,010	6.3	6,737	2.7	17,273	13.3
No piped water	169,919	44.7	73,819	29.5	96,100	74.0
Toilet facilities:						
Flush toilet	154,170	40.6	143,866	57.5	10,284	7.9
Other toilet facilities or none	225,619	59.4	106,116	42.5	119,503	92.1
Bathing facilities:						
Bathtub or shower	151,881	40.0	142,823	57.1	9,058	7.0
No bathtub or shower	227,908	60.0	107,179	42.9	120,729	93.0

Source: United States Census of Housing, States and Small Areas, Mississippi 1960.

In summary it may be said that housing is far from satisfactory as a factor in the material well-being of the State's people. This is especially noticeable in the nonwhite places of residence. The high figures on crowded occupancy, dilapidation, and lack of water and toilet facilities indicate that they contribute to other and broader problems such as public health and public safety.

WELFARE STATUS

Another indicator of the well-being of the State's people may be found in the statistics on the extent and distribution of the program of public assistance. Since this program is administered by professionally trained workers it should provide a reliable index to the poverty of the population.

TABLE 15.—*Condition of occupied housing units by color of head of household for the State, urban and rural—1960*

	All units		White		Nonwhite	
	Number	Percent of all units	Number	Percent of white units	Number	Percent of nonwhite units
THE STATE [1]						
Sound	346,821	61.1	276,997	76.8	69,824	33.6
Deteriorating	145,012	25.5	64,838	18.0	80,174	38.6
Dilapidated	76,237	13.4	18,624	5.2	57,613	27.8
Total	568,070	100.0	360,459	100.0	207,611	100.0
URBAN						
Sound	165,419	70.9	132,448	85.2	32,971	42.4
Deteriorating	44,979	19.3	19,037	12.2	25,942	33.3
Dilapidated	22,862	9.8	3,951	2.5	18,911	24.3
Total	233,260	100.0	155,436	100.0	77,824	100.0
RURAL						
Sound	181,402	54.2	144,549	70.5	36,853	28.4
Deteriorating	100,033	29.9	45,801	22.3	54,232	41.8
Dilapidated	53,375	15.9	14,673	7.2	38,702	29.8
Total	334,810	100.0	205,023	100.0	129,787	100.0

[1] As defined by the Bureau of the Census: *Sound* housing is that which has no defects or defects so slight as to be corrected in the course of regular maintenance; *deteriorating* housing is that which needs more repair than would be provided in the course of regular maintenance and which must be corrected if the unit is to continue to provide safe and adequate shelter; *dilapidated* housing is that which does not provide safe and adequate shelter and in its present condition endangers the health, safety, or well-being of the occupants.

Source: United States Census of Housing, State and Small Areas, Mississippi 1960.

Table 16 shows the Mississippi public assistance cases and payments by type and race for the month of September 1964. The total number of persons receiving assistance, 161,138, represents about 7.4 percent of the population (as of 1960). It will be noted that, including all types of assistance, 61.66 percent of the cases are nonwhite and 38.34 percent are white, although whites constitute 57.7 percent of the total population and nonwhites 42.3 percent. This disparity is noted in all types of assistance but is particularly great in the category of aid to dependent children where 81.16 percent of the cases are nonwhite.

Table 17 is further illustrative of the pattern of public assistance. This table shows the program by type of assistance, by race, and by amount of monthly payment. One will note the near uniformity of the monthly payments, not only as between races but as between the different types of assistance. For example, the average monthly payment to persons in the old age assistance group is $37.20 while the payment to each case in the dependent children category is $39.34. The significance of this comparison will be seen when it is remembered that each case of dependent children is a household or a group and that the 20,898 cases represent 66,574 children, or an average of 3.18 children per case. Thus the average monthly payment per child in this type of aid is $12.37.

TABLE 16.—*Mississippi public assistance cases by type, by race, September 1964* [1]

Type of assistance	White		Nonwhite [2]	
	Number of cases	Percent of cases	Number of cases	Percent of cases
Total	44,272	38.34	71,190	61.66
Old age assistance	32,089	43.52	41,641	56.48
Aid to the blind	955	34.46	1,816	65.54
Aid to dependent children	3,937	18.84	16,961	81.16
Aid to the permanently and totally disabled	7,291	40.37	10,772	59.63

Mississippi public assistance payments by type, by race, September 1964

Type of assistance	White		Nonwhite [3]	
	Amount of payments	Percent of payments	Amount of payments	Percent of payments
Total	$1,693,153.00	37.86	$2,778,862.00	62.14
Old age assistance	1,198,354.00	43.70	1,544,096.00	56.30
Aid to the blind	41,852.00	34.19	80,541.00	65.81
Aid to dependent children	138,755.00	16.88	683,326.00	83.12
Aid to the permanently and totally disabled	314,192.00	40.02	470,899.00	59.98

[1] Compiled from report of Division of Research and Statistics, Mississippi State Department of Public Welfare.

[2] Includes Indians and Chinese.

[3] There was a total of 66,574 children in the 20,898 cases of which 10,567 were white, 55,738 were Negro, and 269 were Indian or Chinese.

A comparison of these statistics with those of 5 years ago reveals little change in the general picture of the State's recipients of public assistance. Figures [6] for September 1959, compared with those for September 1964, show an increase of only 0.1 percent in the total number of cases. Over the period the white cases decreased 2.4 percent and the nonwhite cases increased 1.5 percent. In certain types of assistance the racial difference is more important. In old age assistance the number of white cases decreased 5 percent while the number of nonwhite cases increased 11.1 percent. The number of white dependent children receiving

[6] These percentages are taken from Memorandum No. 1447, Mississippi Department of Public Welfare, December 30, 1964.

assistance decreased 24.2 percent while the number of nonwhite children receiving such assistance increased 27.4 percent during the period. There was a large increase in the number of disabled persons receiving assistance in both categories, with the number of whites going up 91.4 percent and the number of nonwhites increasing 89.3 percent since 1959. Obviously, the presence of a large indigent group in the population is a continuing problem.

Naturally, serious questions may be raised as to the adequacy of the public assistance program, particularly as to the amount of payments. To a very large degree, however, the amounts are geared to the State's ability to pay and thus, are another indicator of the economic conditions which prevail.

TABLE 17.—*Mississippi public assistance by type, by race, by amount of payment, September 1964*[1]

Type of assistance	Total cases		White		Nonwhite[2]	
	Number of cases	Average monthly payment	Number of cases	Average monthly payment	Number of cases	Average monthly payment
Total	115,462	$38.73	44,272	$38.24	71,190	$39.17
Old age assistance	73,730	37.20	32,089	37.34	41,641	37.08
Aid to the blind	2,771	44.16	955	43.82	1,816	44.36
Aid to dependent children	[3]20,898	39.34	3,937	35.24	16,961	40.29
Aid to the permanently and totally disabled	18,063	43.46	7,291	43.09	10,772	43.72

[1] Compiled from report of Division of Research and Statistics, Mississippi State Department of Public Welfare.

[2] Includes Indians and Chinese.

[3] Of the 20,898 cases there was a total of 66,574 children of which 10,567 were white, 56,007 were nonwhite.

TABLE 18.—*Years of school completed by persons 25 years and over by color, Mississippi—1960*

Number of years of education	Total population 25 years and over		White		Nonwhite	
	Number	Percent of total	Number	Percent of white	Number	Percent of nonwhite
No school years completed	40,640	3.8	8,444	1.2	32,196	8.4
Elementary:						
1 to 4 years	160,015	15.0	40,274	5.9	119,741	31.3
5 to 7 years	202,383	19.0	90,315	13.2	112,068	29.3
8 years	145,737	13.7	98,287	14.4	47,450	12.4
High school:						
1 to 3 years	199,101	18.7	156,554	23.0	42,547	11.1
4 years	184,331	17.3	168,058	24.6	16,273	4.2
College:						
1 to 3 years	73,496	6.9	67,504	9.9	5,992	1.6
4 years	59,273	5.6	52,523	7.7	6,750	1.8
Total	1,064,976	100.0	681,959	100.0	383,017	100.0
Median years of school completed	8.9		11.0		6.0	

Source: United States Census of Population, General Social and Economic Characteristics, Mississippi 1960.

EDUCATIONAL ACHIEVEMENT

A final aspect of the welfare of a State's population is the level of education. A definite correlation between education and income can be easily established. Table 18 gives data on the level of education of people in Mississippi. It shows that only 3.8 percent of the people have no schooling and that the median years of school completed are 8.9. When broken down into white and nonwhite groups, there is a large variation. While only 1.2 percent of whites have had no schooling, the proportion of nonwhites without schooling is 8.4 percent. The median years of school completed are also in marked contrast, showing 11 years for whites compared to 6 years for nonwhites. Other comparisons show much the same contrast. For example, the percentage of whites with 4 years of college education is 7.7 percent while for nonwhites it is 1.8 percent.

TABLE 19.—*Employment status of males 14 to 34 years by school enrollment and color for the State, urban, rural-nonfarm and rural-farm—1960*

	All persons	White	Nonwhite
THE STATE			
Total	300,747	186,047	114,700
Enrolled in school	117,950	67,686	50,264
In labor force	33,605	20,676	12,929
Unemployed	(2,179)	(1,290)	(889)
Not in labor force	84,345	47,010	37,335
Not enrolled in school	182,797	118,361	64,436
In labor force	166,107	110,214	55,893
Unemployed	(9,166)	(5,124)	(4,042)
Not in labor force	16,690	8,147	8,543
Percent out of school and out of work [1]	8.6	7.1	11.0
URBAN			
Total	118,258	82,927	35,331
Enrolled in school	40,900	27,642	13,258
In labor force	13,925	10,295	3,630
Unemployed	(1,083)	(713)	(370)
Not in labor force	26,975	17,347	9,628
Not enrolled in school	77,358	55,285	22,073
In labor force	73,022	53,115	19,907
Unemployed	(3,645)	(1,597)	(2,048)
Not in labor force	4,336	2,170	2,166
Percent out of school and out of work [1]	6.7	4.5	11.9
RURAL			
Total	182,489	103,120	79,369
Enrolled in school	77,050	40,044	37,006
In labor force	19,680	10,381	9,299
Unemployed	(1,096)	(577)	(519)
Not in labor force	57,370	29,663	27,707
Not enrolled in school	105,439	63,076	42,363
In labor force	93,085	57,099	35,986
Unemployed	(5,521)	(3,527)	(1,994)
Not in labor force	12,354	5,977	6,377
Percent out of school and out of work	9.8	9.2	10.5

[1] Nonenrollees who are unemployed or not in the labor force as percent of the total.

Source: United States Census of Population, Detailed Characteristics, Mississippi 1960.

It is natural that the level of education has a relation to employment in the modern economic system. Table 19 shows this relationship in the economy of Mississippi. It will be noted that 8.6 percent of all males between the ages of 14 and 34 are out of school and out of work. Rural residents show a slightly higher percentage (9.8 percent) than urban residents (6.7 percent). Males out of school and out of work constitute 7.1 percent of the total white group. But in the nonwhite group 11 percent are in this category. Only 4.5 percent of urban white males are out of school and out of work but 11.9 percent of the nonwhites are so reported. This disparity between whites and nonwhites is considerably smaller among rural males. In the rural areas 9.2 percent of white males are out of school and out of work and 10.5 percent of the nonwhite males fall in this group. The growing scarcity of rural occupations, as well as the type of education offered in rural areas, may account for the higher percentage of unemployed and out of school white males in that category.

Chairman HANNAH. Mr. Taylor, do we have another guest?

Mr. TAYLOR. Yes, Father Nathaniel.

Chairman HANNAH. Father Nathaniel, we thank you for being here. Will you have a chair, sir.

Reverend MACHESKY. Thank you, sir.

Chairman HANNAH. Mr. Finkelstein?

TESTIMONY OF FATHER NATHANIEL MACHESKY, LEFLORE COUNTY, MISS.

Mr. FINKELSTEIN. Father Nathaniel, we have asked you to come here today to give us a little more flesh and blood picture about what some of the statistics mean for at least one Negro community in Mississippi. I understand that you worked in Greenwood for a number of years, principally with the Negro community. Perhaps you would like to tell us something about your work and some of the problems which that community faces.

Reverend MACHESKY. That is correct, Mr. Finkelstein. I have been in Greenwood since 1950. At that time I began as an assistant at the so-called uptown parish and worked there for a year. And then I was part of a team that established a mission outside town. Ours is not a Negro parish in any sense. We are a Catholic parish. However, it so happens that our parishioners are predominantly Negro.

In 1952, a very fine lady, a native Mississippian, was instrumental in establishing St. Francis Center, staffed by members of Pax Christi, which hopes one day to be a secular institute. This was prompted because of a frightful need among the people in our community and she was instrumental in inaugurating a program known as the Exercise of the Corporeal and the Spiritual Works of Mercy. Unemployment is very, very high. Poverty is present. And our program is one that emphasizes a social program of the works of mercy. The ladies now number something like 13 actually present at the Center, and other centers have been established in Clarksdale and Meridian.

During this time, we also found a great need to establish a voice for the Negroes of the community. The local newspaper, for example, would very, very seldom publish a death notice for Negroes. Our newspaper was established to emphasize the importance of human dignity and also to encourage community projects. There was no sense of community solidarity. The newspaper that we established violated some of the local taboos. I think the ladies and gentlemen of the panel are aware of those. We say "Mr." and "Miss" in our newspaper. And this encouraged local wrath in that, several months ago, a sheet was published known as the Delta Discussion in which advertisers in our paper were warned not to advertise. As a result, all the advertisers abandoned us. Somehow or other we have been able to continue because we feel there is a need for this newspaper. We feel that it is important for establishing human dignity. We feel also that it was instrumental in inaugurating several community projects.

We have a man and woman of the year award toward the close of the year. We have a home improvement campaign in the spring. We feel we were instrumental in inaugurating a very substantial recreational program for youngsters, little boys baseball. We also have an extensive educational program at the center. We have an adult education program known as "Life, Literacy and Instruction for Everyone." Approximately 80 percent of the people that we deal with were functional illiterates. And during all this time we feel like we were making a substantial contribution to people as people because we wanted to emphasize human dignity.

Our population is not strictly Catholic. We ask no questions about what their beliefs are. We simply recognize them as individuals. In order to emphasize human dignity we inaugurated this program. I would like to say also that from the very beginning we have had the encouragement and assistance of the bishops of this diocese, and we also had a great deal of encouragement from others throughout the State. We have had very little local encouragement.

Mr. FINKELSTEIN. Can you tell us anything about the problem of medical care and what you are doing in this field?

Reverend MACHESKY. This program was largely started because Miss Kate and the others with her visited what, at that time, was the Negro hospital. There were no facilities in the local hospital for Negroes. A doctor operated a private clinic. In a visit to this private clinic, Miss Kate and the other ladies were convinced that something had to be done. Now there is a wing at the Greenwood-Leflore Hospital for Negroes. But there is a frightful number of people who are without medical attention because they are either unaware of the facilities at the local welfare office or they are simply unable to obtain it. We have three nurses now who give home nursing classes and who also do a great deal of nursing in the homes.

Mr. FINKELSTEIN. In your opinion, what does the Negro community in Greenwood need most at the present time?

Reverend MACHESKY. Jobs. They need jobs. They need employment opportunities. This is basically an economic problem. Almost 25 percent of the families in Leflore County—twenty-two point something percent earn an income under a thousand dollars. 59.7 percent of the families in Leflore County have an income under $3,000.

There is also a very, very great need for communication. We have made several attempts to encourage communication, but each time we were rebuffed. This may seem facetious, but they say, "We talk to them all the time." But, of course, there is no real communication. There is a very, very serious wall between whites and nonwhites in the community.

Mr. FINKELSTEIN. You say that there is heavy unemployment among the Negroes in Greenwood. What about welfare payments? Are those adequate for these periods of time? Are they available?

Reverend MACHESKY. Welfare payments are available, but certainly these are not adequate, especially where the family is large. We have come across many, many cases where the welfare payments have been discontinued because of an illegitimate birth or because of other circumstances. So this is no solution at all to the very real proverty that exists.

Mr. FINKELSTEIN. No further questions.

Chairman HANNAH. Father Hesburgh?

Commissioner HESBURGH. Father Nathaniel, are you going to try to tie into any of the poverty programs?

Reverend MACHESKY. Yes, Father, we are making an attempt right now.

Commissioner HESBURGH. I think there are a number of things they could do to help. Also, is this hospital facility you speak of getting Federal aid?

Reverend MACHESKY. The Greenwood-Leflore Hospital?

Commissioner HESBURGH. Yes.

Reverend MACHESKY. I believe it was a Hill-Burton hospital.

Commissioner HESBURGH. Well, a Hill-Burton hospital has to serve Negroes. It is part of the Federal law. It might be good to look into that. We are both in the same league, so I am a little more sensitive at times. You say you are taken care of by a group called Pax

Christi, which means the Peace of Christ. If you haven't had Latin, you don't know that. And secondly, they want to be a secular institute. This sounds like something out of the blue, but I think the audience might like to know what kind of people these are and what a secular institute is.

Reverend MACHESKY. These are people who lead a life of total dedication. They remain laymen, but they live a life of consecrated service to the church. After 2½ years of training, they make promises very much like religious servants do, promises of poverty, chastity and obedience. This little group has grown so that they now number some 15 consecrated members and 6 trainees. There are two phases to the work. One is the group apostolate where they live and work together and the other is the individual apostolate where they seek to Christianize the atmosphere in which they live.

Commissioner HESBURGH. Good. I think that makes the shorthand clearer. Thanks a lot.

Chairman HANNAH. Any other questions? Thank you very much, Father. We are very grateful to you. We will take a 10-minute break, and at 10:30 we will have our economic panel.

(Whereupon, the Commission took a short recess, after which it proceeded with the Economic Panel.)

ECONOMIC PANEL, FEBRUARY 20, 1965

The Commission met with the Economic Panel in the Recreation Hall, Veterans Administration Center, 1500 East Woodrow Wilson Drive, Jackson, Miss., at 10:30 a.m., Saturday, February 20, 1965, the Hon. Eugene Patterson presiding.

———

Present: John A. Hannah, Chairman; Eugene Patterson, Vice Chairman; Mrs. Frankie Muse Freeman, Commissioner; Rev. Theodore M. Hesburgh, C.S.C., Commissioner; Robert S. Rankin, Commissioner.

Panel Members: Owen Cooper, President-elect, Mississippi Economic Council; Robert Ezelle, President, Jackson Chamber of Commerce; E. J. Palmer, President, Mississippi Manufacturers Association.

PROCEEDINGS

Vice Chairman PATTERSON. The hearing will come to order. We are privileged today to have with us as guests three distinguished men from the State of Mississippi, businessmen who are distinguished not only in their own businesses but in the business organizations of this

State. I would like to introduce them at this point. On my left, Mr. Owen Cooper, president-elect of the Mississippi Economic Council. On my right, Mr. Robert Ezelle, president of the Jackson Chamber of Commerce. And on the left, Mr. E. J. Palmer, president of the Mississippi Manufacturers Association. Gentlemen, for the record would you briefly give us the composition of the organizations of which you are presidents. Mr. Cooper?

Mr. COOPER. Mr. Chairman, the Mississippi Economic Council is an organization of the business and professional men in Mississippi. It is in reality the State Chamber of Commerce, has members in every county of the State, and speaks as the voice of organized leadership in Mississippi. May I say for the record, however, that no individual speaks for the MEC. I will read a portion of action taken by the MEC and therein the MEC speaks. Otherwise, I will be speaking as an individual.

Vice Chairman PATTERSON. Thank you. Mr. Ezelle?

Mr. EZELLE. The Jackson Chamber of Commerce is an organization of business and professional leaders here in Jackson. There are over 1,500 members. This organization has been on record on some of these issues and that is one of the reasons that we are here today. It does express the business leadership or interest of the city. But I am in the same position as Mr. Cooper. I don't speak for it other than the statement that has been made.

Vice Chairman PATTERSON. Thank you, we understand. Mr. Palmer?

Mr. PALMER. The Mississippi Manufacturers Association is the organization in the State of manufacturers and consists of approximately 650 members. We, of course, are interested in all matters which affect manufacturers, such as legislation, education, and any other concern that might come in to affect our operations.

Vice Chairman PATTERSON. Thank you, gentlemen. The Commission's purpose in being here is to find the facts as they exist today, and not yesterday. We, of course, have found in the testimony before this Commission some evidence of change, some evidence that people are shouldering new commitments in Mississippi, the business community among them. We would like you to express whatever you would like to place into the record of this hearing. We will begin with Mr. Cooper. What role do you see for business in this difficult time, Mr. Cooper?

Mr. COOPER. Mr. Chairman, following the passage of the Civil Rights Act in 1964, many responsible citizens in Mississippi began an agonizing period of reappraisal. It was hard for us to recognize certain things. But we have recognized that the Civil Rights Act is now the law of the land; that we lost the battle. And probably the tactics used during the battle have to change. We may not have always used the very best of tactics during the battle, but this carried on for more than 1 year, as you know. Great adjustments had to be made. And these adjustments affected patterns that covered the past 2 centuries and the habits of yesteryear had to be cast aside. These things are not done easily. But Mississippi is not the same today as it was 6 months ago.

Now social changes take time. I think those of you who work with individuals recognize that sometimes it takes months or even years to rehabilitate or change the pattern of life for an individual. And it may take even longer for a society, or group of individuals. I remember back in my ROTC days we were marching along, the commanding officer would give us "About face," and in two steps we would be walking in the other direction. It was relatively simple. But society does not move with that degree of rapidity. We have an operation on the Gulf Coast down at Pascagoula. We are next door to the refinery that has been built. Somtimes they bring in these tremendous tankers, and our plant happens to be right on the turning basin. It takes a great deal of care and time to turn one of these tankers around in this small area. I think we need to keep in mind that it is going to take time on these things.

But there needs to be a beginning, a starting point, a Jamestown, or whatever you would have it. And the business and professional leaders in Mississippi sometimes begin to talk among themselves. And one of the wholesome signs in Mississippi is that it no longer is taboo to talk about this problem; it is at least out on top of the table and that is a helpful sign. As concerned men began to talk among themselves, they found out other people were thinking about this problem with an equal degree of concern, and they were not alone, as one of the Old Testament prophets found out when he thought he was alone, when he found there were 7,000 in his community that felt like he did. And he found there were many people in Mississippi that were concerned about this. And simultaneously, the political leaders of Mississippi, notably Governor Johnson and Lt. Governor Gartin and State Treasurer Winter and Attorney General Patterson began to speak out as our political leadership hasn't spoken in years. I know it has been called to your attention that even during his inaugural address, Governor Johnson made some statements that have been a source of encouragement and background and probably the foundation on which some of our recent actions have been predicated.

Now, these concerned Mississippians turned to what they considered to be Mississippi's most influential professional and business organization, the Mississippi Economic Council, which is our State Chamber of Commerce. And on February 3, 1965 this State organization adopted and released the following statement which I would like to read. The first portion is somewhat a preamble to the statement, but it reads as follows:

The Mississippi Economic Council, since its organization in 1949, has been concerned with the economic and social well-being of our State. This means that it is concerned with the peace and tranquility of our State.

The recent passage of certain Federal legislation creates monumental problems for Mississippi. The Council opposed the passage of the Civil Rights Act, but as a leadership organization it cannot bury its head in the sand and ignore its existence.

In the past, the Mississippi Economic Council has faced up to its responsibility in dealing with major public problems. It has also spoken out for principles in the field of Federal affairs. For instance, it has repeatedly declared its position: first, for constitutional government and States' rights, and in opposition to any legislation that would destroy the constitutional function of our State and Federal governments; second, for the proposition that education for all citizens is indispensable, and the education provided by public schools is essential; and third, upon the right of controlled public schools as guaranteed to the States by the Constitution of the United States and to finance them without additional Federal funds; fourth, that public schools, colleges and universities must remain open and maintain their integrity, quality, instructional standards and full accreditation.

Then, on February the 3rd, the Council's Board of Directors, in a special session, reviewed these developments and adopted the following statement:

As concerned Mississippians are aware of the monumental problems facing our State, we advance with pride the fact that Mississippi is not an island unto itself but is an integral and responsible part of the United States. We recognize that the Civil Rights Act of 1964 has been enacted by Congress into law. It cannot be ignored and should not be unlawfully defied. Resistance to the law should be through established procedures in the American tradition of resort to enlightened public opinion, to the ballot box, and to the courts. We should adjust ourselves to the impact of this legislation regardless of personal feelings and convictions and limit our resistance to the stated methods.

For the purpose of furthering justice, harmony, and continued development in Mississippi, we respectfully urge the following:

First, order and respect for law must be maintained. Lawless activities in the State by individuals and organizations cannot be tolerated. The penalty of law violations should be fairly and equitably applied to all law violators. Second, communications must be maintained between the races within the State. Third, registration and voting laws should be fairly and impartially administered for all. Fourth, support of public education must be maintained and strengthened.

Mississippians have the capacity and courage to face the problems of this State and to create conditions favorable to their solutions. We call upon all Mississippians to take positive action toward these ends.

Now you have come to get a balanced picture and we hope you get one. We would be the first to admit that there are some dark spots in the picture. And we are not proud of these. We wish they did not exist. But there are some hopeful signs, one of which I have just read: the position of business and professional leadership. And incorporated in this statement, which we would like to make a part of the permanent record, are statements on problems that have not hitherto been made by any group in Mississippi. Another hopeful sign of commitments being made are certain public officials in Mississippi. I know these men and I believe them to be men of sincerity. I believe they will stand behind the commitments that have been made. And then action by certain groups in Mississippi, particularly related to the registration of voters. The circuit clerks and the sheriffs have made statements which I think are most encouraging.

We haven't solved all our problems, and there will be other problems. All of our people will not change at the same pace. Many of them do not feel change should be made. So we haven't solved all of our problems from this day out. And part of the problems will come from within. And we also feel that part of our problems in the future will come from without. There are those who come to our State, some to foment trouble because they represent subversive organizations who thrive on trouble, others to create incidents because on incidents they raise money, and some to raise trouble because they get a kick out of raising trouble. And I believe a fellow that goes into a place trying to get in the jailhouse can find ways to get in there.

But now that the civil rights bill has become law—has been so recognized—now that there is a growing feeling that we are not an island unto ourselves and that our image is important, now that the avenues for discussion of this problem are being opened within race groups and between races, now that business and professional leadership has expressed itself by a statement which we think is positive and comprehensive, and now that our political leaders have expressed themselves, I personally feel that we are at the starting point of a new and a more progressive day in Mississippi in this area as well as other pertinent economic and social matters. Thank you.

Vice Chairman PATTERSON. Thank you, Mr. Cooper.

Mr. Ezelle?

Mr. EZELLE. Thank you, Mr. Patterson. The Jackson Chamber of Commerce was the first business organization that had a statement that went to the public in regard to the Civil Rights Act of 1964. This statement was made on July 3, immediately after the Act became a law. I would like to read this statement for the record:

In view of the passage by the Congress and the signing by the President of the Civil Rights Act, the Board of Directors of the Jackson Chamber of Commerce makes the following statement: 1. The Board of Directors of the Chamber, acting as a policy-making body for this organization of business and professional people, officially opposed the civil rights bill and encouraged opposition to it during the period that it was under consideration in Congress. 2. Now that the bill has been passed, the Chamber Board recommends that business affected comply with the law pending test of its constitutionality in court.

The citizens of Jackson have earned a reputation as a law-abiding community, and the business and professional leadership of the city and our elected city officials have always encouraged all of our people of both races to abide by the law of the land. We may not be in sympathy with all the laws of the land, but we must maintain our standing as a community which abides by the law.

Now the reason for this statement is that at the time of its passage, there were many business and professional people, particularly small businesses, that were affected by it immediately in the transportation and eating field. These people needed guidance. They asked us for guidance. We took the position we have always taken: that a law must be abided by if you are to have a law-abiding community. We feel that this statement at that time when issued was a helpful instrument in helping us get over a rather tough period of time and that it did a lot of good at that time.

On February 3 of this year the Chamber of Commerce held a meeting for its members to discuss Title VII which comes under the Civil Rights Act in July. This meeting was well attended by over a hundred people; in fact, there were several hundred people. And information on this subject I think will be most helpful to the business people in complying and working under this law. On February 5 our Board endorsed the Mississippi Economic Council's statement which had gone further than our position of the previous summer as far as civil rights are concerned. Now I think that these actions show good faith and intent as far as the Jackson business community is concerned in complying with the law. I think that these statements have been helpful in our present situation and have certainly shown a desire to be in the mainstream of American life.

I do not think that we can discuss this situation primarily in the present, Mr. Patterson. I think you need a background of the progress that this State has made over the last 30 to 35 years in 2 fields. And that is the field of economics and the field of education. I believe that these two fields are the general basis of our real problems. I would like to submit for the record a little information that I have collected here which I feel will show progress that has been made in those fields and should be considered in any discussion of problems in Mississippi. This progress can be best shown from an economic standpoint. For example, when you go back to the per capita income of 1933—this is less than 35 years ago—our per capita income at that time was $131 per year. And on a per capita income of that amount, a State has a very difficult time of maintaining any type of adequate educational facilities. This has changed considerably over the years and in 1963 we had a per capita income of $1,390. It is estimated that this will rise to $1,500 in 1964. There is an increase also in percentage of per capita income in the United States. Back in the 1930's our percentage was 34 percent. It is now approximately 56 percent.

Back in 1936 the Mississippi road program was started. In 1936 we had only 992 miles of paved road throughout the entire State. Now if we had wanted to consolidate our schools at that time to the extent we have now, we couldn't have done it because we couldn't have transported the children. In 1965 we now have over 25,000 miles of paved road throughout the State. This represents a tremendous change in the economic situation and the ability of the State to do a better job in this field.

The educational activities of the State of Mississippi receive 65.09 percent of the total appropriation of funds aprpopriated from the general fund appropriation of the State. We were fifth in the Nation as far as expenditures per pupil in elementary and secondary schools are concerned, in comparison with our percentage of per capita income. This means we were giving a lot to education, as far as our abiltiy to pay is concerned. Now, in 1941 and 1942 the average salary of the classroom teacher for whites was $735 per year, and for Negroes it was $232 per year. So you can see, when we checked in 1963 and 1964, the average salary for white was $4,010, the average salary for Negro was $3,565. This is primarily that of teacher qualification rather than a difference primarily in pay. There has been a tremendous stride made in narrowing this gap and in developing proper educational facilities. With that progress that has been made in both those economic and educational fields, with the attitude of business toward complying with the civil rights law, and with these strides forward that we have made in these two important fields, I think we are on the road to a better future.

Vice Chairman PATTERSON. Thank you, Mr. Ezelle.

Mr. PALMER. Many of the members of the Mississippi Manufacturers Association are also members of the Mississippi Economic Council and, as individuals, work very closely. In fact our Board met on the same day that the MEC came out with this statement, and we were the first to endorse it. In addition, we said at this time—and I would like to read the addition of our statement:

As employers of relatively large numbers of people, manufacturers are concerned with the implementation of Title VII of the Civil Rights Act of 1964, the equal employment opportunities section. In the opinion of many, Title VII represents the most far-reaching labor legislation since passage of the Taft-

Hartley Act. We recognize the problems inherent in the implementation of this law for employers everywhere, including Mississippi. We call on all employers in the State to become familiar with its provisions. We urge all Mississippians to understand the facts concerning the law so their opinions and actions may be based on its facts rather than suppositions. We, in turn, pledge our efforts to the dissemination of factual information as a catalyst to objective action.

We respectfully submit to the people of Mississippi, and to their political and civic leadership that Mississippi's future progress in all areas of economic and social development depends greatly on our ability to educate and train our citizenry, young and old, in the most effective manner possible. To that end we urge that all our actions, the actions of all Mississippians, be made in the knowledge that ours is a continually changing society; that technology in agriculture, industry and the trades is constantly changing; and that with this change comes the need for special types of education, training and skills which Mississippi has only recently begun to prepare to provide. Progress in this area of endeavor cannot be stymied by short-sightedness.

We submit that the greatest gain to all of the people of Mississippi comes through gainful employment—in a useful occupation, in an expanding economy in which all citizens, all Mississippians, have the equal opportunity to enjoy the fruits of their own individual labors.

We call on those who lead, and who seek to lead, the destinies of the people of Mississippi to use their every influence in the quest for a solution to the problem facing us. We submit that Mississippians have the capacity to seek the advantages inherent in any adversity. Let us not overlook in the months ahead the many opportunities to be gained through positive and progressive attitudes and actions.

Now, preceding this statement which accompanied our endorsement of the MEC, we had had the opportunity to appear before the ANI board in early November to discuss with them our plans for the implementation of Title VII. At that time we disclosed our plan for a seminar which was held in late November, which was attended by some several hundred representatives of employers. We have underway six additional seminars in various areas of the State. The purpose of this is again to be sure that the Title VII is thoroughly understood, that employers and their representatives know what their responsibilities are in detail and, in addition, to discuss with them a program for orderly implementation. Such implementation will in most cases include discussion with their management and supervisory employees of the facts of this Title VII and what it will mean to them as individuals, and in turn, a discussion of these matters with all of their employees. And we feel that in this manner, in each community where there is a manufacturer, he will be communicating facts to a great broad spectrum of the community. If people contact many of the different activities in the community with facts and with knowledge and with preparation, we sincerely hope this will lead to orderly implementation. I think also it is well to point out that many of the larger manufacturers in the State have already proceeded with implementation and have opened up job opportunities to Negro citizens, which have not previously been open to them, before this Title VII, in fact, becomes the law.

I think we should also point out specifically here, the efforts of manufacturers—and we all are hopeful for a continuing expanding economy because it will be helpful to all of us—through the development of available skills. We have a gap in Mississippi that is evident whether the individual be a white citizen or a Negro citizen. And that gap comes in our technological training—not at the professional level, necessarily, but at the technician or skilled level. We are only, as I have indicated, beginning to touch that. It needs much, much more impetus to be able to cope with our present needs as well as what we hope will be our future needs in that particular area—to be able to place citizens of Mississippi in those jobs that are now open and will come open.

Vice Chairman PATTERSON. Thank you, Mr. Palmer. I can only regard the statements of you three gentlemen and of your organizations as encouraging. Many of us in the South have had growth figures in other States like those in your State, Mr. Ezelle, but a question has occurred to businessmen during these years of racial difficulty. What are we missing along with the growth we are enjoying? I would like to hear what you feel are the factors involved in the economics of harmonious race relations. Is it good economics?

The average Mississippian would look to you for leadership, for economic advice as to whether the training of a pool of Negro manpower, for instance, would be good for the State, would be good for the working man as well as the businessman, or whether the image of a Mississippi which is in more peaceful accord with the civil rights law has now become in fact good business affecting the economic growth of your State. And if so, what are the factors involved. Mr. Cooper?

Mr. COOPER. I would not want to identify the communities, Mr. Chairman, but I was in a community not long ago in which they were discussing the matter of industrial expansion. It was generally conceded that based on the current employment practices, the community had reached a saturation point, and that it could not even hope to bring in any substantial additional industry. Now the current pattern is not different from that generally prevalent in Mississippi. Any additional industry that came in would have to depend largely on Negro workers, of which most of them would be unskilled. In fact, most of our employed white workers are unskilled. So that I think is a concrete illustration that there is some way to combine both. Good race relations alone will not provide the skilled worker. It will help open the door to follow up on the things that Mr. Palmer has said.

In another instance there was a textile operation that had a plant in the community, one of the most efficient plants that they have in their whole system. It employed only one race and the hiring pattern was such that it was deemed wise not to change that, although they would have liked to have doubled that plant. But they thought they had employed all the available workers that they had. So in those two instances I think we probably have some concrete instances there. We have several industries with jobs. Jobs mean payrolls and payrolls mean solving some of these housing problems and educational problems and many others that come along.

Vice Chairman PATTERSON. I see. And in order for that community which you used as an example to have such a plant, it would have had to supply the skilled labor. Therefore, you feel that whether skilled labor is Negro or white, the supply of skilled labor controls the rate of growth for that community?

Mr. COOPER. That's right. And it is more than just race relations. That is part of it, but part of it is training people to get the job done.

Vice Chairman PATTERSON. I see. Mr. Palmer, do you have any thoughts on that?

Mr. PALMER. Well, I think the same as Mr. Cooper. Certainly we have experienced relative indications that where there were people who had ideas of changing, business has changed it. We need to change that pattern. And I think these steps will attempt to do that. Certainly, in addition, it would mean there would be less apprehension on the part of certain skills that various industries would be looking for. They would no longer be hesitant to come here and participate as employees in manufacturing where they are sorely needed. Certainly this whole matter of the upgrading of our available people and skills, I think, would make it easier for these things that we hope to come about.

Vice Chairman PATTERSON. Mr. Ezelle?

Mr. EZELLE. I go along with the statements which have already been made. I do know in talking with some manufacturers that they had felt that the labor market was pretty well saturated at the present time. But that is because in their particular field the saturation was in white labor and there was an untapped source that might still be tapped if we worked out the proper race relations.

Vice Chairman PATTERSON. And if that were tapped, do you think it would create some economic growth in the State?

Mr. EZELLE. Very definitely.

Vice Chairman PATTERSON. But it would have to be skilled labor. It could not be unskilled?

Mr. EZELLE. It could be some semiskilled and some skilled.

Vice Chairman PATTERSON. Mr. Cooper, what has been the reaction around the State of Mississippi to the statement by the Mississippi Economic Council which you entered into our record? Have any of the communities in the State identified themselves explicitly with this statement?

Mr. COOPER. There have been 24 organizations, 17 or 18 of which are local chambers of commerce, that more or less spontaneously acted favorably. My feeling is that many more will act in time. Many of them have monthly meetings. Many of them need to give some thought to it, but the response has been most gratifying.

Vice Chairman PATTERSON. I would like to get the views of all of you, if possible, on a trend that has shown up in testimony before this Commission this week. We have heard testimony from different communities with different problems. Some had very tough problems of law enforcement. Others, like some of those on which we heard testimony yesterday, have had considerable tranquility. But in nearly every case the sheriff or the police chief has said that the attitude of the business leadership, of the community leadership which gentlemen such as you represent, has a direct effect on his ability to enforce the law. Do you agree with these sheriffs and police chiefs?

Mr. COOPER. Do you want me to start it off?

Vice Chairman PATTERSON. If you like.

Mr. COOPER. I don't know about being first every time. Yes, I do. I feel that maybe it is improper that it should be so, but a person in the community that has an organization that employs a large number of people probably has an influence he is not aware of, and probably one he would rather not have. But it rests on his shoulders just the same. And my personal feeling is that if the business community identifies itself positively and frankly on the side of law and order, as was done in the statement by the MEC, and lets it be known in the local community along with the other business leaders in the community that this is not lip service only, that this is really a conscientious feeling on his part, that it will give a backing to the sheriff. He needs the backing, too, because there are lots of people that subscribe to what has been done. Some of those people still live in Mississippi. The substantial responsible leadership needs to identify itself with law and order in a positive manner and let the law enforcement officials know that that is their attitude. I think it would be most helpful.

Vice Chairman PATTERSON. Mr. Ezelle?

Mr. EZELLE. That is true. I think that we have tried to do that here. And I think that has been helpful to the Jackson situation. I think it was very helpful last summer.

Vice Chairman PATTERSON. Do you have any thoughts on that, Mr. Palmer?

Mr. PALMER. Well, only, I think, that the whole experience has been one of a realization that hadn't existed, perhaps, before by many individuals of their interdependence upon each other as individuals and as groups, and the effect that they had by what they said or did or failed to say or do. And I think much has been gained from many of the problems in that area.

Vice Chairman PATTERSON. Mr. Rankin, do you have questions?

Commissioner RANKIN. Well, I know that all of you have read Frank Morgan's article of February 2, the feature article in the Wall Street Journal about Mississippi. I notice that in that article he says this: "The State Legislature also has appropriated $5½ million to match Federal funds for technical training courses in public schools." I gather you approve of that action heartily?

Mr. PALMER. Very definitely.

Commissioner RANKIN. And I wondered, also, if this could be an indication of what is going to take place? If the legislature does this, can all the school boards do likewise insofar as accepting Federal grants for the purpose of education? Could they follow the leadership of the legislature and do likewise?

Mr. PALMER. I think all of the things that are happening today and a week or two weeks ago will certainly make it more likely that they will. And certainly they can.

Commissioner RANKIN. These hearings help and the action of the legislature also helps.

Mr. PALMER. Yes.

Mr. COOPER. Of course one of the dilemmas we are faced with is technical education which is very expensive.

Commissioner RANKIN. It certainly is. But all education is expensive.

Mr. COOPER. Well, I realize that. But one English teacher can take about 30 pupils and have 5 classes. You can't do that with vocational training. So we are faced with less money and probably the biggest task of technical education, which makes it more important that we seriously consider all sources of funds to provide this technical education. But in all candor, we are going to look at what strings are tied to these funds, and they will be evaluated in light of the local situation. I think that I would expect you would do the same thing. You might accept funds that somebody else might not accept, but you would want to know what you are doing when you accept them anyway.

Commissioner RANKIN. Yes, I would look the gift horse in the face. But if it helps education, I certainly wouldn't look too hard. I would take the money.

Vice Chairman PATTERSON. Gentlemen, one final question for the panel. I would welcome the response of any of you. Governor Paul Johnson, before this Commission on the opening day of this session, asked that Americans "get off our backs and get on our side." If this Commission's report to Congress and the President and its information to the American people says, "All right, let's get off Mississippi's back and get on her side," what are we going to get on your side for? What is it that you plan for this State?

Mr. COOPER. May I answer that?

Vice Chairman PATTERSON. All right, sir.

Mr. COOPER. I think, fundamentally, that our aim for Mississippi is expressed by the Mississippi Economic Council's program that they call "75 by 75." That is a broad economic program that has as its objective attaining a per capita income so that by the year 1975 we will have 75 percent of the national average. And Father, if you will forgive me, I am going to leave aside the spiritual values, because that is another subject.

Commissioner HESBURGH. We will get to that in a minute.

Mr. COOPER. Fundamentally, I think that is what we all need first, but we are talking about some of the other things now. In the economic field we need to increase our per capita income to where we will be more nearly the national average. Maybe by the year 2000 we could get to be the national average. When you bring up the per capita income, everybody will tend to get some benefit under that umbrella. So in the economic field I think all of us in Mississippi want industry because it provides jobs, like the Father from Greenwood said. Fundamentally, our people need jobs, and jobs mean industry, and we've got to get industry in here. Therefore, we need folks on our side to talk about locating industry down here, not keeping industry away from us, because we penalize the very people we would help and we destroy the very objective that we would accomplish if we could create these jobs and build this up. But this thing alone is not enough.

I stand on this statement that the Mississippi Economic Council has made because it covers the four vital areas. Now our public officials have said that we are for order and respect of law. Lawless activities ought to be stopped by all individuals and organizations. The penalty of the law should be fairly and equitably applied to all. Personally I stand on that and I believe our people do. But that is not going to be accomplished overnight. We want you to help us move toward this and not get by our side and say "Presto, the millenium has come in Mississippi." It hasn't. We want to help bring about the millenium, and we want other people to help us.

Vice Chairman PATTERSON. And that includes progress in the civil rights area.

Mr. COOPER. That's right. And the registration and the voting laws should be impartially administered. As far as I know, that is the first time an organization has made that statement and gone that far. I will stand with the Economic Council on that, and I believe most people in Mississippi will do that although that is not going to be a transformation that will come overnight. And we need the strength and support of our public education system. So when we say get by our side, it is like saying we want you to get by our side over in Vietnam. The very fact that you get by our side doesn't mean that we are going to solve that problem overnight. It means that we think, with sympathetic understanding and help, that we can go down this road faster than we can otherwise. But it is still some time off before a situation may exist in our State that is comparable to that which you desire and probably comparable to that which many people in Mississippi desire.

Vice Chairman PATTERSON. Thank you, Mr. Cooper. Mr. Ezelle?

Mr. EZELLE. Yes. I would not attempt to speak for the Negro race in regard to what their desires are, but I have an opinion of what their basic desires are. And I would give you my opinion at this time. I think their first desire is the ballot. I think their next desire is job opportunity. And I think their next desire is educational opportunity. And then there should be communication between the races, which has been very poor up to date. Going in that order the Mississippi Economic Council's statement touches on each of those. And I feel that if we are to provide this job opportunity and the educational opportunity, which I feel are so important, if we are to do this job, then we are going to have to work within the mainstream of America and expect the mainstream to work with us.

Vice Chairman PATTERSON. Thank you, sir. Mr. Palmer?

Mr. PALMER. You asked in what manner we would want people to get on our side, and I feel that it would start with a cessation of belaboring the past. If you have the feeling that there has come through to you an expression of a change in attitude and action which is of a positive note, then make that known that it is positive and that it is different. Because I believe that certainly the most significant value to be gained from history is to let sufficient time pass before reexamination of it to see what the significance of its impact was. And I don't feel that there would be anything to be gained by anyone by continuation of what has occurred up until now by belaboring the past. Certainly we have—as expressed here and many times—we need additional education, we need additional upgrading of our people in order to take advantage of the additional opportunities that we hope we will be able to bring before them.

Vice Chairman PATTERSON. Thank you, gentlemen. I want to express again the appreciation of the Commission for your appearance before us today. We will have a 10-minute recess and reassemble at 11:30.

(Whereupon, the Commission took a short recess, after which it proceeded with the Religious Panel.)

RELIGIOUS PANEL, FEBRUARY 20, 1965

Commissioner HESBURGH. Reverend gentlemen, and ladies and gentlemen, we come to our final panel, a group of religious leaders from this community. I would like to begin by introducing each one of them. On my far left and your right, we have the Most Reverend Richard O. Gerow, Bishop of the Catholic Diocese of Natchez-Jackson, Mississippi. Next to him we have the Reverend S. Leon Whitney, Pearl Street African Methodist Episcopal Church, Jackson, Mississippi. Next, the Right Reverend John M. Allin, Bishop Coadjutor, Episcopal Diocese of Mississippi, Jackson, Mississippi. On my immediate right and your left, we have additional help for the Presbyterian church because Commissioner Rankin is an elder in the Presbyterian church in North Carolina. On my immediate right and your left, we have Rabbi Perry E. Nussbaum, Temple Beth Israel, Jackson, Mississippi. Next to him we have the Reverend Edward J. Pendergrass, Bishop of the Jackson area Methodist Church, Jackson, Mississippi. And next to him we have the Reverend William P. Davis, President of the Mississippi Baptist Seminary, Jackson, Mississippi. And, finally, we have the Most Reverend Joseph B. Brunini, Natchez-Jackson Diocese, Jackson, Mississippi.

I think I should say on behalf of the panel and on behalf of the Commission, that in coming to Mississippi, as in coming to many of the other States we have visited as a Commission on Civil Rights, we have, without exception, in our public hearings called upon all segments of the community which we thought could bring some vision, some imagination, and some courage to bear upon the vital problem of civil rights, which three successive Presidents have said is the most pressing domestic problem of the United States. We have received great help all over this country from the religious segments of our society, which in conjunction with the other segments of our society—the businessmen, professional men, lawyers, doctors, leaders of industry and people of good will everywhere—take responsible action within the community to bring the full weight of their good will and the full courage of their leadership to bear upon this problem. We are delighted this morning to have all of these gentlemen with us. We are here to hear from them primarily, not from me.

I would like to make one or two primary observations which have grown out of the hearings thus far. The first observation is that we have found one of the most necessary elements in the moving forward of any society—and this is not something unique to Mississippi, it is unique to this problem throughout the United States—that is the element of communication. I think it is simply a matter of history that in the whole life of this Nation, as well as in the life of many other great nations, it is the religious sector of society—the religious leaders of society—who have been able to facilitate that communication, who have been able to draw together separated parties within a community and have been able to stand up clearly, forthrightly, and courageously for that which is just against that which is unjust and erroneous and deleterious to the building of a great society. I think, also, that it is the duty and obligation of religion in our time, as in any time, to be relevant. We have had some serious criticism in many of our hearings, including these, to the effect that there have been times when religion was not relevant. It followed rather than led. It has seemed to follow the course of expediency rather than the course of courage. It has not been clear in outlining those principles which are at the base of our society, which are derived, as you know, from the strong religious base of Judeo-Christian culture.

I believe that many of you have heard the leaders of the business community today. They indicate, as did the leaders of the legal community yesterday, that there seems to be a turning of the road in this State, as there is a turning of the road throughout this country, and that people today are beginning to see the importance—the moral importance—the moral imperative of solving this problem. I think it is particularly relevant to this panel that it makes very little sense to say that half of the educational system, for example, in Africa, which is a continent of colored peoples, that half of the education in elementary and secondary schools is provided by missionaries from this country and then to say that in our own country we have problems that are not being solved.

So, I'm delighted to be associated with all of the gentlemen on this panel this morning. I would like to begin by setting up, as we have in our other panels, one or two questions to which each of you may address yourselves. The first question I would like to ask—and I think everyone on the panel should have an equal opportunity to answer these questions—the first question I would like to ask is this: What is the religious community doing to make manifest to this Commission, to this whole State, and to each particular community of this State what they think should be done about this most pressing problem—the problem which has brought us to Mississippi?

The lawyers have come out with several statements and the business leaders have come out with several statements. The governor and the attorney general this past week have made statements on this problem. I think it is important that we hear from all of these religious leaders regarding their statement or what statement they might make, either separately or collectively, about the possible answers to this problem. I would like to begin with Bishop Gerow, and just let them take turns in saying whatever they might wish to say.

Bishop GEROW. Yes. I'm very happy to speak on this question. During the year 1963 there gathered in St. Andrews Rectory, or St. Andrews Hall, a small group of religious leaders, and we discussed what we should do. This group then grew, it grew to the point where our meeting place was not sufficiently large. So we moved to our diocesan chancery where we have ample accommodations. And about once a month we had a meeting consisting of prominent religious leaders. Each meeting would consist of about 10 white leaders, religious leaders, and about 10 colored religious leaders, one of whom was Dr. Whitney here beside me. In these meetings we found a beginning of communication amongst ourselves. We learned to understand each other. We learned to appreciate each other, to respect and really to love each other.

I enjoyed those meetings. We would sit around and in an informal way we would talk. We finally came up with this thought. The question of communicating between the races was an important question and we resolved to do something about it. So the group of us arranged to meet with one of our prominent local organizations of men. I would prefer not to mention names or identify organizations. Somehow or other we didn't get very far on that occasion. They just didn't understand us, and we didn't understand them. We tried again to get communication with one of the civic officials. We didn't get very far there. And we felt that if we could establish communication, if we could get together and sit down and talk things over in a very cordial, friendly, and informal way, we might come up with something that would better the situation.

Those conditions that I speak of were conditions that existed probably a year or little less than a year ago. I think things have grown a little bit better now, but still they are far from being what they should be. Now, does this answer your question?

Commissioner HESBURGH. Thank you very much, Bishop Gerow. Now, I would like to ask Reverend Leon Whitney to say a few words on the same subject.

Reverend WHITNEY. Yes. I think that perhaps with Bishop Gerow and the rest of the members of the community, we have had some communication. But there is no communication with the Negro and white church *per se*. This is definitely a fact. I think of reevaluating what Mr. Ezelle said a few minutes ago, his categorizing of the Negroes' need. I think perhaps the first thing we need is communication across the line. These must be all inclusive and the question as to when we should start, we start now. We work on all these things as we go along. Unfortunately in Mississippi we have extended the invitation to any ministers in the white community to just come and talk with us about the problem, but even this has been not done. A few of us, as stated by Bishop Gerow, have talked about it but we have not gotten beyond the point of talking about it. But the church has not faced up to its moral responsibility in solving the race problem in Mississippi.

Commissioner HESBURGH. Thank you. I would like to ask the Right Reverend John M. Allin, the Bishop of the Episopal Diocese, to speak.

Bishop ALLIN. The key word has been communication as Bishop Gerow said. We started more than 2 years ago, and found that in the worst of circumstances there are some benefits and good fruits. One of these was the discovery of the persons, and perhaps many more religious leaders have come, as the Bishop said, to know each other and maintain communication throughout this period of 2½ years or more under great difficulty. It was difficult, for example to find a place to meet. I remember at the outset in speaking to one of the public officials we were told that the white clergy exercised perhaps a 10 percent influence and the Negro clergy a 90 percent influence. I rather think that was an accurate estimate and it was a good lesson in humility, too, which we learned.

In terms of how confused or how scattered the people were, we debated and discussed at length the matter of making pronouncements. There were a great many pronouncements. I remember the feeling expressed on a number of occasions that to make a statement simply presented something that was then to be placed amidst the confusion and the lack of communication to be distorted and misused by those whose efforts sought to separate us. As the Bishop said, we made an appeal to a prominent board. Some of the men on that board received us and heard us. There were some who would have moved to remove us immediately. But our whole purpose at that point was to find some way to communicate. I might add that one of the problems of communication which I think is perhaps still before us is that of pressures from both inside and outside. These have changed in some regard, but I remember listening to one of the city officials respond to our request by saying we are never sure whom we are talking to on the other side. If we could talk to people in our own community—now I'm fully aware that the argument has been presented many times that we don't want outsiders and I'm not referring at this point to that. But I am saying people with common problems many times come closer to solving them if given a chance to discuss them and I could appreciate—I couldn't entirely agree with him—but I could appreciate his fear and the anxiety that was expressed.

I think in addition to communication the greatest need we had was for perspective. There are many blind spots in the picture. We could spend a long time in talking about our failures and, as I know the men that are present here and others who have met with us, I don't know anybody who has made any boasts about our accomplishments. But in trying to get the perspective to understand a very complicated problem that faced us, there was a move, for example, by one group—an appeal to the laymen in churches that said in effect, "If your clergy doesn't behave we will meet with you and show you the means of reforming the church."

I remember 2½ years ago making what I thought was a rather innocuous speech to a civic club to which I was asked to speak on prophecy. I talked about the need to gather around a problem, to attempt to define a problem, to isolate the factors, to coordinate an attempt to solve it. I was told later by one of our laymen that on the way down somebody said to another man on the elevator, "You know, if he had been one of our boys, we would cut off his groceries." You know, this gives pause for thought. But the greatest need, I think, still is communication and perspective. While I'm willing to admit that in the face of all the difficulties and the complications I never have lacked real hope, I felt there have been many things that have been bad. It could have been worse, and the reason it wasn't worse is because there were many factors and indeed many, many people in the State of Mississippi who are concerned with seeking the truth and are concerned with fair play.

Under the pressure of group anxiety, under the pressure of blown-up fears of what might happen, these people frequently retreat. But I have seen too many times that when persons do meet, there is a courtesy that comes through. And I don't think this should be discounted. So we make no claims for great accomplishments, sir, but we at the same time must say we feel deep concern. There has been what feeble effort we could make to reach out and communicate with one another.

Commissioner HESBURGH. Thank you very much, Bishop. I would like to ask Rabbi Nussbaum to say a few words.

Rabbi NUSSBAUM. Mr. Chairman, I'm often disagreeing with my

very good friend Bishop Allin when we get together, and I'm disagreeing again.

Bishop ALLIN. It makes it an official meeting.

Rabbi NUSSBAUM. It makes it the kind of meeting that we have been having over the past 2 years at the Catholic Diocesan office. I don't think the key word is communication. I think the key word is brotherhood, and I mention that deliberately because we are beginning a brotherhood week. This whole idea, this concept, is still missing from so many parts of our country and from these parts. I think that not until religion in general will go from the preaching in the pulpit to implementing in the pews what the fatherhood of God means and the brotherhood of man also means in the real sense, will we ever accomplish more than this creeping progress.

Yes, we have made some progress. But it has been my feeling as a Jewish teacher that not until we rise to our responsibilities, religiously speaking, will this basic problem of our times, this crisis in human relations in our times, ever be met. I think it was Mr. Patterson who asked a question in the last panel to the industrialist and others who were here. He wanted to know is it good economics? Now, the question that I have been asking for years, is, "Is it good religion?" I am one of those naive people who think that religion is at the core of our life—our national life, our State life, and our community life—and that it should not be on the fringes. Bishop Allin's quotation from a very distinguished public official, I think, expresses the attitude of most people. But I do not agree. I think that if we can call ourselves worshipers of one Father, then this must be part of our life and every facet of our living.

Now, your question is what are we doing. You have heard what we have tried to do in the past years. I think we have made certain progress, but much more has to be accomplished. There's no question. We need interfaith programs. We are just beginning that in this State and for most of the State the idea is unknown. We need to make understood what the word "brotherhood" means in terms of various religious groups, in terms of the racial groups. If religion is to be a force in this State, we need councils and committees and organizations on human relations which will not be afraid of the term "human relations." For too long a time we have run away from the canards about the concepts of human relations. We have run away from these rhetorics, these distortions of all of the ideas and the values which, as religious people, we believe in and we are called upon to teach. I am very hopeful for our State. We have made progress. But if patience is a virtue, I think procrastination is very much of a vice and a religious sin. And since 1954 there has been a good deal of procrastination in this whole area of the brotherhood of man under the fatherhood of God.

Commissioner HESBURGH. Thank you, Rabbi Nussbaum. As you can see, this is like a lawyer's panel. We are getting a little disagreement. But that is all to the good because it is out of this basic disagreement that we find a common unity. Next we have the Rev. Edward J. Pendergrass, Bishop of the Jackson Area Methodist Church.

Bishop PENDERGRASS. Mr. Chairman, ladies and gentlemen. Thank you very much for the privilege of coming. I have no desire to disagree with anyone. I'm a Johnny-come-lately to Mississippi. I only came last August. I came from the State of Florida, and I came with my eyes open and my heart heavy and my hopes high. And I have found here one of the finest groups of people with whom to work that I have known.

I represent a church that is connectional. We number more than 10 million people, if that means anything at all. We meet every 4 years to develop our program for the denominational group. I came in light of the fact that much of the program of the church had been enacted this year that was controversial. It affected some of the churches in Mississippi as it has affected some of the churches elsewhere who are in disagreement. While the program was enacted in a democratic way, it was not fully accepted. Our people are episcopal in their form of government. Some of them have not learned that fact, even though they have avowed themselves to the principles of the church. They want to be congressional in their worship and, therefore, are doing some things that are not in keeping with the total program of the church.

With the things we are attempting to do here, we are in the process in our religious community of trying to effect communication between the races. There is, out of the four conferences representing the white and the Negro races in Mississippi, committees in each of these conferences to communicate with each other. This is, as you can see, a biracial group to discuss our problems and how we can solve them among ourselves. Then the second thing that we have done is to try to thwart the purposes of those who come in and try to tell us how to do our job. We have had a number of people come into areas of our work in Mississippi that have frustrated our people, who have not understood their problems, who have been in some instances hindering the work that we could do if this interference had not taken place. We developed the missionary program that will take effect. This is biracial in that the committee who forms the program will be both from the central jurisdiction, which is the Negro division of our church, and the southern jurisdiction, which is the white, until such time as this can be rectified. These will develop a program to help us in our missionary activity in the Delta system that has created such a great problem for all denominational groups in Mississippi.

In addition to that, within the last several hours, we have at our State, denominational schools, signed Federal compliance on education, which I think is a tremendous step in doing something here to meet the issues that confront us.

Now we do have pressures from within. We have people who are differing with those who are attempting to follow the patterns of the church as a whole. These have created a great deal of problems both for the bishop and his cabinet who work out the affairs of our Methodism in Mississippi. But I think in many, many instances we made progress. We tried as best we could, and I hope the others would say the same thing, to be as faithful and even more so if we can, to cooperate with the denominational groups in this State as they have with us. These gentlemen who are here with us on the platform today have given me the privilege of chairing the Committee on Concern. And I have had delightful experiences in that and have had an opportunity to share any sort of ability that I have and any sort of influence that I have to ask people to share in that. I think, Mr. Chairman, if I were to analyze things in Mississippi from August of 1964, until this moment, I think that great progress has been made, notwithstanding the fact that much information has been to the contrary.

Commissioner HESBURGH. Thank you very much, Bishop Pendergrass. I want to say a special word of thanks to the next gentleman who is going to speak since he was very helpful in getting this panel together this morning. Also, although he was officially scheduled for a much longer statement I would like to ask him to make this statement as a matter of record. I am very happy to present to you the Reverend William P. Davis of the Mississippi Baptist Seminary.

Reverend DAVIS. Mr. Chairman, I would like for the printed copy to become a part of the official record. The press has a copy and will handle it as it thinks best.

Commissioner HESBURGH. It will be copied into the record as if read.

STATEMENT OF REV. WILLIAM P. DAVIS, MISSISSIPPI BAPTIST SEMINARY

I have been invited to discuss the Committee of Concern—its background, when and how it was formed, what it has accomplished, and its purposes for the future.

The tragic background has been told by news media in many ways. But the concern of a small group of religious leaders has been overlooked. The leaders of that group have met from time to time for many months to seek some way out of the confusion and misunderstanding and to offer guidance for the common welfare. Some who expressed their concern resigned their places of leadership and left the State because of pressure. Many other religious leaders courageously challenged their people to consider the judgment, justice, and mercy of God in every movement of history. They restrained the surging tides of brutality and death, thus making it possible for leaders on the battlefront to make advances in good will for better human relations. These have been Jewish, Catholic and Protestant.

Since 1957 many of these leaders have sustained my place of leadership as Secretary of the Department of Work with Negroes of the Mississippi Baptist Convention Board and President of the Mississippi Baptist Seminary and have enabled me to have biracial communication throughout Mississippi. The small group of religious leaders inspired me with their confidence. Their concerns as early as 1960 gave me the idea of a Committee of Concern to help resolve racial tensions.

The Mississippi Baptist Seminary was organized in 1942 with an interracial faculty and board of trustees. Constant growth has been its history. It is now operating a system of 22 schools with 15 extensions. The enrollment last year was 1,923. Through these 22 schools and 15 extensions, the Sophia Sutton Mission Assembly, Baptist student work on college campuses, scholarship aid for college students, Bible institutes, conventions and conferences, I have had biracial lines of communication with thousands of people. This vast work has been made possible by the concerned leadership and support of the Mississippi Baptist Convention, and hundreds of National Baptist leaders as well as by many other religious and civic leaders in Mississippi. This work is jointly financed by the Mississippi Baptist Convention, which allocated $80,166 for this work, and the National Baptists in Mississippi, which gave $34,804. White Baptist churches gave $15,192. Teachers donated $1,124 in professional services. Allocation of MBC for 1965 is $94,386.

Naturally, the burning of crosses and churches and other injustices and indignities heaped upon Negroes became my supreme challenge, likewise my greatest problem. How I have thrust myself into the midst of the struggle for the welfare of all people is well known in every section of the State.

On July 18, 1964, I stood in the ashes of a burned church. The smoke of burning Bibles, hymn books, the playthings of little children, pulpit and communion furniture drifted over my head. I said, "I must and I will challenge the religious leaders of my State, my Nation and my world to create beauty from ashes by building a community of good will."

A few days later two of my best friends, Dr. Chester L. Quarles, executive secretary-treasurer of the Mississippi Baptist Convention Board, and Dr. Joe T. Odle, editor of the Baptist Record, called me for a conference. They expressed their concern and discussed how best to challenge Mississippi Baptists to manifest their concern. On August 9, 1964, Dr. Odle wrote a lead editorial, "Smoke Over Mississippi," that stirred concerned people to action. Shortly, in a second editorial and a news release, he announced that the Department of Work with Negroes would receive funds to help rebuild the burned churches and made an appeal for funds. Other religious journals called upon their people to support this worthy cause.

On September 9, 1964, the most important step was taken in helping to rebuild the burned churches. The Committee of Concern was formed in the chapel of the Baptist Building to "make it possible for men, women and children of good will to respond to violence, hatred, and destruction with concern, compassion and construction." The committee was interfaith and biracial—Jewish, Roman Catholic and Protestant.

The Friends Committee for Church Construction and Reconciliation (Quakers) and the Mennonites had been working in Mississippi making an on-the-scene study of the burned churches. Members of the committee offered to cooperate with the Committee of Concern in helping rebuild the churches. The Committee of Concern welcomed their offer. The Society of Friends of Philadelphia and New York sent Lawrence Scott to work with the Committee of Concern. The Mennonite Disaster Service sent volunteer workers. Contributions from individuals, organizations, churches, and synagogues have been received from almost every State of the Union and from 16 foreign countries. Contributions since October 5, 1964, have totaled $58,099.54. Over half of this amount has come from Mississippians. The Mennonite Disaster Service has contributed $15,000 of skilled labor. Many others have donated labor and materials, both inside and outside of Mississippi. Architects in Jackson have donated their services. The Council of Churches of Southern California has raised the money to rebuild and furnish the St. Matthews Baptist Church. Eighteen of the 38 burned churches are under construction. The Christian Union Baptist Church was dedicated January 24, 1965. Six churches are almost completed. The Committee of Concern will help the remaining 20 burned churches, if funds are available.

Students from Oberlin and other colleges, in cooperation with the local congregation, rebuilt the Antioch Baptist Church and raised the money for the construction and furnishing of the building. Students from Queens College, New York, spent 2 weeks, from January 29 through February 12, working on three churches. A number of college students, both inside and outside of Mississippi, have indicated a desire to help. At the YWA House Party, Gulf Shore Assembly, over 400 high school and career girls gave $184.30 and expressed a deep concern in helping rebuild the churches. If the remaining 20 burned churches are to be rebuilt, the Committee of Concern must have an additional $100,000.

The immediate and future purpose of the Committee of Concern was clearly stated by a spokesman for the Quakers in explaining their role in the church reconstruction program:

"As we see it, the most important thing about this entire effort is not so much the buildings being replaced as the manner and fact of their reconstruction. Thus, we have endeavored to explore the opportunities which a cooperative building program might provide for bringing the white and Negro communities into a more meaningful relationship. We have chosen to work with the Mississippi Committee of Concern because we have felt this constructive new response to violence and hatred might serve as an appropriate vehicle for the establishment of new bridges of interracial understanding."

In addition, let it clearly be added that anarchy, bigotry, demagoguery and violence shall not be allowed to prevail in Mississippi—that we, the people of Mississippi, will not stand for it. A new sunrise of interfaith and biracial good will stands at the gate of the morning in Mississippi "to bind up the brokenhearted and give unto them beauty for ashes, and to build the old waste places, the desolations of many generations. Let no man's heart fail." Indignities and injustices shall not prevail. Tyranny must go! A power structure designed to deprive citizens of their voting rights and to discriminate in the administration of justice because of race or creed is tyranny. It is not treason to challenge tyranny. It is the highest act of patriotism and obedience to the eternal command of Almighty God: "Let My People Go."

Any citizen worthy of the name is entitled to his civil rights. Intimidation or discrimination used to deny a citizen his civil rights should not be tolerated in Mississippi or anywhere in the United States of America. There should be no place for such practices in the wide, wide world. Human beings matter more than empty tradition.

Reverend DAVIS. I would like to say that I am not a Johnny-come-lately. I have spent most of my life in Mississippi with the exception of about 14 years during which time I was abroad visiting our mission fields and other places of interest—studying humanity. I returned to Mississippi in 1948 and have been officially connected with interracial mission work in Mississippi almost since that time. I have seen this work grow from infancy to a position which today covers a State like—as one of the newspapers described its spread—the dew. We have 1,900 students enrolled in our seminary system, 22 schools, 44 extension centers of those schools. So it was easy for the department, which I am trying to lead, to become identified with the leadership of the Committee of Concern which was organized September 9, 1964, in the Baptist Building of the Mississippi Baptist Convention.

It has been, since its beginning, interracial and interfaith. There isn't anything fraternalistic about the Committee of Concern. Presently we are engaged in rebuilding 18 of the 38 burned churches. Six of the churches have been completed and if we have the money we intend to rebuild or help rebuild the remaining 20.

I think that because of the efforts of the Committee of Concern, we have created a different situation in Mississippi. The lawyers supported the Mississippi Baptist Convention, the covention board, the executive committee. And these gentlemen here on the panel with me and thousands of Mississippians not here this morning, but who probably are listening to this panel discussion, have been most helpful in making this work a reality.

Now, I would like to say as a final word, let it clearly be added that anarchy, bigotry, demagoguery, violence shall not be allowed to prevail in Mississippi—that we, the people of Mississippi, will not stand for it. A new sunrise of interfaith and biracial good will stands at the gate of the morning in Mississippi to bind up the brokenhearted and to give unto them beautiful ashes and to build the old waste places the desolation of many generations. Let no man's heart fail in dignity and injustices shall not prevail. Tyranny must go. A power structure designed to deprive citizens of their voting rights and to discriminate in the administration of justice because of race or creed is tyranny. It is not treason to challenge tyranny. It is the highest act of patriotism and obedience to the eternal command of Almighty God. "Let My People Go."

Any citizen worthy of the name is entitled to his civil rights. Intimidation or discrimination used to deny a citizen his civil rights should not be tolerated in Mississippi or anywhere in the United States of America There is no place for such practices in the wide, wide world. Human beings are more important than empty tradition. I think we are establishing lines of communication and good will by racial lines of communication. And for that we are dedicated and in that direction I believe we are moving.

Commissioner HESBURGH. I think we ought to give him a cheer.
[Applause.]

Reverend DAVIS. I thank you and I think you ought to give me a lot of prayers too. These gentlemen have helped me so sacrificially in bringing these things to pass. I claim no credit for myself. The committee in return has received contributions from every State in the United States and 17 foreign countries, $58,000. You have it on the record there. Please put it in the press. We need a hundred thousand dollars more, though.

[Applause.]

Commissioner HESBURGH. I think these good people in the audience would expect that now is the time to pass the hat, but we are not going to.

[Laughter.]

I would like to ask Bishop Brunini if he would like to add a few words to this.

Reverend BRUNINI. Mr. Chairman, I would like to accept all the fine things that have been said up here this morning and early afternoon. It has been a pleasure for me to be associated with all the men of religion of this panel. You ask what we should do. First of all we must basically continue to teach the Christian principles for the dignity of all men as children of God and brothers of Christ. We must move into actual integration. The time of talk is past. We say with protection of the law and the courts there should be no difficulty. We do have communications of course in the Catholic Church, Negro priests, Negro sisters and brothers in Mississippi and over 6,000 devoted self-sacrificing Negro Catholics. We are happy to assist all races in attaining full citizenship rights both as citizens of this world and as members of the church.

This is a moral problem. This racial problem, this problem will be with us in our part of the world for many years. We are keenly aware of the deprivation, the suffering, the hardship of our Negro citizens and indeed of our white citizens, also, here in Mississippi. Thirty years ago, I believe, President Roosevelt said that the South is ill-fed, ill-housed and ill-clothed. We can hardly say in 1965 that there is much progress that the South is well-fed, well-housed, and well-clothed. We are very much interested in the antipoverty program and all programs to benefit all of our people. We have many very, very poor people, white and Negro, here in Mississippi. The situation is desperate. The Catholic Church has gathered priests, brothers, sisters and money here in Mississippi from various parts of Europe and from all parts of the United States to teach Christian principles and to educate the Negro and our white people also.

The Catholic Church is not a Johnny-come-lately in helping the American Negro. And I might add that like the authority of J. Edgar Hoover, the reputation of our Catholic institution in keeping out communistic influence is well established. Here in Mississippi at the present time we operate 28 Negro schools, educating over 5,000 students. Our interest is not limited to our Catholic people. Sixty-five percent of these students are not of the Catholic faith. We have assembled 170 teachers. And besides this program on the elementary and secondary level we operate a seminar in St. Louis. Bishop Gerow and myself, these men there, have assisted in educating and ordaining over 40 Negro clergymen. At the present time, according to public school costs, the cost of educating in our Catholic schools is $1,154,-515, not including the cost of the land and buildings involved. The amount of this money, 65 percent representing those who are not of the Catholic faith, would come to about $700,000. So we are happy to have this panel here in Mississippi and that you came, Father Hesburgh—and the other members. It has been rather salutary. We are ready to roll up our sleeves and make progress. God bless all of you.

Commissioner HESBURGH. Thank you. Now, Commissioner Rankin said he wants to put in a plug for the Presbyterians, and I think we ought to give him that opportunity.

Commissioner RANKIN. I am completely out of place up here. I should be down with you because each Sunday I listen to men like these. But I think we have a secret insofar as really making better race relations. They preach to me and tell me, "Do unto others as you would have them do unto you." If we members of the different churches represented here really followed that admonition, we could solve most of these problems that we have. It's not a question of a gap in a civil rights law. It's really a question of treatment. It's really carrying out this admonition that is given us.

The other day I was down in eastern North Carolina attending a Presbyterian church that had very fine race relations. I asked this young minister how he accomplished this. He said. "Well, I added a new tenet to the Presbyterian doctrine. To election and predestination I added reincarnation. I preached a sermon not long ago in which I said, 'All of you are coming back to the Earth, and you are coming back as a cotton cropper out on the plantation here, earning $2 a day with inadequate medical attention, education not further than the fourth grade, and so on and so forth.' And it really worked. It started those people thinking. I find that here in my church, race relations have been much better." So all I can say is to remember the admonition of these men, "Do unto others as you would have them do unto you," and most of our race relations problems will be solved. [Applause.]

Commissioner HESBURGH. Thank you very much, Mr. Rankin. I think everyone has had a chance to say something. I would like to put a hypothetical question to this group since it represents a wide sweep of the religious element in Mississippi. We have heard a number of times during the course of this week and, of course, on other occasions—and we heard it from the good Bishop Allin this morning when he spoke about getting the groceries cut off—what would happen to the clergymen of this State if they really came out for the things that have been spoken about this week—the things Mississippians yearn for in this new day.

If they came out with the statement that every registrar in the State of Mississippi should act on what has been said by the business community and by the legal community and by many of your fine leaders who have spoken here, including your Governor; if they said that they believe every capable citizen of this State should have the right to vote, not 20 years from now, not 50 years from now, but right now, even if we have to keep the registration places open all night long to register people who are qualified; if every single religious representative in this State came out and said he believes that equal opportunity in education is important because no State moves forward without education and he thinks we all ought to put our shoulder to the wheel and come out for adequate education right now so that every single citizen of this State would have a much greater opportunity to be educated to the full extent of his talents; if they said they think that every citizen of this State should have an equal opportunity to a decent place in which to live, so far as that is possible, and should be accepted as a human being on his own personal capability and his own personal dedication, his performance as a human being, not his color; if they went beyond that and said they are going to try to invigorate aspiration among all people, white and colored, that they are going to make of this State a kind of new South which people haven't seen before. And are going to do it quickly, ignoring those people in their congregations who think this is a bad idea. Because part of religion is prophecy, and part of prophecy is having the courage to stand up and say what is right, what is right today, not next year or when it is easy to be right, not what is right because it is popular or what is right because it is profitable, but right because this is the will of God for His people, and we are His people. What would happen if every religious person in this state would sign such a statement?

They can't drive all the ministers and all the priests from the State. There wouldn't be any religion here, and I think there is a great deal of religion here. As a matter of fact, I think there is a lot more religion here in Mississippi than in many other States of the Union. We have heard some wonderful people during this past week who said, "I'm afraid to go into that booth alone, but I am not really alone because I have prayed, and God is with me. But I have been afraid. And yet I realize all I can do is die. And if something is right, you should be willing to be a martyr for it as evidenced by others who have gone through great indignity and great injustices." Vice chairman Patterson asked one little old lady about 80 years old, "Do you like the white people."

And she said, "of course I likes them. I loves them. I wouldn't be Christian if I didn't."

I think I would like to ask the panel this question, and I would like a little open discussion on it. What would happen if every religious leader in this State came out in one swoop and said, "This is our manifesto, and this is what we believe. We are going to begin preaching this doctrine day in and day out. We are going to live it in our church associations and our church activities. And if you don't like it you are going to have to drive out every one of us." I just don't think that's going to happen.

Reverend WHITNEY. Mr. Chairman, I think this is hypothetical.

Commissioner HESBURGH. That is all right.

Reverend WHITNEY. But I think really that you have a situation here which is much deeper than most people recognize because there are a lot of persons who preach the Gospel who don't believe it, who really believe that God made several groups and put some groups here and other groups there and there should be no communication between these groups. I don't think you could get the ministers of this State to really come out with a statement stating that this is the will of God, and we should follow it. I think Mr. Golden, in his book, "Mr. Kennedy and the Negroes," talks about it very beautifully when he says the society is sort of moving on the middle class and most of the ministers are no longer leading the people but the people leading the ministers.

I think this is the problem we have, for example, in our congregation. I have said to the people when a white man or woman cannot come into our congregation and worship with us, then I am not going to accept this church as my pastorate. I am not going to work with you. This is my conviction, that any person who wants to come to X church can. A person comes to worship God and I don't think we should deny him the right. I believe this, but I'm not sure whether or not the men in the other denominations really believe that we should be together as children of God.

Commissioner HESBURGH. Well, I think we have that problem confronting us when the good Lord says, "Whatsoever you do to one of my least brethren, you do to me." Bishop Allin, I think you have been doing some scribbling, and I would love to hear what you have on that paper.

Bishop ALLIN. I think that if the supposition you said came about that we would be able to adjourn and have harp practice. I think we would all be in heaven at harp practice. A man of my color skin has no right to ask for patience or for delay and there's a keen awareness of how little we understand the longer we live in this situation.

But, by the same token, to attempt to wish in something or oversimplify something or to ignore the facts is meaningful. Let me put it this way. Gradualism as a doctrine or a theory is here identical and doesn't make sense. To oppose it from a governmental situation is no longer reasonable. But by the same token the literal meaning of the word, steps, conditions, stages, are processes which cannot be ignored. When you find yourself lost, to the degree that in a sense we have been lost or confused, it simply takes steps to get back. These are tedious; these are painful. I wish it were not so. I wish it were possible to say what you have said. But one of the illusions which we the clergy have labored under in many periods in this country's history is that somehow we are the only voice or the infallible voice.

You said that if all of the clergy were driven out then we would have no religion. You didn't really mean that. I have always remembered the question that a theology professor put to me in the seminary. He said, "Gentlemen, if the garbage collector and all of the ministry went on strike at the same time, which would the society ask to come back to work first?" We have a voice and a voice of reason, and we have a responsibility to reach out. There is such a thing as integrity and sometimes integrity means that you have to admit that you're identified with people who may hold the wrong position.

Now, to say I no longer agree with you and I won't have anything to do with you any longer I think oversimplifies it. I become very leery of anyone who begins a sentence with "It's simply a matter of . . . ." There's nothing simple about it. Indeed, the fact of complexity requires that as one race or one group of people or one church we cannot alone solve the problems.

It would be a great deal easier if we could look to one person to answer the question and that's why the—indeed we have got to develop within this community and within this country and I think in this world, strength enough to disagree without becoming violent about it. True, it is only through disagreement and maintaining communication that we learn. And so while I wish, sir, it were possible to say, "yes," and I sincerely think that the majority of the clergy do say or would say what you say. There's also the question of hearing. And we have been concerned with the hearing and tried desperately at times to keep so many people from adding to the confusion by one more pronouncement.

I would say just in conclusion that very many times I have felt the deepest pain, indeed have admitted cowardice in not speaking. But by the same token I have discovered that the clergy are not the voice of the community alone but that you only have a voice when it is a voice in concert in the same sense as you only have a whole community when the various agencies and people, businessmen, labor, governmental agencies as well as clergy come and speak together. And I think this is where we must continue to struggle. It's not going to be tomorrow. We have had some casualties, incidentally, in our clergy ranks. But, I still think that it's an attempt to talk with one another, and to do this honestly and realize it is not going to be solved simply—if we are going to find our way out. And I am convinced we are going to find our way out.

Commissioner HESBURGH. I am certainly glad to hear that. Rabbi Nussbaum?

Rabbi NUSSBAUM. He has seen me scribbling. And you will excuse my theological difference here, but the Episcopalian said we would be in heaven if everything happened according to your long rhetorical question.

Commissioner HESBURGH. All my questions are long.

Rabbi NUSSBAUM. My answer is that we have a little heaven on this earth, and this is what we need.

[Applause.]

As you always point out, we agree with each other; we say it a little differently. I should have wished—and I don't think it's too late—we are doing it now by our very presence on this panel because this is the first time this has happened, and Heaven help some of us, perhaps——

[Laughter.]

One or two of us are not the bosses. This is the first time it has happened. I don't think it's too late for united religions to speak out. Now, it has happened in other parts of the Deep South. This isn't the business of just going on in the North. And wherever it has happened in the Deep South, whether it has been on a State level or a community level, where the voice of religion has said, "This is what we believe in. This is what we think is the teachings of our

Bible," there has been encouragement for people. And there are thousands of similar people in this State who have been looking for some kind of leadership.

Mr. Chairman, this morning—and this is the first time I have been here because I have been out of town—this morning I heard certain industrialists say some things about what's going to happen and the hopefulness now. Mr. Owen Cooper, who is the past president of a Mississippi Baptist convention board, tried not to talk religion but was talking religion all the way through here. He was trying to talk as an industrialist. And Mr. Cooper, I think, reflects the dilemma that has been in existence here for many, many years, and not just since 1954—the exact roll of religion in the going problems of living, and this is every facet of living.

I think the time has come for the teachers of religion to say this is what we believe in. This is what we think is God's word. Now, Bishop Brunini said that. I think the time has come for us to say that in a united voice—if only for the sake of somebody like myself because that old song about hanging together or hanging separately is very true—if only for the sake of the Negro preacher on this issue. And to me, it's the greatest challenge that has confronted our State and our Nation and it's a challenge that we all know is going to be with us for the rest of our lives. In this issue we as religious leaders must do some teacher work and, if you please, then some leading without deprecating all the fine sacrificial efforts that people on this panel here—that people in this room have been engaged in for all these years.

If there is one thing that I resent—and I'm going to say this in public—I don't think Bishop Allin was strong enough and here I agree with you, John. I resent the image that has been created by our colleagues in other parts of the country that we are the weaklings, that we have accepted the status quo. I resent it. I resent the type of clergymen who have come into Mississippi and on an overnight investigation has become an expert on the problems of Mississippi and all of these areas in which this Commission is concerned. I have the highest respect in the world and I have met hundreds of those who have come into the State to make witness, and to make witness is something else besides coming in and becoming an expert on a 24-hour basis. I had a young rabbi come this past summer. He called me up on Monday morning with one foot on the plane and said to me he came in on Sunday. And he had came down to take a look-see. And he had seen and he called me up and said, "Rabbi, I admire you. I know what you are going through." My answer to him was—Well, I can't give it in public.

[Laughter.]

You haven't the faintest idea what is happening in Mississippi. There have been too many such clerical experts who have come down into our State. Come down and share with us—not as the voice of the North telling us simple-minded folk of the South what to do.

Commissioner HESBURGH. I think one thing is coming through. They aren't dead yet.

[Laughter.]

I would like to wind this up in about 10 minutes. I don't want to arbitrarily say who should speak or not speak, but I think we have something rolling here and I think it's terribly important. Would you like to say something again, sir?

Reverend DAVIS. Well, I would like to say, sir, that the roll of the minister is in behalf of the welfare of all the people of the State and of the Nation. That is his primary concern. The concern of God is not for things but for people. And, our concern likewise becomes a concern for the total welfare of humanity in this State. I think that more ministers and more leaders have been aware of that and working in that direction than we have recognized. We are fellow laborers in a common cause; I see no defeat—I see victory. I think that we will resolve our tensions. We will settle our disputes and difficulties. We will come through to victory. I don't think we are going to do it tomorrow, but I think we will do it. I think we shall do it.

Commissioner HESBURGH. Thank you very much, sir. Now, would you like to say something again, Bishop Pendergrass?

Bishop PENDERGRASS. May I say this. Since 1940—these are facts that people do not altogether understand—the church that I represent has been totally integrated at the upper level. We have representatives on the major boards of our church. We have bishops in the Methodist church. And when I spoke a moment or two—and this is in rebuttal— that I'm a Johnny-come-lately, I meant by that, that while I have come to Mississippi as a Johnny-come-lately, I have not been totally unaware of the problem that exists. And with my deep and sincere appreciation for Rabbi Nussbaum's presence here, if he will permit me, I would like to say just this one word. Almighty God has never done anything overnight. In the beginning he made a world and spoke unto chaos and said, "Let there be light, and there was light." He put a perfect man and a perfect woman in a garden and they could not deal with the problem—there were problems of disobedience and an unwilling-ness to abide by the principles of God. Then He gave us the patri-archal fathers, but they were not enough. He then gave us the law giver, but he was not enough. He then gave us the prophets, but they were not enough. And then He reached in the coffers of love, as we Christians say—and for this I apologize to my friend here.

Rabbi Nussbaum. Why apologize?

Bishop Pendergrass. I do it in deference to my own faith and to the position I hold. He gave us his Son. The scripture says, "in the fullness of time," it is upon that principle that I build my hope for total integration. In the fullness of time God will do this thing and He will help us to do it in the way that we are trying to do it to the very best of our ability. I do not apologize for any of the ministers in my connection.

We have had them to do exactly what our chairman has said to do, and they have done it without fear. Fear of being hungry. Some of them have left the State because of that. I do not think simply for the group of ministers represented here today to stand up and make any sort of a pronouncement that we will do so and so is the answer to this problem. Because what good will it be to try to lead a parade if you have nobody following it? And that's exactly what would happen to us. We have got to win them by love. And I think we are doing it. And I think we are doing it with some degree of success. And while I'm sure that my Negro friends are impatient with us, I hope that that impatience will not be destroyed or destroy our hope. And make us understand that we are trying to be as faithful as we can. God knows that the things that have been represented by this panel in the discussions that I have been in with them have been an eagerness to do what we believe is the right thing under God to do. And Mr. Chairman, I think that that's the thought that all of us have.

Commissioner Hesburgh. Thank you, Bishop Pendergrass. Who else would like to speak?

Bishop Gerow. I want to agree with Bishop Pendegrass that the religious leaders of this locality are doing everything possible. Now, fortunately I occupy a position somewhat different from the position of the Rabbi and some of the others. I'm not going to lose my job when I speak. And this is what we have done briefly. We have worked from time immemorial upon the principle that the church building is the house of God and—anyone who comes sincerely to worship Almighty God is welcome. And in our Catholic churches it is not a bit unknown or uncommon to see a Negro or small group of Negroes—I'm speaking of what you might call the white churches. I don't like to call them by that name, but you'll understand better when I speak of them in that way. It is not all uncommon to see a Negro or small group of Negroes attending Mass or another devotion and coming to the Communion rail with the rest of the congregation to receive Communion.

There was an occasion on which I was very, very happy. On the day of the burial of President Kennedy we had a memorial service to which we invited leading ministers of the city and the high officials of the city, county and State. We had a nice congregation. In fact, someone who couldn't get in, told me there were over a thousand turned away who couldn't get in. But we did have a nice representation of ministers and civic officials. What pleased me most at that time was when Communion time came there was a nice group of Negroes that came up to receive Communion and knelt at the Communion rail right beside the rest of the congregation. There was no resentment. It was just a normal thing because it had been normal in the past.

Now, I feel that then another thing, we have integrated our schools, as Bishop Pendergrass said, not entirely, but on a gradual basis. We sent out word last year that our schools were to be integrated starting with the first grade this year and, of course, an increase in years to come, because we felt we had a problem there that we had to solve and if we tried to take too great a step at one time we might be set back. I was surprised at the fine reaction I got from a number of our Catholic people. I can't say that that same reaction was found in all cases. I did get some pretty bad reaction. In fact, a few, not many, of our parents were withdrawing their children from the Catholic school. However, this was to be expected.

But, I feel that we are making progress. Now, I feel that I say this because I think this represents the intention and the desire of the ministerial body of Mississippi—at least of Jackson. I know, I have gotten to know these people. We have been meeting together. We have gotten to know each other and trust each other. And I know them and they want to do the same thing. And they are doing a good job, I think. And they are trying their best to do it. And I want to tell them that I appreciate what they are doing. May God bless you.

Commissioner HESBURGH. Yes?

Reverend WHITNEY. One word. I think that perhaps among the many things the people misunderstand is that the segregator is more victimized than the segregated, and that religion here seeks to save the total man. And that as long as the Negro is not really free, then none of us is free. This is the problem we are grappling with. And to say that God is going to work this thing out—but you see God's not going to work it out apart from us. He will work it out through us. We are the instrument through which God will solve this problem. I think it is good to put it in the hands of God, but I think our lives must be dedicated to the proposition that we are going to do the will of God in our day and in our time. We can't just say, "Well, it will happen after a while." We must be the instruments through which God must work.

Commissioner HESBURGH. Ladies and gentlemen, we have used up our time but I promised Rabbi Nussbaum I would let him close with an aphorism famous among the rabbis.

Rabbi NUSSBAUM. Well, everybody has gotten in a lick for their religion and I want to say something in behalf of mine. When the children of Israel came to the Red Sea and they heard about the Egyptian hords pursuing them, as we are all aware, they got scared and started crying to the Lord. And according to a rabbinic comment, the Lord said, "Moses, you tell those people to get up from their knees and stop praying and let them do something." This is what we have to do. We have a rabbinic aphorism that says, as I remember most of it, "The day is short, the work is much, the matter is urgent. It's not up to you to complete the work. But, neither are you free to desist from it." And I say thanks to the Commission for being here to give us the kind of encouragement that we need to continue with this work that has gone on for many years in this State of Mississippi which we all love.

[Applause.]

Commissioner HESBURGH. Ladies and gentlemen, on behalf of all of you and, I presume, on behalf of all those who are seeing us on television, I want to thank each and every one of these gentlemen for the wonderful hour they have given us. I think it has taken courage on their part to say what they have said. I think we have tried to blend courage with realism, but also with idealism which, after all, will get us where we are going. It is customary at both the beginning and the close of Commission meetings to have an official statement from our Chairman who, as you know, is Dr. John Hannah, president of Michigan State University.

Chairman HANNAH. Thank you, Father Hesburgh.

As we bring this Mississippi hearing to a close the Commission on Civil Rights extends its appreciation to the U.S. District Court in Jackson. And then I want to say a few words about the hearing. First we want to express our appreciation to the Federal district judges who made possible the use of the Federal courtroom for last week's executive session. We are very grateful to the director of the Veterans' Administration Center and his staff members whose cooperation greatly facilitated the conducting of this week's public sessions. We are also grateful to Chief U.S. Marshal Jack T. Stuart and his deputies who have ably assisted us during all sessions of the hearings.

A special measure of appreciation must go to the members, past and present, of the Mississippi State Advisory Committee to this Commission who have worked so patiently and courageously to help awaken the consciences of their fellow Mississippians. Their work has been performed under conditions which have sometimes been extremely trying. It is reassuring that so able and dedicated a group of Mississippians will remain in constant communication with us and will be continuing their important work long after the Commission has left Mississippi. We thank the many members of our own staff who have worked so hard in making this hearing possible. In the view of all the Commisisoners, they have done very well indeed.

Most of all, we should like to express our appreciation to all those who have appeared before the Commission during these hearings. It was encouraging to us that the Hon. Paul B. Johnson, Governor of Mississippi, not only came before the Commission to discuss the problems and progress of his State but urged other responsible Mississippians to seize upon this hearing as an opportunity to put the facts about Mississippi in perspective. We are grateful to State Attorney General Joe T. Patterson and Mayor Allen C. Thompson of Jackson and to the scores of other private citizens and public officials from whom we have sought information during the past 2 weeks.

For some of these, it was not an easy experience to testify before the Commission, but we would assure them that our sole concern has been to elicit facts, not to cause any person discomfort or embarrassment. We are aware, too, that some of those who testified here had already paid a substantial price in physical suffering or economic loss for speaking their convictions or attempting to exercise their rights. It is a tribute to Mississippi that such citizens have been willing to appear at this hearing and the Commission hopes, with them, that the climate of opinion in Mississippi is now such that people can speak the truth as they see it without risking reprisals or abuse.

When the Commission opened these hearings 2 weeks ago, we announced that we intended to call a broad range of witnesses so that we might examine allegations of racial discrimination in voting and law enforcement objectively and in context. We have conscientiously sought to do this, both in the executive session and in the public session. Since the beginning of the hearings, the Commission has heard the testimony of some 100 Mississippians of both races, representing a wide spectrum of experience and opinion. The hearing itself was the outgrowth of months of preparation and research, including many field trips by staff members and the sifting of voluminous records and complaints in an earnest attempt to examine as fully as possible the conditions which have produced civil rights problems, in certain parts of this State, of a kind and intensity rarely encountered elsewhere. It was determined long before the Commission arrived here that our major interests would be the present status and future prospects of civil rights in Mississippi rather than an exhaustive and largely profitless review of past injustices.

We have not presumed to come to Mississippi either as sanctimonious critics whose own home States are perfect havens of racial equality or as all-knowing physicians equipped to prescribe instant cures for Mississippi's social ills. We are simply attempting, as best we can, to fulfill an obligation which has been ours since 1957 when the Congress first charged us with finding and evaluating facts and recommending corrective action in the complex and difficult field of civil rights. Though final decisions must wait till a later time, it is probable that the Commission, after it has studied the transcripts of this hearing, will issue a report, including recommendations, to the President and Congress. A somewhat broader gauged report on the status of civil rights in Mississippi will follow at a later date.

It is too early to assess fully the testimony we have received here, but some tentative observations may be in order. First, it seems clear that, despite some encouraging signs of change, many of Mississippi's Negro citizens continue to face extremely serious and unwarranted denials in voting and law enforcement. In most parts of the country citizens of both races take the fundamental right to vote for granted. It has been very disturbing to realize that there are still places in Mississippi where merely seeking to register, much less to vote, requires considerable courage. Some white Mississippians in far too many counties are still seemingly bent on denying the vote to Negro citizens by the application of discriminatory standards, intimidation, and violence. It is hoped that thoughtful and conscientious white leaders in this State will take every necessary step to guarantee the free exercise of this fundamental citizenship right throughout Mississippi.

The Commission has been heartened during this hearing by signs of a developing consensus among many responsible white Mississippians that it is poor economics, poor law, and poor morality to encourage or permit racial violence and injustice. Physical security is basic to all other rights and the Commission is appalled to find that there are many citizens in some Mississippi communities who fear for their lives.

The people of Greenville, Miss., have been able to develop a community in which Negroes as well as whites feel that they will receive fair and just treatment and adequate protection from law enforcement officials in their town. What was possible in Greenville we are sure is possible throughout this State. Business and political leaders of other communities from which we heard testimony would find it no less beneficial to insist on well-trained, impartial officers of the law. Violence and disorder are certainly less likely to occur in any community, North or South, where fair and equal administration of justice acts as a curb on distrust of, and contempt for, the law.

Although education was not a primary field for consideration at these hearings, the testimony of witness after witness pointed to the need for improved educational opportunities as a key to many of Mississippi's problems. Certainly Mississippi cannot achieve the economic growth so many of her leaders see as a crucial requirement in the decades ahead without a determined effort to increase the amount and quality of training available to her young people—especially those coming from Negro and poor white families. Attempting to maintain a segregated system that results in lower quality and higher cost will not advance the long-term best interests of any group of Mississippi citizens. It is encouraging to note that school authorities in some Mississippi communities have apparently recognized that Mississippi can ill afford to shortchange its children by rejecting Federal aid to education as it becomes available in ever larger amounts.

On these and other matters the best decisions for Mississippi are likely to flow from frank and open discussions, shared in by Negro Mississippians who constitute almost half of the State's population. It is a matter of common sense, as well as simple justice, that Negro citizens be allowed a larger voice in the decision-making process. More than one witness indicated the need for free and open exchange between white and Negro citizens in Mississippi. It would seem that the possibilities for improved communication between the races are better now than at any time in the past 10 years. Hopefully, the voices of moderation now being heard, after a long silence, will begin speaking clearly and forcefully for a progressive Mississippi.

As Governor Johnson said in his appearance before the Commission, Mississippi is, and must be, an integral part of America. It is not good for this State or for the rest of the Nation to assume that Mississippi is a place outside the normal flow of American life and culture. As Mr. Leroy Percy of Greenville said yesterday, sitting in the chair, which I now sit, "The people want to be in the mainstream of America and not in the backwater. They are tired of being led by the dead hand of the past * * * they want a change and I believe they are going to get it."

And finally, 10 days ago, at the opening session, the Commission announced that it hoped to conduct the hearings that we now close in a manner which would assist Mississippians in finding solutions to the problems in their State. We have tried as best we knew how to keep that pledge. We sincerely hope that we have in some measure succeeded.

These hearings stand adjourned.

[Applause.]

(Whereupon, the hearings of the U.S. Commission on Civil Rights were concluded at 1:50 p.m.)

U.S. COMMISSION ON CIVIL RIGHTS

MONDAY AFTERNOON SESSION, FEBRUARY 15, 1965

The Commission met in the Recreation Hall, Veterans Administration Center, 1500 East Woodrow Wilson Drive, Jackson, Miss., at 2:00 p.m., Monday, February 15, 1965, the Hon. John A. Hannah, Chairman of the Commission, presiding.

Present: John A. Hannah, Chairman; Eugene Patterson, Vice Chairman; Mrs. Frankie Muse Freeman, Commissioner; Erwin N. Griswold, Commissioner; Robert S. Rankin, Commissioner.

Also Present: Howard W. Rogerson, Acting Staff Director; William L. Taylor, General Counsel; Michael O. Finkelstein, Assistant General Counsel.

PROCEEDINGS

Chairman HANNAH. Ladies and gentlemen, the Civil Rights Commission is in session this afternoon for the purpose of receiving certain documents that have been subpenaed.

Let the record show that I am John A. Hannah, the Chairman of the Commission.

On my right is Mr. Eugene Patterson, the Vice Chairman; on his right is Dr. Robert Rankin; and on my left is Mrs. Frankie Freeman, all members of the Commission.

We will ask the audience to remain quiet and to terminate any of their activities with reference to arrangements that they are making for wires until this session has been concluded. Mr. Taylor, will you call the first witness.

Mr. TAYLOR. The first witness is Sheriff Jack Purvis, Sheriff of Humphreys County.

Chairman HANNAH. Mr. Purvis, will you raise your right hand?

(Whereupon, Mr. John D. Purvis was duly sworn by the Chairman and testified as follows:)

Chairman HANNAH. Have a chair, sir. Mr. Purvis, who is the gentleman accompanying you?

Mr. PURVIS. Mr. James T. Bridges.

Mr. BRIDGES. I am an attorney at law and his counsel.

Chairman HANNAH. All right, Mr. Taylor, will you handle the proceedings?

TESTIMONY OF JOHN D. PURVIS, SHERIFF, HUMPHREY'S COUNTY, MISS.

Mr. TAYLOR. Mr. Purvis, you are currently the sheriff of Humphreys County, is that correct?

Mr. PURVIS. Yes.

Mr. TAYLOR. And you are here pursuant to a subpena which calls for the following documents:

"All records, documents and memoranda in your possession or control including, without limitation, all records of complaints, affidavits and warrants, records of arrests, booking sheets and investigative reports pertaining to the arrest of Mary Thomas on or about September 4, 1964, in Belzoni, Mississippi, and the arrest of Aline Hunter on or about January 8, 1965, in Belzoni, Mississippi."

Secondly, "All photographs of applicants for voter registration, or of persons entering or leaving the courthouse or any office therein, taken by you or any officer, agent, deputy, or assistant under your supervision during the period from August 1, 1964, to date."

I will ask you to produce the documents.

Mr. PURVIS. I have some copies of these, and I would like to——

Mr. BRIDGES. We don't have copies of those.

Mr. PURVIS. We don't have. Well, I would like to have them back, because they are part of my records.

Mr. TAYLOR. Yes, sir. All of the documents you produce will be returned to you.

Mr. PURVIS. Oh. Well, good, sir.

Mr. TAYLOR. The clerk will give you a receipt for them.

Mr. PURVIS. This is the warrant and the mittimus and the cost bill on Mary Thomas.

Chairman HANNAH. Are you giving these numbers?

Mr. FINKELSTEIN. No, sir.

Mr. TAYLOR. They will be listed on the receipt.

Mr. PURVIS. This is the entry on the jail docket. It is a photostat copy of it.

Mr. TAYLOR. In the case of Mary Thomas.

Mr. PURVIS. And also a receipt for the bond from Step and Hopkins.

Mr. TAYLOR. Good.

Mr. PURVIS. This is a certified copy of the Mississippi Privilege Tax License that she bought on the 12th day of February for her beer items. It is a certified document. I believe that is all I have on Mary Thomas.

Mr. TAYLOR. Those are all the documents you have with respect to Mary Thomas?

Mr. PURVIS. That's right.

Mr. TAYLOR. Do you have documents concerning the other matters?

Mr. PURVIS. This is a bench warrant and affidavit for a bad check, and a check. I got this from the justice of the peace, and it has to go back into his files.

Mr. TAYLOR. Yes, sir. It will be returned to you.

Mr. PURVIS. This is a photostatic copy of the jail docket.

Mr. BRIDGES. I have a verifax picture of the affidavit for the bad check, which we would like to substitute in lieu of the affidavit which I have to carry back to the justice of the peace. It is just a verifax picture of the affidavit showing the bad check and so forth that you have the original of.

Mr. TAYLOR. Yes. We have an original stating under the heading "Affidavit for Bad Check."

Mr. BRIDGES. Yes. I have a verifax picture of that which I could leave in place of the original which I have to return. That's all right; you can keep it to examine, but when we leave I would like to have it back.

Mr. TAYLOR. You can have them now and we will take the verifax. That does not contain a copy of the check, does it?

Mr. BRIDGES. It has the face of it, and I have the endorsements on the back written below it there.

Mr. TAYLOR. I see.

Mr. BRIDGES. We will be glad for you to have the original as long as we can carry it back. It is not a part of our records; it is a part of the records of the justice of the peace court.

Mr. FINKELSTEIN. May I see the original again?

Mr. BRIDGES. Yes, sir.

Mr. PURVIS. Now there has been a good many to take the voter test, but I only have six pictures of those people.

Mr. TAYLOR. I see. The documents you just gave us are all the documents that relate to——

Mr. PURVIS. Those two cases.

Mr. TAYLOR. Aline Hunter and Mary Thomas?

Mr. PURVIS. Yes.

Mr. TAYLOR. And now these are photographs?

Mr. PURVIS. Yes. I only have six of those pictures.

Mr. TAYLOR. Mr. Purvis, are these all of the documents in your possession that are called for by the subpena?

Mr. BRIDGES. Yes.

Mr. PURVIS. I believe, yes.

Mr. TAYLOR. That is Mary Thomas, Aline Hunter and the photographs.

Mr. PURVIS. Yes.

Mr. TAYLOR. These documents will be marked and a receipt given to Sheriff Purvis. Mr. Chairman, I recommend that the witness be kept under subpena until Tuesday, February 16, at 1:30 in the afternoon, during which session the documents will be returned to him.

Chairman HANNAH. Is this all that you need from Sheriff Purvis?

Mr. TAYLOR. Yes, sir.

Chairman HANNAH. Thank you, gentlemen. You are excused. We will see you again tomorrow afternoon. If you are here by 1:45 tomorrow, it will be time enough because I think that we will go through until about 12:30 and therefore may not be back until about 1:45.

Mr. BRIDGES. All right, sir.

(Witness excused.)

Chairman HANNAH. Call the next witness.

Mr. TAYLOR. The next witness is G. H. Hood, Circuit Clerk for Humphreys County.

Chairman HANNAH. Mr. Hood, will you raise your right hand?

(Whereupon, Mr. G. H. Hood was duly sworn by the Chairman and testified as follows:)

Chairman HANNAH. Mr. Hood, would you introduce your counsel?

Mr. BRIDGES. James T. Bridges of Belzoni, Miss., counsel for Mr. Hood.

Chairman HANNAH. Mr. Taylor, will you handle the proceedings?

TESTIMONY OF G. H. HOOD, CIRCUIT CLERK, HUMPHREY'S COUNTY, MISS.

Mr. TAYLOR. Mr. Hood, you are currently the Circuit Clerk or Registrar for Humphreys County, is that correct?

Mr. HOOD. I am.

Mr. TAYLOR. You are here pursuant to a subpena which calls for the following records:

"All written applications for voter registration submitted to the Registrar, Humphreys County, during the period from August 1, 1964, to date."

I ask you to produce the documents called for.

(Documents handed to Mr. Taylor.)

Mr. HOOD. They are numbered on the top, sir, right under that clip.

Mr. BRIDGES. Mr. Chairman, these records are a part of the permanent records of Mr. Hood's office, and we can't leave the originals here except for a short time. We have to have them back.

Chairman HANNAH. Can we keep them until tomorrow and return them then?

Mr. BRIDGES. Yes, sir.

Chairman HANNAH. That will be satisfactory.

Mr. TAYLOR. Mr. Hood, are these all of the documents called for in the subpena?

Mr. HOOD. That's right.

Mr. TAYLOR. They are. In that case, the clerk will give a receipt to Mr. Hood for the documents. I recommend that the witness remain under subpena and be excused until tomorrow, February 16, at 1:45.

Chairman HANNAH. Thank you very much, gentlemen. You are excused until tomorrow.

(Witness excused.)

Chairman HANNAH. Mr. Recorder, will you indicate on the record that Dean Griswold, another member of the Commission, is now in attendance.

Mr. TAYLOR. Mr. Chairman, the next witness is Dan C. Thompson, Chief of Police, Canton, Miss.

Chairman HANNAH. Mr. Thompson, will you raise your right hand?

(Whereupon, Mr. Dan C. Thompson was duly sworn by the Chairman and testified, as follows:)

Chairman HANNAH. Will you introduce your counsel?

Mr. GOZA. Mr. Robert Goza, city attorney, Canton.

Chairman HANNAH. Mr. Taylor, will you proceed.

TESTIMONY OF DAN C. THOMPSON, CHIEF OF POLICE, CANTON, MISS.

Mr. TAYLOR. Chief Thompson, you are currently the Chief of Police of Canton, Miss., is that correct?

Mr. THOMPSON. Yes, sir.

Mr. TAYLOR. You are here under subpena to produce the following documents:

All records, documents and memoranda in your possession or control including, without limitation, all records of complaints, affidavits and warrants, records of arrests, investigative reports medical reports, and statements pertaining to the beating of Mirza Hamid Kizilbash, in Canton on or about May 29, 1964.

Secondly—

All records, documents, and memoranda in your possession or control including, without limitation, all records of complaints, affidavits and warrants, records of arrests, investigative reports, and statements pertaining to the following matters:

(a) All incidents of violence at the building known as the Freedom House, 838 Lutz Street, Canton, Miss., from January 1, 1964, to date, including, without limitation, the bombing on or about June 8, 1964, the attempted bombing on or about July 11, 1964, and the shootings on or about May 7, 1964, May 20, 1964, and August 2, 1964.

(b) The bombing of Joe and Barb's Grocery Store, Canton, on or about September 5, 1964.

(c) The attempted bombing of a grocery store owned by George Washington, Sr., in Canton, on or about September 5, 1964.

(d) The bombing of the home of Mrs. Alberta Robinson, 315 Second Firebaugh Avenue, Canton, on or about June 12, 1964.

(e) The bombing of Pleasant Green Church, in Canton, on or about June 12, 1964.

(f) The burning of the Christian Union Church, near Ridgeland, on or about July 20, 1964.

(g) The burning of the Willing Workers' Meeting Hall, Gluckstadt Community Church, Gluckstadt, on or about August 11, 1964.

(h) The burning of St. John's Baptist Church, Valley View, on or about September 17, 1964, and

(i) The burning of the Cedar Grove Church, Route 43, near Canton, Madison County, on or about September 17, 1964.

I ask you to produce the documents.

Mr. THOMPSON. In regard to No. 1, I have nothing on that. I have no information on that.

Mr. TAYLOR. You have none of the records called for in the case of Mirza Hamid Kizilbash, is that correct?

Mr. THOMPSON. It was not reported to my department. This is a report of W. R. Cook, a police officer, of May 20, 1964. That is in regard to that alleged shooting, May 20, at 838 Lutz Street.

Mr. TAYLOR. Right.

Mr. THOMPSON. The next one is a report on the bombing of the Freedom House, which happened June 8.

Mr. TAYLOR. Right.

Mr. GOZA. Under Item (d), under No. 2, that date is incorrect. It is June 12, 1964, instead of July 12. Now I don't know what your procedure is in that regard. Would you like to correct your error and receive our report for that day, or leave it like it is and let us report to you that we have no report of a bombing on July 12?

Chairman HANNAH. Correct the error.

Mr. TAYLOR. We would be glad to make that emendation and accept the document for that date.

Mr. GOZA. Here is the report of that date; that satisfies your requirement. And (e) is the same thing. Both those incidents happened on June 12 instead of July 12.

Mr. TAYLOR. All right. The record will be corrected in that respect.

Mr. THOMPSON. Next is a report on September 5, in connection with the bombing of Joe and Barb's Grocery, and attempted bombing of George Washington's grocery.

Mr. TAYLOR. That relates to both items, (b) and (c)?

Mr. THOMPSON. Right.

Mr. TAYLOR. May I inquire with respect to the document that relates to the bombing of the Pleasant Grove Baptist Church whether there is a signature or any indication of the identity of the person who prepared the documents? It does not seem to appear on the document itself.

Mr. GOZA. I noticed that myself, that it had no signature on it. It is the report of Officer Allen Halbert. It is unsigned.

Mr. THOMPSON. Items (f), (g), (h), and (i) were not reported to our office.

Mr. TAYLOR. If I may, I would like to review this for a moment. With respect to Item 1, the Kizilbash case, you have no records on that.

Mr. THOMPSON. No.

Mr. TAYLOR. With respect to (2), you have given us all the document with relation to (a) : incidents of violence at the building known as the Freedom House.

Mr. GOZA. With the exception of the shootings on May 7 and August 2, which were not reported to the police department.

Mr. TAYLOR. Therefore, you have no documents on that.

Mr. GOZA. We have no documents on that.

Mr. TAYLOR. You have given us a document with respect to item (b), Joe and Barb's Grocery Store. Those are all the documents you have on that matter?

Mr. GOZA. That is correct.

Mr. TAYLOR. You have given us a document with respect to item (c), the bombing of the grocery store owned by George Washington. And that is the same item, I take it, as the——

Mr. GOZA. That's correct.

Mr. THOMPSON. Same date.

Mr. TAYLOR. With respect to (d), you have given us a document with respect to the bombing of the home of Mrs. Alberta Robinson, on or about June—rather than July—12, 1964.

Mr. GOZA. That is correct.

Mr. TAYLOR. And that is all the documents you have on that; is that correct?

Mr. THOMPSON. Yes.

Mr. GOZA. That is correct.

Mr. TAYLOR. With respect to (e), the bombing of Pleasant Green Church, in Canton, on or about July 12—or June 12, again, you have——

Mr. GOZA. They are both in the same documents, I believe.

Mr. TAYLOR. And with respect to the rest of the items, (f), (g), (h) and (i), you have no documents in your possession or control.

Mr. GOZA. That is correct. We have, further, the jail docket of the Canton police department which pertains to the attempted bombing on

July 11, 1964, and arrests that were made in connection with that bombing. And that is the only further information we have.

If I may make a request of the Commission, that is a permanent jail docket and we would certainly like to have it back as quickly as possible.

Chairman HANNAH. Would tomorrow be soon enough?

Mr. GOZA. Yes, sir, Mr. Chairman, it would. One of those documents has nothing whatsoever of interest to this Commission in it, and if we may take it back with us, we would appreciate it.

Mr. TAYLOR. Mr. Chairman, I would recommend that we copy the relevant portions of these documents and return them before the witness leaves today, and the other items can be returned on the return date of the subpena, which is later in the week. Would that be satisfactory?

Mr. GOZA. That will be satisfactory. Could we have a determination by the Commission or its representative that one of the dockets has nothing of interest in it; the little black book is merely a log which could be probably photostated. Could we have such a determination at this time?

Mr. FINKELSTEIN. Well, we will have to examine the books.

Mr. GOZA. Fine. But will we have that determination before we leave?

Mr. TAYLOR. We will return the books to you.

Mr. GOZA. Fine.

Chairman HANNAH. Anything further, Mr. Taylor? When are these gentlemen to return?

Mr. TAYLOR. Well, the clerk will give a receipt for the aforementioned documents, and I recommend that the witness be kept under subpena and excused until Friday, February 19, at 9 a.m.

Chairman HANNAH. You are excused.

(Witness excused.)

Mr. TAYLOR. The next witness is Sheriff Jack Cauthen, Sheriff of Madison County.

Chairman HANNAH. Sheriff, will you raise your right hand?

(Whereupon, Mr. Jack Cauthen was duly sworn by the Chairman and testified as follows:)

Chairman HANNAH. Will you introduce your counsel, sir?

Mr. CAUTHEN. This is Mr. W. S. Cain.

Chairman HANNAH. Mr. Taylor, proceed.

TESTIMONY OF JACK CAUTHEN, SHERIFF, MADISON COUNTY, MISS.

Mr. TAYLOR. Mr. Cauthen, are you the Sheriff of Madison County?

Mr. CAUTHEN. Yes, sir.

Mr. TAYLOR. You are here pursuant to a subpena calling for precisely the same documents as I read with respect to Police Chief Thompson.

Mr. CAUTHEN. Yes.

Mr. TAYLOR. Unless you would like me to, I will not repeat——

Mr. CAUTHEN. I heard it all, so that's all right.

Mr. TAYLOR. I ask you to produce the documents called for in the subpena.

Mr. CAUTHEN. Can I start with No. 1, please?

Mr. TAYLOR. Yes, sir.

Mr. CAUTHEN. There was no complaint made. I have no records or documents pertaining to No. 1.

Mr. TAYLOR. That is the——

Mr. CAUTHEN. This is Mr. Kizilbash.

Mr. TAYLOR. Yes, sir; proceed.

Mr. CAUTHEN. No. 2(a), I have no records. All this is pertaining to the city, what happened within the city of Canton. Everything there was more or less handled by the police and—just a second. Any records that I have would be contained in this jail docket of arrests, convictions and so forth pertaining to that.

Mr. CAIN. We would submit this jail docket, if it please the Commission, but we would like to have it back as soon as we can get it, under the same conditions that the marshal of the city submitted his.

Mr. TAYLOR. With the Commission's permission, we can copy any relevant information from the docket and make it available tomorrow morning if someone wishes to claim it at that time.

Mr. CAIN. Thank you, sir.

Mr. CAUTHEN. That will be available tomorrow morning?

Mr. TAYLOR. Yes, sir, at our office in this building.

Mr. CAUTHEN. Would that be this same office?

Mr. TAYLOR. That is Room C–125.

Mr. CAUTHEN. Is that the address on the subpena?

Mr. TAYLOR. Yes.

Mr. CAUTHEN. All right. That's fine.

Mr. TAYLOR. You may proceed.

Mr. CAUTHEN. Pertaining to (b), that will be the same answer.

Mr. TAYLOR. The only record you would have of (b) is any record contained in the jail docket that you have already submitted?

Mr. CAUTHEN. That's right. And there will be no record in there because there was no arrest made by my office. As for (c), there was an investigation by the Canton police, one representative of my office, the Mississippi Highway Patrol, and the FBI. I have no records on (c).

Mr. CAIN. If the Commission would wish a statement from this witness, we would be glad to give his name.

Chairman HANNAH. Would you like this information, Mr. Taylor?

Mr TAYLOR. Yes, sir, if a written statement could be received on this matter, we would be glad to receive it.

Mr. CAIN. All right, sir; that is on (c).

Mr. TAYLOR. Do I assume correctly that when you say there are no records in your possession or control, that means there are no records in possession or control of the deputy or agent to whom you refer?

Mr. CAIN. Yes, sir; we mean the office.

Mr. TAYLOR. You may proceed.

Mr. CAIN. Unfortunately, up to now, I might say for the benefit of the Commission we have kept too few records. We don't make records, except under normal conditions where there are arrests, the warrants and mittimuses and so forth are all in the justice of the peace's office. They are not retained by the sheriff. The sheriff keeps only investigative reports and statements. That would be about all he could possibly have in the way of records, that you have asked for.

Mr. TAYLOR. And you have no investigative reports or statements prepared?

Mr. CAIN. No, sir; not prepared for you at this time. But we would be very glad to prepare one and submit it.

Mr. TAYLOR. All right. You may proceed with the other items.

Mr. CAUTHEN. That completes (c).

Mr. TAYLOR. Yes, sir.

Mr. CAUTHEN. Items (d) and (e) will be exactly the same answer as we have just completed on (c).

Mr. TAYLOR. The same answer as (c)?

Mr. CAUTHEN. Yes.

Mr. TAYLOR. That is, that an investigation was made by one of your employees?

Mr. CAUTHEN. Yes, sir, deputy sheriff from my office.

Mr. TAYLOR. You have no document reflecting that investigation, but you will submit a report on it?

Mr. CAIN. We don't have any written documentary evidence whatsoever of the investigation. We will prepare one and submit it to you, yes, sir.

Mr. TAYLOR. All right. Fine.

Mr. CAIN. These, I would like the Commission to understand, were all made in conjunction with the Highway Patrol and the city, in some instances concurrently. The FBI, the Justice Department, and other agencies made concurrent investigations of these matters, and in some instances the Sheriff's office was not only hampered in its investigation, but was almost forced to discontinue its investigation because one person was running over another one.

Mr. TAYLOR. You may proceed with the other items.

Mr. CAUTHEN. I take for granted we have given you the answer down through (e).

Mr. TAYLOR. Yes, sir.

Mr. CAUTHEN. Item (f) the burning of the Christian Union Church, near Ridgeland, that was the first church to burn in Madison County. I have a report tendered me by an investigator of the Highway Patrol.

Bear in mind that when that church burned I was relatively new in office. I called for assistance from the Highway Patrol and the Fire Marshal's office. There were investigative agents from both offices on this and the other church burnings in Madison County. I requested them to submit a report to me of the investigation that we conducted together. I have that report. It is not complete. It was submitted to me, but that is not my report. That report is in my office. I do not have it here for the reason that it was not my report.

Mr. TAYLOR. In this case, the subpena called for all documents and memoranda in your possession or control, whether or not made by you. But I would simply recommend that the Commission take this matter under advisement at the present time.

Chairman HANNAH. Would it be possible for you to furnish us a copy of what you do have?

Mr. CAUTHEN. Yes, sir.

Chairman HANNAH. Well, that would satisfy our needs, would it not, Mr. Taylor?

Mr. TAYLOR. Yes, sir.

Chairman HANNAH. There is other information he is going to get for us, so he could include that statement.

Mr. CAIN. Yes, sir; we can do that. But I thought, myself, and advised the sheriff that the Highway Patrol would furnish you with an identical document, I'm certain of that.

Mr. TAYLOR. Well, if the Commission has no need for it, we can so advise you. But unless you are so advised, I would recommend that you produce the document.

Mr. CAIN. We would be glad to.

Mr. TAYLOR. You may proceed.

Mr. CAUTHEN. May I ask when and how to submit that report?

Mr. TAYLOR. I would like you to submit it at the same time that you reclaim the jail docket, if that is possible.

Chairman HANNAH. Do you have some duplicating machine so that you can photograph it?

Mr. TAYLOR. Yes, sir. Next item is (g), I believe.

Mr. CAUTHEN. The burning of the Willing Workers' Meeting Hall at Gluckstadt was investigated by a member of my office, a member from the Fire Marshal's office, at our request, and two investigators from the Mississippi Highway Patrol. Practically the same answer there.

Mr. TAYLOR. All right.

Mr. CAUTHEN. And for the last one, same thing.

Mr. TAYLOR. Will you submit that report also?

Mr. CAIN. We will have to prepare them. You understand we don't have them. We are going to prepare them.

Mr. TAYLOR. The report of your own investigation.

Mr. CAIN. That's correct.

Mr. TAYLOR. And you have no other documents in your possession?

Mr. CAIN. No.

Mr. TAYLOR. All right. Proceed.

Mr. CAUTHEN. Exactly the same answer for the others, (h) and (i).

Mr. TAYLOR. Investigations were made by persons under your supervision along with other investigative agencies.

Mr. CAUTHEN. Yes, sir.

Mr. TAYLOR. Do I understand your answer is that you have no documents relating to this, but you can submit a report to be prepared by an investigator? Is that correct?

Mr. CAUTHEN. That is correct.

Mr. TAYLOR. You have no documents of your own or of any other authorities such as the Highway Patrol?

Mr. CAUTHEN. We do not.

Mr. TAYLOR. In that case, the clerk will give you a receipt for the document submitted. I recommend that the witness be kept under subpena and excused until Friday, February 19, at 9 a.m.

Chairman HANNAH. Mr. Cauthen, you indicated that you had recently come into office when some of these incidents occurred. When did you assume the office of sheriff?

Mr. CAUTHEN. January 6, 1964.

Mr. TAYLOR. My last statement was that you were excused for the time being but are still under subpena and are to return February 19—that's a Friday—at 9 a.m.

Mr. CAUTHEN. At the same place?

Mr. TAYLOR. At the same place, yes, sir.

Mr. CAIN. We will bring in the report from the Highway Patrol tomorrow morning. We will bring in these others Friday morning, if that meets with your approval. We will have to prepare them.

Chairman HANNAH. But he will bring in copies of what you now have tomorrow. And where you are getting reports prepared by deputies or others, you will have them on Friday when you come in.

Mr. CAIN. Yes, sir.

Mr. CAUTHEN. The reports that are coming in tomorrow are not my reports.

Chairman HANNAH. I understand. They are photostats of what you have in your office submitted to you by the Highway Patrol or someone else.

Mr. CAUTHEN. Yes, sir.

Chairman HANNAH. Are you finished, Mr. Taylor?

Mr. TAYLOR. Yes, sir.

Chairman HANNAH. You are excused, gentlemen. Thank you.

(Witness excused.)

Chairman HANNAH. Mr. Taylor, call the next witness.

Mr. TAYLOR. The next witness is Sheriff Odell Anders, Sheriff of Adams County.

Chairman HANNAH. Sheriff Anders, will you raise your right hand?

(Whereupon, Mr. Odell Anders was duly sworn by the Chairman and testified, as follows:)

Chairman HANNAH. Will you introduce your counsel, sir.

Mr. ANDERS. This is Joseph Zuccaro. He is an attorney in Claiborne County.

Chairman HANNAH. All right, Mr. Taylor, proceed.

TESTIMONY OF ODELL ANDERS, SHERIFF, ADAMS COUNTY, MISS.

Mr. TAYLOR. Sheriff Anders, you are presently sheriff of Adams County, is that correct?

Mr. ANDERS. Yes.

Mr. TAYLOR. And you are here in response to a subpena calling for several documents. This is rather a long list, and if it is satisfactory, I will simply read them one by one and you can respond to each of the items.

"All records, documents, and memoranda in your possession or control, including, without limitation, all records of complaints, affidavits and warrants, records of arrests, investigative reports, and statements pertaining to (a), the burning of Mt. Plains Baptist Church, on or about September 21, 1963."

Mr. ANDERS. I didn't take office until January 6, 1964. So we don't have anything whatsoever which was, you know, before we took office in '64.

Mr. TAYLOR. Are there no records in the sheriff's office pertaining to that matter which may have been filed by one of your predecessors?

Mr. ANDERS. If there are, I haven't found them, no, sir.

Mr. ZUCCARO. They may be in the possession of the counsel of the previous sheriff. That's possible. We don't have them.

Chairman HANNAH. What's the name of the former sheriff?

Mr. ZUCCARO. William T. Ferrell.

Chairman HANNAH. And who was his counsel?

Mr. ZUCCARO. He is not under subpena, Mr. Chairman, and I don't know whether he has counsel or not. I think of all items—and the sheriff may correct me if I am incorrect—which occurred prior to January 6, 1964, the day on which this sheriff took office, there are no records in the sheriff's possession.

Mr. ANDERS. I think that would be through (d); (a), (b), (c) and (d).

Commissioner FREEMAN. Mr. Zuccaro, are you saying that the sheriff's office maintains no records?

Mr. ZUCCARO. There are some records, but nothing pertaining to those incidents. The sheriff, of course, then, was William T. Ferrell.

Commissioner GRISWOLD. Mr. Chairman, I wonder if the answers ought not to be given by the witness, who is under subpena and under oath, and not by his counsel.

Mr. ZUCCARO. The lady asked me; that's why I proceeded to answer.

Commissioner GRISWOLD. I think that is true. Nevertheless, it is only the witness who is under oath. And if we are taking answers that documents are not available, it seems to me they should come from the witness.

Mr. ANDERS. If there were records in the sheriff's office, I didn't find them. Now there might be; I don't know. But if there are any records on these four things before January 6 of '64, I don't know where they are. Now here's one I see, that Leonard Russell—this is (d), in Franklin County, which wouldn't be in Adams County records anywhere.

Commissioner GRISWOLD. Mr. Sheriff, have you made a search for these records?

Mr. ANDERS. In the Adams County office, yes, sir.

Commissioner GRISWOLD. And you have not found such records?

Mr. ANDERS. No, sir; we have no records at all on these things.

Commissioner GRISWOLD. When you took office as sheriff, did it appear that all or most of the papers and records had been removed by your predecessor?

Mr. ANDERS. Sir, I don't—I don't know how many had been removed or, you know, that hadn't been removed in the sheriff's office. I don't know what was there prior to January 6.

Commissioner FREEMAN. Were there any records in the office when you took office?

Mr. ANDERS. There were some records in the office. But what they are—I went through those and I didn't find anything pertaining to these records. I see one—you take (b) in this report, was in Port Gibson, which is outside the boundaries of Adams County, in Claiborne County. And I doubt that the previous sheriff has any records on those.

Mr. TAYLOR. Well, Mr. Anders, we understand that some of these relate to events that occurred outside of Adams County, but we are asking whether there are any documents in your possession or control relating to these matters, whether or not they took place in Adams County.

Mr. ANDERS. No. No, sir; and I say if there are any records, why I don't know where they are. And I'm sure there are no records on this.

Mr. TAYLOR. That answer applies to items (a), (b), (c), and (d) is that correct?

Mr· ANDERS. Yes. Right.

Mr. TAYLOR. Let's go to item (e).

Mr. ANDERS. I don't have anything on the burning of six crosses on April 24. The crosses were burned there. We don't have any investigation of them. I mean we answered all calls, but as far as investigating, when you come to where a cross is burning, possibly in the middle of a road or something like that, there is nothing left, no report, nothing to be made on it.

Mr. TAYLOR. So the answer is you have no records of telephone calls or investigations?

Mr. ANDERS. I have no records on that, no, sir.

Mr. TAYLOR. Next, go to item (f), "the vandalizing of St. Mark's Baptist Church, on or about June 6, 1964."

Mr. ANDERS. Yes, sir.

Mr. ZUCCARO. Mr. Chairman, these files here are active investigatory files of the sheriff's office. I am not seeking here to testify, Mr. Griswold, but I just want to point out that this information in here, this matter is still being investigated. I don't say extremely actively, but if things come up, this file is still open. These matters have been turned over—and Mr. Anders can—you can ask him about this when I'm through—to the Federal Bureau of Investigation and to the Mississippi State Highway Patrol.

Mr. ANDERS. I doubt that this was turned over, this St. Mark's Baptist Church. Actually, it looked like the work of some children, but the rest of them have been turned over, but this is actually all it was on the vandalizing of that church there.

Mr. TAYLOR. As in the case of the other witnesses, sheriff, these files will be returned to you at an early date.

Mr. Zuccaro. Let me ask you, Mr. Taylor. Are these files to be kept confidential, you know, because some of these matters are confidential and as I say, these matters are still under investigation.

Mr. Taylor. I can give you no assurance, sir, that the files will be kept confidential.

Mr. Zuccaro. Are these files going to be public matters now? I will ask the Chairman that. Mr. Chairman?

Commissioner Griswold. Well, I think this would lie within the judgment and discretion of the Commission. The Commission is not required to make everything public, but I think it is entitled to make it public if that is its judgment.

Chairman Hannah. I take it you are making a request that this particular document or some other documents you may produce not be publicly disclosed.

Mr. Zuccaro. That's right, sir, because, as I say—and I am certain that if I were an FBI attorney here, I would make the same request. The sheriff is still working on these matters.

Chairman Hannah. The Commission will certainly take notice of your request, and we will formally act on them before there is any public disclosure. I will advise you as to what the decision is.

Mr. Zuccaro. Thank you, sir.

Mr. Taylor. The next item is (g), "incidents of violence at the Dumas Motel since March 1964, including, without limitation, the burning of a cross near the motel, on or about June 20, 1964."

Mr. Anders. Now let me explain that anything that happens in the city of Natchez, that the chief of police does the entire investigation, and if we are called to help or if we find any information that might help in the investigation, then it is turned over to the chief of police. So anything that has happened inside the city limits, I don't have any records whatsoever pertaining to it.

Mr. Taylor. Then your answer is that on this specific item there are no records in your possession?

Mr. Anders. On this one, yes, sir; I was called and I did see it. I went down and did investigate it, but the things that I found were turned over to the chief of police in Natchez.

Mr. Taylor. And you do not possess a copy of any information you had?

Mr. Anders. No, sir; I surely don't.

Mr. Zuccaro. Mr. Taylor, I might state that Mr. Robinson, of course, has been subpenaed here and I suppose he will be next.

Mr. Taylor. Yes, sir.

Mr. Zuccaro. And we have gone over with Mr. Robinson these several items, and I think between the two, the sheriff and the chief, you will get everything that we have.

Mr. TAYLOR. Fine. Now the next item is (h), "the burning of the Jerusalem Baptist Church, Natchez, on or about July 12, 1964."

Mr. ANDERS. We have those. Since they were both burned on the same night, both in the same community, we wrote up the same report on (h) and (i), that is, the Bethel and Jerusalem Churches.

Mr. TAYLOR. Yes, sir. Those will be received.

Mr. ANDERS. And the FBI, Highway Patrol and the State Fire Marshal's office was called immediately on this. In fact, the Fire Marshal's office was there by noon on that date.

Mr. TAYLOR. We can proceed to item (j), "the throwing of molotov cocktails at the home of Willie Washington."

Mr. ANDERS. Which is in the city.

Mr. TAYLOR. So your answer is the same as with respect to the Dumas Motel.

Mr. ANDERS. Yes.

Mr. TAYLOR. In that case, let's proceed to (k), "the burning of Mt. Pilgrim Baptist Church, Natchez, on or about August 5."

Mr. ANDERS. And again may I say the FBI, Highway Patrol and Fire Marshal's office were called immediately after this report came in.

Mr. TAYLOR. Yes, sir; these documents will be received.

The next item is (1), "the burning of the Jake Frishman's Tavern, Natchez, on or about August 14."

Mr. ANDERS. That was within the city of Natchez. I believe you will find the next four, the Jitney Jungle Stores, and (n), the Cadillac Car Agency, and (o) Mayor Nosser's house, were all within the city limits.

Mr. TAYLOR. So you have no records of any of those?

Mr. ANDERS. No, sir, none whatsoever.

Mr. TAYLOR. And (p), your answer is the same?

Mr. ANDERS. (p), that's right, Willie Washington.

Mr. TAYLOR. (2), "all records, documents and memoranda in your possession or control, including, without limitation, all records of complaints, affidavits and warrants, records of arrests, investigative reports, medical reports, and statements pertaining to (a), the beating of Albert Whitley, on or about February 6, 1964."

The documents you are submitting are all the documents that you have in your possession on this matter?

Mr. ANDERS. That's right, yes.

Mr. TAYLOR. The next is "the beating of Archie Curtis and Willie Jackson on or about February 15, 1964."

Mr. ANDERS. Yes, sir.

Mr. TAYLOR. And those are all the documents you have with respect to that matter?

Mr. ANDERS. Yes.

Mr. TAYLOR. And the next one is "the beating of James Winston, on or about February 15, 1964."

(Documents handed to Mr. Taylor.)

Mr. TAYLOR. All right. Now we go to Item 3. "All records, documents, and memoranda in your possession and control, including, without limitation, all records of complaints, affidavits and warrants, records of arrests, investigative reports, medical reports, ballistic reports, and statements pertaining to: (a), the killing of Clifton Walker whose body was was found near the Poorhouse Road, Wilkinson County, on or about February 28, 1964."

Mr. ANDERS. That is outside the boundary of Adams County and I know nothing whatsoever about it. I have no records at all.

Mr. TAYLOR. And (b) "the shooting of Richard Joe Butler, on or about April 5, 1964, in Kingston, Adams County?"

Mr. ANDERS. I did not bring the jail record. I did bring the affidavit of arrest on the one arrest that we made there, and I brought that along.

Mr. TAYLOR. All right. Those documents will be received.

Mr. ANDERS. I would, if possible, especially on this one—on the others, too, but on this one more especially, I would ask that it be kept in strict confidence, because some of the things—this is the Richard Joe Butler case—some of the things that we have in here we hope will break the case, and we certainly don't want it to get out.

Chairman HANNAH. The Commission will certainly take that into consideration, Sheriff.

Mr. ANDERS. Thank you, sir.

Commissioner GRISWOLD. I think we have complete sympathy with you. But not having seen this, we simply aren't in any position to make any judgment.

Mr. ZUCCARO. I think you will, Dean, when you see it. So we are satisfied.

Mr. ANDERS. We are as interested in the case as you are and we wouldn't want anything to get into the wrong hands.

Mr. TAYLOR. Those are all the documents that are called for by the subpena?

Mr. ANDERS. Yes.

Mr. TAYLOR. In that case, I recommend the witness remain under subpena and be excused until Thursday, February 18, at 9 a.m.

Chairman HANNAH. You are excused, sheriff, until February 18, at 9. Thank you very much.

(Witness excused.)

Chairman HANNAH. Proceed, Mr. Taylor, with the next witness.

Mr. TAYLOR. The next witness is Police Chief J. T. Robinson, of Natchez.

Chairman HANNAH. Chief Robinson, will you raise your right hand.

(Whereupon, Mr. J. T. Robinson was duly sworn by the Chairman and testified, as follows:)

Chairman HANNAH. Will you introduce your counsel?

Mr. ROBINSON. This is Hon. Claude Pintard, from Natchez.

TESTIMONY OF J. T. ROBINSON, CHIEF OF POLICE, NATCHEZ, MISS.

Mr. TAYLOR. Chief Robinson, you are presently the police chief of the city of Natchez, is that correct?

Mr. ROBINSON. Yes, sir.

Mr. TAYLOR. And you are here pursuant to a subpena which calls for records which are precisely the same as those I read with respect to Sheriff Anders. So if you will, let us proceed in order with the documents called for.

First is 1(a).

Mr. ROBINSON. This was in the county, and the sheriff issued you the documents that he had on this. I don't have anything on (a), (b), (c) or (d), or (e).

Mr. TAYLOR. You have no records within your possession or control on any of these items, (a) through (e)?

Mr. ROBINSON. No, sir.

Mr. TAYLOR. All right. The next item is (f), the vandalizing of St. Mark's Baptist Church.

Mr. ROBINSON. This was also in the county, and I don't have anything on it either.

Mr. PINTARD. Mr. Taylor, I might add that Sheriff Anders is sheriff of Adams County, and Mr. Robinson is the chief of police of Natchez municipality. Mr. Anders' duty and investigatory work lies outside the municipality in any crimes, violence, or anything that occurs outside the city. We can give you (g), (j), (l), (m), (n), (o), and (p).

Mr. TAYLOR. In other words, with respect to all of the items other than those you have just mentioned, you have no documents within your possession or control.

Commissioner GRISWOLD. Mr. Chairman, I think we ought to get the witness' statement as to those——

Mr. ROBINSON. All right, sir; for everything that happened inside the city, I have the documents that you requested.

Mr. TAYLOR. All right. In that case, let's proceed with item (g), which is the first item for which you have a document.

Mr. ROBINSON. This is the "violence at Dumas Motel since March '64 including, without limitation, the burning of a cross near the motel, on or about June 20, '64."

Mr. PINTARD. Mr. Chairman, I likewise would like to make the same request as Mr. Zuccaro did for Mr. Anders, that these records be kept confidential, because they are still being investigated and we hope to conclude these matters in the future.

Chairman HANNAH. Gentlemen, the Commission will certainly take your request into consideration. And we will advise you of our decision. We will certainly not disclose them without advising you.

Mr. ROBINSON. Thank you, sir.

Mr. TAYLOR. You have submitted all the items in your possession under (g), is that right?

Mr. ROBINSON. Yes, sir.

Mr. TAYLOR. New we proceed to (j), is that correct?

Mr. ROBINSON. "Throwing of molotov cocktails at the home of Willie Washington, 1144 North Pine Street, Natchez, on or about July 12, 1964." I might add the FBI was called in on these cases, each one that we have had. And we have some information and some crime lab reports back in this file.

Mr. TAYLOR. All right, sir. You may proceed to item (1).

Mr. ROBINSON. "The burning of Jake Frishman's Tavern, Natchez, on or about August 14, 1964." I believe we have two in this one. No, sir; this is just one report·

Mr. TAYLOR. You may proceed.

Mr. ROBINSON. That is (m), isn't it? "The vandalizing of two Jitney Jungle Food Stores owned by Mayor John J. Nosser, on or about September 15, 1964." This is all under one report, too, (m) and (n), which was "the vandalizing of the Cadillac Car Agency owned by Orrick Metcalf on or about September 15." This happened the same night.

Mr. TAYLOR. Both of those reports are contained in the same volume you just handed us?

Mr. ROBINSON. Yes, sir.

Mr. TAYLOR. All right. You may proceed to (o), then.

Mr. ROBINSON. This (o) and (p) is contained in the same report, as this happened the same night, just a few minutes apart. And that is the bombing of Mayor John J. Nosser's home on or about September 26, '64, and the bombing of the home of Willie Washington, 1144 North Pine Street, on or about September 26, 1964. Both of these are under the same report.

Mr. TAYLOR. That will be received. What you have submitted now are all the documents within your possession and control pertaining to all of these items, (g), (j), (1), (m), (n), (o), and (p)?

Mr. Robinson. Yes, sir.

Mr. Taylor. Do I understand correctly that with respect to the remaining items under No. 1, you have no documents within your possession or control?

Mr. Robinson. No, sir, I do not.

Mr. Taylor. And your answer is the same to the items called for in 2 and the items in 3?

Mr. Robinson. Yes, sir, 3(a) and (b). I don't have anything on them at all.

Mr. Taylor. In that case, the clerk will give you a receipt for the documents that you have submitted. And I would recommend that this witness remain under subpena and be excused until Thursday, February 18, at 9 a.m.

Chairman Hannah. Gentlemen, you are excused. Mr. Robinson, we will expect to see you Thursday morning at 9.

Mr. Robinson. All right, Mr. Hannah. Thank you.

Chairman Hannah. Thank you very much.

(Witness excused.)

Chairman Hannah. Proceed, Mr. Taylor.

Mr. Taylor. The next witness is Mr. T. B. Birdsong, Commissioner of Public Safety.

Chairman Hannah. Mr. Birdsong, will you raise your right hand?

(Whereupon, Mr. T. B. Birdsong was duly sworn by the Chairman and testified as follows:)

TESTIMONY OF T. B. BIRDSONG, COMMISSIONER OF PUBLIC SAFETY, STATE OF MISSISSIPPI

Chairman Hannah. Will you introduce your counsel, please?

Mr. Birdsong. This is Mr. Lyell.

Mr. Lyell. Garland Lyell.

Mr. Lyell. Mr. Chairman, I believe I might clarify Colonel Birdsong's position if you allow me to make a short statement about the Highway Patrol and the Department of Public Safety and the function it plays.

Chairman Hannah. Proceed.

Mr. Lyell. Colonel Birdsong is the Commissioner of Public Safety, and as such, has charge of not only the Highway Patrol, but the other various Departments of that Commission, which includes, the Safety Responsibility Bureau, the Drivers License Division, and cattle theft, auto theft, and a separate investigation division consisting of 24 trained investigators, who are the only ones that play any role in this type of thing.

The Highway Patrolmen as such—there are a couple of hundred of them—their authority is limited to the enforcement of the traffic laws on the State highway. They do not have general police power. And it was only in May of 1964 that these 20-odd investigators were vested with full police power. Now they don't initiate investigations; they only operate when they are called in by local authorities, as has been indicated by some of the testimony you heard here this morning. And I believe that will help you to understand the role that they play in criminal matters in general, and in particular, the things about which you are inquiring here. Not being like a municipal police department or sheriff's office, they have no jail dockets; they have no permanent documents or records of any kind; nothing, but investigative files.

Colonel Birdsong has been directed to produce certain investigative files here which, particularly in the light of the Chairman and the Vice Chairman's remarks here today, as well as counsel's, with all deference and at the same time with a desire to cooperate with this Commission, we must respectfully decline to furnish. They are wide-open cases. They have unconfirmed rumors, defamatory material, incriminating material about various and sundry people, scores of people. And to furnish those files with any possibility of any leakage at this time would compromise many, many months of investigation. And we must respectfully decline to furnish them.

Chairman HANNAH. Mr. Taylor?

Mr. TAYLOR. Mr. Chairman, if I may proceed, I believe the record should reflect the documents called for in this case. Mr. Birdsong is here in response to a subpena which calls for the following records:

1. All records, documents, and memoranda pertaining to any request for assistance in law enforcement received by the Highway Patrol concerning incidents of racial violence from January 1, 1964, to date, in Adams, Madison, or Pike Counties, Miss.

2. All records, documents and memorandum in your possession or control including, without limitation, all records of complaints, affidavits and warrants, records of arrests, investigative reports, medical reports, ballistic reports, and statements pertaining to:

(a) The shooting of Richard Joe Butler on or about April 5, 1964, in Kingston, Adams County, and

(b) The killing of Clifton Walker, whose body was found near the Poorhouse Road, Wilkinson County, on or about February 28, 1964.

Let me go back a minute. Do you decline, Mr. Birdsong, to produce the documents called for in No. 1?

Mr. BIRDSONG. That is the records that we are talking about. Yes, sir.

Mr. TAYLOR. Do you decline to produce the records called for in No. 2?

Mr. BIRDSONG. We don't have those records to produce. We don't have any records to produce on that.

Mr. TAYLOR. Let me understand. Are we dealing with Item No. 1, all records, documents and memoranda pertaining to any request for assistance in law enforcement received by the Highway Patrol concerning incidents of racial violence from January 1, 1964, to date, in Adams, Madison, or Pike County, Miss.

Mr. BIRDSONG. If we had any, they were verbal. We have no records of such.

Mr. TAYLOR. You have no records under Item 1 ?

Mr. BIRDSONG. No, sir.

Mr. TAYLOR. Now we go to Item 2: Do you decline to produce the documents listed in Item 2 ?

Mr. LYELL. Those are the ones of which I speak, Mr. Taylor. I hope that surely counsel and the Commission should understand that these are serious, very serious cases, homicides and things of that kind. These investigators have worked many, many months in close cooperation with the FBI and others to try to solve these cases so that they can be presented to a grand jury for prosecution. Had they been completed, they would have been presented by now. Surely you realize how seriously you would compromise these things if there was any possibility of any leakage.

I am not on the witness stand, but when this subpena was served on Colonel Birdsong, he asked me and one of my colleagues to come look at these files. I can assure you gentlemen it would never do for any risk to be run at this time of any of the information in those files, or these unconfirmed rumors and unrundown leads—for there to be any possibility of any leakage at this time. They are working on these cases constantly.

Mr. TAYLOR. Well, let me proceed, so that I can understand Colonel Birdsong's answer to all of these requests.

No. 3 is "all records, documents, and memoranda in your possession or control including, without limitation, all records of complaints, affidavits and warrants, records of arrests, investigative reports, medical reports, and statements pertaining to the beating of Mirza Hamid Kizilbash, on or about May 29, 1964, near Canton, Madison County." Do you decline to produce those documents, Colonel Birdsong?

Mr. BIRDSONG. We don't have any documents pertaining to this beating.

Mr. TAYLOR. All right. Let me proceed then to item 4: "All records, documents, and memoranda in your possession or control including, without limitation, all records of complaints, affidavits and warrants, records of arrests, investigative reports, and statements pertaining to (a) the beating of Bruce Payne, on or about October 31, 1963, in or near Port Gibson, and (b) the assault of Bruce Payne and George Green, on or about November 2, 1963, in Jefferson or Claiborne County." Do you decline to produce those documents?

Mr. LYELL. For that reason.

Mr. TAYLOR. Colonel Birdsong, do you decline——

Mr. BIRDSONG. That would be the same status. I might explain this——

Mr. LYELL. But you have no record on it.

Mr. TAYLOR. I am not sure I understand your answer to it.

Mr. BIRDSONG. Sir?

Mr. TAYLOR. The answer to the question on the documents in Item 4 is that you decline to produce them?

Mr. BIRDSONG. I don't have them to produce.

Mr. TAYLOR. You say you have no records?

Mr. BIRDSONG. No records.

Mr. LYELL. Mr. Chairman, I am not too familiar with your procedures. As I say, we want to cooperate to the fullest. I don't know what relationship there is between this Commission and perhaps a Federal District Court, but I would be happy to recommend to Colonel Birdsong that he let a Federal district judge determine if that can be done.

Mr. TAYLOR. Mr. Chairman, I would recommend that the Commission take this matter under advisement. I would simply like to have Colonel Birdsong understand that this is a hearing pursuant to the Commission's duties to investigate allegations in writing, under oath or affirmation, that certain citizens of the United States are being deprived of their right to vote and have that vote counted by reason of their color, religion, race, or national origin, and further, to study and collect information concerning legal developments constituting a denial of equal protection of the laws under the Constitution because of race, color, religion or national origin, or in the administration of justice; that the documents are sought here because there are allegations that there have been denials of equal protection of the laws and the administration of justice in various areas in this State, and particularly the areas named in the subpena; that specifically, there have been allegations of failure by law enforcement officials to investigate or to investigate properly several of these matters.

The Commission has reason to believe that in the matters named in this subpena, the Highway Patrol did investigate or conduct some investigation or assist in an investigation in the cases, and therefore these documents are pertinent to our inquiry.

Chairman HANNAH. May I ask the counsel for Mr. Birdsong a question. In the event that the Commission should determine, as you requested, that these documents and records be kept confidential, would you advise Mr. Birdsong to permit the Commission to look at them?

Mr. LYELL. Well, Mr. Chairman, that is a hard question to answer right now in view of the fact that neither you nor the Vice Chairman could give any assurance that these things would be kept confidential. I take it, from the nature of your statement, that you could hardly assure that. Can you?

Chairman HANNAH. I think you didn't hear my question. As I worded the question, assuming that the Commission determined that it needed access to some of those specific records that have been called for in this subpena, and assuming that the Commission would assure you that the perusal of these records was for its own information, not for public disclosure, would you then make these records available to the Commission?

Mr. LYELL. I would like a little time to answer that question.

Chairman HANNAH. Do you have further questions you would like to ask, Mr. Taylor?

Mr. LYELL. May I ask this. If that was done, would you want copies of these things, or would you just want the perusal of them?

Chairman HANNAH. I ask only for an opportunity to look at them. This is a decision that will have to be made by the Commission; one the Commission will undoubtedly reach either this evening or later on this week. I recognize it is a hypothetical question, but I am asking you whether if that request were made, would you consider it and what would your answer be. I take it you will consider it if that request were made.

Mr. LYELL. If you tell us when we can have another audience with the Commission, I will give you an answer to that.

Mr. TAYLOR. We will take it under advisement and be in touch with counsel and Colonel Birdsong. I would recommend that Colonel Birdsong remain under subpena and be excused until Friday, February 19, at 1:45.

Chairman HANNAH. Thank you, gentlemen. We will see you, Colonel, on Friday, at 1:45. If the Commission decides that it would like to follow the procedure that I have suggested, we will get in touch with you, sir.

(Witness excused.)

Chairman HANNAH. Call the next witness, Mr. Taylor.

Mr. TAYLOR. Next witness is Mr. Walter Dell Davis, State Fire Marshal.

Chairman HANNAH. Mr. Davis, will you raise your right hand?

(Whereupon, Mr. Walter Dell Davis was duly sworn by the Chairman and testified, as follows:)

Chairman HANNAH. Will you introduce your counsellors?

Mr. DAVIS. This is Mr. Rubel Griffin, Assistant Attorney General, and Mr. Maurice Black, attorney for the insurance department.

Mr. DAVIS. Mr. Chairman, my true title is Commissioner of Insurance of the State of Mississippi, and ex officio Fire Marshal by reason of that office.

Chairman HANNAH. Thank you, Mr. Davis.

Will you proceed, Mr. Taylor.

TESTIMONY OF WALTER DELL DAVIS, COMMISSIONER OF INSURANCE, STATE OF MISSISSIPPI

Mr. TAYLOR. Mr. Davis, you are here pursuant to a subpena which calls for certain documents and records: "All documents, records, and memoranda including, without limitation, investigative files and any records of communications with or requests from State or local law enforcement officials, in your possession or control, pertaining to fires occurring at the following locations on the dates given:

"(a) Jake Frishman's Tavern, Natchez, Adams County, on or about August 14, 1964." Do you have documents?

Mr. DAVIS. Mr. Taylor, I am here. I am perfectly willing to submit the information requested, except for one slight technicality; that is, a conflict with the laws of the State of Mississippi, which I will ask Mr. Rubel Griffin, Assistant Attorney General, to explain for the benefit of the Commission.

Chairman HANNAH. Mr. Griffin.

Mr. GRIFFIN. Before I commence, I think it should be pointed out for the benefit of the record that Mr. Lyell, who appeared here with Colonel Birdsong just now, is also an Assistant Attorney General. Certainly the Attorney General's Office, as well as the Commissioner of Insurance, are willing to cooperate with this Committee, on our own, as well as in accordance with the statement given earlier to this Commission by the Governor.

We have written out Mr. Davis' response to the subpena and have entitled the same "Response to Subpena to Produce Records, and so forth, in the Custody of the State Fire Marshal." I will read this and then we will file it with the Commission:

Now comes Walter Dell Davis, Commissioner of Insurance of the State of Mississippi, and ex-officio State Fire Marshal and in response to subpena to produce records of the State Fire Marshal as scheduled by attachment thereto, dated January 28, 1965, says as follows:

1. That he has custody, as State Fire Marshal, of some of the records scheduled by attachment to said subpena, but that he has such custody and can produce same only when authorized to do so under the Law of the State of Mississippi, and particularly only as authorized by and to those persons to whom same are authorized to be produced by the terms of House Bill No. 398 of the Mississippi Legislature of 1964, same now appearing as Chapter 471 of the General Laws of Mississippi 1964; that by the provisions of said law any record of fires investigated by him or deputy are required to be "maintained" in his office, and are not authorized to be taken therefrom, and in his office are subject to inspection only by a party of interest in the fire loss. Such inspection is further limited by the requirement that no record or report of an investigation is subject to inspection pending such investigation or while same is in progress, and after completion of an investigation same is further subject to inspection, if it contains any evidence of arson or other felony, only by the district attorney and county attorney of the county in which it is indicated such offense may have been committed, except upon the written approval of such district attorney or the order of a court of competent jurisdiction. A copy of said act is attached hereto, numbered exhibit A and made a part hereof as if fully incorporated herein.

2. That the investigation of all of the fires scheduled by attachment to the subpena are either pending or in progress, in that all of the facts surrounding same have not been obtained, and some evidence in each indicates that arson or other felony may have been committed, and the district attorney of none of the counties involved has given the State Fire Marshal written authorization to permit inspection of any of such records to any person.

3. That the production of any of said records to this Commission would be a violation of law and of the legal duty of the State Fire Marshal, and that same would impede the further investigation of said fires and the subsequent enforcement of the criminal laws of the State of Mississippi.

Therefore, Respondent respectfully declines to produce or permit inspection of any of the records scheduled and in his custody, and prays that the aforesaid subpena be quashed.

"Respectfully submitted," signed by Maurice Black as attorney for the Insurance Department, and Peter M. Stocket, Jr., as Special Assistant under Joe Patterson.

Mr. TAYLOR. Commissioner Davis, in order that our Commission may understand the basis of your objection, and the cases in which you have no documents, I would like to go one by one and obtain the basis for your objection to each one, and if there are no records, the fact that there are no records.

Mr. DAVIS. Mr. Taylor, we have no objection to producing the records and testifying in support of the records. It is simply that the State law of the State of Mississippi prohibits my surrendering or placing these records before you until you have a directive of the consent of the district attorney in the district in which the offense occurred or else a court order. We have no objection whatsoever.

Mr. TAYLOR. Well, I meant your objection in a legal sense—I was not talking about a personal objection, sir.

Mr. DAVIS. No. I believe that that is set forth amply in the answer that was read. I know of no better way to express it.

Mr. TAYLOR. Well, you did say, as I heard it, that there were some cases in which you had no documents.

Mr. DAVIS. Yes, sir; and in order to conserve your time, I will say with the exception of No. 1, or (a), which is Jake Frishman's Tavern, Natchez, I am not certain that we made an investigation of that, but I am certain that all church fires were investigated. And I think I can safely say that the remainder of those enumerated were investigated by my office and we do have a record in those instances. It is possible that (a) could have been reported. If so, it was also investigated.

Mr. TAYLOR. All right. Now, with respect to (a), do you know of any records in your possession?

Mr. DAVIS. I am not certain.

Mr. TAYLOR. With respect to (b), as I understand it, counsel's objection was predicated on section 5699 of the Mississippi Code, is that right?

Mr. GRIFFIN. I forget the section number. We have a copy of it attached to the response there, Mr. Taylor. It was last amended in 1964.

Mr. TAYLOR. 5699, Mississippi Code.

Mr. GRIFFIN. The title of it would probably give you the section number there.

Mr. TAYLOR. And then succeeding sections 5702 and 5704. There are diverse grounds provided in those sections, and I would like to understand what the grounds are with respect to each of these cases.

Mr. DAVIS. I think the same answer would apply to each, Mr. Taylor.

Mr. TAYLOR. Well, you stated, for example, Commissioner, that you were not permitted, if I am correct—to reveal records where there is physical evidence of arson or other felony.

Mr. DAVIS. I think I could answer you by saying that in our opinion, there is physical evidence of arson in each of the church fires.

Mr. TAYLOR. Is it also true that each one of these cases is under active investigation?

Mr. DAVIS. Not a single case has been closed. And I might further add that we have worked in conjunction with the Federal Bureau of Investigation I believe on every case. We communicate with each other, and no case has been closed where they are concerned and they are still under active investigation.

Mr. TAYLOR. Am I correct, then, in saying that no case has been closed; therefore, no case has been solved?

Mr. DAVIS. That is exactly right, sir.

Commissioner FREEMAN. Mr. Davis, did you indicate that the records could be available for inspection upon the approval of the district attorney?

Mr. DAVIS. Yes, ma'am; yes, indeed.

Commissioner FREEMAN. In line with your efforts and offer of cooperation, have you inquired of the district attorney whether he would approve the inspection of these records by the Commission or someone on its behalf?

Mr. DAVIS. No, we have made no effort along that line. We thought perhaps the Commission could best handle that situation.

Chairman HANNAH. Any further questions, Mr. Taylor?

Commissioner FREEMAN. Would you, Mr. Davis, recommend to the district attorney that he grant approval to the Commission for the inspection of these records?

Mr. DAVIS. Frankly, I would make no recommendation under the circumstances. I feel that the Commission is amply able to make a request. If the request is not granted, they have the right and authority to go to the Federal court or any other court of jurisdiction.

Mr. TAYLOR. In that case, if there are no further questions, I would simply like to explain for the benefit of Commissioner Davis and his counsel that the subject matter of the Commission's hearing is an investigation into denials of equal protection of the laws because of race, color, religion, or national origin under the Constitution of the United States or in the administration of justice; that the pertinency of the documents to our inquiry is that allegations have been received that there has been indeed a denial of equal protection of the laws in the areas specified, and specifically, in the failure of law enforcement officials to investigate or investigate properly; that we had reason to believe that is the case where there were investigations of fires by the Fire Marshal. Therefore, these documents are pertinent to our inquiry.

I would simply recommend that the Commission take this matter under advisement and that the witness be kept under subpena and excused until Friday, February 19, at 1:45.

Chairman HANNAH. Thank you, gentlemen.

Mr. DAVIS. Mr. Taylor, if I might make one statement, more or less in answer to Mrs. Freeman's question, where I stated that I would not request or encourage. I likewise would not discourage or oppose. It is a matter in which I would be entirely neutral. You people are interested in seeing justice be done.   I am also interested in seeing that injustice is not done.

Mr. TAYLOR. All right, sir.

Chairman HANNAH. Thank you, gentlemen.   I am sure you appreciate that the Commission is after the facts.

Mr. DAVIS. I regret that it would not be possible, Mr. Chairman, to take you or your counsel and show you our files.   It would save both our office and your own Commission quite a bit of time and would show you actually the lack of information, you know, that appears there.   But nothing, of course, would suffice other than these records be subpenaed in your regular and orderly manner.   And we will cheerfully submit to any court order or any instructions by any district attorney in any county in which the offense was committed, sir.

Chairman HANNAH. Let me ask one further question.   The Assistant Attorney General that appeared with Mr. Birdsong indicated a willingness at least to give consideration to the possibility of making these records available to the Commission if the Commission would pledge itself to keep them confidential.   Your failure to produce them is based on the fact that you consider this to be a violation of the State law of Mississippi and for that reason you feel it is impossible for you to make them available even for inspection without a court order?

Mr. DAVIS. Mr. Chairman, that is my sole reason.   I do not have the further reason that Colonel Birdsong might have had.   I have no fear of incriminating any party as far as our records are concerned. These matters are all totally unsolved.

Chairman HANNAH. Thank you very much, gentlemen.

(Witness excused.)

Chairman HANNAH. Are there further witnesses, Mr. Taylor?

Mr. TAYLOR. No, Mr. Chairman, that concludes the subpenas which are returnable today.

Chairman HANNAH. We will convene tomorrow morning in this room at 9:30.   The meeting is adjourned.

(Whereupon, at 3:35 o'clock p.m., the Commission was recessed until 9:30 a.m. the following day.)

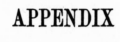

APPENDIX

EXHIBIT NO. 11

STAFF REPORT OF INVESTIGATION OF INCIDENTS OF RACIAL VIOLENCE, PIKE COUNTY, MISS., 1964

INDEX

[1] Believed to have occurred in the city of McComb.

[2] Arrests have been made.

STAFF INVESTIGATION REPORT: PIKE COUNTY, MISS.

The following is a report of incidents of racial violence in Pike County, Miss., during 1964 which have been investigated by the staff of the Commission.

1. On January 25, 1964, between 25 and 50 crosses were burned throughout Pike County.[1] On March 19, 7964, numerous crosses were again burned throughout the county.[2] These incidents came to the attention of the sheriff.[3] No arrests were made on either occasion. (Cross burning is not a crime in Mississippi.)

2. Curtis C. Bryant is a middle-aged Negro who works as a craneman for the Illinois Central Railroad, and as a part-time barber. He is president of the local NAACP and has lived in Pike County most of his life, and in McComb for the past 25 years. He lives with his wife and two children in his own home in the Beartown section of McComb. Mr. Bryant is a deacon of his church and chairman of his union local of the railway clerks.

He has suffered repeated acts of violence or intimidation.

(a) On January 25, 1964, between 7 and 8 p.m., a cross was burned on his front lawn. The incident was reported to the police. No arrests were made.

(b) On April 28, 1964, between 8:30 and 9 p.m., someone threw a firebomb into his barbershop, next to his house. No one was in the building at the time. The interior of the building was damaged and a chair, destroyed. The incident was reported to the police. No arrests were made.

(c) On June 22, 1964, about 10 p.m., Mr. Bryant's son, Curtis, Jr., was on guard in a car outside his father's house. He saw a truck pass several times and on the third time, a bomb was thrown, which exploded on the lawn. This attack was reported to the police. No arrests were made.

(d) On the evening of July 24, 1964, four shots were fired at Mr. Bryant's house from a passing car. The shots did not hit the house. He gave a description of the car to the police. No arrests were made.[4]

3. On June 8, 1964, Louis Asekoff, Andre Martinsons, and Rene Robert Jonas, all white men, were travelling in the South for the purpose of obtaining information for publication of a magazine article. They arrived in McComb about 2 p.m. Shortly after their arrival Police Chief Guy came up to them and asked them what they were doing in McComb. The men talked with Chief Guy for a short while and then went to city hall, where they interviewed him and Mayor Gordon Burt. They then interviewed various Negroes in the community. Their movements were observed by police officers.

About 9 p.m. they left McComb. About 10 to 15 miles north of McComb they were forced over to the side of the road by cars which had been following them. Seven to nine men jumped out of the cars and one man said: "This is the law." One man with a revolver ordered the driver out of the car and directed him to the side of the road where he held him at gun point. Another man told the two passengers to get out of the car. When they refused, he struck them repeatedly with brass knuckles. The assailants apparently feared discovery by passing cars, and drove off. Asekoff and his friends drove to Jackson, where the two had been injured were treated for their injuries. Jonas required about 20

---

[1] Department of Justice files (hereinafter referred to as "DJ files").

[2] Ibid.

[3] Affidavit of Edwin D. Wolf, staff attorney, Dec. 18, 1964, of interview with Sherin Warren.

[4] Signed statement of Curtis C. Bryant, Nov. 23, 1964; affidavit by Curtis C. Bryant, Jr., Dec. 26, 1964.

stitches. One of the men called Chief Guy and told him what had happened, but was unable to give him the license numbers of the car or any other identification. No arrests have been made.[5]

4. Ivey Gutter is a 54-year-old Negro who had until recently lived in Pike County all of his life. He is married and has five children. He worked for the Illinois Central Railroad for 18 years. Mr. Gutter is a member of the NAACP and the Masons. He has not been involved in any civil rights activities, except attendance at meetings of the NAACP.

On June 11, 1964, Mr. Gutter arrived home from work at his accustomed time, about 4:30 p.m. As he walked from the road to his house, he was stopped by three men wearing black hoods, armed with pistols and shotguns. The men said that he was a member of the NAACP and that they had him now. Mr. Gutter did not think they meant any trouble and laughed at them. He told them that he was not a member of the NAACP. They began to hit him with what appeared to him to be homemade metal clubs. He fought back and kept trying to get to his house, but they would not let him. They then tried to force him into their car, but he resisted. They finally knocked him out with blows of a club, and when he came to, he was lying on the floor of the back seat of the car with one of the men astride his legs and another astride his shoulders. In the car they kept talking to him and threatening him. They drove him about 6 or 7 miles and then ordered him out of the car. They made him face away from them and said, "Now you are going to talk." They took his wallet from his back pocket and looked into it. One of them said, "The damn Nigger isn't lying." When Mr. Gutter tried to look back, one of them said, "Don't you look back or I'll shoot you in two." They told him to walk away, and then got into the car and drove off. Mr. Gutter found the home of a Negro whom he knew and tried to call his wife to have her drive him to the doctor. The telephone wires at his home had been cut and he had to call a neighbor. His wife finally came and drove him to the infirmary, where he was X-rayed and had eight stitches in his scalp. He was treated by Dr. Mayer, who stated that Mr. Gutter was badly beaten.

When Mr. Gutter went to the infirmary, the nurse asked him what had happened. He said that he did not want to tell her because the men had warned him not to tell anyone about the beating. She said that she could not treat him unless she knew what had happened, so he told her. She called the sheriff, who came with a deputy to talk to Mr. Gutter. Mr. Gutter told him that the car was a 1954 or 1955 two-door Chevrolet, with a black top and white bottom. He saw that the license plate was from Mississippi, but could not see what county. The sheriff kept asking him if it was an out-of-state license, but Mr. Gutter insisted it was a Mississippi license. He also told the sheriff that the men had called the driver "Charles," and that he had done most of the talking.

The sheriff never talked to Mr. Gutter again. Mr. Gutter called him on June 12 to tell him that he had heard that someone over in Walthall County had a car of that description and that he had heard the man was the kind of person who might be involved in this kind of incident. Mr. Gutter wanted the sheriff to go look at the car because he thought there would probably be blood on the inside. The sheriff never called him back. Mr. Gutter did not call him again because he thought the sheriff was not interested. There have been no arrests.[6]

5. Wilbert Lewis is a 45-year-old Negro who worked as an automobile mechanic in a garage owned by a white man in McComb. He moved from Louisiana to

---

[5] Affidavits by Andre Martinsons, Jan. 18, 1965 ; Rene Robert Jonas, Jan. 15, 1965 ; and Louis Asekoff, Jan. 18, 1965.
[6] Affidavit of Ivey Gutter, Dec. 21, 1964 ; affidavit of Dr. W. T. Mayer, Dec. 21, 1964.

Pike County 6 years ago and lives with his father-in-law. He is not a member of the NAACP and has never been involved in civil rights activities.

On June 19, 1964, Mr. Lewis was told by his boss to go with a white customer to fix a car which had broken down on the road. Mr. Lewis went with the man, whom he had seen before, but whose name he did not know, to a spot where another car was parked with its hood up. As he bent over to begin work on the motor, a man who appeared to have been working under the hood of the car put a gun to Lewis' head. He said, "Don't try to look me in the face." At this point, two other men with black hoods on came out of the bushes; they, too, were armed. The men put a tarpaulin bag over Lewis' head, ordered him into the car, and forced him to lie down on the floor of the back seat. Because his head was covered, he does not know what happened to the other car. He was driven for almost half an hour. The men then took him from the car, tied his hand together around a tree and began asking questions about the NAACP and COFO. They asked him the names of the lieutenants of the NAACP and then the name of the secretary of the NAACP. He told them that he did not know and that he did not attend any meetings. They told him that he was lying and asked him about the meeting places of the NAACP. He said again that he did not know, so they whipped him with a "cat-o'-nine-tails" until he told them who he thought was the secretary and who the members were and where they met. The men were not satisfied with the information he gave them, so they put a rope around his neck, threatened to hang him, and whipped him some more. They kept asking him questions, and when he refused to answer or did not answer to their satisfaction, they whipped him. They told him to tell his friends that this was only a sample of what they would get if they engaged in civil rights activities. And they told him to tell his father-in-law—who is a minister—to stay out of Amite County. Finally he was untied and told to "get running." He was driven home by a Negro he found about 3½ miles from the scene of the beating. He was treated by Dr. Howard.

Lewis was questioned by the police and by the sheriff's office immediately after the beating. He was afraid of them and therefore did not speak freely. He did, however, identify the car at that time, and subsequently identified one of the men to the FBI by pictures shown to him by them. He also stated that he recognized another of the men. There have been no arrests.[7]

6. Mr. Freddie Bates is a 45-year-old Negro service station owner who lives in his own home at 928 Summit Street in McComb. He has lived in southwest Mississippi all of his life, and in McComb for more than 25 years. He has been very active in civil rights activities in McComb, but has not attempted to register to vote.

On June 22, 1964, about 10:30 p.m., a woman teacher who was boarding in Bates' house came running to the back of the house and warned Bates and another man who was with him that she had seen a white man throw something on the porch. The bomb exploded half a minute later, breaking seven windows and two doors, destroying the porch, and venetian blinds inside the house, and cracking some of the walls inside the house. The cost of the repairs was over $1,000. The incident was reported to the police. No arrests have been made.[8]

7. Mrs. Corine Andrews is a 52-year-old Negro who has lived in McComb all of her life. She lives with her 11-year-old son in a house which she owns in

---

[7] Affidavit of Wilbert Lewis, November 1964; letter from Dr. Howard, Jan. 14, 1965; DJ files.

[8] Affidavit of Freddie Bates, Nov. 23, 1964; affidavit of Edwin D. Wolf, staff attorney, of interview with Sheriff Warren and Police Chief Guy, Dec. 18, 1964.

McComb. Mrs. Andrews works as a maid for a white family. She has never been involved in civil rights activities.

On June 22, 1964, between 10 and 11 p.m., her three dogs began barking. She went to her front door and saw smoke on her porch. She ran into the back of the house, taking her son with her. The dynamite exploded, tearing a hole in the porch, knocking other boards loose and shattering glass in the front door. The incident was reported to the police. No arrests have been made.[9]

8. Early in the summer of 1964 the city of McComb hired two Negro policemen, Vernel Felder and Artis Garner, to patrol the Negro neighborhood. On July 8, 1964, about 10 p.m., Felder and Garner were on duty in front of The DeSoto, a Negro hotel. A car containing four whites drove past and a shot was fired at them. Garner fired two shots back. Shortly thereafter, four young white men were arrested and charged with disturbing the peace. The police found a .22 caliber pistol in their possession and determined that it had recently been fired, despite the denial of the four men. The men pleaded guilty to disorderly conduct. Three of them were fined $22.50 and one was fined $47.50.[10]

9. The congregation of the Zion Hill Baptist Church was organized in 1876. Some of the original families are still members. In 1962, the congregation built a new wooden church 7 miles west of McComb, near the Percy Quin State Park. The church was never used for civil rights activities and no members of the congregation participated in the civil rights movement in McComb.

Sometime after midnight on July 17, 1964, the church was destroyed by fire. Local law enforcement officials have concluded that the fire was the result of arson. The incident was reported to the sheriff. No arrests have been made.

The church was insured for $8,800, but the insurance has not yet been paid. Replacement of the church will cost $16,000, and $5,000 of the insurance money must be used to pay off the mortgage on the old church.[11]

10. The congregation of Sweet Home Baptist Church was organized in 1895 and today numbers over 400 persons. The present church building in southeast McComb was constructed 7 years ago; an annex to the building was being added this year. The church building has never been used for civil rights activities, although some of the members have participated in such activities.

During the evening of July 18, 1964, an attempt was made to burn the church. The floor carpeting was soaked with kerosene, but a fuse leading to a pan of black powder burned out before reaching the pan. No arrests were made.[12]

11. The Mt. Vernon Missionary Bapist Church was a wooden building constructed 65 years ago. The church stood on Highway 48, 5 miles west of Magnolia. There are 150 Negroes who worshipped at Mt. Vernon; this summer they were renovating the church. The building was never used for civil rights meetings and none of the congregants had been involved in such activities.

About 10:30 p.m., on July 21, 1964, the Mt. Vernon Missionary Baptist Church burned to the ground. The fire was reported to Sheriff Warren. No arrests were made. The congregation plans to rebuild the church at a cost of $20,000. Insurance will cover $5,000.[13]

12. The Rose Bower Baptist Church is located in Amite County on Highway 24, about 9 miles west of McComb. It is a wooden building and has a congregation of 120 members.

[9] Affidavit of Edwin D. Wolf, Dec. 18, 1964, of interview with Mrs. Andrews.
[10] Affidavit of Artis Garner, Dec. 30, 1964; affidavit of Edwin D. Wolf, Dec. 18, 1964, of interview with Police Chief Guy, and of inspection of police records.
[11] Signed statement by Rev. Daniel Walker, Nov. 24, 1964.
[12] Affidavit of Rev. W. H. Tobias, Jan. 13, 1965.
[13] Signed statement by Rev. Harry McKnight, Nov. 23, 1964.

On July 23, 1964, the church was damaged by a fire. Rugs and a chair were burned and a hole about 3 feet in diameter was burned in the floor. The repairs cost $300, which was paid by insurance. No arrests were made.[14]

13. Mrs. Bryant is a 51-year-old housewife who is married to Charles A. Bryant, who was a carpenter in McComb. She had lived in McComb all of her life. She was very active in civil rights, as was her husband, who had been a member of the NAACP for 20 years.

On July 26, 1964, about 1 a.m., Mr. Bryant was asleep and Mrs. Bryant was awake because she had difficulty sleeping. She noticed a car parked in front of their house with some white men in it. About 2 minutes later, the lights of a passing car lit up the parked car, and it drove away. Mrs. Bryant thought the car might be dangerous, so she got her gun and waited. About 15 minutes later, the car came back and stopped in front of the house. She took aim at it with her shotgun. Something was thrown into the yard from the car, and she fired. The car then drove away. She ran to the back of the house to wake her husband, and heard a popping sound. She woke Mr. Bryant, who took the gun from her and ran out the back door. Mrs. Bryant took a rifle and went to the kitchen door. The car drove by again and two shots were fired at the house. At that moment there was a loud explosion. The dynamite landed about 12 feet from the house. The explosion blew out all the front windows, tore the asbestos siding off the house, ripped screens, blasted a large hole in the lawn and uprooted shrubbery around the house. Following the attack, Mr. and Mrs. Bryant took turns standing guard over the house every night. In September they moved to California. Arrests were made in this case.[15]

14. The Mt. Canaan Baptist Church is a wooden structure built about one hundred years ago when the congregation was formed. It is located in Smithtown, about 15 miles east of McComb. The congregation numbers over 300. The church had not been used for civil rights meetings, and none of the congregants had participated in civil rights activities.

In the early morning of August 6, 1964, the church was damaged by fire. The fire was caused by an explosion of some kind of fuel oil. The interior of the building was badly burned, benches and chairs were destroyed, and a piano was ruined. The repairs to the church will cost $2,500. There was no insurance.

The incident was reported to the sheriff, who investigated and concluded the fire was the result of arson. No arrests have been made.[16]

15. Dr. W. T. Mayer is a 41-year-old white physician who has lived in Mississippi for 15 years. On August 12, 1964, a cross was burned in front of his home. He reported the incident to the police.

The only reason that Dr. Mayer can think of for the burning of the cross was that he made a contribution to a fund to rebuild various Negro churches which had been destroyed in McComb, and his name was on the list of contributors that was published in the paper on July 27.[17]

16. On August 12, 1964, a cross was burned in front of the home of G. T. Vaccarella, Jr., a white resident of McComb. The incident was reported to the police. The Vaccarella family owns several stores in the McComb area, and, according to the police chief, had been subjected to pressure to fire some Negro

---

[14] Affidavit of Rev. A. Holmes, Dec. 31, 1964.

[15] Signed statements by Mr. and Mrs. Charles Bryant, Nov. 23, 1964.

[16] Signed statement by Rev. Earnest Landrew, Nov. 23, 1964.

[17] Affidavit of Dr. W. T. Mayer, Dec. 21, 1964 ; McComb Enterprise-Journal, July 27, 1964.

employees who had attempted to register. According to Sheriff Warren, the men arrested in November admitted burning these crosses.[18]

17. Mr. Pete Lewis is a 65-year-old Negro who has lived for 48 years in Pike County. His wife died one year ago. He is retired from the Illinois Central Railroad where he had worked as a fireman for 49 years. He is a stockholder in a Negro corporation which opened the Burgland Market at 630 Warren Street in 1956. The market corporation went into debt and Mr. Lewis agreed to take over the debts and operate the market until the debts were repaid, when it would return to the stockholders. The store has about $7,000 worth of stock, appliances, and equipment. It is in a two-story, cinder-block building owned by a Negro Masonic lodge, which occupies the second floor.

Mr. Lewis has been registered to vote for over 10 years. He is treasurer of the Citizens League and has supported COFO activities in McComb. He has been active in other Negro community affairs as well. The Masonic hall was used for a freedom school during the school walkout in 1961, and executive meetings of the NAACP have been held there regularly for 10 years.

On the night of August 14, 1964, a bomb was thrown at the store building. Mr. Lewis was not in the store at the time and was called by an employee. The bomb tore a hole in the sidewalk about four feet from the building where it hit. It also blew a double door from its hinges into the store, broke every window on all four sides on both floors, destroyed a wooden awning, and broke windows in Mr. Lewis' house 200 feet away. The building itself was shaken and long cracks opened in the interior walls. Mr. Lewis thinks the building is no longer structurally safe. He lost about one-third of his stock, mainly fruits, vegetables, breads, and cakes, from flying splinters. One counter was broken and a cigarette machine damaged. The lost stock was valued at $1,200 and the cost of replacing windows at $500. Mr. Lewis' equipment was insured by him, but the Masons carried no insurance on the building, so Lewis had to pay for those repairs himself. The store reopened for business the next day. He received no threats before the blast and one afterwards. The incident was reported to the police. No arrests have been made.[19]

18. On August 22, 1964, in the evening, Pat Cleborn Martin, a white man, was being driven home by three Negroes. Near his home, the road was blocked by a log. Five armed and masked white men stepped out of the bushes, ordered the Negroes not to move, and told Martin to come with them. They drove him some distance and then took him out and hit him several times with a strap. They told him he had been talking too much with Negroes. Martin asked the sheriff not to investigate the case. No arrests have been made.[20]

19. Mr. Willie Dillon is a 42-year-old Negro who has lived all of his life in Pike County. He was formerly employed as a mechanic by the McComb Scrap Iron Co., and now repairs cars at his home. He lives with his wife and three children in his own house in McComb. Mrs. Dillon has been a member of the NAACP for about a year; her children went to freedom school this summer, and COFO workers have been around their house frequently. In August 1964 she attempted unsuccessfully to register. She has been active in all aspects of the civil rights movement in McComb.

According to Mr. Dillon, on August 28, about 1 a.m., a detonator cap exploded in his front yard, 20 feet from the house. Nine sticks of dynamite failed to

[18] Affidavit by Edwin D. Wolf, staff attorney, Dec. 18, 1964, of interview with Police Chief Guy and Sheriff Warren.
[19] Signed statement by Peter Lewis, Nov. 23, 1964.
[20] DJ files.

explode. At the time of the explosion, Mr. Dillon was washing up after repairing a car, Mrs. Dillon was asleep in the front bedroom, and the three children were asleep in the back bedroom. Mrs. Dillon called the FBI, who arrived with the police and the sheriff. The sheriff questioned Mr. Dillon closely about a car which was parked in front of his home. Mr. Dillon told them that he had repaired the car, that he did not know the name of the owner, but knew that it was from COFO. The police searched the car to determine its owner. Mr. Dillon was then arrested by the sheriff and charged with operating a garage without a permit, and stealing electricity by attaching an electric wire outside the meter. (The wire was attached to a floodlight which had been recently installed because cars had been circling the house at night.)

Mr. Dillon was taken to jail in Magnolia about 4 a.m., and appeared in justice of the peace court in McComb the next day. He pleaded guilty. He was sentenced to $100 and 3 months in jail for stealing the electricity and $500 and 5 months for operating a garage without a permit. He was not represented by counsel and saw no friends from the time of his arrest until after he was sentenced, when he was permitted to see his wife for 15 minutes.

According to Mr. Dillon's understanding, appeal bond was set at $1,200, and was raised by Mrs. Dillon, with the help of COFO. When she presented the bond to the sheriff however, the amount was raised to $2,000 and Mr. Dillon was not released. Subsequently, District Judge Mize ordered Mr. Dillon released on $500 bail. The appeal bond was posted on September 28, 1964.

According to Sheriff Warren, bond was originally $2,000 and he then lowered it to $1,000 before he was ordered to release Dillon on $500 bond. No arrests have been made in connection with the bombing.[21]

Mr. Dillon's sentence has been appealed for trial de novo; the case was removed to Federal court, where Judge Mize reduced the appeal bond to $500 and then remanded the case to the State court. The remand order is now on appeal to the Fifth Circuit.

20. Presiding Minister Hugh Washington is a Negro contractor who lives in Summit, Miss. He is a Jehovah's Witness and for this reason has not participated in any civil rights activities.

On September 7, 1964, about 1 a.m., dynamite was thrown on the roof of his home. The explosion blew a hole in the roof of the carport and tore away parts of the wall of the house. The door leading from the carport was slightly damaged. Washington, his wife, and their five children were in the house at the time; none of them was injured. Washington called the Summit city police, who notified the sheriff. No arrests have been made.[22]

21. Allen Coney is the principal of the Consolidated School in Magnolia. He has lived in Pike County all of his life. He has never been involved in civil rights, but he is registered to vote. He has a Master's Degree from Atlanta University. He lives with his wife and two daughters in his own home in Magnolia. Mr. Coney also owns a farm several miles east of Magnolia, near Rose Hill community. On that farm there was a wooden building used for cookouts. It had a large fireplace and chimney.

On September 7, 1964, soon after midnight, dynamite exploded in the cookout building, completely destroying the structure. Parts of the building were scattered several hundred feet away. The damage amounted to $300. The sheriff was notified. No arrests have been made.

[21] Signed statement by Willie J. Dillon, Nov. 24, 1964; affidavit by Edwin D. Wolf, Dec. 18, 1964, of interview with Sheriff Warren.
[22] Signed statements by Jeanette and Hugh Washington, Nov. 23, 1964.

After this incident, Mr. Coney's brother and sister installed floodlights at their homes and at a store owned by his brother. On September 17, two of these lights were shot out by a shotgun. The shells were recovered, but no arrests have been made. According to the sheriff, the six men arrested in November admitted their responsibility for the shooting.[23]

22. Booker T. Gutter is a Negro construction worker who lives in Ruth, near Summit, where he and his wife also operate a grocery store. He has not been involved in civil rights activities.

On September 7, 1964, between 1:30 and 2 a.m., dynamite was exploded under the front portion of the store, and the front room was ripped from the structure. Items inside the store were damaged. The loss amounted to $1,000. Insurance covered $400. Mrs. Gutter called the sheriff. No arrests have been made.[24]

23. Reverend James Baker is a 51-year-old Negro who is married and has five children. He has lived all of his life in Pike County. He works as a mechanic, and a part-time minister at two churches in the area. Reverend Baker and his wife own their home, near Summit, and 51 acres of farmland. He is registered to vote and is president of the local Negro PTA. Mrs. Baker is an invalid. Although it was rumored that Reverend Baker was active in civil rights, neither he nor his wife has participated in civil rights activities, and Reverend Baker had taken the position that membership in a civil rights organization was inconsistent with membership in either of his churches. On January 25, a cross was burned on his lawn.

About 12:30 a.m., on September 9, 1964, Mrs. Baker and Mrs. Bessie Forrest, a friend, were asleep in the Baker's home. Reverend Baker was in the hospital. Mrs. Baker was awakened by a car driving away from the house; immediately thereafter there was an explosion. The blast broke windows and glass in the front door, tore shingles and wooden eaves from one place in the roof and blasted a large hole in the front lawn. Arrests were made.[25]

24. Mrs. Aylene Quin is a familiar figure in the Negro community. She has lived in McComb for 11 years, and has run a cafe at different locations in the Negro section. She was married and has four children. During the summer of 1964 Mrs. Quin's cafe was a meeting and eating place for civil rights workers. Her daughter was involved in the school walkout in 1961 and she herself attended civil rights meetings. She registered to vote in Harrison County in 1952, but has failed the test in Pike County several times.

On the evening of September 20, Mrs. Quin was at her cafe, while a 19-year-old babysitter looked after her two youngest children, 4-year-old Anthony and 9-year-old Jacqueline. Shortly before 11 p.m., her home was bombed. Anthony was pinned to his bed by the fallen ceiling, but was not injured. Jacqueline suffered injuries to her ears from the explosion. They were carried from the house by neighbors who rushed to the house and broke down the front door.

The damage to the house was severe. The front wall of the children's room was blown in. The estimated cost of repairing the damage is $6,000. The house was insured for $5,000, and Mrs. Quin's claim has been paid. Arrests were made.[26]

---

[23] Signed statement by Allen Coney, Nov. 23, 1964; affidavit by Edwin D. Wolf, Dec. 18, 1964, of interview with Sheriff Warren.

[24] Signed statement by Booker T. Gutter, Jan. 4, 1965.

[25] Signed statements by James and Aline Baker, Nov. 23, 1964.

[26] Signed statement by Aylene Quin, Nov. 23, 1964; and signed statement by Johnnie Lee Wilcher, Dec. 16, 1964; letters from Dr. Howard, Jan. 14, 1964; letters from Dr. Janes, Jan. 16, 1965.

25. The congregation of the Society Hill Baptist Church was organized in 1910. At present it includes 275 members. The church building is a frame building over 50 years old, on Route 51, just south of McComb. The congregation refused to permit COFO meetings to be held at the church during the summer, but many members of the congregation, including Curtis Bryant, were active in civil rights, and the church was used for mass meetings of the NAACP and for weekly voter registration classes.

On September 20, 1964, a bomb was thrown at the church, causing severe damage. The entire center portion of the roof caved in and brought the walls with it. The church was a total loss. The church was insured for $11,000, which has been paid. Contributions were received from the North to rebuild the church. The sheriff was informed of the bombing, but no arrests have been made.[27]

26. Matthew Jackson is 59 years old, a Negro who has lived in Pike County since 1919. He has worked for the Illinois Central Railroad for 35 years. He has 5 children and 19 grandchildren. He owns his own home, southeast of McComb, and shares 40 acres of farmland with his brother. He has never registered to vote, but has been a member of the NAACP for several years.

On September 23, 1964, between 11:30 and 12 p.m., he and his wife were asleep when they were awakened by an explosion in the front of their house. Some dynamite had torn a hole in their lawn, 45 feet from the house. There was no damage to the building. The sheriff came when his deputies heard the explosion. No arrests have been made.[28]

27. Artis Garner is a McComb Negro who was hired at the beginning of the summer to act as a policeman in the Negro section of the city. Mr. Garner worked for about 2 months, and then left around August 20. Shortly thereafter, he began to receive threats against his life. On August 26, the other Negro policeman, Vernel Felder, warned him to get out of town. On September 16, 17, and 18, two white policemen drove around the house which Garner rented on Wilson Street, shining lights in the windows. On September 19, Garner was asked to come down to the police station. He went to the station and was arrested by a deputy sheriff on unspecified charges. He was held in the Pike County jail at Magnolia from 2 p.m. that day until the afternoon of the next, when he was released without any charges. On September 23, Mr. Garner made preparations to leave McComb. He arranged for his wife and child to go to Jackson while he went to Greenville to testify at a hearing of the Mississippi State advisory committee to the U.S. Commission on Civil Rights.

He testified publicly concerning alleged Klan influence in the McComb police force and to a number of incidents involving the police. That night a bomb exploded at his house in McComb, about 1 hour after his wife and child boarded the bus for Jackson. The Garners have never returned to McComb. No arrests have been made.[29]

28. There were several incidents of violence directed against COFO workers.

(a) On July 8, 1964, a bomb was thrown at the Freedom House, blowing away the outside wall of one of the bedrooms. One of the people sleeping in the bedroom was cut by flying glass, others were not injured. The incident was reported to the police, but no arrests have been made.[30]

---

[27] Affidavit by Rev. Ned Taylor, Dec. 26, 1964.
[28] Signed statement by Matthew Jackson, Nov. 24, 1964.
[29] Affidavit by Artis Garner, Dec. 30, 1964; see transcript of SAC meeting in Greenville, Miss., Sept. 23, 1964.
[30] Signed statement by Jessie Harris, Nov. 24, 1964.

(b) On July 19, 1964, Mendy Samstein, a white COFO worker, was assaulted in the street. He was not seriously hurt. He reported the incident to the police. There have been no arrests.[31]

(c) On September 2, 1964, Robert V. Stone, a 25-year-old white philosophy student working with COFO, was knocked to the ground and kicked by a white man on a street in McComb. He telephoned the police and described his assailant. The officer did not ask any questions about the beating or the assailant and did not ask Stone to come to the police station. Chief Guy later came out to the COFO office to talk to him. No arrests have been made.[32]

(d) Rev. Russell Bennett is a 27-year-old white minister of the United Church of Christ, a graduate of Occidental College, where he was elected to Phi Beta Kappa, and of the Harvard Divinity School. He now lives in California. On September 2, 1964, he drove another white COFO worker, Brian Peterson, into the center of town to the Western Union office. When Peterson went into the office, the car was surrounded by six white men. One man stuck his head into the car and asked what he was doing in McComb. He replied that he was a minister working for COFO. This man then told Bennett to take off his glasses. Bennett complied and was struck in the nose by the man's fist. He was then pulled from the car and was kicked and beaten by the group of men. The beating lasted for about 2 minutes, after which the men drifted away. Bennett got back into the car and waited for Peterson, in order to return to Freedom House. When Peterson got back into the car, he, too, was hit. As they drove back to Freedom House, they noticed that they were being followed by a police car. This car followed them back to the Freedom House. It turned out to be Police Chief Guy, who was on his way to investigate the assault on Robert V. Stone. When they got out of their car, Chief Guy pulled up behind them. They reported the incident to him, and he expressed surprise. Peterson asked Chief Guy to go to the scene with them, so that Bennett might try to point out one of the assailants. Chief Guy refused since he thought that the men would have left. Bennett was then taken to the hospital for treatment. He was treated by Dr. Janes. He was interviewed by the FBI the same day and signed an affidavit. There have been no arrests and the police never talked with him again regarding this incident.[33]

(e) On October 27, 1964, a white man pulled a gun on a white Canadian COFO worker named Malcolm Campbell who was working with COFO, and threatened him. The man was arrested, but Campbell was in jail when the trial came up, and the case was dismissed for lack of prosecution.[34]

29. Beginning on September 30, 1964, 11 local white men were arrested in connection with the violence in Pike County. Charges against 1 of them were dismissed, and the other 10 were indicted by the grand jury in connection with the bombings at the home of Charles Bryant on July 26, at the home of Reverend Baker on September 7, and at the home of Mrs. Quin on September 20. They were charged with violation of section 2143 of the Mississippi Code, which carries a maximum penalty of death.

Nine of the men were tried on October 23, before Judge Watkins in Magnolia. Six of them pleaded guilty to the substantive crime of illegal use of explosives. Two of the men had been charged with all three of the bombings, and the other four had been charged with one violation. Each of these six men was sentenced

[31] Affidavit of Julius Samstein, Feb. 3, 1965.
[32] Affidavit of Robert V. Stone, Dec. 21, 1964.
[33] Affidavit of Rev. Russell Bennett, Jan. 6, 1965.
[34] Affidavit of Edwin D. Wolf, Dec. 18, 1964, of interview with Police Chief Guy.

to 5 years on each charge, the terms to run concurrently. The sentences were then all suspended and each man was placed on probation for 5 years. All nine of the men pleaded *nolo contendere* to charges of conspiracy. They were given the maximum penalty for the crime—6 months in jail and $500 fine. The jail sentences were then suspended. It was stipulated that the 10th defendant would plead *nolo contendere* to conspiracy and receive the same sentence.

Judge Watkins cautioned the defendants that they were not to possess or own any firearms, dynamite, or combustibles during the probation period. Another condition of the probation period was that if at any time violence or crimes or unlawful acts occur or erupt in Pike County to such an extent that the court is persuaded or satisfied that a systematic plan has developed for crime and violence, such as to endanger people's health, lives, or property, then the probation is subject to being revoked by the court, whether the defendants actually individually are involved or not.[85]

30. On November 4, 1964, six white men were arrested by Sheriff Warren. They were implicated in four recent incidents of violence in McComb. Some of these were racial in nature, and others, while typical of Ku Klux Klan activity, were not racially directed.

The first incident involved a white man named J. K. Wallace. On October 26, 1964, four men attacked him, threw household ammonia in his face, and beat him. Four white men were charged with assault with intent to maim in connection with this incident.

On October 29, 1964, shots were fired at Charles J. Hughes, an Englishman who has lived in McComb for 10 years. Five white men, including the four above, were charged with pointing, aiming, and discharging a firearm at a human being.

On November 1, shots from a 20-gage shotgun were fired into the home of G. T. Vaccarella on Highway 51 in McComb. One of the men charged in the two above incidents and another white man were charged with pointing, aiming, and discharging a firearm at a human being in connection with this incident. The same night, steel balls were shot into the window of the Shop-rite at the intersection of Routes 24 and 51 in McComb. The store is owned by the Vaccarella family. One of the white men was charged with malicious mischief in connection with this offense.

Five of the men pleaded guilty to these incidents and were sentenced to 1 year in the county jail; the sixth is to be tried in March.[86]

---

[85] Affidavit of Edwin D. Wolf, staff attorney, Dec. 18, 1964; of interview with Robert Reeves, county attorney; copies of indictments in Commission files. A copy of the terms of the probation, as reported in the McComb Enterprise-Journal, is included as an appendix thereto.

[86] Affidavit of Edwin D. Wolf, staff attorney, Dec. 18, 1964, of interview with Sheriff Warren; inspection of county court records.

EXHIBIT NO. 12

"STATEMENT OF PRINCIPLE," ENTERPRISE JOURNAL (McCOMB, MISS.), NOVEMBER 17, 1964

(OMITTED IN PRINTING)

EXHIBIT NO. 13

STAFF REPORT OF INVESTIGATION OF INCIDENTS OF RACIAL VIOLENCE, ADAMS COUNTY, MISS., SEPTEMBER 1963–JANUARY 1965

INDEX

[1] Arrests were made.
[2] Believed to have occurred in the city of Natchez.

STAFF INVESTIGATION REPORT: ADAMS COUNTY, MISS.

The following is a report of incidents of racial violence connected with Adams County from September 1963 to the present which were investigated by the Commission staff. The report is based upon affidavits of victims and witnesses, interviews with law enforcement officials, information in Government files, and staff observations.

1. The Mount Plains Baptist Church was a wood building built about 65 years ago. The congregation had 45 members. The church was near Kingston Community. The pastor was Rev. Shead Baldwin, who was also pastor of Jerusalem Baptist Church in Kingston.

On the night of September 21, 1963, the church burned to the ground. The sheriff was notified. The State Fire Marshal's office told Reverend Baldwin that the fire was deliberately set. The church was insured for $2,000; the insurance company has paid the full amount of the policy. The church was rebuilt at a cost of $5,500. No arrests have been made.[1]

[1] Affidavit of Rev. Shead Baldwin, Nov. 18, 1964.

2. On October 31, 1963, Bruce Payne, a white student from Yale University, who was working in the Aaron Henry Freedom Vote campaign (an effort to stimulate Negro interest in registration and voting) ; George Green, a Negro worker with the Student Nonviolent Coordinating Committee (SNCC) ; and Ella Baker, a Negro Southern Conference Education Fund (SCEF) consultant, were followed during most of the day in Natchez by two carloads of white men. Late in the day, the Payne group left Natchez for Jackson, followed by the two cars. Payne stopped at a gas station in Port Gibson and the two cars pulled in behind him. One of the men struck Payne and then said to him : "You've been making trouble in Adams County. If you come back, you'll get worse."

On November 2, 1963, Payne and Green were driving at night north of Natchez when they were forced off the road by a car driven by a white man. The car was also occupied by one of the men involved in the previous incident. Shots were fired and a high-speed chase ensued. Payne and Green managed to escape. They made positive identifications of their assailants to the FBI shortly thereafter.[2]

About a year later, on October 22, 1964, the FBI and the Investigations Division of the Mississippi Highway Safety Patrol arrested four men on charges of assault and battery with intent to kill Payne and Green. Another man was arrested shortly thereafter on the same charges. All of the men are residents of Adams County. Charges against the first four arrested were dismissed when the case came before the grand jury in district court in Claiborne County on January 5, 1965. Charges against the other man were dismissed at a preliminary hearing. Neither Payne nor Green were asked to testify at the grand jury proceeding.[3]

3. Leonard Russell is a 49-year-old Negro, who presently lives in Natchez. He was born in Bude, in Franklin County, Miss., and has lived either in Franklin or Adams County most of his life. He is employed at the International Paper Co. plant in Natchez and is a former president of the Negro Pulp and Sulfite Workers' local at the plant. He has not been involved in civil rights activities.

On November 21, 1963, about 11 :15 p.m., someone called from outside Russell's house and asked for help in getting a car started. Russell and his wife got into their car and drove out to help push the stalled car. His wife drove. Russell noticed that the stalled car was a light colored, 1957 Plymouth with an Adams County license plate. They drove by the car in order to turn around and, as they did so, Russell saw a man wearing a hood. He told his wife to head back home. The other car drove off. An hour later the same car and another returned to the Russell house. Russell was waiting with a shotgun. The men in the car shot an incendiary or smoke grenade through the window of the house. The projectile knocked a hole in the screen, the window pane, and another window pane across the room. The grenade set fire to the curtains. Russell shot once at the car and once through his front door at a possible assailant, and then put out the fire in his living room. A white neighbor called the sheriff. A deputy came out and remained on watch all night. The sheriff came the next morning and told Russell that his attackers had not intended to kill him. He returned a few days later and told Russell's wife, "I was wrong, they did intend to kill you." Russell left Meadville the morning after the incident. No arrests have been made.

---

[2] Affidavit of Bruce Payne, Dec. 29, 1964 ; affidavit of George Green, Feb. 2, 1965.
[3] The Jackson Clarion-Ledger, Jan. 7, 1965.

(Several months earlier Russell had filed a grievance with the Pulp and Sulfite Union complaining that work traditionally performed by Negro laborers had been given to whites. About the time of the incident the company abolished separate pay lines for whites and Negroes over the objections of some white employees. Russell lived near Meadville in Franklin County in a neighborhood where several Negro and white employees of the IPC lived. The investigation did not establish, however, that the above facts had any direct bearing upon the violence against Russell.)[4]

4. Alfred Whitley is a 52-year-old Negro janitor who has worked at the Armstrong Rubber Company in Natchez for 18 years. He lives on his farm about 10 miles from Natchez with his wife and two children. He has not been involved in civil rights activities.

On the night of February 6, 1964, after finishing the 4 p.m. to midnight shift at Armstrong, he started to drive home on Highway 61, a four-lane highway. At the Bar-B-Que Pit, about 3 miles from Natchez, he tried to pass a car. This car speeded up to prevent him from passing. He recognized the driver as a white man he knew at Armstrong. A second car drove up behind Whitley's car, with the other car continuing in front. When Whitley turned off the highway onto the dirt road leading to his house, the car behind him followed. As he neared his home, he saw two cars with headlights on blocking the road. He stopped his car. A number of men wearing white hoods got out of the three cars. They forced him from his car into one of the other cars and tied his hands. He was not blindfolded.

Whitley was driven to a spot in Homochitto National Forest on a route leading through the town of Washington to Cranfield Community on Highway 84, then over back roads to the Liberty Road in the forest. Whitley was forced to strip off his clothes. He was beaten with a bull whip and a shorter whip. After the beating, one of the men accused him of being a member of the NAACP and the Masons, and of "wanting to be with white folks." He does not know the number of persons involved and could not identify any of them. They were wearing hoods made of sheets which came to their waists.

The men left him where he was beaten. He could not find all of his clothes. He walked until he came to an oil well area where he found a truck loading oil. The driver picked him up and took him to a refinery in Cranfield, where his wife came to get him. He was treated by Dr. Philip Springer. He was hospitalized for 3 days and remained home from work for 10 days. Whitley's wife notified Sheriff Anders the morning after the beating. Later that day a ranger in Homochitto Forest brought the rest of Whitley's clothing to the sheriff's office. No arrests have been made.[5]

5. Archie Curtis is a 56-year-old Negro undertaker. He is married and has two children. He has lived in Mississippi for 40 years. He is a graduate of Natchez Junior College and a registered voter. He has been chairman of the voter registration drive of the Natchez Business and Civic League for a number of years.

Willie Jackson is Mr. Curtis' 45-year-old helper. He has not been active in civil rights and is not a registered voter.

On February 15, 1964, shortly after midnight, Mr. Curtis received a call from a person who sounded like a white man, to come to Palestine Road to pick up a "Harry Gooden's" wife who, according to the caller, had suffered a heart attack.

---

[4] Signed statement of Leonard Russell, Feb. 18, 1965.
[5] Signed statement of Alfred Whitley, Nov. 21, 1964; copy of hospital medical record, submitted by Dr. Philip Springer.

(The name turned out to be fictitious.) The caller gave directions to the house. Curtis picked up Jackson and they drove the ambulance to Palestine Road. Curtis did not see any lights and began to think that the call was false. At that moment a car drove up behind the ambulance and Curtis pulled to the side of the road and motioned the car to drive alongside so that he could ask directions. The car stopped and four men wearing hoods and carrying guns stepped out. Curtis and Jackson were forced out of the ambulance and blindfolded. Both men were placed in one of the cars and driven a short distance to the Humble oil field. Curtis was made to walk about 20 or 30 feet and told to take off his coat. He did and was whipped twice on the shoulder and once on the legs. A man asked for his NAACP card and Curtis answered that he did not have one. The men told him to drop his pants. He was whipped on his lower torso on the front and back sides and on both legs. Jackson was forced to strip and was whipped on his back. One man said he wanted to kill them both, but another said, "No, just leave them here." Curtis and Jackson walked back to the ambulance, but could not drive it because the battery had run down. They walked to the home of Norman Bell, who drove them to the sheriff's office. Curtis was able to identify the make of one car and to give physical descriptions of two of the men by size and clothing. Curtis was treated for his injuries by Dr. E. L. McAmis, a white Natchez physician. No arrests were made.[6]

6. James Carter Winston is a 40-year-old Negro who was employed at the time of the incident by the Pickett's Cafeteria at the International Paper Co. plant in Natchez. (He was transferred by the Pickett's chain after the incident to its cafeteria in the Texarkana Ordnance plant.) Winston attended Bay St. Louis Seminary for 7 years and the St. Mary's Missionary House in Techny, Ill., for 4 years. In the early 1950's, he was in a mental institution for a period of time.

On February 15, 1964, at 9 p.m., Winston left work and began walking down the road by the plant to go home. As was his usual practice, he attempted to hitchhike a ride home. A car stopped and a hooded white man carrying a rifle got out and ordered him into the car. Winston was ordered to lie down on the floor and a hood was placed over his head and tied around his neck. There were two other white men in the car, one of whom put a rifle against his head. During the ride, Winston was asked if he were a member of the NAACP. When the car stopped, he was forced to crawl to a spot where other hooded men were waiting. His clothes were stripped off and he was whipped. He was forced to drink a bottle of castor oil and beaten a second time. Then he was forced to run naked down the road.

Winston wandered about until he found a house where the people took him in. They gave him clothes and drove him to Natchez a few hours later. Later that day, a deputy sheriff who had been notified of the incident came to his home and was informed of what had occurred. Winston did not go to a doctor, and he went to work the next day. No arrests have been made.[7]

7. Clifton Walker was a Negro laborer who worked in the woodyard of the International Paper Co. in Natchez. He had worked for the company since 1950 and was considered a good employee who was regular in his attendance. He lived in Woodville in Wilkinson County. He was married and had children. He drove to work in a car pool with another Negro and three whites.

.On February 28, 1964, he worked his regular shift, from 3 p.m. to 11 p.m. He never returned home. About noon the next day he was found dead in his car

---

[6] Affidavit of Archie Curtis, Nov. 20, 1964.
[7] Signed statement of James Carter Winston, Dec. 21, 1964.

near the Poor House Road in Wilkinson County. He had been shot in the back with buckshot and rifle slugs. Sheriff Charles T. Netterville of Wilkinson County investigated. No arrests have been made.[8]

8. Richard Joe Butler is a Negro farm laborer who lived in the Kingston Community. He had not been active in civil rights and his whereabouts at the present time are unknown.

Sometime in March 1964, Butler's car was stopped by two cars driven by white men. He managed to escape. A few days later, the Identification Division of the Mississippi Highway Safety Patrol in Natchez was notified of a threat against Butler. Nightly surveillance of Butler's home was set up by the Patrol and the Adams County sheriff's office. The surveillance generally ended about 2 a.m.

On April 5, 1964, about 8 a.m., Butler was shot four times with a shotgun on the property of his employer, H. B. Drane, near Kingston. He was seriously injured and taken to Jefferson Davis Hospital in Natchez. That same day he named five men as those who shot him. On April 7, 1964, the Highway Patrol arrested two men and charged them with assault with intent to kill. Charges against one were dropped when a lie detector test indicated his probable innocence; charges against the other man were dismissed on December 18. On October 27, 1964, two other men were arrested and charged with the shooting. Charges against both were dismissed without prejudice on November 17, 1964. County Prosecutor Edwin Benoist gave lack of sufficient evidence as the reason for the dismissal in all the cases.[9]

9. On April 24, 1964, six crosses were burned in Adams County, as part of a statewide demonstration by the Ku Klux Klan. No arrests were made.[10]

10. St. Mark's Baptist Church is a small wooden church near Natchez, built about 80 years ago when the congregation was founded. The present pastor is L. L. Miller of 1017 North Union St., Natchez. The church had never been used for civil rights meetings and no members of the congregation had participated in civil rights activities.

On the morning of June 7, 1964, the assistant pastor, C. W. Cain, went to the church and found the benches overturned, profane words (including reference to race) written on the blackboard, the Bible torn in half and thrown into a shallow pond in back of the church, chair covers ripped, and one window broken. Damage was about $200. Sheriff Anders was called. He investigated, but never spoke to the pastor. No arrests have been made.[11]

11. The Riverview Motel is a modern brick motel built by Michel O. Dumas, a Negro businessman in Natchez, who is a graduate of Fisk University and a registered pharmacist. It was opened for business for Negro guests only, about March 1, 1964. Before the motel opened, vandals cut down a billboard advertising the motel, and shot out the motel sign. On June 20, 1964, between midnight and 1 a.m. a cross was burned on the property next to the motel. Mr. Dumas did not call the sheriff. In addition, since the opening of the motel, the sign has been shot at on three occasions. Each time, Mr. Dumas has notified the police.[12]

12. The Jerusalem Baptist Church in Kingston Community, southeast of Natchez, was a wooden building constructed about 70 years ago. The congrega-

---

[8] DJ files.

[9] DJ files; affidavit of Staff Attorney Edwin D. Wolf, Feb. 9, 1965, of interview with County Attorney Edwin Benoist.

[10] DJ files.

[11] Affidavit of Rev. L. L. Miller, Nov. 20, 1964.

[12] Signed statement of Michel O. Dumas, Nov. 21, 1964.

tion was founded in the 1860's and now has about 79 members. The congregation planned to build an addition to the church costing $1,400, and about $1,000 had been collected for this purpose before the fire. The pastor of the church is Rev. Shead Baldwin of 105 Georgia St., Natchez.

On July 12, 1964, the church burned to the ground. Reverend Baldwin learned of the fire early that morning. He reported the fire to the sheriff's office. The sheriff investigated and called the State Fire Marshal to assist him. The sheriff believes the fire was the result of arson. No arrests have been made. Reverend Baldwin has no idea why the church was burned. It was never used as a civil rights meeting place and none of the members was active in civil rights. The building was insured for about $8,000. The insurance company has paid the full amount of the policy. The congregation plans to build a modern structure costing about $25,200. The white community of Natchez has contributed $2,500.[13]

13. The Bethel A.M.E. Church was a wooden building located on the Kingston Road about 8 miles from Natchez. The building was more than 50 years old and had been remodeled in 1962. The congregation now numbers 28 members. The church was never used for civil rights meetings and none of the members took part in civil rights activities. The pastor of the church was Rev. James Manley who lives at 125 Dinwiddie Street, McComb, Miss.

On July 12, 1964 (the same night on which Jerusalem Baptist Church burned), the church burned to the ground. The sheriff and the State Fire Marshal investigated. The sheriff could not discover the cause of the fire, but he believes it was deliberately set. The congregation intends to rebuild the church and expects that rebuilding will cost about $12,000. It has collected $3,000 from the insurance company, and expects to receive $2,700 from the white community.[14]

14. Willie Washington is a Negro contractor who has been a successful bidder on municipal jobs in Natchez. He is 57 years old, married, and does not have any children. He has lived in Mississippi all of his life. He is a registered voter and a member of the Business and Civic League. He is not active in the civil rights movement.

On the night of July 12, 1964, while sitting in his living room, he heard the sound of breaking glass on the front steps of his porch. He went to the door and saw a car pulling away from the curb. He called the police who discovered that a glass bottle stuffed with a rag wick and filled with kerosene had been thrown at the house. The bottle was broken and the fluid did not ignite. The fragments were sent by the police to a police laboratory. No arrests have been made.[15]

15. The Mount Pilgrim Baptist Church was a wooden building built on Duck Pond Plantation, 3 miles from Fenwick, Miss., some 50 years ago. The congregation numbers about 70 persons. Early in 1964, a new roof was put on the church. Rev. R. J. Johnson, 59, of 34 Wilson Lane, Natchez, has been pastor of the Mount Pilgrim congregation for more than 20 years. On August 5, 1964, the church burned to the ground. The sheriff investigated. No arrests have been made. The building was insured for $4,000 and the full amount has been paid. Plans have been made to rebuild the church.[16]

---

[13] Affidavit of Rev. Shead Baldwin, Nov. 18, 1964.

[14] Signed statement of Rev. James Manley, Nov. 23, 1964.

[15] Affidavit of Willie Washington, Nov. 19, 1964.

[16] Affidavit of Rev. R. J. Johnson, Nov. 19, 1964; affidavit of Staff Legal Assistant Jonathan W. Fleming of interview with Sheriff Odell Anders, Feb. 4, 1965.

16. Jake Frishman is a 58-year-old white man, who has lived in Adams County for 40 years. He operated a Negro tavern called "The Wall Street Grocery" behind 609 Wall Street, in Natchez. The tavern was in a frame building, next door to a house rented and used by civil rights workers last summer.

On the night of August 14, 1964, about 60 persons were inside the tavern. About 11 p.m. a boy came in and said that the building was on fire; the tavern was evacuated. Within a minute there was an explosion and flames shot through an open window. The fire spread rapidly and gutted the interior of the building. The fire department was called, put out the fire, and assisted the police in setting up a guard around the building. Investigating law enforcement officers discovered evidence of arson at the rear of the building. The sheriff believes the fire was set by whites.[17]

17. On the night of September 15, 1964, stink bombs were thrown into two Jitney Jungle food stores owned by Mayor John J. Nosser, and bricks and a stink bomb were thrown into a Cadillac car agency owned by Orrick Metcalfe and his son. The bombs were thrown after pro civil rights statements attributed to both men appeared in an interview published by the Chicago Daily News. No arrests have been made.[18]

18. On September 26, 1964, at about 9:23 p.m., dynamite was thrown at the home of Mayor John J. Nosser. The mayor and his wife were sitting in the living room at the time of the explosion. The blast cracked every wall in the house and knocked the columns askew. Total damage was over $10,000. The police investigated. No arrests have been made.[19]

19. On September 26, 1964, the home of Willie Washington was attacked again. About 9:30 p.m., while Mrs. Washington was home alone, a bomb exploded in front of the house. The blast damaged the roof, gutters and woodwork, cracked plaster, and broke two windows. Prior to the bombing, Mr. Washington had received a number of threatening phone calls. After the bombing, a crowd of 200 to 300 Negroes gathered near his house. The police asked Washington to tell them to disperse and he refused. The police did not make any other effort to get the crowd to leave. No arrests have been made. The house was insured and all the damage paid for.[20]

20. George Metcalfe is a 53-year-old Negro who works for the Armstrong Tire Company. He lives at 9 St. Catherine St., Natchez, Miss. He is president of the Adams County chapter of the NAACP.

On the night of January 25, 1965, a shot was fired at his house, striking a window frame and shattering the window. Metcalfe was in the house at the time. He looked around and saw a car down the street near a street light but was unable to get the license number or a description. He called the FBI and the police, who arrived that night and investigated. The police returned the next morning and continued the investigation.[21]

Other incidents during the period covered by this report have affected white citizens of Natchez. None of the persons affected were willing to testify at the hearing because of fear of reprisal. In addition to these incidents, there were others reported which we were unable to confirm because of the victims' unwillingness to be interviewed.

[17] Signed statement of Jake Frishman, Nov. 23, 1964 ; DJ files.
[18] Affidavit of Staff Legal Assistant Jonathan W. Fleming of interview with Mayor John J. Nosser, Feb. 4, 1965.
[19] Affidavit of Staff Legal Assistant Jonathan W. Fleming of interview with Mayor John J. Nosser, Feb. 4, 1965 ; DJ files.
[20] Affidavit of Willie Washington, Nov. 19, 1964.
[21] Affidavit of George Metcalfe, Feb. 5, 1965.

Several white citizens of Natchez related to us that they had received threats following actions on their part indicating sympathy for the Negro community. Several persons received anonymous telephone calls—usually in the middle of the night. Another person was warned of an impending bombing of his house. Another person reported that he was under surveillance and that his car had been followed by a car occupied by a group of white men. One family's home was watched on New Year's Eve by an occupant of a car and then guests were followed by several cars when they left at 4:00 a.m.[22]

There were also threats of economic boycott and actual boycotts against persons who hired Negroes or were otherwise identified as favorable to Negroes. Finally, the Catholic clergymen in the area were attacked by extremist literature as a result of visiting a Negro in jail.[23] This literature is in appendix B to the staff report.

---

[22] Affidavit of Edwin D. Wolf, staff attorney, of interviews with white citizens of Natchez, Feb. 15, 1965.

[23] *Ibid.*

EXHIBIT 14

NEWSPAPER ADVERTISEMENT OF CIVIC ASSOCIATION, "WE BELIEVE,"
DEMOCRAT (NATCHEZ, MISS.), DATED OCTOBER 18, 1964

PAGE FOURTEEN—B   NATCHEZ (Miss.) DEMOCRAT   SUNDAY MORNING, OCTOBER 18, 1964

WE BELIEVE

1 That this community is on the threshold of a great economic, cultural and industrial development period and to assure such growth we must have a reputation as a law-abiding community of people fully aware not only of the privileges, but more urgently of the responsibilities of living here.

2 That violent and unlawful acts of a few, determined to impose their will upon us, not only endanger our personal security but threaten the hopes and whole future of this area, and such acts must be met with overwhelming determination by all of us to end them.

3 That "fear of being involved" by responsible people is the very blood on which these hoodlums thrive, and we must not only put aside such fear, we must seek ways to participate actively in bringing to our governing officials and law enforcement officers, local, State or National, any fact, matter or suspicion which might help them in their efforts to protect us.

On these beliefs, we the undersigned local organizations, urge every individual to join our law enforcement bodies in giving notice to any and all who would destroy the highly respected and widely known image of this great southern city, that these patterns of criminal malice will not be tolerated here.

Natchez-Adams County Chamber of Commerce	Natchez Lodge No. 353, Benevolent and Protective Order of Elks	Loyal Order of Moose	Natchez Rotary Club
Natchez Civitan Club	Post Presidents Council Natchez-Adams County Chamber of Commerce	Natchez Garden Club	Natchez Y's Men's Club
American Association of University Women	40 & 8	Natchez Historical Society	Natchez Trace Association
Altrusa Club of Natchez	Natchez Junior Chamber of Commerce	Natchez Area Ministerial Association	Natchez Toastmasters Club
American Legion	Natchez Junior Auxiliary	Newcomers Club	Young Men's Christian Association
Civic and Welfare Club of Natchez	Natchez Kiwanis Club	Pilgrimage Garden Club	Women For Constitutional Government
Natchez Community Concert Association	League of Women's Voters of Natchez	Pilot Club of Natchez, Inc.	Veterans of Foreign Wars
Kiwanis Club of East Natchez	Lions Club	Adams County Chapter American Red Cross	Natchez High Twelve Club
	Natchez Little Theatre, Inc.		

The following resolution was adopted at the regular monthly meeting of the NATCHEZ AREA MINISTERIAL ASSOCIATION at the Eola Hotel at noon, April 6. It was subsequently mailed to all the local law enforcement officials and published in the local paper. In our meeting on October 5, WE VOTED TO REPUBLISH IT IN ORDER to emphasize our opposition to violence within our community.

THE NATCHEZ AREA MINISTERIAL ASSOCIATION is deeply concerned over the tension and high feelings in our community over the racial problem. This problem is immensely complicated, and we do not profess to have all the answers.

But as Christians, and as ministers, we are convinced that violence of any description is not an answer. For the sake of every individual in our community, and for the sake of the community itself, both spiritually, economically, and culturally, we feel that a strong statement to the effect that no violence or mob action will be tolerated by any of the responsible citizens of this community, is badly needed. Such positive leadership will surely elicit the whole-hearted support of the large majority of our people. Such a statement might well avoid further incidents in our community that would destroy lives and families and give a black mark on our city and county that none of us would want.

THE NATCHEZ AREA MINISTERIAL ASSOCIATION earnestly requests that all concerned persons and all of the legal authorities of our community exert such positive leadership in these tense days. We pledge to you our prayerful support in such an endeavor for the good of our people, and the good of our community.

NATCHEZ MINISTERIAL SOCIETY

EXHIBIT NO. 15

STAFF REPORT OF INVESTIGATION OF INCIDENTS OF RACIAL VIOLENCE, JONES COUNTY, MISS., 1964

INDEX

[1] Arrests have been made.
[2] Believed to have occured in the city of Laurel.

STAFF INVESTIGATION REPORT: JONES COUNTY (LAUREL), MISS.

The following is a report of the staff's investigation of incidents of violence against Negroes and others attempting to use public accommodations under Title II of the Civil Rights Act of 1964, and violence against members of Local 5–443 of the International Woodworkers Association in Jones County, Miss. The report is based on affidavits of victims and witnesses, interviews with law enforcement officials, and information in Government files.

1. On July 11, 1964, Larry McGill (age 11) and several other Negro youths decided to eat at a previously segregated lunch counter at the S. H. Kress Store in downtown Laurel. Larry and his group were driven downtown by his mother, Mrs. Bertie Mae McGill. When they arrived in the downtown area, the children got out of the car, went into the Kress store and sat at the lunch counter. Mrs. McGill parked her car and followed. The police chief of Laurel, L. C. Nix, was present. Before the Negroes could be served two white men armed with bats who had been in the store attacked the Negroes as they sat at the counter. Jessie Harrington was struck on the head and blood ran out of his mouth. Larry McGill was hit across the back and knocked down as he was leaving his seat. The police chief stopped the attack and arrested one of the assailants. The Negroes were taken to the hospital, treated and released.

The police did not interview Mrs. McGill or any of the victims of this attack. The person arrested forfeited an appearance bond of $25.[1]

2. On the afternoon of August 15, 1964, Larry McGill and other Negro boys went again to the S. H. Kress Store. A group of white men were standing in the store with baseball bats when they entered. As they sat at the lunch counter, Larry was approached by a white woman who pointed a pistol at him and ordered him to leave his seat. His mother, who was in the store and observed the incident, was also threatened. Another of the youths was struck on the back of the

[1] Signed statement of Larry McGill, Dec. 16, 1964; signed statement of Mrs. Bertie Mae McGill, Dec. 16, 1964; affidavit of Jonathan W. Fleming, staff legal assistant, of interview with Chief of Police L. C. Nix, Feb. 4, 1964.

neck with a baseball bat by one of the white men. The Negroes left the store and reported the incident to a policeman. They also swore out warrants for the arrest of their assailants. Both were subsequently tried on charges of assault and found not guilty.[2]

3. On the morning of August 11, 1964, Eugene Keys, an 18-year-old Negro resident of Laurel, went to the S. H. Kress Store to buy a notebook. A white man whom Keys did not know approached him from the front of the store. The man accused him of eating at the lunch counter, threatened him, and then took brass knuckles out of his pocket, and tried to hit Keys two or three times. Keys grabbed the man's arm and was not hit. Keys fled when the white man took out a knife. The incident was reported to the police. A few days later Keys pointed out his assailant to Federal officials. No arrests have been made.[3]

4. On August 14, 1954, Sharon Diane Jefferson, a 13-year-old Negro girl, was accosted by three white men as she sat at the lunch counter in the Woolworth Store in downtown Laurel. One of the men pulled her from the stool and another kicked her as she was being pushed out of the store. No arrests have been made for this assault.[4]

5. On the afternoon of November 28, 1964, two civil rights workers, John T. Foster, Jr., white, and John Handy, Negro, went to the S. H. Kress Store in downtown Laurel. They sat at the lunch counter and were served. About half-way through their meal, a white man came up behind Foster, spun him around and hit him on the nose and the back of the head with his fist. The man then walked away. After the assault, Foster and Handy went to the police station and swore out a "John Doe" warrant for the arrest of the man based on a description given to the desk sergeant. No arrests have been made.[5]

6. On December 16, 1964, six persons, four Negroes and two whites, went to the Pinehurst Cafe in the Travel Inn and attempted to obtain service. They entered the cafe and sat in two groups. They were not served. There was no crowd or disturbance. When they refused to leave upon requests of the management they were arrested by the police chief on warrants sworn out by the attorney for the management. Some of the group went limp and were carried out of the cafe and dragged up the steps of the city hall. The others walked to jail. All were charged with breach of the peace. The four demonstrators who went limp were also charged with resisting arrest. No trial has been held.[6]

7. On December 24, 1964, a second integrated group of 20 persons were arrested on charges of disturbing the peace and resisting arrest during an attempt to integrate the Pinehurst Cafe. No trial has yet been held.[7]

8. Ottis Matthews, a 41-year-old white native Mississippian, is the assistant business agent of Local 5–443, International Woodworkers of America. He has held this position for the past 6 years. In March of 1964 he was the Union officer who worked directly with management in integrating seniority lists and facilities at the Masonite plant. Members of the Union who Mr. Matthews believes are members of the Klan opposed these integration efforts. Klan literature was

[2] Signed statement of Larry McGill, Dec. 16, 1964; signed statement of Mrs. Bertie Mae McGill, Dec. 16, 1964; signed statement of Charles Nelson Hartfield, Dec. 16, 1964.
[3] DJ files.
[4] DJ files.
[5] Affidavit of John T. Foster.
[6] Signed statement of Gwendolyn Robinson, Dec. 16, 1964; signed statement of Marian Burchard Davidson, Dec. 17, 1964.
[7] Signed statements of Johnny Lewis Smith, Nancy Margaret Grogan, Jessie James Smith, and Gwendolyn Delores Robinson, Dec. 28, 1964.

distributed at the plant and in the fall union elections, a group challenged the Union leadership on racist grounds.

On the evening of November 16, 1964, while Mr. Matthews was driving home from a Union meeting, he was stopped by a parked car which blocked the road. Three men with woolen mufflers over their faces forced their way into his car at gun point, blindfolded him and drove him to a side road. He was taken out of the car, tied, stripped from the waist down, forced to lie face down and beaten with a leather strap. Several times during the beating his attackers poured a stinging liquid into his cuts. The men threatened Matthew's life and warned him not to talk against the Klan. Following the beating his car was disabled so that he could not follow his assailants. He went home and called the sheriff. The following night, after a Union meeting, he was followed again but he returned to the parking lot at the Union hall.[8]

The Masonite plant in Laurel employs about 2,800 men. Prior to 1964, the plant was entirely segregated. In March 1964, the signs over the drinking fountains and at the restrooms were taken down, and the seniority lists at the plant were integrated. Four Negro employees at Masonite were the victims of Klan violence during March and April. Two of them had crosses burned at their homes after they used formerly white drinking fountains. The other two Negro employees had been promoted to new nontraditional jobs. One man had a cross burned on his lawn and received a telephone threat, "You got your warning and you had better straighten up at Masonite." Another Negro had a cross burned on his lawn. Two weeks later, three rifle shots were fired at his home. The following day he reported the incident to the sheriff and shortly after he returned home, two shotgun blasts were fired at his home.[9]

EXHIBIT NO. 16

MATERIAL SUBMITTED BY CLAUDE RAMSAY, PRESIDENT, MISSISSIPPI AFL–CIO

(OMITTED IN PRINTING)

---

[8] Affidavit of Jonathan W. Fleming, Staff Legal Assistant, of interview with Ottis Matthews, Feb. 4, 1964; affidavit of Edwin D. Wolf, Staff Attorney, of interview with Ottis Matthews; DJ files.

[9] Affidavit of Edwin D. Wolf, Staff Attorney, of interviews with four victims.

EXHIBIT NO. 17

STAFF REPORT OF INVESTIGATION OF INCIDENTS OF RACIAL VIOLENCE AND THE ASCS ELECTION, MADISON COUNTY, MISS., 1963-64

INDEX

[1] Arrests have been made.
[2] Occurred within the city of Canton.

STAFF INVESTIGATION REPORT: MADISON COUNTY, MISS.

The following is a report of incidents of racial violence in Madison County, Miss., occuring during the latter part of 1963 and during 1964, which have been investigated by the staff of the Commission.

1. On June 25, 1963, five young Negroes were hit with birdshot from a shotgun fired at them by a middle-aged white man as they were walking home on West Peace Street in Canton, at 9:30 p.m. The Negroes were not involved in civil rights, but a registration rally was being held near the gas station at the time of the shooting. Local officials assumed that the shooting was in response to civil rights activity in Canton. A white man was arrested several days later on a warrant signed by city authorities. After four continuances of his trial he pleaded *nolo contendere*, and was fined $500; half of the fine was suspended upon good behavior. The mayor and president of the chamber of commerce publicly

condemned the shooting and announced that the city would not permit violence against any of its citizens. A copy of this announcement is an appendix to this report.[1]

2. In January 1964, the Madison County Movement, a local Negro civil rights organization, announced an economic boycott against white merchants in Canton. The aims of the boycott were to obtain jobs for Negroes and more respectful treatment for Negro customers. At its peak the boycott was about 90 percent effective. Within weeks, three white businesses closed and business in a large white-owned supermarket dropped by 40 percent. At the same time business in Negro-owned stores increased by 100 percent.[2]

In early February, the Madison County Herald reported the reorganization of the once dormant White Citizens Council under the steering committee of 40 prominent white men. These included the sheriff, chief of police, mayor, city attorney, a State senator from Madison County, a former sheriff and deputy, as well as bankers, lawyers, physicians, industrialists, and businessmen. The policy of the Madison County White Citizens Council, as determined from staff interviews with members and from public announcements of the Council, was to avoid violence and to present a unanimous white resistance to the Negro majority of the county.[3]

3. On February 28, 1964, the first Freedom Day in Madison County was held. About 200 Negroes marched from the Negro section of Canton to the county court-house in the center of town. They were placed in a single line around the court-house square by sheriff's deputies, city police, and auxiliaries. During the entire day only four Negroes were permitted to complete the registration applications. Police preparations included putting 75 special Highway Patrolmen on standby alert at Jackson about 23 miles away.[4]

4. On May 7, 1964, at about 8:50 p.m., a man wearing a white hood drove by the Freedom House at 838 Lutz Street. He waved a pistol and fired a shot towards the house. Several Negroes saw the car and were able to read the license number. The number and description of the car were given to the Canton city police by George Washington, Jr., a witness to the incident. Washington alleged that he recognized the car as belonging to a member of the Canton police. No arrests have been made.[5]

5. On the night of May 20, 1964, Theodis Hewitt and James Collier, Negro civil rights workers, were sleeping in the Freedom House when a white man knocked on the door and demanded to be let in. They refused. The man went back to his car, returned with a pistol, and fired several shots at the house. Hewitt called the police, reported the incident and furnished descriptions of the man and his car. No arrests have been made.[6]

6. A second Freedom Day was held in Madison County on May 29, 1964. Armed deputies and city policemen prohibited any marching. Negroes remained massed at two Negro churches which served as headquarters. Fifty-three per-

---

[1] Affidavit of Attorney Roy Littlejohn of interview with Shirley Dotson Gunn and Agnes Nell Dotson ; DJ files.

[2] Affidavit of George Raymond.

[3] Affidavit of Assistant General Counsel Michael O. Finkelstein of interview with Phillip Mullen ; affidavit of Staff Legal Assistant Jonathan W. Fleming of interview with Mayor L. S. Matthews ; report of Rev. Wofford Smith, Feb. 28, 1964.

[4] Report of Rev. Wofford Smith, Feb. 28, 1964.

[5] Affidavit of George Washington, Jr. ; DJ files.

[6] Affidavit of Theodis Hewitt ; DJ files.

sons were arrested during the day. A Negro youth was knocked unconscious and arrested by a city policeman whom he had taunted with curses.[7]

7. On the evening of this day (May 29), Mirza Hamid Hasan Kizilbash, a Pakistani who teaches sociology at Tougaloo College, drove Chaplain Ed King, Mrs. King, Miss Joan Trumpauer, and Eli Hochstedler, all members of the Tougaloo faculty, to Canton to attend a voter registration rally. Canton was still patrolled by armed police and auxiliaries and tensions were very high. Attendance at the rally was poor and it ended early. As Kizilbash and his friends drove out of town they were followed. On the edge of town, at the access road to Interstate 55, his car was stopped by three vehicles. It was dark by this time. A group of 10 to 15 white men approached his car and Kizilbash rolled down a window to talk with them. One of the men reached into the window, pulled up the doorlock and opened the door. He grabbed Kizilbash by his shirt collar, pulled him out of the car, and hit him on the head with a club. They were all told that they would be killed if they ever returned to Canton. Kizilbash was then allowed to drive away. One of the intercepting cars followed them.

Near the entrance to Millsaps College, in Jackson, some Tougaloo faculty members recognized Kizilbash's car and saw that it was being followed. They followed in their car and were able to obtain the license number of the car following Kizilbash.

At the time of the attack, Kizilbash believed that he was able to identify some of the men involved. He made a complaint to the Highway Patrol in Jackson that night, but a patrol spokesman said it lacked jurisdiction to investigate, and refused to escort Kizilbash back to Canton to make a complaint to Sheriff Cauthen of Madison County. Later that evening Highway Patrol officers questioned Kizilbash extensively. Three days later, Kizilbash, in a letter to Sheriff Cauthen, described the incident and reported that he had the license number of one of the cars that had followed him from Canton. At the same time President Beittel of Tougaloo called Sheriff Cauthen and gave him the same information. Kizilbash never returned to Canton to make a formal complaint. He was never interviewed by the sheriff. No arrests have been made.[8]

8. On June 8, 1964, at about 1 o'clock in the morning, a bomb was thrown at the Freedom House. The explosion damaged the sidewalk about 12 feet from the house. The explosion was not reported to the police until the following morning. George Washington, Jr., who guards his father's property at night, saw the bomb thrown. A few days after the incident he gave a general description of the car to the police. No arrests have been made.[9]

9. On the morning of June 8, 1964, George Washington, Sr., landlord of the Freedom House, was picked up in his grocery store by Officer John Chance for questioning about his failure to report a bomb explosion at the Freedom House earlier in the morning. (When the bomb exploded, Washington, who lives nearby, woke up, investigated, saw no damage, and went back to sleep without calling the police. When daylight came, his wife noticed a broken window in the Freedom House and called the police.)

Chance took Washington to the Canton police station.

Washington alleges that as he walked through a doorway, Chance struck him in the eye with his fist. He was put in a cell for about 15 minutes and then

[7] Affidavit of George Raymond.
[8] Affidavit of Mirza Hamid Hasan Kizilbash; affidavit of Mrs. Pat Hutchinson.
[9] Affidavit of George Washington, Jr.; DJ files.

taken into a room for questioning. The interrogation lasted four hours. During this time he was slapped in the face twice by Chance. Washington was threatened with prosecution for failure promptly to report the bombing. He was asked to evict the civil rights workers and to help the white community in driving them from Canton. He refused. Washington says he did not mention the injury to his eye during the interrogation because Officer Chance was present. Chief Dan C. Thompson and City Attorney Robert L. Goza came into the room but did not see the slappings or take part in the questioning. Two or three days later he complained to Chief Thompson that Officer Chance had hit him. He also called Mayor Matthews about a month later and reported the incident to him. He assured Washington that it would not happen again.[10]

10. Shortly after midnight on June 12, 1964, a bomb was thrown at the home of Mrs. Alberta Robinson of 315 Second Firebaugh Ave., Canton. The bomb landed on the corner of her lawn and did little damage. Mrs. Robinson is not active in civil rights. The bomb may have been intended for her next door neighbor, Mrs. Marian Robinson (no relation), who helped to organize a school boycott in March 1964.[11]

A few minutes later a second bomb exploded on the lawn of the Pleasant Green Church of Christ on Walnut Street. The church, a brick structure, was used for civil rights meetings. The bomb blasted a shallow hole on the lawn and cracked a window.[12]

11. On July 11, 1964, about 7 p.m., a firebomb or molotov cocktail was thrown at the Freedom House from a light green Volkswagen. A number of Negroes were on the street at the time and some of them were able to read the license number. The number was given to city police and to the Special City Prosecutor W. S. Cain, who came to investigate the incident. The number was traced and three white youths were arrested. All three pleaded *nolo contendere* to a charge of breach of the peace and were fined $50 each. This fact was concealed from the Negro community by Prosecutor Cain. He stated to Federal investigators that he did not want members of the civil rights movement at the Freedom House to know of the arrests.[13]

12. On Sunday, July 19, 1964, Michael Piore and William Carney, two white civil rights volunteers, were assaulted by a local white man as they walked past his gas station on West Peace Street. They were returning from an unsuccessful attempt to attend services at the First Methodist Church. They swore out a warrant for the arrest of their assailant. Piore and Carney asked that the trial be postponed one week because they were not able to appear in court on the day scheduled for trial. Subsequently, the city requested a continuance and later the prosecutor, Robert L. Goza, left for summer military duty. In late August both Piore and Carney returned home. The city attorney then dropped the prosecution because the complaining witnesses had left Canton.[14]

13. On July 19, 1964, sometime in the night, the Christian Union Baptist Church in Ridgeland burned to the ground. The church had never been used for civil rights meetings. Sheriff Cauthen investigated. No arrests have been

[10] Affidavit of George Washington, Sr., affidavit of Staff Legal Assistant Jonathan W. Fleming of interview with Mayor L. S. Matthews; DJ files.
[11] Affidavit of Mrs. Alberta Robinson; affidavit of Mrs. Marian Robinson; DJ files.
[12] Affidavit of George Raymond; affidavit of Mrs. Marian Robinson; DJ files.
[13] Affidavit of Staff Legal Assistant Jonathan W. Fleming of interview with Michael Piore; affidavit of George Raymond; DJ files.
[14] Affidavit of Staff Legal Assistant Jonathan W. Fleming of interview with Michael Piore; affidavit of Staff Legal Assistant Jonathan W. Fleming of interview with City Attorney Robert L. Goza.

made. The church has been rebuilt by a Committee of Concern at a cost of $14,000, at a new location. The building was dedicated in January 1965.[15]

14. On August 2, 1964, a car containing a group of white teenagers drove by the Freedom House at 8 p.m. Someone in the car fired a shot at the Freedom House. George Washington, Jr., who was sitting on his front porch with a pistol, fired back. The youths fired again and drove away. Washington gave a description of the car to the police, but did not tell them that he had returned the fire. Two days later, he was arrested for unlawful possession of a firearm. No other arrests have been made in this incident.[16]

15. On August 11, 1964, around 11 p.m., the meeting hall of the Willing Workers Society of the Mount Pleasant Church in Gluckstadt burned to the ground. The hall was being used as a Freedom School and contained a Freedom Library. Sheriff Cauthen investigated the fire. On August 28, 1964, he arrested Joe Lee Watts, a Negro civil rights worker, on suspicion of arson.[17] Charges were never brought against Watts and he was released the same day. The basis for the arrest was a statement made by Watts on the day after the fire when he tried to investigate for COFO. He had said to the sheriff and other officers that he was there "to interview [sic] the building we burned." No other arrests have been made.[18]

16. Shortly after 1:30 a.m. on September 5, 1964, five sticks of dynamite exploded inside Joe and Barb's Curb Market on West North St., Canton. The explosion damaged the interior of the store, some appliances and merchandise. The business is owned by Joe Ferguson, who is white. The store is patronized almost exclusively by Negroes. It had been on the boycott list of the Madison County Movement until April 1964, when Mr. Ferguson complied with the Negroes' demands. His was the only white store taken off the boycott. The sheriff's office and the city police investigated. No arrests have been made.[19]

17. Shortly after the explosion at Joe and Barb's had awakened the Negro neighborhood, George Washington, Sr., inspected his store. He found a 5-foot fuse leading from the cinder block foundation of the store. The police were called. A deputy sheriff found a package of eight sticks of dynamite under the store. He could find no explosive caps and the fuse was not attached to the dynamite. The fuse had been burned completely through. No arrests have been made.[20]

18. On the night of September 17, 1964, two Negro churches that had been used for civil rights meetings burned to the ground. At 10 p.m., St. John's Church in Valley View, about 10 miles northeast of Canton, was discovered on fire by local Negroes. The church was destroyed within a few minutes. Sheriff Cauthen was called and he investigated.[21] About two or three hours later Cedar Grove Baptist Church, on Highway 43, several miles southeast of Canton, burned. Sheriff Cauthen investigated. No arrests have been made.[22]

---

[15] Affidavit of George Raymond; DJ files.

[16] Affidavit of George Washington, Jr.; affidavit of Staff Legal Assistant Jonathan W. Fleming of interview with Michael Piore.

[17] Affidavit of Staff Legal Assistant Jonathan W. Fleming of interview with Joe Lee Watts.

[18] Ibid.

[19] Affidavit of George Raymond; affidavit of Staff Legal Assistant Jonathan W. Fleming of interview with Joe Ferguson; affidavit of Joe Ferguson; DJ files.

[20] Affidavit of George Washington, Sr.; affidavit of George Raymond; affidavit of Staff Legal Assistant Jonathan W. Fleming of interview with Sheriff Jack Cauthen; DJ files.

[21] Affidavit of Staff Legal Assistant Jonathan W. Fleming of interview with Sheriff Jack Cauthen; DJ files.

[22] Ibid.

MADISON COUNTY ASCS ELECTIONS

The following is a report of incidents of violence occurring in connection with the Agricultural Stabilization and Conservation Service elections held in Madison County on December 3, 1964. Under Department of Agriculture regulations any person may be present at the polls. Representatives of the Department had agreed to allow civil rights workers to be present and had communicated this agreement to local ASCS officials and to local law enforcement officials.

19. Community "A" (so designated by the Department of Agriculture) is the town of Flora and its environs in southwestern Madison County. The polling place was in Hawkins' General Store and was patrolled by a deputy sheriff and town police from Flora. Miss Euvester Simpson, a Negro coed from Tougaloo College, was a civil rights worker who was acting as a poll watcher.[23] She arrived at the polls at 1:30 p.m. Twice she was forcibly ejected from the store by a white man. After conferring with other COFO workers, who were standing outside the store, Miss Simpson entered the store a third time. She was told to leave and refused. A person in the store called to a Flora policeman and asked that Miss Simpson be arrested. The policeman entered and arrested Miss Simpson for disturbing the peace. She was held overnight in the Flora jail. The following morning she was transferred to the Madison County jail in Canton. She was released on $500 bond that evening.[24]

20. Community "B" is the town of Madison in the southeastern section of Madison County. The polling place was the Madison County Health Center and was patrolled by Constable Carl Holley.[25] Marvin Rich, a 34-year-old white man, who is a national officer of the Congress of Racial Equality, was in Madison County to observe and assist in the ASCS election. In the morning he canvassed Negro farmers. In the afternoon he went to the polling place in Madison. Miss Martha Rose McAvoy and Miss Catherine Lucido, civil rights workers, were poll watchers inside the building. Rich stayed outside to assist Negro farmers coming to vote. During the afternoon a small group of white teenagers hung around the polling place making derisive remarks. Constable Holley ordered the civil rights workers to move a car from the area. Rich moved it to a Negro church where he parked with the permission of the minister's wife. He returned to the polling area.

About 3:30 p.m. Rich became concerned at the growing size of the gang of whites. He went to telephone the civil rights office in Canton and his national office in New York. After completing his calls Rich tried to enter the Health Center Building, but two white youths blocked the doorway. He sat down on a bench outside the building. Some of the whites began tossing stones at him. He protected himself with his arms and elbows. Finally the stones forced him to try again to enter the building. The two white boys were still standing in the doorway, which was the only unlocked entrance to the building.[26] Rich started to call to Constable Holley, who was inside the building. Before he could call out, one of the young men standing in the doorway punched him in the face and another person slashed him in the face with a belt buckle. His nose was broken in two places as a result of this attack.

---

[23] Affidavit of Staff Legal Assistant Jonathan W. Fleming of interview with Tom Ramsey, Feb. 5, 1964. (Hereinafter cited as Ramsey Interview.)
[24] Signed statement of Miss Euvester Simpson, Dec. 18, 1964.
[25] Ramsey Interview.
[26] Affidavit of Marvin Rich; signed statement of Miss Catherine Lucido, Dec. 14, 1964; signed statement of Miss Martha Rose McAvoy, Dec. 14, 1964; DJ files.

Constable Holley came out of the building. The beating stopped. Holley asked Rich if he wished to make a complaint, adding that he did not think the boy would have hit Rich unless he were provoked. Rich answered that he did not want to make a complaint, but that he wanted to see justice done. One of the girls inside the building called to Canton civil rights headquarters for assistance. A car was sent to pick them up. As they drove away stones were thrown after the car by members of the gang.[27]

Sheriff Cauthen knows of this incident, and the identity of the boy who struck Rich. No arrests have been made.[28]

21. Community "C" is in Canton. The polling place was Ballard's Gin and was patrolled for part of the day by Deputy Bill Noble.[29] Eric Orr, a white civil rights worker, was punched in the face by a white man as he walked up the steps of the Gin. The man was arrested on a warrant sworn by Orr. Orr failed to appear at the trial, which was scheduled on December 5, 1964, and the charges were dismissed.[30]

22. Community "D" consists of the locality of Farmhaven and surrounding area. The polling place was McDonald's Store. Two civil rights observers of the election, Miss Anne Draper and George Raymond, were arrested here.[31]

23. Community "E" is in the Gluckstadt area of the county. The polling place was the office of the R&N Grocery.[32] The civil rights worker who observed was Miss Elayne DeLott, white. Space in the office was crowded, but ASCS Manager Robert Hodges arranged things so that Miss DeLott could observe the balloting and assist any Negro farmer who requested her help.[33] Sometime after 9:30 a.m. Sheriff Cauthen arrived and asked Miss DeLott to leave the store. She was told that she could see all she needed to see from the outside. She complied with his order. After the sheriff left, an ASCS committeeman asked her to come back inside the store. An hour or so later Sheriff Cauthen returned. He discussed the situation with the ASCS committeemen and, over their objection, ordered Miss DeLott to leave the store. He told her that he was in charge of keeping the peace, and that if she remained in the store four or five white men might decide to "rough her up." He advised that she would be safer outside. Miss DeLott left the building. Later the COFO project director, George Raymond, told her to go back inside the store. She did. About 11 a.m. Sheriff Cauthen returned to the store and arrested her.[34]

Miss DeLott had been accompanied that morning by Eartis Crawford, a Negro civil rights worker, who remained outside the store with a walkie-talkie. After Miss DeLott was arrested Crawford attempted to enter the store. A group of white men who were inside stopped him at the entrance. One of them got a gun from behind a counter, but was restrained by two other white men. Crawford was hit on the back of the head by an unseen assailant and pushed out of the store. His radio was thrown after him. He made no complaint to law enforcement officers.[35]

---

[27] *Ibid.*

[28] Affidavit of Staff Legal Assistant Jonathan W. Fleming of interview with Sheriff Jack Cauthen, Feb. 5, 1964 (hereinafter cited as Sheriff Cauthen Interview).

[29] Ramsey Interview.

[30] Ramsey Interview ; Sheriff Cauthen Interview.

[31] Signed statement of George Raymond, Dec. 14, 1964 ; Ramsay Interview.

[32] Ramsey Interview.

[33] Hodges Interview ; signed statement of George Raymond, Dec. 14, 1964.

[34] Signed statement of Miss Elayne DeLott, Dec. 15, 1964 ; Sheriff Cauthen Interview.

[35] Signed statement of Eartis Crawford, Dec. 15, 1964.

EXHIBIT NO. 18

LETTER FROM MR. MIRZA HAMID KIZILBASH TO JACK S. CAUTHEN, SHERIFF, MADISON COUNTY, MISS., DATED JUNE 2, 1964

June 2,1964

The Sheriff of Madison County
Canton,Mississippi

Dear Sir:

On Friday May 29,1964 some friends of Mine and I were returning in
my car from a meeting in Canton when we were stopped by three cars
full of white people. These people cursed and threatened us and
I was beaten with a billy club on the head. As a result of the beating
I had to get medical attention and had to stay in bed for a day.

One of the cars involved in the beating followed me all the way to
Jackson and we were able to get its Mississippi license-plate number.
I am a citizen of Pakistan and have informed my Government as well
as the Governor of Mississippi of this incident. I have reported the
incident to the Mississippi Highway Patrol in Jackson.

If you would like further details, please get in touch with me.

Sincerely Yours,

H. K.

(Mirza Hamid H. Kizilbash,
Assistant Professor,Social Science Div.)

Feb. 2, 1965
I certify that this is a true copy
of the letter I sent to the Sheriff
of Madison county.
H. Kizilbash

EXHIBIT NO. 19

JAIL DOCKET SHOWING THE ARREST OF MISS ELAYNE DeLOTT, MADISON COUNTY, MISS., DATED DECEMBER 3, 1964

(OMITTED IN PRINTING)

EXHIBIT NO. 20

REPORT OF JACK S. CAUTHEN, SHERIFF, MADISON COUNTY, MISS., DATED FEB. 18, 1965

> Sheriff of Madison County,
> *Canton, Miss., February 18, 1965.*

CIVIL RIGHTS COMMISSION,
Recreation Hall,
Veteran's Administration,
Jackson, Miss.

DEAR MEMBERS: In response to your request and the subpena duces tecum received by the undersigned, the following report is made, to wit:

1. As to paragraph No. 1, having reference to the alleged assault on Mirza Hamid Kizilbash, near Canton, on or about May 29, 1964, the undersigned advises that no formal complaint was ever made to the sheriff's office of Madison County, Miss., and that this office has no official records pertaining to this incident. Approximately one week after this incident allegedly happened, the undersigned received a call from Dr. Beidel [sic] of Tougaloo College who made inquiry as to whether or not there had been arrests and what progress, if any, had been made. The undersigned advised him that no formal complaint had been made and that this office had been unable to acquire any tangible evidence in connection with the alleged assault. Further investigation led to no arrests and to no tangible information concerning this incident. This office is advised that several other law enforcement agencies were advised of the incident. The undersigned has never seen the accuser and has never seen any persons allegedly in his presence at the time of this incident.

2a. A representative from the sheriff's office accompanied city authorities in connection with investigation of the alleged bombings of the Freedom House at 838 Lutz Street, Canton, Miss., and does not have any written reports concerning paragraph No. 2a in the subpena. All investigations were conducted by other authorities including the FBI, the Justice Department, the city of Canton, and others, and all evidence acquired, if any, or pertaining to the alleged incidents was obtained and kept by authorities other than the sheriff's office of Madison County, Miss.

2b. This office had a representative assist the FBI in the alleged bombing of Joe & Barb's Curb Market in Canton, Miss., on September 5, 1964 and any and all evidence, if any, was taken into the possession of the FBI or other investigative authorities and this office does not have any evidence, physical or otherwise, in it's possession, nor does it have any suspects, and made no arrests.

2c. An officer of this office assisted the FBI at the scene of the attempted bombing of a grocery store owned by George Washington, Sr., on September 5, 1964 and any and all evidence, physical or otherwise, was taken and retained by the FBI and this office has no evidence in connection with this bombing, no reports, no records of complaints, and made no arrests.

2d. An officer from this office acompanied the FBI, the city authorities and other investigating authorities in connection with the alleged bombing of the home of Alberta Robinson, 315 Second Firebaugh St., Canton, Miss., on June 12, 1964. All evidence acquired at this scene was taken into the possession of and kept by other authorities, and this office has no evidence, records of complaints and made no arrests in connection with this alleged incident.

2e. An officer from the sheriffs' office of Madison County, Miss., accompanied the FBI in the investigation of the alleged bombing of the Pleasant Green Church, on or about June 12, 1964, and all evidence, if any, which may have been acquired was taken into the possession and retained by the FBI. This office has no records of complaints, made no arrests and has no copies of investigative reports or statements pertaining to the incident.

2f. We attach to and make a part of this letter a case report on the alleged burning of the Christian Union Baptist Church near Ridgeland, on or about July 20, 1964.

2g. This office has previously turned in a report of the alleged burning of the Willing Workers Meeting Hall near Gluckstadt, Miss., on or about August 11, 1964.

2h. This office has previously turned in a report of the alleged burning of St. John Baptist Church at Valley View, on or about September 17, 1964.

2i. This office has previously turned in a report of the alleged burning of the Cedar Grove Baptist Church, near Canton, Miss., on or about September 17, 1964.

As to paragraph 2h and 2i above, the writer has prepared a supplemental report and attaches and submits the same with this letter.

Respectfully submitted,

JACK S. CAUTHEN,
Sheriff of Madison County, Miss.

CASE REPORT

Burning of: Christian Union Baptist (Negro) Church, Madison County, July 19, 1964

This church is located approximately 2 miles north of Natchez Trace and about the same distance east of U.S. Highway 51. The church was of frame construction with asbestos shingles. The church was situated 40 feet west of a blacktop county road which runs generally north and south. There was a mortgage on the church and it was insured for $5,500 with Shackleford Insurance Agency of Canton, Miss. The church was equipped with a one-year-old piano valued at $800 and a $300 pulpit. This church is at least 60 years old but was kept in a good state of repair. There is no evidence that this church has ever been engaged in any civil rights activities. There is also no evidence of this church having ever had an integrated congregation.

This building stood on brick piers approximately 18 inches in height. There were eight piers on either side of building with the same number running down center of building. Building faced east. A square five-gallon can was found in the debris 18 feet from rear of building at the center row of piers. This can is now in possession of Investigator Jack Smith. It was noted that fragments of asbestos shingles were to be found 100 feet in all directions from the building.

Canton Police Department received a call around 2:30 a.m. stating that a church was burning but the caller did not give his name. This information was passed on to Sheriff Cauthen but the caller gave a location in which no church is located. Sheriff Cauthen found the burned church at 7 a.m. This information will be checked out with the Canton police.

Officers of church: E. D. Hogan, Jackson, Pastor. Deacons: Herbert Jones, Jackson; Eddie Clark, Jackson; Harry Gray, Jackson, 2514 Idaho St.; Albert Washington, Tougaloo; Arthur Kelly, Madison; Ellzey Jones, Tougaloo, also custodian.

Interviews

Elizabeth Gibson, Route 1, Madison, lives 250 yards due east of church. This Negro female, age 45, awoke sometime before daylight on morning of July 19, 1964, and saw church afire. Afraid to go to church. Popping of shingles woke her. Saw no one, nor any vehicles around church.

L. F. Palmer, Negro, male, Route 1, Box 272, Madison. Lives ¼ mile south of church. Palmer's wife woke him at 3 a.m. and told him that a car was running back and forth on the road which runs in front to their house and the church. Stated car was blowing horn. Palmer got out of bed and saw a car going north. Stated car was going slow. This car had a white tail light on left rear with a red tail light on right rear. This car drove by church slowly but did not stop. He states this car passed his house twice. When Palmer first noticed the fire it was in the extreme front of the church in the bell tower. He states that roof burned first and fell into church before walls burned. Palmer returned to bed at 4 a.m. and states positively that no cars stopped at church between 3 and 4 a.m.

Arthur Courtney, Negro male, lives ½ mile northwest of church. Courtney was awakened at 4 a.m. by popping sound and saw glare from burning church. Church cannot be seen from his house.

Clarence and Katie Mae Palmer, Negroes, Route 1, Box 23, Madison. Katie Mae received call at 2:30 a.m. from Jessie Pate's wife, Ollie, stating that church was burning.

Elzie Jones, Negro, male, 62, Tougaloo. Deacon and custodian. Employed by Faulkner Concrete Pipe Co., Moody St., Jackson. Jones has been custodian of the church for 30 years. He states that Agnes Jopeins or Hoskins, a Negro female, who lives at Turkey Farm, called Georgia Gray, wife of Deacon Gray in reference to church burning. Georgia then called him at 3 a.m. and advised him of the church burning. Jones states that the square can definitely does not belong in the church, but that he did keep a round can (5-gallon size) in the storage closet.

It should be noted that Carl Roberts, white, male, of Ridgeland, woke Paul Adams, who operates Pak N Sak store of Ridgeland, at 3:20 a.m. and reported the fire. Investigation continuing.

Burning of: St. John Baptist Negro Church and Cedar Grove Baptist Negro Church

On the morning of September 17, 1964, the writer, Jack Cauthen, accompanied by two fellow officers, continued the investigation of two church burnings of the past night. We proceeded to the St. John's Baptist Church and the building had been completely destroyed by fire. A thorough search of the scene failed to disclose any evidence as to how the fire started.

While we were at the scene a Negro named Mathew Brown, one of the deacons of this church, drove up and he stated that they did not owe anything on the church, and they didn't have any insurance on the church. He said they had tried to get insurance about a month before but was unable to get any.

On further questioning, Mathew Brown advised the writer that a Freedom School was conducted there, at this church, all summer long, by a Mr. and Mrs. Levine. Mathew Brown gave the writer the names of the other deacons of the church and several of them were contacted. The ones contacted admitted the Freedom School, but seemed unwilling to cooperate.

We then went to the Valley View Freedom House, and as we drove up two white girls were driving off. The writer stopped them and asked their names; one stated she was Karen Duncan, and the other Nancy Jerris. The writer advised them we would like to talk to them, and they invited us to come in the Freedom House; Charles Prickett, white, male, was the only other person there at this time. The writer asked if they would agree to an interview one at a time, to which they agreed.

Interview with Karen Duncan, white, female, age 19, 1390 Joice Street, Novato, Calif.; mother and father Mr. and Mrs. Jack Duncan; father runs the A & A Planting Co., San Francisco, Calif.

She stated that she was staying at the home of Rev. Eleigh McCullok (Negro preacher), and she had been here since June 28, 1964, trying to teach the colored people to vote.

She stated that about 10:30 p.m., the past night, September 16, 1964, that Andrew Green came to get her to go to the Freedom House to answer the phone and radio. Green said there was a carload of white men in the area and he was going to investigate.

The church was not on fire at that time: 30 minutes to one hour later Green reported the church was burning. Karen stated she notified the Canton Police Department, Highway Patrol, Fire Department, and FBI.

Interview with Charles Prickett, white, male.

He stated the night before Andrew Green and Honor Williams came to the Freedom House and told him to dress and go with them to see about a fire. He said while he was dressing Green and Williams went to get Karen to come answer the phone. When they got back with her, he got in the car with Green and Williams and they [sic] past the church which had already fallen in, they then turned around and went back to the Freedom House.

Charles Prickett stated that Green had called George Raymond the night before and told him he was uneasy and felt that something was going to happen.

Writer and a fellow officer then returned to jail in Canton, and writer picked up Andrew Green for questioning. Then I (Sheriff Cauthen), sent a deputy around to the Roger School to get Honor Williams, but Dave Dennis (a COFO worker) had picked him up about 10 minutes before the deputy got there. The sheriff's department was unable to find Honor Williams that night. The next morning George Raymond brought him to the sheriff's office.

Interview with Andrew Lee Green, Negro, male, 1005 Country Club Road, Hattiesburg, Miss.; stays at Lizie Welch home, Valley View community.

Green stated that he and Williams had been to Pickens to see their girl friends, [sic] come home and went to bed. About 15 minutes later Williams came over and told him something was on fire. He said his car had a flat, and he told Williams to change it while he was getting dressed.

He said he got dressed and was helping Williams change the tire when two cars came by. The front car was a 1958 brown Ford with red lights, on or near the bumper, and the car behind was a Chevrolet or Plymouth. We got the tire changed and went over to the Freedom House and picked up Charles and drove toward the fire. Green said at the third bridge across the creek, they met the same two cars. He said they drove on past the church and turned around at Earl Smith's house and drove on past the church and back to the Freedom House.

We told Green that his story was different from that the other had told. Then he told us that on the way back from his girl friend's house they had met a blue Pontiac, and that Honor Williams said, "There is Mr. Billy Noble." He also admitted that he called George Raymond and told him they had visitors. He said George asked him who is was, and he told him Mr. Billy Noble.

This writer told Green that in view of the conflicting statement, he would like for him to come to the Mississippi Highway Patrol Headquarters and take the polygraph test, and Green agreed to do that. So, the next morning, August 18, 1964, the writer and Billy Noble brought Andrew Green and Honor Williams to Highway Patrol Headquarters and both were given polygraph tests.

Witness Arthur Lee Green and Honor Williams were both later interviewed separately and together and both stated that they had not seen a 1958 brown Ford with red lights, on or near the bumper, and had not seen the other car herein mentioned, being a Chevrolet or Plymouth. Both of these witnesses stated that they had not seen anyone resembling Mr. Billy Noble at any place on the night of the fire.

All witnesses interviewed in connection with this fire were at first very arrogant, [sic] antagonist and reluctant, and did not care to impart information to the investigating officers.

The file in this case is still open.

This fire was also investigated by the FBI and the State Fire Marshal's office.

EXHIBIT NO. 21

STAFF INVESTIGATION REPORT ON FINES AND SENTENCES IMPOSED BY LOCAL COURTS IN GREENWOOD, MISS., 1963–64

STAFF INVESTIGATION REPORT ON FINES AND SENTENCES IMPOSED BY LOCAL COURTS IN GREENWOOD, MISS.

The following is a report on an analysis of city court records in Greenwood, Miss., which was conducted by the staff of the Commission. The purpose of this analysis is to determine whether civil rights workers appearing before the court received more onerous fines and sentences for the same offenses than other persons not involved in civil rights.

SUMMARY

The city court docket of Greenwood shows that during 1963 five civil rights workers were charged with blocking the sidewalk, running a stop sign, operating a car with improper equipment, and reckless driving. All were found guilty. Except for the worker charged with reckless driving, all received fines which grossly exceeded fines given to other persons during the year. Court records also show that during 1963 approximately 35 persons were arrested during demonstrations in connection with attempts to register to vote. They were charged with breach of the peace, disorderly conduct, and disturbance in a public place. The majority received fines of $200 and jail sentences. The fines were 15 to 20 times greater than the average fine imposed for similar violations of city ordinances during the preceding year.

In 1964 the Department of Justice filed an action under the Civil Rights Act of 1960 against Greenwood city officials and others alleging, among other things, that persons engaged in voter registration activity were given substantially heavier sentences than other persons for comparable offenses. The Commission staff analyzed the city court docket pertaining to the period in 1964 after the institution of the Attorney General's action. The analysis shows that during the last six months of 1964 civil rights "offenders" still received discriminatory sentences and fines, although to a lesser degree.

During the last half of 1964, four civil rights workers were charged with profanity and driving without a proper license. All were found guilty. They were required to post a cash bond or were fined amounts which were greatly in excess of fines given to other persons during this period. Court records also show that approximately 130 persons were arrested during demonstrations at the courthouse in connection with attempts to register. They were charged with a variety of violations of city ordinances. All were found guilty. The majority were fined $100 and sentenced to 30 days on the county farm. These sentences were substantially more severe than sentences imposed on all other persons for violations of city ordinances during the same period.

I

Analysis of Docket Entries for 1963

Blocking the Sidewalk (scheduled fine [36] $5) :
COFO Cases:
$100 fine suspended, two years probation (two cases).
Other Cases:
$5 fines (four).
Running Stop Sign:
COFO Cases:
Jane Stembridge, $50, October 28, 1963.
Other Cases:
$10 or less (58) ; $15 (one) ; $25 (one).
Improper Equipment (scheduled fine $15) :
COFO Cases:
Jane Stembridge, $50, October 28, 1963.
Other Cases:
$15 or less (23) ; $25 (two) ; $100 suspended if damage paid (one).
Reckless Driving (scheduled fine $50) :
COFO Cases:
Samuel Block, $100, October 22, 1963.
Other Cases:
Reckless driving is often charged in lieu of DWI [37], but the fine imposed is equal to a fine for DWI. This change in the charge is noted on the docket. Taking this factor into consideration, no fines were discovered greater than the scheduled fine of $50.
Civil Rights Arrests
March 29, 1963
Disorderly conduct (eight), $200 plus four months. (In the preceding year there had been 19 convictions for disorderly conduct. The average fine was $7.37. Two defendants were sent to jail.)

---

[36] For explanation of "scheduled fine" see appendix.
[37] Driving while intoxicated.

April 3, 1963

Disorderly conduct (12), $100 plus 30 days.

June 25, 1963.

Breach of the peace (10), $200 plus four months. (Average fine during preceding year was $6.66, excluding fines against COFO workers.)

Parading without a permit (three), $200 plus four months.

June 26, 1963

Disturbance in a public place (two), $500 plus six months.

II

Analysis of Docket Entries, June 1 to December 18, 1964

Profanity (scheduled fine of $15) :

COFO Cases:

Silas McGhee,[38] $200 cash bond, $100 fine, docket 55450, September 28, 1964.

Other Cases:

$50 suspended (three)

$35 fine (one)

$15 fine (seven)

No Driver's License (scheduled fine of $25) :

COFO Cases:

Jake McGhee, $200 cash bond, $25 forfeited, $175 returned, docket 55078, August 21, 1964.

Jake McGhee, $50 fine, docket 55060, August 18, 1964.

Jessie Harrison, $35 fine, docket 54829, July 21, 1964.

Other Cases:

$25 fine (10)

$15 fine (one)

$15 suspended (one)

$10 fine (one)

In several other categories of offense there were no patterns of significant discrimination against COFO personnel. These results appear below.

Running Red Light (scheduled fine $10) :

COFO Cases:

Silas McGhee, $10, docket 55700, November 2, 1964.

Other Cases:

Reading by staff attorney did not reveal a pattern varying from the norm established by the schedule.

Running a Stop Sign (scheduled fine $10) :

COFO Cases:

Jessie Harrison, $10, docket 54828, July 21, 1964.

Other Cases:

Reading by staff attorney did not reveal a pattern varying from the norm established by the schedule.

Speeding (scheduled fines, simple : $10; aggravated : $25) :

COFO Cases:

George L. Green, $50, docket 55147, August 27, 1964.

Silas McGhee, $10, docket 55700, November 2, 1964.

Lonnie McGhee, $10, docket 55050, August 17, 1964.

---

[38] Profanity in this case probably involved the city ordinance of June 21, 1964, making it unlawful to curse at city policemen, punishable by a $100 fine and 30 days in jail.

Other Cases:

Reading by staff attorney did not reveal a pattern varying from the norm established by the schedule.

Reckless Driving (scheduled fine $50):

Reckless driving fines were not applied in a discriminatory manner. It was a regular practice of the court to accept a plea of guilty to reckless driving in lieu of trying the defendant for driving while intoxicated, an offense which can result in loss of license, and to impose a heavy fine up to $200.

COFO Cases:

George Albertz, $50, docket 54845, July 23, 1964.
George Albertz, $50 forfeit, $25 returned, docket 54904, July 29, 1964.
Esau McGee, $50, docket 55035, August 17, 1964.

Other Cases: (Other than DWI originally charged):

Reading by staff attorney did not reveal a pattern varying from the norm established by the schedule.

Improper Parking (scheduled fines, double parking: $5; parking: $2):
COFO Cases:

Silas McGhee, $10, docket 55284, September 10, 1964.

Other Cases:

Reading by staff attorney did not reveal a pattern varying from the norm established by the schedule.

Improper Left Turn (scheduled fine $5):
COFO Cases:

Peter Kaiser, $10, docket 55320, September 14. 1964.

Other Cases:

None

Displaying License of Another (scheduled fine not listed):
COFO Cases:

Jake McGhee, $50, docket 55058, August 18, 1964.

Other Cases:

$75 (one—no others found).

Civil Rights Arrests

March 31, 1964
Disorderly conduct (14), $500 cash bond, removed to Federal court, where bond was reduced to $200 and $100.

July 16, 1964
Unlawful picketing of a public building.

Docket numbers 54681–54794 (110 persons, excluding some multiple charges), fined $100 plus 30 days.

August 3, 1964
Disorderly Conduct

William Hodes, $100, docket 54928.
Fred Harris, $50, docket 54927.

John Hardy, $50, docket 54926.
Walter McGlothin, $25, docket 54929.
Mary Anne McGlothin, $25, docket 54930.

August 12, 1964
Disturbance in a Public Place
COFO Cases: [39]

Charlie McAfee, $25, docket 55011.
Nadine DeLaney, $150, county farm, docket 55012.
Emma DeLaney, $25, county farm, docket 55013.
John Hardy, $75, county farm, docket 55014.
Mary Austin, $50, county farm, docket 55018.
Barbara Edwards, $75, county farm, docket 55019.
Catherine Edwards, $25, county farm, docket 55020.
Gary Harper, $100, county farm, docket 55022.
Eddie Henderson, $25, county farm, docket 55023.
Booker Nelson, $100, county farm, docket 55024.
Mamie Parker, $75, county farm, docket 55025.
Ernestine Pruitt, $50, county farm, docket 55026.
James Williams, $25, county farm, docket 55027.
Tom Harris, $150, county farm, docket 55028.
Jessie Harrison, $200 cash bond, removed to Federal court, docket 55044.

APPENDIX

Schedule of Fines in City Court [40]
Greenwood, Mississippi

Assault	$15.00
Assaulting an Officer	50.00
Assault and Battery	25.00
Assault and Battery with a Deadly Weapon	100.00
Begging	100.00
Concealed Weapon	100.00
Destroying Public Property	50.00
Disorderly Conduct	25.00
Displaying a Deadly Weapon (1)	50.00
Displaying a Deadly Weapon (2)	100.00
Drunk	15.00
Drunk and Disorderly	40.00
Indecent Exposure	25.00
Interfering with an Officer	50.00
Malicious Mischief	Twice value of property destroyed
Petit Larceny	100.00
Possessing Whisky	100.00

---

[39] COFO elected to refuse to pay the fines and to go to the county farm.
[40] Until 1964 the maximum fine which could be imposed by a City Court for violation of any City Ordinance was $100 or 30 days or both. This sta[s] was amended in 1964 to permit City Court to impose fines of $300 or 90 days or both. See [Miss.] Code 3374-137. The maximum fine for violation of the Greenwood City Traffic Ordinance is $100 and 30 days. Traffic Ordinance, City of Greenwood, Mississippi (1954), Sec. 137. When a warrant is required, the judge charges an additional $5.

Profanity _____ $15. 00
Resisting Arrest_____ 50. 00
Shoplifting _____ 100. 00
Trespassing _____ 50. 00
Vagrancy _____ 100. 00
Unauthorized Person Driving a Motor Vehicle _____ 25. 00
Blocking an Entrance_____ 5. 00
Double Parking_____ 5. 00
Driving While Intoxicated—first_____ 100. 00
Driving While Intoxicated—second_____ 200. 00
Expired License_____ 15. 00
Revoked License_____ 100. 00
Failure to Dim Lights_____ 5. 00
Car Not Under Control _____ 10. 00
Failure to Yield Right-of-Way_____ 10. 00
Hit and Run_____ 100. 00
Improper Equipment_____ 15. 00
Improper Left Turn_____ 5. 00
No Driver's License_____ 25. 00
Parking _____ 2. 00
Reckless Driving_____ 50. 00
Running Red Light_____ 10. 00
Running Stop Sign_____ 10. 00
Speeding—Simple _____ 10. 00
Speeding—Aggravated _____ 25. 00

Add $5 if warrant is required.

EXHIBIT NO. 22

STATEMENTS ON LAW AND ORDER ISSUED BY OFFICIALS IN GREEN-VILLE, MISS.

(OMITTED IN PRINTING)

EXHIBIT NO. 23

RESOLUTION OF THE MISSISSIPPI STATE BAR ASSOCIATION, DATED JULY 15, 1964

RESOLUTION

Whereas, rapidly occurring, recent and, in many instances, regrettable events and incidents have taken place on many fronts—national as well as local—as to make our great State the focal point of unfavorable and unjust publicity and to create tension, divisions and prejudices among our peoples;

Whereas, by the spoken and printed words and by acts, various groups outside our Commonwealth have unfairly and unjustly stated or intimated that the courts—the last refuge or bulwark of a free people—and particularly the Mississippi courts, State and Federal, and the Mississippi Bar, as arms or officers of said courts, are recreant to their oaths and duties and cannot, and will not, accord to "strangers within their gates" or others whose philosophy or beliefs are contrary to the traditional beliefs or mores of our State, a fair and impartial trial in our State because of alleged inability to obtain competent and courageous counsel;

Whereas, despite their beliefs as citizens, and the assertion of such beliefs, in the political or legislative domain, State or Federal, the lawyers of Mississippi have never shirked their duty or violated their oaths in the representation of persons charged with crimes or who sought legal redress of their grievances, for the Mississippi Bar has at all times been ready to discharge their duties and comply with their oaths as attorneys in behalf of all persons, of low or high estate, rich or poor, resident or nonresident, popular or unpopular, and regardless of race, creed, color or of national origin, and the history of jurisprudence of our State attests such fact;

Whereas, one of the most basic of constitutional or human rights is that every person, in defending or prosecuting a civil cause [Section 25] or in "all criminal prosecutions" [Section 26] shall have a "right to be heard by himself or counsel, or both" [Sections 25 and 26 aforesaid, Mississippi Constitution of 1890] and through the years all Mississippi courts have been "open" and have afforded a "remedy by due course of law" where "right and justice" has been "administered without sale, denial or delay", as guaranteed by our Mississippi constitution [Section 24]; and all Mississippi courts and lawyers have at all times not only been cognizant of those fundamental rights, but have diligently sought to accord them to all citizens; that since 1817, the above constitutional guarantees have been the organic law of this State, and need no support from *Gideon* v. *Wainright*, 372 U.S. 335 [1963] [which declared that under the 14th amendment to the U.S. Constitution the sixth amendment thereto [the latter of which vouchsafes "(I)n all criminal prosecutions, the accused shall . . . have the assistance of counsel"] was made applicable and obligatory upon the States] ;

Whereas, despite the tensions and emotions which currently prevail and regardless of whether a person charged of crime, or who seeks legal redress of civil grievances, or the cause he or she is espousing, is popular or unpopular or respected or despised, the Mississippi State Bar, acting through its governing authority [Section 8687, Mississippi Code of 1942] or executive agency, [By-Laws, Art. III, Section 1] to wit, its board of bar commissioners, in its organizational, due and regular session, properly convened, desires to reaffirm its stand and the time-honored traditions of the bar of our State and to provide a liaison committee from its members to be available for consultation with the courts, State and Federal, and for all persons who have any grievances as to representation of counsel : Now, therefore, be it

Resolved, by the board of bar Commissioners of the Mississippi State Bar, in its organizational, due and regular meeting, properly called, That :

1.

It is the sense of the Mississippi State Bar that all the courts of Mississippi, State and Federal, and all of the members of the bar who practice in said courts have been, and will continue to be, faithful and true to their duties and oaths in according to every person, of high or low estate, resident or nonresident, rich or poor, popular or unpopular, respected or despised, and regardless of race, color, creed or of national origin, a fair and impartial trial, with assistance and protection, where sought, of competent counsel;

2.

It is the sense of the Mississippi State Bar that, true to finest traditions, the practicing attorneys of our State, members of our unified bar, should take, as it is the sense of this body that they have taken, the representation of a person charged with crime or who seeks legal redress of grievances, unless there be present a conflict of interest or other compelling ground or cause, or, where unable to pay a fee, when appointed by the court, in which his cause is, or where the same should be, lodged; provided, however, that this shall not prohibit a lawyer from charging and collecting a reasonable fee where it is ascertained by him that the accused is able to pay such fee.

3.

That the president of the Mississippi State Bar is requested to appoint a special committee to act as liaison committee from the membership of our bar to be available for consultation with the courts, State and Federal, of our State, and for or with all persons who might have any grievances as to, or lack of, representation of counsel, such committee to be a large and representative one, with sections thereof—because of geographical proximity to courts, State and Federal, and persons within the area—being preferably appointed for each division of each of the northern and southern districts of Mississippi;

4.

That said liaison committee be requested to work with the conference of local bar associations and with the different county or other geographical-area bar associations in the discharge of their duties, as well as all judges of all courts in the State;

5.

That copies of this resolution be mailed by the executive director of the Mississippi State Bar to: (a) the president of the conference of local bar associations; and to (b) the president of each county, or other geographical-area, bar associations; Be it further

Resolved, That the attorney general of Mississippi be requested to notify all judges of courts of record in this State of the content of this Resolution; Be it further

Resolved, That newspapers be furnished a copy of this resolution for publication, and that a copy of said instrument be furnished all members of the Mississippi State Bar;

Thus done and resolved, This July 15, 1964.

CERTIFICATE

I, Mrs. Alice Nevels, executive director, secretary and treasurer of the Mississippi State Bar, do hereby certify that the above and foregoing is a true and correct copy of that certain resolution adopted by the board of bar commissioners of said Mississippi State Bar, by a unanimous vote of those present, at the duly called and regular meeting of said board on July 15, 1964..

Witness my hand, This July 16, 1964.

MRS. ALICE NEVELS,
Executive Director, Secretary and Treasurer, Mississippi State Bar.

INVESTIGATIVE REPORTS PRODUCED IN RESPONSE TO SUBPENA

ROBERT R. WARREN, SHERIFF, PIKE COUNTY: INVESTIGATION REPORT OF THE
BEATING OF MR. IVEY GUTTER, DATED JUNE 11, 1964

Ivey Gutter — C.M.
6-11-64 — 4:30 Pm
Hospital 7:30 P.m.
Ivey Rides To Work With
W___ L___ F___ —
Got out of Car & 3 men Wearing
Hoods came out of woods —
Hit Gutter 4 or 5 times Knocked.
Down 3 times. Then Put him in
Car. The Three Hooded men
Were young 19 or 20 About 140#
The driver of Car Was older, After
Putting Gutter in Car A Hood was
Placed over his head & her.Was
Carried Into Woods. One of
The men Said you & CC Bryant
goes To Lunch Everyday Together.
Gutter's Discription of weapons
used By The men Mere
22 Auto Pistol
38 Pistol
20 gauge Shot gun
He believed The Car was A
57 Chev .Blk. No Tag number
was. gotten.
Gutter's Wife had gone To Gro.
Store when This happened.

INVESTIGATION REPORT OF THE ATTEMPTED BOMBING OF THE HOME OF MR. WILLIE
J. DILLON, DATED AUGUST 28, 1964

Willie John Dillon

8 - 28 - 1964

An Explosion was heard About
1 Am. got Call from FBI That
Explosion had Occured but Wasn't
Certin of Location. Agreed To
Meet Agent Intersection 51 & 24
South McComb Met Frank Ford
Agent with FBI About 1:15 AM
date. We Proceeded in direction
of Explosion And found it To
be in yard of Willie John Dillon.
Upon Arriving At Scene We
Started An Investigation.
Willie Dillon Was in house
when Explosion Occured And didnt
See Anything. He Stated he had
Been Working on An Automobile
until 12:30 And had gone in house.
In Checking This Auto which Dillon
Said hadnt been Out of his yard
Ford & myself found The Motor
& Tires was Still hot.
The Explosion had Knocked A Small
hole in yard with no Other damage
Our Opinion Was That A dynamite
Cap had Exploded Then nine Sticks
of dynamite Was placed on The ground
within Six Inches of The hole in
ground.
In making The Investigation it
Was noticed That Dillon Was
Jumping his Electric Meter & Was
Also Operating A garage Without
A License. Dillon Was Placed

Under Arrest for These Violations
About 3AM date.
Dillon Was Carried To J.P. Court
The Same date About 1 P.M. After
being Advised of his Rights he
Pled Guilty As Charged on Both
Counts.

INVESTIGATIVE REPORTS PRODUCED IN RESPONSE TO SUBPENA

JAMES ODELL ANDERS, SHERIFF, ADAMS COUNTY: INVESTIGATION REPORT OF THE
BEATING OF MR. ARCHIE C. CURTIS AND MR. WILLIE JACKSON, UNDATED

J. ODELL ANDERS

SHERIFF AND TAX COLLECTOR
ADAMS COUNTY

NATCHEZ, MISSISSIPPI

OFFICE PHONE 442-2752

On the morning of 16 February 1964, Sunday, at approx. 6:30 A. M. David
Blough, Chief Deputy Sheriff, Adams County, Miss. received a call to come to
the Adams County Jail to investigate a report by two Colored Males that
they had been beaten by four or five masked men.

Upon reaching the jail, deputy Blough met Deputy Guy T. Smith and they
met in the interrigation room with A.C.Curtis and Willie Jackson.
A.C. Curtis reported that he had received a telephone call late Saturday
night to send an ambulance to pick up a person who had had a heart attack.
Curtis reported that he was told to come to the end of the Palestine road
and there he would be met by a man with a lantern who would take him
to the house of the person suffering the attack. Curtis further reported
that he went by the house of Willie Jackson to get Willie to make the
call with him and to do the ambulance driving.

The two men when questioned gave the same account of the incident which
was:

They answered the call as asked and went to the end of the palestine Rd.
and there they were met by a man with a light and they stopped the
ambulance and got out and they were then ordered not to get back into
the ambulance, but four or five hooded men made them get into their car
and they were driven several miles down the road and then forced to get
out of the car and to lay down on the gravel road with their pants pulled
down and parts of their clothing removed and they were then beaten with
whips. The two men were only able to give one clue on the car and that
was that it was a 1959, dirty ford galaxie. It was a four door car.

The two men were left in the woods and they hooded men drove off and
the two colored men were forced to walk some several miles to a telephone
and a ride back to town. When they returned to the city the Sheriff's
Office was notified and an investigation was immediately started. The
City Police and the F. B. I. along with the state investigators were
notified at once and asked to help in the solution to this incident.

Deputies Blough and Smith talked with the men in search for clues.
The two deputies and the two men went back over the route of travel
of the two man, went to the scene where the ambulance was left, helped
get ambulance started and they later drove the ambulance back to town--
that is, Curtis and Willie Jackson drove it back to town. The deputies
and the two colored men went out to the scene of the beating, which turned
out to be on the property of Miss. Bessie Bailey. The area was searched
for any possible clues. One piece of red cloth used so they said for
masks was recovered. There were no traces of tire tracks that could be
lifted. The scene of the beating with on a well prepared oil field
gravel road. There were marks on the bodies of the two men to show that
their bodies had been beaten.

All authorities were given what information was available to help in the
search.

Investigation Report of the Beating of Mr. Alfred Whitley, Undated

SHERIFF'S DEPARTMENT
NATCHEZ, MISS.

CASE REPORT

CASE NO.	DATE	CITY Natchez	COUNTY Adams

Subjects	Dates worked on case This Report:	Unit Making Report:
Albert Whitley		Sheriff Anders
	Title or Description of Case:	

KETCHINGS, NATCHEZ

On Feb. 6th, 1964 at 7:40 a.m. we were called to the Jefferson
Davis Hospital by hospitalppersonnel. Albert Whitàày was a patient
in the hospital, being treated by Dr. Phil Springer.

Deputy Smith and I talked to Whitley who said he worked at
Armstrong Tire and Rubber Company and left work at twelve midnight.
He told of seeing some men he knew and worked with at Armstrong Tire
and Rubber Company on the way home. He lived on a gravel road off the
Airport Road. A man who he named as a Mr. _____ passed his car and
slowed him down and remained in front of him until he got to the Airport
road turnoff. Mr _____ proceeded norkh on Highway 61 North and Whitley
turned left on to the Airport Road. He proceeded on the Airport Road
approximately 1/2 mile and turned to tje right on to a gravel road where
he lived, but was stopped by a car in the middle of the road with the
lights on, before he reached his house. He was forced out of his car
into the parked car by four or five hooded men, the model of the car,
Whitley thought to be an Oldsmobile. He was forced to lay on the floor
of the car and was driven to an unknown place and there taken out of
the car and whipped. He was left in the woods, and caught a Miller
Transport Truck to Cranfield. There he called his wife and she brought
him to the hospital. We followed every lead and found nothing.

Five days later, an article of subject's clothing and his glasses
case were found on a forestry road off the Liberty Road where the alledged
whipping took place. It had rained in the meantime, and any evidence
that might have been there was washed away.

Investigation Report of the Burning of Jerusalem Baptist and Bethel A.M.E. Churches, Adams County, Miss., Undated

SHERIFF'S DEPARTMENT
NATCHEZ, MISS.

CASE REPORT

CASE NO.	DATE	CITY Natchez	COUNTY Adams

Subjects	Dates worked on case This Report: July 12, 1964 - Continuas	Unit Making Report: Sheriff Anders
	Title or Description of Case: JERUSALEM & Bethel Churches - Burning	

KETCHINGS, NATCHEZ

The burning of the two churches. The Sheriff's office was
notified at 6:00 a.m. on July 12th, 1964 that these two churches
burned the night before. I went to the Kingston neighborhood and
found both churches burned to the ground and still smoking.

I returned to Natchez and contacted the Mississippi State Fire
Marshall's office, the Mississippi Highway Patrol office, and the
Federal Bureau of Investigation. ~~_____~~ people were contacted.
No motive was ever established. No one saw anything. No evidence
was found around the churches. Cases are still open and being
investigated.

INVESTIGATION REPORT OF THE BURNING OF THE WILLING WORKERS MEETING HALL
IN GLUCKSTADT, DATED AUGUST 11, 1964

MISSISSIPPI
LIVESTOCK THEFT BUREAU
CASE REPORT

Date 8–11–64   County Madison State Miss.
DATE WORKED ON CASE   UNIT MAKING REPORT
THIS REPORT   Unit 9—Jack Smith
8–11–64   Unit 70—WEEMS
TITLE OR DEFINITION OF CASE: WILLING WORKERS SOCIETY
BLDG. OWNED BY MT. PLEASANT CHURCH, SOMETIMES
CALLED the WOMANS MEETING HOUSE, OR PRATT
HOUSE, MADISON CO.

August 11, 1964: Writer heard conversation between the Hinds County sheriff's
office and Constable Bruno Holly reference the burning of this house in Madison
County. We proceeded north on Highway No. 55 to Gluckstadt Crossing, turning
west on gravel road for two miles; we were shown how to get there by unit 161—
Billy O'Neal.

Soon after arriving, we were assisted by Bruno Riley arriving on the scene,
accompanied by Justice of Peace Levon Hawkins; all assisted us in this case.

The building measured 25 feet by 32 feet (25′ x 32′) it was rough, unpainted,
frame building, covered with tin. About all that was left at 8:30 a.m. when
we arrived was the tin from the roof. It was completely burned clean.

Shortly after our arrival, there were three Negro men, two white men, and one
white female arrived on the scene in a 1964 Belair Chevrolet, radio equipped, tag
42049, registered to National Car Rental, Jackson, Miss. The car parked and
all six came from the public road onto the church grounds.

Rudolph J. Lombard, Negro male, driver's license No. 1629787, who stated he
was a field secretary for CORE and working for CORE out of Meridian and
Canton headquarters, seemed to be in charge of this crew, being Jerome Smith
W/M, Robert Watkins W/M, James Ohls W/M, Robert Stout W/M, and Arlene
Brock W/F.

Rudolph Lombard stated the burned building was called a meeting hall and
was being used as a Freedom School for the past two months. The school at
present was being run by Robert Stout W/M, and Arlene Brock W/F. As soon
as we got this information these persons left the scene immediately.

Page 2

Mt. Pleasant Church Building Burned in Madison County, Early a.m., Aug. 11,
1964

This building is located directly across the road from the Mt. Pleasant Methodist Church, the gravel road is known as the Mansdale Road; and according to
information that we could get this property is owned by the Mt. Pleasant Church.

The Mt. Pleasant Church had been torn down and is in the process of being
rebuilt.

The statements by the Negroes in the area was that the burned building was
being used as a temporary church until the new one was ready for occupancy.

At about 12 a.m., Mr. C. B. Lowe from the Fire Marshal's office arrived at the scene to assist us. Constable Holly received a call to go to Judge Leroy Hawkins' home and he left.

About this time a 4-door, 1958 brown Chevrolet, tag 45-5408, registered to James C. Ohle W/M, 838 Lutz St., Canton, Miss., and originally from Callacoon, N.Y., car occupied and driven by the owner listed above, arrived at the scene, and with him was Mark R. Lepper W/M, Leo Bouldin C/M, Sears Buckley, Jr., C/M, Joseph Lee Watts C/M. Subject Watts seems to be in charge of this crew, he and Sears Buckley, Jr., were the first down the hill to the burned site.

I (Jack Smith) approached Joseph Lee Watts and asked him "What do you want?" His answer, in the presence of Officer Weems #70, and Mr. C. B. Lowe was, "We come down to interview the building we burned." My statement was, "Repeat that answer again," and his answer was the second time, "We come down to interview the building we burned."

Although he made this statement two different times in the presence of we three officers, he denied having made this statement. He stated he was a Task Worker with COFO, working out of the Canton office for the past two years.

The white boy by the name of O. C. Ohle, stated that for sixty (60) days they had been holding a Freedom School at this building owned by the Mt. Pleasant Church. The school was conducted from 9 a.m. to 1 p.m. each day by Robert Stout and Arlene Brock. The school was first taught by Peggie Gunn and Vickie Chute, white. They went north around July 9, 1964. Vickie Chute came down to work only during the month of July, and Peggie Gunn was arrested in Canton and her parents forced her to return home.

Page 3

Mt. Pleasant Church's Building Burned in Madison County, Early a.m., Aug. 11, 1964

Subject Ohle stated further that permission for this school was granted by Rev. N. O. Taylor and the deacons in the church. So far, we have not been able to make contact with Reverend Taylor or any of the deacons.

Constable Holly stated he received information on the burning of the building from Percy Campbell at 7:30 this morning. Percy Campbell owns or operates a feed mill in Madison, and some of his Negro help reported the burning of the church building to him on arrival for work this morning.

INVESTIGATION CONTINUES

By: ————————————————————

Unit #9—Jack M. Smith, Investigator

By: ————————————————————

Unit 70—D. Weems, Officer MMP

INVESTIGATED: Aug. 11, 1964

Typed: 8-12-64

JACK S. CAUTHEN, SHERIFF, MADISON COUNTY, MISS.: A. INVESTIGATION REPORT
OF THE BURNING OF ST. JOHN'S BAPTIST CHURCH AND CEDAR GROVE BAPTIST
CHURCH, DATED SEPTEMBER 16 AND 17, 1964

MISSISSIPPI BUREAU OF IDENTIFICATION

CASE REPORT

Case No.   Date 8/17/64   County   Madison   State   Miss.

Subjects:	Dates Worked on Case This Report: 15 and 17, Sept. 1964	Making Report Unit 9—Jack Smith Unit 70—Dewey Weems
	Title or Description of Case: Burning of Two Negro Churches in Madison County, Mississippi, Night of 18 Sept. 1964 #1—St. John Baptist Church #2—Name of this church unknown at this time Cedar Grove Baptist Church	

At approximately 11:45 p.m., the writer received a call from the radio operator that the St. John Baptist Church located thirteen (13) miles north of Canton had been burned. This report was called in by Karen Duncan, COFO worker.

Units 9 and 70 went 10–8 and were met in Canton by Sheriff Jack Cauthen and proceeded to the scene. The church is located approximately five (5) miles northeast of Highway 51. This church was completely destroyed by fire.

While we were checking on this church, we received a second call from the Canton police department, stating that Mrs. Harold Hillbery, who lives on Highway 43, five (5) or six miles south of Canton reported a Negro church just below her house was on fire. We proceeded to the scene. This church was also completely destroyed by fire, but no one was up or present anywhere near the church, this being approximately 3 o'clock, we did not wake anyone and was unable to get the name of this church. The name of this church will be obtained this morning.

We returned to Canton with Sheriff Jack Cauthen and went to the Freedom House located in Canton to see where they had received their information concerning this fire. Apparently they did not know about the second church and we did not tell them, but as we got out of the car in front of the Freedom House in Canton, three (3) Negroes jumped out of a car parked in front of the house next door to the Freedom House. Two of them came toward us at a brisk pace and wanted to know who we wanted and what we were looking for. These three subjects were identified as George Raymond, George Washington, Jr., and Jack Melton. Melton called George Washington back to the car. George Washington was shielding something on his side with his shirt tail and returned to the car and was seen to place something inside the car. He was called back to the Freedom House and was in our sight all this time and on his side was a holster for a snub nose pistol. The sheriff asked him if he owned a pistol for the holster and he stated he did not. We all walked back over to the car and Sheriff Cauthen opened the front door and in under the front seat where George Washington was seen placing something, he removed a 6 shot .38 Colt pistol. He arrested George Washington and at 3:30 a.m. he was placed in the Madison County jail.

George Raymond made the statement to us there, and by that time, four city policemen had arrived at the scene, that this Karen Duncan had called him and notified him about the burning of the church and George also made the statement that a local police officer was seen at the church just before it was burned and was seen leaving the church after it had burned. We attempted to get George to give us this information as to who this police officer was. He stated he would find out for us.

Sheriff Jack Cauthen is to attempt to contact District Attorney Bill Waller this date to see if any charges can be placed on George Raymond for this accusation.

Investigators are returned to Canton this morning to get with the Sheriff and the Fire Marshal and investigate further on these two burned churches.

> Jack Smith
> Dewey Weems
> *Investigators*
> *Cattle Theft Bureau*

JS fc

(Information received from Investigator Jack Smith via public service.)

DAN C. THOMPSON, CHIEF OF POLICE, CANTON, MISS., INVESTIGATION REPORT OF THE
BOMBING OF THE FREEDOM HOUSE, CANTON, DATED JUNE 8, 1964

REPORT ON BOMBING AT THE FREEDOM HOUSE ON JUNE8th. 1964

Rembret Washington reported to the police Department, by telephone
at 7:15 AM on June 8th. 1964, that someone threw a bomb at the freedom
house, 838 Lutz St., between the hour of 1:00 AM & 1:30 AM. (reported
about six hours after explosion). I ask Rembret why she didn't report
when it happened, she said she thaught that James Collier had reported it.

I went to the freedom house and talked to James Collier, and asked
him why he didn't report it to the police. He stated he only had three
dimes and he used them to call(first) Charlie Bone , who is an FBI agent
in Jackson, but did not get in touch with him.(second) C.O.F.O. office
in Jackson and advise them as to what had happened.(third) the Justice
Department in Washington. He stated he could not call the police because
he didn't have another dime.

Upon investigation I found out that George Washington owned the
building, known as the freedom house, and that he xxx knew about the
bombing and was on the scene very soon after it happened.

We braught George to the station and questioned him as to why he
didn't report it to the police, he would not give any reason at all.
He was releaced after questioning.

Special Investigator Gynn Cole of the MHP was call in to help
with the investigation.

An investigation was made at the scene and all evidence appered
that the window which was broke out, had been broke from the inside,
also at the spot where the explosion was suppose to have been there was NO
evidence of any kind od powder burns or smoke stains. The area was
searched very closely and no kind of ávidence was found to determin what
made the marks on the side walk.

(2)

James Collier stated he received a telephone call about 11:30 PM on the 7th of June, The voice on the phone said "We are going to get you tonight " He also stated that the explosion happened about 12:30 AM but later changed it to about 1:30 AM. Collier also stated he received another phone call about 2:30 AM. the voice on the phone ask him " How many niggers did we get?

The case is still under investigation.

WILLIAM R. COOK
Asst Chief of Police

INDEX

A

505

F

G

H

POLICE IN AMERICA

An Arno Press/New York Times Collection

The American Institute of Law and Criminology.
Journal of the American Institute of Law and Criminology:
Selected Articles. Chicago, 1910–1929.

The Boston Police Strike: Two Reports. Boston, 1919–1920.

Boston Police Debates: Selected Arguments. Boston,
1863–1869.

Chamber of Commerce of the State of New York.
**Papers and Proceedings of Committee on the Police Problem,
City of New York.** New York, 1905.

Chicago Police Investigations: Three Reports. Illinois,
1898–1912.

Control of the Baltimore Police: Collected Reports.
Baltimore, 1860–1866.

Crime and Law Enforcement in the District of Columbia:
Report and Hearings. Washington, D. C., 1952.

Crime in the District of Columbia: Reports and Hearings.
Washington, D. C., 1935.

Flinn, John J. and John E. Wilkie.
History of the Chicago Police. Chicago, 1887.

Hamilton, Mary E.
The Policewoman. New York, 1924.

Harrison, Leonard Vance.
Police Administration in Boston. Cambridge, Mass., 1934.

International Association of Chiefs of Police.
Police Unions. Washington, D. C., 1944.

The Joint Special Committee.
**Reports of the Special Committee Appointed to Investigate
the Official Conduct of the Members of the Board of Police
Commissioners.** Boston, 1882.

Justice in Jackson, Mississippi: U.S. Civil Rights
Commission Hearings. Washington, D. C., 1965.

McAdoo, William.
Guarding a Great City. New York, 1906.

Mayo, Katherine.
Justice to All. New York, 1917.

Missouri Joint Committee of the General Assembly.
Report of the Joint Committee of the General Assembly
Appointed to Investigate the Police Department of the
City of St. Louis. St. Louis, Missouri, 1868.

National Commission on Law Observance and Enforcement.
Report on the Police. Washington, D. C., 1931.

National Prison Association.
Proceedings of the Annual Congress of the National Prison
Association of the United States: Selected Articles.
1874–1902.

New York City Common Council.
Report of the Special Committee of the New York City
Board of Aldermen on the New York City Police Department.
New York, 1844.

National Police Convention.
Official Proceedings of the National Prison Convention.
St. Louis, 1871.

Pennsylvania Federation of Labor.
The American Cossack. Washington, D. C., 1915.

Police and the Blacks: U.S. Civil Rights Commission
Hearings. 1960–1966.

Police in New York City: An Investigation. New York,
1912–1931.

The President's Commission on Law Enforcement and
Administration of Justice.
Task Force Report: The Police. Washington, D. C., 1967.

Sellin, Thorsten, editor.
The Police and the Crime Problem. Philadelphia, 1929.

Smith, Bruce, editor.
New Goals in Police Management. Philadelphia, 1954.

Sprogle, Howard O.
The Philadelphia Police, Past and Present. Philadelphia,
1887.

U.S. Committee on Education and Labor.
The Chicago Memorial Day Incident: Hearings and Report.
Washington, D. C., 1937.

U.S. Committee on Education and Labor.
Documents Relating to Intelligence Bureau or Red Squad of
Los Angeles Police Department. Washington, D. C., 1940.

U.S. Committee on Education and Labor.
Private Police Systems. Washington, D. C., 1939.

Urban Police: Selected Surveys. 1926–1946.

Women's Suffrage and the Police: Three Senate Documents.
Washington, D. C., 1913.

Woods, Arthur.
Crime Prevention. Princeton, New Jersey, 1918.

Woods, Arthur.
Policeman and Public. New Haven, Conn., 1919.

AMERICAN POLICE SUPPLEMENT

International Association of Chiefs of Police.
Proceedings of the Annual Conventions of the International Association of Chiefs of Police. 1893–1930. 5 vols.

New York State Senate.
Report and Proceedings of the Senate Committee Appointed to Investigate the Police Department of the City of New York. (Lexow Committee Report). New York, 1895. 6 vols.

THE POLICE IN GREAT BRITAIN

Committee on Police Conditions of Service.
Report of the Committee on Police Conditions of Service. London, 1949.

Committee on the Police Service.
Minutes of Evidence and Report: England, Wales, Scotland. London, 1919–1920.

Royal Commission on Police Powers and Procedures.
Report of the Royal Commission on Police Powers and Procedure. London, 1929.

Select Committee on Police.
Report of Select Committee on Police with the Minutes of Evidence. London, 1853.

Royal Commission Upon the Duties of the Metropolitan Police.
Minutes of Evidence Taken Before the Royal Commission Upon the Duties of the Metropolitan Police Together With Appendices and Index. London, 1908.

Committee on Police.
Report from the Select Committee on Police of the Metropolis. London, 1828.